FIERCER THAN TIGERS

FIERCER THAN TIGERS:
THE LIFE AND WORKS OF REX WARNER

BY
STEPHEN E. TABACHNICK

MICHIGAN STATE UNIVERSITY PRESS
EAST LANSING

∞ The paper used in this publication meets the minimum requirements of ANSI/
NISO Z39.48-1992 (R 1997) (Permanence of Paper).
Michigan State University Press
East Lansing, Michigan 48823-5202

Printed and bound in the United States of America.

07 06 05 04 03 02 1 2 3 4 5 6 7 8 9 10

LIBRARY OF CONGRESS CATALOGING-IN-PUBLICATION DATA

Tabachnick, Stephen Ely.
Fiercer than tigers : the life and works of Rex Warner / by Stephen E. Tabachnick.
       p.   cm.
    Includes index.
    ISBN 0-87013-552-X
1. Warner, Rex, 1905- 2. Authors, English-20th century-Biography. 3. Translators-
Great Britain-Biography. 4. Classicists-Great Britain-Biography. I. Title.
  PR6045.A78 Z9 2001
  828'.91209-dc21

                                                    2001003707

Cover design by Heidi Daley
Book design by Marilyn "Sam" Nesbitt

Visit Michigan State University Press on the World Wide Web at:
www.msupress.msu.edu

To Sharon, Daphne, Orrin and Laurie
always

CONTENTS

ACKNOWLEDGMENTS

Probably the greatest pleasure of working on this project was making the acquaintance of so many helpful and generous people, including some of the most important British and American intellectuals of Rex's generation. If his friends are any indication of Rex's personality, then he was a kingly person indeed. I would like to offer heartfelt thanks to the following individuals, living and deceased, and I can only beg pardon if I have inadvertently left out anyone who has been of assistance to me. For the sake of convenience, I have omitted academic titles from the following lists, but I want to state that a large number of the people who aided me are academics.

Mrs. Frances Warner has been able to help me enormously with her memories and Rex's letters and manuscript materials, including the unpublished beginning of Rex's autobiography. Rex's younger son, George Warner, and his family, Monica, Tamara and Daniel, have also been extremely helpful. Rex's second wife Barbara Rothschild (nee Hutchinson, and later Ghika), Lucy Penna (Rex's daughter with Barbara Rothschild), and her husband Richard Penna have been very forthcoming. So has Mrs. Katherine Chapple. Basil Goode, of the Warner family, and John Luce, of Rex's mother's family, have also supplied valuable information. The Morris family and Paul Ryan have been generous with their memories and their letters from Rex. But none of these people has in any way tried to influence the writing of this biography.

Rex's schoolmates at St. George's School, Harpenden, were able to help me with his life there; and his classmates at Wadham College in the 1920s have been very good about answering my requests for information. Nonetheless, as might be expected, there was much less information available for the earlier chapters than for the later ones. Beginning with the 1930s, we have the published work as well as the letters to editors C. J. Greenwood (held at Michigan State University) and John Lehmann (at the Harry

Ransom Humanities Research Center, the University of Texas, Austin). For the late 1930s, 1940s, and onward, the letters to publishers and friends Pam and John Morris and their children (held by Mrs. Anne [Morris] Ambrose), are very revealing.[1] The only problem with all of these letters is that they are largely undated; much like Christopher Isherwood's circle and the young Cecil Day-Lewis, Rex seems to have had a vaguely disdainful attitude toward dating letters.[2] I have done my best to cross-check and order them, and hope that I have succeeded. The middle 1940s saw the inception and development of Rex's friendship with poet George Seferis, and their mutual correspondence (held at the Gennadius Library and by Mrs. Frances Warner). This correspondence continued throughout Rex's marriage with Barbara Rothschild and beyond, right up to the time of Seferis's death in 1971. In the 1960s, Rex began writing to Paul Ryan, a colleague in classics at Bowdoin College, and that correspondence continued through Rex's retirement. From 1964 until his death in 1986, Rex maintained a correspondence with scholar Alan McLeod (held at the Rare Books Room, Pennsylvania State University Libraries), who in 1965 and 1985 published essay collections devoted to Rex's achievement. Rex continued writing to me, his doctoral advisee for two years, after I graduated from the University of Connecticut in 1971, up until the time of his death fifteen years later.

My debt to the following people, some of whom consented to lengthy interviews, or were willing to write long letters to me, or to translate from the Greek, is very great. But owing to their number, I have been forced to express my appreciation in alphabetically ordered lists.

Those who knew Rex: Anne Ambrose, Dame Peggy Ashcroft, the late Sir A. J. Ayer, Jill Black, Tony Bland, R. F. Bretherton, John Malcolm Brinnin, Francelia Butler, Joseph and Edie Cary, David and Marjorie Clark, Frank Coventry, Mrs. Edie Coxe, Irving and Hildy Cummings, Elizabeth Curry, Narayan Cutting, Jack Davis, Jill Day-Lewis, Sean Day-Lewis, Leonard Dean, Harriet and Leslie Duer, Mrs. June Fenby, Jeremy Fisher, Marcus Fyfe, Lance Garrard, Graham Greene, Lawrence Hall, Frank Halliwell, Stuart Hampshire, Edward Hanson, Sheila Hines, Robert Hodges, Stephan Hopkinson, Petter Juel-Larssen, Mrs. Leto Katakouzinos, Edmund Keeley, Francis King, Tony and Barbara Knowland, William Lannon, G. K. Laycock, Patrick and Joan Leigh Fermor, J. C. B. Lockyer, A. L. McLeod, Alan Milton, Pam Morris, Sir Claus Moser, William and Ruth Moynihan, Balaji Mundker, the late Michael and S.H. Oakeshott, Charles Owen, Mariella Piggott, Mrs. K. M. Raymond, Max Reinhardt, Charles A. Rivington, Mrs. Enid Roberts, Robert Robinson, William Rosen, the late Sir Steven Runciman, Paul Ryan, George Rylands, Tassos Sagos, Shan and Roxaine Sedgewick, Mrs. Maro Seferiades (Seferis), the late Sir Stephen and Natasha Spender,

Milton Stern, Taqui Stevens, Paul Vaughn, Geoffrey Warnock, Denis Watts, James Will, Gwyn Williams, Ken and Marilyn Wilson, and Charles Wrinch.

Those who supplied valuable information or documents: L. L. Baker, Michael Bott, Gabriel Carritt, Roy K. Close, Jacqueline Cox, Stephen Crook, Peter Daniel, Paola Daniele, A. M. Davies, Adrian Gaster, Michael Grant, Francesca Hardcastle, Peter Harris, Norman Hoare, Richard Hough, Peter Neumeyer, Donald Nicol, Daniel F. Poffenberger (a professional genealogist), Michael Richardson, Richard Schimmelpfeng, R. Scott, Bruce Stark, Olwen Temes, Ann Tracey, and Pam Weatherley.

Those who translated: George Economou and Jody Morgan.

Those who helped in other ways: Calvin Byre, Allan Chapman, R.M. Davis, Clayton and Gail Reeve, and Donald Shojai.

I would also like to thank the Research Councils of Tennessee Technological University and the University of Oklahoma, and the National Endowment for the Humanities Travel to Libraries Program, for helpful economic assistance.

I thank Mrs. Frances Warner for permission to quote from all of Rex's letters, books, and manuscripts. I also thank Mrs. Maro Seferiades for permission to quote from her husband's unpublished letters; Mrs. Valerie Eliot for permission to quote from an unpublished letter of T.S. Eliot; Edward Mendelson for permission to quote from an unpublished letter of W. H. Auden; and Jill Day-Lewis for permission to quote from several unpublished letters of C. Day-Lewis. I thank the Bodley Head (an imprint of Random House Group Ltd.) for permission to publish extracts from Rex Warner's *The Wild Goose Chase, Poems, Poems and Contradictions, The Professor, The Aerodrome, Why Was I Killed?, The Cult of Power, Men of Stones,* and *Men of Athens.* I thank Blackwell Publishers for permission to publish extracts from Rex Warner's *The Kite.*

The following libraries and archives have allowed me to see and/or publish items from their holdings: BBC Written Archives, Caversham; Berg Collection, New York Public Library; Betty Radice, Hamish Hamilton, and Penguin Archives, Bristol University Library; the British Council; Bodley Head and Hogarth Press Archives, Reading University Library; Special Collections, Brigham Young University Library; Gennadius Library, Athens; Harry Ransom Humanities Research Center, University of Texas, Austin; Special Collections, Michigan State University Library; Archives and Special Collections, University of Connecticut Library; Special Collections, State University of New York at Buffalo Library; Rare Books Room, the Pennsylvania State University Libraries; St. George's School, Harpenden; Wadham College Library, Oxford University.

Martha Bates of the Michigan State University Press has been the best editor that any writer could ever hope for. I will always be grateful for her support and assistance.

My children, Daphne, Orrin, and Laurie, had to give up a part of me during the more than ten years that it took me to research and write this book. I thank them for their warmth, humor, comfort, and support. My wife Sharon deserves my deepest thanks for urging me to do this book, for her encouragement and patience while I was doing it, and for her very excellent suggestions.

INTRODUCTION

Rex Warner's fellow Oxford student and friend W. H. Auden averred that "Time . . . worships language and forgives/Everyone by whom it lives." In other words, people who create memorable utterance will be remembered, whatever their personal foibles. The time has come for all those who care about language and literature to appreciate Rex. As a creative writer, he was a "legend" in the 1930s and 1940s, as Stephen Spender told me. In the 1950s and 1960s he published four historical novels, one of which (*The Converts*) Spender called the best example of that genre that he had ever read. Many readers know Rex Warner better as an eminent translator of the Greek and Latin classics, and his Penguin Thucydides has sold nearly one million copies. But even if Rex had not been a writer, he would have been worth remembering as a very big man physically and mentally—a "Rex" or king. As a person, Rex was refreshing because he had little tolerance for pretentious theories and pompous people, and could so easily adapt to new environments. He loved football and bourbon as well as Rugby and Scotch. While he would have enjoyed more fame, he never sought it. This book represents my attempt to bring Rex Warner the recognition that he deserves as an important yet neglected member of what has been termed "the Auden circle," and to assess the artistic and personal legacy that he has bequeathed to us. It is my contention that Warner should be included in future discussions of this circle on an equal basis with Stephen Spender and Cecil Day-Lewis, its most prominent members outside of Auden himself.

When I was Rex Warner's doctoral student, I looked forward to my biweekly visits with him no less for his good humor and companionship than for the excellent literary advice that he would inevitably provide. But I had no knowledge of the depth of experience that lurked behind his wry comments. Because he was born in 1905, he lived through the major events of almost the entire century and confronted them with integrity. He faced the tensions of being in school in England during World War I, and experienced the postwar gaiety at Oxford in the 1920s. Out of a concern for social justice and opposition to Hitler, he became a Marxist sympathizer in the 1930s when he and his wife Frances lived in near-poverty, but he remained one only until he was disillusioned by the Molotov-Ribbentrop Pact of 1939. He and Frances suffered through the raising of a disabled child at a time when little help was available and disabilities were considered a stigma. They lived through the Blitz in London, and he went on to witness the aftermath of the Nazi concentration camps, the Greek civil war, and life in postwar Germany.

There followed great personal luxury and a move up the class ladder in the early 1950s when he was married to Barbara Rothschild (nee Hutchinson and later Ghika), and great personal poverty and dogged literary struggle in the late 1950s and early 1960s after he was separated from her and was living in Scotland with Liz Fyfe. Then, almost miraculously, came a very happy personal and professional period in America, at Bowdoin College and at the University of Connecticut. This permanently rescued him from want and finally enabled him and Frances, now remarried, to retire close to their grandchildren in Wallingford, a pleasant English village. His return to a place much like Amberley, where he had grown up, marked the completion of a painful great circle voyage with some deviations en route.

Philosophically, too, Rex Warner seemed to journey in a great circle voyage. He set out with certain values—belief in Christianity, respect for the individual, love of nature, pride in athletic prowess, and interest in the past as revealed in the Greek and Latin classics. Under the pressure of politics in the 1930s he seemed to deviate from these traditional beliefs, and became a Marxist sympathizer. Beginning in 1939, he started to return to a less extreme, if still liberal, mental posture.

The turn to Marxism was never a true deviation for Rex, because even when he seemed extreme he was less than a convinced Marxist, and viewed Marxism only as a practical way to oppose fascism and to realize his social ideals. Rex himself stated in later life that even during his most radical phase in the 1930s he still respected tradition, but that he had pretended not to. Following this clue, I find in the very style of his first serious novel, *The Wild Goose Chase*, skepticism and balance as well as ostensible Marxist radicalism. I agree with Christopher Isherwood and Samuel Hynes that the reader of *The Professor* remains more sympathetic to the Professor's love of the past, Socratic method, and reasoned arguments than to his critics' complaints about the Professor's views. So even when he ostensibly advocates Marxist activism and a dismissal of the past in this novel, Rex Warner actually defends the classics as valuable in themselves and as a way of judging the present. He would in time become one of the most important popular advocates of classical study. I see Rex's later translations and historical novels not as betrayals of radical politics or as signs of a literary decline, but as an overt coming home to what was always his true allegiance: a belief in individual dignity and in literature (especially classical literature) as its repository. I feel that it is their dogged defense of freedom, justice, and reason in a world gone mad, rather than a superficial allegiance to Marxism, that will keep his 1930s (and later) novels alive.

Ultimately, the conflict in Rex Warner's mind was less between Marxism and his original beliefs, than within his original belief system itself. C. Day-Lewis, his best friend, wrote in his autobiography *The Buried Day* that the system of values under which both he and Rex were educated contained "an opposition between Christianity and the Greek thought, the Greek way of life which was, as it were, our unofficial religion."[1] This conflict can be more broadly defined. In some form, Rex Warner was haunted by an unreconciled tension between what the Victorian writer Matthew Arnold termed "Hebraism" (which he defined as too-earnest belief and attention to duty) and "Hellenism" (which he saw as encompassing skepticism, tolerance, and appreciation of worldly things). Barbara Rothschild, Rex's second wife, suggested that Rex took to drinking because it was the only way that he could still the inner conflict between these two basic forces, which showed up in many ways. He believed in social justice and fairness, but was not averse to living well himself when the chance presented itself, and may have felt guilty for having done so. He tried to escape the Evangelism of his mother's family, the Luces, and the more progressive Christianity of his father's, the Warners, and probably felt guilty about that until, at the end of his life, he admitted to a respect for his father's beliefs. In order to satisfy a felt need, amounting almost to a duty, to write, he was ready to return to a gloomy England when his two-year stint as director of the British Institute was over, even though he loved Greece and the good life that he led there. Fortunately, this tension was artistically productive. In his important novels *The Wild Goose Chase, The Professor*, and *The Aerodrome*, the philosophical and dramatic action occurs when a rigid political system demanding obedience is confronted (and only sometimes vanquished) by a more tolerant, life-loving, and all-too-human protagonist.

But while this opposition between rigidity and love of life emerges frequently in different forms in Rex Warner's life and writings, I have refrained from highlighting it constantly. Nor have I felt the need to describe Rex's times as well as his life, aside from some basic necessities of historical context. Numerous writers, most notably Samuel Hynes and Valentine Cunningham, have covered "the writers of the 1930s" and their times very well, and good histories of the following decades are readily available. Since Warner's life story has not previously been told and since the materials relating to it were so abundant and so unexplored, I have felt justified in making this a "life and works" rather than a "life and times." I have tried to write a straightforward, accurate story based on eyewitness testimony (including my own), literary and historical documentation, and Warner's texts themselves. I have presented, as objectively as possible, his personal and literary faults as well as his strengths, so that the reader can arrive at his or her own assessment of them.

I am painfully aware that Rex Warner's ideal biographer would have been a marvelous classicist with a thorough knowledge of English literature, an Englishman who had lived in America and in Greece for a long time, someone brought up in Christianity who had also flirted with paganism, and a person who had known him all his life. I realize my distance from this model of the ideal Warner biographer. But I comfort myself with the thought that few people could fulfill that ideal, and that owing to sixteen years of personal study and acquaintance with him, more than ten additional years of close reading of his published writings, unpublished manuscripts, and letters, and travel in America, England, and Greece and many interviews in all of those places, I have succeeded (as I often doubted that I would ever do) in covering some of the gaps in my knowledge. Rex, *ave atque vale*—hail and farewell.

CHAPTER ONE

BIRMINGHAM AND AMBERLEY, 1905-1913

I. REX AND AMBERLEY

In the beginning, there were the Warners and the Luces, and there was Amberley, a village in the Cotswolds. Hilly and well-forested, in the green and rolling Gloucestershire country near the town of Stroud, it had (just as it does today) shady streets and pleasant stone houses. In an "Essay on Gloucester" that he wrote in July 1917 at the age of twelve, Rex reported that "Gloucester is surrounded by the most beautiful country and picturesque villages with old English cottages and flower gardens. One of the most beautiful villages round Gloucester is Amberley."[1] The Amberley Inn continues to function, in the same central location on the village green, much as it did at the beginning of the twentieth century. With a population of 1,250 around 1905, it was a close, warm, safe community at a time when World War I was not yet a whisper.

During his life, Rex Warner met and worked on an equal basis with many intellectual celebrities. But this hobnobbing with the great never turned his head, and the English countryside and village, and particularly the English pub, provided him with a lifelong democracy of feeling. As a child, Rex was delighted to be in the country and was encouraged by his mother in his prayers to thank God for the great gift of being allowed to live there, made even greater by its distance from the unsanitary and harsh industrial cities of the British midlands. Rex lived the nostalgic Edwardian dream, rather than the more prevalent smoky reality of Birmingham,

5

where he was born on 9 March 1905. In his unfortunately brief and incomplete autobiography, begun after his retirement in 1974 and limited to his early childhood, Rex wrote that he remembered nothing of Birmingham and that although he bore no grudge against the city, he was always reluctant to name it as his place of birth.

On the other hand, the few pages that exist are full of references to the countryside around Amberley: "In these early years the presence of God, or of something divine, was evident in hills, woods, meadows, birds, butterflies, flowers + perhaps particularly in sunsets. He was certainly out of doors, though it had to be admitted that He must, at least sometimes, be present in Church."[2]

He felt this attraction to the earth and its creatures even though when he first moved with his family from Birmingham to his new home in Amberley at the age of two and a half, he found that nature could be treacherous. He exuberantly flung himself, lightly dressed, into a patch of stinging nettles and then, amidst many tears, had to be rubbed down with some dock leaves. From this incident, Rex learned as a child not the usual religious explanation that God sends pain to try people, but rather that "when God sees fit to cause pain, He will immediately supply an antidote, even if it is not a very effectual one." This philosophy of realistic optimism seems to have stayed with Rex all of his life.

II. REX'S FATHER AND THE WARNERS

Rex learned the love of the countryside and of literature not only from personal experience, but from the Warner and Luce families, and particularly from their male members: the gentle father and enthusiastic uncles whom Rex never ceased to respect. His earliest memories were of butterfly hunting with his father, and near the time of his death when he was asked by the local vicar which person he most admired, he answered, "My father."

Frederic Ernest Warner, born on 24 March 1868, was a progressive clergyman of the Church of England. His tall, austere, and frail appearance expressed a genuine seriousness, but also disguised a gentle, kindly, thoughtful nature. Frederic[3] obtained a B.A. at Trinity College, Dublin, in 1890 and served as a curate of St. Simon Church, Portsea, Hampshire, from 1892-96, becoming ordained as a priest there in 1893. From 1896-97 he held a curacy at St. Peter's, Islington; and at Christ Church, Summerfield, Birmingham, from 1897-1905.

On 5 April 1904, when he was thirty-six and she was twenty-four, he married Kathleen Luce (born 17 September 1879) at Saint Nicholas, Gloucester, the church of her father, the very respected and somewhat fearsome Reverend John James Luce.

While his father Frederic was still curate of Christ Church in Birmingham, Rex was born at the couple's home at 344 Gillott Road. Rex was baptized Reginald Ernest, Ernest being a very popular name around the turn of the century in England, when earnestness was admired, and satirized in the title of Oscar Wilde's famous play, *The Importance of Being Earnest*. But the family adopted the nickname "Rex" very early, possibly after a child of that name who had died earlier, and it stuck. Certainly it suited him very well, because given his large size, keen intellect, and daring spirit (especially on the sports field), he was indeed a "Rex," or king.

Soon after Rex's birth, Frederic became vicar of St. Barnabas Church, also in Birmingham, where he stayed until 1908. But in that year, before Rex was three, Frederic and Kathleen moved into the old rectory (now gone) of Holy Trinity Church in Amberley. The rectory in which Rex grew up was an old, rambling building with a stone-flagged floor and oil lamps. At the age of twelve, Rex wrote of it, "It is a typical old English country house with a beautiful garden. There is a large vegetable garden attached to the Rectory, also some stables which are not used."[4] Holy Trinity was built in 1836 entirely with funds provided by the son of the famous economist David Ricardo, who lived in the area. It is not a handsome or unusual church; Rex himself wrote, "Amberley church is not as picturesque as it might be as unfortunately it was built at a period when nobody minded what the church looked like and cared less."[5] Frederic loved the church because of its parishioners rather than for the building itself. He remained here for almost twenty-seven years, becoming the parish's second longest serving rector. He was inducted into the living at Amberley on Wednesday, 10 June 1908. He signed the church's burial book for the first time on 18 June 1908 and for the last on 22 October 1934.

At the annual Whit Monday gathering of the Sunday school in 1908, the new minister thanked his parishioners for the warm welcome that they had shown him and his family. He recalled being told by the previous rector, Reverend Summerhayes, that he was coming to a unique place. Frederic told the congregation that as far as he could tell it most certainly was unique, and very different from his previous parish in Birmingham. It was a warm, close-knit group, and it included some interesting people. The church's cemetery contains the grave of Percival Christopher Wren (d. 1941), author of the romantic novel about the Foreign Legion, *Beau Geste*, as well as the grave of Maj. Gen. Sir Fabian Ware (d. 1949), who in 1919 became permanent vice-chairman of the Imperial War Graves Commission. Sir Fabian is remembered for his heroic attempt to memorialize every single fallen British and Allied World War I soldier. It was he who advised Rex's family to send Rex to St. George's School, Harpenden, at the age of eight, and who presented

Rex with a complete set of Gibbon's *Decline and Fall of the Roman Empire* in March 1926, on his twenty-first birthday.

At a special ceremony held at the Sunday school on 17 January 1935, Frederic and his wife were presented with a silver salver, a silver rose bowl, and a check as signs of appreciation for their service. The only recorded rough spot in this long career occurred during a church council meeting in May 1917, when Frederic was criticized for allowing lay members of the church to help with the 8 A.M. communion. He had done so because he was without a curate during wartime; undoubtedly, he was eventually excused for this innovation, which is common today in the Church of England. The most conspicuous high points of his career were the dedication of memorials to soldiers who had been killed in action during World War I. The first memorial, a church plate donated by a local artist, was dedicated in the presence of the bishop of Gloucester, Bishop Frodsham. The second dedication occurred during the unveiling of the Amberley War Memorial on the Common by Sir Fabian Ware circa 1920. No other special events or problems are recorded, but the war changed Amberley greatly. Not only did some big munitions plants spring up nearby, but old customs that existed when Rex was a child were no longer in place after the war. Rex himself remembered that "Before the war 'May Day' was kept regularly by all the children in this or that village dancing round the village May-pole with sticks hung with garlands of flowers etc. Then it was put to the vote as to who should be 'Queen of the May.'"[6]

Frederic's final service in Amberley was held on 19 January 1935. He had decided to go to a smaller church where his then-weaker voice would be heard more clearly. According to local historian Roy K. Close,[7] Frederic was regarded as a man of "wide cultural attainment, kindly and sympathetic. . . ."[8] John Luce, Rex's younger cousin on his mother's side, told me that Frederic Ernest was not outstanding intellectually, but was a gentle person—a typical country rector. This is confirmed by Rex's own autobiography. Rex wrote there that he preferred being told Old Testament rather than New Testament stories at bedtime, because he could visualize them better. But he recounted that his father was shocked by some of these Old Testament stories, and could never believe, for instance, that "Abraham could have been told by God to sacrifice his son + that he should actually be prepared to do so." Frederic also "would point out that the story of the creation, excellent as a story, conflicted with known facts."

Frederic's progressive views caused him frequent, if mild, trouble. Rex remembered:

> In those days perhaps the majority of churchgoers still believed in the literal truth of the
> Bible + my father's modernistic ideas, as I discovered later, offended some of his

parishioners + scandalised a few of my aunts. But, as he never expressed his opinions with arrogance + was always ready to listen to the point of view of others, any offence he caused was seldom lasting. He was loved even by those who most resented what they considered his unorthodoxy. Such people were disarmed by his gentle tolerance, his way of treating every point of view, if sincerely held, with respect + perhaps by his genuine interest in + love for anything odd or eccentric.

To the end of his life Rex, like his father, loved odd historical facts which he cited with glee as if announcing the finding of treasure.

From 1935 until his death on 17 October 1937, Frederic served as the minister of the Church of St. John the Baptist in Great Rissington, about twenty-five miles from Amberley, also in the Cotswolds. He and Mrs. Warner were welcomed to their new parish by the lord and lady of Great Rissington manor, Maj. and Mrs. W. J. Paley Marling. When Frederic died in 1937, his annual stipend was £726; in Amberley it had been £553. Neither salary testifies to any great love of money, and for most of his own life, Rex never had much money either. Simultaneous memorial services were held at both churches, and again somewhat unusually for the time, Frederic was cremated in accordance with his own wishes.

This easygoing, nature-loving, liberal, gently progressive, and humane man was also a passionate butterfly and moth collector and, according to Rex's autobiography,

> He subscribed to Wordsworth's view that Heaven lies about us in our infancy + he, like Wordsworth, had spent his childhood in the country. One of my earliest memories is of being shown, + reverently handling the drawers in the cabinets that contained his fine collection of British butterflies + moths. Their names, particularly those of the butterflies, were an enchantment: Queen of Spain's Fritillary, Red Admiral, White Admiral, Camberwell Beauty, Purple Hair-Streak, Lulworth Skipper + many more. The moths, much more numerous than the butterflies + usually rather duller, were still fascinating enough + especially the top drawer of the cabinet which contained specimens of the Death's Head + other Hawk moths.

Rex learned not only passion for nature but also moral lessons from his father's collecting activities:

> There were specimens of nearly every variety of British butterflies in the collection, but strict moral or scientific rules governed their acceptance as full members. We had, for example, one specimen of the Camberwell Beauty + several of the Large Copper butterfly. These were said "not really to count" because the Camberwell Beauty was thought to

have been caught on the Continent + the Coppers had been bought from a dealer + given to my father without evidence of origin. Nothing "really counted" except specimens that had been caught or bred in the British Isles by a member of the family or a friend of known integrity.

Despite his father's rules, Rex sometimes became overenthusiastic in his desire to collect:

> But the discovery of a Purple Emperor was a dream never to be fulfilled, nor had we a specimen in the collection. I had been told that these magnificent + rare creatures could be attracted by the rotting carcase of a sheep + I would tentatively suggest that we could save up to buy a dead sheep in a suitable stage of decomposition, carry it to some remote glade, perhaps in the New Forest, + watch it day after day in the hope that some time we should see descending from a great height perhaps a speck, perhaps one or two, perhaps in the end a cloud of these great purple insects. But my father, while sympathising with the idea, foresaw difficulties not only with regard to the expense but also the transport involved + my mother considered the whole enterprise "a wicked waste. . . ."[9]

Rex later realized that

> this abortive plan for securing a Purple Emperor seems to indicate already something of the ruthlessness which is so common among collectors. I never gave a thought to the sheep or to the pollution of the fresh air. And I had forgotten, though only temporarily, the pleasures that surrounded me every day in finding + recognising other species just as beautiful as the Purple Emperor + which, though less rare, were new to me. In those days the sunny turf along the southern Cotswolds was full of butterflies + flowers.

For Christmas in 1910, when Rex was just five, he gave his father a "Book of Butterflies" containing colored drawings of various species.

Despite his mother's misgivings and insistence upon warm clothes, Rex's father liked to take him on nighttime excursions to hunt moths by means of "treacling," which involves painting a mixture of black treacle and rum on a few trees to attract the creatures. They could then be snared in the light of a lantern. This was exciting enough, but Frederic

> shared the common belief at that time that there was nothing small boys liked better than to listen to blood-curdling ghost stories, particularly in appropriately dark + mysterious surroundings. He was very good at telling stories + on our way through the dark woods I

would clutch his hand as I listened to such sentences as: "It had a big body + moved rather like a toad, but much faster. It had NO FACE + it came silently from behind trees. . . ."

When he heard such stories, Rex would "keep on looking back or around + would try to think of someone really brave like Achilles or Sir Richard Grenville, even though neither of those heroes, to my knowledge, had ever confronted the danger of faceless apparitions in the woods." Here we have the beginning of Rex's love of well-told stories and his attraction to epic heroes. This love was no doubt augmented by the presence around Amberley of many fossil beds and of two old deserted manor houses. One of these, Rodborough Manor, had greenhouses "all over-grown with ivy, convolvulus and weeds." The Woodchester Park deserted house had "most beautiful surroundings, a large wood with all kinds of trees and fine, large lakes."[10] At the age of twelve, obviously under the influence of these houses and his father's penchant for scary tales, he would concoct his own bloody ghost story centered on a deserted mansion, entitled "The Story of an empty house."[11] Despite his father's interest in telling him scary stories, Rex remembered most "the constant presence + support of his gentleness + understanding. I cannot remember ever hearing a harsh or unkind word from him + it was easy + natural for me to follow where he led."

Despite Frederic's gentle and relatively unambitious nature, he was from a very successful family. Originally, a "warriner" was someone who supervised the control of rabbits and other animals for the owners of large estates. But the first known Warners of Rex's family were country gentlemen, one step below aristocracy, owning large estates themselves, and living in a large house near the town of Botley in Hampshire.

Because Rex's great-grandfather Isaac Warner was a younger son, he did not inherit the property; Isaac's older brother William kept it. Isaac's twin brother (also named Frederic, as Rex's father would be) became a doctor, and Isaac entered a well-known firm of solicitors in Winchester, eventually becoming a senior partner. Isaac Warner married twice. His first wife, Susannah Witt, was the daughter of a merchant in the shipping business in Southampton. She had seven children. The most famous of these seven children was Rex's great-uncle George Frederic Warner, who became Keeper of the Manuscripts in the British Museum in 1904, was the author of numerous books, and was knighted upon his retirement in 1911. He used to send Rex some presents at Christmas, and died at the age of ninety-two. Isaac Warner's second wife, Mary Thring, had four children, three of whom entered the medical profession; one of these, Eleanor, was among the first women doctors in England.

The eldest of the seven children of Isaac and Susannah was Frederic Isaac Warner, Rex's grandfather, who followed his father Isaac Warner in becoming a solicitor in Winchester. His wife, Isabel Eastall, had been born in India. Frederic Isaac and Isabel also had seven children, one of whom died in infancy. Frederic Isaac did not like the law, and so prevented his sons from going into it; they chose the clergy, another solid occupation in the Victorian and Edwardian periods. The family firm of Warner and Richardson, however, still exists in Winchester. Law, medicine, teaching, and the clergy were to be the primary occupations of Rex's solidly professional extended family.

Of the six surviving children, Rex's uncles and aunts on his father's side, George Johns Stratton (1874-1966) was Rex's favorite. He was ordained, but never had a parish, and spent his whole career as a chaplain at a boys' school, Trent College. When a history of Trent College was written, a whole chapter was devoted to "Some activities of Mr. Warner."[12] He came to Trent in 1901, the year of Queen Victoria's death. George immediately collected a group of snakes, including the eight-foot boa constrictor, Barnabas, to eat rats and mice. He held classes in bird-skinning, a now almost defunct skill. He once organized a hike for the boys and himself, complete with a push-cart containing tents and blankets, from Trent to the Land's End, a distance of 350 miles. In addition, he instructed the boys in building a working, 200-foot bridge across the Trent River. During World War I, he became the commanding officer of the Officers' Training Corps at Trent, and instructed his men in drill and trench digging. This uncle took Rex camping in the Malvern Hills, about thirty miles southwest of Birmingham, and taught him how to catch and skin adders and to make bookmarks from their skins. He also took Rex on long bird-watching trips. The love of birds stayed with Rex throughout his life. At the age of twelve, he remarked about the country around Amberley that "In certain seasons large flocks of wild geese (generally gray leg geese) and Wild Ducks fly down over Gloucester to the Severn."[13] Rex would remember this when it came to titling his first important novel. George knew a lot about trees, and expected children, including Rex, to recognize 100 different species.

But unlike Rex, Uncle George was also a devoted fan of new technology. Even before it became popular to do so, he led school bicycle trips, much like the hero George— possibly named after him—of Rex's first serious novel, *The Wild Goose Chase*. He became addicted to motorbikes as soon as it was possible after World War I, motoring thousands of miles on them. Uncle George remained a bachelor all his life and also loved a good beer; Rex may have formed an attraction to alcohol based on George's influence.[14]

III. REX'S MOTHER AND THE LUCE FAMILY

Rex's mother's side of the family was just as rich in unusual uncles, and indeed aunts. John Luce reports a legend that the Luces were descended from Joan of Arc; that a substitute was burned at the stake, and she herself came over to Jersey, where the Luce family is from. The name given her by the King of France was Jean du Lis, and Lis was supposed to have become "Luce" in Jersey. Rex's mother Kathleen was an intelligent, organized, and disciplined person, much given to good works. In the 1920s and 1930s she gave Scripture and mathematics lessons at Gloucester High School for Girls, and was a moral influence on the whole school.

Kathleen was also a much stricter and more dominating person than Rex's gentle father. She never approved, for instance, of Frederic's occasional visits to the pub after services to meet his parishioners, when they lived in Great Rissington and the pub was near the church. (These visits were for socializing only, because Frederic never drank himself.) On at least one occasion, Rex's evangelistic aunt Dora Luce, who was visiting, caught Rex in the pub while Uncle George and his father—whose very presence in the pub would have shocked Aunt Dora—got away without being seen. Rex's own son George, now a biologist, remembers that once as a child he saw a fox near his grandmother Kathleen's house in Great Rissington and ran in excitedly to tell her. Instead of being delighted as he expected she would be, she phoned the Marlings' gamekeeper or Master of Fox Hounds to come and catch the fox. The animal was never caught, which made George very happy because he would have felt guilty otherwise. (In Kathleen's defense, it should be said that she probably thought that the fox would kill the neighborhood chickens.) He was also told that in the late 1930s his older brother Jonathan was riding in the back seat of her little Jowett car, and her window was open and snow was pouring in onto his lap. He complained, but she said that she needed to give hand-signals, so he had to continue freezing with a snowdrift building in his lap. She was a very strict person in George's remembrance, and Rex had difficulty dealing with her when she was older. She had the manner of a schoolmistress, that is, she was very idealistic, methodical, and principled. For instance, she would drive into Gloucester every day when she was teaching there in the 1930s, even when it was snowing hard. In her early days, she rode a motorbike, which was a very modern thing for a country vicar's wife to do.

No doubt Rex imbibed a certain discipline but also guilt from his mother's side, while his father's family tended more toward the tolerant, if not pleasure-loving. We can see a lifelong division in Rex between Hebraism and Hellenism, duty and enlightened hedonism, which was developing here, but it was not pronounced yet. And of course Kathleen may have been more tolerant when she was young and Rex was a child. John Luce feels that she had more energy than her husband (who sometimes suffered from severe migraine headaches) and may have felt restricted in the role of vicar's wife; he feels she would have made a good lady of the manor instead, which might account for some of her bossiness. (In fact, her best friend toward the end of her life was "Aunt" Helen Marling, the Mrs. Marling of the manor in Great Rissington.) She died on 11 May 1958 at a nursing home in Gloucester.

Kathleen was the daughter of a very devout and very strict churchman, John James Luce, and Alice Charles Stubbs, who were married in Islington on 9 April 1872, by Alice's brother Stewart Dixon Stubbs. They had thirteen children, two of whom died in their early childhood, as was common in those days. Alice Stubbs's cousin was the bishop of Oxford, and her brother Stewart was a vicar. John James, Kathleen's father, first worked in a poor parish in London as a curate. From 1872-78 he was at Cheltenham Parish Church, and after that he went to St. Nicholas in Gloucester, where he remained. In his "Essay on Gloucester," the boyish Rex described the circa-twelfth-century St. Nicholas church as

> extremely ancient . . . . At one time, this church was a place of sanctuary. It was attacked in the revolution under Cromwell and the tower bears marks of the bombardment to the present day. It has an extremely ancient knocker which represents the devil carrying away a drunkard on his back. The interior of the church has some exceedingly fine carving and a beautiful font.[15]

The atmosphere in Kathleen's parents' house was solemn.The whole family grew up in a repressed atmosphere, full of inhibitions; several of the children eventually reacted against John James and his views. Gordon Luce, Kathleen's brother and a very gifted man, told his son John, Rex's cousin, that as a child he was very frightened of his father, and that John James would spank him if he wet his bed. On one occasion when he was told at dinner that children should be seen and not heard, Gordon stood on his head on his chair and then calmly resumed the proper position, without saying anything.

John Luce recalls asking Rex why he had to write allegorically rather than directly, and Rex simply answered that he felt he must write that way. John believes that it might have been easier for Rex to write allegorically because, in view of the repressive upbringing that was transmitted from the Luce side, allegory masked his true feelings and presented them in code. Certainly Rex's writings, like those of most writers, presented personal events masked as public ones.

Of his mother Kathleen, Rex writes in his autobiography,

> The affection I felt for my mother at this time was, I think, of a more physical kind. I remember being held in her arms, clinging to her + covering her face with kisses for as long as I was allowed to do so. And I would say 'I love you, I love you' over + over again as I embraced her or was being embraced. I thought of her as being extraordinarily

beautiful + indeed she must have been beautiful at this time. It was a shock to me when (+ this happened on several occasions) I was taken to see her in bed, having been told that she was ill, + finding her with a flushed or strained face + somewhat dishevelled hair lying among the medical smells of a sick room.

Rex later learned that those "illnesses" were the aftermaths of several miscarriages. When his parents asked if he would like to have a little brother or sister, he found the question "acutely embarrassing." But Rex remained an only child, which was unusual in those days of large families; and he also had a happy childhood, which challenges the theory of those who claim that an unhappy childhood is essential for a writing career. It must have been very difficult for Kathleen Warner to let her only child go off to a boarding school at the age of eight, but she did so. Always interested in Rex's advancement, she was intrigued and proud when he began writing.

Three of her brothers—Frank Mowbray Luce (1878-1962), Arthur Aston Luce (1882-1976), and Gordon Hannington Luce (1889-1979)—were very close to Rex, and Arthur and especially Gordon became distinguished scholars. One sister, Rex's aunt Ethel (nicknamed "Lucy"), was a brilliant medical student and the first, or one of the first, female recipients of the Rockefeller scholarships for study in America. She eventually married the dean of the medical school at the University of Rochester, Samuel Clausen. She herself became a professor of medicine after receiving her M.D. at Trinity College, Dublin. When Samuel Clausen died and the McCarthy era began in America, she went back to England and took a house on the island of Jersey, although she retained her American citizenship. Despite her scientific bent, Lucy was fond of discussing religion with Rex. John Luce relates that at one point when Rex was already mature he told her that "what I really believe is that love is God and God is love, and in that sense I believe in God." Aunt Lucy was cremated in the Golder's Green crematorium, and her ashes were deposited in the family cemetery in Treadworth, Gloucester.

Two other sisters, Rex's aunts Dora and Grace Luce, were kind but strict religionists who lived in an "incredibly stuffy Evangelical atmosphere," as John Luce put it to me. They did not allow Rex to go to the movies on Sunday when he would visit them in Gloucester. Even the piano performance of Beethoven's "Apassionata" by Rex's cousin Sandra Luce was thought contrary to the solemn spirit of the day.

Arthur Aston Luce was a distinguished professor of philosophy and eventually (from 1946) vice provost of Trinity College, Dublin, where Rex's father had received his degree much earlier. In his *Views of Attica and Its Surroundings*, Rex recalled standing on the banks of the river Wye near Tintern Abbey,

> where once, as a boy, I listened to a philosophic uncle [undoubtedly Arthur] declaiming the famous words of Wordsworth. When he had finished, he paused and regarded me gravely. "Space-Time," he pronounced. "It is all a continuum." Only dimly apprehending his meaning, I gazed with new eyes on the dripping mossy walls and the green grass. Yet still that monkish and ruined past seemed indefinitely remote. Only the water there and the vegetation possessed for me the qualities of a vigorous permanence.[16]

Arthur became obsessed with George Berkeley's philosophy, and produced a major edition of his works and a biography. He also wrote on the turn-of-the-century French philosopher Henri Bergson, and wrote a book with the wonderful title *Fishing and Thinking*. Bertrand Russell referred to Arthur affectionately as "Rifleman Luce" because in World War I Arthur had disdained the role of chaplain and instead served as a captain in the 12th Royal Irish Rifles. Arthur said that he would not die, but would merely "immaterialize," and later wrote a book about this entitled *The Dialectic of Immaterialism*.

In 1964, a meeting of Trinity College Fellows was held to discuss whether or not women could become Fellows. Arthur Luce led the opposition to the acceptance of women; his cause failed, however, despite his wit. This was only one of many academic disputes in which Arthur was involved, sometimes to the point of obstinacy.[17]

Arthur Luce had a complex history, which accounted for his crankiness. Indeed,

> in the First World War he suffered severely from the psychological disturbance then known as shell-shock, and this probably inclined him towards extreme views and controversial attitudes; and in 1940 on a family fishing outing his wife and daughter were drowned almost before his eyes—a blow which he overcame by an impressive exercise of will-power, and which helped to mellow him. Most men contain some qualities which seem inconsistent with each other, but in Luce the opposites were to be seen in conflict almost every day.[18]

Arthur's opposite sides, with which Rex, too, had to contend, were

> The courteous host and the frosty disciplinarian; the conscientious and devoted servant of the College and the tenacious fighter for his rights and emoluments; the single-minded seeker after truth and the master of a repartee based on unfair pseudo-logic; the stern moralist and the very unorthodox churchman; the man of the world and the ill-informed

provincial; the stylist in words and the ignoramus in the sphere of the fine arts—what was one to make of such a mixture? At his best there were few men in College who commanded such respect and admiration; at his worst he drove his colleagues mad.[19]

Rex undoubtedly acquired his interest in Greek philosophy from Arthur, but he never at any point in his life took to trout fishing, perhaps because of its morbid associations. He may have learned to avoid some of Arthur's less admirable traits. Interestingly, the only novel of Rex's that Arthur—a staunch conservative—approved of was his boys' book, *The Kite*. John Arthur Luce, Arthur's son, also became a philosophy professor at Trinity College and later tutored Rex's oldest son, Jonathan, there. Like his father, John Arthur Luce served as vice provost of the university.

Rex's uncle Gordon Luce was a prodigy who read Greek at the age of six and was able even as a child to participate in those wonderfully literate Victorian parlor word games demanding that one decipher an anagram, or construct a poem out of a random question and a random noun. When barely the age of six, Gordon was given the question, "What is the time?" and the noun "pear" to weave into a poem. His on-the-spot response was

> The time is six
> I'm in a fix
> Mother says I'm to go to bed
> For to rest my weary head.
> But I said, "No, no, ma mere
> I would rather eat a pear."
> And so to my delight I ate,
> A nice ripe pear upon a plate.
> Now I am stuffed, said Gordon Luce,
> Now I shall waddle like a goose.
> So he went waddling down the street
> Eating pears; what a delightful treat![20]

Not many six year olds then or now—but there would be fewer now—could accomplish this. Rex's later admiration of the London *Times* crossword puzzle champions may have been based in part on his knowledge of Gordon's precocious mastery of words.

At Cambridge, Gordon Luce had become a member of the Apostles, hobnobbing on equal terms with students who would become the poets James Elroy Flecker and

Rupert Brooke, the novelist E. M. Forster, the economist John Maynard Keynes, and the Orientalist Arthur Waley. He knew the whole Bloomsbury set intimately, including writer Virginia Woolf, critic and writer David Garnett, and artist Duncan Grant, who painted Gordon's portrait. Once, Gordon came back to his room at Cambridge and found on his door a little poem from Lytton Strachey, the historian and member of the group, as follows: "Who is it that has tied/ his punt my punt beside?"—a punt being a pole-propelled small boat popular on the Cam River and in Oxford. When Gordon set sail for his first teaching job in Burma in 1912, he was accompanied as far as India by his friends R. C. Trevelyan (the brother of the important historian G. M. Trevelyan) and E. M. Forster, who used that very trip as the basis for his *Passage to India*. As a teenager Rex was scandalized that Gordon could shrug off Rupert Brooke's poetry, which Rex idolized. Gordon was very fond of Rex, and once when at Oxford Rex asked for money for a weekend in Paris, Gordon sent the money along with this ditty: "What else is an uncle for, but to pay for his nephew's whore?" He thought all of Rex's novels wonderful, and they would discuss literature together.

In Burma, Gordon Luce at first taught English but was told in 1920, when the University of Rangoon was formed by the British, that since he had married a beautiful Burmese in 1915 named Ma Tee Tee, he was no longer "English" enough for that position. Gordon had betrayed his "race" in the eyes of the orthodox. His own family was shocked by his marriage at first, but they came to love "Tee Tee" (a sound children make in Burma when they summon animals), especially since she was educated as a Christian, although her father's Christianity was a bit eccentric, something like Quakerism. She was not only very talented, but also generous, and therefore fit very well with the Luce family. Rex was generous himself, loaning money without stint to friends and relatives, even when he did not have much himself. When Gordon died, Rex was ready to pledge £2,000—then a large sum—to support Gordon's family if necessary.

With typical energy and because he came to love Burma, Gordon paid no attention to the insult of being fired and returned to England and France, where he studied Oriental languages at the London School of Oriental Studies and at the Sorbonne. He then returned to Burma where he received a position in the department of history at the new university. Subsequently, Gordon Luce became one of the greatest scholars of Burmese history in the twentieth century, while Tee Tee transformed herself into the beloved headmistress of a home for orphaned boys. She started the home because she and Gordon had sent their own children to be educated in England (in the English manner) and she felt the lack of them. Dressed as a man, she visited the slums of Rangoon and brought some poor boys back; those were her first students. Tee Tee became the first woman magistrate in Burma as well as the women's national tennis champion. She would say jokingly that she preferred France to England because in England everyone would stop to watch her play tennis, while in France people were more xenophobic and would not bother her when she was playing.

During World War II, Gordon and Tee Tee barely escaped the invading Japanese army because he insisted on photographing all the important Burmese artifacts while there was still time. He deposited these photographs in the national library before he left, but they were burned during the war. After the war, when Gordon and Tee Tee returned from India (to which they had fled on litters carried by tribesmen), he had to redo all of his previous work.

All visiting celebrities in Rangoon came to Gordon and Tee Tee, including Golda Meir and Edwina Mountbatten. Despite their services to the country, however, they were forced out of Burma in 1962 by a military dictatorship that did not like their criticism. They moved to the island of Jersey, ancestral home of the Luces, where Gordon completed his major life's work, the three-volume *Old Burma-Early Pagan*, published by New York University in 1969-70.

Ma Tee Tee was one of Rex's favorites, but although she liked his originality, she felt that at least during his Oxford years he was a bit wayward, and drank too much. Gordon provided him with a model of what genuine scholarship could be. When Gordon died on 3 May 1979, New York University's Institute of Fine Arts published a lengthy obituary, as did London University's School of Oriental and African Studies; previously in 1959, a Burmese publication devoted an entire issue to his career.[21]

Uncle Frank, while less distinguished than the other two Luce uncles, was also an enthusiastic outdoorsman and bird watcher and delighted in taking Rex on excursions. Rex expressed a candid, but loving, view of Uncle Frank on 12 December 1975 in a letter to an American friend, Paul Ryan:

> It was my uncle Frank Luce who was driven out of doors by his . . . wife . . . + read Homer in an air-raid shelter. He had played Rugger + cricket for Oxford + for Gloucestershire. He had been in the Indian civil service + was much incensed when, after spending three sleepless days + nights trying to organise flood relief in his district, he read in an Indian newspaper that, at the height of the emergency, he had been seen on a raft in a lake, playing the violin, an instrument of which he knew nothing. Of course he was compared to Nero. He was very keen on pig-sticking + used to send back to my mother huge stuffed + mounted heads of boars, which she didn't like at all. He also delighted me by giving me great chains of "tushes," the kind of thing that killed Adonis. He retired early, + devoted himself to betting on horses, cricket + birdwatching.

From all of the Warner and Luce uncles and Aunt Lucy, as well as from his father, Rex learned one essential lesson: that enthusiasm for a subject, whether it be butterfly collecting, bird watching, literature, medicine or Burmese history, makes life incomparably richer. He also learned that this enthusiasm, however great, must be practiced with absolute integrity. He retained his enthusiasm for bird watching, sports, and literature—if not for pig-sticking, medicine, or horse racing—right up to the end.

In the company of his extended family or by himself, the very young Rex spent many happy days searching for butterflies and watching birds and taking walks, until he went to a boarding school at the age of eight. He had a dog named Fido, a cat named Queenie, a hen, and a duck. There is no record of any extraordinary childhood deed or feat of intellect, although Rex had begun writing poetry by the age of nine.

Rex undoubtedly enjoyed roaming the hillsides and woods in the company of various friends, and certainly he took part in the Sunday school. He had a beautiful voice, and sometimes assisted his father as reader during the Sunday service when he was older. But from childhood on, he loved sports the most. When Rex was at Oxford and shortly after, he played Rugby for the Stroud Rugby Football Club, and was known as the "most dangerous man in the West of England," an epithet of which he was prouder than any other all his life. Once, John Luce says, he was passed the ball three times and got three tries in one game, which was quite a feat. During his teenage years at school, he was very strong and big for his age. As photographs from this time show, he was also very handsome. His face was rugged and he had a powerful frame that eventually reached six feet.

But not all was blissful in Amberley. Disease was a problem, and even measles could be deadly, causing the whole Amberley school to be closed during an epidemic. A printed Luce family poem written by John James, accompanied by a solemn family photograph, and dated Christmas 1912 when Rex was seven, first recounts the Luce family's triumphs for the year: a tour of Egypt and the Holy Land by father, mother, daughter Edith and nurse; Arthur Aston becoming a Fellow of his college; Gordon "fresh from Cambridge forthwith to Burma goes"; Ethel's love of physics and chemistry; Frank and his wife Cecily's work in India. The poem goes on, however, to state: "But life is not all sunshine, 'tis ever mixed with shade,/And we have sorrowed with dear Kath., while joyous for the aid/To her and Ernest brought; and glad are we to know/That Rex to them and us is spared, his cheery face to show." This undoubtedly refers to some terrible childhood disease from which Rex barely recovered.

Yet when Rex thought of Amberley, it was with unalloyed pleasure. This feeling is clear in one of his earliest recorded poems. Complete with childish typographical errors, it appears on a loose-leaf in a manuscript anthology notebook of poems[22] dedicated to his mother on her birthday, 17 September 1914, when he was nine and beginning his second year at St. George's:

Amberly, Amberley, place that I love
Place where I played with rapture and joy
At the sea there are cliffs around and above
But amberley is the true home for a boy

Fair waves the golden corn
The birds around do sing
The leaves away are born
By the soft wind of spring
In spring and earley summer
Amberley's like this
Cupid sends down in rapture
His arrow of sweet Bliss

Amberley the Fairest
The finest place I've known
Amberley the sweetest
That ever I've been shown.

CHAPTER TWO

HARPENDEN, 1913-1923

I. EARLY DAYS AT ST. GEORGE'S SCHOOL

Rex Warner began studying at St. George's School, in the pleasant town of Harpenden about twenty miles north of London, in the autumn term of 1913 at the age of eight. Sending children to a boarding school had been the established custom among the middle and upper classes in England for some time. Rex's parents chose St. George's because Sir Fabian Ware had recommended it and because it fit their own progressive but still religious educational leanings. During his ten years at this school, notwithstanding the trauma of World War I, Rex would progress from a homesick child to a prefect and finally to a confident head boy who had won many honors. These were crucial years for the formation of Rex's attitudes, and by the time he graduated, he had already become something of an athlete, a dandy, a socialist, and a writer. But whether or not he was always aware of it, he would also retain the respect for tradition, including Christian tradition, inculcated by the school.

No longer a private institution limited to paying customers, St. George's is now a state comprehensive school that also accepts some boarders. The boys' dormitories in which Rex was housed are gone, and there is a new wing in uninspired modern school architecture. Yet reminiscences of a more elegant past remain. The original Victorian main building and beautiful wooden chapel still stand, and the rear playing field looks out on the same miles of verdant rolling hills and woods. Rex spent ten years of his life, except for vacations, in this pleasant academic setting.

The influence of St. George's on his life was very great. Here he met contemporaries who would later become important cultural figures: social philosopher Michael Oakeshott (a few forms ahead but a great boyhood friend) and Kenneth Horne, famous during World War II for his radio show "Much Binding in the Marsh." Lennox Berkeley the composer was also a St. George's student a few forms ahead of Rex, and both were in the Debating Society. Here Rex also met Marion and David Grove, the sister and brother of his wife-to-be Frances, who herself began Form Ib of St. George's in the winter term of 1916. The students were mainly the children of doctors, solicitors, clergymen, teachers, and engineers, and destined to take their places in the professions and cultural life of England (and America) in their turn. Much later, when she was with Rex at the University of Connecticut, Frances would teach in a Montessori school there; Maria Montessori herself visited St. George's in 1919 and 1925, and "on each occasion was accorded an overwhelmingly enthusiastic welcome from pupils and parents alike."[1]

At first the new pupil was homesick, as his letter of 25 September 1913 to his mother, who was staying at St. Nicholas Vicarage, Gloucester, her parents' home, reveals:

> Dear Mother, what day do you go back to Amberley. I feell a bit homesick I will write a letter each day. Pleas do to. pleas dont give me my pocket money this year. and by a cake with it for G[small g crossed out]race and Ethel do all you can for Fido, Qeeny and her kitten and dont kill her kitten.
> Love from Rex
> P.s. dont forget about the cake.

An undated letter written very soon after this one repeats the themes of the first in a similarly touching way:

> Dear Mother, Mrs Grant gives us sweets every day and reads to us on Sundays. Pleas be affuly kind to Fido + co. I cant think of much to say, but dont forget about the cake I really mean it, and dont kill the kitten. I hope you are getting on well and that Daddy has no more headaches. Love from Rex[2]

Rex himself seems to have been ill frequently. Although gas lighting and hot water radiators were installed in the school in 1913,[3] substantially improving its physical comfort, the children were required to sleep with windows open, and temperatures got very cold. (The habit stuck. When he was teaching at the University of Connecticut in the 1960s and 1970s, students remarked that his first act upon entering the seminar room was to open the windows, even in winter.) In one undated letter, Rex wrote that the milk was frozen at breakfast. There was also a typical problem with bullying: another early letter home states that "cadwallider is not at all a nice boy he is bullying allover the place I cant think of anything to say because I am in bed I was second in the formlist." Yet there were exciting things, too, during this first school year, like a lecture by one of the men in the Scott polar expedition.

During the ten important years that Rex was at St. George's, he was grounded in values from which he could never quite escape, for good and for ill. The school instilled ideals of friendship, trust, fair play, and duty, but also guilt for lapses from these ideals. The central feature of St. George's, architecturally and morally, was its chapel. In 1914, Rex's first academic year at St. George's, skilled pupils were carving the oak panels for the chapel walls under the guidance of a master.[4] The high quality of these panels shows how important the job was to the students. The children would attend the Anglican service during Morning Chapel for fifteen minutes and Evening Chapel for ten minutes every day. Chapel was of course required on Sunday, and long sermons had to be endured. Yet the repetition and beauty of these rituals also undoubtedly inscribed them and their message forever in Rex's mind. Rex's own father would give a guest address in that chapel during the winter term of 1921.

Self-development along Christian lines was the school's basic philosophy, with the arts playing a prominent role. In a manuscript notebook[5] entitled "Poems. 1917-1918, '19," Rex has a poem (probably written in early 1919, when he was 14) to "St. George's school Chapel," clearly revealing his affection for this impressive building:

> A beauteous place wherein the painter's art
>   Unites with music's glorious harmony,
> The carver's work with other crafts take part
>   In making God's house beautiful to see.
> Then let us worship God with fuller heart
>   In such a house of love & peace & ruth,
> Where all around us we see glorious art
>   And Beauty dwelling in the house of Truth.

Keatsian influence is obvious in the last line, which echoes the "Ode on a Grecian Urn." The poem probably expresses a genuine feeling of piety on Rex's part at this early age, which would endear him to the headmaster.

The person filling that role during Rex's day was Cecil Grant, M.A. (1870-1946), a gaunt, reserved, and rather forbidding-looking Church of England cleric who exemplified Victorian earnestness. The biggest influence on him, apart from Christian doctrine, was John Ruskin, the Victorian apostle of the Gothic and of hard work, but there were other influences as well. According to the memoir of one St. George's alumnus, "The Bible . . . the Greeks, and English literature, especially English poetry, were the food of Grant's inspiration" and so, it must be noted, of Rex Warner's as well. Moreover, Grant felt that the best profession for a Georgian was the Church, but if a student felt inadequate for that, he might become a schoolteacher. The memoir writer adds that Grant claimed "that the best things in life do not come to the rich, and that his advice to a young man would be to choose his career quite regardless of money considerations and even to face poverty for a time."[6] Clearly Grant influenced Rex, who became a schoolmaster after graduation from Oxford, and was poor for most of the thirties and forties, even though he didn't particularly want to be.

Grant's high moral tone was typical of pre-World War I schools, but St. George's had some unique features, particularly coeducation. Owing to the influence of "Keck" (as Grant was known to the pupils), St. George's was one of the first three coeducational schools in England. Pam Weatherley, the school historian, tells us that he had "become very interested in co-education" after a "visit to America where it was a fairly common practice."[7] In fact, coeducation would become the "cornerstone of St. George's School where children could live in an atmosphere closely related to family life, based on sound Christian principles."[8] The sexes mixed very well and there was even a certain camaraderie. According to one alumnus, the boys "always referred to the girls as the 'Stags' and the girls referred to the boys good humouredly as the 'Louts.'"[9] There was very little, if any, dalliance between the sexes, and never a pregnancy.

In *The Case for Co-Education*, which he coauthored with Norman Hodgson and published in the year that Rex entered the school, Cecil Grant set forth his philosophy of education, including the ideas that "without moral security intellectual brilliance is but a useless and dangerous toy" and that "above all . . . it is the individual who matters, and not the school or the community."[10] These principles would be important for Rex throughout his life. Rex rose from the ranks to become head boy on the field in his last year, while Stephen Luke, later knighted, became head boy in the house. A photo shows Rex standing right next to Grant, a sure mark of distinction. And in a telling sign of Grant's strong influence on him, Rex went on to Wadham College, Grant's own alma mater.

II. REX THE ATHLETE AND AESTHETE

No doubt the respect Rex felt for Cecil Grant while he was a student at St. George's was mutual. In his last two years, Rex won every conceivable honor the school could bestow: school prefect, captain of football, captain of cricket, and essay writing prizes. It is hard to overestimate these honors. The professor and writer Donald Shojai, who went to St. George's in the 1950s and was a prefect there, said that he could never again rise so high in life. Being head boy carries an enormous status: the head boy would eat first, leaving second choice to all the rest; the head boy would also bathe first, bequeathing his dirty water to those who followed in the same bathtub. These were only some smaller perks of the position.

An important factor that allowed Rex to attain a high position in the school was his athletic ability. Rex was later to comment that the school was notable for its attention to sports, if not for winning. In this very sports-conscious school, Rex was noticed for his prowess in Rugby, cricket, and running. By 1923, he was clearly an exceptional athlete. "Fox," as he was known to his friends, was captain of football from 1921 on, and made a powerful impression as a forward. (Of course football in England means Rugby, not the American game.) In a game against Mill Hill on 10 December 1921, "The best feature of the match was the brilliant forward rushes led by Warner, which often took the ball more than half the length of the field. Grove played a great game forward and deserved his cap." David Grove, later his brother-in-law, was Rex's vice-captain.[11] The description of the 1st XV, the best team, in the football retrospect for 1919 includes "R.E. Warner, Captain (1918-19).-Forward, 9 st. 12 lbs. [134 pounds]. Has set a great example of keenness and humility. Always a dangerous forward who often scores through his pace. Handling excellent, and tackling and kicking much improved. Must develop his qualities of leadership, think out his plan of attack, and make his presence more markedly felt."[12] Rex improved his leadership, because the final football retrospective for the 1922-23 season reads:

> So far we have not mentioned our Captain. The reason for the omission may have been guessed. On paper he is among the forwards, and certainly he is there pushing the hardest, following up ahead of everyone, conspicuous at line-outs; but he is also to be found giving inspiration to the three's, bucking up ready for a pass, or serving as our last line of defence, and saving our lines with really brilliant tackles. He is ubiquitous. He has been, as we expect him to be, the inspiration of the whole team.

And the critique lists him as a forward weighing 10 st. 6 lbs. [146 pounds] and adds, "The mainstay and inspiration of the XV. A most dangerous follow-up; tackles with deadly certainty. Being fast and always in good condition he can cover up mistakes whenever they occur. Has over and over again saved our lines and made tries possible by closely backing up our 'threes.'"[13] Rex was later to admit that as a student he had prayed for success on the sports field rather more than he had for academic success. To some degree, the powerfully built Rex remained a boy all his life who never again, in his own eyes, equaled his achievements as a Rugby player in his late teens and early twenties.

Cricket was also a good game for Rex, although he did not favor it as much as Rugby. In 1917, he wrote a beautifully precise essay describing the rules of cricket, accompanied by a superb diagram of the positions of the players.[14] Already in July 1919, the school reporter informs us that "Warner and Langdon-Davis have shown themselves invaluable bowlers ["pitchers" in baseball parlance], who have on several occasions saved the side from defeat. . . ."[15] By 1922 he had received his cricket colors, and the Georgian noted that he is "without doubt the team's best bowler, maintaining an excellent length. Batting improved considerably."[16] The final cricket "character" for Rex reads "R. E. Warner (Captain). Led the School team during this last and most successful season. Had developed an eye for the field. He proved our most successful bowler, and made full use of his discovery that few school boys of to-day will hit the well-tossed-up ball. His run, serve, and action all helped him. Made runs when the side really needed them." In his last year, St. George's beat Dunstable Grammar School in "The most sensational match of the season, possibly in the history of St. George's."[17] Rex was not only strong and well coordinated, but fast too. In the display case in the school dining room there are still several cups with Rex's achievements in running inscribed on them. His first victory in this area, in the under-12 boys' 100 yards, is listed in the *Georgian* for July 1916.[18] In 1919 he came in third in a 220-yard race. In 1921 he came in first in the under-16 100-yard dash, with a time of 11 4/5 seconds. But perhaps his finest achievements occurred during 1922:

> Warner ran extremely well in all flat races, and won the 1/4 Mile, 1/2 Mile, and Mile. In the Mile he made a magnificent finish, his time being equal to that of the School record. This was one of the finest races ever witnessed at St. George's; all the runners kept so well together that it was impossible to foresee the winner until the last lap was half spent. At the finish the first four to reach the tape were within a few yards of one another.[19]

In the 440, Rex's time was 58 seconds, and he completed the 880-yard race in 2 minutes, 20 and 4/5 seconds. He also took part in boxing, winning the under-10 stone [140 pounds] competition in 1921, because of "greater experience and longer reach."[20]

Rex's appointment as full school prefect, undoubtedly the result of his qualities of leadership, is announced in the summer 1921 issue of the *Georgian*. It is not an easy job to instill discipline and serve as a model in a school of boisterous young boys and girls. A student's letter of March 1929 to his parents reveals the crudity of life in a boys' dormitory at the school, including pranks that probably occurred during Rex's years there as well:

> Something really funny happens in the lavs sometimes. I don't know if I ought to tell you; you might be shocked. But I'll risk it. The cubicles are side by side, ten of them, and are all served by one cistern at one end. No plugs to pull. When the cistern is full, there's a gurgle and a whoosh and water rushes along underneath you whether you're there or not. When it's full again, the same thing happens. Well, after breakfast there's usually a full house, so a boy bags the top cubicle, pulls off about half a roll of paper and crumples it up ready. Then just before the whoosh he lights it with a match and the water takes the fire down the row of bottoms. It's funny to hear the squawks, one after the other. Sorry Mum. Hope you aren't too shocked.[21]

Undoubtedly, Rex was respected as prefect because in addition to being a "hearty" (or athletic) type he was also something of a rakish teenage "aesthete," interested in style. One classmate recalls that Rex liked to have his shirt hang out slightly, and that other boys who admired him did the same. John Brandon-Jones, however, does not see this in an entirely positive light:

> My only clear memory after some seventy years, is that Warner was, in those days, a bit of a "dandy" and more conscious than most of us of sartorial propriety. He would make cutting remarks about the clothing of boys whose shorts were too short or too long or whose shirts were too loose or too tight. Teachers and parents thought that our shirts should be tucked tightly into our shorts but Warner tried to persuade us to follow his example in wearing his shirt slightly pulled out, in the way that the girls wore their blouses![22]

This is probably an accurate memory, because during his time at Oxford he was a full-blown dandy, as his wife Frances remembers. He thus exemplifies the "children of the sun" phenomenon of the 1920s described so well by Martin Green, with attention to the body beautiful as one of its most important features. Rex's sartorially extravagant touch, so typical of the 1920s, represented a reaction to the difficult 1914-18 war years.

Outside of his desire to impose conformity in clothes, Rex is remembered as having been kind to the younger boys, and not a bully. He was a strong model, noted for all-around prowess in school activities. One alumnus recalls that Rex made excellent drawings of men in armor; another that he sang in choir. Michael Oakeshott (now deceased) wrote me that "He was, even in those days, a remarkably thoughtful boy +

a strong, very self-contained character. I remember . . . we used to talk together about books we were both reading eg. Keats' poems + Tolstoy's *Childhood, Boyhood + Youth*."[23] Oakeshott's memory was very good: as the school magazine shows, Rex read a paper on Keats when he was head of the literary society, and we have seen the influence of Keats on his poetry. Rex also had a good sense of humor. During a Gilbert and Sullivan concert, in a deliberately off-key voice, Rex sang the solo from *Patience* that includes the line, "If you walk down Piccadilly with a poppy or a lily in your medieval hand," which caused an uproar from the audience, since "Poppy" was the nickname of a very sedate housemistress.[24] Rex's sense of humor would also carry over into his writing.

A letter of 22 January 1916 to his mother proudly revealed the beginning of his career as a published writer: "We have got our Georgians now, and a letter of mine is in it. When I send you the *Georgian* you will know it because it is the only letter signed R. E. W."[25] The published letter's quiet but effective wit points to things to come:

> Dear Sir,-I see no reason why the Lower School (or at least IIIa) [Rex's form] should not do War work; even the lowest forms could employ themselves by brushing away leaves and such like accomplishments. Each form could do War work in the period which the majority of the form liked least. War work could certainly be done in Geography time, as Europe will be very much altered at the end of the war.

The editor's answer is, "Though R.E.W. seems to have a curious idea of the purpose of war work, the demand of the Lower School to be included in the scheme is to be commended, and the Editor promises to consult the official of the Labour Bureau on the matter."[26]

This publication was preceded by much unpublished writing. Since a prolific output is the surest sign of a writerly future, it is significant that while at school Rex seems to have consistently written poetry as well as letters and short articles. Over the course of his school writing career, he progressed from traditional themes and forms to a Swinburnean aestheticism.

The cover of the 1914 manuscript anthology that also contains Rex's loose-leaf "Amberley" poem reads,

> This book of Poems is
> Entirly Dedacated
> To My Mother.

From REX.
Wishing her many happy
Returns for her birthday.
September 17, 1914

This anthology provides testimony about Rex's abilities and tastes at the age of nine. It includes, among other budding efforts (some of which were undoubtedly influenced by children's books and rhymes), the following: "The Eagle" ("King of Birds invincible./Thou well art called a king;/ No Kite nor any bird of prey/Can beat thee on the wing."), "The Birds" ("O little birds that fly about/And sing in every tree/Tell me the secret of your song/And I your friend will be"), and "Black Panther" ("Black Panther, Black Panther,/Thou strongest of all,/Black Panther, Black Panther,/Thou never shalt fall,/By the hand of any man.")

A common theme in almost all of these poems is the love of nature, especially bird watching, which Rex learned from his father and uncles. In a letter of 11 June 1916 to his parents he mentioned that

When Eurich and I were going out for a walk today we caught 19 caterpillars, they are all the same kind though vary a *little* in marking and feed on hazel leaves. They are crimson and black and white with a hump near were their head ought to be and covered with hairs. I have drawn what Eurich would call a very rough sketch of one. Radford has caught two small fish whitch he says he is going to feed on Horlicks malted milk tablets till they come to the size of whales when they will be consumed. If they do not thrive then Beecham Pills will be administered and after that Carters little liver pills.

In addition to nature, patriotism and war are important themes in these writings. An early but undated letter to his mother states that he has been "making some more poetry" and this example follows:

Sons of the Empire for Englands sake,
Still fight and fall together,
A still greater Empire our sons must make
United we stand for ever.
O God our mighty Lord
Be with us as of old
Lift up thy awfull sword
and make our nation bold

III. THE WAR

The presence of martial poems in Rex's reading and writing during 1914-18 is not merely an affirmation of a typical boyish interest. The beginning of Rex's second year at St. George's coincided with the start of World War I in August 1914. Although Grant was against militarism and tried to maintain a normal atmosphere, Rex's next four years, from age nine to thirteen, were inescapably full of war.

An undated letter home says that "there is a lot of soldiers staying here and also at Harpenden we make great freinds with them we had a football mach with them on Saturday."[27] In fact, between 4,000 and 5,000 troops were stationed near Harpenden at the beginning of the autumn term in 1914. The *Georgian* notes, too, that

> Maps of the area affected by the war are up in the form rooms, and the positions of the respective armies are marked out from time to time with small flags on most of them. "Weekly Questions," too, have been devoted to explaining the causes remote and recent of the actual outbreak, the reasons for Germany's rush forward, and the importance of ending the struggle as soon as possible. It would seem that the war has permeated every side of school life, and even if the results are not at first very obvious, its influence is always felt working beneath the surface. H.R.

A poem blaming the Germans for the conflict and vowing revenge follows this statement.[28] Yet in the July issue before the war began, the Georgian also carried an approving review of an antiwar book, showing that there was some balance in the school.

On unattached sheets in Frances Warner's possession we find more war poetry, this time obviously much more mature-perhaps written when Rex was fifteen or sixteen, and accompanied by very good drawings. The spelling and grammar are much improved, but the heroic theme continues to prevail.

> A Viking's Song
> Our home is on the ocean,
>   Our swords are in our hands,
> We love to have the notion
>   Of finding distant lands.
>
> We give all cities to the sword,
>   And then, when rich with gold

We'll sail onward, ever onward
  Till we land with wealth untold.
        so we'll sail in the swans bath
        We'll follow the whales path
        Till we find the distant lands.

Our home is on the ocean,
  Our swords are in our hands,
And we love to have the notion
  Of finding distant lands.

There is also a two-page prose piece "Vae Victus" ("Woe to the Vanquished"), singing the praises of an English victory over the Norsemen.

The heroic tone of such poems, which Rex wrote during and shortly after the war years, shows only one side of his feelings. He could not be oblivious to the pain as well as the bravery caused by the war. The chapel walls at St. George's are filled with wooden plaques carved by the students themselves, each giving one or more names of "old boys" who were killed. Older alumni still remember the grim 1914-18 years, during which Cecil Grant would deliver a somber sermon every week and, when necessary, read the names of the former St. George's boys killed since the previous memorial service. Out of sixty-four Georgians who fought in World War I, nineteen died. Rex did not have an older brother about whom to worry, as no doubt several of his classmates did. But his uncle Arthur, in the Irish Rifles, was a combatant in constant danger who eventually became severely shell-shocked.

The war's profound blow to the Victorian and Edwardian ideal of progress becomes clear in Grant's sermon of 1917:

> We believed above all in the gradual penetration of Christian standards and Christian ideals, and argued that to live in the twentieth century after Christ must somehow be better than to have lived in the fifteenth or tenth or fifth, and a *fortiori* better still than to have lived in the benighted centuries before the incarnation of God among men.

> Well! we were wrong; and now we are *proved* to have been wrong. . . . In fact we are quite unable to establish our superiority at any point in life conduct or morals over the citizens of imperial Athens or republican Rome.[29]

Terrible incredulity and disappointment resonate beneath every word.

But perhaps fortunately, children seem to listen very little or very selectively to sermons, and the full force of Grant's demoralization may not have been clear to the young Rex sitting in his audience. In an essay of 1917 entitled "Effect of the war on England. (assuming we win)," Rex sounds more hopeful than Grant did:

> There will be . . . less distinction of classes after the war, and also the war will be of great moral and social value. There is some talk that there will be a league of nations that have signed a treaty not to go to war again. . . . The shipbuilding trade will flourish after the war as all the ships that have been sunk will have to be rebuilt. . . . This war will bring America and France and our other allies closer to England. . . . Munitions workers will of course lose their jobs but owing to thousands of soldiers killed in the war there will be no lack of labour. . . . For years Englishmen will remember with pride the retreat from the Dardanelles . . . and the subsequent capture of Baghdad.

There follows a patriotic poem about a knight and his son.[30] Apparently, Rex was shielded by youth from the full impact of Grant's intellectual shock and grief.

On Armistice Day, 11 November 1918, Cecil Grant danced publicly, and a day holiday was declared. Despite the dampness and chill of the day, sports events were held as a celebration. Rex was there in some large, dirty football boots that deterred a girl from wheeling him in the wheelbarrow race. A poem in the 1917-19 manuscript notebook is entitled "August 4, 1918"; by this date the Allies had won significant victories on the Marne and the end of the war could be glimpsed. The poem clearly expresses Rex's patriotic schoolboy sentiments on this day as well as a widely shared hope for a new world.

> Now four long years of dreadful war have passed,
> Four years of misery and endless wrong
> And men cry out "How long O Lord, how long
> Shall tyrants prosper and oppression last."
>
> With clouds the sky of Europe is oercast,
> And these long years of endless loss of life
> Have made us long for peace and end of strife
> But ever in our minds let this stand fast—
> We went to war for freedom, let us fight
> To the last man for liberty and right,
> Till this is gained let warfare never cease.

Then, when the day is ours, the battle won,
When strife is finished and the long war done,
Then let a new world rise from the long-sought peace.

All was not well, however, when the war ended. The war was followed by the fear caused by the great influenza epidemic of 1918. Although St. George's seems to have been spared deaths, there was no issue of the *Georgian* in December 1918 because the editor had the disease. A few short months after the armistice, on 8 February 1919, Grant preached a sermon indicating his wariness of the tentative new political world that was coming into being: "But suppose the League of Nations successfully constituted, will the world be at peace? What of Russia? What of Poland, where the Poles have begun their new career as a nation by a wholesale murder of Jews?" Did Rex's horror upon viewing the Nazi concentration camps, which he visited immediately at the end of World War II, have its dim precursor here? The students' "Near East Relief Group," whose secretary was Marion Grove, Frances's sister, was well aware of the Armenian massacres, as this July 1919 *Georgian* entry indicates: "The war-sufferings of Belgium and France, grievous as they were, cannot be compared with those of Serbia and Armenia, which moreover in Armenia's case, followed hard upon the blackest record of oppression in modern history."[31] Rex took his turn serving on this committee.

Surprisingly, Rex may have imbibed socialism as well as Christian charity at St. George's. An essay in the following issue of the *Georgian* on "Socialism as It Is!" claims that "The truly inspired men of all ages, such as Langland, and all those who have served their fellows best throughout history, are to be numbered in the roll of true Socialists."[32]

Moreover, Rex's form in 1919 was known as "the form where the budding politicians live," and was studying home affairs rather than other areas of the world. A report on these studies in the *Georgian* states, "It is noticeable that the majority [of the form] has gone very strongly over to the Left. The Government of our own country has come in for far more criticism than support. It has been difficult sometimes to adjust the balance of opinion, especially, for instance, in the matter of our policy in Russia. The Russian delegates have shown a marked tendency to support Bolshevism. . . ."[33] Certainly, the reason for this political shift is that Grant had implanted Ruskin's proto-socialist ideas and harmonized them with Christianity, and after several grim years of war and moral failure, the Russian Revolution seemed to bring hope for genuine change. Rex would later describe himself in his twenties as a religious Marxist.

Very explicit indications of Rex's interest in social justice can be seen in some poems of 1919 in the "Poems. 1917-18, '19" manuscript notebook, particularly in one obviously modeled on Blake's "London," and entitled "A Reproach":

> In the dim back streets of the London slums
>> There is endless misery.
> No ray of cheer or comfort comes
>> To these dens of poverty.
>
> They have lost all hope of help or release,
>> These slaves of poverty.
> Slaves, that dwell in a land of ease,
>> A land that is called free.

IV. REX'S LITERARY GROWTH

Perhaps the clearest sign of Rex's purely literary tendency at a precocious age is a one-act play entitled "A Venetian Tragedy" that we find in his manuscript notebook, and which dates to 1919. Although brief, it is skillful in that it is written in blank verse and divided into scenes. The plot, however, is clichéd: Lorenzo, a poor Venetian, is in love with the Lady Dolorosa, whose rich father, Norbert, is blocking their romance because of Lorenzo's poverty. Dolorosa's monologue in scene two, "A turret in Norbert's house," is typical of the stagey, pseudo-Shakespearean language of the play:

> [The Lady Dolorosa spinning]
> *Dol* O woeful sorrow of the prisoner!
> Withheld from love & all that life holds dear.
> I would that I were free, & I might feel
> Lorenzo's arms about me & could hear
> The whispered protestations of his love.
> But never more his face will bless my sight.
> For I am an unhappy prisoner.
> O cruel, grim + blank grew walls
> That hold me from the essence of my life!

* * *

Yet even here I feel his love with me
And even hence my heart can fly to him.

But the song that immediately follows shows some lyrical talent:

Though prison walls ourselves do part,
    Though miles of distance do us sever,
Thy love will dwell within my heart,
    For love lives on for ever.

Nations, powers & cities too
    Pass away remembered never,
Always I'll remember you,
    For love lives on for ever.

Rex also gives Lorenzo a beautiful expression of the idea of afterlife:

We cannot disbelieve in future life,
Seeing around us Nature's parables.
Mark thou the worm that only eats & sleeps
Until it seems to die—then does it rise
Up beautiful & free as air, not worm
But butterfly. E'en so are we on earth
As worms without true thought, but when we
die
We rise transformed into some lovely thing.

The idea of life after death is the only comfort conveyed by the play's tragic action. Lorenzo and his friend Pietro smuggle a rope to Dolorosa and she climbs down to them. Just when they are about to take her off in a boat, Norbert and his three sons enter. Pietro is killed, as well as Dolorosa's brothers. She springs between Norbert and Lorenzo and Lorenzo stabs her by mistake. He then kills Norbert and throws himself into the canal. The action of this tragedy occupies only ten and a half small notebook pages. While scarcely original, it is deftly handled. This little play shows that even as a schoolboy of fourteen or probably fifteen, Rex had mastered the conventions of Elizabethan drama.

A poem immediately following the end of this play in the manuscript notebook is dedicated to the appearance and reality motif and a reverse view of the beautiful butterfly transformation that Rex used in the play to express the idea of an afterlife.

The Glowworm.
During a cold & wintry night
    I saw a radiance by the way,
A shining piece of heavenly light
    That told of happiness & day.

I picked it up & guarded it,
    To see it in the light of day,
Wond'ring what beauteous form was fit
    To shine with such a glorious ray.

Day came, & full of joy & awe
    I looked upon the wondrous thing.
A great & ugly worm I saw,
    Without a light, without a wing.

Given Rex's age (probably fifteen), these examples show a surprising maturity. Even more impressive is another play entitled "Thomas a Becket; a short drama." Probably written a few years after "A Venetian Tragedy," it contains twenty-five pages of blank verse and very creditable dialogue.[34]

Rex's similarly skillful, and probably more original prose writing can be seen around the same time, in his 1919 review of *The Shaving of Shagpat* by George Meredith, the now-unread (but then, celebrity) novelist:

This book is utterly different from all others by the same author; it is far less difficult to read and, in fact, is so engrossing that when once taken up it is difficult to lay down. It resembles the Arabian Nights stories, but in my opinion, is far more beautifully worded, and contains deeper wisdom and fresher humour. It is an allegory, but does not forcibly strike our attention as such; and its fruits of wisdom and advice are surrounded by flowers of humour and excitement. The prose is interspersed with short verses which offer both variety and pleasure to the reader.[35]

Rex here outlines the very direction that he would take as a mature writer. He himself would be committed to allegory, which "does not forcibly strike our attention as such"; and his novel *The Wild Goose Chase* would intersperse prose and verse. The review also shows a critical mind, for Rex comments that what he dislikes in the Meredith book is that the main character is predestined to succeed, and the impossibility of him ever failing "detracts a great part of our pride in him with the deed accomplished. We feel that it would have been far more glorious fighting against destiny than with it." With regard to fantasy, with which allegory is so closely associated, a library note of 1923 mentions that William Morris's *Roots of the Mountain*—also a favorite of T. E. Lawrence's—and Morris's other romances "seem popular in the upper part of the School. The mingling of the fairy story with adventure and high romance of chivalry should appeal to many more" students.[36]

Given his literary precocity, it is not surprising that in 1922 Rex became president of the Literary Society, whose terminal report states,

> It was decided that the activities of the Society this term should be confined to the Elizabethan period of Literature, although general papers might be read. Although the discussions have not reached their usual standard this term, the two papers on "The Appreciation of Poetry" were exceptionally good. Papers have also been read on "The Sonnet," "Shakespeare's Originality," and "Elizabethan Lyrics." The following Plays have also been read:- "Antony and Cleopatra," "Dr. Faustus," and "The Merchant of Venice."

It is undoubtedly the latter, already read a few years earlier by Rex, that contributed to "A Venetian Tragedy."

Rex was interested not only in modern, but also in ancient literature. In his "Memories," Maurice Bowra says that when Rex arrived at Wadham College, it was clear that he had been badly taught in the classics. Rex himself later echoed this opinion, and the fact that it took him three tries to get a scholarship to Wadham may be proof of that statement. He almost got one the first time; then he failed completely; and only on the third try did he succeed, earning 80 pounds, almost sufficient to pay all his costs.

But whether or not St. George's training in the classics was excellent, the school did instill a love of literature in Rex, and love of one's subject is perhaps the best result of any education. In his address at Rider College, New Jersey, upon receiving an honorary doctorate in 1968, Rex said,

> When I look back upon a largely mis-spent youth, I find much to reject, much to be ashamed of. I regret that I either could or would not learn anything but the crudest elements of mathematics; I regret that under our rather antiquated system hardly anyone studied biology; I wish that I had been kinder to the French teacher; + I am deeply ashamed to think how fervently I used to pray to God that He would ensure my personal success in football, cricket or on the track. This seemed to me, I blush to say, very

important to the nature of things. But there are one or two things which I do not regret + of which I am not ashamed. One is that I always loved literature (+ of course English literature was the most easily accessible.) The other is that I managed rather painfully to acquire some small knowledge of Greek + Latin.[37]

A testimony to the importance of the classics at St. George's is that in Rex's personal library one finds *Scriptorum Classicorum Bibliotheca Oxoniensis*, edited by Gilbert Murray and published in London by Humphrey Milford, 1913; it was awarded to Rex in July 1923 because he was "leaving as a School Prefect" and for "Ten Years at St. George's." One of the books in the set was his lifetime favorite, Thucydides' *Peloponnesian War*, of which he would become perhaps the finest modern translator.

Rex had his teachers to thank for these lasting enthusiasms. They were not, after all, a usual lot. Madame Reider, the French teacher (to whom Rex regretted not having been kinder), was an original member of the League of Nations, and acquired from Prince Feisal, Lawrence of Arabia's associate, a flag of the new (and short-lived) Sherifian Arabia for the school museum. H. W. Howe later left to become headmaster of Keswick School, but while at St. George's reported on American sport, thus perhaps planting an interest in America in Rex's mind.[38] Mr. (later Dr.) Arthur Watts was a wonderful English teacher, and read a paper to the Literary Society when Rex was head of it. His favorite sayings were: "Never two words where one will do," "Use Anglo-Saxon terms where possible," and "If you use Classical words they should enrich and not debase the meaning."[39] In his later life Rex was not without failings, but wordiness and pretension were not among them. Teachers such as Arthur Watts were undoubtedly responsible for that. Finally, Dr. Clarke, one of Rex's classics masters, was very erudite, as Rex himself would one day become.

Many Greek plays were performed by the children, which may have led to Rex's eventual desire to translate Euripides and Sophocles. The *Georgian* for December 1917 carries an eloquent defense of the study of the classics, basing it on the opinion of Macaulay, who is cited as an eminently practical man and a lover of Greek and Latin literature.[40] Rex told me that when he was young the study of classics had carried great status, and that over the course of the century it had become much reduced in prestige; he voiced the hope that English studies would not go the same way. The need for a defense in the *Georgian* shows that despite the strength of classical study in 1917, its importance in the curriculum had already begun to wane.

Of all the classical writers, Thucydides held the highest place in Rex's affections. The writer of the *Georgian* essay quotes nineteenth-century historian Thomas Macaulay as saying that the retreat from Syracuse in Book VII of *The Peloponnesian War* is the finest thing he ever read in his life, and that Thucydides is the greatest historian who ever lived. Such opinions certainly worked on Rex during his early years.

The Bible was also important in Rex's curriculum, and in 1920, along with Lennox Berkeley and Michael Oakeshott, he was one of ten students to obtain a Certificate in the Diocesan Scripture Examination held during Easter. In another sign of intellectual distinction, Rex received awards for Classics, English, and History in 1921, while other outstanding students received awards in one or at most two subjects.

All of his reading in older and more recent literature had a beneficial effect on Rex's own writing. By the age of fifteen, he could write a technically excellent, if conventional, Shakespearean sonnet:

> Once 'neath the stars I stood + all around
> Throbbed in immensity the heart of Night,
> And huge rose up the trees + every sound
> Spoke of something far beyond my sight.
> Ah! then how very little were the things
> That seemed so great + big in daily life
> How poor the thoughts, how frail the joy that brings
> But biting sound in its train + strife.
> But then I knew that far beyond the trees
> that rose up huge against the dim moonlight,
> Yet nearer to me than the clinging breeze
> And holier + vaster than the Night
> > Was One that knows our joys + sorrows all,
> > And loves us though we be so very small.[41]

The ababcdcdefefgg rhyme scheme is correct, and Rex handles iambic pentameter naturally and well. This poem is also notable for the strength of its religious feeling.

By his last year, when he was about seventeen, Rex was composing something like fin de siècle "aesthetic" poetry that strongly resembled Swinburne's in its vowel and consonant orchestration and its reliance on classical themes. His control of the sonnet had advanced, too; innovatively, he combined the Petrarchan abba abba form with three Shakespearean couplets:

> Pan
> In dewy coverts where the grass spreads green,
> > Where honeysuckle twines dishevelled hair

Through blushing roses, and the drowsy air
Falls sweetly, oft have lonely wanderers seen
The God, goat-footed, gazing on a stream
    That gurgles low along its sinuous bed,
    Or crowning his uncouth mysterious head
With wine dark ivy shade, or lost in dream
    Of Syrinx loved too well and lost too soon.
    And when the shadowed woods reach to the moon
In night-time, through the valleys far and near
    Swells tremulously upon the listening ear
    A passionate piping, the unending smart
    Of his eternally frustrated heart.
                    R.E.W. (VIth)[42]

Although from the beginning Rex's prose always seemed more sure and less imitative than his poetry, the "eternally frustrated heart" of Pan is a wonderful touch, recalling Tantalus; and this poem is a fine imitation of the dreamy music of the late Victorian poets.

In his last year, Rex displayed quiet wit in summing up the activities of the Literary Society: "Our work does, I feel sure, progress; but it is beyond doubt that members have lost that 'first fine careless rapture' with which they used to plunge into discussion. There is a strange fear of making the proverbial 'fool' of oneself. It is salutary to remember that in all cases this is quite unnecessary."[43] Here we see something of the aplomb and good nature that enabled Rex later to run the British Institute in Athens very successfully. St. George's had prepared him not only for writing, but for administration.

According to a report in the *Luton News and Bedfordshire Advertizer*,[44] on Speech Day in July 1923, her Grace the Duchess of Hamilton and Brandon distributed the awards, and Hon. E. Lyttelton, D.D., late headmaster of Eton and chairman of St. George's governing board, officiated. Cecil Grant, celebrating his semi-jubilee (St. George's having been founded at Keswick in 1898), stated that "Co-education is no longer regarded as doubtful and dangerous" and in this he was supported by the duchess.

After Dr. Lyttelton's sermon in the chapel in the morning and then lunch, the speeches and awards ceremony took place in the Big Hall. First the assembled school sang the "Song of Remembrance"; this was followed by Thomas Morley's madrigal "My Bonny Lass She Smileth." The poem "London," "with which Christopher H. O. Scaife, a sometime Old Georgian, has this year won the Newdigate Prize at Oxford, was feelingly recited by the school captain, R. E. Warner," according to the newspaper report.

Then Cecil Grant summarized the school's success in education reform and pointed to its prowess in sport as "a welcome proof of good health." But important as these successes and the number of Old Georgians' university distinctions were, the real test of the school's success for Grant was as follows:

> How did the Georgian meet a crisis? How did he bear adversity, or (what is more testing) prosperity? Was he loyal to his school, faithful to his friends? Did he put the cause above the reward, honour before honours, duty before life itself? Did he in all places and under all circumstances play the game?

The honors-including recognition of Rex's ten years, School Prefectship, Classical scholarship, the Halley Stewart "League of Nations" essay award, and sports records-were distributed. The Duchess of Hamilton and Dr. Lyttelton were "accorded a vote of thanks, proposed by Maj. R. Bennett Sidebottom (who was accompanied by the Hon. Mrs. Bennett Sidebottom)" and then, at the call of R. E. Warner, three rousing cheers were given by the school.

The event ended with eurhythmic dancing-an early form of aerobics-based on Schumann's "Études Symphoniques," a performance of country dances, in costume, and a gymnastic display. It was to be Rex's last affiliation with St. George's, except for some visits during Old Georgian reunions.

The school had bequeathed him responsibility, Christian traditionalism, a love of classical and modern literature, enthusiasm for sports, and even a future wife, but it also imparted an interest in socialism, in America, and in breaking free. These clashing interests would come to the fore at Oxford.

CHAPTER THREE

OXFORD, 1923-1928

I. WITH DAY-LEWIS AND BOWRA AT WADHAM COLLEGE

At the beginning of the fall or Michaelmas term of 1923, Rex Warner sat in Wadham College, at a long Scholar's Table (reserved for the best scholarship winners) in a fine oak-paneled hall beneath the portraits of famous alumni, including the great eighteenth-century architect Sir Christopher Wren. Nearby, at the dons' High Table, set above all the other tables, Warden "Juffie" or Joseph P. Wells, known for the editing of Herodotus and for his work describing the architecture of the college, banged hard with his trencher for silence. A Scholar said Wadham College's Latin grace, which was charming and long and ended with the hope that all assembled 130-odd Wadham men should enter into the Resurrection together with Nicholas and Dorothy Wadham, the founders of the college. At the Exhibitioner's Table, also wearing a gown, sat future Poet Laureate Cecil Day-Lewis, who was to become Rex's best friend. As an "Exhibitioner" he received £60 a year but would not be among those who could publicly recite grace; as a Scholar Rex received £80 and could have that honor.

The Reverend T. W. Griffiths, who was finishing Oxford in 1923-24 when Rex came up, recalls him as a tall, athletic man who played Rugby with him and Day-Lewis. He also recalls that Rex was serious but fortunately "not so gloomy-looking" as Day-Lewis.[1] G. K. Laycock confirms this impression of Day-Lewis's appearance: "I remember entering his room once and remarking that Hardy was well represented on his shelves. His face lit up with a glow: 'He's wonderful!' But usually his face wore a look of profound melancholy, especially in hall at dinner when he sat munching silently with the commoners. So much so that one night I sent my compliments to him by the Head Waiter and told him to cheer up as things would turn out all right in the end."[2] Tom Hopkinson, later the editor of the *Picture Post*, remembers in his autobiography, *Of This Our Time*, what Cecil, Rex, and Charles Fenby looked like at this point:

> Cecil Day-Lewis was handsome and elegant, with a fine speaking and singing voice. He had already published poetry and his intention in life was simply to be a poet, an ambition he planned to subsidize by schoolmastering. His close friend, Rex Warner, tall, pale-faced and black-haired, had a passion for games equal to my own but was also a scholar with a wide knowledge of the classics; his was a special kind of wit combining the flippant and the pedantic. "In a future radiant with the purple of fame and the rose-pink of innocuous love," he wrote in a letter, "gleams the brown and green of one pound sterling which I hope shortly to repay.". . . Unlike the others [Fenby] was completely careless of appearance, and indeed always looked so ill that every time I met him I was surprised he should be walking about at all. His face was white and his weak eyes rimmed with red, he suffered continually and painfully from boils, and at twenty was already going bald. Since I would know him for the next fifty years, I was able to observe how he reversed the normal process of decay, changing from a sickly youth with one foot in the grave into a large, rosy-faced elderly man.[3]

In his memoir *The Buried Day*, Day-Lewis tells us that the generation of men who had fought in World War I had just gone down from Oxford. He mentions that Charles Fenby, later to become an important newspaper editor, was given the task, some time around 1925, of hosting Robert Graves for a literary society that he, Rex, and Cecil (roommates at 22 St. Giles) had formed. (This was named "The Jawbone," and had as its emblem the actual jawbone of an ass, procured on their order by Selfridge's department store.) Graves stood silently listening at a window to a piano that was playing. Graves explained that it was the same melody that a young officer invalided to Wadham (like Graves) during the war had played for Graves then.[4] Although it could never be completely forgotten by Rex's generation, the war atmosphere had dispersed by 1923, and Oxford was returning to its old ways.

Evelyn Waugh, who came up to Oxford in 1922, offers the picture of a comfortable, traditional institution in the first volume of his autobiography, *A Little Learning*. He writes:

Oxford then was very much closer to my father's (and, indeed, my great-grandfather's) university than to my children's. There was no feverish competition for admittance.... The town was still isolated among streams and meadows. Its buildings proudly displayed their grey and gold, crumbling ashlar, now condemned by the pundits as "leprous" and renovated at prodigious cost. Its only suburb comprised the Ruskinian villas and well-kept gardens round the Woodstock and Banbury Roads. The motor works at Cowley existed, but were far from sight or sound of the university. During term tourists were few. The surrounding woods and hills were those the Scholar Gypsy haunted and could be reached on foot in the middle of the road. We walked up the tow-path and practised sortilege at Binsey, as we believed our predecessors had done. In the quiet streets predatory shop-keepers waited on the university and tempted the young into debts.... At Canterbury Gate and in the Broad hansom-cabs and open victorias were for hire. Bicycles and clergymen abounded and clergymen on bicycles were, with the cattle coming to market, the only hazards of traffic. I doubt if there were thirty cars in the university owned by dons or undergraduates. Telephones were never used. Correspondence was on crested cards delivered by college messengers on bicycles.[5]

Cars were allowed only in a student's last year, and were identified by a special green light. College gates were closed at 9 P.M., but admission was granted to college members returning—there was no possibility of leaving—until midnight. Having been shaped during this period, Rex in later life never liked cars, telephones, or typewriters. He always wrote by hand, using the ampersand favored by his Oxford tutors as well.

Most of the entering Wadham students came from a few private schools—Dulwich, Clifton College, and St. George's, among others; just as in Compton Mackenzie's Oxford novel *Sinister Street* (1913) they hail from Exeter and Winchester. Although not as prestigious as some other colleges, Wadham had a unique, positive atmosphere during the years Rex was there. There was a scattering of Jews, some Americans, and one Indian among the undergraduates resident in any one year during Rex's period. Wadham was noted for law, and was socially well balanced in that it was free from cliques. Apparently, there was no snobbery among Wadham men toward one another, no matter which school they came from.[6]

The faculty was quite good. In addition to Warden Wells, the soon-to-be famous classics scholar Maurice Bowra came to Wadham in 1922, and by 1925 he was dean. H. T. Wade-Gery, the history tutor, was eccentric and brilliant. Lord David Cecil, the historian and literary critic, was a celebrity among the tutors. The works of these men are still read and respected in their fields.

The faculty's intellectual prowess, however, was not matched by the accommodations. There was no central heating and no hot and cold water. The bath house was near the kitchen and college scouts brought students a jug of hot water and lit a fire in the sitting room in the morning. G. K. Laycock remembers that Rex's rooms in his first year were not in the main quad, but

> in one of the three old 18th century houses running continuously from the front of the college to the King's Arms Inn at the corner of Holywell St. In our time this largish untidy area rather resembled a scrap-heap with the odd bush or tree and Wade-Gery, sandal-footed, could be seen at times shifting soil and sods with a spade. Warner's rooms were on the ground floor of one of those dirty old 18th century houses. . . . I remember entering once his gloomy and desperately untidy room and found not an intense probing discussion of the minutiae of the poetic art in progress but some pretty rough horse-play and as I'd come in with my golf clubs on my shoulder I seem to remember contributing my bit by practising a shot or two.[7]

R. F. Bretherton, a classmate, remembers that Rex regretted the division between private school and grammar school boys that existed at Wadham despite the lack of overt snobbery. Even more to Rex's credit is an incident of spring 1925 concerning an Irish student, John Roche. As recalled by Lance Garrard, another classmate (eventually principal of Manchester College, Oxford), the following occurred:

> One night going to the bathrooms (a primitive affair, remote from our rooms), I found that Roche had beaten up an off-beat Jewish Communist who enjoyed shocking the more orthodox. After doing what I could to patch him up, I went round to Rex and was glad to find Day-Lewis and Fenby with him. When I told them what I had seen we all went back to do what we could for the victim, and as soon as we had returned Rex immediately took charge of things and led us to the Junior Common Room, where he drafted an admirable letter of protest, which we all four signed. Day-Lewis whispered to me "I never thought of Rex as a man of action!" We found it interesting to see which men added their signatures at once and which held back until they saw which way the wind was blowing. Soon afterwards we took Honour Mods, Rex getting a 1st, Day-Lewis and I a second.[8]

Day-Lewis writes that "Rex . . . kept his more earnest side well concealed. A son of the rectory, he was now beginning to revolt against many of the things he had been brought up with, to swing more and more wildly between ideal and real, his brilliant brain often at the mercy of emotional pressures which it imperfectly understood and reacted to feverishly."[9] The Roche incident shows that Rex was ready to defend a Communist. Moreover, while he had begun to reject his father and mother's religiosity, he clearly remembered the basic human decency they taught, as well as the leadership learned as head boy under Cecil Grant.

Rex's strong character probably saw him through Maurice Bowra's eccentric influence also. Bowra, who died on 4 July 1971, has attained almost legendary fame. His memoirs are strangely stiff, but he was known as a witty and malicious talker, completely unrestrained in his barbed comments. Anthony Powell, like Rex a habitué of the Bowra dinner parties for undergraduates, comments in his memoir, *Infants of the Spring*, that there was always a sense of danger at these parties. One never knew what sexual or other personal innuendo, true or false, might be directed one's way, and Bowra delighted in overstepping the normal bounds of teacher-student distance.

Homosexuality was part of the 1920s culture at Oxford, and Day-Lewis admits that he was initiated at school into homosexual activities which he later rejected. According to Anthony Powell, Bowra "always talked as if homosexuality was the natural condition of an intelligent man." Powell also points out that Bowra's innovation was to

> proclaim the paramount claims of eating, drinking, sex (women at that early stage somewhat derided, homosexuality and autoerotism approved), but to accept as absolutely natural, open snobbishness, success worship, personal vendettas, unprovoked malice, disloyalty to friends, reading other people's letters (if not lying about, to be sought in unlocked drawers)—the whole bag of tricks of what most people think, feel, and often act on, yet are ashamed of admitting that they do, feel, and think.[10]

But Bowra was to become interested in women later on. One apochryphal story has it that Bowra, giving a wedding talk about one of his former students, said, "Both Bob and Barbara are excellently matched mentally and physically—I know because I've slept with both of them."

Another story has been repeated more often and so may have more truth to it. At Parson's Pleasure, a nude sunbathing area for men along the Cherwell River in Oxford, Bowra and a colleague, John Sparrow, were sunning themselves. Local women knew that when they came by on punts they had to avert their eyes when they got near this point, but on this occasion a boat full of tourists approached, and the women did not do so. Sparrow jumped up and covered his midsection with a newspaper, while Bowra covered his face with his newspaper. After the gaping tourists had gone by, Sparrow said, "Maurice, why did you do that?" Bowra replied, "I don't know about you, John, but most people know me by my face."

Privately, Rex expressed contempt for homosexuality, but he was never publicly impolite to anyone on this score. Certainly Rex's dislike of academe, demonstrated in *The Wild Goose Chase* in particular, was partially attributable to his distaste for Oxford homosexuality and what he saw as an effete atmosphere among university intellectuals. Day-Lewis testifies that during his Wadham period, Rex was overly fond of wine and women, leaving song to Day-Lewis himself. Rex, however, would comment to interviewer Andrew Cramp in the 1980s that Day-Lewis's comments about him were "all wrong. He likes to say nice things about his friends but it's all untrue. He talks about me spending my time with wine and women. Well I couldn't afford any wine, and I was too shy for women so he was wrong. It was Cecil's idea of being nice."[11]

Evelyn Waugh notes about Oxford,

> It was a male community. Undergraduates lived in purdah. Except during Eights Week girls were very rarely to be seen in the men's colleges. The proctors retained, and in my day on one occasion at least asserted, their right to expel beyond the university limits, independent women who were thought to be a temptation. The late train from Paddington was by tradition known as "the fornicator," but it was not much frequented for that purpose. Most men were well content to live in a society as confined as it had been before the coming of the railway and to indulge in light flirtations during the vacation and deep friendships during the terms. . . . I am sure that fewer than ten per cent of my contemporaries had what Dr Gibbens means by "girl friends." Some had made a single, pleasureless adventure with a prostitute abroad. Few had any serious interest in women, but . . . very few have developed into homosexuals.[12]

Waugh concludes that "We were in some respects more sophisticated than our successors, but in others barely adolescent."

Rex's main occupations seem to have been wine, sport, and classical and modern literature. He must have had money for wine, because he was a developed drinker by the time he was married soon after graduation, and was used to spending some time in the pub every day; he became a heavy drinker in the 1930s and remained one until his doctors ordered him off drink in the 1970s.

Regardless of Bowra's ambiguous sexual proclivities and his interest in wild parties, he was known for his classical scholarship and exerted considerable spiritual authority over the students because he had served in the Great War. Powell likens coming into contact with Bowra to one's first reading of Nietzsche. "The Bowra delivery, loud, stylized, ironic, usually followed by those deep abrupt bursts of laughter, was superlatively effective in attack."[13]

Rex must have overlooked Bowra's homosexuality but he was influenced by him intellectually, and always spoke of him with great respect. Although Rex was in contact with Bowra throughout his career and especially during Rex's marriage to Barbara Rothschild, Bowra devotes only two sentences to Rex and Day-Lewis in his *Memories 1898-1939*:

> In my first years I was fortunate in having a number of lively and gifted pupils—. . . Rex Warner, whose remarkable gifts and promise were hampered by a breakdown in his third year, when he was said to see the transcendental deduction of the categories lying in solid blocks across the room, but who was, when I taught him, the ideal pupil, since he had been badly grounded at school and found in Greek and Latin all the charms of novelty; Cecil Day-Lewis, who was already a poet and applied his literary gifts to the translation of classical texts with an adventurous originality.[14]

Rex's competitive instincts were aroused by Bowra; and probably because of that he was able to break away from him, if at the cost of pushing himself too hard academically. Powell comments that one had to get away from Bowra, much as Day-Lewis says that one had to get away from Auden. Superbly intelligent, both were also too overpowering, too cutting, too cynical, too insistent that things be done their way.

H. W. Parke recalls what a Bowra lecture was like during Rex's first year. Rex was probably at the lectures, also, although he would not take Mods, the all-important series of examinations, until spring of 1925. Parke writes:

> In 1923/24 I also attended Bowra's first course of university lectures. His subject was Sophocles' *Philoctetes*, and as the play was one of the set-books for classical Mods in 1924, he was sure of a large audience. He was to lecture in the College hall and prompt on time he strode to the dais and started in a loud commanding shout. Of course in those days there were no such things as microphones for university lectures, and Wadham hall was acoustically difficult. But it was partly also an indication of his nervousness. Behind his bow-wow manner even in ordinary conversation lay a certain element of high-strung self-consciousness.

Parke also remembers an occasion when students who had taken Classical Mods in 1924 were hosted by Bowra and they acted charades based on Pindar's *Pythian Odes* while Bowra himself wore a "top hat to impersonate Zeus, with outstretched arm hurling Ixion to his doom."[15]

J. M. Ross remembers,

> To be tutored by Bowra for Honours Mods was a wonderful experience. It is not always recognized that Bowra was not only a wit and a master of literature and culture but also a first-rate classical scholar who knew that you could not understand the Greeks until you could understand their prepositions and enclitics. . . . I learnt from him to respect the text of every classical author, and to try to understand it from a Greek or Roman point of view and not to rush into amending it or forcing it to yield a sense in accordance with some modern fashion.[16]

As much as Rex respected Bowra's scholarship, it seemed to force him into a spirit of competition. He was fond of remarking that his score of thirteen alphas and two alpha betas in classical Honours Moderations examinations was better than Bowra himself had received, even though Bowra, according to Christopher Hollis's *Oxford in the Twenties*, had "got a brilliant First in his Mods, receiving, we were told, a record number of Alphas in his papers."[17] Bowra himself was the tutor for Honours Moderations at that time, and his preparation methods undoubtedly helped Rex achieve this outstanding result. While we have no record of exactly which papers Rex wrote, it is obvious that his level of performance was exceptionally high: out of fifteen papers ranging over almost the entire field of Greek and Latin literature and composition, it was amazing to receive thirteen "A's" and two "A-/B+" grades.[18] Perhaps the reason for Rex's success is that he was a far better writer than his tutor.

II. SPORTS, LITERATURE, AND POLITICS

Although his exam performance was inferior to Rex's, Cecil Day-Lewis was more advanced as a poet, self-publishing his first book, *Beechen Vigil and Other Poems*, in June 1925. Lance Garrard describes an occasion when he was "permitted to share a punt with Warner's trio" and was presented with a copy that Day-Lewis autographed and then unfortunately dropped in the river (it was subsequently rescued). Garrard also mentions one Francis Giveen, who knew how to climb into college when the gates were locked, and performed such pranks as climbing the Martyrs' Memorial and leaving a chamber pot on top. Rex's group, he hastens to add, was not involved in such activities. Garrard also remembers that in April 1926, Rex was present at a party for Garrard's twenty-first birthday. There was much noise and glasses were thrown into the street, earning Garrard a hefty fine from the proctors. Day-Lewis enjoyed all the excitement, but Rex disapproved of the whole affair.[19] The picture of Rex that emerges is that of a balanced person, aesthetic and hearty but not rowdy.

In addition to his superb "First," Rex's main achievements during his undergraduate years were in the areas of sports and extracurricular literary activities. Rex became captain of the Wadham Rugby First XV by 1926 and was a forward in the Hockey First XI by 1924. Rugby did not fare particularly well, which was not Rex's fault. The *Gazette* for summer term 1925 noted, "The Rugby XV has had a chequered career, winning some of its matches and losing others. The main difficulty has been to get the same team to play together, as some of the best men were tempted away by Hockey, and the river claimed a large share both of old and of new talent" (201). L. W. Ridley, who was on the team, remembers that Rex was an excellent captain, popular, and also scholastically respectable.[20]

The Hellenic Society at Wadham, founded only in 1921-22, was quite strong in Rex's time. In addition to Bowra, Gilbert Murray, the Regius Professor of Greek, then fifty-seven years old and still very active, attended it quite often. At the annual dinner of the Hellenic Society on Friday, 13 June 1924, Murray responded to a toast to "the Classics" by N. C. Brook. He said that the classics were an educational necessity, and that Oxford was regarded in some quarters as the rectifier of the vagaries of modern education which was in the hands of "intellectual rough-necks" who did not honor Greek and Latin study. Rex respected Murray enormously, and forty years later would write of the beauty of listening to him read Greek during his lectures. On 27 October 1923, the noted historian Arnold Toynbee read a paper, "The Greek View of History," which was followed by a vigorous discussion. At the last meeting of the year, the members read Aristophanes' *Clouds*, with Day-Lewis taking a tenor role and Rex a bass part in the chorus.

Charles A. Rivington, who was president of the society when Rex was secretary in 1924 or 1925, recalls that the menu-card was "entirely in Latin and Greek, the menu itself (in Greek) being I think composed by Maurice Bowra (who would have been Rex's tutor at this time)."[21] These years were perhaps the high point of the prestige of classical study. It is difficult to conceive of that prestige today, when classics departments are relegated to the backwaters of the humanities in most universities, which are dominated by science, engineering, and business schools.

On 23 November 1924, Rex gave a paper, "A Woman Homer Sung," to the College Literary Society; other topics that term were "Moralism and the Creative Spirit," "Malory," "The Decay of Poetry," "Naturalistic Fiction of England and France," and

"Programme Music." In 1925, Lord David Cecil joined the college, and on 22 November of that year gave a talk on "Bad Poems by Good Poets." When Rex returned in the fall of 1927 after a break and decided to take his degree in English, David Cecil would be his tutor.

In addition to sports and literature, politics would become an important undergraduate activity. The big event of the 1925-26 academic year was the General Strike, which lasted from 3-12 May 1926, and was preceded by Red Friday, 31 July 1925. The Conservative Government under Stanley Baldwin was pitted against the Trades Union Congress, which controlled most of the workers in Britain, and which had decided to strike in solidarity with the coal miners, who were demanding fewer hours and higher pay.

Julian Symons points out that what people first noticed on the opening morning of the strike was peace and stillness in the streets because of the absence of buses; not one of the 4,000 buses of the London General Omnibus Company moved. "Fifteen out of London's three hundred and fifteen Underground trains ran, and those for short distances."[22] Then came bicycles and cars as people tried to get to work, with huge traffic jams. Food supplies were imperiled, and some members of the Cabinet, such as Churchill, advocated harsh measures for ending the strike. Baldwin did not want violence, however, and called instead for volunteers. Symons writes, "The volunteers came in their thousands: not only the thousands of respectable middle-aged professional men who were queuing outside recruiting stations, but medical students, law students, and undergraduates from Oxford and Cambridge, to whom the strike was an exciting joke. The attitude of the University authorities varied."

In one case, according to an eyewitness at Exeter, "The sub-rector and the Vice-Chancellor caught the fever early, the latter, urged undergraduates to enrol themselves, the former gave a discourse to a crowded and thrilled audience who were exhorted to come and sign on between 10 and 1 tomorrow. . . . Most of the College put down their names, including many who were doing schools [exams] which they hoped to avoid."[23] This was the situation at most of the colleges, including Wadham—although Lance Garrard testifies that they were told not to go strikebreaking in Oxford itself. Christopher Hollis states that he asked Bowra what he did during the strike and Bowra answered, "I stayed here and went on with my work."[24] Hollis comments, however, that this was not quite true. In fact, Bowra had collected some signatures in support of the Archbishop of Canterbury's plan to initiate negotiations to bring the strike to an end. Hollis points out that what really interested Bowra politically was the freedom of the intellectuals and the middle classes. Not until Bowra's anti-Nazism surfaced did he express very specific and deeply felt political beliefs.

C. Day-Lewis, however, who had been moving steadily leftward, joined a group led by the pro-strike committee and organized by G. D. H. and Margaret Cole (leftist economic historians who also wrote detective stories). He drove cars on liaison work for the Trades Union Congress for a day or two according to his memoir, and then moved on to pro-strike newspaper work, but the strike was over before he could get the newspaper going. Garrard remembers that Warner, Fenby (whose father was an important editor and who later edited *Picture Post* and the *Oxford Mail*), and Day-Lewis wanted to get out an unbiased paper, but never managed to do so.

Cecil Day-Lewis testifies that Rex participated, on a lark, in breaking the strike by conducting a tram in Hull. When Day-Lewis reproached him, Rex replied that the authorities were bound to win anyway, and so the quicker they could be helped to win, the better![25]

Day-Lewis's 1938 novel *Starting Point* contains a character, Anthony Neale, who although his father is a Liberal member of the government rather than a clergyman, is very much like Rex in many ways: a rugger player, and straightforward yet brainy. During a conversation between four friends in their rooms in Oxford, Anthony announces that he will join the strikebreakers although he is in sympathy with the strikers. The Socialist science student John Henderson asks, "What's your motive then? Do you want excitement? Join the blacklegs and see the world?" and the conversation continues with Anthony's response:

> "No, it's not that. It's just common sense. You see, from what I've heard of Ramsay, Thomas + Co. [TUC leaders], I don't believe they dare carry the thing through. They're no Lenins. They'll want to arrange a gentlemanly compromise, as soon as it's decently possible. Whereas a large section of the Cabinet, so my father says—and he's pretty knowledgeable—is determined to seize this opportunity of smashing Labour. Well, when you have two fighters, and one is pulling his punches and the other is determined to win by a knock-out, which do you back?"
>
> "It's a matter of what you believe in, I suppose," said John.
>
> "Exactly. I sympathize with your lot; but I don't believe in the Cause enough to make me go and fight in a forlorn hope."
>
> "In that case, I should have thought neutrality was the honourable course. . . ."
>
> "No," said Anthony. "Neutrality's all right for a nation, but impossible for an individual. I shouldn't be able to do any work here if I did stay. . . . And besides. The longer this strike goes on, the worse the unions will come out of it. The best way of stopping a war quickly is for neutrals to enlist in the big battalions. Not that my course of action is of any great importance to the world," Anthony added, grinning apologetically.[26]

Day-Lewis seems to have captured here from memory the complexity of the actual conversation he had with Charles Fenby and Rex at the time of the strike. Rex-Anthony's argument has the same subtlety in the defense of an unworthy cause as did his letter to the *Georgian* when he was fifteen asking to be relieved of homework so he could help the war effort. It is apparent why Day-Lewis would later write that Rex was the "hawk-faced man who could praise an apple/In terms of peach and win the argument." Rex delighted in brilliant but specious argument just for the sake of winning, and his social views were far from settled at this point, although Marxism had begun to make inroads.

Anthony in the novel becomes a navvy, unloading food ships in a seaside town, possibly Hull, where Rex was posted. Rex, however, like Larkin in Day-Lewis's novel, became a tram conductor. Larkin recounts that he and the scab driver diverted a bus from its usual route in order to take a pretty girl home. Whether or not this was based on a story of Rex's, we cannot know, but it would not be beyond him. As a tram conductor, Rex would have received very light training, and a large share of unpleasantness on the road. Policemen would ride on the front and back platforms of each tram because there were frequent attempts to stop them, including the breaking of windows and other violent measures. Rex's actions during the strike show that he was not yet a convinced leftist or very serious about social issues, but that his usual physical courage had not deserted him. On the other hand, it could well be that, like Anthony Neale, who is converted to Socialism as a result of witnessing the workers' plight during the Strike, Rex underwent a similar conversion at that time. Charles Fenby, described as an "old fashioned liberal," just stayed at Oxford working.

W. H. Auden came up to Christ Church in 1925, and met Cecil Day-Lewis and Rex at some point during the 1925-26 academic year; in a memoir of Auden written with Gabriel Carritt, Rex says that he met Auden toward the end of his second year, but it must have been in the third since Auden did not begin until Rex's third year. Day-Lewis describes Auden as an aesthete, complete with a bizarre cloak and starting pistol, who enjoyed sitting in the artificially illuminated dark like Poe's Dupin, even during the day. He fails to mention, however, that by this time Rex was not much different. Mrs. K. M. Raymond, who was five years behind Rex at St. George's, wrote me that she "literally bumped into him coming out of a cafe in Oxford one afternoon. I was amused to see that he had become the complete aesthete-black cloak, + a large black sombrero!"[27] Frances Warner confirms this style of dress, and whether it was inspired by Auden or inspired Auden, who knows? It fits very well into the "Children of the Sun" period, as described by Martin Green in his book of that name.

Cecil Lightfoot, a classmate, testifies that Rex was "never intellectually arrogant: he had a good sense of humour and we shared many jokes about the rather peculiar post-World War I atmosphere e.g. 'Oxford bags' (wide trousers) and all that."[28] Rex's dress included longer than average hair, a suit, usually brown, instead of "bags," and a bow tie, which Cyril Davies recalls invariably indicated bohemian tastes.[29] Edmond Johnson, another contemporary, remembers that Rex was "a most gifted man who seemed quite unaware of his powers—not the Balliol tranquil acquiescence of an effortless superiority—but far more impressive—sheer ability and a wide friendliness that even Bowra's snobbish influence did not tarnish."[30]

Stephan Hopkinson, who came up to Wadham in the fall of 1927, remembers that Rex invited him to breakfast with Auden and Stephen Spender. Rex and Auden and Spender were more or less on the same track from the beginning, passing poetic enthusiasms among one another without any clear precedence. As Rex wrote, Auden "was writing incessantly. For some weeks on end, T.S. Eliot would be the model, then Gerard Manley Hopkins or Anglo-Saxon verse."[31] Rex's own work is notable for the influence of Hopkins, which he may well have picked up from Auden, or which Auden may have picked up from him. Eliot was a towering presence for all three, a figure to whom each had to react.

Auden was also invited home to Amberley to meet the Warners. Rex remembered, "His considerate behaviour to old people who came to tea-parties won him golden opinions and more than atoned for some minor eccentricities, such as wandering about in the middle of the night to raid the larder or take down the curtains to pile on his bed. I think my parents realized earlier than I did, that Wystan had, to a marked degree, what Jane Austen would call 'right principles.'"[32]

III. BREAKDOWN

Although Rex seemed to fare well, mental competition was not good for him, as the nervous breakdown mentioned by Bowra shows. Rex was not the only Oxford undergraduate to suffer a breakdown owing to overstrenuous study; L. A. G. Strong, a wartime Wadham man and later a published writer who was to help both Cecil Day-Lewis and Rex secure their literary start, also experienced this fate.[33] Rex's breakdown was so severe that he went home for all of the 1926-27 academic year. Day-Lewis attributes it to the strain of Rex's brilliant academic performance—according to him, Rex "read philosophy to such effect that one day he saw the Absolute walk in at his door, and taking the hint, saved his sanity by having a nervous breakdown, leaving Oxford for a year, and returning to read for a quiet Pass in English."[34]

Rex always denied that story. He later told Frances something about the precise nature of this breakdown: that he went to a physician, and that when his leg was struck with the rubber hammer, it jumped violently because he was very nervous. He could not concentrate or collect his thoughts. He actually hallucinated, although he denied Bowra's version that Rex saw "the transcendental deduction of the categories lying in solid blocks across the room." The reasons for the breakdown are not hard to guess. Strong testifies that his own breakdown was caused by overwork, and philosophy in particular seems to produce those results in many people; thinking about thinking is not a safe occupation for the obsessive student. In his letter of 30 August 1989 to me, Lance Garrard tells a new version of the breakdown story and testifies to his own mental difficulties with philosophy: "The story I heard, which may be quite untrue, was that he [Rex] had become obsessed with the theory of Solipsism (everything but one's own existence is a figment of the mind). Oddly enough I had quite a turn myself after speculating on this and was saved by a friend who gave me some strong coffee and told me to snap out of it."

Since Rex was a competitive type—a head boy—he would work far too hard. Rex would also, like Day-Lewis, have to face the rigors of Final Schools, or final B.A. examinations, during the following academic year, as well as the prospect of finding a job—probably as a poorly paid schoolmaster. Students nearing the end of their studies typically become anxious about the future, with good reason. After a carefree few years, the reality of impending graduation begins to glimmer even in the most alcohol-soaked brain.

Rex commented later that he had already done all the work for his final examinations when he had his breakdown. Perhaps that is an exaggeration, but it seems clear that during the summer term of 1926, at the end of his third year, he pushed himself too hard, undoubtedly in the hope of repeating his brilliant Mods performance and again surpassing Bowra in the Final Schools, still a year away. After the breakdown at the end of the 1926 summer term, Rex went home to Amberley for a time. He was fortunate in that his father's friend, W. J. Paley Marling, the lord of the manor at Great Rissington, gave him 50 pounds for a trip. With this money, Rex went abroad to Morocco to rest for two or three months in the late summer and fall of 1926. He traveled on his own, and loved it there. Perhaps because of this experience, he was ready to take a job in Egypt after graduation. A letter of about 1939 to C. J. Greenwood contains one of Rex's few reminiscences of this trip, including "a church warden with whom, ages ago, I went round the brothels in Algiers."[35]

He was back in England by late November 1926 and possibly still planning to take his Final School in Classics the next summer. Since he did not have to be in residence for that, and because he was not ready to resume full-time study, he needed a job, which meant letters of recommendation.

Dean Bowra wrote a positive but brief letter that does not allude to any problems. It is not dated, but it is obviously from around fall 1926 because it says that Rex is studying for Greats rather than for English as he decided to do around the fall of 1927: "R. E. Warner has been a scholar of this college since October 1923. He is one of the ablest men we have had for some time, getting a very good First Class in Honours Mods. in 1925. He is now working for Greats. He has also been President of Junior Common Room, Captain of the Rugby XV, & President of the Olympic Club. Personally he gets on with all sorts of men & has a very engaging manner."[36]

The letter Warden Wells wrote for Rex, dated 27 November 1926, alludes circumspectly to a breakdown. He writes,

> Mr. R. E. Warner came up to Wadham as a scholar in October 1923, & obtained a good first class in Classical Moderations in March 1925. He is now reading for the Final Classical School, & should, without question, get a First Class in it next summer. My only anxiety is that he has had some trouble with his eyes, & although this is now being mastered by proper treatment, it has interfered somewhat with his work.

He continues,

> Mr. Warner has been one of the leading members of College both intellectually & athletically. He is full of interest in all modern developements [*sic*], & at the same time is most loyal in supporting the authorities of the College. He is a thorough gentleman, a man of the highest character, & very pleasant to work with. I am quite sure he will be a valuable helper in whatever work he undertakes, for he will be acceptable to those above him, & influential with those he is to lead.

This letter shows that although Rex was still planning to read Classics (or still saying that he was planning to read Classics), he had already experienced a serious problem: Wells's allusion to eye trouble (perhaps written on the basis of what Rex told him) no doubt masks Rex's mental breakdown. Another recommendation letter written by Wells in 1928 speaks openly about a previous, serious breakdown in health, but again does not mention mental problems.

The 1926 letter of recommendation from Wells (and possibly that from Bowra) was effective in landing Rex a job, and he became employed by a very wealthy American family. The Pells were hereditary lords of the manor of Pelham, New York, under a grant from King Charles II, according to a *New York Times* obituary, and sold part of the land in 1688 to Huguenot settlers, who then founded New Rochelle. Clarence

C. Pell, Rex's employer, was the younger brother of Herbert Claiborne Pell, the congressman from New York and diplomat, and he was an uncle of Sen. Claiborne Pell, Democrat from Rhode Island.

Clarence Pell was also the American amateur racquets champion. He was in England in 1925, when he became the only foreigner ever to win the British amateur singles championship. He returned to England with his wife, the former Madeline Boland, and their two young sons and little daughter, in 1926. These were the luxurious 1920s, and the Pell family was abroad just to buy bulldogs. By late 1926 or early 1927, Rex had become the tutor to their three children, and went with them to Paris and St. Jean de Luc. They were a very charming family, and indulged Rex in everything. He was very fond of the children, and they liked him. Rex confided to Frances that when he first met the Pells, he talked about sports and boasted a little about his own prowess; but when he found out who Pell was, he felt small.

According to Allison Danzig's *The Racquet Game*,[37] Pell was the champion of the Tuxedo Club (perhaps the premier American racquets institution) from 1912-30, and held the national American championship twelve times between 1915 and 1933. Danzig writes, "Pell comes as close to the ideal perfect racquet player as any amateur developed in the United States has come. Some of the professionals who have watched the parade for thirty years rate him as the greatest of all American players. . . ."

As good as Pell's game was, his sportsmanship was even better. Danzig tells us,

> No finer sportsman ever stepped into a racquet court than Clarence Pell. In a game in which the spirit of noblesse oblige is so cherished and universally prevalent, his scrupulous fairness stands out as a shining example of sportsmanship to the nth degree. He plays the game to the hilt and shows no mercy, but he would rather lose a championship than take any point about which any question was raised. . . . No player has more thoroughly deserved the honors he won than has Pell and none has worn them more nobly or been held in higher regard by his contemporaries in the racquet court.[38]

Pell, who had been taught racquets by Robert Moore of Cambridge University, was well-disposed toward England and Englishmen, and Rex would be influenced by Pell to like America, about which he had already heard much at St. George's.

Rex probably stayed with the Pells until he returned to Oxford in fall 1927, so he worked for them for a total of approximately eight months. Frances, by then his girlfriend, recalled that the Pells treated them both very well, taking them to Noel Coward plays and to expensive restaurants. Rex's interest in athletics would ensure good rapport with Pell and the contact with wealth probably excited him and made America seem even more attractive.

IV. RETURN TO OXFORD

Rex returned to Oxford in the fall of 1927 refreshed and ready to work, as a second letter of recommendation for him written by Joseph Wells, dated 22 September 1928, attests:

> He obtained a good First Class in Classical Moderations, & is fully qualified to prepare candidates for Classical scholarships at Oxford; he would do this the more effectively as he is not only a good scholar in the strict sense but keenly interested in the life of antiquity & also in modern literature.
>
> We had expected him to do as well in his final examination as he did in Moderations, but a serious breakdown in health ruined his work. His health is now completely restored, & he has had the advantage of a good deal of foreign travel while recovering. Mr. Warner is a thorough gentleman & a man of the highest character.[39]

Rex's last year at Oxford, 1927-28, was very uneventful academically. Rex told Andrew Cramp in the early 1980s that only his classics work at Oxford mattered to him and that "I don't count the English [studies] at all. I did all the work for my final classics exam, then I had some sort of nervous breakdown or something and went away for a year. When I came back, I got a third in English. Auden did as well."[40]

Things had changed by the fall of 1927. Joseph Wells had retired as warden. Day-Lewis, who would graduate with a fourth in Greats,was no longer living in Oxford but was in the vicinity teaching. He pointed out that Rex returned to take a "quiet third" in English, for which he was badly prepared by the eccentric Lord David Cecil. It is ironic that three of the leading lights of modern British literature received low marks in the humanities, including literature, at Oxford! Is this a comment on academic study, or on them?

Charles Fenby had moved on to join the editorial staff of the *Westminster Gazette*. S.H. Oakeshott, Michael Oakeshott's brother, who had been with Rex since St. George's, had graduated with a B.S. in June. But as if in compensation for these departures, Rex enjoyed increased friendship with Auden.

Rex recalled in 1974 in the *Wadham Gazette*, "We used to go for long and talkative walks in the neighbourhood of the gasworks, a locale already sanctified by a phrase in *The Waste Land*, and I can remember expeditions in canoes with Wystan and Cecil up evil smelling tunnels." In response to Andrew Cramp's question about whether he had spent much time with Auden, Rex in the early 1980s answered, "Quite a lot, yes. I knew him very well. Certainly toward the end when C. Day Lewis left University. The last year I was there about the only person I did see was Auden." He also commented that they were "constantly arguing about one thing or another and I think we were all influencing one another in various ways."[41] Auden wrote in his 1929 "Verse-letter to C. Day-Lewis" that Rex "looked at much and much saw through."[42] Frances remembers Auden very early on—maybe from 1927, when she met Rex—as always a very boyish-looking person who gave one the impression of being clever, but who was not showy at all. Undoubtedly, Rex's association with Auden and Day-Lewis and his turn toward English studies were influential in convincing him to become a professional writer, and so his breakdown may have had beneficial effects.

The *Wadham Gazette* for the summer term of 1928 included the notices of Day-Lewis's second book, *Country Comets* (1923), and of *Oxford Poetry* (1927), edited by Auden and Day-Lewis. Rex had been included in this journal for 1926 (when Auden and Charles Plumb edited it), with four poems: "A Kitchen Garden," "Friends," "Odyssey," and "Manifesto." Auden himself had only three poems included and Day-Lewis, four. One of Day-Lewis's poems was entitled "Naked Woman with Kotyle," leading Tom Hopkinson to remark facetiously, "Lucky man, that Kotyle." (A *kotyle* or *cotyle* is an ancient Greek cup.)

Rex had not yet written any serious prose, and his poems remain testimony not only to his artistic ambitions and style, but also to his personality at that time:

Manifesto
I laugh at all women excepting three,
 And out of ten
 I mock nine men,
Because they are dissimilar to me.

Snail-like within an egoistic shell,
 Day after day
 I will inveigh
Against this earth's amusing heaven and hell.

When all the stars are shining I will cry
 Out for the moon,
 And at broad noon
I will demand a different sun and sky.

Against the world I ride to break a lance,
　　And challenge it
　　To match my wit
With situation and circumstance.

This shows a young man's discontent and also his pride in his intelligence. The poems are not formally innovative or daring, but they are witty, intelligent, and understandable. Rex's writing career had begun.

V. FRANCES CHAMIER GROVE

In the 1927 volume of *Oxford Poetry*, Rex has five poems, more than either Auden or Day-Lewis. The poems are shorter than before and of lesser quality, but still playful and witty:

Impression
Here is my hand. Yours
Is one foot from it.
Twelve inches in this foot
　　Are all infinite.

If I wrenched space awry
　　And touched you in play,
The universe would squawk
　　And go flap away.

Is this about Frances? Perhaps. He met her during the summer of 1927 when her brother David had just been sent back on leave from Lagos, Nigeria, where he had found work with the British colonial government. He was a sensitive man with whom Rex as a student liked to talk about what was meant by God. He could not stand his job of prison inspector, and resigned immediately after this leave and eventually joined the Communist Party.

During David's leave in 1927 he brought Rex, then in good spirits after his year off, home where he met Frances, who had been some years behind him in school. (She had left St. George's in 1919 when her parents moved to London, and had attended a day school there, but had retained good memories of St. George's.) The first sign of Rex's interest was not long in coming. In the late summer of 1927, not long after David had brought Rex to her house, Frances, David, and Rex went to a reunion at St. George's. In the assembly room, David told Rex to sit on one side of him, but Rex said, "No—I want to sit next to your sister." Later on, David and Frances went up to Oxford to see Rex, and they would also have lunch with Cecil at the George.

Frances, who was born on 15 November 1910, was only about seventeen at this time and had just started at the Royal Academy of Dramatic Arts. With her youth, slim figure, gray eyes, and brown hair, it is no wonder that Rex was immediately attracted to her. Moreover, she liked poetry, and remembers that during these outings with Cecil they discussed Yeats, Rupert Brooke, and Shelley. Alone, she and Rex discussed poetry and politics. From 1923, Cecil was in love with Mary King, whom he married in 1928. Frances never became really friendly with Mary, but there is a photo showing the two couples on the lawn at Amberley Rectory in 1927 or 1928.

The Groves were a widely traveled family. Frances's mother, Daisy Chamier, of French Huguenot descent, had been born in Australia and had gone to Germany to study music at age nineteen. She then returned to Australia, where she met Frances's father, Frank, who was fifteen years her senior. She fell in love at first sight, and the two were married in Tasmania in 1902. Frances's parents went to England where her brother David was born in 1904. They then spent twelve years in China (Frank was a civil engineer who built railroads), where Frances was born. When Frank, in government service, was recalled to England from China in 1916, they traveled on the Transiberian Railroad. They first lived in Manchester, where Frank directed munitions factories, and then in Bournemouth. (Frank was later awarded the OBE, or Order of the British Empire, for his munitions work during World War I.) Frank went off to Persia to do more surveying for railway work, and the children were put in St. George's. During the 1920s, the family came to London and got a house in Kensington; later they moved to 36 Landsdowne Road, Holland Park.

Rex visited the Landsdowne Road house. He was undoubtedly impressed with the cosmopolitan, religiously exploratory, and aesthetic atmosphere. Frances's mother, Daisy, had been an admirer of Annie Besant, the Theosophical movement's guru after the Madame Blavatsky period. Daisy wrote a book entitled *The Mystery Teaching of the Bible* and another, for the Theosophical Society, called *The Apocalypse Unseen*, and did a great deal of lecturing about these things. (Daisy became disillusioned with the Theosophical Society at the time of the Krishnamurti scandal in the late 1920s, and became a Roman Catholic in her old age.) She also lectured widely about music. Daisy was a very lively speaker who used to illustrate her lectures on Wagner, for instance, at the piano. David, Frances, and their sister Marion (some years older than Frances) sang part songs and madrigals, while her father had a good bass voice and liked operatic arias and popular songs of the time.

Marion went to the London School of Economics and received a degree in Economics. She worked for Nonesuch Press, David Garnett's publishing house, and knew the poets Vera and Francis Meynall and would visit them at Toppersfield in Essex. Among other landmarks, the Nonesuch Press produced the *weekend book* series of puzzles and short stories, and also Joseph Conrad's novella *The Secret Sharer*.

Marion became very left wing and gave up her school friends when she got married. She had one child with her first husband, Wells Coates, a Canadian—a daughter named Laura born at the same time as Rex and Frances's first, Jonathan—and two with her second husband. She was a very brilliant and beautiful woman, and her parents were disappointed when she became involved with politics.

Rex got on fairly well with Frances's family, but he was never to become a member of their circle or of the Bloomsbury group, because he was in London very little. Rex and Frances knew each other for eighteen months, including a year's engagement, before getting married, because her parents insisted on a long engagement.

Before he could think of marriage, Rex had to get a job. The letters of recommendation written by his teachers, mostly in 1928, tell us a lot about him at this time. Percy Simpson, M.A., of Oriel College, Oxford, joint editor of the Oxford *Ben Jonson*, wrote on 27 March 1928:

> Mr. R. Warner, of Wadham College, tells me that he is applying for a post as an English teacher in an American university. I have much pleasure in supporting his application. He is a good classical scholar, as his First Class in Honour Moderations shows. He has also read for the Greats School but he had to shorten his Oxford course, & so he changed over to English. He is taking the Honour School in English this summer—a two year's [*sic*] course—after one year's reading. Whether it is possible in so short a time for him to secure a First Class I am not sure, for the range of reading is wide; but I am certain that his work will be first class in quality. He is a very good critic, & writes excellently & with literary appreciation. And I think he would do well as a lecturer. He is keen & alert & has sound judgement.[43]

The influence of St. George's and the Pells shows up in Rex's American hopes, which were not to be realized for another thirty years. Simpson is very accurate in predicting that Rex would not be able to gain a first in English, but offers the information that Rex had done two years' reading in one for the exam.

The *Gazette* for the Michaelmas Term, 1928, carries two interesting notices under "Educational Appointments": first, that Paul Roberts who had entered Wadham in 1908 would become headmaster of the Frensham Heights School, a coeducational boarding school founded in 1925; he would hire Rex when Rex came back from Egypt in the 1930s. The other notice is that R. E. Warner "is at present doing Preparatory School work at Harecroft Hall, Gosforth, Cumberland." He was not to work there long. The school was strange: the staff drank bad port out of dirty mugs, and a teacher who was about to be ordained got so drunk on his last day as a layman that he had to be carried home.[44]

A letter of 26 November 1928 from R. A. Vallance, headmaster of Harecroft Hall, gives the official reason that Rex decided to leave after only one term there:

> Mr Warner came to us at the beginning of the present term well recommended from Oxford, and also by a previous employer. His work here was to teach Latin as a main subject, general form-work to some of the boys, and to take charge of the School Rugger. It was a great disappointment to me when Mr Warner informed me a few days ago that circumstances compelled him to leave us, solely in order to take up work in or near London. I had asked him to return here permanently after the holidays.
>
> Mr Warner is, first and foremost, a gentleman. It follows that we find him an agreeable member of the household, and that the boys like and respect him. I shall be delighted to hear that he has been able to secure a suitable post.[45]

Rex had been launched on his career, not as a professor at an American university, but as a classics master. Frances, by this time a serious girlfriend, was certainly the compelling circumstance for Rex to want to be near London, but the poor conditions at the school also helped.

He might also have wanted to be near London for literary reasons. His serious writing career began around this time. In a biographical sketch that he filled out in 1958 for the *Atlantic Monthly Press*, Rex wrote, "I started writing early. . . . I wrote my first novel when I was about 23 [that would be in 1928] + immediately destroyed it."[46] This is the only semi-official mention he ever made of this first early novel. Frances remembers that he told her that it was a more realistic kind of novel than he was later to publish. No trace of it remains, but it points toward the successful attempt, in *The Wild Goose Chase*, that was to come soon enough.

CHAPTER FOUR

SONNING, MINIA, AND ALEXANDRIA, 1929-1934

I. FIRST STEPS IN MARRIAGE AND CAREER

After an eighteen-month courtship, Rex, twenty-four years old, and Frances, eighteen, were married on 31 July 1929, by Rex's father in his church in Amberley. Rex's clergyman uncles Arthur Luce and George Warner were also in attendance. Rex's parents put on the wedding, because Frances wanted to be married in the country. On the marriage certificate, Frank Grove and Kathleen Warner are listed as witnesses.

The two sets of parents met during the wedding for the first time, and discovered that they had little to say to one another. Although Frederic and Kathleen Warner had traveled in France, Switzerland, and Ireland, unlike the Groves they had never been as far afield as China and did not concern themselves much with music and theater. So Rex's parents did not have much to discuss with Frances's literary sister Marion, with her mother Daisy, given her musical and residually Theosophical opinions, or with her father Frank, who played the cello and had worked in very distant lands. Because Frances's brother David had been at St. George's and Wadham with Rex, the Warners probably knew him better than the others, but he was not among Rex's closest friends. Frances had met the Warners before, but only superficially. When Frances first met them, she was at RADA, the Royal Academy of Dramatic Arts, and had told them that her studies included fencing. They asked if she studied fencing so that she could act in *Hamlet*, and she said no, just to learn how to be graceful. They may have considered her involvement in acting slightly disreputable, as did Dora and Grace, Rex's "low" church evangelistic Gloucester aunts on his mother's side.

The young couple looked very handsome: Frances in a blue dress that was made especially for the occasion in London, and Rex in a fashionable suit. Among the guests were Day-Lewis and Mary King. Cecil was the best man and wrote a marriage poem praising them both. On that day, Rex vowed that when he was fifty he would stand before his favorite old oak tree near the rectory again. He later told Frances, with typical self-deprecating humor, that in 1955 (when he was married to Barbara Rothschild) he stood there meditating for one full day until he realized that he was only forty-nine because it was before his birthday in March.

Six months before the wedding, Rex had left the eccentric Harecroft Hall for a new job at the Oratory School outside the city of Reading. Soon after the wedding, the young couple moved into a small house at 2, Thames Cottages, in the nearby Thameside village of Sonning. Rex was making only £300 a year teaching, and even paying the rent was a difficult task.

Fortunately, they had some help from their parents. They were allowed to use all the furniture Frances's parents did not store when they gave up their London house and went off to New Zealand on one of Frank's engineering jobs in the fall of that year. The furniture was not Frances's preferred style because it was old-fashioned and heavy for such a small house, but with that and the wedding presents of glass and china, they were able to manage.

The house itself was not ideal either. It had no bathroom—the bath was under the kitchen table, and the lavatory was outside. It also needed painting, and in the time-honored fashion of young couples starting out, they painted the walls themselves. Frances remembers that the modern idea then was color wash in light pastel shades. Rex was not very good at all this, and never much of a handyman. As a result, Frances's sister Marion, her first husband Wells Coates (who later became a known architect), and Frances's brother David often visited to help. For her part, Frances barely knew how to cook then, and had to learn that art painfully.

It was a honeymoonish time. Rex and Frances did not have the money for restaurants, but they could eat out at the White Hart, a very inexpensive little country hotel. They would go to Reading for shopping and amusement. They also went to Oxford often and visited and were visited by Charles Fenby, who had become an editor at the *Oxford Mail* (begun by his uncle). Rex and Charles corresponded often, usually writing nonsense or comically exaggerated descriptions of what they were doing. With Cecil, they delighted in saying outrageous things to and about one another. Charles did not marry until 1941. Like many other journalists and writers, he was to become an alcoholic.

Frances's father gave them a car—a two-seater Fiat with a "dickie" or rumble seat—and Rex used it for driving to school, where he taught English and Scripture. The Oratory School was Catholic and during one of Rex's classes, a boy put up his hand and said "Please, sir, isn't that a heresy?" But it was still early in Rex's schoolmastering career, and he enjoyed teaching. Moreover, he was doing the same work as Day-Lewis and Auden, so perhaps there was a sense that it was bearable despite the low salary. A touch of Cecil Grant's occupational idealism probably helped as well.

It was during this period, from 1929 until his departure for Egypt in 1932, that Rex began writing the prose that would bring him public attention. With Day-Lewis, who visited them often and was visited in his and Mary's cramped flat at Belmore House in Cheltenham, Rex discussed some of the ideas that would go into *The Wild Goose Chase*. These were heavily political as well as aesthetic conversations, and one friend told Rex and Frances that theirs was a "conspiratorial" downstairs sitting room. Day-Lewis was full of Communist ideas and used to take the *Daily Worker*, which Mary hated to see around their house. Rex never subscribed, nor did he join the Party, but he sympathized with and did some work for it.

Like most other people, Rex and Cecil were more intense when they were young than they would be later on. At this time, Rex in particular was dismissive of the older generation and of ideas he did not like. One can empathize with the distress of Frederic and Kathleen Warner concerning Rex's turn to radicalism. Frances recalls Kathleen telling the couple that they were trying to destroy everything that she and Rex's father believed in.

Jill Day-Lewis, Day-Lewis's second wife, says of a later time (but it was undoubtedly true earlier too) that Rex and Cecil "sparked each other off" and built on one another's witticisms. They would tease each other without pity. Rex, for instance, was ruthless about mocking Day-Lewis's earliest poems, which he could quote from memory. Cecil would retaliate with, "What about your sonnet that said 'a touch of flesh is worth a pound of thought?'" This indicates a friendly but sometimes strong rivalry, which also manifested itself in sports. Sean Day-Lewis remembers when he was a child seeing a rather intense tennis match between Rex and Cecil. He was even sent away because it got so hot and dangerous, with very fast balls whizzing around. Jill also remembers in the early 1950s that Rex, by then a very experienced bird-watcher, was furious because Day-Lewis, also a bird-watcher, saw a spoonbill first. But despite all of the mutual teasing, Cecil admired Rex's writing enormously, and Rex felt the same way about Cecil's. Mutual support was very important at this time, because neither Day-Lewis, who was published, nor Rex, who wasn't published at all outside of Oxford journals, had made any impact on the literary world.

Among the couple's visitors in late 1929 was Maurice Bowra. At that time, Frances was pregnant with their first child Jonathan, and she may have felt, like so many others, that she was being sized up by this sophisticated and naughty mind, whose most lasting saying may be "Never explain." Frances had met Auden in Oxford, but he never visited at the cottage in Sonning. Stephen Spender did not visit because he and Rex had met only once or twice at Oxford via Auden and they barely knew one another before World War II. But Rex, Charles Fenby, and sometimes Frances would meet at the George pub in Dorchester, where there were sides of bacon hanging up, and the bartender was the very fat Joe Jordan, who would appear as the character Joe in *The Wild Goose Chase*.

On 10 July 1930, Rex and Frances spent the whole afternoon on a punt on the river at Sonning. Soon after, birth pangs began, and Rex drove Frances to a small nursing home on Bath Road in Reading. Jonathan was born the same night, and Rex entered the world of adult responsibility. Soon after the birth, Auden came to visit them when they were in Amberley and enjoyed pushing Jonathan around in a carriage.[1] About eighteen months later, in December 1931, Auden would send the Warners the manuscript of a poem about Jonathan, who is hailed as the new leader who will cure society's ills: "John, son of Warner, shall rescue you." The poem continues, in part:

> The few shall be taught who want to understand,
> Most of the rest shall live upon the land;
> Living in one place with a satisfied face
> All of the women and most of the men
> Shall work with their hands and not think again.

Without mentioning them by name, the poem goes on to mock figures identified in Auden's notebook as Wyndham Lewis, Robert Graves, and T. S. Eliot, all of whom he considered, with some justice, reactionary.[2] Although Rex had no share in writing it, this poem may have contributed to a literary dispute between Rex and Graves that erupted much later, if Graves recognized that he was attacked in the poem.

II. WRITING *THE WILD GOOSE CHASE*

Despite the Depression and the couple's lack of money, this was an exciting period in Rex's life. John Luce, Gordon's son, remembers the precise occasion when *The Wild Goose Chase* was begun. Rex was at Amberley Rectory during a vacation, perhaps the Christmas break of 1930, and came down, ecstatically, from his room with the first few pages in his hand and read them to the assembled family. Those present, including Rex's parents, received it well, and it remains a clear family favorite, with Rex's younger son George as well as Frances preferring it to all of Rex's later work. Perhaps because this was the first novel he wrote, Rex always felt something special toward it. In 1983, he wrote me that "I still like the book, though it's obviously full of youthful faults, exaggerations, etc."[3] It is undoubtedly one of the most important British novels of the 1930s. Since this complex and exciting novel would not be published until 1937, the story of its revisions, publication, and impact appears in my discussion of Rex's career in the late 1930s. Here I will limit myself to a brief synopsis of the novel and to tracing Rex's progress in writing and publishing it in the overall context of his life during the 1929-34 period.

Essentially, *The Wild Goose Chase* tells the story of three brothers—the heroic George, the intellectual David, and the daring Rudolph—who set off on bicycles on a "wild goose chase," which symbolizes, among other things, a quest for the right way to live. Their journey takes them across the border into a new country, where they find a dictatorial regime. Rudolph and David fail in their quest, but after much struggle George succeeds in vanquishing the dictatorship and in attaining an honest, authentic existence as a man of the people. The novel's unnamed narrator, however, remains in doubt about the reliability of the old man who has recounted the brothers' adventures after they left on their journey. So the reader can never be sure if the story happened as it has been related either in its details or as a whole. The most famous incident in the novel is a "fixed" football match in which a science fictional field is made to twist and tilt to unfairly favor the regime's side against George's.

Like most first novels, the book owes much to events taking place in the life of its author at the time. George might be named for Rex's uncle, while the academic David might be Frances's brother. But a more definite connection between life and art exists. At the end of the summer term of 1931, Rex was sacked for taking the side of a rather wild Irishman named Rudall who claimed that he was a former member of the IRA and frequently talked of the revolutionary spirit, and who was accused of Communism by the Oratory School headmaster, Father Henry Tristram. The charge against Rudall also included subverting the older boys politically. Father Henry dismissed Rudall, but he would not go away, and paraded around the grounds with two large Chow dogs and spread scandal about the staff and headmaster. Father Henry called the faculty together and wanted their help in "excommunicating" or shunning Rudall, but Rex wouldn't comply. Rudall would frequently visit Rex and Frances in their cottage during this period.

Appropriately, Rudall became the character Pushkov, who speaks in Rudall's conspiratorial tone: "You may laugh at me, but if you knew what I know you would do something else. I will tell you for why. Certain measures may at any moment be taken against certain people and there are other people who are always ready to provide the right moment for the taking of those measures. Ah-ha, it cuts both ways, though."[4]

Rex felt that faculty should not be dictated to and he would not abandon his friend Rudall to save his own career, even though jobs were very hard to come by and he had a child to support. Here, as with the case of the Jewish Marxist at Wadham, Rex demonstrated personal integrity at some risk to himself. The trouble over Rudall is reflected in a letter of 1 November 1931 from Wystan Auden at Larchfield Academy, Helensburgh (where Auden was teaching, having replaced Day-Lewis): "What you tell me about yourself is absolutely scandalous. Can I do anything. I'll write to Father D'Arcy if you like. . . . Your headmaster wants a good hiding and I'm itching to give it to him."[5] But Rex may have felt that Father Tristram did not deserve a hiding, because Tristram's letter of recommendation is highly laudatory:

> Mr R. Warner came to this school in January 1929 and left in July 1931. He was senior classical master, and prepared his pupils mainly for the . . . School Certificates of the Oxford and Cambridge Board. He also took the fifth form for the English of the School Certificate. For such work he is exceptionally well qualified, and he has given us every satisfaction. Further he took a great interest in the Rugby Football, and coached the first XV. He got on well with his pupils and his colleagues in general, and I can recommend him for a similar appointment elsewhere.[6]

Rex would have difficulty finding another job because of the Great Depression, which had begun with the New York stock market crash on 29 October 1929. This had been followed by enormous unemployment in England, reaching over twenty percent of the work force (some two and a half million people) by 1932. Rex had tried to write for money even while employed, with only limited success. He published just two pieces during this early period of his marriage, his first works in a non-Oxford and non-school journal. On 22 February 1930, a poem entitled "Exile" appeared in the *New Statesman*:

These sympathetic cobwebs are soon broken,
>   Since from abroad no humane words are spoken,
>   Nor rigour of any iron girds heart to heart
Which any silly wind will not dispart.

From now on bar the gateways of the mind
In face of everything that's undefined;
And if there's voice of translunary things,
Oh, clip that bird of Paradise's wings.[7]

The occasion for this piece is unknown, but one catches a hint of John Donne's poetry ("translunary"), and perhaps Rex's youthful contempt for those who rejected the new ideas of Marxism, which may have appeared more metaphysical then than they do in retrospect.

The second piece, a short story entitled "Holiday" also from the *New Statesman*,[8] displays the taste for biting caricature combined with fantasy that would mark Rex's later work. One character, Mr. Bean, has a huge lip, which frightens the other two characters, Mr. and Mrs. Bat: "But Mr. Oliver Bat was frankly startled by the lip. What would happen, he wondered, if it did break. What fearful fleshy inundation would overwhelm Mr. Bean's projecting waistcoat! It might even wash away their chairs."

While his wife flirts with Mr. Bean, Mr. Bat floats off on daydreams reminiscent of J. Alfred Prufrock's claws scuttling across silent seas: Bat has a vision of perfect beauty, "some divine composition where words fail, an accidental union of sight and sounds, whose static perfection is beyond the arts, an eternal moment thrown instantaneously, negligently, by a god for a satisfying mirage on the desert plain of existence."[9] The telling sentence comes from the mouth of the vulgar Bean, who says "'Steady, Bat, or you'll be having a nervous breakdown.'" We cannot know, but Bat's dream of beauty may contain something of Rex's vision during his breakdown. Bat's brief moment of reflection out of this world constitutes his only "holiday," and the story's title therefore becomes very striking after one has read it.

Rex was already unemployed when he visited the Day-Lewises from 25-30 July 1931, and played shove half-penny, a pub game, in the dining room with Cecil and Lionel Hedges, an amateur actor and irregular cricketer (who was soon to die of the flu). This was one of Rex's favorite games, and he was very good at it. Each player tries to slide his coins across a 24-inch by 15-inch polished mahogany board into indentations on the other side, in a kind of miniature shuffleboard.

According to Sean Day-Lewis's biography of his father, the three men also took a drive to A. E. Housman's Bredon, and went to the cinema on this occasion. Here they likely saw a German film such as *The Student of Prague* or Fritz Lang's *Metropolis*, a Russian masterpiece by Eisenstein or Pudovkin, or a lighter American film. During the 1930s, they would grow into fanatic fans of the Marx Brothers and Fred Astaire and Ginger Rogers. On this occasion, Rex was visiting to give support to Cecil as he waited for his wife to give birth to their first child. Rex went home, and Sean was born on 3 August 1931. Rex visited them again on 17 August and 22 August; and Rex and Frances together on 17/18 October.

When fired by Father Tristram in July 1931, Rex received one term's salary as compensation; when Frances turned twenty-one in November of that year, she received a gift of £100 from her parents. Rex used these two sources of income to write much of *The Wild Goose Chase* during the summer and fall of 1931. Unfortunately, the manuscript cannot be studied because Rex later gave it to the Friends of the Soviet Union to sell in an auction. In response to Andrew Cramp's question about whether or not Kafka's symbolism was more ambiguous than Rex's, Rex replied,

> Yes, but my symbolism used to be very complicated. In *The Wild Goose Chase* I tried to lay down everything so that every figure could be understood in a philosophical, historical and political way. That was the idea anyway. I had notebooks about it which I've lost now. Of course, the original book was much longer. In some ways it was modeled on Fielding's *Tom Jones*. There were diversions and essays.[10]

What were Rex's political leanings at this time? According to Frances Warner, Rex was idealistic, but he was never a Communist Party member nor quite as enthusiastic about Marxism as Day-Lewis was. On the other hand, he was seen selling the *Daily Worker* in the streets of Reading.[11] In his interview with Andrew Cramp, Rex said, "I wasn't actually a member but I was doing things with them and generally working for them which I probably would have done much more if I hadn't gone to Egypt at that time."[12] In answer to Cramp's question about whether or not he was influenced by Marxist theories of literature, Rex responded,

> Well, I wasn't really—not the theories of literature but I certainly studied Marxism a good deal. I think because it appeared to be a sort of alternative to the bumblings in an idiotic way of what was going on in the liberal left which one would normally have belonged to you see. They seemed to be letting the side down constantly, so a more rigid thing like Communism made sense and was more practical. And of course at the beginning

everyone had great great hopes of Russia. I'd imagine very much like Wordsworth did at the time of French Revolution—really hoping for the future.[13]

So Rex's lack of respect for liberal waffling, Christian sympathy for the poor, antipathy to the rise of fascism, and idealistic hopes for the future easily coalesced into a great respect for, if not a totally firm intellectual commitment to, Marxism.

Rex's work throughout the 1930s shows that he remained strongly involved with Marxist ideas during that decade. Like many other people, he did not abandon Communism completely until the time of the Molotov-Ribbentrop Pact of 23 August 1939. This nonaggression pact between Stalinist Russia, the standard-bearer of Communism, and Hitler's foreign minister, seemed to many idealistic Communists and sympathizers like a complete betrayal of their cause.

Marxist ideas are certainly present in *The Wild Goose Chase*. Around October 1931, Rex was able to give Day-Lewis a look at the first four chapters of *The Wild Goose Chase*, as Day-Lewis's previously unpublished and important letter,[14] reveals:

I have just read through the allegory for the first time, & must write at once to tell you how good I think it is. I cannot put it more adequately than by saying that you make one believe you really do know a thing or two about the Wild Goose. So let me adjure you (quite unnecessarily) to let nothing stop you, & if your money runs out, finish the book here. I think the prose is lovely, except for a few awkwardnesses which I will mark, & which may be justified. The plot seems to me clearer & more coherent than that of "the *Castle*," & the incidental stuff more robust. Two things I don't feel sure about:—i] the Chap & Pyrrha incident: I can't find much connection between the Chap & Christ, & I think their joint connection with Graeco-Roman civilisation too strongly represented. C's & P.'s reunion after the death of the Don suggests some external historic event—but what? the Reformation? Modernism? God forbid. But if so, one is surely entitled to know more about their subsequent existence. If on the other hand that scene simply intends to show George's private separation of GK.-R. civ. & Christianity, a cleaning of his mind, then his immediate departure from C.&C. for the frontier seems to be sketchily motivated. I think that scene should receive more attention (all the first part, with the Don, will do; I see what you mean now). ii] re. The interludes: the form is justified, comes off excellently. But I detect in the matter (only occasionally) a reaction—sometimes contempt, sometimes defiance—towards emotions & states you have outgrown or experienced only an intellectual contact with. I don't think, in the last resort, that contempt or defiance will do: there is contempt (positive) on the one side, & defiance (negative) on the other; & both are death sooner or later: between them, possibly, a strip where you may walk in safety—pure, good emotion; not something abstract, "scientific," meteoric, philosopher-in-a-basket; but a correct & so far nameless attitude. I don't think you have this (which being a perfection, it is not unnatural.) But when Fielding, for instance, in his interludes shows contempt, he laughs—not the frightened destructive laughter of your police force, but a personal amused laughter: your contempt is, I think, too serious, too we-are-not-amused-almost, in fact, the laughter of your own policemen, except that it is a private rather than a social defiance. This does not necessarily detract from the form of the book or from its didactic value; but somehow it must detract from your own authority. I agree that pure destruction can be a good thing; but in so far as contempt & defiance is your method, it must destroy yourself as well—an unnecessary self-sacrifice, one hopes. I don't know if I have been clear about these things. I shall read the m.s. again tomorrow, & put down anything further that occurs to me, before I send it back: also, go into the amatory question, about which I think you are very sound, though you have had rather a hilarious & one-sided account of it. Couldn't you come here for a few nights? Sonning is impossible, much as I should love to come, as I am working all Saturdays & most Sundays this term.

Another page dated "Tuesday" is included:

I've read the M.S. a second time & put down a few pencil comments on the side. There is little criticism to add to what I put in my last letter; I've put a cross against one passage where the English seems badly involved; the other passages I had in mind justify themselves on a second reading. I like bits of the interludes very much, & they are obviously a good device, but I don't feel the certainty in them that I feel in the story itself. Whether this is a failure of yr. expression or my comprehension I can't say. You get so much of your personal quality into the objective story, that to a person who knows you the interludes must seem rather superfluous; but this is, of course, no argument against them. I am struck again by your mythopoeic faculty—you do extract the maximum significance out of people & incidents, & apart from anything else you tell a good story— to put it at its least common denominator. If you can keep this up, & I've little doubt you will surpass it, the book must be first-rate: it seems to me already one of the best things I've ever read in prose. I envy you the middle of it: I'm full of the usual desperation & aimlessness, having finished a piece of work, with no idea what is going to happen next. I might reorganise the satire, but I feel it has the wrong end of the stick somehow.

The reference to Rex's running out of money in the first part of the letter shows that it was indeed written around October 1931, when his compensation money from the school was running out and Frances's £100 gift had not yet arrived. This letter also proves that Day-Lewis and Rex had both read Kafka's *Castle* by this time, and while Rex was still working on *Wild Goose Chase*. Willa and Edwin Muir's translation of Kafka's novel appeared in 1930, and Kafka must be seen as an influence on Rex, although Rex later downplayed that.[15] Day-Lewis is quite right in seeing that the Don Antonio, Pyrrha, and Cleobyle incident of chapter two was and remains quite obscure. Also, the degree to which Cecil was willing to confide in Rex is apparent, since in a paragraph I have omitted the letter responds to Rex's advice concerning one of Cecil's extracurricular love affairs.

Another page of the same letter dated "thursday" reads:

> Your postcard just came: I'm sending the book back tomorrow. I've put an O in pencil against some of the things I don't like in the interludes: but, though I feel the substance of my contempt-defiance criticism to be true, the actual example scarcely seems now to call for anything so serious. Let me see the fuck chapter soon; the sentence you sent me is lovely; & the fuck comes rather near home at present. As the past romance, "A pretty girl that naked is/is worth a million statues."

> Sean [Day-Lewis's son] puts on 6 oz. a week, & in 1953 will wrest the Heavy Weight Championship of the World from Jonathan. Wystan is very pleased with my book & writes, "If your child is a daughter (*sic*) I shall have to use Rex's." I've also had most enthusiastic letters from Maurice [Bowra] & Strong: what the bleeding reviewers will say remains to be seen.

Cecil obviously refers to his own book *From Feathers to Iron*, which was published in September 1931. The Auden reference, then, is to Auden's composition of the poem (Ode IV of *The Orators*) that was eventually dedicated to Jonathan Warner, and shows that around October 1931 he was wondering whether to dedicate it to Day-Lewis's child (whose sex he did not know) or to Jonathan; he sent the Warners the manuscript of the poem around December 1931, when it was published in the *Adelphi*.

The "fuck" chapter must be chapter five of Part I of *The Wild Goose Chase*, in which George makes love to Joan; if so, the sentence that Day-Lewis praises might be: "Then he turned and saw Joan huddled up on the bed, her hands covering her face, in an attitude of utter desolation, and he ran to her, throwing wildly his arms round her, covering her cold body with his kisses, still crying: 'The wild geese! Oh the wild geese!' and she looked up at him doubtful, in need of reassurance, then gladly turned to him, crying out in joy, close clinging."[16]

So we know from this letter that by October 1931 Rex had finished the first four chapters of Part I of his novel, and had begun on the fifth. Another very enthusiastic letter from Day-Lewis shows that Rex had finished at least the introductory sections and Part I (or the first volume) of the book at some point, probably in December 1931 or January 1932, before he left for Egypt in February 1932:

> I've just finished reading the volume, & I like it very much indeed, particularly the Rugger match, which I found deeply moving: more of it later. Believe me, the whole thing inspires—that, as a professed teacher, must be the quality you most want to be found in it. I can't help feeling though, like Lawrence's work, it will be ignored at first; perhaps reviled; if praised, praised by the wrong people for the wrong reasons; yet it must, like his work, gain a foothold somewhere & penetrate & spread. One can only hope that some of the right people will see it.[17]

When in Egypt, he finished the novel before October 1932—but to no avail, for it would not be published while he was in Egypt nor for several years after that.

III. EGYPT

Why did Rex go to Egypt? The Depression (and perhaps his political opinions) made it difficult for him to get a job in England, and his money had run out. Perhaps Bowra or another of his Oxford contacts helped him find something abroad. When Rex left on 19 February 1932 aboard the S.S. *Rawalpindi*,[18] Frances went to stay with Rex's parents at Amberley Rectory, where the couple's second child, Anna Joan, was born on 2 October 1932. Frances had to wait behind because she was pregnant and they did not know about conditions in Minia, where Rex was sent. Happily, she felt close to Rex's parents—even addressing them as "Father Ernest" and "Mother Kath"—which made a long stay with them possible. She saw Rex off at the train station in London, and would join him in Egypt about a year later, in January or February 1933. The trip to Port Said took two weeks. Rex would return from Egypt around early July 1934,[19] while Frances would go back to England in early spring 1934.

Egypt had gained independence in 1922, but until 1936 the British kept military forces dispersed all over the country, and continued to supply English teachers for the school system. Rex had secured a job in the Egyptian Government P.I., or Public Instruction service.

He first taught at the Minia Government Secondary School in El Minia, about 150 miles south of Cairo, and then at the Ras-el-Tin School in Alexandria. In 1932 Minia was a very pleasant city, known for its friendliness. There was a beautiful tree-lined street along the Nile where people promenaded at night, and an island off the shore where cattle, herded by farmers in boats, grazed. Some of the most interesting ruins in Egypt are within a radius of less than fifty miles, including Hermopolis—the city of Thoth, the scribe of the gods and the inventor of writing—as well as many tombs of various dynasties.

Rex told Andrew Cramp that he regarded the job as "a kind of Foreign Legion. I was teaching English in public schools. There were some jolly good people. A percentage of defrocked priests, and drunkards—things like that."[20] He also mentioned that "there was a group of people there who were Marxists but not very active."

A letter of Cecil's postmarked 3 October 1932 from Cheltenham, is addressed to Rex at "Secondary School, Minia, Upper Egypt." This previously unpublished letter is very revealing of the relationship between Day-Lewis and Auden, and provides details concerning Rex, Frances, and *The Wild Goose Chase*:

£5 will do very well: Marion [Frances' sister] has paid the rest—she says she owes it to you. I am having Wystan's book sent tomorrow: it is very good [possibly *The Orators*, published in 1932]. I was rather depressed about my writing lately: Wystan so clearly has the makings of a great poet, & I can't be more than a good one; I felt that I was simply queering the pitch of himself & any book of his . . . there may be by persevering. With forty one ought to be first-rate or drop it. That is to say, drop publishing. Yet I don't fancy the Captain Oates [self-sacrificing Scott polar expedition hero] act very much. And with poetry that is at least half propaganda, the more the better, I suppose. God knows what anyone else can do it for now, except that. It's all very well to say that one writes because one wants to make something: but it's not as simple as all that: when you have made a chair somebody can sit in it—& who is going to sit down on a piece of poetry in 1932— a few bloody juveniles in Bloomsbury—they'd be better sitting on the floor. Anyway, whatever happens after, "the Magnetic Mountain" will go to a publishers: it is good poetry, pretty good propaganda, I think, & it is sufficiently lively to get me chucked out here to make withdrawal an act of funk. Christ, what a country: Hedges & Osborne—not myself, funnily enough—were put on the mat for pubbing, the nub of the indictment being that they were "lowering themselves by playing darts with the school sergeants." No, anything one can do to smash that way of thinking must be done. I shall enjoy it when we move into our house—a vegetable environment is thing for yours truly I suspect. No news yet about Francis [*sic*] or your book: I'm keeping this letter open till tomorrow in case it comes.

Just heard the glad news [the birth of Rex's daughter Anna]: congratulations, old boy: you & Frances ought to settle in Italy, you'd get quite comfortable living out of the bonuses which Mussolini gives for fecundity. . . .Wystan is teaching at a rather good Quaker prep. school near Malvern.[21]

The letter shows that by October 1932, when Anna was born, *The Wild Goose Chase* was most certainly completed and being sent around to publishers. It is also fascinating for its revelation of Day-Lewis's desire to "smash" the "establishment's" way of thinking.

In the meantime, Rex's life as a schoolteacher in Egypt went on. Gwyn Williams, a Welsh poet and author and later head of the English Department of Farouk University, met Rex at an exam session in Cairo in 1933 or 1934 and explained in a letter to me what it was like to teach and examine in Egypt. The main examination session would take place in June and then there would be a retest in September. It would be a public examination for the certificate in English, and would be open to all Egyptian schools. The test itself would be given in different centers around the country. The Education Department of the Egyptian Government would then pay examiners' expenses for a trip to Cairo and a small remuneration for their marking of the exams. Scores of examiners would read thousands of examination papers in a large hall in Cairo. In summertime after the exams, many of the British teachers who could afford to do so would go home to England. This took about ten days, perhaps five if the trip were carried out partly by train. Leave would be three months. Everyone worked very hard marking the exams in order to get away as soon as possible, whether to England or simply for summer holidays. Salaries were a bit better than a British salary—maybe £300 annually; in Britain it was about £250. At first it seemed that the salary was good, but teaching school was hard work, and £300 was not really much in any case. Teachers would do private tutoring to make extra money because parents would want the students brought up to the proper level for the exam, especially during spring and summer.

The schools were well run and classes were no larger than those in England. The Egyptian headmasters were strict disciplinarians, and the result was that the level was fairly high. During the school year, supervisors visited schools quite regularly; in Rex's time, the inspector of English was Gilbert Smith, a very easygoing and civilized man. Rex did not get into any difficulties, having learned from his previous experience. According to Gwyn Williams, however, Rex seemed more interested in cricket than in teaching, and even wanted to help improve the British cricket team in Cairo. Moreover, his main interest in Egypt was bird-watching, and the pair went to Fayum just for that. Egypt was a marvelous place for wild ducks and geese, but Rex did not like Egyptian kites very much, as his poem with that title reveals:

> Verminous aeronaut, leaflight turkey, kite,
> smothering an airpuff with heave of shoulder,
>   fingering
> delicately with stretched flight plumes your sky,
>   or crucified
> in calm you float, wheeling symbol of an old world
> in the reeling blue serene, looking for something dead.[22]

Williams feels that many of Rex's poems, also written about this time, capture the feeling of Egypt very well. There are certainly some excellent poems about Egypt in Rex's first volume, published in 1937:

> Blown up the Nile in hot gusts a wind
> of dead dust, breathing of lions from waste of
>   sand,
> from Thebes, Abydos, Meroe, from miles of drift,
> vegetable wreck and wrack, reeds and plaited raft,
> a south wind vain for sails, laden with dust.[23]

> Sun is torn in coloured petals on the water,
> the water shivering in the heat and the north
>   wind;
> and near and far billow out white swollen cres-
>   cents,
> the clipping of feluccas, seagull sails.[24]

After *The Wild Goose Chase* was finished, at some point before October 1932, Day-Lewis kept doggedly sending the manuscript out to publishers for Rex. One false alarm may have been particularly painful. From Belmore House in Cheltenham on 17 October (undoubtedly 1932), before Frances had joined Rex in Egypt, Cecil wrote that "it's all right about the book so far. Eliot liked what he read of it, + another director who wrote to me is clearly favourable. But apparently the whole board of directors has to see it before they come to a decision: the only doubt, apparently, is over it's [*sic*] saleability. Wystan has a job at a Quaker school [Downs] near Malvern.

We are seeing Frances on thursday, I hope, when I shall claim my £5. Love Cecil." On 16 November, however, Cecil reported the following:

> I interviewed Faber + the american partner Morley yesterday: they fired questions about you + the obscure points of the book: like a Greats viva [Oxford oral exam]. The upshot is this. They say that allegory is almost always a commercial loss, + that the loss over a book the length of Wild Goose-Chase would be excessive for them. But if the book was cut down to the average length of a novel—75,000 to 100,000 words—they would in all likelihood publish + risk a loss. They admire it very much, + so did the other partners who read it; but they can't afford to lose several hundred pounds at the present juncture. I fought hard against the idea of reducing but the buggers—though affable shits—were adamant: + they said that no firm would take it at it's [sic] present length—I think they are [honest crossed out] right about this, because they have a reputation for taking risks on unpopular work. So I think it would be better for you to cut it, if you could face the task, than for me to hawk it around to other publishers. I also tried hard to make them promise to publish if you did cut it down, but it was no good: they could go no further than to say they would make every effort to publish it in a shortened form. As to the actual cuts, they would leave that to you, but suggest I that opening chapters might be speeded up—they felt that the duplication of towns, the town from which the brothers start, + the capitalist town, is very confusing: II that some of the stories inside the main story could be omitted or shortened: III that the country section in the middle, when George clears the pigsties, is rather tedious: + that the planning for the revolution is left too much to the imagination. They also wanted to know whether you would be going on writing + if so what sort of stuff: I said yes, but probably stuff no more best-selling than Wild Goose Chase: they said, if they took this book in it's [sic] new form would you agree to an understanding that you should give them first refusal of following work: I said I thought you would. So that, I'm afraid, is that. I do feel terribly disappointed about it + only hope you won't take it to heart very much more severely than I do. It's such a hell of a good book as it stands.

Cecil goes on to mention politics and then Michael Roberts's forthcoming *New Country* anthology, whose 1933 publication is now seen as a landmark of 1930s writing:

> But I suppose one can't expect these chaps to finance propaganda they don't agree with out of a pure love of art. They are returning the M.SS. to me: I'll keep it for a fortnight + if I don't get a cable from you in that time telling me to offer it elsewhere I'll send it out to you. I am sending on the poems to [Michael] Roberts—he is rather a one for

making Statements: I still like the Hymn best of your verse + the Vices least: "It is not asked . . ." is fine + very salutary. I like the chorus from the Dam very much too—who is this Col. Humphries? When will the Dam be finished—I believe Faber would be quite likely to publish it—perhaps before the Wild Goose Chase. I've done all but the last two poems of the Magnetic Mountain—it's going very well—I'll send you some as soon as I have time to type them out. We went over to see Frances on Sunday but found she had been ill.

On 16 February 1933, Cecil wrote Rex about *The Wild Goose Chase* that

Putnam's have returned your book, God rot them. However, I have discovered the reader whom Faber mentions in the postscript, + he is going to send them in a cracking good report; so it's just conceivable they might change their minds. In the meantime I am sending it to Gollancz—[L.A.G.] Strong is going to tell them to sit up + take notice: + if they are stupid about it, to Barker—a good new publisher, for whom Strong is the novel reader. So there is still plenty of hope for it. If all these sods won't take it—+ if you felt favourable, I would like to approach Faber again + see if they would publish it as it stands + I guaranteed £100—I've got no better—or nearly as good-use for the money I hope to get out of Blackwell [for *Dick Willoughby*, his contribution to Strong's adventure series].

Cecil's offer to subsidize the book at his own expense is certainly generous. This letter shows too that by February 1933 Rex had not yet cut the book down and was trying to get it published in its original form. The whole process of submission and rejection was undoubtedly very painful, although Rex tried to take it in stride.

Rex did eventually cut the book, but apparently only to have it rejected again since it was not published by Faber or Putnam, the publishers mentioned by Day-Lewis. According to Frances, at least two chapters were excised, including a Greek-like description of the regiments in George's army. Gwyn Williams remembers that *The Wild Goose Chase* was completed while Rex was in Alexandria. Since a letter from Day-Lewis indicates that it was completed and circulating in England by October 1932, when Rex was still apparently living in Minia, Williams probably refers to Rex's cutting down, or editing of the work to comply with publishers' demands. As we have seen, Rex resisted this demand initially but finally complied with it when faced with repeated rejections. The final editing or revision was probably done while Rex was in Alexandria, to which he had been transferred at some point between October and January or February 1933.[25]

Gwyn Williams also recalls that during one summer trip when Rex came to Cairo probably in 1933, a friend of Gwyn's, Bernard Rice, a wood engraver, introduced Rex and Gwyn to Stener and Miriam Vogt, the Norwegian consul and his wife. They invited Rex, Gwyn, and Bernard to dinner in a lovely country house at Bulac Durcrur a few miles northwest of Cairo. Miriam asked Rex how his book was going—was he sending it to publishing houses? Rex said that he had finished and had sent it to 40 publishers. Miriam encouraged him to keep sending it out, and Williams claims that owing to this urging Rex "tried once more, sent it to Boriswoods and the book appeared as *The Wild Goose Chase*." But Williams's memory has deceived him, for the connection with Boriswoods came about after Rex left Egypt, in the manner described in the next chapter. Williams also remembers that Miriam took them out to the garden to celebrate what must have been *The Wild Goose Chase*'s possible future acceptance and said that if you climb these trees you'll see Cairo, and he, Rex, and Bernard climbed the trees and saw Cairo.[26]

In his letter of 16 February 1933, Cecil also discusses his work on Michael Roberts's *New Country*, and mentions a newly completed work by Rex: "As to 'the Dam.' Will you send it to me, + I'll get it typed here: then I could offer it to Faber—or to the Hogarth Press: I'm certain they would like it for their new series. I've been correcting the proofs of M. Roberts' anthology today—the first two choruses in it out of 'the Dam' seem to me terrifically good."

Four choruses from Rex's never-published short play "The Dam" were published in March 1933 in *New Country*. I have not been able to locate a manuscript or typescript copy of "The Dam," but a letter of 28 December 1935 from Rex offers John Lehmann the play.[27] Another letter, of 11 January 1936, from Rex to Lehmann seems to indicate that Lehmann had wanted to publish it, but also possibly why in fact Lehmann did not do so: "'The Dam' is fairly plain sailing. It was written four years ago, + since then some of the jokes in connection with R.[amsay] McDonald have become rather hackneyed. I should probably have altered them if I'd had time; so, if you think fit, make any omissions or alterations you like."[28] Ramsay McDonald had been elected Prime Minister in 1929, but by 1935 had resigned. Other parts of the play may have been very topical, also.

The overt Marxist polemics of "The Dam" choruses are sometimes parallel to similar sentiments expressed in *The Wild Goose Chase*:

> And yet our sons
> won't agree with your guns,
> They will desert your ranks,

not owe you thanks,

will flood your basements

and erase your emplacements,

while we like shrieking roots shall rise

and run up our red standard to the skies,

watching delighted the devastated plain

invested again with shifting corn, the windy grain.[29]

The "Colonel Humphries" to whom Day-Lewis referred earlier, in his letter of 16 November 1932, appears in a line echoing the rhythms of T. S. Eliot's *Waste Land,* "What has happened to Colonel Humphries? Will he come?"[30] From the published choruses, he appears to be a positive figure who will help in the building of the Dam (possibly by protecting it from the workers' enemies), but who has possibly been waylaid by various capitalist snares. The Dam itself no doubt reflects the giant public works projects favored by Communist leaders such as Stalin, and may also symbolize the workers' ability to erect a wall against poverty and fascism.

The fourth chorus contains a hope for a "great leader," and participates in the futurist poetry of machinery so much a part of Auden's and Spender's work at this time as well.

we will turn back this river to land which long time or ever has waited for the life of water and for our great leader who already has scored the desert with steelwork of expert.

This vaguely characterized "great leader" will, perhaps paradoxically, usher in a golden age of more individual freedom and happiness:

We shall listen to our own voices and shall mind our business, some leaders to command, others happy to lend a hand, all able to enjoy women and the company of men, not needing tarts and beer as we needed them before when without work we became hard and our beds were hired. With those fit for us among the great masses we will set up house.[31]

Rex's style here is the same as in *The Wild Goose Chase,* and is especially evident in the proletarian leader George's speeches. References to sandstorms and kites show the influence of Egypt on Rex. In contrast, the "Hymn," which is similarly political and also included in Roberts's anthology, could have been written anywhere:

Come then, companions. This is the spring of blood, heart's hey-day, movement of masses, beginning of good.[32]

New Country also contains work by Auden, Spender, Edward Upward, John Lehmann, and Day-Lewis, among others. Day-Lewis obviously did Rex a favor by sending his poems on to Michael Roberts for this collection, which would become one of the most famous of the period and which grouped him with his contemporaries.

During the marking period after the exams in the summer of 1933, Gwyn and Rex spent some time together in Cairo. They had meals out, and Rex drank beer, but not heavily. They lived in a cheap European boarding house, and had no contact with Egyptians. But dysentery was a problem. Williams recalls a story Rex told him about another teacher, a Welshman named Tommy Gittens, who became ill and had a bottle of orange drink instead of his usual alcoholic beverages because that was the only drink he could keep down. When a mutual friend, Ivor Ajax, another Welshman, came to visit, he did not know Tommy's condition and, appalled by Tommy's apparent switch from alcohol to orange juice, warned him, "Good God! Tommy, you've got to be careful of that. It pits the linings of the stomach."

The Wild Goose Chase does not shed light on Rex's own view of Egypt and his life there, since he had completed at least half of that novel before he left England. For Rex's experience of Egypt, we must look to *The Kite*,[33] which he wrote in just four weeks[34] upon his return to England. This boys' adventure book was number eight in a series, "Tales of Action by Men of Letters," edited by L. A. G. Strong, who awarded him the contract at Cecil's prodding. Cecil had already done one of these boys' series volumes, *Dick Willoughby*, himself. *The Kite*, which is about the apprehension of a drug smuggler, draws on Rex's own experience of Egypt and in some of its details seems to provide an accurate picture of his life at this time. The "Government secondary school in Minia" is mentioned early on.[35] Referring to dwelling places, a character says, "That's where most of the English live. . . . Not that there are many of us here: about six in the school, several in cotton, two bank managers, a few on the railway, and occasionally we have a missionary." There is also a "native quarter, although this 'quarter' really comprised practically the whole town."[36] The Copts have English names and are richer than the Muslims. Rex describes how one gets from Cairo to Minia by train.

The Kite also offers a description of someone smoking hashish, and Rex in his much later *Views of Attica* mentions trying it once without specifying when—likely during this Egyptian experience. Abd el Kader, one of the heroes of the book, says, "Hashish is not so bad."[37] Rex's entire plot turns on the apprehension of the European drug smuggler, the Kite, who has two identities, but he smuggles heroin, not hashish. The policeman Morris says that "In 1929 it was estimated that out of the fourteen millions in Egypt there were half a million addicts. . . . On October 1st, 1931, we had in prison over 4,000 traffickers and near 3,000 addicts, but by the same date in 1934 these numbers were reduced to 2,600 traffickers and only about 400 addicts."[38] Rex also offers the information that a kilogram of pure heroin was worth £3,000. He had obviously done his homework, using some official source of statistics.

The inroads in drug smuggling made by the British are one point in their favor. The Rex who wrote the following passage was anticolonialist, but not rabidly so. After all, he had taken a job in what was still to a large degree the colonial system. "Uncle Frank," no doubt modeled on Rex's own Uncle Frank who had worked in the British civil service in India, gives a very balanced view of British activities to his teenaged nephew, John:

> England has given Egypt some very fine men, and the Egyptians give us credit for that. No Englishman is unpopular here because of his nationality. But, although they are perfectly willing to have us here, they do want to control their own country. That seems to me perfectly right and proper. As for "doing good," it's just humbug to suppose that the English take jobs in Egypt in order "to do good." They take jobs in order to earn their bread and butter, and may or may not do good incidentally. Given the technical skill and resources, the Egyptians have more powerful motives for "doing good" here than we can ever have. What I admire about the Egyptians is their level-headedness about all this. When I meet some of the Englishmen out here I wonder at the fact that as a general rule Englishmen are respected. You know the type I mean. Wretched little people, with all the airs of royalty, despising almost everything, because they find it difficult to understand, arrogant as turkey cocks, and about as intelligent. That sort of person is a greater menace to England than the most extreme politician among the Egyptians. Actually, it is people like Abd el Kader that we ought to take most seriously. There really is a sort of renaissance going on here, just as it is all over the East. I think that if we come to terms with the right people in that movement we should save ourselves a lot of trouble and bitterness. As it is, we are blamed for everything that goes wrong. If we were to leave things alone for a bit, the Egyptians would soon find out that it's not only the English who in the past have made money out of poverty and bad conditions of labour and unorthodox pressure on politicians. . . . [39]

This is, as Marian McLeod claims, "rather liberal thinking for the pre-1936 era,"[40] but it is further balanced by Rex's realistic view that the English are not the only ones to blame for the situation. In fact the British government was working with the Egyptians during this period to achieve a balance between complete Egyptian independence and maintaining certain British interests (such as the defense of the Suez Canal), so things were moving in the direction that Rex describes as desirable. In

1936, all British troops in Egypt would be withdrawn from most of the country and confined to the Canal Zone. In Minia, Rex was teaching the English language and did not get involved politically, although he was obviously sympathetic to the Egyptian movement toward complete freedom from the British.

Rex's view of a possible "renaissance" taking place in Egypt, seen in the following passage about the schoolboy Abd el Kader and his secret society, reads perhaps too much of English liberalism and Marxism into the Egyptian nationalist movement. As of 2001, more than sixty years after *The Kite* was first published,[41] and over forty years after the 1956 Anglo-French-Israeli Suez Campaign (the upshot of which was complete Egyptian freedom from European control), the goals enunciated by Abd el Kader remain largely unrealized:

> The object of the society was no less a thing than the regeneration of the whole country. "Of course, we do much in politics," Abd el Kader explained, "but not only that; we aim at being more advanced than the politicians. For our independence the whole country is united, but we go farther than this: we believe in equal rights for women, equal pay for equal work, and such things that many of our people do not yet believe in. Our aim is to place Egypt in the first rank of nations." So he went on speaking, and John was thrilled with the enthusiasm and imagination of the boy who spoke of replacing mud huts with stone houses, giving leisure and education to the peasants, using, for the first time in history, the great wealth of the country for the purpose of making a happy and self-reliant people.[42]

Islam is notably absent from these objectives, which shows that Abd el Kader's speech is more the result of Rex's secular thinking than a recapitulation of widespread indigenous Egyptian sentiment. Rex's model for the new Egyptian society is Marxist, and this passage reads more like George's program in *The Wild Goose Chase* than anything else.

Another important element here, in addition to Rex's imposition of his own liberalism and to some degree socialism on the Egyptian situation, is Rex's genuine cosmopolitanism. This was always one of his strongest points, and it appears clearly as the moral of the whole story: Uncle Frank "was pleased to think that in the future John would have more reason to respect and like boys of other nations, and would never be likely to slip into that stupid and intolerant attitude which is too common among English boys and grown-ups, the attitude that leads a person to inquire about another person's school, income or nationality and then to adopt prejudices about that person's character."[43] It was his rejection of that narrow attitude that later enabled Rex to have success in Greece and in the United States. Rex possessed the rare combination of love of provincial British mores and an ability to get on with people of many cultures.

An envelope postmarked 18 July 1933 in Alexandria from Day-Lewis in Cheltenham, is addressed to Rex at 18 Rue General Wilson, Mustapha Pasha, Alexandria, where he had moved to take up a post at the Ras-el-Tin School between October 1932 and February 1933. The type of apartment he lived in is perhaps indicated by *The Kite*'s description of the policeman Morris's apartment at Clinton, #19 (which seems very close to Wilson, 18): "And they went into the large block with the road to Ramleh on one side of it and the sea on the other."[44]

Rex's attitude toward the city of Alexandria was mixed. When I discussed Lawrence Durrell's *Alexandria Quartet* with Rex in the early 1970s, he responded that Alexandria had been nothing like the exotic, hothouse place described there, but a good deal more mundane. Yet the description in *The Kite* shows that he felt something positive for the city:

> In that tender blue morning light, which is so soon ripped and scorched through by the summer sun, Frank Cartwright was approaching Alexandria. From the boat he could see the whole splendid sweep of coast from Montaza to Ras-el-tin. To his right as he looked from seaward was a dark patch of pine woods and palms, and among them rising the towers and steep roofs of that incongruous summer palace of the king. Then stretched out the long white sands of Sidi Bishr. Small headlands broke the sweeping line of the Corniche road, and Frank could pick out the position of Stanley Bay, the small and crowded bathing beach with a line of red buoys across its mouth and rows of bathing cabins behind. Here Greeks, Syrians, French, Italians, and English showed off their dresses in summer mornings, and here in other times there may have been other displays of fashion, when Cleopatra was entertaining Julius Caesar or Antony, and when Napoleon's generals, their fleet destroyed, were enjoying the north wind and the distractions which make tolerable an Egyptian summer. From here the coast curved on proudly to the Old Harbour, where Caesar's ships had ridden at anchor and which was now bordered by the tall frontage of hotels and, behind them, the rising ground on which the commercial centre of Alexandria was built.[45]

Rex's interest in the classical connection is very apparent. We can only imagine the delight with which he first contemplated this harbor.

E. M. Forster's *Alexandria: A History and a Guide*, which Rex was surely aware of at the time, and which he would mention in his own subsequent British Council pamphlet on Forster, explores all the layers of the city: the Ptolemaic period, including Cleopatra, the Christian period, the Arab period, and the modern period. He discusses the great Pharos lighthouse and the library of ancient times, but moves to more depressing remarks on the present (that is, 1922) town. After the first flush of excitement wore off, Rex might well have agreed with Forster's views of the modern city, expressed here:

> Her future like that of other great commercial cities is dubious. Except in the cases of the Public Gardens and the Museum, the Municipality has scarcely risen to its historic responsibilities. The Library is starved for want of funds, the Art Gallery cannot be alluded to, and links with the past have been wantonly broken—for example the name of the Rue Rosette has been altered and the exquisite Covered Bazaar near the Rue de France destroyed. Material prosperity based on cotton, onions, and eggs, seems assured, but little progress can be discerned in other directions, and neither the Pharos of Sostratus nor the Idylls of Theocritus nor the Enneads of Plotinus are likely to be rivalled in the future. Only the climate, only the north wind and the sea remain as pure as when Menelaus, the first visitor, landed upon Ras-el-Tin, three thousand years ago; and at night the constellation of Berenice's Hair still shines as brightly as when it caught the attention of Conon the astronomer.[46]

Forster mentions Ramleh, "the straggling suburb where the British and other foreigners reside" and Stanley Bay, "a fine bit of coast scenery and a favourite bathing place"[47] of the British. This contrasts with Rex's view in *The Kite*, that it was a "small and crowded bathing beach" where the foreign women showed off their dresses.

Frances, with Jonathan and Anna, then three months old, joined Rex in Alexandria in January or February 1933. Everything was fine at first; Frances and the children enjoyed the new, warmer environment. During the summer, they, too, went to Stanley Bay. There were other English couples and children for company; these were the days when there was no contact between Europeans and Egyptians. They secured a Jersey girl, Iris Crosby, as a nursemaid, and made friends with the Collies, who had a comfortable place and enjoyed entertaining younger English people. But in December 1933, about ten months after they had arrived, a tragedy occurred that was to mark the family's life to the present day. In that month, Rex and Frances took a plane from Alexandria to Cairo for a holiday. The couple stayed at a hotel and went to see the pyramids and the latest film. But as soon as they got back to their hotel there was a telegram from Iris Crosby. The children and Iris had been staying with the Collies while Rex and Frances were gone. Iris Crosby summoned them back urgently. When they arrived via the most readily available transportation, a train, they were told that Anna had had sudden, prolonged convulsions at night. The two available English doctors came in but could do nothing. The Collies, however, succeeded in bringing in a Greek doctor who performed a lumbar puncture, which enabled an examination of the cerebro-spinal fluid and may also have saved Anna's life. Anna had had convulsions for six hours, and when she came round her whole right side was paralyzed. It was encephalitis.

According to recent medical encyclopedias, the disease is an inflammation of the brain cells caused by a viral infection. It is common in Europe and the United States as well as in other regions of the world. In mild cases, it resembles any brief viral infection, but in severe cases such as Anna's, there can be loss of muscular power in the arms or legs, double vision, impairment of speech and hearing, and even coma and death. Only a small number of cases have serious consequences, but Anna's, involving permanent brain damage, was one of those. Today we have steroid drugs to counter inflammation, and respirators for helping with breathing. Physiotherapy can also aid in relearning lost skills such as clear speech. But in 1933 none of these aids existed, and even today they are not entirely satisfactory.

After the attack, Anna recovered slowly, but never completely. She was able as a girl to swim, participate in the "Girl Guides," go camping, play chess and go to regular school, but one side of her body was permanently affected. During her teenage years, epilepsy (a possible result of encephalitis) set in. She would have both "grand mal" and "petit mal" fits. During a petit mal, her speech would often be slow and slurred, and she would sometimes droop off her chair, and have to be alerted back to consciousness. While today she has a good memory, a sense of humor, and is able to enjoy novels and poetry, she lives in a nursing home owing to the effect of the medication that she has to take.

Frances and Rex had nothing for which to reproach themselves. If they had been present, they could not have prevented the disease, nor its toll. It might have happened in England as well. But the feelings of parents caught in such a situation are rarely entirely rational. There was certainly guilt over having come to Egypt with a small child in the first place, not having watched the child sufficiently (impossible in any case), and having been absent when the disease began.

In addition to the psychological burden, the young and impecunious couple would have to deal with a disabled individual in their house, only three years after they were married. Jonathan would have to live with a disabled sister, and Rex and Frances would be concerned about the psychological impact on him. It was not an auspicious beginning for a marriage, but the couple overcame it—for a while.

The blow might have been exacerbated by the sharp intellect of both mother and father. Rex and Frances were used to quick intelligence, not mental disability. Rex was fond of Anna but must have felt pain and possibly guilt in her presence. Caring for her fell entirely to Frances. Rex and Frances had intended to go down the Nile and to enjoy all that Egypt had to offer, but now they would never be able to do so. Frances returned to England early that spring with the two children so Anna could be taken to a specialist, and Rex followed later that summer, after the grading in Cairo was over. By early July 1934 he was back in England.

If Rex did not have a substantial reason for pub crawling before, he did now. Anna is not mentioned in his work of this period, but his ambiguous feelings about Egypt appear in "The Straits," number 18 in his 1937 *Poems*. This poem was originally published in 1935 but seems to have been written in 1934 just before he left for England:

> Oriental Cairo! Splendid Alexandria!
> I leave you gladly for meadows of grass,
> the whitening wash of willow, corn's winding
>   waves,
> fleet water, flying birds.

CHAPTER FIVE

FRENSHAM HEIGHTS, 1934-1939

I. THE FRENSHAM HEIGHTS SCHOOL

By publishing two permanently important but subtly ambiguous novels of ideas, *The Wild Goose Chase* and *The Professor*, Rex dramatized the tensions between Communism, liberalism, and fascism better than any other writer of the 1930s. Driven by the extreme political events of the decade, he obsessively explored the essence of these three opposed philosophies as he uneasily tried to think through his own choice between liberalism and Communism. He also had to adjust to life in an increasingly tense England torn between these same divisions. But first he had to get settled.

When Rex returned in the summer of 1934, he first went to Amberley and then joined Frances in Jersey, where her parents had retired. He was soon in touch with Day-Lewis as well.[1] The immediate problem was finding a job; then he must work on getting *The Wild Goose Chase* published. A letter from 1934 (month unknown) from Cecil at Wesco, W. H. Auden's family cottage near Threlkeld, asked if Rex would consider taking on Day-Lewis's job at Cheltenham, which he wanted to leave at Christmastime. The headmaster was decent, and would not make a fuss about Rex's leftist political views if he kept them to himself. In a second letter from Wesco about this time—June or July 1934—Day-Lewis expects Rex on the 16th or 17th and says he will push *The Wild Goose Chase*.[2]

It turned out that Rex did not need Day-Lewis's help in finding a job. Paul Roberts, a St. George's master during Rex's study there, was then headmaster of the Frensham

Heights School in Surrey. Rex later recalled that "Paul (or 'Bobs,' as he was then called) was the hero of the small boys [at St. George's]. In rugger, we used to credit Bobs with super-human strength and agility . . . I was extremely timid, and I, along with many others, owed a lot to Paul for the confidence with which he gradually inspired us."[3] Paul remembered Rex well too, but perhaps was unaware of how much trouble hiring someone of Rex's outspoken political opinions would cause the school.

A few miles outside of Farnham, surrounded by rolling hills, fields, and forests, the Frensham Heights School occupies several acres. One of its main buildings is a Victorian mansion with a ballroom. The visitor receives a feeling of peace and well-being in an elegant but not ostentatious setting. In Rex's time, among the people sending their children there were writer Aldous and scientist Julian Huxley and the film star Clive Brook. Yet Frensham Heights was always somewhat poorer than older, better-known schools. School life was rather harsh by our present standards, with chilblain a common problem for the students in the winter. But essentially the atmosphere was easygoing, with a tendency for students not to work too hard to acquire knowledge.

Working against the mild academic climate, however, was a large influx in the later thirties of German and Austrian Jewish children, mostly boys, who had barely escaped the Holocaust. From 1935-39, they made up nearly ten percent of the student body. According to Peter Daniel, Frensham was "one of the few schools that would accept children who knew no English."[4] Several of the children had been orphaned by the Nazis; almost all had had traumatic lives before they arrived. Rex was undoubtedly influenced by their reminiscences of persecution.

These students not only gained freedom, but also a more benign school environment than they were used to in Germany or Austria, even in the best of times. Sir Claus Moser, one of those boys, is now the Warden of Wadham College. He finds it a touching coincidence that Paul Roberts, Stephen Hogg (another Frensham teacher), and Rex Warner had all been at Wadham. Moser recalls the following of Frensham:

> I came to the school in 1936 straight from Berlin, where I was just one of thousands of pupils who were the objects of . . . discipline and regimentation. What a contrast to come to Frensham! I still remember my first days there for the spirit of friendliness and happiness which seemed to pervade the school atmosphere . . . at no time did I find my complete ignorance of the English language the slightest handicap to making friends or being accepted into the general community . . . the secret of Frensham's unquestioned success as a school lay in the peculiarly happy association between staff and pupils, the essence of which was co-operation rather than mere obedience and which consequently created *real* respect . . .

the thing that counted at the school was not whether you were a Jew or a Gentile, a German or an Englishman; but whether you were a good member of the community. . . .[5]

Moser was at Frensham from 1936-40 and studied Latin and Greek with Rex. He remembers that Rex's conversation was like *The Wild Goose Chase*, with a succession of good stories and ideas going off in all directions. He also recalls that Rex was a great sportsman and warm human being as well as an intellectual, and he claims that Rex was probably the most popular teacher in the school. His impressions tally perfectly with my own as Rex's doctoral student thirty years after he left Frensham, especially with regard to the complete attention that he paid to each student's remarks. Rex even shared his writing with some of his students at Frensham Heights. Richard Hough, later a prolific author, remembered that "He read aloud the opening chapter of *The Aerodrome* in manuscript to a few of us."[6] Rex gave at least one memorable reading of Smollett as well.

Despite his own skepticism about Marxism and the conservative bent of the school's governors and many parents, Paul Roberts was very tolerant of Rex's political views, which Rex did not hesitate to express at this time. There was a strong leftist tendency among teachers and students, if not parents and governors, and Rex fitted into that very well. But he caused trouble.

On 7 November 1935, when he had been there for about a year, Rex and Lewis Weedon (another leftist master) led a party of seniors, three boys and one girl, to a Conservative meeting in nearby Rowledge. Peter Daniel reports that at the meeting, Sir Arthur Samuel, the sitting member of Parliament for Farnham, gave a boring talk; and the chairman of the meeting, who was also the school doctor, told the students that they were not allowed to vote. He then asked the audience to sing the national anthem to show their unanimity, but the Frensham Heights party did not do so. This was noticed by a Conservative parent of two children at the school. Sir Arthur indignantly told Rex's group that "You ought not to have a flag" and other members of the audience told them that they ought not to have a country either. The Frensham students were also involved in jeering. The result was that local popular feeling was offended and in Daniel's words, it "was not to be assuaged till in 1940" the school became the headquarters of the local Home Guard battalion. The chairman of the school's board wanted to close the school but was dissuaded by Paul Roberts. This would not be the only time that Rex would cause him dangerous trouble.[7]

Rex and Frances belonged to the local group of the Left Book Club. This now-famous club was founded by publisher Victor Gollancz, and by June 1936 could count 9,000 subscribers, each of whom were paying 2s. 6d. a month for six months, for which they received one "progressive" book a month, which they then discussed in local groups. When a friend of Rex's ran for election as the Labour Party candidate, Rex supported him although to no avail. During the period he was at Frensham Heights, Rex also took part in demonstrations against Japanese militarism, shouting the slogan, "Don't buy Japanese Goods. Japanese Goods mean Japanese Bombs!" through a megaphone from a car that drove through Farnham, a very sedate district, in late 1937 in response to a public campaign organized by a newspaper and the Co-operative Societies.

Peter Daniel notes that in the late 1930s, a complaint was made to Gavin Hamilton, acting chairman of the governors, about the fact that in one of Rex's poems in *Poems* (1937), "king" was not capitalized, though Rex explained that "It never occurred to me that anyone would think I meant the king of England." Rex went on to say that "At first, Paul took the whole thing lightly. He told me that he'd point out to the Governors that many more subversive things were said in the Gospel of St Matthew in reference to scribes, Pharisees and hypocrites. However, if he did raise this point, it cut no ice with the Governors, and Paul was very upset when they insisted on my dismissal." Roberts then threatened to resign himself, and Rex's job was saved.[8] Roberts was later to write of Rex that "his value to us lay . . . in the love of life, the feeling for style and quality, whether in learning, thinking or writing, the directness and gaiety which were so much part of his character, and which he was able to impart to others."[9] But he was not an easy poet or teacher to defend to a conservative board of governors.

The poem in question must have been Rex's "Hymn," a plainly Marxist work, first published in 1933 in Michael Roberts's *New Country* anthology:

> There is no need now to bribe and to take the bribe.
> The king is flying, his regiments have melted like ice in spring.
> Light has been let in. The fences are down. No broker is left alive.
> There is no pretence about the singing in the streets and the dancing.
> Come then, you who couldn't stick it lovers of cricket, underpaid journalists,
> lovers of nature, hikers, O touring cyclists,
> now you must be men and women and there is a chance.
> Now you can join us, now all together sing All Power,
> not tomorrow but now in this hour, All Power
> to Lovers of Life, to Workers, to the Hammer,
> the Sickle, the Blood.
>
> Come then companions. This is the spring of blood,
> heart's heyday, movement of masses, beginning of good.[10]

Whether or not Rex meant "the" king, which he may or may not have, it is easy to see how the poem could be understood that way. With or without the line about the king, the poem would be bound to offend any conservative person. It also gives clear insight into what Rex is getting at in *The Wild Goose Chase* with which it is exactly contemporary: the hope for a society that would consist of people like Rex—nature-loving, brainy yet athletic, sensitive aesthetically yet not effete, and underpaid—and treat them well. Rex's vision of what Marxism could give is molded largely in his own image. By this time Marxism had largely replaced his early Anglicanism with a vision that was so idealistic as to be a religion. Yet for Rex at least, belief in Marxism always carried with it some ambivalence.

Rex and Day-Lewis came closer together on some political issues around this time. In 1936 when the Frensham Heights student council decided to help the South Wales unemployed, Cecil Day-Lewis was among the guests. Mary Day-Lewis's diary reveals that Rex visited them on 13-14 July 1934 and again on 15-17 September 1934, 12-14 January 1935, 6-9 April 1935, and on 22-26 April 1936, and Day-Lewis was a frequent visitor at the Warner house. But despite this proximity and mutual influence, Rex never adopted Day-Lewis's absolute Marxism.

A small stone building, Middle Park Cottage, was to be home to Rex, Frances, Jonathan, and the somewhat disabled Anna for several years to come, while Rex did his writing in a little hut behind the house. He was to enjoy many a drink and game of shove half-penny from about 6-7:30 P.M. every day at the Hare and Hounds pub in the nearby village of Rowledge. It was there that Rex found the old men weeping on 11 December 1936, the day that King Edward VIII announced his abdication to marry Mrs. Simpson, as they asked: "How could he leave us?" Richard Hough recalls that during this period, Rex also enjoyed "gentle walks in the woods with Cecil Day-Lewis, pausing to study the bird life through binoculars."[11]

II. RECOGNITION BY LEHMANN AND GREENWOOD

During his years at Frensham Heights, Rex's writing career became public. John Lehmann, who himself had three pages of poems included in Roberts's *New Country*, wrote Rex at some time late in 1934 about an anthology, *The Year's Poetry 1935: A Representative Selection*, that he was editing with Denys Kilham Roberts and Gerald Gould for John Lane the Bodley Head. He must then have written a second letter to Rex after he read Rex's "Sonnet" ("How sweet only to delight") in *The Listener* of 23 January 1935. Rex's response to this second letter, the first of a long series from Rex to Lehmann, is dated 18 July 1935:

I owe you an apology for not having answered the letter you wrote me last year. . . .
I'm glad you like the "sonnet" I had in the Listener sufficiently well to wish to
include it in The Years Poetry, + am perfectly willing for you to do so.

The only other poem I have had published in your period are (i) "Lapwing" in the
Listener [13 March 1935] (also in Janet Adam Smith's anthology)[12] (ii) "Light + Air,"
three so-called sonnets in the London Mercury of about February, I think [February
1935, pp. 331-32]. I'm afraid I haven't got a copy by me. And (iii) 4 poems in New
Verse No 15 [June 1935, pp. 12-14].[13]

Rex quickly followed up this opportunity with a letter of 30 July from Seabright, La
Roque, Jersey, Frances's parents' house, offering Lehmann three unpublished poems. He
adds, testifying once again to his inveterate inability to coexist with technology, that "In
the one called 'Truth,'[14] by the way, I'm not intending to produce a typographical effect by
putting the words 'lips' + 'true' in lines by themselves. It's only that I can't manage the
marginal adjustment of my typewriter." (Perhaps Rex referred to a typewriter at school,
because Frances remembered that they did not own one.) Rex mentions that he will be at
La Roque for the next six weeks or so. On 10 September he mentions that he is leaving
Jersey in a day or two to return to Frensham Heights, and that he is pleased Lehmann likes
"the poems well enough to include in the book. The chough poem hasn't appeared anywhere.
No one seems to think much of poems about birds, + I was glad that you liked it. . . ."[15]

Rex's poems of 1935 are less explicitly political than the choruses from "The
Dam" and "Hymn" (originally entitled "the first lesson"), but the political undercurrent
is always there, as in these lines from "Sonnet" (I): "Nor will my mind permit me to
linger in the love,/ the motherkindness of country among ascending trees,/knowing
that love must be liberated by bleeding,/ fearing for my fellows, for the murder of
man./ How should I live then but as a kind of fungus,/ or else as one in strict training
for desperate war?"[16] Today in hindsight such lines may seem strident or melodramatic,
but viewed against Japanese aggression in China, Mussolini's threats to Abyssinia,
the rise of Hitler, and intimations of the Spanish Civil War, which began in July 1936,
Rex's political poetry seems both apropos and admirable, if not great poetry. A short
unpublished topical poem, undoubtedly written at some point after Mussolini's invasion
of Abyssinia in October 1935, is entitled "Epitaph for Abyssinians":

Stranger, report as follows to the powers of the West:
Obedient to your wonderful words we lie
blistered by gas which you helped to supply.
Words may be wonderful, but deeds are best.[17]

While powerfully biting, this is not very subtle poetry and Rex (or his editor C. J. Greenwood) rightly decided not to include it in his revised poetry volume of 1945, *Poems and Contradictions*. But one can only sympathize with Rex's anti-Mussolini sentiments here.

On 1 July [1936], just before the start of the Spanish war, Rex wrote from Frensham Heights, offering Lehmann a poem entitled "Peace," which had been neglected by the periodical *Janus* to which it had been submitted. The poem was indeed published in *The Year's Poetry 1936:*

Over the hills, over the austere hills,

not in this country or the nearest town

but far away we learn to think of Peace,

children who were shaken by shock of shells,

and boys who watched the summer sky

be stained with puffs of smoky down,

who knew the soaring lark

sang in between the bursts of a gun,

that the gold shone

to make more easy murders for the day,

and in the dark death did not cease.[18]

"Sonnet" (IX in the 1937 *Poems*), which appeared in Lehmann's anthology with "Peace" and "Spring Song," is overtly Marxist in its closing lines, "For blight in the meadows, for our master builders/let sickle be a staggerer and hammer heavy." In its use of medieval expressions ("master builders," "staggerers") and alliterations, this is Marxist Hopkins.

On 11 January 1936, Rex had sent Lehmann some extracts from *The Wild Goose Chase*, and on 18 June he wrote Lehmann that he was glad that Lehmann preferred "The Football Match," adding "I think myself its the best of the extracts." In the letter of 1 July, he writes that "The heading you suggest for 'The Football Match' + the money seem to me quite all right."[19] This passage, found in chapter 15 of the novel, probably remains its most famous single episode. George attempts to referee an unfair Rugby game on a field made of rubber, which is constantly adjusted so the King's side cannot lose.

Lehmann, then editing *New Writing*, explained in his memoir how his interest in *The Wild Goose Chase* came about:

When I went to see Cecil Day Lewis at his country home, to persuade him to write for us, he told me that his friend Rex Warner had written a novel, *The Wild Goose Chase*, in a fantastical or allegorical manner, and was finding great difficulty in getting anyone interested in it. We persuaded Rex—whom I did not meet personally for some years— to pick out one or two more or less self-explanatory episodes for *New Writing*, and I remember feeling, when they came in, that an entirely new event, comparable with Edward Upward's *Journey to the Border*, was taking place in the imaginative writing of our time.[20]

On 20 August 1936, from La Roque, Rex asked Lehmann for the extracts to be returned, because "There is a faint hope of some publishers getting interested in the book again," but he does not specify to whom he is referring.[21] "The Football Match" was published in *New Writing* II (Autumn 1936) in October.

In August 1936 Rex also composed "We're Not Going to Do Nothing," a response to Aldous Huxley's pacifist pamphlet, "What Are You Going to Do About It?: The Case for Constructive Peace," which had appeared earlier in the year. Writing a few months after Italy's conquest of Abyssinia, Hitler's army's entry into the Rhineland, and the beginning of the Spanish Civil War, Rex argued for a "People's Front" between the Communists and the Labour Party, which would be modeled on the "Popular Front" recently set up in France. The idea was to form a union of interested people (including pacifists) and governments to resist Italy, Germany, and Japan. It is hard to disagree with Rex's conclusion that in 1936 something still might be done against fascism and that "we must act *act at once*" if anything positive were to happen.[22]

In the November issue of *Left Review*, Stephen Spender did his best to help Rex get published. In a review of Lehmann's *New Writing* II (as well as works by Auden and Isherwood), he wrote that "to my mind the most remarkable story in this volume is Rex Warner's *The Football Match*, which is only an incident from his novel *The Wild Goose Chase*. It strikes me that this little sketch of the match between the teams of the Pros and the Cons, in which the result is decided (against the Pros) before the match begins, and when the Pros show signs of winning the football field expands enormously, is the best political allegory I have read since *Erewhon*. I am told that *The Wild Goose Chase* has found no publisher, since none is persuaded that he could sell it: if the rest of the novel is up to the standard of this fragment, this is a very serious comment on the state of English publishing."[23]

Barbara Morris, one of Rex's pupils, was the daughter of John and Pam Morris, who were among the directors of Boriswood along with C. J. Greenwood. This was a new and experimental publishing company. (The company had, for instance, published James Hanley's sexually explicit novel *Boy* in 1931, and Greenwood had consulted T. E. Lawrence with regard to possible governmental prosecution of the book for indecency.) Through Barbara, Rex met Pam and John, probably at some point in late 1936. According to Julia Greenwood, C. J.'s wife, the Morrises had first introduced Rex to C. J., who was the editorial director of the company.[24] Possibly, Greenwood had read the *New Writing* extract, or Spender's November review of it. Whether Rex or Greenwood contacted the other first, Rex gladly supplied him with some poems and the whole manuscript of *The Wild Goose Chase*. Julia Greenwood writes that "I remember C.J.G. admired the poems but what really excited him was the grubby-looking MS of a novel, *The Wild Goose Chase*, which R.W. had written two or three years back and which had been turned down by Faber."

She went on to describe the publishing house for which she and C. J. worked:

> Boriswood was run on a shoestring. It operated in four rooms of an old house off Soho Square, and the whole firm consisted of C. J .G. (editorial director, production, and advertising), John Morris (accounts), Fred Littman (traveler), Pamela Morris (scout and translator), me (typist and dog's body) and Jim (packer and office boy). Boriswood published the Poems, The Wild Goose Chase and The Professor and then went into liquidation in 1938—as did many small publishers at that difficult time—and was absorbed by John Lane, the Bodley Head. C. J. G. only, moved to the Bodley Head, becoming its managing director. The chairman of the firm was Sir Stanley Unwin, a life-long teetotaler.

Richard Hough adds further details to this subsequent history of Boriswood when he writes,

> Times were hard, and Boriswood went into liquidation along with several contemporaries at the same time as the Bodley Head. Stanley Unwin, aided and abetted by W. G. Taylor of Dent and G. Wren Howard of Cape's, collared the lot and put C. J. in to run them under The Bodley Head name and collophon. This amalgam was housed in an old fruit-and-veg warehouse an apple's throw from the British Museum and even nearer to Unwin's hallowed premises of George Allen & Unwin Ltd in Museum Street.

He adds that Greenwood was a thin man "with a schoolboy's face, uptilted nose, sleek head of hair and a smile—and manner—of the utmost charm."[25]

In 1936, therefore, while Boriswood was an ongoing concern, there began a long and very close literary and personal friendship between Greenwood and Rex. Julia Greenwood wrote, "C. J. G. was Rex's greatest admirer, and also they never tired of their jokes about shove ha'penny, darts, cricket (R. W. supporting Gloucester[shire],

C. J. G. Lancs [Lancashire]), and above all the availability or otherwise of liquor in the war years."[26] Another reason for the friendship was that Rex became "about the only Boriswood author who made the firm any money."[27]

In obvious answer to a letter from Greenwood after he saw the manuscript, Rex wrote on 9 December 1936:

> Dear Mr. Greenwood: thank you very much for your letter.
>
> Its tremendously encouraging to know that one's writing has given pleasure to people whose opinion one respects, + I'm particularly grateful for encouragement where the Wild Goose Chase is concerned. I put a lot into it when I wrote it, + have been rather dismayed at the attitude of, for example, some of the people in Fabers, who, while admiring the book, were most reluctant to take a risk over it.
>
> I shall get down to the job of improving the second part as soon as I can. If you noticed any particular parts which seemed to need re-writing, I should be very grateful to hear of them.
>
> Many thanks again for your letter.[28]

This letter must have accompanied the contracts for *The Wild Goose Chase* and the *Poems*, which are in the Reading University Bodley Head Archive, dated 9 December 1936, and made out between Rex at Middle Park Cottage and Boriswood, 59, Frith St., London W1.[29]

On 28 December [1936], Rex was able to write to Lehmann from Great Rissington Rectory, "Before I got your letter asking me to inform you of any steps I might take with regard to the W.G. Chase I had signed a contract with Boriswoods. They are going to publish a small book of my poems followed by the W.G. Chase some time next year."[30] Rex later stated that he went with Boriswood rather than another publisher because it had never turned him down. Most likely he was delighted simply to take the first definite offer at last.

On 22 January 1937, Rex wrote Greenwood from Frensham Heights about the poems: "I like very much indeed your suggested order for the poems, + I quite agree with you about the ones to be left out. . . . By the way, 'Truth' was published the other day in Twentieth Century Verse[31] + the second line misprinted 'drunk by moonlight.' I think that this is an improvement, as 'drunk by midnight' seems to imply a pretty serious toping effort from, say, eight o'clock onwards. 'Drunk at midnight' might do: but I rather lean towards the misprint." In any event, the misprint "drunk by moonlight" was retained.

In this letter, Rex suggested keeping a poem about the wild goose for *The Wild Goose Chase* rather than including it in the *Poems* volume; as the published volumes prove, Greenwood accepted this request. Rex hoped that Greenwood would approve the unspecified changes he made in the novel manuscript. He added, "Isn't it the case, by the way, that someone or other has published recently a book called *Wild Goose Chase*? Would this matter? I'd hate to change the title of mine, particularly as I thought of it first." *Wild Goose Chase: a novel* by one Luard Lawson was in fact published by Collins in 1937, so Rex's worries were justified.

III. THE PUBLICATION OF *THE WILD GOOSE CHASE*

Rex's letter of 6 February 1937 is worth quoting at length because it reveals some of the details of the changes in the *Wild Goose Chase* manuscript, which is probably no longer extant (although the typescript is):

> Dear Greenwood. . . . Thank you very much for your good opinion of the book. To me the Wild Goose Chase means much more than the poems, perhaps because I've consciously tried to put much more into it than I have into the poems.
>
> Now then for the points you mention.
>
> 1. I quite agree about Antonio. But there are a few suggestions as to the exact working of the alterations.
>
> P.39. "spitting at the dead man's face" I think should be left, though "face" could be left out on p. 40. It seems to me that the first spit needs a definite target. (I don't feel terribly strongly about this).
>
> P.40. Instead of "properly" I'd suggest "the girls can't even speak our language, + yet . . ." P.41. I'd suggest "Pyrrha still squatting on the floor, + by her side an axe, some savage instrument which she had taken from the wall." (This to avoid the definite pause at "floor" rhyming with "door")
>
> P.42. I've made a slight alteration in the MS.
>
> 2. I must say I don't much like the idea of changing the first page, particularly as it seems to me that the sentence which is most likely to tie up the ordinary reader is the one about the gannets, + I rather like it. Also, since the book does demand some intellectual effort from the reader, I don't see why it shouldn't advertise the fact right away. Would a heading more attractive than "Introduction" meet the case? "Far on Bicycles"? "Leave on Bicycles"? "Adventure"? If you absolutely insist, I'll do something about it, but, as I say, reluctantly.

3. I'm enclosing a few sentences to go in on Page 203. I'm not sure that they are satisfactory, because I haven't got the MS with me + have a feeling that I've written something rather like them earlier on. I scrapped the original epilogue because it seemed to drag a bit. If you don't approve of the bit I'm sending I'll have another go at it.—As to the dedication, I'd like it to be just "To Frances." What about having either before or after the Wild Goose poem, the following:

[the original Greek, then the English translation as follows]:

for our contention is not with the blood + the flesh, but with dominion, with authority, with the blind world-rulers of this life, with the spirit of evil in things heavenly." Ephes. 6, chap., 12

—I got this out of the Nonesuch edition of Blake. It's the superscription to "The Four Zoas," but whether the English translation is Blake's or someone else's, I don't know. It seems to me rather an apt quotation, + might capture the Church of England vote for the book, though this is unlikely. I'd like to have it (the quotation, not the Church).

The epigraph, first page, and pages 68 and 70 of the 1937 Boriswood and 1990 Merlin editions[32] show that Greenwood accepted all of Rex's suggestions except that the epigraph be given in Greek as well as English. He even accepted Rex's reverse attribution—it should be Ephes. chapter 6, verse 12, not verse 6, chapter 12 as Andrew Cramp has pointed out. Rex seems to have been reading Blake, whose exuberance might be seen as an influence on *The Wild Goose Chase*.

Greenwood did not, however, accept a second stanza that Rex inserted into the "Wild Goose" poem that begins the book:

> The publishers admitted that you were interesting,
> but hardly to the taste of the general public.[33]

The typescript of *The Wild Goose Chase* exists as part of MS 49 at Michigan State. The deletions on page 116 of the typescript show that Rex was certainly cognizant of Eliot's "Waste Land," Yeats's "Innisfree," and Lewis Carroll's *Alice in Wonderland* and was not above parodying them all in some pretty bad verse:

> I met you at Davos and sat upon your knee
> We talked of the wattles that grow in Innisfree.
> I'll meet you this evening when the stars are shining
> and shall we shan't we, well I don't know, yes we will tonight.

Right after the paragraph on page 440 near the end of the published text of *The Wild Goose Chase*[34] that concludes "the sea of faces, the joy," Rex originally had the poem "Hymn."[35] He wisely decided instead to omit this didactic poem, whose too-certain tone does not fit the context and which would have been unsuitable for the end of the story. The passage to be inserted on page 203 of the typescript that Rex mentions in the letter of 6 February is the paragraph on pages 441-42 of the published novel. This is the novel's final paragraph, and Rex added everything from "Now to him all the future" to "and it was dead calm."

There are many other differences between typescript and published novel. The following poem was in the typescript and would have appeared in the mouth of the comic musician Bob on page 40 of the published novel after the words "recognize you," but Rex omitted it:

> Some people have sunny days,
> Some people have funny ways.
> Some people have money, some people have none.
> But, honey, this is what I say:
> You can take away the sunny day,
> Take away the sunny skies
> And leave me this:
> The feeling, that's so appealing, of a kiss,
> And leave me too
> Your wonderful eyes.
> Yes, wonderful sweetheart, leave me your wonderful
> wonderful eyes of blue.[36]

This is Rex's attempt to imitate the popular 1930s film music of which he would remain fond all of his life. The reader must decide whether Rex's decision to omit it from the final novel is justified.

We find Rex's Hollywood tendency in another omitted passage. The description of Pyrrha's killing of the philosopher Don Antonio reads as follows on page 70 of the published novel:

> On the way downstairs Bob, white-faced, wide-eyed, ran into him and clung to his arm, almost sobbing, such was the state of his terror and agitation. "Sir! Sir! Let's go away. I can't bear it, this house." George went to the dining room and, on opening the door, saw Pyrrha still squatting on the floor, and by her side an axe, some savage

instrument which she had taken from the wall. She looked up at George, then, for the first time smiling, said "Had good time?"

In the original version in the typescript (pp. 41-42), however, this incident was a good deal more bloody:

> On the way downstairs Bob, white-faced wide-eyed, ran into him and clung to his arm, almost sobbing, such was the state of his terror and agitation. "For Christ's sake, sir! For Christ's sake! Let's go away. I can't bear it, this house." He pointed down to the dining room and whispered in George's ear: "She's chopping the old man up," and was then sick, with disgust or fright, on the carpeting of the staircase. George went to the dining room and, on opening the door, saw what he could scarcely have imagined, Pyrrha still squatting on the floor, her face smeared with blood and between her teeth what appeared to be the severed and gnawed finger of Don Antonio. By her side was an axe, some savage instrument which she had taken from the wall, and with which she had cut off the philosopher's nose and ears, hacked at his lips and chopped away the fingers, sexual parts, and toes, all of which were arranged on the floor in separate piles. and by her side an axe, some savage instrument which she had taken from the wall. She looked up at George, like a beast surprised, then for the first time smiling, said: "Had good time?"

Rex resisted the sensationalist temptation although indulging it might have helped increase his sales.

Rex wrote again on a Tuesday probably during March correcting Greenwood's spelling of the name Frances and stating that he was going to think of "suitable titles," possibly because Greenwood had asked him to think of substitutes for "*The Wild Goose Chase.*" With great relief, Rex added "Its fine to think of all those much perused + dirty pages at last getting under way."

Rex's letter to Greenwood of 6 April 1937 from Frensham Heights stated that

> I'd like to keep "Wild Goose Chase" if possible, but you'll know better than I do how far that would injure the book's chances of success. If you think it would be a mistake to keep the title, I'd suggest "Follow the Bird" as an alternative. It isn't so good as the original one, but it doesn't seem to me a bad one. If we do change to "Follow the Bird" I'd suggest that the Introduction (about 2 chapters) should be called "The Wild Goose Chase." For Part I I suggest "The one Remains," for Part II "The Many Change." What do you think of this? I'll leave the question of the title entirely to you, only stating that, if its not going to make a lot of difference anyway, I'd prefer "Wild G.C."

A postcard from Great Rissington Rectory dated 16 April [1937] follows up the previous letter with "What about 'Chase of Geese'? Or is it too late?"

The question over the title apparently ended well, and Rex was able to proceed with proof-reading. On 12 May 1937, he wrote from Charlton Kings to Greenwood, "here are the proofs. I couldn't find many mistakes. What about the headings for Introduction + Part 1? I don't do anything about these, not knowing what type would be used. I'll be back at Great Rissington on Saturday or Sunday. Am leaving here today." Undated notes reveal that he was sending the proofs back in batches. A longer letter dated only Saturday from Frensham Heights during that May states "here is another lot of proofs. The printer's reader caught me out this time, but I hope they'll get the 'red integration' right. I got the money for the Poems this morning + see you've made me a present of the extra copies. Very many thanks. One of the girls here has an aunt who has expressed the intention of buying my Poems, + that is all I know about how the sales are going." So the *Poems* were out in the last half of May, while *The Wild Goose Chase* would be published on 14 September 1937.

Finally, on a Thursday, probably 13 May, he wrote Greenwood,

> here's the last lot of proofs. It's a pity about that page. I had an idea that the missing one came just before it does, in a part that would be easy to replace. Actually I wrote this part on loose paper + probably threw it away after I'd typed it out, so I doubt whether a journey to Gt. Rissington, the only place where it could possibly be, would be worth while. I've written a substitute passage, but am by no means sure that its as good as the original. I didn't type it, as this would mean missing a post. I hope you'll like it, + agree with me that the book really does look better in print.

On 3 May he sent Greenwood, certainly in response to a request for information useful for publicity, an important description of his philosophy and the influences acting upon him:

> My father is a clergyman in the Church of England. My mother is a schoolteacher. I have spent most of my life in the country + have always been interested in country matters; also in poetry, sport + philosophy. My favourite poets are Shakespeare, Homer, Aeschylus + Lucretius. My favourite novelists are Tolstoy, Dostoievsky, Fielding, Smollett + Cervantes. The only modern novelist I like is Kafka, but the best prose I have read is by T.E. Lawrence. I like the poems of my friends C. Day Lewis + W.H. Auden, but I haven't got any theories of poetry of my own, + rather dislike such theories as I have come across. I have, on the other hand, a few theories about the novel. What I

dislike in most modern novels is their triviality. I should like to see the characters of a novel invested with the level of poetic quality that makes them in their own way, more, not less, impressive than the characters of everyday life. I should like to see epic + allegorical qualities in place of the photographic methods which now seem to be popular.

Rex's reading influenced his own attempt in *The Wild Goose Chase* to capture something akin to the epic sweep of Homer, Virgil, and Tolstoy, the psychological understanding of Dostoyevsky, the picaresque characters and plot surprises of Fielding and Smollett, the social satire of Swift, the fantasy of Kafka, and the rhetorical prose of T. E. Lawrence.

Around this time Rex wrote an unpublished biographical chapter about T. E. Lawrence[37] (who had died in 1935) as well as one about the explorer Fridtjof Nansen. In the early 1980s, referring to the entire generation of thirties writers, Rex said that " . . . I remember one person who influenced all our writing and that was T.E. Lawrence. A hero, and, as we thought, against the establishment."[38] Moreover, as Day-Lewis tells us in *The Buried Day*, his own career took off largely as a result of Lawrence's intervention, so both Day-Lewis and Rex owed him a literary debt of gratitude.[39] In his chapter on Lawrence, which is largely elevated hackwork, Rex praises him for his anti-imperialism, his superb prose, and for his *Odyssey* translation, which had also been praised by Bowra. In his chapter, Rex does not mention Christopher Caudwell, who wrote that Lawrence "halted on the nearside of achievement so that instead of becoming the communist hero, which his gifts and his hatred for the evils of capitalism fitted him for, he became a bourgeois hero who miscarried."[40] Rex probably had not read Caudwell when he wrote his chapter, and unlike Caudwell he presented Lawrence as an unconsciously Marxist man of the people defeated by the forces of imperialism and class.

Although T. E. Lawrence does not appear directly in Rex Warner's fiction, Rex did produce several notable heroes who rise above the mundane, including the proletarian leader George of *The Wild Goose Chase* and Roy, the rebellious son in *The Aerodrome*. Was Rex aware, perhaps through biographies by Lowell Thomas (1924) or Robert Graves (1927), that the young Lawrence in 1906-8 rode a bike through the remnants of feudal France? If so, did that influence Rex's creation of George's bicycle adventures among foreign kings and tyrants? Had Rex read Lawrence's prose in *Revolt in the Desert* (1927) before he began writing his own novel? Did the rebellious airman Lawrence of the R.A.F. linger in Rex's consciousness when in the late 1930s he decided to write about fascism in the Air Force in *The Aerodrome*? We cannot know because there are no letters affirming this, although Chris Hopkins has pointed to the possible influence of Lawrence's *Mint* on *The Aerodrome*.[41] Rex probably read Christopher

Caudwell's essay only after he finished his own Lawrence chapter, but Caudwell's distinction between the positive and negative hero in that essay was possibly somewhere in Rex's mind when in the late 1950s he wrote his historical novels *The Young Caesar* and *Imperial Caesar*,[42] as N. H. Reeve has pointed out.

Lawrence was not the only possible influence on *The Wild Goose Chase*. In a letter of 14 November 1983 to me, Rex reiterated that

> In "The Wild Goose Chase" the main influences are, I think, Swift, Fielding, & Dickens, together with Plato's myths (in the Republic, Gorgias & Phaedo). Also Dostoievsky & Bunyan. Also, in aspects of the "atmosphere," Kafka's "The Castle." I doubt whether I'd read "Brave New World" when I was writing the book. That book of essays of mine—"The Cult of Power"—is fairly close to my view at the time.[43]

Rex was clearly attracted to fantasy and epic rather than to the usual photographic "proletarian novel" reproducing drab mundane lives. Not only did he not know much about the life of a factory worker, but he refused to be forced to follow a narrow aesthetic philosophy based on politics alone. In the 3 May letter to Greenwood, Rex commented on the Communist Alec Brown, whose turgid *Daughters of Albion* (1935) had just been published by Boriswood. Rex politely indicated his desire to depart from the everyday and not, like Brown, to reinforce it. A sentence about Brown's philosophy of style stands out from Rex's diplomatic overenthusiastic praise of this justly now-forgotten book: "Its the only modern novel I've read which reminds me of Tolstoy. I don't mean that it's as good as 'War + Peace,' but he has that exceptional seriousness + sincerity + sympathy which just don't seem to exist in other modern novelists. I thought it a magnificent bit of work, though I don't agree with his ideas on language. I don't see why prose should be colloquial any more than poetry (+ look at Wordsworth)." Brown advocated writing based on spoken English only, a typically "proletarian" literary philosophy of the period exactly contrary to Rex's.[44]

Rex was to regret his polite enthusiasm for Brown, which probably led Greenwood to introduce him to Brown. Rex expressed that regret humorously in a letter to Greenwood of 13 October with no year given: "Had rather an unsuccessful evening with Alec Brown. He read his novel aloud for 2 hours, + then in desperation I rose to get some whiskey. Apparently I had got to my feet at the very moment when the climax was reached. I hadn't observed it."

Rex's disagreement with Brown's linguistic philosophy goes right to the point of Rex's own achievement in *The Wild Goose Chase*. It has been praised for its socialist ideas, attacked for its lack of organization, but not fully analyzed in terms of its style. The story is certainly important, since it says much about Rex's views; but the style is perhaps Rex's unconscious statement of what he was really about. As several writers at the time pointed out, Day-Lewis, Auden, Spender, and Rex (like Alec Brown) were middle class and not at all comfortable with the proletariat. Despite their best intentions, they were unable to completely throw over their educations and middle-class affiliations in their rush to champion a working class revolution. In Rex's case, his style contains a distance, balance, polish, and skepticism learned from his study of the classics, and it often has the effect of subtly taming the excessive fervor that informs much of the novel's prorevolutionary subject matter. It shows that Rex, deep down inside, was not fully convinced by Marxism.

IV. AN ANALYSIS OF *THE WILD GOOSE CHASE*

Rex's plot in *The Wild Goose Chase* certainly reveals his overt socialist convictions circa 1930-33. Three brothers, Rudolph, David, and George, set off on bicycles to chase the wild goose beyond the frontier, cheered by the crowd at a seaside town. Rudolph is overly adventuresome, David an effete intellectual, and George the perfect mesomorph, resembling Rex himself, or his uncle George—smart but also good at sport, commonsensical and down-to-earth. Each brother goes off in his own direction. Before he crosses the frontier, George has an encounter with Don Antonio,[45] a windbag philosopher who is murdered by one of the two women he has kept enslaved. After George crosses the frontier, he experiences various forms of oppression by the government of a village. He proceeds to the capital and finds his brother David, who has become an androgynous member of the Convent, which symbolizes the university. The capital reveres a stuffed goose, and is ruled by three kings representing technology, religion, and fascism. George is also reunited with his empire-building bluff brother Rudolph, who was first taken in by the kings, only to be blinded by them. George leaves the capital, where he almost was assassinated, goes back to the village, and in concert with other revolutionaries, forms an army. The revolutionary army fights a major battle against the national government, which is armed with technological monstrosities such as robots made of human flesh, and succeeds in defeating it. The subtitle of the second major part of the book, "The Many Change," clearly shows Rex's intentions: revolution against the old order. He almost always portrays workers in a positive light, while intellectuals are corrupted by a brutal and fascistic bureaucracy.

Marxism is never overtly mentioned, but the wild goose chase of revolution and societal change seems to be caught, and the novel ends on a cautiously optimistic note:

Now, looking upwards, they saw the whole blue sky and the sun, and across the sky streaming the white shapes of flying birds, a horde, from horizon to horizon; nor was their number more to be wondered at than the size and splendour of each one of them; for these creatures were altogether uncommon, with wings wider than playing-fields, bodies like boats, and straight extended necks like a flying forest. . . . Never for long had he lost sight of a purpose that had been always powerful and sometimes distinct. But now, at the top of the temporary avenue up which his present triumph had led him, he could only envisage vaguely the shapes of difficulty, success and danger that were to come. . . . Be the future as it might be, and no doubt that complete success was distant still, he knew that something not unworthy had been achieved already. . . .[46]

The wild geese clearly approve of this outcome.

Yet even as the plot seems to be clearly resolved in favor of revolution, we should notice that the entire tale is told by an unnamed narrator who has heard it from an old man purporting to be George, which throws some doubt on the whole story. Given this unreliable narration, is it all a false tale, a wild goose chase after all? Rex's epic glorification of George and the proletariat and disparagement of the kings[47] seems to show that it is not, but some skepticism lingers. Indeed, the title may ultimately derive from Yeats's skeptical political poem "September 1913," which includes the lines "Was it for this the wild geese spread/The grey wing upon every tide;/For this that all that blood was shed . . . ?" Yeats's poem implies that political sacrifice may be only a wild goose chase after all.

Like *The Wild Goose Chase*'s possibly unreliable narration, Rex's style takes back what it gives, from the first sentence on. Rex seems to praise the three brothers, but actually undermines our certainty that their chase was a good thing. The retrospective narrator's modifications and balances seem to indicate that he cannot now (any more than he could when the brothers originally left) make up his own mind as to the basically heroic or foolish quality of their adventure:

It seems, though it was many years ago, only yesterday that we citizens of a seaside town, standing in ranks along the esplanade, watched, cheering at the same time with all the force of our lungs, the outset of the three brothers who, with the inconsiderate fine daring of youth, were prepared, each in his own way, to go far on bicycles, distinguishing our town by an attempt which even the brothers only dimly understood and which seemed to most of us who stood spectators vociferously cheering impracticable, to some even ridiculous.[48]

The narrator's prosaic beginning, "It seems . . . only yesterday," is immediately offset by the casually inserted "though it was many years ago," which subtly indicates that all is not what it seems. The repeated description of the cheering ("with all the force of our lungs"; "vociferously cheering") becomes ludicrous when we arrive at the end of the sentence and learn that the cheering spectators, including the narrator, did not know what to think of the quest they were cheering. In retrospect, the phrase "inconsiderate fine daring" also has something of the foolishly reckless about it, and near the end of the sentence it becomes evident that the brothers themselves only "dimly understood" what they were up to. Even the phrase "to go far on bicycles" seems faintly deflating and ridiculous, since its heroic ring describes not sports cars or horses (fiery, fast things) but only mundane bicycles. The narrator does not rule out the heroic possibilities of the adventure either—there is fine daring, even if it is inconsiderate. But the very hesitations and reluctance of the narrator's style, the rhythm broken up by commas and impeded by an almost over-conscientious desire for accuracy ("each in his own way"), force us to think carefully about the matter in contrast to the original cheering audience.

Even when Rex is glorifying revolution through the mouth of the heroic George, he speaks with the clarity, distance, and rationality learned from Thucydides rather than with a wild enthusiasm. On 29 May 1984, in reply to a query of mine about that possible source, Rex wrote, "Incidentally, you're probably right about Thucydidean influence on 'The Wild Goose Chase,' though at the time I believed myself to be a kind of religious Marxist." In this statement, Rex himself notices the opposition between the restrained and antithetical style of Thucydides and the emotion implied in being a religious Marxist—an opposition which, however unintended by Rex, saves the novel from an excess of ideological fervor and grants it lasting interest. It demonstrates Rex's commitment to classicism and tradition no less than to revolution. *The Wild Goose Chase* is unique for combining tradition and revolution.

The voice most clearly heard in George's final speech (and in all earlier speeches by all characters, and in most of the narrator's own comments) is the voice of Rex's own later Thucydides translation. Here is Hermocrates' address to the Syracusans:

> Let us therefore make our preparations here in a spirit of confidence. We must send to the Sicels, in some cases to make sure that we can depend on them, in others to attempt to make treaties of friendship and alliance with them. We must send representatives to the rest of Sicily to point out that the danger threatens all alike, and we must also send to Italy so as to gain alliances there for ourselves or else to see that they do not receive the Athenians.[49]

And here is George speaking:

We shall choose our own way of living and it will not be the way of kings or scientists. We shall keep the routes clear and welcome travellers. We shall make use once more of time and space and shall be particularly attached to the earth and to the sun. . . .

Comrades, let us think no more of our dead friends, or of the wasted portions of our lives, since we are on the way to create a new civilization, something which has not existed for a long time, if ever.[50]

George's speech is more sententious than Hermocrates' and rather like some of Pericles' utterances in *The Peloponnesian War*, but regardless of content, the use of classical rhetoric remains the same. We notice the use of the collective imperative ("let us") in both speeches, the resort to anaphora ("We must . . . we must . . . we must"/ "We shall . . . we shall . . . we shall") and the balanced parallels and antitheses ("in some cases . . . in others," "send representatives to the rest of Sicily . . . and we must also send to Italy," "so as to gain . . . or else to see"/our own way and it will not be the way of kings . . . ," "keep the routes clear and welcome travellers," "think no more of our dead friends or of the wasted portions of our lives"). In both speeches we have the use of parallels or antitheses composed of two elements to imply authority and finality.[51] In his introduction to his Thucydides translation, Rex approves of "what seems an overdoing of antitheses or an unnecessary roughness in the transitions of the syntax"[52] in Thucydides' style. George's speech employs many other rhetorical figures known to Thucydides and to eighteenth-century neoclassical writers such as Swift.[53] The novel remains unique for its application of classical rhetoric to proletarian subject matter, but its cumulative effect, combined with the doubt about whether or not the story ever happened the way George tells it, is to subtly declare Rex's allegiance to tradition and skepticism at least as much as to revolution.

That skepticism remains a subtle hint in the novel itself—as if part of Rex does not fully believe his own glorification of George and revolution. It would be fully expressed only in a letter of 2 September 1937, five years after the novel was written. From La Roque, Rex wrote Greenwood that "I've been thinking over all sorts of ideas for a new book,—ideas ranging from a story about a whale to a story about a gentleman—, but so far haven't fixed on anything + am not sure that I shouldn't do better to continue the W.G. Chase. I think I could do something good by giving the other brothers a run, + letting George suffer from the corruption of power. . . . The second part of Don Quixote isn't half as good as the first."

So Rex himself conceived of George becoming corrupt! Although this is two years before the Hitler-Stalin pact, we see some doubts about Stalin and other "heroic" leaders expressed here through Rex's projection about George. His reading of *Don Quixote*, a satire on excessive idealism, is also telling here. Did George now strike him, five years after he had written the novel, as too idealistic and self-deluded, like Don Quixote?

V. THE RECEPTION OF *THE WILD GOOSE CHASE*

The Wild Goose Chase was finally published on 14 September 1937. Rex's stylistic mastery was noticed even by Marxist critics such as China scholar Joseph Needham who, though more interested in the novel's ostensibly prorevolutionary message, found a "likeness to Bunyan" which "is reinforced by occasional faint echoes of a seventeenth century prose."[54] The less ideological writer of the London *Times* review found that Rex's allegorical method offered "freedom to read for pleasure without being required to absorb instruction," but that "The chief beauty of the book is very properly the prose, since it never forsakes clearness of meaning to make an effect, but strides on in large and lovely periods that are nowadays most often hard to find."[55] Similarly, in the *New York Times Book Review*, Harold Strauss praised "Mr. Warner's magnificently cadenced, eloquent prose style—a style that is as fresh and original as the narrative itself."[56] This stylistic praise has been echoed by more recent commentators.[57]

In contrast to this praise of his style, his subject matter won only mixed reviews. On one hand, V. S. Pritchett in the *New Statesman* noticed the arrival of a new talent, stating that *The Wild Goose Chase* was satire at its "caustic, hilarious and immoral best" and "a remarkable and original piece of imaginative writing."[58] (Rex wrote Greenwood on 24 September 1937, "I'm glad Pritchett liked the book, because I thought his short story in New Writing one of the best I'd ever read.") But on the other hand, Alick West, a Marxist reviewer, found that Rex's hero George "has not thoroughly revolutionised himself" and saw in him a middle class individualism which isolated George from those who should be his "comrades, and belies his supposed development."[59] The important leftist novelist Edward Upward told Andrew Cramp in 1982 that when he first read the novel, he felt that ". . . it was too indulgent. The fantasy proliferated in a wild way. There is no kind of measure in it at all. I felt that carried little weight. You've got to believe these things are really happening at some stage or another."[60] These Marxist critics sensed that Rex, even at the time of his greatest attraction to Marxism, was less than fully convinced.

Day-Lewis, who was pushing Rex's novel at the time, remembered in *The Buried Day* that around the mid-thirties Rex's "mind was . . . going through an anarchic phase that had elements both of Communist and Fascist thought, but in general was violently heterodox and anti-establishment—a kind of seismic disturbance within himself rather than a planned programme of his own life or anyone else's."[61] N. H. Reeve echoes these comments today, finding that in this novel, Rex's "Marxism was a heady brew, and had a number of potentially fascist elements mixed in it . . . even in this novel, where his socialism is most ostensibly committed, it is easy to sense that one of the reasons his works project so powerfully the imaginative appeal of fascism is that he was himself strongly attracted to it."[62] Here Reeve also notices Rex's lack of full Marxist conviction in this novel, and like Day-Lewis even sees an attraction to fascism.[63] While Day-Lewis and Reeve are right about Rex's less-than-exclusive commitment to Marxism, it is important to stress that nowhere in his hundreds of letters or in any of his other writings does Rex ever express anything but a strong distaste for fascism, and that his actions accord with his words. To place too much weight on a far from obvious unconscious attraction would therefore be unfair. Unlike Auden, who in his poem to Rex's son perhaps found that "Mussolini, Pilsudski and Hitler have charm," Rex never overtly praised fascist dictators. Furthermore, at least by 1937, he was worrying that his socialist character George had too much power.

Rex's poem "Arms in Spain," which appeared in the *Left Review* for April 1937, and which has frequently been republished, is only one of many examples of his clear opposition to, for instance, Mussolini's fascism:

So that men might remain slaves, and that the little good
they hoped for might be turned all bad and the iron lie
stamped and clamped on growing tender and vigorous truth
these machine guns were despatched from Italy.[64]

The tone is very decisive, and nowhere in the poem is there anything but a distaste for dictatorship. On the other hand, Rex's decision to volunteer to fight in Spain in the early 1930s was made only halfheartedly because he was worried about supporting his family then. He was quite pleased when he was turned down, ostensibly because he had a wife and children, but he suspected that the real reason was that the interviewers thought him some kind of spy.[65]

Probably the best formulation to describe Rex's political views during the 1930s is that he was never right wing, but that he was less than fully convinced of Marxism, even when he tried to convince himself that he was. He wanted to find clear solutions to the pressing problems of the period, and tried to convince himself that Marxism was synonymous with his own liberalism. The critics of *The Wild Goose Chase*, whether ideologically or aesthetically motivated, are reacting to the disparity between Rex's overt desire to praise revolution and the subtle indications that he could not quite convince himself that revolution would be a good thing.

In 1961, Rex himself was to call *The Wild Goose Chase* a "mad" novel. How does it stand up today? Rex acknowledged on 24 October 1983 to me that the novel has its flaws, as first novels will: "I still like the book, though it's obviously full of youthful faults, exaggerations, etc." Some of these are a picaresque plot that relies more on momentary inspiration than on strategic planning, imperfectly differentiated minor characters, and a tendency to divide the world into good guys—George and friends—and bad guys—the "kings and scientists" and effete intellectuals whom he opposes. But fortunately George's values do not cook the novel's artistic goose, for it is Rex and not George who has the final say in the writing of the book. Thus, despite George's dislike of technology and the uses to which it is put by a wicked ruling class, Rex's best scenes are those revealing a fascination with the science-fictional possibilities of technology: the unfair elastic yet "fixed" football game (first published in *New Writing*), the tubes connecting live peasants' bloodstreams to those of dead kings, the telescreen (shades of Orwell's later *1984*) used to breach individual privacy and, most impressive perhaps, the concentration-camp-like robots made of human flesh and the use by the defending police of gas canisters, both of which predict the near future with horrifying accuracy. And in spite of George's orthodox Marxist dictum that "Words are dug from mines and grow in fields. Critics, but not poets, sit at tea tables," Rex has written his novel—including many of George's own utterances—in a style owing far more to the tea table of Oxford classical study than to mines and fields. The rhetoric of fiction of the artistic Rex proves at least as powerful as the rhetoric of ideology of the revolutionary Rex; as a result, *The Wild Goose Chase* remains alive even today.

VI. ESSAYS AND *POEMS*

By the time Rex wrote his essay, "Education," in Day-Lewis's *Mind in Chains* anthology, published in June 1937, he may have seemed on the surface more clearly committed to Marxism than when he wrote *The Wild Goose Chase*. But in fact he was far from "liberated" from the liberalism of his teachers. The essay is particularly interesting for Rex's judicious opinion of, even lament for, the status of education until World War I destroyed his teachers' confidence:

In those Victorian days of optimism education was, with far smaller resources than it has at present, a thriving concern. Teachers were proud of their culture and quite confident that it was their culture which was going to change the world. Correspondingly, in the world outside the school the teachers' valuation was accepted. Both the reason and the morality of the schools were assumed to be put into practice by those who left school. Apparent inconsistencies, such as the unequal distribution of wealth and the forcible government of blacks by whites, were admitted to be departures from the strict creed of liberalism, but were nothing to worry about. In the one case, wealth soon would be more or less equally distributed as the benefits of science became accessible to all; in the other case, it was for their own good that the blacks were being governed by the whites. Those whose fortune or education was better than the average were firmly told that these advantages entailed responsibilities. . . . [66]

Rex refuses to casually countenance inequality as some of the last generation's liberal educators had. But far from denouncing the Victorians, including people like his own headmaster Cecil Grant, Rex praises them. He feels that socialism has merely inherited liberalism's mission: "Nowadays, as has often been pointed out, one need not be a Marxist, one need only be an ordinary decent person, to approve the immediate practical aims of Marxism."[67] Montagu Slater, reviewing *The Mind in Chains* in the *Left Review*, called Edward Upward's essay on literature and Rex's education piece "the most valuable essays in Marxist criticism the movement in England has yet produced."[68] But Rex's essay simply restates longtime English liberal beliefs in tolerance and moral rectitude and even moderation while calling them Marxist.

It is also worth noticing that in Rex's essay, "Jonathan Swift: Defender of Liberty," published in the *Left Review* in June 1937, he singles out as permanently valuable two distinctive and definitely anti-authoritarian traits for admiration: Swift's "intense and undeviating respect for human integrity" and Swift's respect for "government by consent, if not self-government. . . ."[69] Even during his most Marxist period, Rex remained committed to English individual and democratic values. For him, Marxism seemed the only way to maintain those things at the time.

In the meantime, the *Poems* were also getting a mixed reception, although they were being noticed. Rex's letter of 13 August 1937 to Greenwood refers to two reviews by Spender: "Have you had any more reviews of the poems? I'd rather like to see what Spender said in 'Fact.' He seems to me the only intelligent critic I've had, though he's a bit priggish. I'm glad Knopf are keen on the W. G. Chase, + hope their cheque will be along before the end of the holidays. So far I've been in Cornwall, catching congers + reading Don Quixote (a damned good book)."

What Spender had written about Rex's *Poems* was far from complimentary. In a group review of George Barker, Charles Madge, Auden, Ezra Pound, and Rex in the *Left Review* (3, 6) for July 1937 (358-59) he began by saying that "Rex Warner is serious, honest, observant, passionate (and an important prose writer, to judge from what I have seen of the *Wild Goose Chase*), but he does not seem to trust sufficiently either his own intuitions or his own perceiving eye: he has the schoolmaster's habit of hammering in his moral with prodigious anvil strokes." The precise problem, according to Spender, is that

> Rex Warner's poetry suffers from the excess of the poet's conscious will. He never looks at a bird or a berry or cracks a joke without one feeling behind his lines the pressure of a conscience determined to draw a moral and exploit a meaning. . . . No poetry could be more arrogantly individualist, more the product of a Public School and Oxford education, with holidays on the moors, than Rex Warner's. Because he puts his will before his imagination, he never succeeds in breaking down the barriers of a social class and special environment, as Auden has sometimes done.

In *Fact* (in an issue devoted to "Writing in Revolt: Theory and Examples"), also published in July 1937, Spender said essentially the same thing, using Rex's "Poem" as an example of "bad Marxist poetry" while praising his "Nile Fishermen" as an "excellent Marxist poem." What Spender has against the third stanza of "Poem" is that "We feel that a way of looking at things, a theory, a habit of mind, have been translated into an idiom and substituted for the poet's unique and authentic experience."[70] He is not wrong about "Poem":

> But what most moves my mind
> is torture of man by man;
> how hearts in every land
> are stamped upon like stone;[71]

Rex's heart may be in the right place, but the moral is obtrusive. As a redeeming feature, however, "Poem" begins with some rather good stanzas about nature:

> What I watch most is moss
> or leaves in alleys of air,
> the rasping blade of grass,
> tiny berries on a huge moor;

the sparkling black bill
of stonechat on a spine,
water tumbling from a pool,
or a hawk in the sky alone.[72]

"Nile Fishermen" today seems no more or less overtly hortatory than "Poem," but it
too has some good lines about nature:

Sun is torn in coloured petals on the water,
the water shivering in the heat and the north wind;
and near and far billow out white swollen crescents,
the clipping wings of feluccas, seagull sails.[73]

Two American critics seem to have an understanding of Rex's poetry. Commenting
in the *Nation*, poet Louise Bogan found that although Rex's poetry was "rather smugly
hortatory, and deriving from C. Day Lewis and Hopkins, it has moments of simplicity
and beauty."[74] The anonymous *New Yorker* reviewer wrote that "Mr. Warner is young,
English, and Comrade-exhorting. A seizure of Gerard Manley Hopkins unfortunately
attacks him from time to time. He is sometimes good at expressing simple things in
his own words."[75]

While Spender's similarly contemporary criticism shows that even Marxist poets
could criticize each other for moralism, we may feel that the line dividing a "good
Marxist poem" from a bad one is difficult to see today, and that his singling out Rex is
a bit unfair. Marxism means moralizing, and it is difficult to find much genuinely
Marxist poetry, including the 1930s work of Spender and Auden, that does not have it.
Some of Auden's best poems, "Musée des Beaux Arts" and "In Memory of W.B.
Yeats," manage to transcend Marxist didacticism only because they contain very subtle
and very few lines referring to Marxist doctrine. Spender's criticism at the time may
have struck Rex as territorial only: advice to stick to prose because poetry was already
his and Auden's bailiwick. Could this review have been the beginning of the slight
distance from Spender that Rex felt even in later life?

On the other hand, it seems that the *Left Review* specialized in attacking leftist writers;
in the April 1936 issue[76] Edgell Rickword attacked Day-Lewis's *Noah and the Waters*
because "his poetry is still infected with the feeling that struggle is transitory," just as Alick
West had taken *The Wild Goose Chase* to task partially because George's method of
organizing his revolutionary army was not specified. (In fact, the typescript of *The Wild
Goose Chase* shows that Rex excised several passages dealing with the actual organizing,

no doubt because he wanted a more universal or allegorical picture.) It was hard for committed writers to strike a balance between the demands of politics and a purely aesthetic approach; they were damned if they went "too far" in one direction or the other, and who was to say where the line was? Given the fundamental ambivalence toward Marxism of many of them, like Rex, it was all the harder to toe a line, whether political or aesthetic.

VII. THE GENESIS AND COMPOSITION OF *THE PROFESSOR*

On 11 October 1937, Rex wrote Greenwood from Great Rissington that he had been there five or six days because his father was very ill. Rex's father died at the rectory on 17 October 1937 at the age of sixty-nine. There was a small funeral, which was attended by family and local people. His father was cremated. This was an unusual act and an unusually liberal view for a Church of England clergyman at that time. The "Directions for Funeral of Rev. F. E. Warner" give insight into his principled and modest character, specifying his rationale for desiring cremation and insisting upon a simple service.[77]

Despite their disagreements over politics, Rex loved his father dearly and near the end of his own life, in answer to a clergyman's question about whom he admired, answered, "My father." In Rex's next novel, *The Professor*, the Professor is presented very well in his fatherly role, undoubtedly as a reminiscence of Rex's own recent bereavement. *The Professor* and his son disagree, but clearly love one another. Tellingly, Rex began thinking of the new novel right after his father's death, writing Lehmann on 27 October, probably 1937, that he was trying to develop new ideas for a prose work and hoped to get started during the Christmas break.

Another motivation for writing a new novel was Rex's chronic need for money. On 19 November he wrote Greenwood from Musbury that he was offering to sell the manuscripts of *Poems* and *The Wild Goose Chase* to Eric Allen Osborne for £6 and £20, respectively. Osborne was the editor of a Communist anthology, *In Letters of Red*, published in March 1938, that included one chapter excised from the published *Wild Goose Chase*, entitled "Visit to a Mine,"[78] along with contributions by Auden, Day-Lewis, Edward Upward, and Lion Feuchtwanger, among others. Osborne does not seem to have bought either manuscript.[79]

Another sign of the new prose project mentioned to Lehmann in October comes in a letter of early January 1938 from the rectory at Great Rissington to Greenwood:

> [S]o far I've spent the whole time nailing up packing cases, + doing pretty well every kind of job that could be done better by someone else. Most people in the Rectory are ill,—

conspicuous maladies being a duodenal ulcer + gall stones. My aunt, a strict teetotaler, presides at meals, + I drink surreptitiously over sinks or in cellars. I don't see any chance at all of getting away to a pub by myself, but I think I may be able to secure a few days at the Rectory next week, + have got, I think, something like an idea for another book.

In a letter of 11 January 1938 to Greenwood, showing his contact with writer Naomi Mitchison, Rex reports more progress: "I think I shall come up to town in the morning on Saturday [15 January]. . . . Am going to dinner with Naomi Mitchison in the evening. I've just had a pretty severe reprimand from my aunt for going into a pub on Sunday; but this bracing atmosphere is enabling me to get on quite nicely with a plan for a book." While he was still in London on the 17th of January, Rex also met John Lehmann in person for the first time.[80]

In a letter to Greenwood, dated only "Wednesday," but probably also of January 1938, Rex again mentions a new novel: "I've started on a new idea for a book, having found that my letters were getting duller + duller. So far its going on all right. Its about a Professor." In February, he reported to Greenwood that "I've written about 12,000 words of the new book, but may have to alter some of what I've written. I don't like writing in short disconnected periods of time."

VIII. REX ON THE ALLEGORICAL NOVEL

Teaching and speaking to leftist literary groups interfered with progress on *The Professor*. In an undated letter to Greenwood, probably from around this time, Rex writes that he had nearly finished three chapters in a week, and "If I only had six clear weeks I'd finish the book. School is an absolute bugger, + I'd really like to be shut up (with reasonable liberties) in an office or anywhere else." In another letter, of 3 February [1938] to Greenwood, Rex writes

I've just heard from Julius Lipton that they've started a Left Book Club group of writers + readers (sounds inclusive enough), + that they want me to address them on the W.G.C. on Feb. 11. He answers me that this "will be very helpful both for yourself + your readers." If they're all like Alec [*sic*] West I think I can help them more than they can help me, but perhaps it will be worth while attending, so I think I shall come up to London on the 11th.—I told Penning-Rownell that I couldn't do anything about books until I'd finished the one that I'm on at present. This is going on all right, + would be better if I had any time.

What Rex said on 11 February is fortunately available in manuscript form in the Michigan State University library Greenwood collection (MS 49). Although undated, the manuscript is entitled "The Wild Goose Chase," is four handwritten pages long (talk length), and tackles the problem of realism in the novel. It is an early version of "The Allegorical Method" of 1945, and shows what was in Rex's mind just when he was writing his important novels. It also gives a sense of what Rex was like as a speaker, and so is worth reprinting in full:

"The Wild Goose Chase" is an allegory; that is to say that it is not only a story but is intended to *mean* something, is intended to present a view of life.

"Why then not say what you mean straight out?" it may be asked. The answer is that no one, on any subject of vital interest, ever has been able to say what he meant straight out. We know + feel things not as isolated objects, easy for the eye + tongue, but in their relations to ourselves + to each other; + our truest descriptions come not through the camera or medical text book, but through painting + poetry. I do not mean to belittle the camera or textbook; such apparatus is the most important thing of all, because our bread + butter depends on it. I am only concerned with truth.

The scientist in his writing must use words with their minimum connotation. His aim is to be so perfectly understood that no one can go wrong while applying his methods. The poet's aim is different. He loads his words with meaning + seeks an accuracy which is of quite a different kind from scientific accuracy. Poetry is not to be "applied" but to be experienced.

The philosopher is the most unfortunate kind of scientist. He tries to explain + co-relate what he is apt to call "phenomena," meaning people's thoughts + lives. He used to have a big field in which to disport himself with his "substances" + "accidents" + "transcendentals"; but now his field is, owing to the encroachments of science, much reduced in area. The best philosophy is no longer a pursuit of first causes, but a method of thinking.

Plato in some of his dialogues found himself in the same awkward situation that "metaphysicians" are in today. All the arguments are neatly recorded, but when they are set up against real fact (the actual death of a friend, for example) they have a way of looking rather foolish. On these occasions Plato took refuge in a "myth," + in his myths he aimed at the truth of poetry rather than the truth of science; he put, as it were, into his words more, not less, than they would hold.

"The Wild Goose Chase" started as an attack on the idealist philosophy, on "the spirit of evil in things heavenly." I was not concerned much with the esse:percipi [being:perceiving] stuff, but wanted to show the cruelty + despair of idealism in the fabric of human lives. Idealism is not something pushed on to us by Plato: it was a way of thinking which grew out of our economic relationships, a system of thought most appropriate to oppression. So together with idealism I was led to attack the oppression of one class by another. But "idealism" + "oppression" are abstractions. I had to show them as real influences on a human personality. This is where the story comes in, because a human personality is always changing + moving in time + space. And yet I had to have something typical or universal about this "human personality." I did what Plato did in the "Republic" + Dostoievsky in his "Brothers Karamazov." I copied Plato's "tri-partite division of the soul" + adapted Dostoievsky's three brothers. The three brothers in "The Wild Goose Chase" are, in a sense, all part of George who is, as it were, the dominant partner. They are also separate, representing the forces of intellect (David) + imagination (Rudolph) when these are unrelated to the body + to the lives of other people.

The three brothers are chasing the wild goose. That means that they are trying to live. They discover that life is impossible without a consciousness of themselves as bodies + minds intimately related to the bodies + minds of others. And since the most obvious connection between people is the sexual relation I have made much use of the idea of sex with its possibilities for denial, perversion, or acceptance.

Though it may be said in general that the theme of the book is the revolt of matter against spirit, body against intellectualism, the masses against their exploiters, it is not so simple as that. The revolt is a dialectical one + does not solve every difficulty. "Freedom is the knowledge of necessity" we read—a great + profound statement; but, recognising this, we may be tempted to go further, + to question "So what?"

If it had been possible to provide a "key" to all the characters in the allegory there would have been no point in writing the book as it has been written. I can only assure the reader that the key, though unprovided, does exist, + that if the general meaning of my allegory is not much clearer than a textbook of metaphysics, then I am a Dutchman.

This is Rex's only interpretation in writing of his first serious novel. At last, we know from his own mouth what he meant by the "wild goose chase," what the brothers are supposed to mean, and what the direct influences on their creation are. The depth of Rex's philosophical engagement also becomes clear, but also his recognition that when philosophy is embodied in characters, it must become more emotional and less logical. (We recall, for instance, that the wild geese first appear when George experiences love with the steadfast Joan.) We also learn that at least at the point when he wrote this lecture, Rex thought that revolution would not solve all problems. This feeling comes out fully, however, only in *The Professor*, which of course was also being written at this time.

The group that Rex addressed was apparently unimpressed, as a letter to Lehmann of 19 February makes clear. Rex first writes that he was interested in (i) replies to pacifist arguments and in making pleas for (ii) "less realism in the novel." He goes on to remark about the meeting that

I made a speech on (ii) to the Writers and Readers Left Book Club group + got the impression that most of the audience thought I was rather an ass, + that such things as "The Wild Goose Chase" were damned as soon as anyone called them "allegorical." I was rather irritated by this, + particularly by the fact that none of my critics had read the book. But I might be able to make a better show of my argument in writing. Another thing I might do is to enter the controversy on "Should poetry be political?" But I'd like to learn what your ideas are, + whether [it] is intended as an open forum or as a means for getting across a "general line."[81]

Rex's interest in finding answers to pacifist arguments was woven into *The Professor*, because one character there, an old cobbler, is a Christian pacifist and is given a surprisingly strong role.

Rex's ambivalent feeling about the relationship of Marxism to writing comes out more strongly in a letter of 14 March, probably 1938, to Lehmann:

I'm very sorry to have offended you about the articles. Let me explain about them. They are both "contract work" + done to get money. The International Literature one[82] I did at the request of Day Lewis, + probably won't even get any money for (unless "valuta" implies caviar + fur coats). I'm very ashamed of the article + would like it to appear in New Writing anyway. The one on "Socialism + Literature" is for a man (Cohen) who seems to be getting together a book like "The Mind in Chains." This I'm doing partly for money + partly from a sense of duty as a socialist propagandist. I haven't started to write it yet, but if (which I doubt) it turns out at all good, I'll enquire from Cohen whether I can send it to New Writing first. I don't see why I shouldn't, if the aim of the book is propagandist. The truth is that I don't like writing essays + never have written one unless the subject has been prescribed for me. If you'd like to commission one from me (to be done by a certain time + on a certain subject) I'll do it; but I don't really think that my ideas in that abstract form are any better than most other people's ideas.—But I'm sorry to have conveyed an impression that I was deserting New Writing for other fields.[83]

Here Rex states openly his commitment to Marxism, but at the same time reveals his intense embarrassment over the propagandist's role. Again, this is a sign of how uneasily

Rex and Marxism coexisted, even when he seems convinced by it. The idea of writing Marxist articles to make money also seems a contradiction, at least superficially.

Rex's political activities continued in and around his work on *The Professor*. On 3 May 1938, he wrote Greenwood[84] that "I may be coming up to London next Tuesday to see Stephen Spender + others. He's organising a kind of discussion on plays, + asked me to come along. . . . I'm getting rather stuck in my new book. Sometimes I think it is quite good, more often bloody awful. What I want is to get a few weeks continuous work on it." Spender's *Trial of a Judge*, which appeared early in 1938, features a liberal, pacifistic, and indecisive judge, and shows the fascists gaining ascendancy over the judge and over defeated Communists. Either seeing this play or hearing about it at that discussion must have helped Rex formulate his own ideas and accelerate the completion of his novel.

On 22 July 1938, Rex and Day-Lewis (who was making his first trip abroad) left England for a rally in Paris "For Peace and Against the Bombardment of Open Cities." John and Rosamond Lehmann, Goronwy Rees, the spy Guy Burgess, and Stephen Spender were there also, as were Louis Aragon, André Malraux, and Ilya Ehrenburg. Rex recalled that Cecil had forced him to come to the conference and then had been unsociable to the French writers by refusing to speak a word of French. It was a point of pride to Rex that his own French was not bad. They were back home by 26 July.[85]

IX. THE PUBLICATION AND MEANING OF *THE PROFESSOR*

Rex made good progress with *The Professor*, because on Monday, probably 8 August, he wrote to Greenwood,

> I've finished writing the book today, + feel like a piece of limp discarded rag. On Friday I'm coming up to London to stay for the week end with an aunt from America. So shall I bring you the MS. which I should have revised by then, on Friday morning? If you're busy I'll just leave it at the office. Would this cottage be any use to you as a week end retreat? I'm going away certainly this week-end, probably the next one, + undoubtedly for several after that . . . If its any good to you, do say so. Is "Attempting to Escape" a possible title?

On 10 August [1938], he was able to write to Lehmann that "Actually I did get started on an article on Realism + the Novel, but while I was writing it I found that my views were beginning to alter rather rapidly + so left off, waiting for a solidification. Now that I've finished my novel, I hope I'll be able to start on something else."[86]

In a letter dated Saturday, probably a week or two later, he writes to Greenwood, ". . . I'm very glad that you were impressed favourably by a second reading of *The Professor*. I'm by no means ashamed of it myself, though I should like to write something less bitter if I could do so sincerely. But at present one really seems to be living in an environment which is almost worse than a mad house. Is there any news about the book from America?. . . Have you + John [Morris] yet struck a blow for internationalism by joining the Wine Society?" How right Rex was about the insanity of a world torn between Hitler and Stalin, with the weak democracies in the middle; wine helped maintain sanity.

Things moved very rapidly, probably because Greenwood saw how topical the novel was and felt that it should be published quickly. On 10 September 1938, Rex wrote to him, "I'm coming through London on Monday on my way to Jersey, + will look in at the office at about lunch time. . . . I'll bring the corrected proof copy of 'The Professor.' You've certainly got it through at an astonishing speed. Am reading, with interest + admiration, 'The Dynasts.'" Hardy had in common with Rex a love of the rural, and Rex was obviously interested in Hardy's way of presenting the Napoleonic wars.

Rex regretted that he could not be any more optimistic about politics than Hardy had been. On 27 September 1938, he wrote to Pam Morris, "I was very glad that you think well of 'The Professor.' I agree that it would be a better book if there was something beside despair in it, + if the times were not the present times there would have been more gaiety, or at least hope."[87] Of the years from 1936-39, Frances recalls: "We were not very happy. He was preoccupied. The war in Spain, the awareness of the Nazi menace were always there. We had very little money. These were difficult years, and in *The Professor* he expresses his unhappiness and pessimism."[88] But the publication of the book made him happy.

Already on 20 October 1938, he could offer Greenwood "many thanks for the copies of 'The Professor.' I like the look of it, slender as the volume is. . . ."

At this time, he was very interested in working out his own, unique literary philosophy. On 16 November 1938, he stated his fictional aesthetic to Lehmann:

You seem to have felt much the same about it as I do myself. Its on a much smaller scale than 'The Wild Goose Chase,' +, though concentration has some advantages, it can hardly make up for a severe limitation of scope. It was meant to be a kind of cross between epic + Platonic dialogue rather than a novel, if by 'novel' one understands a slice out of an arrangement of 'real life.' Instead I try to act out + exhibit nakedly forces + ideas that control 'real life,' + for this method a certain artificiality of style seems necessary. I must be, I suppose, a sort of Platonist, as I am constantly trying to see the soul in things, + tend to claim for my creations a kind of reality that is epic rather than scientific. It is all a question of keeping a very delicate balance, pushing one's world just a little further than the real world, but in the same direction + not too far. A vague enough theory, + inadequately explained, I fear![89]

So Rex aimed for the "soul" of things, in this case politics, rather than its superficial manifestation. He captures some of the eternal truths of politics in the long speeches in *The Professor*, but on the other hand the novel is very tied to immediate events. Hence, in this new work, Rex arrives at a form somewhere between allegory and realism.

Michigan State University Library's MS 47, undoubtedly written in response to Greenwood's request for blurb material, gives Rex's own précis of what *The Professor* is all about:

"The Professor" is a study of a middle-aged classical scholar, who, at a crisis in his country's history, is given the office of Chancellor + who attempts in this position, by pursuing a course of strict legality, to justify those ideals of individual freedom + of democracy on which, in his view, civilisation is based.

His country is threatened with foreign invasion + with internal disturbance. *The Professor* is unaware, when he takes office, that his Chief of Police is already in the service of the enemy + that the majority of his colleagues are inefficient to the point of worthlessness.

His plan for a plebiscite, his reasoned appeal to the whole people over the radio are forestalled by the machinations of the Chief of Police, + the Professor, after narrowly escaping assassination, is pursued through the streets + takes refuge in the house of an old cobbler, an advocate of non-resistance + of a type of love which springs from disgust + disillusion.

Plans are made for an escape, but the Professor refuses to leave the city without the lady to whom he is engaged + whom throughout his misfortunes, he imagined to be faithful + understanding. Here also he is doomed to disappointment. He is arrested, subjected to various indignities in prison +, in the end shot "while attempting to escape."

Of this leading character the author writes: "He believed, scholar though he was, not only in the existence but in the efficacy of a power more human, liberal + kindly than an organisation of metal. He believed not simply in the utility, but in the overriding or pervasive power of the disinterested reason. Metal was to be proved harder than his flesh, stupidities + fanaticism more influential than his gentlest syllogisms; + yet, easy though it is to name the man a pedant + dismiss him as misguided, his contribution to a civilisation that may one day be organised or given room to flower will be found, perhaps, to have been not altogether nil."

Other characters in the book include the Professor's son, a revolutionary who is yet seen to be developing those ideas on which his father's political theory is based: an assassin who is the propagandist for a new system of morality: the Rev. Furius Webber, a pacifist: nudists + cabinet ministers.

The book is not as much "political" as a study of the ideas behind politics. But the book is not, as was "The Wild Goose Chase" allegorical. Nor, though the narrative is direct enough, could it be described exactly as "realistic." It is preeminently a study of one man in one situation, + other characters + events are so organised as to throw into the sharpest relief this main object for study.

Perhaps the most important thing that Rex says is that the novel is a study of the "ideas behind politics." As always, Rex attempts to penetrate to the "soul" of the situation, in this case the clash between fascism, liberalism, and Marxism, and to show what is at stake. In a generalized form, without naming any country, Rex writes about the urgent political situation in Austria before and during the time of writing— first the assassination of Chancellor Engelbert Dollfuss on 25 July 1934 by Nazi agents because he had tried to keep Austria independent of Germany, and then the unrelenting pressure by Hitler on the government of Kurt von Schuschnigg, resulting on 14 March 1938 in the Nazi takeover of Austria and the arrest of Schuschnigg. The Nazis also constantly threatened invasion of Eduard Beneš's Czechoslovakia from 1935 until 1939 when the German army occupied the country; Beneš fled in 1938 to London, where he set up a government in exile.

N. H. Reeve finds in Rex's novel a very precise parallel to political events involving Franz von Papen, Hitlerite chancellor of Germany, and the Austrian pro-Nazi Arthur Seyss-Inquart: "The Ambassador's threats to Dr Tromp [the Professor's predecessor as Chancellor] recall von Papen's bullying of the Austrian government; Grimm, the Chief of Police and covert Nazi, plays a similar role to Seyss-Inquart's; the Professor's plan for a plebiscite on national independence, though not his economic programme, invites comparison with Schuschnigg's; events both in Warner's fiction and the Anschluss turn on the dramatic developments in a radio broadcast." He finds, moreover, that "Schuschnigg, in his reckless trusting of Seyss-Inquart and Glaise von Horstenau, and in his appeal to the Western powers to make sufficiently strong representations of support for Austrian independence to deter a German invasion, while stopping short of actual intervention themselves, could be regarded as having been every bit as naive and credulous as Warner's hero, without having the latter's liberal decency and integrity. . . ."[90]

In addition, Rex's novel seems to reflect the intra-Austrian events that Stephen Spender mentions in "An Open Letter to Aldous Huxley on his 'Case for Constructive Peace,'" when attacking Huxley's pacifism in 1936.[91] Spender decried the dictatorial Dollfuss regime, which crushed the Socialist unions in order to ingratiate itself with Italian fascist leader Benito Mussolini, only to have the fascists assassinate Dollfuss himself. The Schuschnigg regime was no better, according to Spender, because it also attempted to suppress the Left.

In early 1938, Schuschnigg, who had been Dollfuss's lieutenant, announced a plebiscite which would decide the fate of the country. Hitler cancelled the plebiscite with his invasion, and Schuschnigg belatedly tried to gain the support of the Socialists, but it was all too late.[92] This grim scenario was taking place just prior to and during the time that Rex was writing *The Professor*. In Rex's novel, the liberal Professor refuses to arm, but does not suppress, the Left. Only when his country has been invaded by the fascists does the Professor realize that his son's call to arm the Left was correct, because the Left offered the only organized answer to the invasion.

The lack of a manuscript hampers our understanding of the evolution of *The Wild Goose Chase*. But the manuscript (in two large notebooks) of *The Professor* is at Michigan State, so we can witness to some degree how Rex shaped the work from fairly early on in the writing process.[93] As is usual in Rex's manuscripts, there are relatively few emendations. He will cancel a phrase here or there and substitute another for it, but on the whole his manuscripts attest to a Mozart-like clarity and decisiveness of thought. The ideas and even the sentences seem to come fully formed from his brain to paper with no stumbling or false starts. The manuscript we have, consisting of 204 pages, is probably the fair copy from which Greenwood (or Rex) had *The Professor* typed. But given Rex's fluency of thought and writing, it may well be the only manuscript of the book that ever existed despite its relative lack of emendations.

Yet there are a few substantial changes that show us what Rex was aiming to do. On page 20 of the manuscript, which is page 40 of the novel,[94] right after the sentences "And yet his son, like they, was in opposition to the Government, had declared openly that the community did not exist. Where was his support?" there follows this excised paragraph: "Not, certainly, among the Legionaires who, though they asserted their respect for law + order, based their programme on a political theory that would not stand a moment's rational examination, + their propaganda on an appeal to forces that the Professor himself would never dream of summoning to his aid." Then comes the sentence that exists in the published novel, "Who were the men of good will?" Rex may have felt that he had shown so clearly that fascism (represented by the Legionaires) was irrational, that he had no need of such overtly anti-fascist statements.

From the manuscript it also appears that Rex may have felt that too much anti-pacifism was overkill, although the novel as a whole makes it clear that he remained as convinced of the need for action as he had been in 1936 when writing (or participating in) the pamphlet in answer to Huxley, who had also (as we have seen) provoked Spender to a reply in the *Left Review*. On page 25 of the manuscript, which corresponds to page 47-48 of the novel (1938 and 1986 editions), in place of the block beginning, "As a matter of fact" and ending "Hrumph! Hrumph!" Rex originally had an excised paragraph:

> . . . an awful bore. You know, I think that what we need isn't a lot of dry formulas, but perhaps a little more loving kindness. And we people in the P.T.S.M. [Peace-Through-Spinning Movement] don't have to go about arguing all the time, because really, you know, everyone's a pacifist. What a jolly fine thought that is! You know, I don't believe that anyone really wants to be killed. That's my idea anyway. So why not join in with us? What we're trying to do at present is to get everyone to take up spinning. Its really awfully good fun; + then there are a lot of other jolly amusing handi-crafts like raffia-work. Those are the lines along which the P.T.S.M. would solve that beastly unemployment problem. No party bitterness. Nothing like that at all. And as for international affairs, of course we ought to have a World Economic Conference quite soon, I think. Get people round a round table. It makes no end of a difference to dis-, Hrumph! Hrumph!, to dismay.

Here Rex ridicules the ineffectiveness of Aldous Huxley's pacifism once again, but of course the Professor's liberalism fares no better. Only the son's revolutionary Marxism seems to have force, with the Professor finally understanding that his son's dictum, "I hate because I love," is the only effective idea in the anti-fascist fight. It appears that the second chapter, "The Orators," was particularly difficult for Rex to write, judging from the number of excisions it contains, although most of them were small. After that, he seems to have hit the right tone and the novel just flowed.

X. THE CHARACTER OF THE PROFESSOR

In *The Wild Goose Chase*, a classically restrained and balanced style was at odds to some degree with an enthusiasm for Marxist revolution. Almost unconsciously, George's—Rex's—enthusiasm was being held in check by a more conservative upbringing and education. In *The Professor* the struggle between Rex's education and the contemporary politics of the 1930s—the "modern world"—continues in more overt form: the "Professor" is modeled on Gilbert Murray, as Rex stated in his conversation with Andrew Cramp. As we have seen, Rex deeply respected Murray as a scholar of the classics. Murray was someone who attempted to apply Sophocles' balance, moderation, and reason to the insanity of post-World-War-I Europe; he was a founder of the League of Nations and a believer in the old and much-battered Victorian hope that the world could be made a better place. Who wins in *The Professor*—Murray, with his wonderful, old-world belief in reason, or the son of the Professor, with his belief in Marxist revolution?

In *The Wild Goose Chase*, Rex was undoubtedly on the side of George against all of the anonymous kings and generalized forces of evil; he was the rebellious son. In *The Professor*, however, while Rex is overtly on the side of the Professor's son, he has unusual sympathy for the Professor himself, and we can see Rex divided between his old teacher and his education on the one side and the need for action such as the son recommends on the other. In all of the early novels, the rebellious sons—George, the Professor's, Roy in *The Aerodrome*—do well. Perhaps Rex stopped writing such rebellious works when he could no longer see himself as a rebellious son and, as his own children Jonathan and Anna grew during the 1930s and George was added in the 1940s, began to be a somewhat more conservative father himself. Or perhaps he stopped writing such works when he realized that he was a liberal, like the Professor, rather than the radical that he had forced himself to be in response to fascism.

In *The Professor*, even while taking the part of the rebellious son, Rex could still see things from the father's—Murray's, his former headmaster Cecil Grant's, and perhaps his own deceased father's—point of view. So this is a "war" between two parts of himself as well. In *The Professor*, the conflict between Rex's classical education and Murray's traditional liberalism on the one side and the horrible events then taking place in Austria and Czechoslovakia on the other is very overt indeed. Rex openly scrutinizes the value of classical literature as it had been taught to him, that is, as a source of moderation and reason and a way of understanding the present.

Rex sets this conflict in motion in his description of the Professor on the novel's first page:

> Those who knew the man seem to have admired him, though pity rather than admiration is likely to be the feeling by which those who peruse his history will be most affected; for we shall see a man quite unfitted for power, in his day the greatest living authority on Sophocles, rich in the culture of many languages and times, but for his own time, not through irresolution or timidity but rather, as it seems to us, through a pure kind of blindness, most inapt. He believed against all the evidence, scholar though he was, not only in the existence but in the efficacy of a power more human, liberal, and

kindly than the power of metal. He believed not simply in the utility but in the over-riding or pervasive power of the disinterested reason.[95]

This is not just the Professor who is being described here, but Rex himself to some degree; he too believed in reason and humanity and as a teacher himself, in teaching.[96] Rather than a sarcastic condemnation of the Professor's naiveté and his own liberal instincts, we have a regretful feeling of "Goodbye to All That" as Rex saw Europe hurtling toward war once again and understood that Murray-like League of Nations ideals of cooperation and moderation were inadequate.

In fact, until close to the very end, the Professor continues to believe in the wonderful abstractions in which Rex himself was taught to believe at St. George's and possibly at Oxford:

> Let me say that there is much—very much—in the programme of your party with which I am in agreement, whereas to the programme of the National Legion I am entirely opposed. But there is one thing more important than my own point of view. It is the Idea of Democracy. It is the Idea of Justice and Legality. I can never arm one faction of my own people against another faction. Believe me, my dear boy, that even at this hour persuasion may be proved more powerful than violence. . . . Democracy. . . is a faith, and the faith is based on the goodness of man. (161)

Rex treats this Platonic argument somewhat wistfully here as a pleasant position that can no longer be maintained. Seeing the bumbling of the Chamberlain government, which took office in May 1937 and promised "Peace in our time," Rex felt that stronger measures to counter fascism were necessary.

The Professor's liberalism and belief in universal values are simply no match for the fascist philosophy, brilliantly presented in the resentful Julius Vander's speech in chapter 5:

> I ought not to have been surprised . . . to find you still harping on those frayed and worn-out strings. Peace, democracy, culture—all that clap-trap, I expect you believe in it.

> . . . all these "ethical ideals" of yours are mere clap-trap, schemes, like marriage, to enslave the strong man in the interests of communities of second-rate pedlars, dreamers, twisters, and things that are still wanting to be back in mother's womb. . . .

> . . . Will I put anything in place of your ideals? Yes, I will. I will put their direct opposites in their place. And, what is more, people will like it.

. . . our great strength comes from the fact that we represent the morality which is older, more vital, and more specifically human than yours. Our love is the emotion not of a dutiful intellectual but of a warrior in battle. It depends on hatred for the enemy. . . . We show our followers how to regain their self-confidence as individuals by hating their enemies. You offer them a whole world to love: we give them a tangible minority to hate. We do not pretend that all men are equal or that women are the same as men. Consequently our audience is not one of castrated intellectuals. Real men have known all along, in spite of the "wider morality," that power over others is the normal flowering of personality, and that women are conquered, not persuaded into lust by a common interest in Euclid. . . . We appeal not to the intellect, or even to immediate self-interest, but to the dark, unsatisfied, and raging impulses of the real man.[97]

Rex clearly understood the nature of fascism and the appeal to the primitive that underlies it.

After his son, in the brilliant chapter "Father and Son," tells the Professor that his girlfriend has been raped by National Legionaires and has committed suicide, the Professor turns to classical literature for solace and understanding, much as Rex undoubtedly attempted to do himself during times of stress. But this resource fails him because he now sees the ancient and modern worlds as very different:

The Professor thought of the lament which Homer, in the 22nd book of the Iliad, puts into the mouth of Andromache. Were such expressions of grief, he wondered, merely the make-believe of a poet, or were they drawn from real life in societies that were differently organised from anything now existing in the world? For in modern society a sufferer will sin against decency and convention if he alludes to, much more if he expresses, his sufferings. He can expect no audience to listen to his laments or to take up with him a sympathetic chorus. To-day the herd will not pause for a weakling, and all grief, in so far as it impairs efficiency, is ranked as weakness. Was this stoicism, or was it inhumanity? (152)

In another passage, the Professor is unable to relate clearly the violence of modern fascists to the violence of ancient ones:

Lists, he thought, proscriptions: a return to the savageries of Sulla or the massacres in which perished the great orator, Cicero. But the historical parallels failed to stir his mind: the actual process of life differed too remarkably from recorded history, and no imaginative insight could bridge the gulf between the living and the dead. (202)

Rex here is painfully voicing his own fear that the classics would indeed fail to provide help in solving the extreme problems of the present.

Like Rex himself, the Professor also finds that no escape into the beauty of art is possible in the face of the present:

> He began, in an effort to calm his mind, to recite to himself the first two or three stanzas of Keats' *Ode to a nightingale*, but, though he seemed to see with great vividness the words printed on shining paper before his eyes, he either missed their sense altogether, or found that when a phrase was understood it gave him no pleasure. For some reason or other he whispered to himself the words "Beauty" and "Truth," but when he had pronounced the words they seemed to bear no reference to the scene which had just been enacted.[98]

So the Professor is progressively forced to realize that all his training and moderation will not do any longer. This is, indeed, the main action of this novel—the stripping away of all illusions. *The Professor* undergoes much the same process as the scholar Kien does in Elias Canetti's *Auto da Fé* (1935), if for a different reason. Like Freud under Nazi tutelage, the Professor realizes that "beneath the apparent surface calm of Christian and democratic civilization wild and dissatisfied forces were waiting for a day of destruction, and now that day was at hand" (260). The Professor is forced (like Rex's headmaster Cecil Grant during World War I), finally, to wonder "whether all the principles by which hitherto his life had been governed were to be proved false" (268). While he rejects that thought, he must admit that "The civilization which, as Chancellor, he had endeavoured to maintain had been, at least in its upper strata and in its direction, generally corrupt," and he turns to his son's Communist organization "as the only possible defenders not only of his own safety but of humanity and the text of Homer" (268). The Communists, maybe even Stalin's Russia, become in Rex's view the defenders of the values of humanistic classical civilization against the forces of book-burning and barbarism. In the thirties Rex discerned few choices other than Communism and fascism. Significantly, however, while Rex tells us what fascism is and what the Professor's liberal ideas are, he does not spell out the Communists' program. In failing to defend Communism in any precise way, or to tell us exactly what it means besides opposition to fascism, he seems to be a revolutionary only by necessity.

Rex's own lack of ease with the choice between fascism and Communism and his lingering love of the Professor's ideals of humanism manifest themselves in the old man Jinkerman's Christian philosophy. Here, perhaps, is another way of understanding. In his letter of 29 May 1984 to me, Rex said that at the time he wrote *The Wild Goose*

Chase he regarded himself as a "religious Marxist," but that position is far more developed in *The Professor* than in the earlier novel. Old Jinkerman's long speech on Christianity and the futility of dealing with economic injustice without attention to the soul of man raises problems that Marxism cannot solve. The key to the change is Anna; in 1932, by which time Rex had written *The Wild Goose Chase*, Anna was not yet injured. By 1938 when he was writing *The Professor*, Rex had over five years to meditate on the injustice of the universe in striking down a helpless young girl for no reason whatsoever. Marxism could not alleviate that situation, and once again Rex reveals his lack of conviction in the new religion even as he seems to advance it in the novel as a whole.

Old Jinkerman tells of an incident concerning a boy's epilepsy that recalls Anna's situation. He says,

> What ideas of goodness or reason could ever justify the sudden and horrible crippling and destruction of beauty and youth and hope? I began to open my eyes farther, and I saw death, evil, pain and disease everywhere. Now I saw that death is not a human institution; pain was not invented by the governing class; evil and disappointment may be alleviated in some cases by material adjustments, but they spring from the soul of man.[99]

Old Jinkerman also comments on his wife,

> Previously I had loved her for qualities which had seemed to me outstanding and exceptional, a more than normal beauty and intelligence. I had watched my love fade away from month to month and from year to year, and had fancied that the reason for its fading was our poverty. But now I saw that no social organization can make the body, born to decay and growing into death, anything but squalid and pitiable.[100]

Marxism, while necessary to combat fascism in the immediate present, offers no explanation of real evil or solution to the deepest personal problems. Old Jinkerman's speeches are Rex's recognition of that fact, even as he feels he must side with the son's revolutionary program as the only answer to fascism.

XI. IS *THE PROFESSOR* AN IMPORTANT NOVEL?

The Professor appeared in England on 24 October 1938 and in America through Knopf on 20 February 1939, and was reviewed widely. The critics, of course, did not know anything about Rex's personal life, including Anna and possible marital troubles, which are sensed in old Jinkerman's words about his wife and in the Professor's difficulties with his mistress. They did, however, appreciate the timeliness of *The Professor*, and its attempt to engage important issues. The *TLS* reviewer, for instance, found the defeat of the Professor "a melancholy conclusion, but Mr. Warner is most persuasive, and the various dialogues between the Professor and representative persons cover most aspects of contemporary morals. Though no one nowadays could call politics dry, they can still be inhuman, and Mr. Warner's achievement is to show them pitiably at work in the lives of human beings without noticeably obscuring the issue."[101]

Like the *TLS* reviewer, most critics understood Rex's love of the Professor even as he seemed forced to show his defeat. Christopher Isherwood, writing in the *New Republic*, found *The Professor* "a very much better book than his earlier novel, *The Wild Goose Chase*," since it is "about a vitally interesting subject—the fate of a liberal in the world of power politics." Isherwood fixes the novel as taking place in pre-*Anschluss* Austria. Clearly siding with the Professor, Isherwood feels that the Professor, although dead, "is still a formidable problem for his enemies, a problem they will never be able to solve. His gentle, persuasive voice will continue to be heard, long after the guns are silent, and the bombing planes have run out of gas. And because Mr. Warner succeeds in making us feel this, his story, though tragic, is heartening and inspiring as well."[102]

One reviewer, Henry Lappin of the *Evening News* of Buffalo, New York, compared the Professor to Gilbert Murray (as Rex was to do later in his interview with Andrew Cramp, admitting that he had not been fair to Murray) and concluded "no Gilbert Murray he! That exquisite scholar, that inspired man of affairs and of state, would—or so one thinks—have superbly handled the situation with which 'The Professor' found himself confronted."[103] The criticism that emerges here is that Rex has stacked the deck against the Professor, who continues to look better than both the Nazis represented by Vander and the Communists represented by his son. Once again, as in the case with *The Wild Goose Chase*, the critics sense that Rex is not quite convinced of the merits of Marxism, that the Professor's turn to it at the end is forced, and that Rex has actually made a very good case for liberalism, at least in the long run. But even the leftist *People's World* found some good words for the Professor himself: the anonymous reviewer in its 11 March 1939 issue called the book "perfect in style and conception" and went on to say that "Something of the Greek beauty and perfection loved by the Professor has entered into his story."[104]

Despite the felt tension between Rex's love of the Professor and his forced condemnation of what the Professor stands for, many critics agreed with Isherwood that Rex's second novel was better because it was more down to earth than the first. In the *New York Times*,[105] Ralph Thompson wrote that, compared to *The Wild Goose Chase*, *The Professor* was a "better managed work in almost every respect, and in its own right a remarkably able one. It is cut from the same piece of red cloth, but the writing is restrained and polished rather than eccentric, while the story itself is relatively compact and, though deliberative in tone, by no means formal."

For readers today, topicality is bound to be the issue: is Rex's book, seen apart from events in Austria or Czechoslovakia, alive now in any real sense? Richard Johnstone implies that it is not, writing of Rex and Edward Upward:

> Neither Warner nor Upward are in the front rank of modern novelists, and there is little to be gained, least of all for the reputation of political literature in Britain, by pretending otherwise. They are, however, in the context of their time, interesting and even admirable for what they attempted. . . . They grabbed onto Marxism with a kind of desperate complacency, convinced of its application to them, yet failing ever to ask any really serious questions about what such a belief meant for the future. There is a profound uncertainty in Warner's and Upward's work, an uncertainty that pervaded the middle-class literary left and rendered it, or so it seems in retrospect, so ineffectual.[106]

Samuel Hynes and Frank Kermode, however, point to the novel's permanent relevance. Hynes writes:

> The position that the novel proposes is absolutely clear: liberalism has created its own destroyers, and is guilty of its own death. Why then does one feel, reading the book, both affection and sympathy for the Professor, a character who represents liberalism? Is it simply because the sins of which he stands convicted—his belief in abstract justice, his faith in human goodness, his philosophical detachment—are the sins of a virtuous man? Not only that, I think, but also because, though the book may persuade us that the Professor's values are obsolete and actively destructive at this point in history, yet they remain moral. We feel that, and so, clearly, does Warner; the Professor dies a good, though defeated man, and his death is not history's execution of a criminally negligent governor, but a murder by fascists, a part of the darkness ahead.[107]

Frank Kermode indicated other permanently valuable features of *The Professor* when he wrote that the novel is "a book that deserves to live, not as another tragedy of liberalism or another indictment of Fascism, but as a study of abstract justice." Here Kermode points to the strength of Rex's semi-allegorical method, which allows the novel to transcend as well as to treat its times. He finds that possibly the "most important encounter" the Professor has is with Jinkerman's father, the religious cobbler, "who wants nothing to do with economic improvement, the amelioration of poverty, or the cure of disease, holding that infinite human wretchedness is the true ground of love." Moreover, Kermode found that "In Warner's novel, classrooms, parks, and streets are merely sets before which long serious debates are staged; though sometimes they are invested with a dreamlike terror. . . . These settings seem exactly suited to the impossible logic of the discussion: book-burning, torture, and rape seem to happen in a dream, but when such dreams invade the waking world the existence of justice is signalled only by its absence, and of love by its present impossibility." Kermode went on to sum up *The Professor*'s value for our time: "This stately, wretchedly noble book, I'm glad to say, is not wholly forgotten. It could not have been written at any other moment, but it still touches the conscience; it expresses very well our interest in justice and our sense of its inaccessibility; and its sincerity is a reproach to our habit of dismissing books merely because we think their surface ideologies dated."[108]

I, too, would make a case for *The Professor*'s permanence despite its obvious weaknesses. The novel retains a cardboard and contrived feeling on the realistic level. Half a century of good thrillers has led us to expect more actual plot work than Rex, somewhat lazily even for an allegorist, offers. But Rex's respect for the Professor, his acknowledgement of Marxism's philosophical limitations, and his simultaneous recognition of the need for Marxism as a counter to fascism, give this novel a surprising depth and tension on the level of character and ideas. In *The Wild Goose Chase*, Rex's subtle commitment to his classical education came through in his style; in *The Professor*, this commitment is embodied in the main character, who is embattled but ultimately admirable. Rex acquitted himself well in facing the pressing political concerns of his period; his heart was always in the right place in the battle against fascism. In the long term, however, his art survives because of his inability to overthrow his own commitment to humanism and the classics.

XII. REX AND BASIL WRIGHT GO FOR A TRIP

Toward the end of his stay at Frensham Heights, Rex had a break from the routine of teaching, family obligations, leftist meetings, and publication. In April 1939 he sailed on a collier in the company of documentary filmmaker Basil Wright and Day-Lewis. (He had met Wright at Day-Lewis's house, and Wright, intrigued by a previous reading of *The Wild Goose Chase*, had taken to Rex immediately, partially because he thought the novel very cinematic.) On 7 April 1939, Rex wrote to Greenwood, "if you do go to

Rowledge this week end, could you possibly collect + send me an oil skin which is hanging behind the front door? On or soon after the 12th I'm going with Day Lewis for a voyage on a collier from London to Newcastle and back. Something to do with a documentary film. We shall probably be sick as dogs." According to Sean Day-Lewis, the Irish director Robert Flaherty had suggested to Wright that it would be a good idea to film the work on the boats that brought coal from the northeast of England to the gasworks near the Thames in London. The British Commercial Gas Association was to sponsor the project, with Wright as producer, Alec Shaw as director, and Day-Lewis as scriptwriter. Cecil suggested that Rex, who was feeling miserable (possibly because he felt an unconscious suspicion of the domestic problems to be discussed in the next chapter), should come along for the ride.

The two left Brimclose on 13 April, and in 1973 Rex recalled that when they changed trains at Yeovil Junction,

> my cautious temperament prompted me to suggest that we should buy half a bottle of whisky for emergencies on the high seas. Cecil wouldn't hear of the idea as we'd both been told by Basil Wright that Captain Tickner of the SS *Wimbledon* never stopped handing out drinks. Rather nettled I said, "All right, I'll buy quarter of a bottle for myself" and did so. At the offices of the Wandsworth Gas Company we were greeted by Captain Tickner (a huge and delightful man) with, "I hope you boys have brought some booze with you, there's none on the ship." We laughed nervously at this and Cecil explained to me afterwards that this was one of the good Captain's little jokes. In fact, it was the strict truth. It was only on the southward run (undertaken by Wright and Shaw) that liquor flowed. Maybe an empty ship needs more careful handling than one full of coal. Anyway we got nothing to drink but incredibly strong tea and I'm sorry to relate that Cecil, instead of allowing me to drink my quarter bottle alone, insisted on having one half of this miserable dram. Once arrived at the Tyne, things changed. Captain Tickner swept us into a pub called The Tram, where he kissed all the fat maids and never stopped drinking for days.

They returned on 18 April. In his script for the film, which was not produced, Cecil recalled Captain Tickner with the line "Three mild and bitters, Alice, and a glass of poison for Mr McCulloch. And don't spill any on the way, lovely."[109]

In addition to alcohol, nature as always retained its place in Rex's affections. When he was not writing, he lived the normal life of a nature-loving teacher. In a letter to Greenwood (dated 13 October, probably 1938), he wrote, "I wish I could have had some nature rambles with you along the Helston estuary (I've caught conger eels there), + compared notes on the Blue Anchor beer." But the routine of Rex's Frensham Heights period was not to last: not only war, but domestic war, already foreshadowed in *The Professor*, would intervene.

CHAPTER SIX

RAYNES PARK, 1939-1945

I. FRANCES, DESPAIR, AND THE SONNETS

From 1939-45, Rex faced serious challenges on the personal and the national home fronts and saw them through victoriously. But these were not easy years. He confronted wrenching domestic discord, the loss of his job at Frensham Heights, and the difficulty of living in Wimbledon, close to London, during the Blitz and the V-bomb attacks. His response was the best writing that he was, perhaps, ever to do. In it, he explored the intricacies of love as well as the possibility or impossibility of a humane existence in the midst of ideological madness.

On 11 June 1939 Rex wrote Greenwood that he'd "done one long chapter of the new novel [*The Aerodrome*] + no more. I don't know when I'll get on with it. Milton is bloody good. If you see [Ken] Marshall or any dart player tell him that I won a game of 301 in eight darts (scores 121, 80, 100). This is the only thing that has given me much pleasure lately." He added as a P.S., "This sounds rather a bloody awful letter, but isn't meant to. I do hope I'll see you soon."[1]

This is one of the first references in the letters to Rex's progress on his new novel, the immediate idea for which he got when a villager in a pub (probably in Great Rissington) complained about the airplanes at a nearby airbase.[2] This is also possibly the first (albeit veiled) reference to Rex and Frances's marital troubles. *The Aerodrome* treats love with extraordinary depth because it (like the sonnets, or "Contradictions" that he wrote in 1938 and 1939) is inextricably related to Rex's love life during this period. In *The Aerodrome* Rex was writing from the heart, not from the mind according to an external ideology, as had previously been the case. Early in June 1939, Frances had confessed to Rex that she had been having an affair with a man on the island of Jersey. This was possible since from 1936 to 1939 she would visit her parents on the island during school holidays while Rex was writing or away with his friends Charles Fenby or Cecil.

The reasons that Frances gave for this affair (which lasted from 1937 until she and Rex were reconciled in 1940, when he began teaching at Raynes Park County School in Wimbledon), when I interviewed her several times during the late 1980s, were clear: Rex had not been a very good husband, preferring the pub, darts, and his friends to his family, and he did not involve Frances in decisions. Moreover, prolonged absences with his friends while she was alone in Jersey with the children were not conducive to a warm relationship. She felt neglected, and Rex's spending on drink strained the family's meager finances. Certainly, it was difficult to deal with a severely disabled child at a time when this amounted to a stigma and no help whatsoever was available; this had to take its toll on the marriage, too. As Frances remembers it, Rex's reaction was one of complete shock and betrayal when she told him about it. He looked at her as if she had burned him, and she spent days crying. (He may well, however, have had an unconscious suspicion of the affair earlier on and expressed it in the Professor's betrayal by his mistress in *The Professor*, and in some moodiness noticed by Day-Lewis.) She remembers that June 1939 was the actual month of separation. She left Rex in Frensham Heights and took the two children to live in Jersey with her parents. John and Pam Morris, whose firm had failed, moved into Middle Park Cottage around August and lived with Rex for much of the time that Frances was absent; they were now fast friends if no longer in the publisher-writer relationship.

An undated letter to John Morris, probably composed in mid-June 1939 as war in Europe was moving from a distant to a near possibility, and sent from the Hotel des Mimosas, Pont-Aven in Brittany, France, reveals Rex's wretched emotional state. It also shows that he was writing poetry and had completed the first chapter of *The Aerodrome*. The Morrises were going to join Rex on holiday in France, bringing their daughter Barbara with them. Rex, alone, discussed a longer separation from Frances: "I feel both indolent + miserable. . . . I lost all my sonnets that night we went to the Moulin. This was a good thing, as I have now reconstructed the good ones + forgotten the bad. I won't send the first chapter, as something may go wrong with the post, but will keep it till I see you. I've told Frances that I'll do nothing about a separation for a bit. This relieves her of a strain, not me. Its a bugger."[3]

In late June, the separation became a long-term reality. It lasted until April 1940. Rex's "reconstructed" sonnets (written during this period, but published in 1945) provide ample evidence of his feelings about this marital rift. In the 1937 poem, "Hymn," Rex celebrated "him and her/who live together now" and asked love's blessing on the couple: "Let natural fidelity/proceed from their sweet unity." He closed by praying "for this sweet unity/perpetual felicity" for his newly married friends.[4] This poem is included in the 1945 *Poems and Contradictions*, but the "Contradictions" directly contradict the poem's positive tone with a bitter perspective on love and marriage.

The *Poems and Contradictions* jacket note says, "Rex Warner's *Poems* were first published in 1937 and have been out of print for the last two years. In the present volume Mr. Warner has retained only about half of the earlier collection, but has added a sequence of hitherto unpublished poems. These new poems consist of a group of sonnets, in various forms, and rather loosely connected together in that they are all concerned with various aspects of adolescent love." A manuscript note (MS 56) in the Michigan State Library adds the information that "The Poems in this edition are selected from the 'Poems' published in 1937. To them have been added a group of sonnets, written, for the most part, shortly after 1937 + entitled 'Contradictions.' Some of these poems were published in 1937. The remainder were written between then + 1939."

The 1939 poems are not about "adolescent love," but about Rex's difficulties with Frances (unless of course Rex meant that until these troubles his view of love was adolescent; the troubles certainly made his writing as well as his perception of life more mature). With this key, these sonnets, all of them in the standard Shakespearean or Petrarchan rhyme schemes, take on added force and meaning. One follows Rex through all of the stormy emotions associated with marital trouble. Seen in this light, they are probably the best poems Rex ever wrote:

> For now like an Egyptian buried king,
> rotten for ages, a ransacked dusty wraith
> blown in the wind about his monument,
> I see that every proud pretentious thing
> is undermined, love most of all and faith,
> by slippery falsehood of the innocent.[5]

Sonnet XVI is perhaps closest to the actual facts, Frances in Jersey in the arms of another man:

> Listen to the gull. Listen to the angry crying.
> He is a lover's ghost. He is like me
> in thought above the shore where you are lying

loose with another by the breaking sea,
and turns away with harsh and bitter cry
from your warm treachery and the easy land,
the pretty lights along the twilit sky,
the voice and the distant thudding of the band;
and over the blackening salt mines he screams
his wasting cry across the drowsy air,
a voice that comes from further than your dreams
he yells against the stars his known despair.
Your head is circled by his wheeling cries,
and if you sleep his feathers fan your eyes.[6]

This sonnet is notable for its bird imagery, which Rex typically uses to express his most powerful moods, and which recalls the circling of the kites in *The Kite*, the wild geese in *The Wild Goose Chase*, and perhaps Yeats's "Leda and the Swan." The cry of the "gull" (undoubtedly a pun) or betrayed lover, is particularly haunting. The poem offers proof that even at this moment of despair, Rex continued to love Frances and felt the pangs of intense jealousy—a jealousy that was to be expressed in the Vicar's attempted murder of his rival Anthony in *The Aerodrome* and a love-despite-all that finally leads the Rex character Roy to marry Bess in that novel despite her infidelity.

In Sonnet XVIII, Rex discusses the difficulty of giving Frances up:

Difficult suddenly to lay down love
Of long standing. Difficult, but must be done
and no more remembered than the time when love was begun
in the spring daffodils and the cherry blossom above,
and above the blossom the windwashed and fleeting sky,
and the clasped hands, and words panted out through
gates of the soul and body both. Then you
loved, I am sure, you loved and so did I.
Then the sun shone and the heart and the lip trembled,
the voice and the eyes and limbs threw spark to spark.
Then we went together: then truly the sun shone,
and the face was true that had not yet dissembled.
O now let the mind's face too rest in the dark.
Let memory be dark. Lay down what is done.[7]

Memory proved harder for Rex to put away than he perhaps imagined. His marriage with Frances was to have many twists and turns in the future, and to grow into a powerful love story.

During this time of trouble, the Morrises were Rex's closest friends. On a Saturday, probably during that fateful summer of 1939, Rex wrote to Pam about it,

> [T]hanks very much for your letter + for your attitude to me before that. I thought that you'ld regard me simply as a bloody fool (which I well may be), but could see that you realised that, fool or not, one's emotions give one hell.
>
> Nothing is being rushed. I rather wish it were. The situation is in one way clarified by Frances having asked her people to find out whether the chap in Jersey had any intentions of getting her to live with him. Of course he hadn't. . . .
>
> The alternatives now seem to be (i) that she should try living by herself for a bit (a thing she'd find very difficult) until her mind gets clearer (ii) that we should separate finally (iii) that we should patch up things dishonestly (iv) (+ most unlikely) that some sort of reality should come into the relationship.

On Thursday, 3 August 1939, just four days after Britain and France tried to warn Hitler off taking Danzig, Rex was considering a legal separation from Frances and he had just received the further bad news that after six years of employment he would be dismissed from Frensham Heights at the end of the coming school year, albeit for economic rather than political reasons.[8] The separation did not become legal, but that did not prevent Rex from consoling himself with another lover.

II. KITTY TREVELYAN, FRANCES, AND *THE AERODROME*

Marital difficulties continued to plague Rex during the year, and the external setting for this trouble was appropriately turbulent, for on 30 September 1939, Britain and France had declared war on Germany. He seems to have decided to visit Frances on Jersey but had trouble getting there, and on 24 December [1939],[9] wrote to Pam Morris from a hotel in Southampton full of mobilized soldiers. This is the only self-pitying letter from Rex that I have ever seen (except for a similar letter that he wrote to C. J. and Julia Greenwood on the same day): "Oh, how miserable life is. And it could be so good."[10]

But Rex also had two reasons for cheerfulness. One was that he was making progress with *The Aerodrome*. "The Dinner Party: An Episode from a Longer Work," chapter one of the novel, appeared in *New Writing* (N.S. III) during Christmas 1939, and he had written several more chapters. The other was Kitty Trevelyan.

During the fall of 1939 he began an affair with Kitty Trevelyan, a divorcée living in Rowledge whose daughters had attended Frensham Heights. Frances and Rex had both known Kitty socially, through the school and the village, and liked her very much, dining at her house and inviting her to theirs. Her former husband was a German, George Gothsche, who had remained in Germany despite the rise of the Nazis, which Kitty as a woman of high principles refused to do. While she was not a deep thinker, she was a genuine spiritual searcher. Kitty was a believer in the methods of Rudolph Steiner, the Swiss educationalist and mystic, and felt, correctly or not, that Frensham Heights offered the closest approach to the Steinerian philosophy to be found in any school in England. She also liked walking in the woods at night, and had other romantic, somewhat Germanic views. It is not difficult to see what she found attractive about Rex. As someone separated from his own wife, he would understand her marital feelings. As a strong opponent of fascism, he would sympathize with her political principles. Moreover, he had not been the immediate cause of the breakdown of his own marriage. Most of all, perhaps, he was handsome, ruggedly built, and intellectual. Perhaps she harbored hopes of a permanent relationship.

The affair between Rex and Kitty lasted from approximately October 1939 to some point in the spring of 1940. Although she had read *The Wild Goose Chase* and admired Rex, they did not really have much in common. While she was good-looking and intellectually inclined, she was upper class and a bit more serious about life than Rex was. She came from a known academic and politically minded family: according to Peter Daniel, Kitty "was connected to the Huxleys by marriage, and was the great-grand-daughter of Lord Macaulay's nephew."[11] As if to further demonstrate how small and tight-knit the English intellectual aristocracy really was, Kitty was also the niece of R. C. Trevelyan, the college friend of Rex's uncle Gordon Luce, and the brother of the noted historian G. M. Trevelyan. The result of the Rex-Kitty liaison was a daughter, Katherine, born on 22 June 1940, since Kitty refused to have an abortion.

When she was sixteen, Katherine's mother informed her that she was illegitimate. Prior to that time, Kitty had told her that she was German, just like her two half-sisters. When in 1956 Kitty decided to tell Katherine the truth, she wrote Rex informing him that she would do so. But Rex wrote that he was having a bad time with his wife of seven years, Barbara, and was not ready to face Katherine then. So Kitty simply told Katherine that her father was a writer, and did not reveal his name. Katherine found out at the age of seventeen, however, when she was staying with a pig farmer named Murford who had been at Frensham Heights. He and his wife told her that Kitty had known Rex and

Cecil Day-Lewis. (Murford actually said that it was terribly unlike Rex to have had a child and not to have stood by her.) To make sure of her father's identity, Katherine set a trap—she put a book of Rex's near her bed and noticed that her mother froze when she saw it. But Kitty did not reveal his name for another few months. Rex did not meet Katherine until 1961, when she was twenty-one years old. She was brought up by her grandmother, the wife of Sir Charles Trevelyan, a baronet and left-wing politician, in a beautiful house in Cumbria, and now lives close to Oxford. Kitty had a bad postnatal depression after the birth, but her family was supportive.

In a letter of 20 February 1940 from Frensham Heights to Greenwood, Rex wrote that "this week I anticipate an interview with Sir Charles," Kitty's father, undoubtedly about his affair with her and her pregnancy, which was now obvious. He also mentioned that "I'm now half way through chapter 10 [of *The Aerodrome*], so I should think that Unwin might send me a case of whiskey." In a letter to Pam Morris from Wimbledon around this time, Rex wrote that "I had another letter from Sir C. [Trevelyan] some time ago, but didn't wish to add to your worries by telling you about it then. It was on the lines you can imagine. I wrote back saying what my income was, + showing that it was less even than K.'s present allowance. I said I'd prefer to talk about the whole thing rather than write, + since then haven't heard again. Did you get any indication of how K. really is? He gave me none."[12]

Simultaneously with Kitty's pregnancy, there was movement toward a possible reconciliation with Frances. On 3 March 1940, Rex wrote Greenwood that "Life pursues its complicated course. It seems like now that I shall be reconciled to Frances. She's coming to England next holidays, either to stay with me or to prepare to do so." He added that he was thinking of sending the second chapter of *The Aerodrome* to John Lehmann for *New Writing*. On 3 March he wrote Lehmann that "I've finished eleven chapters of my book + have about five more to write. I'm hoping to finish it in the Easter holidays."[13]

He continued to make steady progress, and by 18 March [1940] he wrote Greenwood that "I've just written a chapter about women which should convulse the whole sex with shame, were they capable of that feeling. But I must say that I like them really." Rex's chapter—the present chapter twelve—does express his spleen, but after venting it, his personal mood improved.

By 27 April Rex had gotten a new job, left Frensham Heights, and installed himself at Darlaston House, 3 Darlaston Road, Wimbledon. This was a boardinghouse in which Rex, for 25 shillings a week, had a room with hot and cold water, two chairs, and no coat hangers. He wrote Pam Morris, who had moved to Rowledge with John, that he was quite happy with it, because it was only ten minutes' walk from the common and only two minutes from two pubs.[14] He reported to Greenwood that "I only got through one more chapter of the book, what with one thing + another. But I hope to get on with it more quickly now." Rex's writing time would be reduced, however, because he had begun his new job at Raynes Park School.

Around this time, Rex asked Pam for Kitty's phone number and said that he had not worked on *The Aerodrome* for a week, but that he had discovered a "new remedy" for hangovers called Bromo-Seltzer.[15] Clearly Rex had not been doing badly, despite his still-unsettled situation with Frances. He regularly saw Day-Lewis, bookseller Ken Marshall, Greenwood, and other friends, and attended a Wine Lodge in the afternoon and plays in the evenings, including Georg Büchner's *Leonie and Lena*, which he liked. In fact, "Altogether in the last few months I've seen more plays than in the whole course of my life."[16]

At this time the prospects for a reunification with Frances were improving constantly. She visited Rex by herself in April during the Easter holiday. Just before her visit, Rex wrote her,

> I am enormously happy at the thought of being happy. It is like spring coming at last, something real. All opposites seem erect + laughing in my mind. . . . Frances dear, I trust you now, + so I am not afraid of you. I have thought before that I was not, + then discovered some fear still left. But now I am certain. Not seeing you for these months hasn't made me feel that I shall be shy when I see you again. Your letters have made me love + admire you more + more. But the best of all is the death of fear, which is a frightful thing.[17]

Rex wrote from the Cumberland Hotel, Marble Arch, to Greenwood that he had had "very little sleep lately. Between Frances + me things are going pretty well, in fact better than they ever have gone." He asked Greenwood to tell him how "you like or dislike the beginning of the book" and added that "The damned thing has been interrupted all the way through by love affairs, +, as Frances isn't leaving until next Wednesday, I don't know whether I'll finish it these holidays." On 10 April, during the trial reunion, Rex wrote from Cecil's house at Brimclose to Pam Morris, "Too early to say quite how things are going. I'm just trying to be nice, with what results I don't know."[18] Things went well, because they soon were discussing plans for Frances's return.

At some point in the spring, he thanked C. J. for a check and wrote, "This week end I hope to get on some way with the book. If only one could have a little calm!" Part of the calm was achieved by meeting C. J. at the Dog & Fox, the local pub near Darlaston House. By 14 May, he wrote C. J. that he had finished chapter fourteen, and "It only remains to wind everything up, a pretty insuperable task."

But the war cast a threatening shadow impossible to ignore, especially since Frances, Jonathan, and Anna were on the island of Jersey, close to the coast of France. On 30 May 1940, he wrote Pam from Darlaston House that "The war news gets worse + worse. One can imagine an absolute butchery going on in northern France; + I'm afraid that however much people may want to stand outside it all, it will be brought home to us before long." He added that

> I'm still worried about what should be done with Frances + the children. It seems to me now that one place (other than a port) is about as safe as another, + it may be right in times like these to keep families together whatever the risks. Certainly it seems likely that before long the English channel will be almost closed to shipping, in which case Jersey would form a part of France rather than England. I wrote to F. again the other day suggesting that she do all she can to come soon; but the position is as difficult for her as it is for me.

Rex ended his letter by mentioning that he was working on a film with Basil Wright and that "I'm working quite hard at the book, which is some consolation."[19]

At the beginning of June 1940, Rex wrote to Pam from Wimbledon that he had visited Basil Wright on the Channel coast and "We eat + drank + sat in the sun, occasionally hearing gun-fire from Dunkirk. . . . Frances is arriving on the 22nd, or that's her idea; unless there's a sudden alteration in channel services."[20] The evacuation of British troops from Dunkirk was completed on 3 June 1940. Frances, Jonathan, and Anna finally left Jersey on the last ferry before the island's occupation by pro-German forces on 29 June. Ironically, Frances arrived on the day, 22 June, that Kitty Trevelyan gave birth to Katherine. Shortly after that date, Rex wrote to Pam that "I had a pc [post card] from Kitty's mother yesterday, saying that Kitty had had her baby on the 22nd, a girl, not twins. Have you had any news of her? Lady T. just said that both were doing well. I hope this continues."[21]

Frances, Jonathan, and Anna first lived together with Rex at Darlaston House, but the family soon moved to a furnished flat at 3 Denmark Avenue in Wimbledon. Although he complained that he could never find enough time to finish the last two or three chapters of *The Aerodrome*, Rex was emotionally very happy when he wrote to Charles Fenby on 14 July that "Frances came over to England by herself last Easter + our reunion was such a terrific + surprising success that everything has gone like wildfire ever since. It is difficult to imagine now how miserable we both were last year. Indeed the whole thing has been staggering. We are both better off now than we ever have been."[22] Soon after Rex wrote this, the Warners—with the aid of Rex's mother—moved into another house, on 122 Grand Drive, where they were to stay until the end of the war. The house was a double-fronted building whose gables were vaguely influenced by the William Morris-inspired Arts and Crafts movement.

Because of the expense of the house move which would take place around 15 August, in the summer of 1940 Rex was doing extra teaching in a Catholic school. He had gotten the education authorities to recognize his Egyptian service, and so had increased his annual salary from £340 to a still-miserable £346. He was also upset about Kitty's state; she was still suffering from postnatal depression. On 12 August 1940 he wrote John Morris that "I received today the enclosed (which you can throw away) from Sir Charles [Trevelyan]. It was a bad shock to me, as I thought that the danger period was over + I can't help blaming myself for being an accessory. Its evidently no good writing to Kitty, as letters won't be delivered, + in any case wouldn't do any good."[23] This continuing saga of illegitimacy and Rex's renewed love for Frances is particularly important for the composition of *The Aerodrome*, in which Frances figures to some degree as Bess and Kitty as Eustacia. Rex writes in the same letter that "I've done quite a lot of the book, since I spend the mornings here, + at the present rate should finish it in ten days. I'm still uncertain whether it's going to end really well, but hope it will." He might have said the same about his reconciliation with Frances, which was still in its early stages, and about his new status as the father of an illegitimate child.

Around this time, he confessed to Pam that "You'll know that I must feel terribly upset about Kitty, logic or no logic. I wrote Sir C. saying that I was very distressed by his letter + asking him to inform me if there was anything I could do. But of course there isn't anything."[24] He added, a bit optimistically, "I'm getting on pretty well with the book, considering everything + should finish it next week. I think it ought to end fairly satisfactorily, though its an awful job sorting everybody out."

On 25 August he wrote to Pam that he was "very glad to hear the news about Kitty, + agree with you about Sir C.[Trevelyan], though the old chap has probably had a harrassing time. I suppose I'd better not write to her yet, as she's still under medical care." He added: "I saw CJ [Greenwood] on Thursday + handed in the book which I'd finished in a great hurry, but, I think, fairly satisfactorily. Anyway its a terrific relief to have got it finished before term starts tomorrow."[25]

III. LIFE INTO LITERATURE

Although Rex would later tell me that the creation of a masterpiece is largely a matter of luck, the dual saga of Frances and Kitty, as well as the background of the war, allowed Rex in *The Aerodrome* to write a far more accomplished and convincing work than he had hitherto achieved. The book's subtitle is, most appropriately, "A Love Story." It is set largely in a rectory much like the one in which Rex had grown up in Amberley and also like the rectory in Great Rissington, where there was (and is) a large air base nearby. In the novel, there is even a tree that is reminiscent of the tree that stood in Amberley Rectory's yard, and which Rex revisited approximately thirty years after his marriage to Frances there: "In the churchyard there is one tall tree, a libocedrus, which runs up into the air like a black flame, and which, when I was a boy, I used to worship, visiting it regularly after morning service, thrusting my head and hands through its dark foliage, fancying it to be some goddess or divine creature, not uninterested in myself."[26]

The description of the rectory garden resembles, perhaps, the Amberley Rectory of Rex's youth:

> In the Rectory garden the grass is somewhat unkempt; heavy bushes of laurel and laurustinus droop over the paths; there is one tall tree by the disused stable, a lime tree, in the topmost branches of which I once fixed a small platform to be used in my solitary games as a look-out post. I know every inch of this garden; the feel and taste of branches and twigs; the smell of leaves and grass in rain and sunshine; the consistency and colour of the soil in different parts. (16)

No wonder, then, as N. H. Reeve points out, the hero's name "Roy" reminds us of "Rex."

Roy is an orphan who is raised by a vicar, called the Rector, and his wife. The Rector has on his conscience the murder of a rival for his wife's love. Roy falls in love with Bess, who betrays him with a Flight-Lieutenant from the base and whom he writes off. He becomes a member of the Air Force himself and has an affair with Eustacia, the wife of an officer on the base, and gets her pregnant. She refuses to have an abortion and runs off with the Flight-Lieutenant, with whom Bess betrayed him; they are both killed. Roy is reconciled to Bess, and they are happily married. Set against this messy love life is the more logical life of the Aerodrome, run by an Air Vice-Marshal who despises human affections, forbids airmen to father children, and speaks for efficiency and power. But he only appears to represent order and efficiency. In the end, it turns out that the Air Vice-Marshal is the rival whom the Rector had attempted to kill. Unbeknownst to the Rector, he remained alive but as a result of his experiences became determined to root out human passion. He is Roy's father, having gotten his lover, later the Rector's wife, pregnant before the Rector attempted to kill him. The Rector has agreed to raise Roy, knowing that he is not the real father, perhaps as an atonement for thinking that he has killed Roy's father. The Air Vice-Marshal is killed by another illegitimate son of his, the Flight-Lieutenant who had betrayed Roy with Bess, after the Air Vice-Marshal kills the boy's mother (who happens to be the sister of the squire of the village). The Rector is the father of Bess, whose mother is the pub owner's wife. This is a complex web of family relations indeed, and Rex deserves praise for having thought it through clearly.

Speaking through the mouth of Roy, Rex comes to the conclusion that the village life,

> in spite of its drunkenness and its inefficiency, was wider and deeper than the activity in which we were constricted by the Air Vice-Marshal's ambition. It was a life whose very vagueness concealed a wealth of opportunity, whose uncertainty called for adventure, whose aspects were innumerable and varied as the changes of light and colour throughout the year. It was a life whose unwieldliness was the consequence of its immensity. . . . We in the Air Force had escaped from but not solved the mystery. We had secured ease for ourselves, discipline and satisfaction. We had abolished inefficiency, hypocrisy, and the fortunes of the irresolute or the remorseful mind; but we had destroyed also the spirit of adventure, inquiry, the sweet and terrifying sympathy of love that can acknowledge mystery, danger and dependence. (261-62)

Rex here repudiates his own previous Marxist ideology, which had attempted to make the world right through discipline and belief; but more immediately, he admits his own acceptance of what life brings, including betrayal by his wife and the birth of an illegitimate child.

The power of Rex's writing comes directly from his insights into his own states as betrayed (and reconciled) husband (Bess and Roy get married in the end). Using Roy's persona, Rex writes that "it was a shock to me to realize that the Rector's wife, so docile in my experience, had ever been, even if ever so slightly, unfaithful to her husband. I began to see that . . . I had been taking things very much too much for granted. Instead of the orderly and easy system of relationships with which I had fancied myself to be surrounded, I began now to imagine crimes and secrecies on all sides, the results of forces to which previously I had given little or no attention" (43). Because of his own experience, he returns to this theme of deceptive appearances more than once.

About his love for Bess-Frances, Roy-Rex writes with some cynicism, that "When I held Bess in my arms, naked or clothed, I felt assured that I was laying hold of a brilliant, a better, an unexpected world, never thinking that I was doing only what every other man had done and what had finally satisfied nobody" (128), and reflects that ". . . I held her tighter, muttering incoherent words, as people at such moments do, words that seemed to hurt my body as they were dragged through it, words that mean much, but not always what one thinks they mean" (130). Frances's betrayal meant for Rex that a "code of rules" (158) had never really applied to his existence or to anyone else's.

When Roy discovers Bess's betrayal, "my body stiffened and a kind of pain seemed to freeze me and stagger me where I stood" (161); these motions are reminiscent of the shock that Frances noticed in Rex when she confessed her affair to him. Roy's explanation of his feelings also undoubtedly applies to Rex's at the time:

> With no clear idea of what I was doing, I stretched out one hand towards her, and her eyes followed my hand as though fearing it and wishing it away, so that soon I removed it from the space between us and, looking across the space, began to see that now it was most difficult to cross, though all the more I wished to cross it and to hold her in my arms to find comfort there and a kind of explanation for this event that, in reality, held no comfort for me and could never be explained in any way that could cause me any satisfaction. (164-65)

Rex's description of Roy's bitter feelings upon learning of the betrayal seems very authentic: "The very completeness of my love had caused me, most unreasonably, to imagine that Bess must feel as I did. In point of fact her feelings had been entirely different and the very thing which I had taken most for granted, a devotion to myself, was something which she had never felt at all" (170).

Moreover, Roy's feeling of pity for Bess's predicament at having her infidelity discovered is misplaced,

> for maybe she was content with what I knew to be the insincerity of her lover, and I began to suspect that in a love affair sincerity is not of much value, indeed a cumbrous and unexciting quality; that it was I myself who was in the wrong and who, in my desire to give away fully my love and to receive fully the love of another person, must be by nature both awkward and repulsive. To throw myself upon her mercy was what I had done long ago, and with no success whatever. I began now to shrink from her as she previously had shrunk from me. About the nature of the pleasures which she had shared with her lover and which had easily outweighed my love I was not curious. They seemed to me secret things of which I was afraid; and yet still, when I looked at her, my heart seemed to reach towards her, though my mind was clouding over in bitterness and a kind of helpless rage. (170-71)

IV. MEN AND WOMEN

As a result of his marital problems, Rex arrived at a new, more bitter vision of women in general that is not present in his earlier work. Yet balance with regard to women as well as other things remained in Rex's vision in life as in art: Pam Morris was a friend throughout his trouble with Frances; and of course there was Kitty. We recall that although Clara, the Professor's mistress, betrays him with Vander, the Professor's son's girlfriend remains loyal. Rex's bitterness is expressed in *The Aerodrome* largely through the Air Vice-Marshal's brilliantly icy speech that would outlaw love and the desire to procreate, leaving only the satisfaction of lust as a worthwhile objective. The Air Vice-Marshal begins by distinguishing between two types of women:

> You must see women as they are and envisage clearly what it is that you want from them. You must distinguish carefully between a woman as a personality like yourself, and a woman who may be a source of pleasure to you. In so far as a woman is an individual she is bound, as you are, to the future and the past. Indeed the construction of her body must make her much more of a prisoner of time than you are yourselves. And yet there have been many women whose personalities have deserved both the friendship and the admiration of men, at least in many respects. Such women, rare as they are, may be and indeed should be treated as you would treat your own comrades, amongst whom you will of course find, as a rule, much truer and more valuable friendship than you can look for in the opposite sex. (183-84)

Here we remember Frances's complaint that Rex spent too much time with Day-Lewis and other male friends, carousing in pubs. The Air Vice-Marshal continues:

> But if love, not friendship, is your aim, your conduct must be entirely different. In this matter all women, even the best, are irrational and must be treated as such. If you attempt to secure love as you would secure friendship, by honesty, sincerity, openness, you are courting disaster. Believe me, the rules are wholly different and are perfectly well known. Indeed they were summarized by the Roman poet Ovid in the first century of our era, and his prescriptions, with certain modifications, are true today. It is necessary to remember that women's vanity, timidity, and capacity for self-deception are almost illimitable. You must recognize these qualities, try to overcome your disgust for them, and make of them the best use that you can. (184)

The Air Vice-Marshal then embarks on a description of a method of winning women's affections without surrendering one's own; among his many prescriptions is the following:

It is advisable also to pretend that you can observe a great difference between the woman you love and all other women. Assure her of this and you will increase both her self-esteem and her reliance on you; for most women have, when they care to use their minds, a fairly shrewd idea of the defects of their own sex and are inexpressibly delighted if you can persuade them (as it is very easy to do) that they are for some reason entirely immune from the vices which they notice every day in others. A solicitude for her health, a claim for her sympathy, particularly in cases where you can pretend that you have been treated harshly by another woman, a care to arrange cushions in a certain way, a willingness to listen with respect to any kind of stupidity that masquerades either as independent thought or as deep feeling—all this will have the effect of adding to her self-esteem and of making her ready to fall in love with you who have succeeded in convincing her that she is right in looking upon herself as more exceptional than in reality she is. Indeed you now become more and more necessary; for if you were to drop from your hand the mirror which you hold up to her, she would have nowhere to look. By this time she will be speaking of "giving" herself or her love to you. The expression is not unjustified, for, by providing her with a wholly false sense of her own importance both to yourself and others, you have made her dependent on you for the satisfaction of her own vanity, and vanity, with women, is the key to desire. She will like to believe that she exercises over you an exceptional power, and will not realize immediately that the situation is exactly the reverse of this. (184-85)

This remarkable speech continues with more prescriptions by means of which the airmen can protect themselves from love. But it is undercut by the action of the plot, in which it turns out that the Air Vice-Marshal himself is perhaps the most wounded in love, and that his advice to the airmen to root it out of themselves completely is only a reaction to this wound. Moreover, Roy, who had been affected by the Air Vice-Marshal's strictures especially in light of his betrayal by Bess, comes around to love her again, more fiercely than ever, just as Rex came to love Frances once again.

Around the very same time that Rex rediscovered his love for Frances, he discovered that he was to be the father of an illegitimate child by Kitty Trevelyan. In the novel, this takes place in chapter sixteen, when Eustacia reveals that she is about to have a child. How true the details of this episode were to Rex's actual experience, we can only guess, but Roy's description of his feelings upon hearing the news has the ring of authenticity:

Yet together with this horror and shame I could not help feeling at the same time a certain satisfaction. I had never once envisaged the possibility that I might become a father, and it was a pleasant sort of excitement to discover that I was now on the way to being what I never imagined. I thought of the many agreeable hours which I had passed with Eustacia and, when I looked at her, I could see that she herself was pleased with what she no doubt deliberately arranged. "No," I said. "I'm not angry. I'm rather pleased," and as I spoke she left her chair and put her arms around my neck gladly and with a kind of triumph, as though I had surrendered to her something of great value. (248)

Since Rex wrote in February that Sir Charles wanted to see him, that was probably around the time that he learned about Kitty's pregnancy; this would be in advance of the time he reached chapter sixteen, which would have been in the late spring or early summer. So Rex is indeed recording his genuine feelings about illegitimate fatherhood.

At the end of the book, Rex stresses Roy's love for Bess above all other emotions: "We were happy as we had never been, for we were each confident of each" says Roy (301), in words reminiscent of Rex's letter stating that he and Frances were getting along better than ever before. The book ends hopefully: "'That the world may be clean': I remember my father's words. Clean indeed it was and most intricate, fiercer than tigers, wonderful and infinitely forgiving" (302). In language reminiscent of *The Wild Goose Chase*, Rex reasserts his love for Frances and for life. Soon after Frances returned, she became pregnant.

Rex's previous novels had been based on a willed and unconvincing belief in Marxist ideology. In contrast, *The Aerodrome* is formed from his own personal experience, and bitter personal experience at that. The shock to his own self-conception caused by Frances's actions and then by his fathering an illegitimate child liberated the genuine artist in him. Moreover, the decline of his belief in Marxism freed him to choose life with all its messiness over ideology. Although he casts the conflict in terms of air force versus village, he presents us with a clash between any kind of rigid, life-hating set of rules and life itself, which refuses to be confined. This is particularly clear from the manuscript notebook in Rex's own hand,[27] which contains the outline for *The Aerodrome* as well as its first chapter. (The fair copy manuscript from which *The Aerodrome* was set is in Pam Morris's possession; it understandably has relatively few and minor corrections.) The notebook also has a sketch for turning *The Professor* into a play. John Grubb, an English master at Raynes Park, told colleague Frank Coventry that when he had dined with Rex at some point in 1940, Rex had shown him a master plan of *The Aerodrome*—an actual map or plan of the characters' relationships. He must have been referring to the outline and notes in the manuscript notebook.

In his notebook, Rex sets forth the whole plot in outline form. From these notes, it appears that Rex contemplated making Roy think that his father might actually be the king, instead of the Air Vice-Marshal. There are also literary influences. "The meanest of lies—beauty is Truth," an inversion of Keats, perhaps indicates Rex's feelings about Frances as well as Roy's feelings about Bess. There is also a phrase from Dante, "the cult of cruelty,"[28] which is notable because Rex would entitle his 1946 collection of essays *The Cult of Power*, after an essay that he published in January 1942. The Rector, Roy's foster father, is described as representing tradition, and (in a perhaps-unintended echo of Emerson's poem "Brahma") as "The priest who slew the slayer + shall himself be slain." Roy's "pursuit of parents represents reintegration with world."

In this set of notes, we even find the very first draft of the first chapter. As we have come to expect from Rex, this is in a form very much like that of the final version, as in the case of the first paragraph:

> It would be difficult to overestimate the importance, to me, of the events which had taken place previous to that day on which, shortly after ten o'clock in the evening, I was lying on the ground near the small pond at the bottom of Gurney's meadow. . . .

The final version reads:

> It would be difficult to overestimate the importance to me of the events which had taken place previous to the hour (it was shortly after ten o'clock in the evening) when I was lying in the marsh near the small pond at the bottom of Gurney's meadow. . . . [29]

The rest of the chapter shows similarly small changes, and none of any significance for the meaning of the chapter. But his outline for the next chapters shows how carefully Rex worked out this plot. We also have an outline for *The Professor* (in Michigan State MS 52), but it does not go into nearly as much detail because its plot is much simpler than that of *The Aerodrome*. The outline for *The Aerodrome* is spread over several notebook pages with the first chapter interspersed.[30]

The detailed outline and the manuscript of *The Aerodrome* are accompanied by the drafts of the sonnets, undoubtedly written during the 1939-40 period and similarly showing the pain of his rift with Frances. He was never again to achieve the power of *The Aerodrome* or of these sonnets (which might be called the "terrible" sonnets after his favorite poet Hopkins) because he was past his peak as a writer when he suffered a similar personal crisis.

V. SURVIVING THE BLITZ

Sometimes Rex himself seems like the participant in a Greek drama, in which the protagonist's personal conflicts are accompanied by external turmoil. In addition to Rex's private drama with Frances and Kitty was the stress of war and the Blitz. At some point in 1940, he wrote Pam Morris that "Here we get used to continual air raid alarms." Some anti-aircraft guns were installed in the open fields behind Raynes Park, and Rex wrote about them: "The chief improvement lately has been the terrific AA guns. This shakes the house, but makes it impossible for everyone to know whether bombs are being dropped or not, so that one finds it rather soothing. But it would be nice to have a night without any bombs."[31]

For Anna, the war was particularly stressful. During that first year of World War II in England there were many daylight raids. Frances had to walk Anna to and from school every day and once when the sirens went off Anna put her hands over her ears and screamed. After a time she was placed with aunts Dora and Grace in Gloucester and was very happy with the strict routine of their household after the unpredictability of war in London.

During the summer of 1940 Rex was almost hit by a bomb when he was crossing the street near the Raynes Park School at nine in the morning. He heard it coming, quickly laid down in the middle of the street, and then thought better of that and dived into a cigarette store, bringing the elderly owner to the ground as well. The bomb went off nearby and the shop's chocolates and wartime cigarettes, brands such as Ark Royal, Gold Flake, and Senior Service, were scattered around. Because he had probably saved the owner's life, he received a free package of cigarettes from that store whenever he wanted one as long as he remained in Raynes Park. The economics of this situation undoubtedly helped wean him somewhat from his pipe, but he continued to smoke both cigarettes and pipes into his old age.

Smoking was at least one form of relief from the frequent German bombing raids. On 1 September [1940] he wrote Pam Morris:

> In the last two days we've had 11 warnings, with, as a rule, aeroplanes fairly close to us. So much of each day is passed either in the school shelters, where the boys sing at the top of their voices, or else in our larder under the stairs, with the children pulling the bloody kitten about. In the few hours of liberty there's washing up, correcting books, + all the rest to be done. It's a bit of a strain, + you're probably right about the English character up to a point. Its perhaps a method of self preservation to keep one's thoughts on shaving tackle + so on,—one's surface thoughts that is. Its painful to let one's thoughts wander too far.

Rex added that "Our children are standing up to things quite well, though they haven't had an unbroken night's sleep for a week. . . . We've given up entirely the carefree attitude of not seeking cover when we hear the warnings, + I hope you have too."[32] The family would retreat to the larder where they would play games by thinking of animals that began with a certain letter of the alphabet.

On 14 September [1940], Rex wrote to Greenwood,

> Here we get the planes coming over pretty often + last week there was a great air battle over our heads. The nights are very uproarious, the guns making so much noise that one hasn't the least idea whether bombs are coming down or not. After a bit one finds this rather better than the previous state of things. We had one large bomb fairly close, but it didn't go off as well as it might have done + caused hardly any damage. What with this + the guns several of our doors are beginning to stick. I shall be pretty fed up if the house falls down on the day after I've paid the rent.

The worst thing was "having nothing to do except feel like a sort of ant with giants in the air above one." He asked Greenwood to tell him if he liked *The Aerodrome*.[33] In the midst of all this, on 21 September 1940, Anne Morris was born during an air raid.

The days just before 5 October 1940 were full of bombs. On that day, he wrote Greenwood that "we had about 200 incendiaries round us the other night, one of which bounced off the roof into the garden, where we shovelled wall flowers + earth over it. It was an incredible sight at first, though in about 20 minutes nearly all the fires were out." But life went on: he was glad that Greenwood liked the book, and enclosed a blurb.

By Sunday, 24 November 1940, Rex wrote Greenwood that he'd read the proofs of *The Aerodrome* and would do a foreword. Also that he was "trying to add a bit, though this is very difficult. What is the longest time you can give me (remembering necessity of Dec. cash?)." Rex was trying "to cure a cold with whiskey." Rex sent Greenwood the proofs of *The Aerodrome* on 1 December 1940; the previous night had been full of the noise of exploding bombs.[34]

On 27 December [1940], he wrote from Cecil's house in Musbury to Pam that Cecil was "taking his Home Guard activities very seriously." On Christmas Eve, Rex "patrolled the cliffs with him in icy cold watching for invaders till 1.0 in the morning. The whole world seems to be mad."[35]

Back in London, the family had to take in boarders to make ends meet, and there were colds, worries about the meat ration, difficulty finding oranges, and Rex's assignment to firewatching.

An uneasy silence would suddenly be shattered by the anti-aircraft guns at arbitrary moments, and it was impossible to know what would happen or when. Rex reported to Pam on 15 February, probably 1941, that life with its periods of uncertain waiting had come to resemble Chekhov's work. On the positive side, Kitty was now well. And although Knopf had turned down *The Aerodrome*, Macmillan was reported to be interested in it.

VI. MORE POEMS, FILMS, AND ESSAYS

On 22 February 1941, Rex reported to John Lehmann that *The Aerodrome* would be coming out early in March, he hoped that Lehmann would like it, and added, "It's better than 'The Professor' I think." He also sent Lehmann four of his sonnets, stating simply that "They are all on the general theme of love. . . ."[36] Rex celebrated Frances's new pregnancy with one of these sonnets, which shows an obvious debt to Hopkins, possibly to Swinburne, and certainly to the Ira Gershwin song "'S Wonderful":

> IV
> Wonderful, marvelous, after the dark and nuzzling
> to stand on legs and meet surprising day,
> to face huge trees, wide avenues, the puzzling,
> roars, crows and clucks, clashes, barking and bray,
> jangling and stir and splintering of light;
> and to look up as giant faces bend
> bristled and mottled from so great a height;
> for now the lucky death has come to an end.
> Birth swung the child to staggering life: now legs
> push him to peril, grow in strength and drive,
> and force him among phantoms till he begs,
> dazed with lucidity of being alive,
> for the irrecoverable dream, lost eye,
> clinging for posture, milk, and lullabies.[37]

He wrote to Greenwood soon after this from Wimbledon [Monday, undated] that "I'm coming up to London on Friday to have dinner with J. Lehmann who wants me to write an article on something or other, +, incidentally, says he liked *The Aerodrome* very much."

Rex asked if there is "any chance of raising £5 or £10 on a post-dated cheque this month?. . . And when is there a chance of my receiving anything for *The Aerodrome.* The landlord is getting a bit impatient, + the film earnings have gone to pay the coal bill." To earn some necessary money, Rex had begun doing documentary film script writing at some point early in the war, undoubtedly owing to Basil Wright's recommendation. The references to films in Rex's letters increase, but he seems to have regarded film writing as hack work and only rarely named the films that he was working on. During May and June, Rex was preoccupied with writing a film on the Scouts, and early in June he was summoned to the Ministry of Information to write the commentary for a documentary entitled *Airwoman*, about the Women's Auxiliary Air Force. For this film he had to interview people in London every day after school for about a week, and he received £10. Rex commented ironically, "that's what comes of knowing about aerodromes."[38]

In the midst of an air attack on London in the spring of 1941, Day-Lewis had begun what was to become a nine-year affair with writer Rosamond Lehmann, whom he had known since the 1930s. Rex was familiar with Day-Lewis's many escapades with women, and was himself now something of an experienced hand in these matters. On the weekend of 7-8 June they came out to Raynes Park to stay with Rex and see the school play.

By 14 June, Rex reported to Pam that "I'm still absurdly busy. I spent this morning doing the final draft of my Boy Scout film,—very hearty + melodramatic." He commented that "I'm half way through 'Vanity Fair,'—a very good book. There's no doubt that the Victorians knew their stuff all right, though Thackeray isn't a genius like Dickens." Here we have an indication of the strong feeling about Dickens that was to result in Rex's essay in *The Cult of Power* (1946); this essay helped revive Dickens's reputation after World War II. He asked Pam in Rowledge to give Jonathan his love and added, "I hope he's getting on better now at Frensham Heights, + feel rather sorry for him, remembering how I loathed a boarding school for the first few weeks. They are probably bad things altogether."[39] This was not to be his position in the book he would publish on education in 1945.

In August 1941 Rex and the family were in Spring Hill, Malvern Wells, for a vacation and to visit Frances's parents who had also left Jersey just in time. Rex's mother had taken Jonathan for a week, which offered Rex and Frances something of a rest. He wrote Pam, however, that he was growing bored and that he would not mind returning to London itself despite the war, but thoughts of teaching rankled. He added that he would be staying until the 27th when he would have to go for a film consultation in London.[40] By 4 August [1941], as he wrote Greenwood, he was "getting ahead with the articles for Lehmann + might get on to something else when I've finished this," a reference to his articles on subsidizing literature[41] and "The Cult of Power."[42] Frances was beginning to swell up with the baby that was to be George, who would be born on Christmas Day, 1941. Jonathan had to be prevented from sending Pam Morris a box of grasshoppers as a present. By 17 August, Rex had finished the two long articles for Lehmann and for recreation was reading the *Morte d'Arthur* and *Piers Plowman*, as well as a book on Engels by a German Jewish refugee whom Rex had met. The bird-watching was very good, including red starts, sparrow hawks, and wheatears.

Rex may have regretted his desire to get back to London. Around 24 September two incendiary bombs hit Rex and Frances's garden, one of them bouncing off the roof first.[43] In an act of defiance, they planted some cabbages where the bombs fell. Around that time a high-explosive bomb also blew up in the fields behind the house, showering it with soot and blowing the back door open. In an attempt to find calm, Rex recommended Wilkie Collins's Victorian mysteries and Bunyan's *Pilgrim's Progress* to Greenwood for "good reading these days."[44]

VII. A GROWING REPUTATION

Rex's affiliation with the BBC began as early as 5 October 1936, when he readily accepted 5 shillings for a contract for his poem "Lapwing" to be broadcast on the 13 November program to the Empire. His contact for BBC work was probably Walter Rilla, the father of his Frensham Heights pupil Wolf Rilla; Walter was in the European production department. He met Walter several times during the early 1940s, sometimes at the Cafe Royal. On 7 July 1941, in response to a request from a producer named John Glyn-Jones, Rex offered to do some work for the BBC. They had lunch at Broadcasting House on 29 July. In an internal memo of 30 September, Glyn-Jones says that Rex "is a good writer I think and very sensitive, but is a complete novice at writing feature programs."[45] On Sunday, 28 September [1941], Rex was offered work on a BBC program scheduled for 13 October in which John Lehmann introduced British writers to an Indian audience. Rex decided to read from *The Aerodrome*, and his popularity in India, which continues to this day, began then.

At about this time Rex had a £10 payment for the Boy Scouts film in his pocket and he and Frances were able to go up to London to attend the wedding of Charles Fenby, his Oxford roommate who was now working for the *Picture Post*, to a girl named June who also worked for the paper. Rex had hopes that *The Aerodrome* would be published in

America around this time, providing him with some additional income, but that was not to happen until 1946, when it would be greeted with almost universal acclaim.

In 1941 England, however, *The Aerodrome* did not fare so well. An anonymous *TLS* reviewer, writing in the 12 April 1941 issue, was unrelentingly hostile. He accused Rex, "like his exemplar" Kafka, of transforming "every grubby little molehill into a Himalayan range of the soul." Rex could write "good prose of a formal kind when he chooses," but his ideas were "unexceptional" (p. 181). By 1947, however, the book was selling, to quote the *Herald Tribune*, "furiously" in Europe and had "been published in all but four of the European languages."[46] This success made Rex more popular and more highly regarded than ever, but he never did make much money from his writing. *The Aerodrome* was finally made into a movie, albeit only for television, in 1982.

According to his original contract with Lane/Bodley Head, signed on 28 July 1939, he was to receive £70 on acceptance of the novel, 15 percent royalties on the first 5,000 printed, 20 percent on the next 5,000, and 25 percent after 10,000. Although the book did go into several editions, a memo about the fourth impression, dated 31/5/47, lists only 4,750 copies with 12.5 percent royalties. It is no wonder that in his 1941 article for *Folios of New Writing*, Rex called for government subsidies of literature, agreeing with E. M. Forster who in a BBC broadcast had said that the day of the serious professional writer was over.[47]

In another essay written around this time, Rex discussed Christopher Caudwell's idea of "The bourgeois illusion, the belief that the individual is at his best when least connected with other individuals + with society" and concluded that "the world of cash value" had led to a "conscious or half-conscious . . . revolt against . . . the amorphous omnipotence of money." He went on to say that

> the success of Fascist propaganda in Europe is largely due to the fact that the Fascists, for a number of reasons, have appreciated better than their opponents the deep seated desire in modern men + women to escape from the bourgeois illusion of disconnected + aimless freedom. People need a framework of convention in which their lives may be shaped, +, rather than the abstract inhumanity of the cash-nexus they will choose the concrete inhumanity of Fascism + war. The former deprives them of all human value; the latter gives them at least a more credible illusion than bourgeois "freedom."[48]

Rex's Marxist-tinged ideas on the subject of the "cash-nexus" reflect his own inability to earn a decent living since graduating from Oxford. But even twenty-five years later, in his Caesar novels, he was to express the conviction that most people cannot exist without an orderly "framework of convention" outside of sheer materialism.

On 10 October Rex learned that he was to receive only £3. 6s. 6d to read from *The Aerodrome* for the Indian broadcast. Casting about for ways to increase his income, he suggested to Greenwood a verse anthology for boys, to be compiled with the English master at Raynes Park, John Grubb. The project never came off. He asked Greenwood for £5 on a postdated check. Frances, who was pregnant, was "quite well, but enormous," and Rex's mother was coming to stay.[49]

VIII. THE RAYNES PARK SCHOOL

Although Rex's salary was a meager £300-400 a year, he could not have found a better school in which to work. The Raynes Park County School was an exceptional place because it had an exceptional headmaster, and a very amenable and talented staff. Raynes Park was a new and not particularly distinguished suburb of London, and the school, built on former farmland, was surrounded by Bradbury Wilkinson's, a banknote company, and Senior's Fish and Meat Paste factory. The institution was established on 12 June 1935 with John Garrett as its first headmaster. In Paul Vaughan's memoir, *Something in Linoleum*, Garrett is described in 1935 at the age of thirty-three as having a loud voice,

> with a posh accent. He had a large nose, fair hair brushed close to his head, and he would grin with his chin thrust forward, lips pursed a little. He took care about the way he dressed, favouring the kind of clothes that suggested the fashionable thirties intellectual-woollen ties done up in a fat knot, shirts with soft collars, tweedy jackets and suits. When he walked, it was with a swift, tripping stride, shoulders wagging a little from side to side.[50]

He added that "The boys thought he walked like a cissy [sissy], but didn't have much of an idea of what that might mean. We knew he had a persuasive, bullying charm and a knack for getting people to do what he wanted. In due course we learned he had a gift for friendship—particularly if it could prove useful and profitable." Garrett was to remain in this post until Christmas 1942, at which time he took up the headmastership of the Bristol Grammar School. His ambition was to become headmaster of Harrow, which he never achieved; he had an affair with David Skinner, head boy of the Bristol Grammar School, and that ended his career. But that was in the future. When Garrett left Raynes Park, Rex wrote a tribute to him for *The Spur*, the school newspaper, which reads in part,

The Headmaster has never wished the School to be successful in any one department to the exclusion of all others: he has wished it to be successful in all departments. Nor does one remember him for the possession of any one quality pre-eminently so much as for the possession of a great number of qualities in a rare combination. One may remark, for instance, his meticulous and precise attention to detail, but at the same moment will remember his widely human toleration for methods and ideas which are not his own.[51]

This is a positive recommendation, coming from Rex, who was typically reticent about praise for himself and others; if it strikes one as a bit restrained, the reason might be that he had detected Garrett's homosexuality and did not like it. Robert Robinson, a student at Raynes Park, wrote me that Rex "struck me as a very masculine sort of chap in a school where the headmaster was anything but. Indeed, the apocrypha among the boys was that at a Faber and Faber party Rex went into one room where the gentlemen were embracing, then into another where the ladies were embracing, and cried in a voice of thunder 'Is there nobody here who plays rugger!'"[52]

As Peter Harris's history of the school informs us, Garrett was an Oxford graduate and had been an assistant master at Whitgift School. Like most of his students, he had risen from relatively humble origins—his father had been a warrant officer in the Indian Army and later opened a barber shop. He was also exceptional in his love of literature and his ability to attract to the school the very best literary talent England could offer. How many schools, for instance, could boast a school song written by W. H. Auden, which appears on the cover of the first number of *The Spur*, October 1936? The poet was then at the height of his powers, although that is not particularly apparent in this song despite a biting sense of humor that manifests itself in the second stanza of the chorus. Paul Vaughan points out that this song was "one of the school's major selling points, often reprinted in school publications and sung by the boys *en masse* on the first and last days of term, on Speech Days and at House Suppers"[53]:

Time will make its utter changes,
    Circumstance will scatter us;
But the memories of our school days
    Are a living part of us.
Chorus—
So remember then, when you are men
    With important things to do,
That once you were young, and this song have sung
    For you were at school here, too.

Daily we sit down in form-rooms,
    Inky hand to puzzled head;
Reason's light, and knowledge power;
    Man must study till he's dead.

Man has mind but body also;
    So we learn to tackle low,
Bowl the off-breaks, hit the sixes,
    Bend the diver's brilliant bow.

Man must live among his neighbours,
    For he cannot live alone;
Friendships, failures, and successes
    Here we learn to make our own.

Tractors grunt where oceans wandered,
    Factories stand where green grass grew;
Voices break and features alter,
    We shall soon be different, too.

Boys and cities, schools and natures,
    Though they change, like you and me,
Do not simply grow and happen,
    They are what they choose to be.

The music was written by Thomas Wood, who is credited with popularizing "Waltzin' Mathilda" outside of Australia; the tune, described by Vaughan as "Elgarian," was disliked by the boys but stuck despite attempts to replace it. Auden's paraphrase of the Marxist dictum "To each his need, from each his power" was adopted by Garrett as the school's motto after he reviewed for T. S. Eliot's *Criterion* (July 1935) the Auden-Isherwood play, *The Dog Beneath the Skin,* in which the line appears. Garrett and Auden, who were rumored to have had a love affair, co-edited the anthology *The Poet's Tongue* of 1935. Garrett also edited some school readers and an anthology of 1933, containing brief descriptions by sixteen authors from Boswell on and entitled *Scenes from School Life,* which became a standard anthology in many schools, and went through several editions.[54]

    A man of extraordinary energy, Garrett worried over the paint used in the new school, established remedial classes in math and other subjects for those who needed them, and set about building a library. He also instituted a school dinner for teachers and students, and wanted most of all to get as many students as possible into Oxford and Cambridge. On 3 July 1936 Garrett had an open night at the school during which the latest works by the foremost British painters, including Augustus John, Vanessa Bell, and Roger Fry, were displayed; this event was duly noted by the press. He hired Claude Rogers, an important up-and-coming painter, as art master, and was prevented from firing him despite his poor teaching, when W. H. Auden took Rogers's part. (Rogers resigned in 1938, before Rex appeared on the scene.) The school's second play, Shakespeare's *Hamlet*, was reviewed by *The Daily Telegraph* owing to Garrett's Oxford connections. *The New Statesman* frequently took an interest in the school's doings, and critic Raymond Mortimer and novelist Rosamond Lehmann were among the critics who commented on the school's plays.

The 1938 school prize-giving was attended by Lord David Cecil, while the 1939 event hosted T.S. Eliot. By 1938, filmmaker Basil Wright and C. Day-Lewis had become involved in the school. Wright arranged for special film showings at the Rialto Theatre in Raynes Park, including one of his own films, *Night Mail*. According to Paul Vaughan, Day-Lewis was a close friend of Garrett's and remarked once that he was astonished that no one attacked Garrett for homosexuality, or tried to remove him as headmaster because of it. Day-Lewis would visit to read from his poetry or to sing Irish or Scottish folk songs or German art songs. Once when drunk Garrett grabbed Rosamond Lehmann and danced with her, and was not forgiven for this by Day-Lewis. But eventually they made it up, with Day-Lewis and L. A. G. Strong dedicating, in July 1941, their *New Anthology of Modern Verse, 1920-1940*, to the school. (Garrett himself is remembered in a very touching poem, "Trowbridge," by A. L. Rowse, who had been his tutor at Oxford: "Mother's son not one for marrying,/And only I to remember him passing by.") Visitors to the school during Garrett's years as headmaster included Rowse, Stephen Spender, John Lehmann, Benjamin Britten, and Neville Coghill, among others. Michael Redgrave came to the school and sang one of the songs from *The Beggar's Opera*, in which he was appearing.

Rex's employment would follow soon after the inaugural events of Garrett's reign: the school register shows him joining in May 1940 to teach classics, and leaving in September 1945. Certainly Day-Lewis and L. A. G. Strong, who was a school governor, helped Rex get the post, but Garrett also heard about Rex from Bowra. Rex found congenial company: most staff members were in their early thirties and had degrees from the University of London, Oxford, or Cambridge, and the atmosphere in the masters' common room was decidedly leftist.

The boys came in between the ages of ten and twelve and stayed until they were sixteen. The school year had the usual three terms of thirteen weeks each, with three weeks off at Christmas, three at Easter, and seven in the summer. Students studied from 9 A.M. to 12:20 P.M. and from 1:45 P.M. to 3:45 P.M.

Boys "are able to study Religious Knowledge, English, History, Civics, Latin, Greek, French, German, Mathematics, Chemistry, Physics, Botany, Biology, Geography, Music, Art, Handiwork and Physical Training," according to the Raynes Park County School for Boys pamphlet of regulations. Rex's job was to teach Latin but not Greek. The chief classics master was Robert Oates. Rex would take the boys of the Sixth Form through Tacitus, and Oates would then take them through Caesar's *Commentaries*. The students liked Rex very much, although he was a little remote because he was extremely shy. He was also the First XV Rugby coach. Paul Vaughan saw him as a big, shabby, tweedy man with untidy trousers and a cigarette, who would sometimes playfully tap him with a book.

A confidential Board of Education Report of Inspection dated 24-27 November 1942 states that "Latin is taken by all boys during their first two years and subsequently by those in the faster of the two streams leading to the school certificate. The subject is well represented in the Sixth Form. . . . Each of the two Masters who divide between them the bulk of the work is highly qualified, keen, and hard working. . . "(7).

The report goes on to praise "the spirit of frank enquiry animating the School— of which the 'Partisans' Society is striking evidence . . ." (13). The April 1941 issue of *The Spur* (whose title derives from the school's location on the Merton Spur of the Kingston By-Pass Road) explains that the purpose of this society (of which Rex is listed as a founding member) is "to provide an atmosphere in which Sixth Form boys can discuss freely, energetically and profitably anything under the sun" (24). In July 1941 the newspaper reported that the Partisans had met twice at Rex's house and that the discussions were speculations on the state of Britain after the war and on the English Speaking Union (28).

In December 1941 it was reported that the society had met on 19 September 1941 at Rex's house and discussed "Belief in God." Burke Trend, a guest from outside the school, spoke of government, offering the opinion that "'the ordinary man like you or I' knew nothing about politics and therefore should have no part in it." The reporter noted that "Mr. Warner was deeply pained" by this opinion, and that "one wrathful member accused the speaker of being a Nazi." Rex may have left the Communist cause behind, but he clearly had no intention of signing off from politics.

The December 1941 *Spur* reported that Rex had broadcast extracts from *The Aerodrome* on the BBC Overseas Service and had published five [*sic*; should be four] sonnets in *Folios of New Writing* (in the autumn 1941 issue). During the summer of 1941 in the Malvern Hills, Rex wrote his essay entitled "The Cult of Power," which was published in *Daylight* 1 (1941): 59-71 in January 1942, and was eventually to provide the title essay for his collection of 1946. In this strong essay, Rex attempted to explain the rise of Hitler despite the experience of World War I and the postwar religious and Marxist talk of international peace and brotherhood. He felt that "the age of Socrates is nearer to us than the age of Hobbes," because as in that age "there has been a general breakdown in political life accompanied by an uncertainty about moral and intellectual standards." For Rex, the beginning of his age's political problem is unfettered and willful individualism with "the individual asserting himself against general standards that seem too weak to be able to restrain him."[55] The strong individual's rebellion weakens general standards to the point that there is nothing to rebel against, and the masses demand a new system, which he creates, with himself at the head of it. He becomes the God of a new religion.

D. H. Lawrence provides an example of the rebel who tore down the post-World War I gods but who had nothing with which to replace them except "blood, sex, virility, violence." Lawrence's individual revolt, however, never became a system, while Hitler's system—which Rex felt was motivated essentially by the same disgust with the old ideals—did. "The very name 'National-Socialist'" is "the most brilliant of modern political inventions"[56] because it unites the ideal of brotherhood inherent in socialism with the Lawrentian dark forces. But it is also the most sinister: "[W]e have come a long way from the mere individualist, the moral anarchist, who insisted upon the right of the strong man to over-ride constraints, a long way from the polite critic who pointed out the failures and hypocrises of an agreed system of thought, a long way from D. H. Lawrence, whose 'dark' forces were still individual and whose heroes, for all their sympathies with tigers, were horrified by the vulgarity and indiscriminateness of actual war." The one saving grace is that, however strong Hitler appears, "increasing violence, increasing lust for power are the signs of fear, and fear springs from a consciousness of insecurity." If there is to be a reestablishment of law and order after the war, however, "they will have to be a different law and order from those which collapsed so thoroughly in the first act. Mere reiteration of European ideals of universal love and justice will cut no more ice after the war than they did in the time of D. H. Lawrence. . . . The only reply to the cult of individual or racial power and violence is the actual practice of general justice, mercy, brotherhood and understanding."[57]

The problem with all this, of course, is that Rex's prescription of justice and mercy as a cure-all is no less vague or ineffectual than Cecil Grant's hopes after World War I had been. Rex's distaste for power grabbers, dictators, and racial hatred is clear and commendable, but he has no vision of the new world he is calling for, any more than he had been able to predict in *The Wild Goose Chase* what the world of Marxist revolution would actually look like. Notably absent in this essay is any mention of a role for Marxism. In 1941 Rex no longer saw Marxism, and especially not Stalin, as any part of a postwar solution to the world's problems. He was to become obsessed with the theme of the personality cult, returning to it in later life, when he compared Hitler and Stalin unfavorably to Julius Caesar, a pragmatic dictator who, unlike them, formulated no ideology to justify his taking of power.

IX. MAKING FILMS

Despite the dictators and the war, Rex's personal life was very positive. The baby was about ten days overdue, but George Frank Warner was born on Christmas Day, 1941, in the Nelson Hospital, Merton. On Boxing Day, Friday, 26 December, Rex wrote Pam Morris:

> Things started to happen at about 8.15 last night (just as I, being psychic, had returned from the pub). We had to get an ARP ambulance as all the taximen were out, +, sure enough, when I started telephoning, the bloody machine wouldn't work. However it did after I'd given it some hard knocks. The baby (George, I think) was born just before midnight, with some excitement among the nurses, as it was the first Christmas baby, so they said, which they had had. I think Frances had a short but bad time. . . . The baby itself, when last seen by me, was yelling away like one o'clock, + looked rather like those intelligent-seeming monkeys in the Zoo. Tell Barbara that, since the baby has kept us waiting nearly a month, he will be under pretty strict discipline until he has learnt the meaning of the word punctuality.[58]

Around January or February 1942, Rex wrote Pam that "Some film chaps are talking of making a film which will be partly based on the ideas in Kafka's novels, partly on mine in the Wild Goose Chase. This naturally interests me + I'm going to dinner with them on Tuesday to discuss it. Whether there's any money in it I don't know. Probably one talks about it for a year + then gives up the idea."[59] To Greenwood, he wrote on 15 February [1942] saying that he "had the most extraordinary meal with the film chaps. . . . Vast quantities were drunk + I was ill in bed for about a week afterwards (but this I attribute to food poisoning). They seemed to think that some sort of preliminary decisions had been reached, though what they were I haven't the slightest idea." He himself had enjoyed Orson Welles's *Citizen Kane* the day before. He asked if he could get £10 as an advance on royalties or as a loan, because he was in debt for bills.

Despite war, economic adversity, a grinding teaching schedule, and a crowded house, Rex maintained his sense of humor. At some point in February or March, he wrote Pam that "George, after a few nights of waking up at 4.0, has been sleeping till 6.0, + has now started smiling when he sees anything worth smiling at, such as the sinking of a Japanese transport or the inclusion of Sir Stafford [Cripps] in the government. Its still frightfully cold + I'd give anything for a long holiday, sun + oysters. I suppose one may get the sun."[60] Writing progressed. By 4 March he was considering work on a film with Basil Wright, but only if he would receive £20 for the job. This may well have been the beginning of *Why Was I Killed?* which was originally to be a film script for Wright, and which is dedicated to him.

By 29 March, he wrote Pam and John that "The main film job is still uncertain, though I ought to hear something about it this week; but meanwhile I've got a subsidiary film job for the MOI [Ministry of Information],—a production on 'Youth.' Its being run by Calder Marshall who, unlike most of these chaps, seems efficient + to know what he wants; so it may be quite interesting." A BBC job that he was working on with Walter Rilla was "cancelled at the last moment,—I suspect because I had mentioned Lenin."[61] On 6 May Rex apologized to Pam because he "couldn't manage the drink today. I had to go to a conference about this bloody youth film from 5.30 to 6.30, + very dull + unnecessary it was too. Actually I've been rushing up to London for something like this nearly every night for the last ten days + am going on strike now, unless I get some more money."[62]

In a letter dated only Sunday but probably written in late May 1942 to Pam Morris, Rex wrote, "Things are going very busily. I've been rushing up to London several nights this week,—this time getting employment from old Rilla in his 'Blues Gallery' programme. This consists of writing down all the dirt about Nazi leaders. The youth film is approaching its end, thank God, + I don't have to write any more for it." Then he continued, "The other film ('Why was I killed?') is going well, + I enjoy this. I can't work on it except at week ends, + then I write all day (except pub hours). I think it will make a novel in the end, + would like to show it to you."[63] So this is how the novel, published in 1943, began. In a letter to Pam dated 6 June, Rex joked about his film connections that "when I've had a year or two in Hollywood you won't be too proud to come for a trip in my yacht."[64] On 2 July 1942, Rex received 10 guineas for his 12- to 15-minute script entitled "Battle of Youth" for the "London Calling Europe" program. This was supposed to be broadcast on 15 June 1942 but was delayed for some reason.

Despite all his rushing around, Rex found time in July to inscribe a copy of *The Wild Goose Chase* for his colleague, Frank Coventry, as follows:

> If, Coventry, it might at all avail
> In simple words to explicate my tale,
> I'd say the Goose with all his wild alarms
> Was what Jones sought in his Sophia's arms,
> What Christian found at the Celestial Gate
> What all desire to follow soon or late,—
> A glint of meaning in the eyes of fate.
> To Plato then I went for my three men,
> (Though three is one + one is three again).
> But Mind, Imagination + the Normal
> Was what I thought of when the scheme was formal,—
> of that + Dostoievsky's giant three,—
> Though I placed merit in sobriety,
> Not in excess. I thought of them, not me.
> 'The many change, the one remains' I said,
> And saw that what remains is mostly dead.
> I showed the weird fantastic struggling free
> of future life from strong senility,
> The fake gods falling + the new not found,
> Distorted status + enchanted ground,—
> The Pilgrim's Progress,—oh! let grace abound!

Frank Coventry wrote me that after Rex penned this, he complained half-jokingly "that it worked out at too little per line."[65] He noted that the reference to sobriety is probably "due to Rex's reputation for spending all his evenings in the local pub" but he adds that "we never saw him intoxicated." Also, he remembered that Rex was the only teacher who was not reprimanded for working the *Times* crossword puzzle during school hours. Rex's comment about "The fake gods falling + the new not found" explains the problem as he saw it in "The Cult of Power." Marxism had failed, as had liberalism, and there was nothing to fill the gap.

Rex's discussions with the Partisans were interwoven with and led to his own projects. For instance, in *The Spur* for April 1942, the reporter for the Partisans meetings mentioned a speaker about Pacifism who "had become less and less sympathetic towards it because of its apparent impracticability and futility under present conditions"

(14). Immortality was another subject discussed, with consideration of Christianity, spiritualism, and J. W. Dunne's philosophy—as embodied no doubt in his then-popular *Experiment with Time*. These discussions must have influenced Rex, who was then meditating *Why Was I Killed?*—a work that centers on both pacifism and a ghost.

Films provided Rex with most of his work during this period, hackneyed though it might be. The July 1942 report in *The Spur* about the Partisans meeting noted that one of the visitors during a T. S. Eliot discussion was a film director named Nieter, and that

> as the result of his visit, five of the more adventurous and progressive among us sacrificed a long week-end to be subjected to the nervous strain and brilliant illumination of the film studio, where we represented five-twelfths of a cross-section through the youth of the country in a discussion about the war and the peace and so on. The remainder of the cross-section was represented by seven other odd youths. Mr. Warner made his debut in the film world by acting as chairman for the discussion. Apparently our three days' worth of effort is to appear as ten minutes' worth of screen time. . . . Six hours later, the six potential stars, Mr. Rex Warner, B. Meade, P. Crumley . . . J. Carr, R. Forrest and M. Saby, were once again in the Headmaster's study, taking part in a discussion with the rest of the society. (12)

The result of this excursion was *They Speak for Themselves* (1942), which was directed by Hans Nieter and produced by the famous documentary director Paul Rotha for the Ministry of Information. Rex is listed as the scriptwriter. This is a nine-minute, one-reel film with commentary in which, according to the film directory at the British Film Institute, "a group of young people discuss and express opinions on current problems such as the War, the Post-War world, Federal Union, and Education." The "appraisal" of the film states that "Although this film shows that young people have views and sense of responsibility about the community, unfortunately there is no real group leader in the discussion, which results in a mere expression of opinions with no connecting link. It would not be of use to Youth Clubs for discussion purposes, or of particular interest to schools." So much for one of Rex's early films! Another film produced in 1942 by Rotha, *World Without End*, has Rex serving as commentator.

In a letter of 5 August [1942] to Pam, Rex wrote more about his work on *Why Was I Killed?*: "The children went off early yesterday. I'm trying to work like a stoat for the next fortnight, but so far haven't got beyond the stage of sitting in front of a blank sheet of paper + thinking. However I hope a start will be made in a day or two. Its very difficult thinking of this story as a film + as a novel at the same time."[66] It was to be a year before Rex finished *Why Was I Killed?*; it was published on 15 October 1943. He was doing all of this writing while having to teach every day, put up with boarders and visiting relatives in a small apartment, and live with the German raids.

During term time, Rex had six or seven classes a day of about forty-five minutes each, and he was not a terribly good teacher because he was probably exhausted by teaching, the frustration of not being able to write, the lack of good pay, family pressures, and the war. Frank Coventry remembered that Rex would mumble and laugh to himself, and that the boys did not always pay attention. Robert Robinson wrote,

> He was a very mild man when it came to punishments until he got the hang of it, but then would distribute two-hour detentions with a lavish hand. I thought of him as rather distant and vague and not someone who was going to be a teacher in a school for very long. I think if he knew you were any good at it he didn't bother much: he gave me an essay back once when I was quite a small boy and said "You've used a number of words that don't mean what you think they mean. But that doesn't matter."[67]

Whatever Rex's failures as a teacher, Alan Milton, a Caius College, Cambridge, graduate who was a colleague of Rex's and later a high administrator in the Universities of Rhodesia and Ulster, reported that Rex was regarded with reverence:

> Boys and teachers lived in delighted awe at having this splendid novelist, poet, and classical scholar in their midst. The delight was the keener because RW was the easiest, the least "important," the most gregarious and amusing of men. He was physically large . . . and very gentle and warm in demeanour. A lovable man. . . . I am hazy about the political side. To me (a pacifist) RW appeared a congenial spirit, digging deep into questions of power and humanity. I thought of him (in my naive simplification) as a gifted ally on the frontier of power politics. . . .[68]

Rex got on very well with most of the masters, and often expressed himself humorously. Paul Vaughan recounts a story told by physics master Eddie Hanson about chemistry master Peter Smith, who also lived on Grand Drive (calling it "Usher's Alley"). Smith was forty-five and had a beard and gaudy clothes, including an orange tie, and also had a mistress who was seventeen. Referring to both tie and mistress, Rex said "Ah, Smith, natty plunge on today I see." Their positive relationship was not to last. One of Rex's students, Robert Robinson, remembers that in the seedy but convivial pub down the road from Rex's house, he was sometimes allowed to "take chalks" or keep the score of the shove half-penny between Rex and Peter Smith, Rex's biggest rival. Peter and Rex were cronies until Rex published a short story which was a vignette of the pub, and had the chemistry master trying to touch someone for half a crown. Smith was very hurt by this, and told Robinson that although Rex apologized, "He shouldn't have done it."[69] The story must be "Opening Hour: A London Interior," which was published in *English Story, Fifth Series*, edited by Woodrow Wyatt[70] in November 1944. In the story, set in a working-class pub during the war years, a left-leaning chemistry master who condemns "exploitation of the working class and . . . rampant imperialism"[71] unsuccessfully tries to cadge half a crown from the pub owner.

Day-Lewis, however, was a match for Rex's mockery. A bantering debate took place between them at the end of the summer term, 1942, and was reported in *The Spur*.[72] After Cecil read some of his war poems, "someone conceived the happy idea of holding an informal Brains Trust. Mr. Joyce undertook the function of question-master, while Mr. Day Lewis, Mr. Beecroft and Mr. Warner were posted to the unenviable task of answering questions sent in by all present." The first question apparently concerned Day-Lewis's opinion about Rex's acting and translating ability and Rex's opinion of Day-Lewis's poetry. Cecil responded that Rex's "Acting was best summed up as massive and concrete: it must be seen to be believed; and even then, few people would believe it. As for his Latin, he continued, it was sound: Mr. Warner was a good plodding scholar of the Germanic type, unfortunately rather weak on quantities." Rex responded that "it was true that Mr. Day Lewis' poetry was excellent; but he encountered a certain difficulty in dealing with words derived from foreign languages; unfortunately most English words were so derived. Mr. Day Lewis' French was also good, in so far as grammar was concerned, and yet the poet was unable to express himself audibly in this language." (Rex undoubtedly referred here to the 1938 "popular front" rally in Paris during which Cecil had refused to speak French, but the reporter found Rex's thrust noteworthy even without this private knowledge.) During several questions about poetic values, Rex and Cecil agreed that initial inspiration was necessary for writing most poems, and Frank Beecroft suggested that this alone might distinguish poetry from mere verse.

Toward the end of the session, there were more fireworks between Rex and Cecil: "Mr. Warner considered that Mr. Day Lewis' explanation of the lucky horseshoe was mere Celtic superstition. His colleague challenged him, as one who has never remained on a horse above a minute, to improve on this. Mr. Warner's theory about the Canterbury Bell aroused hysterical mirth." Unfortunately, Rex's theory is not reported. But "A feeble joke—why is a mouse happy when it spins?—caused a profound silence throughout the room" and Rex "rose to the occasion magnificently: in Assam, he informed his listeners, the mice spin frequently when performing their nuptial dance (which, Mr. Day Lewis interpolated, is familiar to Mr. Warner if to no one else). He continued with an allusion to the weasel, which, as he attempted to convince his astounded audience, might frequently be observed pirouetting round its prey in order to fascinate it. The session broke up, the experts visibly shaken (save for Mr. Warner, who retained his customary sangfroid) and the proceedings were rounded off by the triumphant question-master."

X. LIFE AND ART IN *WHY WAS I KILLED?*

Even in the middle of World War II, there was at least a minority opinion for pacifism. Huxley's arguments for pacifism and Christianity may have had a delayed influence on Rex, who had included the Christian pacifist's position in *The Professor*. Rex's next novel (begun as a film, as we have seen) *Why Was I Killed?* is indeed a pacifist work, and was extremely controversial at the time—so much so that the BBC refused to broadcast it even though Walter Rilla had asked him to write the script.

Paul Vaughan told me that this was *the* Raynes Park book par excellence, quoted and loved by all members of the student body and staff. The chief character is a dead World War II soldier (now a ghostly presence) who silently confronts a group of visitors to a monument to the "Unknown Soldier" in a chapel. These visitors range from the upper-class Sir Alfred Fothey to Bob Clark, a frustrated member of the working class. The clergyman speaking to the group asks them why they think the soldier was killed, and each gives a different, and unsatisfactory, answer according to his station. As they speak, the soldier envisions their lives, and this gives some detail and visual support to what is a very abstract dialogue. At the end of the visit, the priest concludes with the hope that the horrors of the war will convince all men to be closer to one another and to value life more in the future.

The dead soldier is a composite of all the "unknown soldiers" and is perhaps not traceable to a single real-life person. But at least one character, who appears in chapter VII, which is entitled "The Woman," was based on Roy Barnes. Barnes was a mischievous Raynes Park student who was often in trouble with Garrett; he was caned and finally expelled. He joined the RAF, became a pilot, and was shot down and killed. He was awarded the Distinguished Flying Cross posthumously. At some point after that, Barnes's mother slapped Garrett's face for his previous treatment of her son. In the novel, there is a specific character named Mrs. Barnes, and her husband (rather than her son) is a fighter pilot who is killed. Rex denied that he based the whole novel on Roy Barnes, but Barnes certainly gave him a model for at least this one character. It is possible that Barnes's death motivated him to write this pacifistic novel.

Captain Wallace, a friend of the downed fighter pilot, is definitely based on Alan Milton. In the novel, Wallace tells the airman, whose mother is a pacifist, that "at one time he had been a pacifist himself" but then says "something to the effect that after the war he intended to support some scheme of federalism." Wallace is then killed himself. Rex apologized to Alan Milton for having his character renounce pacifism in his actions and also get killed. Rex did not explain why he did this but Milton certainly accepted Rex's apology and saw him as a political ally. In the December 1942 *Spur* it is reported that Alan Milton spoke to the Partisans on "The Individual and the State," claiming that "one must either suffer State regimentation, and thus lose one's individuality, or else govern oneself and live in chaos." The reporter went on to note that "Lord David Cecil and Mr. Milton preferred the latter course of life, but in recent years many millions have welcomed State control in their anxiety to rid themselves of responsibility" (30). Alan Milton was also known for a notice board he set up called "The Pillory," on which he would post particularly dishonest newspaper articles. At that same meeting, one K. R. Forrest attacked the press, claiming that it "was controlled by advertisers and politicians and contained only a little news, since it was almost completely filled by short stories, crossword puzzles and descriptions of football matches, corpses, actresses, test-pilots and the Royal Family" (30). (Has anything changed?) Certainly, *Why Was I Killed?* would conform to Milton's pacifist agenda.

The composition of *Why Was I Killed?* was far from easy, in my view because it attempts a pacifistic approach to war at the same time that the Germans were trying to bomb Rex, his family, and his students, and he was firing anti-aircraft guns back at them. In an undated letter he wrote to Pam, "The book is being a bloody nuisance. I don't know yet whether it's going to come out all right or not, + actually the theme—Why was I killed?—though impressive at first sight, isn't as marvellous as all that. But I hope I'll feel happier about it soon."[73]

XI. AN ANALYSIS OF *WHY WAS I KILLED?*

Given the wartime atmosphere, it is not surprising that the BBC would eventually refuse to produce *Why Was I Killed?* It is also worth asking why Rex, who actively fought the Nazi attacks on London and despised Nazi ideology, would write such a pacifistic book, although he clearly had been concerned with pacifism since his consideration of Huxley's writings in the 1930s. Because the story is presented through the eyes and thoughts of an unnamed, vaguely characterized "unknown soldier" who witnesses almost equally vague representatives of various British classes trying to explain the reasons for the war, it is more abstract than it might otherwise have been. The difficulties of the allegorical method become apparent here: Rex does not name Hitler or the Nazis, so the war under discussion might be, and sometimes seems to be, especially when wire and trenches are mentioned, World War I rather than World War II. And indeed the two wars are intermingled as Rex shows members of a family dying in both. Rex seems to want to show how bad all wars are, and how little they can be justified in the name of patriotism, a higher standard of living, religion, or even a defense against barbarity. Seen from the point of view of a common soldier who is killed in either war, perhaps there is no difference between them. But from any larger perspective, the differences between the Kaiser and Hitler, between World War I economic interests and Nazi ideology, and between an S.S. man and a British soldier seem all too apparent now.

Rex's allegorical characters, such as the anonymous clergyman, Sir Alfred Fothey and Bob Clark, never come to life (although, according to Paul Vaughan, Rex gave Alfred Fothey a habit that he himself had as a teacher—patting the top of his head with his hand). This kind of cartoon-like rendering of character worked in *The Professor* because Rex adopted a Marx Brothers point of view with respect to the professor's cabinet ministers and gave some brilliant speeches to the characters, including Julius Vander's explanation of fascism. In addition, *The Professor*'s grounding in the actual events of the period enabled the reader to draw parallels between the characters and real-life political figures. *The Aerodrome* has more differentiated and rounded characters than any of Rex's other fiction and also contains the Air Vice-Marshal's remarkable dissection of love. In *Why Was I Killed?* the speeches, like the characters, are not memorable. The unnamed priest is given the longest speech in the book, in the last chapter, but it seems no more special than the vague character himself:

> "I am thinking," he said, "of the enormous goodness and beauty and fascination of life, all the sights and sounds and colours, tastes in the mouth, textures of things touched, the warmth and tenderness of love, the delight of the mind's insight and exploration, the sweetness of some moods, a million things which you will readily imagine. And side by side with this I envisage the most elaborate apparatus for destruction, twisted metal, broken bodies, a whole curriculum of slaughter in which men and women are trained from their early youth."[74]

Rex's talent for the rendering of concrete natural detail seems to have evaporated here as elsewhere in the book, perhaps because he conceived it as a film and thought that the writing would be supported visually.

The soldier's conclusion, following on the priest's defense of the beauty of life, is equally vague:

> But now, through the intervention of another, my isolation was ended, and this fact in itself was to me of such importance that it overrode all else. I looked with new zest on the sweeping hillsides and the distant plains before me, heard more delightfully the rippling of the mountain stream, and stared with a fuller joy into the expanding distance which now appeared to me populated and filled not only with what I had seemed to have lost but with what others might really find.[75]

Through the priest and this final statement of the soldier, Rex makes the point that the result of war may be an increased love of life on the part of those lucky enough to remain alive after it. As the priest puts it, people "might come to realize, just through this destruction, the immense value and distinction of life. If they came to do so there would be at least a certain sense in which it would be true to say that so much death was worth while."[76] The soldier, then, died to make the lives of others more positive and pacific in the future. But this statement, clearly intended by Rex to be climactic, is a much less convincing explanation of why the soldier was killed than the reason urged by the refugee character—that the war exists to stop the other regime's barbarity, which makes perfect sense with regard to Hitler.

However muddy Rex is when trying to explain why the soldier was killed, he is very clear about why he then perceived Marxism as an inadequate political and spiritual philosophy, while continuing to show it some respect. Rex takes the side of the skeptical friend in his dialogue with the Communist, Charles, when the friend, adopting Socrates' own method of questioning, tells Charles, "I forgive you your hasty skipping from Socrates to Lenin, apparently without a thought of how these two great men would have disapproved of each other. But it's really there that the trouble lies. There are plenty of fine sentiments; the difficulty is when it comes to applying them to real life. What, for instance, is the precise meaning of 'the finest cause in the world, the liberation of mankind?'"

Moreover, the friend sees that Leninism will produce only a new ruling class that will dominate the working class again. He also sees that it is a religion, but a spiritually unsatisfying one. As the friend states, "It is a monstrous thing to organize your life round one or two principles, particularly so if they are political principles. . . . Honestly there seems to me something uncouth and vulgar in your preoccupation with people's wages and their standard of living. Certainly these things are important, but they are trivial when compared with the real depth and complexity of life."

Like Jinkerman's father, the old religious cobbler in *The Professor*, Rex through the friend stresses that

> When man has done everything most efficiently, most perfectly in accordance with his highest principles, there will still remain death, the slow corruption of the beauty of body and mind, the million vanities, affections and deceits that are in the best of us. Worse than this: there will always be the underlying inscrutability and horror of things. Behind the most enthusiastic shouting in the streets, the most admirable and antiseptic programmes, behind elegant gestures and conversation, behind the lover's kiss, is an awful nothingness, and men will have lost all their wisdom if they fail from time to time to perceive it.[77]

Rex seems to have penetrated here to a deeper layer than Communism addresses, without quite reverting to the religion of his father and mother. This might be seen as an existential criticism of Communism, but the fact that a priest is later given the near-final say (however inadequate) about why the soldier was killed is significant too, for its indication of the possible importance of traditional religion.

Why Was I Killed? shows the extent of Rex's disillusionment with Communism. He now blames it even for the temporary loss of Frances, as the friend predicts Charles's future:

> Meanwhile, perhaps, you will marry, as enthusiastic about this as about everything else. Almost certainly you will take this step when you have insufficient money to support a home. You will think it contemptible to demand standards of comfort which are much higher than the lowest. After a short time your devotion to "the cause" will lead you to neglect your wife, who, in all probability will have no use for "the cause" at all and will seek consolation elsewhere, and probably with some other man.[78]

Yet Rex remains true enough to his old affiliations to allow Charles, who has served in Spain, to defend the Spanish War, legitimately, as the opening battle of World War II:

> It is true that in Spain and in the relations of other countries with Spain you will be able to find examples of every kind of meanness, cowardice, stupidity, savagery and malice. You may regard our defeat as evidence of the uselessness of our actions. But if you look farther you will see more. You will see, for example ... that our defeat was the first action of a war in which, though you refused to intervene, you will very shortly be involved, when you will have to pay extravagantly for your pretence of impartiality.[79]

Rex's book, then, shows (among other things) his own uneasy political position, and perhaps that of other thirties Marxist or semi-Marxist intellectuals like himself, who had difficulty adjusting to the reality that the establishment that they had mocked and attacked was now fighting not an unjustified World War I, but a just war against a clearly wicked enemy, Hitler. It shows that Stalin was not much easier to defend intellectually than were Hitler, Mussolini, or Franco. Communism might be better than fascism, but it, too, had serious drawbacks.

XII. RECEPTION

Why Was I Killed? fared better than might be expected in the middle of a war, but both Rex's message and his style were in doubt for many English readers. The *TLS* opined that Rex had "given little indication in previous novels of a talent for story-telling, his special slant being a turn of vaguely Kafka-like allegory. This he has dressed up in prose of some deliberation but little vitality; all things considered, he has been ill served by the solemn compliments lavished upon his 'prose style.'"[80] The reviewer goes on, with some justice, to find *Why Was I Killed?* "a nerveless and rather wandering piece of intellectual fancy about the causes and consequences of the war, or of one person's participation in the war." While the reviewer praises Rex's expression of "an intelligible enough mood, for which sympathy may fairly be claimed," he concludes that "Over and above that mood, however, is a great deal of random thought or make-believe that is merely trite and wordy" and moreover that "The intention of the book is transparently honest, but the effect of being lectured to in so drably aimless a fashion is sad." Yet by 1945, five impressions had appeared, and ironically the book was apparently approved for distribution to the Allied forces by 1946.[81]

It was published on 17 March 1944 in America under the title *Return of the Traveller* because, according to the *New York Times* for 26 May 1944, it was feared that American readers would think it a mystery story. Rex wrote the Morrises, offering a different explanation for the change of title. He commented that

> "Why was I killed" is doing pretty well. The Times Lit. Sup., as usual, made a bitter attack on me, but the Tribune + some paper in Huddersfield have shown appropriate respect. More important, its going into a hard edition + has been taken for America. There they insist on changing the title as the Americans aren't interested in being killed, but only in how many Japs they can kill themselves. C.J. is very pleased with results so far, + this has all led to my being able to pay the rent + buy one pair of corduroy trousers.

Despite this American interest that was obvious as early as March 1944 when the book was published there, the BBC refused to broadcast it. The BBC's archives at Caversham explain the full story. On 28 December 1943, Walter Rilla asked to see Rex about making a script out of it. The appointment was to be on Saturday morning, 8 January 1944, at Rothwell House, with Val Gielgud. Apparently Gielgud agreed to go forward, because by 6 April Rilla had Rex's script and wanted to discuss it with him. But problems cropped up, because in a letter of 11 June to Walter Rilla, Rex expresses his disappointment concerning the postponement of the broadcast of the drama. The reason for the postponement appears in a memo of 12 June 1944 from James Langham (assistant director of program planning):

> I think this is well written and moving. Ultimately it leads us nowhere except to contemplation. That may well have been the author's intention, but the script made me anticipate some sort of personal solution by him, which the last page fails to give with its "a new world, to be created or discovered." I think it would be worth broadcasting, *but not now*. I am sorry not to be able to feel that aesthetic grounds are sufficient. Surely many people here would be unhappy to hear it for obvious reasons, and I do not regard the point raised recently by D.F.D. that "listening is compulsory" is valid. I can think of it as "Arts Wavelength, 1945" (or sooner).

The otherwise unidentified D. F. D. has written on the bottom of this memo, "I agree entirely. We decided this morning at Prog[rams] Committee to postpone this for the time being. 15/6"[82] So that was that; one can understand the BBC's concern, because Rex's pacifism in the middle of the war against Hitler was not likely to be popular. Even today, it seems strange given the obvious imperative of defeating Hitler and Rex's own feeling against "the Huns."

On 14 September 1944, Rex wrote Rilla from West Woodhay House, near Newbury, that

> for nearly all the holidays I've been down here with an evacuated portion of our school. I'm hoping to get back soon, but imagine will be here till all the V weapons have ceased, + heaven knows when that will be. I thought you might be interested to know that the American Council of Books in Wartime have arranged for a broadcast of "Why was I killed" (in America its called "Return of the Traveller") over the New York radio network. Possibly the B.B.C. might consider this as evidence that the book doesn't necessarily do anyone any harm.—I hope you've been all right during the flying bomb days. We lost a window or two, but otherwise were very lucky.[83]

On 17 January 1945, the controller for the BBC, despite seeing the American script, refused to allow the work to be produced. And apparently it never was.

The BBC and the *TLS* reviewer were not alone in finding fault with *Why Was I Killed?* There was aversion in America as well. In *The Saturday Review* Norman Cousins stated that Rex "came pretty close to being our favorite contemporary novelist . . . ," but that his new novel lacked "the biting urgency that identified 'The Professor' with the immediate moment."[84] Diana Trilling in *The Nation* opined that *Return of the Traveller* "issues in an attitude which, to some, may be personally consoling but which can scarcely be useful, I think either in avoiding future wars or in comprehending this one."[85]

Given the war situation, however, some of the reviews were surprisingly good, including a front page *New York Times Book Review* piece by Irwin Edman on 28 May 1944. The most favorable review came in the *Philadelphia Inquirer* on 4 June 1944, which concluded that "Mr. Warner has handled a tremendous theme with courage, originality and tenderness. It is hardly too much to say that 'The Return of the Traveller' is one of the great books of our times" (Society section, p. 10). The reviewer for the *Providence Journal* (28 May 1944, sect. 6, p. 6) found that "Its objectivity in the midst of the present war is remarkable. It is, I think, the first postwar novel of World War II."

That comment perhaps explains the favorable and unfavorable reviews—the favorable reviewers found it to be "above" the war, and concerned with healing; those who disliked the book found it strangely neutral in view of the Nazis' nastiness. Today, the reader is likely to agree with the latter party that Rex's neutrality would be admirable if World War II had resembled other wars, but since it did not, Rex has missed the mark. The kind of generalized pacifism that he championed might have been more appropriate for questionable wars, such as World War I, but not for the war against the Nazis. *The Professor*'s desperate mood seems far more admirable to me. But it must be remembered that Rex had not seen the concentration camps when he wrote *Why Was I Killed*, and that the Jewish refugee children with whom he had worked at Frensham Heights had escaped Germany before it was too late, and could not tell of the full horror of the Holocaust.

XIII. WHY DID REX WRITE THIS BOOK?

Since Rex had previously given no indication of anything but full support for World War II, this book remains a surprising one. The manuscript at Michigan State offers no clues to its origins in Rex's mind. The manuscript suggests a rearrangement of some of the scenes for the final version, but no new material and nothing to suggest the germination and development of Rex's thinking appears.

Moreover, other manuscripts and letters from the later war period offer evidence that Rex knew very well why the war was being fought, and that he could have answered the question of why the soldier was killed very eloquently had he wished to do so. Michigan State's MS 55, which contains Rex's essay "On the Freedom of Expression," also has a ten-page (8-inch x 14-inch) outline and text for what is apparently a film script praising plans for postwar reconstruction efforts by the United States, Britain, and Russia through AMGOT, or the Allied Military Government of Occupied Territory. Here, at the top of the first page, Rex writes, "What are we fighting for?" and then indicates that he will give answers for Stalin, for Churchill, for Roosevelt, and for the Atlantic Charter. This was written in late 1943, by which time *Why Was I Killed?* was already published.[86]

Although the Atlantic Charter film script is propaganda to order, it shows that Rex could be an eloquent advocate of the Allies' war aims. On page seven of the Atlantic Charter script, Rex wrote that "Fascism puts the clock back to medieval barbarism. Hitler has set man against man, nation against nation; he has abolished the established liberties of life, the freedom to speak, the freedom to think. He has destroyed food, industry, the means of production. He has brought back slavery to Europe. He has made a wilderness + called it a fortress." Rex concludes with a statement reminiscent of the priest's idea in *Why Was I Killed?* that men are dying in World War II for a better life in the future, but Rex is more definite about the value of freedom here: "The Nations are united in War. But their men are dying for the unity + collaboration in peace to which their leaders have pledged them, + you + all of us. Man was born free. Man is capable of breaking his chains." All told, Rex gives the impression that he has a very clear idea about why the war is being fought. So what about the questioning of the war in *Why Was I Killed?* Which is the true Rex?

Perhaps both. Rex's letters show that a struggle between pessimism and optimism was being waged in his mind. On 1 February, probably 1942, he wrote Pam Morris that

> All that you say about the degeneracy of England + the world + the futility of kindness is quite true + we're suffering for it now. Yet one has to accept, at least outwardly, as much as one possibly can, since it merely weakens one to kick against brick walls. Also there is an infinite amount of good about, tortured, twisted, misguided + helpless though it often is. Its worth remembering that peoples natures have changed very little since the beginning of things. Their virtues + vices have just taken different shapes under different forms of ambition + oppression. Its still true that one can only be free in one's own mind + recent attempts to impose freedom on others rather fortify this view.[87]

In *Why Was I Killed?*, Rex would attempt to express this feeling of the universal nature of mankind, including of course the Germans. In another letter around the same time, however, on 24 February, he wrote about the distress caused by the "Huns"—a word he always used freely in his letters. I feel that in this novel, Rex was trying very hard, probably with his Christian upbringing as a motivating force, to turn the other cheek and to look beyond the present to a postwar reconciliation, which would include the Germans as well. But the idealism of the novel's conclusion outruns Rex's own war-filled feelings and even his own logic as expressed in his Atlantic Charter film script, and *Why Was I Killed?* remains unconvincing.

XIV. TRANSLATION

During his time in Raynes Park, Rex's drive to write novels began to evaporate and essays and translations started to predominate. At first, he saw this type of writing only as a profitable way to spend his time between inspirations. In reality, however, Rex's essays and translations were a sign of his true personality asserting itself after the diversions of Marxism and war. The style of *The Wild Goose Chase* showed that his commitment to classical learning and tradition was as strong as his commitment to revolution; in *The Professor*, the humanistic professor of classics ultimately triumphs in the affections of the reader over the Marxist son as well as over the fascists, and a prominent position is accorded a Christian pacifist; *The Aerodrome*'s satire is directed equally against all totalitarian systems, including Communism; and in *Why Was I Killed?* the pacifist, conciliatory line of Aldous Huxley and old Jinkerman (the pacifist in *The Professor*) surprisingly overwhelms all other perspectives. Now Rex took a great delight in returning to his real self—moderate, non-ideological, humanistic, and traditional—and working his way out of the political commitments that had been forced on him by the Depression and the war.

The move from political novels to translations began innocently enough. Charles Wrinch, his headmaster after John Garrett, remembered this:

> In those days he was very well-known as a novelist. His poems had appeared in anthologies. . . . But I scented his great possibilities as a translator. Finding him reading the *Medea* with his very small group of pupils I suggested that he should translate it for performance at the school. To my amazement he took to the task immediately, and we assembled a remarkable cast to perform it, consisting of boys, masters, parents and, as Medea, a very talented friend of some parents. . . . The School Hall was, of course, blacked out for the performance,

but a violent storm of thunder and lightning at the climax of Medea's giant speech was more effective than any artificial effect and totally unforgettable.[88]

The production of *Medea* took place at 7:30 P.M. on 30 and 31 July 1943. The program notes state that "In the event of an Air-Raid an announcement will be made. Shelters are available." Medea was played by actress Vera Lewington, who was also the first female guest of the Partisans. The review in *The Spur* for December 1943 (p. 15) states that "The 'Medea' of Miss Lewington was both majestic and moving—a very subtle blend of emotions. Her timing and control of movement were professional in the highest sense."

This was the first time that Rex's translation,[89] which was to be published in August 1944 by John Lane the Bodley Head, was heard. *The Spur* reviewer, one U.B., stated that "To write of Mr. Warner's translation last is merely to recognise that it was the foundation-stone of the whole brilliant performance, of which the Chorus was also an integral part. The humanity and delicate violence of his verse could not have given greater pleasure."[90] Rex himself was quite pleased with it.[91]

Yet reviewing Rex's translation on 17 July 1955 in *The New York Times*, the noted American Greek and Latin scholar Moses Hadas found it "less satisfactory" than Richmond Lattimore's work because "fidelity to lexicon and grammar sometimes results in prosiness which is quaint or puerile, made more awkward rather than illuminated by undistinguished verse. In Medea's passionate speeches in particular the dampening of the fire is regrettable." This was Rex's first attempt, and he may have erred on the side of timidity by following the original text very closely. But he always preferred this translation to all his others, except for his Thucydides, and he was avoiding the faults of the Gilbert Murray translations, which often bear no resemblance to the originals.

XV. OTHER PUBLICATIONS

The second half of 1943 was good for Rex in terms of publication. In June a second edition of *The Kite* appeared through Basil Blackwell. His sonnet, "How sweet only to delight," was published in a collection about love edited by Walter de la Mare in September. *Why Was I Killed?* followed on 15 October. Rex wrote Greenwood around that time stating half-jokingly that "having taken a certain amount of trouble in writing a book which is making untold millions for the firm which you represent, I am both pained + surprised that I appear to be about the last person in England to receive a copy of that book?" He added, "I should think that now you might enjoy a well earned holiday if you were to suspend all further publications from the Bodley Head + use the paper thus saved in printing gigantic editions, in various languages, of 'Why was I killed?.'"[92]

In November Rex's essay, "The Uses of Allegory," appeared in *Penguin New Writing*.[93] It is a retrospective defense of his novelistic method, which he had further developed since he began speaking on the subject after the publication of *The Wild Goose Chase*. His main point is that "allegory," broadly conceived, offers an exciting alternative to literary realism, and he cites Bunyan, Swift and, following Edmund Wilson in *The Wound and the Bow*, Dickens as well as Melville, Dostoyevsky, and Kafka as prime practitioners of allegory. In the course of this essay, Rex justifies his own use of a formal, relatively artificial prose style, citing Swift as an example: "A more than ordinary precision of detail and assurance in the reality of what is invented is required, so that fantastic figures like Apollyon or a virtuous horse can be made to appear as 'forms more real than living man.'"[94] He praises, in Dickens and Dostoyevsky, the use of caricature, which he also employs in his own novels. We see where Rex, at least in his own thinking, was coming from as a writer: he combined the matter-of-fact assurance of Swift's balanced style with a taste for Dickensian caricature. Rex's defense of the method is that it is appropriate for those times when a writer is "acutely conscious both of the grandeur and of the insecurity of" the social environment. Moreover, "its aims must be what they have been in the past . . . to throw a bright light on some definitely held but generally unrecognised belief or to extend the use of language so as to uncover or partially reveal aspects of reality which elude, from their very complexity, the ordinary methods of the reporter or the social worker."[95]

Early in the fall, Rex opened the first meeting of the Partisans with a talk on Dickens. The *Spur* reported that "despite a brilliant defence of this author it seemed that the only Dickensians in our midst, were Mr. Warner himself and the Headmaster, who was our guest at this meeting."[96] This "brilliant defense" became Rex's fine essay on Dickens, which was later to be published in *The Cult of Power*. When he sent a copy of it to John Lehmann on 29 January 1944, however, he remarked that "it seems very limited in scope and rather long-winded."[97] Rex begins by finding that "today [Dickens] is not even vigorously attacked but for the most part left unread, elevated on the high shelves marked 'classical' in libraries."[98] Rex defends Dickens on the basis that he created more memorable characters than anyone except Shakespeare, and for his exuberance. Rex comments that Dickens's invention of a whole world is rare today because "today a writer is expected to describe rather than to create a world."[99] He also feels it necessary to defend Dickens against the charge of "Victorianism."

Rex sees little in need of defense, however, either in the period or the author. Authors in Queen Victoria's period "were exceptionally fortunate, since this was the last period in English history during which an author was considered of any account whatsoever."[100] Here we see Rex's consciousness of what we have come to know all too well: the decline in the importance of reading in the face of television, radio, and film. Rex's discussion of the importance to a writer of an audience as well as respect is particularly poignant, given the fact that he was at this time perhaps at the height of his career in terms of recognition:

> And not only does an author like to be regarded as a fairly valuable object, but it is actually good for him when he knows that in the eyes of society he is a person of some weight. He will be in much closer touch with his audience when there is a feeling of mutual respect between him and his readers. Under these conditions he will be tempted neither 'to give the public what it wants' nor to retire in disgust from what he may regard as a world of philistines and hypocrites. Instead he will readily fulfill the functions of a public servant: his work will become a part of history, contributing to and reflecting the changes and the development of life around him. And so long as he is in touch with readers rather than reviewers there will be less danger of his work becoming standardised.[101]

He goes on to point out Dickens's assault on Victorian foibles, and to note, following the Marxist T. A. Jackson, that Dickens was even a radical critic of Victorian society. The fact that Dickens was nonetheless a best-selling author says much for his audience; Rex asks, who now would spend money for social criticism? He admits one fault in Dickens: "Few of us today, unless we are suffering from a severe cold and are fortified by the additional advantages of whiskey and aspirins, can weep as we should over the misfortunes of Little Nell or the protracted death of young Paul Dombey."[102] But Rex defends Dickens against E. M. Forster's statement that Dickens ought to be bad because he uses flat characters:

> These terms "flat" and "round" are misleading if we assume, as Mr. Forster seems to do, that a "round" character is in some way "better" than a "flat" character. It is an odd assumption. No one would maintain that a piece of sculpture is necessarily "better" than a painting. But the modern novel, like everything else, has been profoundly influenced by modern science, and perhaps it is felt to be more scientific to create characters which, because of their psychological complexity and because they can be viewed from many different directions, are assumed to be rounded. This is a fallacy, since it is the effect of the work as a whole that matters, and a thorough-going psycho-analysis may or may not add to this effect.[103]

Rex's lifelong dislike of science and psychoanalysis as opposed to straightforward British "common sense" and Greek intellect is apparent; as is his own feeling of neglect. After all of the considerable fame that he had achieved in intellectual circles, he was still working as a schoolteacher and making very little money, and his books never tapped into popular taste. On 9 September 1943, he wrote Pam Morris about the Dickens essay, admitting, "I don't know enough about Dickens. I don't know enough about anything. But my essay is very dull + pointless. What is really interesting is his great affection for crime + violence, + this I'm not attempting to explain." He asked for Kitty's address, so he could send her a copy of *Why Was I Killed?* Finally, he referred to his own contempt for the Victorian ideal of the "Great Man": "I'm sorry for the Italians, + wish there'd been a real massacre of fascists when Mussolini went. One becomes less + less humane to the power-addicts + wants them wiped from the face of the earth. One thing we have which is good is our distrust of 'the great man.'"[104]

On 3 October he reported to Pam that "I'm getting into a mess with my essays. Having finished one on Dickens I really don't want to write more + yet I have only 30,000 words. I suppose I shall force myself into some piece of sententiousness for the sake of the prize."[105]

Life under siege wore on, but was relieved by the wedding of Barbara Morris and Tony Knowland at St. Martin's in the Field Church on 29 December 1943. In a letter of 5 January [1944], Rex reported that "I've had some sort of an interview with the film boys nearly every day this week + I don't really think I ought to go away for a night just now. We had a terrific cannonade last night + it's only natural for Frances to be rather nervous. I certainly am, as one feels sure that the damned Huns will have a final bloody attack on London one of these days."[106] On 26 March he wrote to John Morris, stating that he had a commission for a book on the public schools and giving "an idea of life in the centre of English civilisation":

Friday: taught all day: on guns at night having cracks at the Hun till 2.30. *Saturday* 2.30-4.30 A.M. sleep. 4.30-5.30 unpacking ammunition. 5.30 breakfast. Mid-day: lunch with a very charming lady + her husband, a Mr. Greenwood. *Evening*: visit from the Marshalls. Sunday 8.15 A.M. Home Guard call-out. Whole morning spent crawling around streets in full battle dress, hoping to be captured, but failing to find enemy. 2.30-7.30 (continuous) Reports. And so it goes on Thank god this is the last week of term.[107]

On 14 February 1944, he signed a contract for *The Cult of Power* with John Lane.[108] On 12 June 1944, he wrote to Lehmann that he had been "trying to earn an honest penny by writing a book about the public schools. I'll be glad when it's over."[109]

XVI. EVACUATION

According to the *Spur*, during the summer of 1944 it became necessary to move the school into the country because of the threat of flying bombs. After 15 June, it seemed as if the early Blitz days had returned, with long stays in the school's shelter. But it was more dangerous than that, and every day children were sent out of the city, although the University of London ordained that the usual Higher and General School Examinations had to be held at the regular time, leaving many candidates to take them in shelters. On a "Special Difficulties Form" for one of the exams at Raynes Park, it was noted that an exam began at 9:30 A.M. and that at 9:45 a bomb "passed overhead and exploded within close earshot." Lunch was eaten outside between alerts.

On 28 June, with the support of the parents, the headmaster decided that since the attacks seemed to be continuing, there would be an evacuation of the school. One group went to Meldreth, near Cambridge, one to Inkpen, and another to Salisbury. Rex went to Inkpen and from there, with the camp, to West Woodhay House nearby. Frances, Jonathan, Anna, and George accompanied him there. Many students and teachers loved the experience of being together in the country, free of parents. On Friday, 30 June, the first children moved to Inkpen. The writer for the *Spur* reports that "Long adventurous hikes were taken during weekends, little tents arose like mushrooms, beds were dragged out under the shelter of the great oaks and elms, even into open fields until the ceremony of saying goodnight took a half-an-hour and entailed a lengthy walk on the part of the duty master; shirts were shed and faces and bodies became brown."[110] Then West Woodhay House was discovered, "and the project of living in a colossal house of strangely mixed architecture, surrounded by impressively large and once well-kept lawns and gardens" seemed possible, since the house had been requisitioned by the War Office.

On Friday, 14 July [1944], Rex wrote Greenwood that he had just heard that he'd have to take a group of children to a country house. He would try to stay at Rowledge until the coming Wednesday, so he could finish the public schools book. He was very pleased with the new, Uniform edition of *The Wild Goose Chase* and *The Professor*. (*Why Was I Killed?* also appeared in the Uniform edition, but only in 1946.) This handsome edition, which never included more than these books, testifies to Rex's intellectual stature at the time, although his actual living conditions never seemed to improve commensurately.

Woodhay was reached by taking the line from Reading to Hungerford, getting off at Kintbury, and then taking a taxi. West Woodhay House had about a hundred rooms, a secret stairway, and also, it was rumored, a ghost. It looked out past large lime trees to a lake, and had a ruined church and churchyard and weedy flower beds. Slowly the school's staff brought the old, neglected building and grounds to new life. There were 80 boys at Woodhay at any one time. The day's routine, according to the *Spur*'s writer, would be "school work in the morning, though the work done differed considerably from the timetable at Raynes Park. For example, there was a survey of the large estate made by boys under the direction of Mr. Gibb. And a great number of boys who had known little of the country received before they left certificates from Mr. Warner to the effect that they were able to identify at least fifty different kinds of trees."[111] Rex was passing on the knowledge and method of his outdoorsman uncle George. "In the afternoons there was gardening (paid and unpaid), visits to Newbury, Hungerford or Kintbury, bathes in the lake, walking and, in the later weeks, a lot of wood cutting. In the evenings, too, activities were varied"[112] and included games of charades and moonlight singing.

Obviously, this kind of camping had its pains as well as its pleasures for the masters and staff. Rex wrote Pam Morris from West Woodhay House, during the summer of 1944, that "this place . . . isn't bad except for one terrible thing. . . . The pubs are only open 3 days a week. So you can imagine the hardships to be undergone. Otherwise, there's lovely country + reasonable comfort on camp beds in this enormous house. I may manage just to get a week of it + then promise to come back later. . . . I hope I'll come out of this waste land soon." He wrote later that he was "going film acting on Friday to Uxbridge," probably for some more war documentaries.

In a letter to Greenwood after he first arrived at West Woodhay, he wrote, "I actually am sorting out some poems, having added a bit to the pub. school thing., + hope I'll be able to get down to an essay or two."[113] But there was almost no beer in the pub, and Rex in an undated letter from around this time therefore wondered "what we're fighting for."[114]

The *Medea* was published in August, while the Uniform Edition of Rex's works was also being published by John Lane the Bodley Head that same summer. *Return of the Traveller* came out on 17 March 1944 in Philadelphia through Lippincott, while *Why Was I Killed?* went into two Lane reprints during the year. Still, life was far from easy from Rex's perspective. Again and again his writing had failed to pay off in any substantial way. Yet he kept working doggedly.

On Wednesday, 2 August 1944, he wrote Greenwood from West Woodhay that he had had a strenuous weekend with the "film chaps" because "they literally work from 9.0 A.M. to 12.0 midnight,—even over the mid-day beer + sandwiches. One day I was rushed to the M.O.I. [Ministry of Information] + back again, + had hoped to call in on you, but it couldn't be managed." He asks if Greenwood could get the public school book typescript sent to West Woodhay.

A month later, he wrote to Greenwood that he had just done two-and-a-half days of hard work. He noted that "The film chaps are coming down here for a bit next week to take me in my natural surroundings. The whole family is here, though Jonathan is going off tomorrow in the chemistry master's party to Stratford to see a few plays. I am left in command here + shall give the boys a few days holiday." Rex complained that "no one knows what the future of this establishment will be, + they've started the appalling habit of playing bridge in the evenings. Also its raining. I'd rather be at your club." George "spends most of his time looking at a bull here + then making extraordinary noises which he describes as 'the song of the bull.'" On the same day, he sent C. J. a newspaper clipping that included *The Aerodrome* on a list of books banned by the Eire Censorship Board in Dublin. He was in good company, since there were books by Gilbert Frankau and Upton Sinclair also on the list. According to Gerald Boland, the minister of justice in the de Valera government, all of the books on the list were "indecent in their general tendency." Rex's response was bemusement. He mock-seriously asked Greenwood, "Cannot a publisher protect his author from the foul breath of slander?" and recounts that someone at Pinewood Studios gave the article to him, "suggesting that the pure air of the film industry was a more fitting atmosphere for my talents than the filthy indecent tendencies of the world of books." On 5 September, he wrote C. J. from West Woodhay suggesting lunch on Saturday the 9th at 12:30 at Long's, because he had to come to London to see a filmmaker. On 25 September, Rex informed C. J. that John Amis of the Philharmonic Arts Club had suggested a reading of Rex's *Medea* at his club; Rex replied that it was "okay by me," using an American Yiddishism no doubt picked up via his film associates. He was waiting for reviews of *Medea*, which had just come out in August, and was particularly interested in Bowra's *New Statesman* response and in the *TLS*, asking if it had "done its dirt yet."

XVII. REX LOOKS FOR A DIRECTION

Back from West Woodhay soon after this, Rex wrote Pam, "I don't know how long we've been back here, but it seems a long time. The evacuation camps have closed down. May it be for the best. Anyway its good not to be in the Home Guard, although some swine are beginning to say that the A.A. guns are insufficiently manned." He goes on to mention the difficulties of caring for Anna in an unsympathetic climate

She had one bad fit while at West Woodhay + we, rather unwisely, mentioned this to the headmistress of her school. She now refuses to have Anna back there, + its very hard to decide what to do. Frances took Anna to Dr. Adams last week, + she gave us a little information about some boarding schools, promising more information. . . . Anna herself has been perfectly well for the last six weeks + is very disappointed at not being able to go to school.

Besides these personal problems, the war was very wearying.

Altogether things are rather gloomy. One had hoped that the war would be over by now. As it is we still get nightly alerts + had one bomb skimming our roof the other night,— though of course its really infinitely better than it was. Frances hasn't been too well. . . . I have to do lots of Rugger + have a heavier time table than usual. However I've proposed to do half the work for half the pay (a 3 day week) for next term, + old Wrinch seems to think he can arrange it. That would be marvellous. George wakes regularly at 5.30 A.M. + leaps into our bed, shouting "I haven't wet my bed" + singing "Loch Lomond."[115]

On 7 January 1945, Rex wrote Walter Rilla that Donald Taylor, a sometime collaborator of Paul Rotha, had mentioned that there was a chance of *Why Was I Killed?* being filmed. On 10 January Rilla wrote him that "I am still working on a film synopsis of the book which, when ready, I shall give to Del Giudice of Two Cities and I should like to know whether your Mr. Taylor and his plans would mean a wash-out of my own?"[116] Despite the popularity of the book, nothing ever came of the film plans.

At the age of almost forty, Rex was now perhaps at the height of his reputation, but with his most important novels and poetry behind him, he was beyond his most creative period (although he would continue to produce distinguished translations, important reviews, and significant historical novels for another thirty years). Some sign of an incipient slowdown appears in a letter of 9 January 1945 from Grand Drive to John Lehmann:

I'm afraid that to your usual request I must make my usual reply,—I have no imaginative prose. I'm hoping against hope that soon I'll be able either to leave the school altogether or else get a half-time job. Then the imaginative prose will flow. At the moment,—very fed up with everything—I've become purely escapist, + am doing a translation of Xenophon's Anabasis. Its a sort of higher form of crossword, + good for the times, innocent, if not very lucrative.—As soon as I do anything worth while I'll let you know.[117]

To what were obviously repeated requests from Lehmann, he wrote on 25 May that ". . . once I've finished my Xenophon (not long now) I hope I'll have something to submit to you." But 1945 shows very little new work: *The Professor* was republished in January by Penguin, in a third edition; he wrote a review of a book by Montagu Slater; *Poems and Contradictions*, which includes the 1937 poems plus the "Contradictions" written at the time of his split-up with Frances, was published; and there appeared a fourth edition of *Why Was I Killed?*

English Public Schools, which appeared through Collins in June 1945, and on which Rex had been working the previous summer, is forty-seven pages long and includes eight color plates and thirty black-and-white illustrations. In the essay Rex (much to his own surprise) found kind words to say about the boarding school system, even though he doubted the value of his own experience. Like many of Rex's essays, it was done basically for money.

Clearly, although he would have many years of writing left, Rex's fictional inspiration had begun to wane. The strain of war, teaching, and family had taken its toll, but most significant perhaps was that the allegorical idea had more or less run its course, as had the conditions of protest that had inspired his best writing. How could one oppose an England opposed to Hitler, or support a Stalin? Political turbulence and war had stimulated his creative faculties, but they had also exhausted him, to some degree permanently. With translation, Rex could retreat into the politics of the past. It was also a return to his true self—to his education, to tradition, and his parents' relative conservatism. And it would eventually cast him in a new role—defender of poetry and the classics in a postwar society that seemed to have little interest in these things.

There is still vigor in Rex's letters of the first half of 1945, and *The Spur* shows him active in school affairs: he received praise for organizing a Christmas carol concert in December 1944, he read his poems to the Sixth Form Society early in the summer of 1945, and was present during a Partisan discussion of the question of how to deal with Germany after the war. This was to be an important question for him, for Rex was soon to be an eyewitness to a bombed-out Germany.

XVIII. A FAREWELL TO IDEOLOGY, RAYNES PARK, AND WAR

Rex gave a broadcast in the BBC Home Service on the evening of 7 May, Victory in Europe Day—the day Germany surrendered. Rex's defense of poetry in "What's the Point of Poetry?" was very relevant to the end of the war. He pointed out that "Intolerance of the arts (or an affected superiority to their appeal) is always stupid and has been one of the characteristics of fascism"[118] and that "Poets don't make good fascists." The reason was that "fascism, with its restricting and mechanical creed, denies just that world of private and individual experience from which poetry creates work that is universal. It's no accident that ideas of liberty and freedom and the images that belong to them occur so often in poetry."[119] Toward the end of his talk, he moved to defend modern poets against the charge of being *too* political: "If this is really true, it shows the difficulties of the present time. Poets who really are 'too political' are attempting, though perhaps too crudely, to re-establish the necessary relation between the poet and the society. Poets who really write 'only for themselves' have despaired of this necessary relationship and have turned back to their art as something more satisfactory than a world where poetry is not valued."[120]

Rex did not attempt to explain, as he might have in the thirties, why Marxist poetry is better than fascist poetry. By speaking of the lack of subtlety of political poetry in general he seems to retreat from his earlier espousal of such poetry. He emerges in this piece as a defender of humanism against technological thinking. But even he must have doubted that he could convince the audience to value poetry as much as it might have done in the Victorian period. So perhaps in the end, the most important thing about Rex's talk is what he tells us about himself: "I myself was fortunate in having parents who not only read poetry to me as a child and encouraged me to read it, but also showed a respect for poetry themselves. . . . I personally never really enjoyed Milton until I was about thirty, though I read and enjoyed the whole of *The Fairie Queene* when I was fifteen."[121]

Although the talk appears to have gone smoothly, in a letter dated "V.E. + 2" or 9 May 1945, to Pam, Rex wrote,

> Altogether the celebrations have been heavy work. I had a nerve wracking time at the B.B.C., never knowing from one moment to the other whether it was I or Churchill who was going to address the nation. Next day our house filled up rapidly. . . . As happens on every day of National rejoicing in this country, the pubs were full of teetotallers swilling down the beer that ought to have been reserved for their betters. It was democracy run wild + one of our two pubs was soon closed. Yesterday I called on the Marshalls + found Ken surrounded with bottles + loot. Today I'm a bit weak.

On a more sober note, Rex continued, "Really, of course, the relief of having this awful business over is enormous. Even now one wouldn't be at all surprised to hear sirens + can hardly get used to the idea of being able to sleep without bothering. Its too early to know what one's felt all the time."[122] Like everyone else in England, he was awakening from the hellish dream of war and finding himself numbed by the experience.

A memo in the BBC Written Archives dated 21 June 1945 says, "Rex expecting to leave for Germany early next week + will be there for at least 3 weeks."[123] Owing to the recommendation of Basil Wright, who wanted to work with him, Rex went on this trip with war correspondent status in order to write a documentary film—never made—on displaced persons. The first entry in Rex's diary of the trip,[124] entitled "Germany 1945," is dated 3 July and the last is 3 August; the diary also includes a proposed film treatment. This trip would bring Rex 4,000 miles in two weeks but an even longer way spiritually: although the trip allowed him some indulgence in good food and drink after the constrictions of wartime London, he would never forget the horrors that he saw.

The first thing that struck Rex, even after the Blitz, was the extent of the destruction in the German cities. At Aachen, where he crossed the border from Belgium to Germany on 4 July, he commented, "worst piece of destruction I've ever seen. Hardly a house standing in Julich either." Soon after they arrived in Dortmund, Rex commented that it was a "city of the dead. . . . Not a single house undamaged in town centre, + nearly all uninhabitable. Strange silence of desolation." Rex was reading Jane Austen's *Sense and Sensibility* during the trip, but its orderliness and civility gave him a "rather odd feeling" by contrast with the destruction he was seeing. With a British correspondent, he talked about Somerset Maugham and T. S. Eliot; certainly Eliot's "Waste Land," with its scenes of a ruined Western civilization, was very much on his mind.

The next horrors that struck Rex so forcefully were the concentration camps and their victims. At Belsen on 8 July, Rex saw a Red Cross train setting off to Sweden with 500 survivors: "Men + women with arms like sticks." He met an old Belgian camp survivor of 60 "with a number tattood on her arm" who had been "arrested by the Gestapo for having a resistance man in the house"; she was "a skeleton with lots of fire still there." A Belgian prisoner of war who had survived a forced march on which the Germans would "'reduce numbers' by fifty shootings a day," told Rex that it had all been a "mauvaise reve" [bad dream]. That night, Rex went to bed at 12, but was not able to get to sleep until 3 A.M., undoubtedly because of what he had seen. During a visit to the camp on 9 July, a Jewish woman from Salonika told him about the gas chambers. On 25 July Rex visited the prisons for the Nazis with a British officer who had once been in charge of a prison on the island of Jersey. He noted that at Altona he "saw political prisoners + war criminals. Strange old woman with cap on back of head, who had been dentist's assistant at concentration camp. Good looking tall sadistic girl. All marching round in circle, wearing wooden shoes,—ex-leaders of Germany." Rex's shock, sarcasm, and disgust are apparent behind his terse comments.

He made these feelings explicit in his letters to Pam and John Morris. On 16 July he wrote, "Atrocity stories have not been exaggerated at all + one sees some terrible things."[125] On 30 July he commented to them that "The chaos and destruction is beyond description,—really horrifying. Nothing however is so horrifying as the concentration camp cases. Among the ruins of towns you still see, surprisingly enough, smiling faces; but the people who have been ruined in the camps must run into millions. Really no propaganda could exaggerate it."[126] Rex never forgot what he saw on this trip, and referred to it often in later years. He mentioned once to me that a British officer who had seen the documentary films from the camps thought that they must have been staged because they were too horrible to be true, but Rex knew they were not, because he had seen it all.

Perhaps the most striking symbolism Rex saw during the whole trip was a pile of 6,000 church bells from Germany, Holland, and Belgium put in a dump near the Elbe River. They probably would have been melted down by the Nazis to be made into cannons. Here was a concrete sign of the depravity of Nazism, as well as of the failure of Christianity to stop it. These bells would reappear in Rex's next novel, *Men of Stones* (1949).

While on the trip itself, Rex wrote the script for a film about Displaced Persons camps. By 17 July he had finished the rough draft, and by 19 July had completed the rewrite. His trip diary includes very complete notes for the film treatment. Rex wrote there that the film would have three aims: "(i) To show the extent of the problem with which MG1 [Military Government] is faced. (ii) To show MG dealing with some of the most important aspects of the problem. (iii) To indicate that MG is still fighting a war to end war, that on its success depends the possibility of peace in Europe." Rex continues:

> 1. The method proposed is to begin the film with a commentary with appropriate visuals designed to show the state of utter chaos, material + physical with which MG was called upon to deal. 2. The main body of this film will consist of commentary delivered by men who are actually concerned with the government of Germany. Between them they will cover (in general terms) food + shelter, administration, law + order, de-nazification, trade + industry—3. In conclusion will come the reflections of a British officer. His point will be that this work is worth doing well, as it is the essential safe-guard for his own children + for the children of his comrades-in-arms.

Rex's conclusion gives a glimpse into Allied thinking about Germany right after the war: he has a British colonel say that "in the end the Germans have got to govern themselves. Otherwise we shall have to occupy the country for ever." Rex continues, "for them to be able to do this they will have to replace the ideals of Naziism by something else" and Rex revised this to read "If they are to become members of a new Europe, they will have to replace the ideals of Naziism by something else." So already it was hoped that a "new Europe" would come into being, and that the Germans, however culpable, would be part of it. (In the conclusion of *Why Was I Killed?* Rex, albeit much more vaguely, had perhaps hinted of something of this sort.) Rex, no longer a "socialist propagandist," as he had sometimes seen himself during the 1930s, had become a propagandist for a democratic, liberal Europe run perhaps on British Labor Party socialist principles. In July Churchill, running as the Conservative candidate, lost re-election despite his magnificent wartime record, and Rex wrote Pam overconfidently on 30 July that "The election has surprised everyone here. If only the Labour chaps do a reasonably good job, I should think there'll never be a Conservative government again."[127]

Rex stayed with Greenwood in London the first night he returned from the trip on 7 August. Upon his return to Wimbledon, Rex found a letter offering him the position of director of the British Institute in Athens. From all indications, his two years in Athens were the happiest of his life. He had earned them.

CHAPTER SEVEN

ATHENS, 1945-1947

I. REX ARRIVES IN A TROUBLED GREECE

Despite an extremely unstable political and economic situation in Greece, Rex experienced there what he would later regard as perhaps the best two years of his life. After the rigors of the war years in London and the unpleasant experience of Germany, he enjoyed relative prosperity as head of the British Institute. He met and was also in a position to host the best British and Greek writers and artists, and was himself lionized. And he was in the center of classical culture.

At first it seemed as if Rex would go to Greece for three or four months, from about November 1945 to February 1946, and he was happy with the idea because it would not place too much of a strain on Frances. Moreover, the political situation in Greece was not without danger, and the country was suffering severely. But the British Council apparently suggested a longer stay, which he accepted.

As Rex recounted the situation in his *Views of Attica and its Surroundings* (1950), one of his finest books,

> The offer was a surprise to me. I had been teaching at a school in London and had no particular desire to go abroad; nor had I ever contemplated the voyage to Greece, being, like most schoolmasters, so badly paid that it would be inconceivable ever to be able to afford the fare there; nor did it seem to me that I was qualified for the post. I had indeed

once translated a play of Euripides into English and had long loved ancient Greek literature; but I was ignorant of the modern language and, moreover, knew nothing of the work of the British Council. Thus it was curiosity rather than ambition which made me reply equivocally to the official who had offered me the post and decide to seek an interview with him.

Rex's remembrance of this interview is very amusing: "When I admitted that I had never had any particular wish to go to Athens, my interlocutor, who had just returned from Greece, looked at me sadly (as indeed he was well justified in doing) as though I had expressed (as indeed I had) a disreputable opinion. He informed me, correctly, that it was impossible not to love the country and the people." Rex declined the kind offer of a preliminary trip because that would be to look too "closely in the mouth of such a gift horse." Rather, "I began to think of the sun, of photographs of the Parthenon, of a life which would at any rate be different from the life of London whether in war or peace. I therefore accepted the post at once. . . ."[1]

Rex's reasons for going to Greece for a year are laid out more precisely in a letter of 29 August 1945 to Pam Morris:

> I think actually there are several advantages. (i) It will be an interesting experience (ii) there will be plenty of money, so that I ought to be able to save some with which to organise a real + final settling down afterwards. (iii) if one can get a governess it will be the best thing for Anna + also save Frances a lot of nervous wear + tear. (iv) one gets from May till September free. (v) I'm only signing on for one year with the option of two.[2]

There were lots of preparations for the journey, which the British Institute wanted to begin on 15 September. Rex held out for 20 September. He had a film dinner on the night of 11 September, and felt he might have to deal with the issues arising there for a few more days. Also, he had completed a translation of Xenophon's *Anabasis* by early September but had not yet got it typed, and he was waiting for approval of the book contract, not knowing that it would not be signed until a year from then. In mid-September Rex wrote to Pam that 9 October looked like the actual departure date, "though one never knows." Rex needed many injections, and had many appointments in London with the British Council. As late as 4 October, he wrote Pam that he was ready to agree to go to Greece only if they "guarantee getting Frances out + back again in the Spring." If they did allow Frances a passage in March and April, Rex hoped that Pam and John could take George for some of the time. Jonathan would remain in school and Anna would be in a convent school on Jersey. Rex wrote that "Everything's very confusing, but at least I shall either get my way or not go to Greece at all. This would be rather amusing, as I've spent a fortune in farewell parties."[3] Apparently, Rex left soon after he wrote this letter.

The situation in Greece at this time was quite complex and unpleasant. The United Nations Special Committee on the Balkans begins its report as follows:

> The decade of 1940-49 was a continuous horror for the Greeks. With the end of World War II in 1945, when the rest of Europe was licking its wounds and beginning its rehabilitation, Greece entered into a second war, more vicious than that fought against the Italians, the Germans and their allies. While 8 percent of the Greek population of seven million had been killed or had died during World War II—ten times the death rate for the United Kingdom for that period—the civil war further decimated the population, bringing the combined toll to almost 10 percent.[4]

According to Francis Noel-Baker's account in his *Greece*, 80,000 Greeks were killed by other Greeks and an approximately equal number, including many children, were made refugees or kidnapped during the civil war.[5]

In 1940 Greece had repelled an Italian invasion, only to fall to the Germans in May 1941 and be partitioned between the Italians, Germans, and Bulgarians. The statistics that emerged from the war years were grim: 75 percent of its forests in some areas were destroyed; 25 percent of all buildings were demolished or damaged; more than 2,000 villages were destroyed; 75 percent of its merchant vessels were sunk; and inflation at times was running at the incredible rate of 170 trillion drachmas to one gold sovereign.

When Greek government was reestablished, it was unstable and corrupt; there were no less than eight governments between the summer of 1945 and November 1946, Rex's first year in residence. To make matters worse, there was an active civil war raging outside (and sometimes inside) of Athens. During World War II, the Communist Party had organized resistance to the German occupation. This took the form of the underground resistance movement EAM (the National Liberation Front) and ELAS (the National People's Liberation Army). There was also a non-Communist resistance movement, EDES (the National Republican Greek League). Even during the German occupation in 1943-44, these right- and left-wing groups fought each other.

In May 1944, as German occupation came to an end, a Greek coalition government was formed; and in December 1944 and January 1945, the Greek army, assisted by the British army, succeeded in destroying most of ELAS, which had attempted to seize power in Athens. This cost "fifty thousand Greeks killed and around two thousand British casualties."[6] On Christmas Day 1944, Winston Churchill and Anthony Eden flew to Athens to bring the civil war to an end by peaceful means; this mission failed, but they gained time to bring in more British reinforcements. On 11 January 1945, the peace of Varkiza brought a temporary lull to the war; it recognized the Communist failure but contained a pardon for Communist resistance fighters. Athens was quiet, but not the rest of the country, because the Greek government under Archbishop Damaskinos continued to actively attack the members of EAM and ELAS, and these organizations never surrendered all of their weapons. EAM and ELAS retreated to the mountains north of Greece, and in December 1946 became the Greek Democratic Army, which was completely controlled by the Communist Party and assisted by the Communist parties of neighboring states—but not, it turned out, by Moscow, which agreed to British control of Greece in exchange for a free hand elsewhere in the Balkans.

During this period in 1946 and 1947, hundreds of political murders were carried out by both left- and right-wing organizations, and there were many arrests without trial. In March 1946 an election supervised by British, American, and French experts was boycotted by the left. There was a parliamentary majority of the right as a result, and in September 1946 the exiled King George returned to Greece. But this did not help. From 30 March 1946 until 1949, there was constant civil war. By the summer of 1947, around the time Rex was leaving, the authority of the government did not extend beyond the suburbs of Athens, while the north of the country was in the hands of the guerrillas. In the end, the civil war probably did even more damage to Greece than the German occupation had.

When Rex arrived in October 1945, the insurgency was not yet at a high level but there was unrest outside of Athens. In this difficult situation, Rex was well-placed to do some good for the artistic community of Greece as well as for himself, and he used his opportunity to best advantage. First of all, he was in brilliant intellectual company on the British side: housed at first in the elegant and appropriately named Grande Bretagne Hotel on Syntagma Square, he lived with high ranking officers, embassy staff, and British Council staff, and worked with many luminaries. The preeminent Byzantium and Crusades scholar Steven Runciman, whom Rex admired greatly, was head of the British Council in Athens, and was therefore Rex's boss. Runciman gave very select dinner parties in a beautiful flat overlooking Athens, during which he would regale the company with superb recitations of Tennyson's "Maud" and other poems.

The outstanding soldier and later travel writer Patrick Leigh Fermor became Rex's flamboyant second in charge. Leigh Fermor had led a commando raid that captured a German general during the war.[7] Leigh Fermor dreamed up the operation and carried it out with Bill Stanley Moss, another British operative, and some Greek resistance fighters. Leigh Fermor parachuted into Crete in February 1944 and Moss followed by boat in April. They disguised themselves as German police and stopped General Kreipe's car as he was returning from a bridge game to his house, Villa Ariadne, which was Sir Arthur

Evans's former excavation headquarters at Knossos. The chauffeur was disposed of and the pair took the general through twenty-two checkpoints and many adventures, eluding patrols along the way, before they got him to Egypt. At one point during the abduction, the general recited the first line of Horace's ode on Mount Soracte and Leigh Fermor completed the remaining twenty-one lines of the poem.

Along with his other qualities, Leigh Fermor is now regarded as one of the finest travel writers of our time. In addition to a love of literature, he and Rex also shared a taste for ouzo, the national drink of Greece. There was one occasion at the British Institute during which Leigh Fermor grew increasingly animated as his own lecture on Anglo-Greek friendship progressed. The audience noticed that he took frequent drinks from the water cup on the podium, but thought nothing of it as he warmed to his topic. After the talk, people realized that the glass held ouzo instead of water.

Rex also met writers Lawrence Durrell (later of *Alexandria Quartet* fame) and Osbert Lancaster, who was the British Embassy's press officer. Lancaster became a good friend of Rex's, and enjoyed spending long evenings with Rex and Leigh Fermor constructing improper poems about mutual friends. Another acquaintance was Xan Fielding, who may later have been Barbara Rothschild's boyfriend and who was to write a book about Crete, *The Stronghold* (1953). On the island of Corfu, Rex also met Robin Fyfe, who would later become the ex-husband of one of Rex's girlfriends, Liz Fyfe.

In 1938 an Institute of English Studies had been founded in Athens to meet the enormous demand for English-language instruction, but it was closed in 1940 on orders from the Greek government, which banned all foreign teaching establishments. On 19 April 1941, all remaining institute staff members were evacuated to Egypt when the Germans invaded Greece. According to a report of N.S. Whitworth, who was sent in April 1945 to revive the institute, it reopened on 8 August 1945 and within seventeen days, 7,815 applications had been received. There was "a scene of unparalleled enthusiasm,"[8] and 3,651 students were accepted. It was decided that the focus should be broadened from elementary English instruction, and so a new, distinct school called the British Institute of Higher Studies was formed to augment the Institute of English Studies. This higher-level school for advanced students, housed at a different address, was to be headed by Rex. As Rex described the situation, "In the summer of 1945 I was offered by the British Council the post of Director of the Institute in Athens, an Institute which at this time did not exist, though the one or two Council officials on the spot were engaged, among appalling difficulties of shifting prices and changing currencies, on the task of purchasing the building and making preliminary arrangements about furniture."[9]

Rex became the first director of the British Institute at personnel grade II and a salary of £740 per annum; this rose to £760 in September 1946, which approximately doubled his salary at Raynes Park. Subsequent directors were Malcolm Welland and the poet Louis MacNeice.

The British Institute was housed in an elegant building at 17 Philikis Etairias (now Kolonaki) Square, not far from Syntagma and Omonia Squares. The building had belonged to a shipping magnate named Petritsis, before the war. Its interior had to be redone, which took a great deal of time in postwar Athens. Rex writes that "there were generous donors of most unsightly pictures. There were almost daily changes in the rates of pay for decorators and electricians."[10] Eventually, there was a reading room with very comfortable sofas, and a large lecture room that held between seventy and eighty people. Rex's policy was to "make the place attractive rather than demonstratively instructive; and we took every possible step to make what we had to offer available to all sections of society." Rex described the square itself, which has changed very little since his day, as full of small shops and cafes and filled at most times of the day "with an assortment of people,—nursemaids and itinerant photographers, men with balloons, women with shopping baskets, priests, soldiers, taxi drivers, idlers, and officials going to and from their offices."[11]

The purpose of the institute was to teach the Greeks about England, and its method was to offer classes on English language and literature, as well as a lecture series and frequent receptions. About 300 people studied there regularly in 1947. Rex's job was to serve as a cultural liaison between the British and the Greeks. Although it has been said that neither Rex, Runciman, nor Leigh Fermor was a very good financial administrator, together they helped to usher in a brilliant series of art exhibits, musical events, and literary readings that left a permanent mark. In 1982 a former Greek minister of culture remarked, "The intellectual life of Athens after the war was formed by the British Council."[12]

The political scene was a threat to the institute's smooth operation, so Rex simply avoided it:

> It was, indeed, a difficult period, and, in Greece, when political passions are high it is not at all unusual for a grammarian, say, who has his own ideas about spelling or about accents, to be, for this reason alone, condemned by one party or another for either fascist or revolutionary tendencies. Thus there were certainly some people on the extreme right who regarded the presence of the *New Statesman* in our reading rooms as an incitement to revolt; and on the extreme left there were others who were convinced that all our activities were a cover for some form of espionage.[13]

Yet Rex enjoyed life to the fullest during this period. Tasos Sagos, who joined the British Institute at the age of twenty, remembered[14] that Rex was jovial and dressed casually, with open-collar shirt and sandals and a pipe always in his mouth. The photos of Marjorie Clark, Rex's administrative assistant at the British Institute, show a handsome man at the height of his powers. After the hardships of the war years, the British in Greece lived relatively luxuriously. Rex was on his own for much of the time while Frances remained in England with the children. He did not womanize, but he did drink. American battleships would pull into port, and there was a lot of black-market whiskey around, but Rex preferred retsina and ouzo because these were the only cheap drinks.

Marjorie Clark remembered Rex's daily routine. A typical day of Rex's would include an 8 A.M. breakfast at the taverna opposite the Grande Bretagne. From 9-10, he would stroll up to Philikis Etairias Square, about a mile away. Until 12:30 or 1 he would stay in his office, perhaps initiating contacts with lecturers or arranging a schedule for a lecture or reception. He would then go to a bar and lunch, and from 3:30-5 he would take a nap, like everyone else. He would then come back to the office from 5:30-7. From 7 to 10 there was more fun; no one dined before 10.

She described Rex at that time as a modest but very outgoing man with a wonderful sense of humor. In the winter of 1945-46, Marjorie's future husband David was twenty-six or twenty-seven (they were married on 26 July 1947 in England, and Rex and Frances attended), and Rex was forty, but David remembered Rex as a great drinking companion, for whom the age difference did not matter at all. (Again and again this comment appears in memories of Rex, including my own; he could see eye to eye with people of any age, even when he was much older.) Marjorie recalled that 1946 was a very quiet year in Athens and therefore a good time to be there; serious insurgency broke out later. The British in Greece were able to enjoy themselves because it was a period of relative peace and quiet following the rigors of World War II, and everyone was quite consciously out for a good time.

In a letter to me, Patrick Leigh Fermor remembered a typical evening's schedule.

These evenings would often begin in one of the two bars of the Grande Bretagne Hotel, not very seriously nicknamed "The Monarcho-Fascist" and the "Communist," though both of them seemed cheerfully undenominational to me. After this, one would move on to one of the tavernas in the Plaka, the old quarter of Athens, between the centre and the Acropolis. These were invariably delightful, rather untidy and cobwebby places, crowded, rather noisy, full of smoke and dominated by rows of enormous barrels, from which the retsina was drawn in straight blue-enamel measures, and plonked down. The retsina, nearly always excellent, was from vineyards that covered Attica from Athens to Cape Sounion. The habitués were working or middle class, heavily tilted in the direction of the arts, letters and sometimes journalism. Violin, accordion and guitar players would move from table to table, and there was much singing. . . . Rex enjoyed this enormously, and was particularly vocal with "Yalo, yalo"—"Along the Beach, Along the Beach"— and "Tria Paidia Voliostika"—"Three Lads from Volo," and, above all, pretty well his signature tune, an island song called "Samiotissa," "The Girl from Samos."

Long after he left Greece, Rex would sing this song with Barbara Knowland (formerly Morris), and his daughter Lucy would join in; and in 1996 George Warner still remembered the words. The favorite tavernas were "The Seven Brothers," and "Platanos," "where one sat out under a big . . . tree in summer, with Corinthian capitals scattered about, and, particularly 'Psarroi,' where an old white-whiskered walrus of a host had his small cork-lined eyrie at the top of a steep pathway of steps on the slopes of the Acropolis." Leigh Fermor added that "if we were determined not to go to bed, we would drive—or be driven—to haunts in the Piraeus . . . or right outside the capital, where soutavy dancers . . . would perform the intricate steps of the Tsembekiko and the Butcher's dance to the Asia Minor refugee music of *bouzoukia*." In such places, some customers might "take a furtive pull at a gurgling hashish-hookah made out of a coconut pierced with a stick of bamboo."

The midday meeting place of Rex, Leigh Fermor, and other literary and institute cronies was a small shop-bar called Apotsos, just off Syntagma Square, "whose walls were covered from floor to ceiling with faded mid- and late-Victorian tin advertisements for biscuits, potted meats, oxo, Barrot and anchovy . . . and various brands of stout and whisky. This haunt of Katsimbalis and ten authors was the setting for pre-lunch ouzo-drinking. Pock-marked vendors of clams and shrimps were always handy with their baskets, and shells mounted up . . . on tables." Rex contributed to this life with his "mixture of robustness and sensitive feeling . . . learning, and frequent and ready laugh."[15] Of Syntagma or Constitution Square itself, Rex wrote that on warm evenings, "the sky will seem pitch-black and beneath the sky hundreds of faces will be illuminated by the artificial light; slow strollers will go between the lines of tables; it will be worth looking closely at the faces, whether eager with argument or in response, to see whether one will meet here some friend who has stopped for a cup of coffee, an ice or merely for a conversation on politics, on literature, on personalities, generalities, or scandal."[16] Rex's job was something of a sinecure, but it demanded an ability to bridge the cultural gap. He was a remarkably good liaison person. He was reticent about himself but very outgoing. He was always laughing and joking, and greatly enjoyed meeting new people. Although he did not know modern Greek at first, he picked up enough to manage. In addition to Marjorie, Rex had a Greek secretary and two embassy servants. Patrick Leigh Fermor was appointed second in charge during Rex's first year, but was rarely present. He was followed in that position by the writer Maurice Cardiff (who would later become British Council Representative in Paris) in 1947.

Rex carried on all the correspondence with London, and had the responsibility of entertaining guests, which he enjoyed. His entertainment was never fancy, but always carried out in tavernas, although major British receptions were held at the Grande Bretagne. Stuart Campbell remembered that Rex was always ready to do anything. He would hire a bus and take five or ten people to Delphi or Daphne; in *Views of Attica* Rex is able to describe the mosaics of the church at Daphne with obvious expertise.

This was before the time of tourism, and the roads were narrow and potholed. But the sea had the same beauty it has today, and its color is what struck Rex: "I remember . . . the deep clear azure" of the sea of the Saronic gulf "and its various and thousand brilliant shades in the evening when the sun sets behind the Peloponnesian mountains."[17]

Although Greece was (and is) beautiful, conditions of scarcity demanded that bread, canned food, and other rations be brought from Athens by the traveler. Rex remembered,

> If one was lucky enough to find food in any restaurant or hotel these rations would always be welcome as gifts or useful as barter. On the occasion that I remember in 1945 there seemed to be no food and little life at all in Levadia [about 15 miles east of Delphi]. We sat at a solitary table in the deserted square eating the bread and tinned meat that we had brought with us and drinking from our own supply of whisky. The one waiter who appeared could provide us only with water and with coffee.[18]

Critic Raymond Mortimer, whom Maurice Bowra was to describe unkindly as a "silk shirt and sharny tie," was one of the guests during this period, as was the artist John Craxton, who later did the jackets for some of Leigh Fermor's books. Dilys Powell the film critic came to Greece, as did many others. In addition to the British guests, there were the Greek writers who very much appreciated Rex's hosting during this difficult economic period. They were very pro-British, and Rex met them mostly through Steven Runciman. Among those who would have a lasting effect on Rex were the poet George Seferiades (or Seferis), and his wife Maro; George Katsimbalis, the famous talker immortalized in Henry Miller's *The Colossus of Maroussi* (whose personality Rex characterized as "somewhat hysterically described" by Miller);[19] and the painter Nikos Hatzikyriakos-Ghikas (known as "Ghika"), who was later to figure prominently in Rex's personal life.

II. SEFERIS, KATSIMBALIS, GHIKA, AND OTHERS

Rex later wrote that he first encountered Seferiades or Seferis in 1945 in Athens at a lunch honoring Greek writers:

> Seferis, then preoccupied with his work in the Cabinet of the Regent, looked at first to be a ponderous and stiff government official. But soon he revealed his nimble, alert mind. He took quick delight in a John Betjeman couplet someone quoted, "I think that I should rather like/To be the saddle of a bike." We became friends and spent many evenings discussing poetry—including the writing of limericks in various languages.[20]

Seferis wrote in the T. S. Eliot modernist style, which had influenced Rex during his own early poetic career. He was a very suave and elegant person, obviously suited to life in the diplomatic corps. Maro Seferiades, whom I met in 1991, was an equally cultured, gentle woman who liked Rex and Frances very much.

In a radio talk that he gave on 27 August 1948 titled "Aspects of Contemporary Greek Poetry," Rex offered a further retrospective view of Seferis and other Greek writers. Of Seferis, Rex said that he is the most European of the Greek writers and yet had an "agonising sense of the depth and weight and variety of the Greek tradition." He singled out, however, Seferis's experience of exile and his engagement with the political realities of his world, as well as his pleasure in Seferis's company:

> Seferis more than any other Greek writer that I know, is conscious of the moral, intellectual, and artistic problems of our age. When I think of him, I recall to my mind some of the happiest hours of my life—hours of conversation with this good, brilliant, and perspicacious man sitting, perhaps, in his small room surrounded by books, with the wine on the low table, listening to his careful and penetrating analyses of the dangers to which culture and humanity are today exposed or to his sudden, quick bursts of unpredictable and peculiar wit, watching his great, domed head that seems to have settled like a rock between his shoulders, and his dark eyes, deep like the eyes of some aquatic mammal yet lit up from time to time with brilliant flashes of intelligence or humor.[21]

In his introduction to Seferis's *The King of Asine and Other Poems*, Rex wrote of his friend that

> Indeed one is at first surprised by the quickness in contradiction to his considerable weight, by the intellectual alertness which suddenly flashes into those large deep eyes,

which somehow remind one, when they are in repose, of a wounded buffaloe or of some biblical figures of speech,—pools or wells or cisterns. Melancholy indeed he looks very often, perhaps when late at night, in some open-air cafe, over an ice or a cup of coffee, he is speaking of the general situation of literature or recalling events in Greek history. But the melancholy is always giving place to his own individual or charming humour. . . . Both his conduct + his conversation are unpredictable, yet they are marked always by simplicity, energy, courtesy + charm. One knows him first as a poet + a diplomat, but cannot know him long without knowing him as a friend.[22]

Rex went on[23] to compare the work of Seferis, Yeats, and Eliot, singling out once again Seferis's political engagement:

Like these last he is acutely conscious of the contemporary situation, having seen much of "the systematic extermination of small nations," of the slogans which replace thought, of the violence + intolerance which lie so close beneath the diseased skin. There is nothing mystical in Seferis' approach to his problems + here he differs profoundly from Eliot. Yet perhaps, after all, he is affected by something which might be described as a different form of mysticism, a mysticism of history + tradition rather than of philosophy or religion.

George Katsimbalis was the editor of the *Anglo-Greek Review*, which began in March 1945 under the auspices of Anglo-Greek Information Services. Then forty-six years old, Katsimbalis was stout and walked with a cane, but was a very cheerful man, who enjoyed perpetually chomping on a cigar.[24] In his radio talk, Rex said of Katsimbalis that "nothing in Henry Miller or from hearsay had adequately prepared me for this large man with egg-shaped head and mouth like a fish who, brandishing his enormous walking-stick or pausing suddenly for a few contemplative sentences, escorted me through the maze of streets to his favourite tavern and never stopped speaking for an instant while hour followed entrancing hour." He went on to comment that Katsimbalis had published very little and was a Greek Dr. Johnson who unfortunately had not found a Boswell.[25]

Born in Athens on 26 February 1906, Ghika was around forty years old when Rex, who was about a year older, became British Institute director. At that time, Ghika was tall and dark and altogether very striking. He was already one of the most important painters in Greece. He had his first one-man show in 1927 in Paris. In 1928, he had his first exhibition in Athens, and in 1941 he was appointed to a professorship in drawing at the National Polytechnic in Athens. In 1946 Rex helped him mount his first retrospective exhibition of forty-two paintings. Ghika's personal life was unusual, for he had early married one of his mother's friends, Antigone

("Tiggie") Kotzia, fifteen years his senior. As a result, his wealthy father had cut him off without a cent, and Ghika had gone from riches to rags until he was able to succeed as a painter. People at parties would ask Tiggie if Ghika was her son. In a strange coincidence, Tony Knowland, Barbara Morris's husband and one of Rex's former students at Frensham Heights, had met Ghika by chance in the South of France in 1937 or 1938 when Tony was sixteen years old. Ghika appeared very lively and young then. He remembered Ghika telling him, "Don't be an academic. They are dead from there [the waist] down."

In 1950 Rex recounted a story about Ghika that was to prove prophetic with regard to Rex's own later relations with him, in that it hints at Ghika's capacity for deception:

> I remember, once at a fancy dress party, which some of us gave, Ghika and I retired with plates of cold meat to my office so that we could eat in greater comfort. As we sat down opposite each other at my desk, Ghika removed the long drooping black moustache which had contributed greatly towards the desired appearance of a Parisian dandy of the 'nineties. He laid the moustache gravely by his plate, and the gesture, followed immediately, as it was, by his own peculiar and staccato laughter, seemed to me not only ludicrous but symbolic. Not that the grave and rigid integrity of his art and thought is at all in the nature of a disguise; but neither is it in the least forbidding.[26]

Another friend was Dora Stratou, a wonderful singer who, according to Leigh Fermor, "later played an important role in rescuing Greek folk music."[27] Rex might have seen these people every other day, and was able to make lasting friendships. He met leftist intellectuals as well, but no politicians came to the institute. Rex himself remained leftist and pacifist in Greece, but not enormously so—indeed that would have been in conflict with his position, since the British government opposed the Communists and the British were in Greece largely to prevent a Communist takeover; in 1944, British General Scobie had done just that. No one discussed politics much with Rex, and he did not often mix with embassy people.

In 1950 Rex wrote the following:

> I cannot blame the Greeks for being unwilling to conform to the Russian pattern or for being, politically, un-English. Unlike some journalists, I did not make up my mind about Greece before I left London, and, in the sense of precisely knowing what is right and what is wrong, I have not made my mind up about it yet. I shall be told, no doubt, that in describing what had delighted me, I am deliberately throwing a veil over what could

delight no one at all. . . . an ability to enjoy oneself is not necessarily a sign of monarcho-fascist sympathies any more than a hatred of injustice is necessarily a mark of communism.

Rex concludes on a liberal, tolerant note: ". . . any picture of Greece that is either unexpected or even not precisely adapted to some ready made political conclusion is apt, I know, to arouse in some sections of the press a kind of priggishness or effrontery or both. Let me admit again, what few journalists are prepared to do, that I am ignorant. Yet not so ignorant as not to see the futility of easy solutions, the inhumanity of learned criticism that lacks love, and the arrogance of impossible advice."[28] Rex later drew a superb distinction concerning politics and art:

> Certainly in Greece and elsewhere there are powerful influences in support of the view that all art, literature and music have not only political importance (which is true) but also a definite political message (which, in the end, if the Gods do not forbid, may become true). Should this view prevail, it will, no doubt, become impossible for people of different political convictions to listen at the same time to the same lecturer on Shakespeare or on Aeschylus. The dead will be pressed into the service of the living and Mozart will be applauded more for his championship of Figaro's legitimate conjugal rights than for the music in which the story and so much else is expressed.[29]

With these prophetic words, which seem to describe much that has happened more recently in the arts, Rex showed how far he had moved from his own position of the 1930s. He was now a social democrat, with no tolerance for rigid ideological positions.

The Greeks with whom Rex came into contact usually spoke English, and genuinely enjoyed British company on the trips they took. There would be no heavy talk on these trips—just fun. Ghika would also go on these trips; he was a very good friend of Rex's at this time, if not quite as good as Katsimbalis and Seferis. Mrs. Leto Katakouzinos, whose husband was an important psychiatrist, ran a salon and Rex was often at their house. He befriended taverna owners George Psaras and the Kanakis brothers. In *Views of Attica*, he writes lovingly of the retsina Psaras served: "Indeed Attica is the place for retsina, and retsina is the drink for Attica. . . . Some will tell you that it is an acquired taste and will describe how they themselves have laboriously acquired it. Others, like myself, will enjoy it from the very first sip. Some unfortunates will never enjoy it at all."[30]

Rex was of course alive to ancient as well as modern Greece. He had a romantic view of ancient Greece, and a genuine interest in the ancient monuments, about which he had read and taught his whole life. At Epidaurus he got up on the ancient stage and declaimed some lines in Greek, possibly from Euripides' *Medea* or from Aeschylus's *Prometheus Bound* (he published the first part of his translation of *Prometheus* in *Greek Horizons* [Athens] in the summer of 1946). In Mycenae he told the company what had taken place there, including the story of Agamemnon's kingdom.[31]

At the same time, he was very aware of the present poverty of the people, particularly whenever he went into the villages. But he noticed how generous even the poor Greeks were, especially when Rex's group on one of these outings came upon a wedding party and the retsina flowed. He also learned Greek folk dances and would perform them at parties in the taverna. Those who saw Rex would find it hard to believe that his father was a staid minister and his mother a rather dogmatic teacher.

This, again, demonstrates the tension that one sees in Rex—the desire to let go completely, to be the artist, the hedonist, the Greek romantic against the pull of duty as the schoolmaster, family man, and loyal son of a minister. Drinking allowed the fun-loving, rebellious side of him to come out, and that is why, some say, he needed drink—that it was even vital to his artistic well being. Or perhaps alcohol allowed him to stupefy the conflict between these two competing sides of himself and attain some peace.

Precisely because of his pleasure there, Greece may have been subtly dangerous for Rex. He had never been lionized before, nor had he possessed the means to entertain as he would have liked when in England; he therefore lacked self-confidence then. In Greece, however, he was the focus and he had the means, and it increased his confidence. He realized that he could move with ambassadors, the rich, celebrities, and government representatives—the level of society to which his intellect had always entitled him. In Greece Rex began to grow restless, although his ostensible goal was to settle quietly in the English countryside, a need cruelly denied him for most of his adult life.

III. FROM ENTHUSIASM TO RESTLESSNESS

The curve of Rex's feelings becomes apparent in his letters to Pam and John Morris and other friends in England. Enthusiasm turned to restlessness and skepticism during the months of his stay in Greece. His first letter to Pam from Greece, dated 14 November [1945], cannot say enough good things about the British in Greece, and the Greeks themselves, but he does not ignore the harsh reality either: "let me say at once that your countrymen, + women, seem to me about the most charming on earth, that the air + landscape are wonderful, + that, if wisely governed, this would be the best country in Europe. . . . A wonderful people! On the other side there's extreme poverty + a very tricky political situation indeed. In the part of Athens where I live one sees nothing of this at all. One is surrounded by every luxury, but one can feel the other side of the picture." He was taking Greek lessons two or three times a week.[32] In an undated but early letter, Rex commented that he had begun "to miss my own children now, though I can't say that I'm broken-hearted about not seeing them for a bit. Its good to escape for a time into a sphere of comparative irresponsibility,—rather like being at the university again, though without one's adolescent worries + loves. Women in particular are interesting when one has (as I have) no special designs on them, + yet gets on well with them."[33]

Despite his good night (and day) life, on 12 December [1945], Rex wrote to Pam that he wished he could join her at the Cherry Tree, the Rowledge pub he favored, but that he might head for Cairo for Christmas, just out of restlessness. He reported again about the riotous life he was leading, but he noted that "There's something slightly sinister about the general situation of all the tavernas being full + yet nobody having any money, of an absurdly unstable political + economic situation side by side with all this revelry. Perhaps it is the 'last days' feeling, + one knows that there are 100 atomic bombs in America." He commented candidly,

> Later on one will have to decide whether to stay on here or not. It's a difficult decision to make. Everything is so much better than Raynes Park, but I still hanker for a house in the English country, from which I could dash off from time to time into foreign parts. One is always a bit uprooted if one is long abroad + I think uprootedness is only good for a fairly short time. At the moment I'm very satisfactorily uprooted, but I know my satisfaction won't last for ever + I doubt whether I should ever write anything here.

Although he did not explain why he could not write much in Greece, Rex might have been like many other writers who have trouble producing once they are outside of their native linguistic area. His drinking and late hours could not have helped, either, since Rex's best working hours were in the mornings, when he would regularly awaken with hangovers. Perhaps too this is another sign of the slackening of Rex's purely creative energies.

He commented finally that "Its rather amusing to find that I have something of a reputation here. Everyone either has read or says he has read my books, particularly the Aerodrome. Literary fame is largely an affair of snobbery, but it is still, with reservations, agreeable."[34] Rex liked being known and liked, perhaps more than he knew. His fame made him attractive to women, but he was not interested in adventures. In a letter of 3 January 1946 (he mistakenly wrote 1945) to Pam, Rex noted, "As for my sexual life, it is blameless. I get on very well with the two most good-looking English women here, + pretty well with all the Greek women of the right centre; but I'm too happily married to the bottle to get involved."

He also reported to Pam that at Christmas he had visited Delphi, which had filled him with "religious awe" but that they had had trouble on the return trip.[35] In *Views of Attica* Rex wrote, "When I first visited Delphi, on Christmas Day 1945, the road was indeed so bad that in England great portions of it might have been condemned as impassable; yet one scarcely resented the fact that a journey that should have taken four or five hours took seven or eight."[36] He also noted that in Delphi on that day, "I joined in an uproarious and hard-drinking party of local Andartes (or guerrilla fighters), and I have often wondered how many and which ones of that agreeable band have been involved, willingly or unwillingly, in the subsequent destruction of so much life, wealth, confidence and security in Greece."[37] They had a political discussion, during which Rex defended Churchill and British policy, adding ". . . it may have been true that our attitude was too irritatingly correct as officials of the British Council";[38] nonetheless, there were no hard feelings, and soon all politics were drowned in drinking and Greek dancing. Later, Rex drank with some officers of the Greek army when his car broke down near Thebes, and commented that "Had they and our friends from Delphi met together in the same room and in the right circumstances, it is possible that amity might have prevailed between them."[39]

Rex was a good defender of British policy in Greece as well as an adept cultural master of ceremonies, and it is not surprising that in his confidential British Council evaluation for the year ending 1945, Steven Runciman awarded Rex fairly high marks.[40]

On Friday, 18 January 1946, Rex wrote Greenwood, thanking him for the return of a £75 loan, and generously offering to lend him more money should he need it in the future. Rex outlined his own financial and literary situation:

> In spite of the prices (which at the moment are gradually falling) I've not spent all my salary here: neither have I saved much: neither have I written much, though I've nearly finished Prometheus Bound, + done one article (unpaid) for the Anglo-Greek review on late 19th century poetry. Its being translated into Greek by the Colossus of Maroussi [Katsimbalis], a very good man, equally + tremendously interested in literature + wine.

But Rex could be critical of other writers, commenting for instance that "arch-impostor Derek Patmore is in Athens persuading them to print limited editions of his own dreary prose."

Rex's anxiety about his own lack of productivity in Greece may have contributed to his criticism of Patmore. On 31 January 1946, he wrote Pam that "I realise perfectly well that a house in England is the objective + that this gay life which I am leading is only an interlude." Tellingly he went on to say that, "I couldn't conceivably write

anything under present circumstances + know well that writing is what I want to do."
Yet the British Council appointment was a posh, easy job and Rex could not easily
resist its blandishments, at least at first:

> Work still eludes me. My Institute is still not ready for habitation. Occasionally I fuss
> about telephones or furniture, but the Greek contractors go their slow way, which suits
> me. Occasionally I write an article on English poetry or take part in some cultural
> functions. It is all a very agreeable change from teaching. Indeed this is culture at its
> best, an ornament to life much more than a profession. Paddy Leigh-Fermor (though
> very charming + mad) does nothing at all, so I've won over to my side a beautiful +
> efficient woman [Marjorie Clark] from the Embassy, who, I hope, will organise
> everything, leaving my mind free for higher things.[41]

But after only half a year on the job, the novelty of his position and even of
Greece itself had begun to wear thin. Rex's letters to Pam begin to detail his feelings
about Greece and his position with a genuine (and elsewhere unexpressed) candor. On
15 February 1946, Rex wrote from British Council Staff A.P.O.S. 433 C.M.F.,

> You'll be glad to hear that I'm getting very slightly tired of it all. I shall enjoy it all again
> when Frances comes here, but I know I couldn't enjoy it permanently. I could never
> write under these conditions, +, though the charm of everything is very great, the
> superficiality of everything is curiously extensive. Without having had any experience
> of Greek love, for example, I can imagine it perfectly,—a riot of sensation in which
> what is really fundamental is given precisely the same exaggerated value as what is
> accessory. Very pleasant, very boring after a bit, + not what the Bronte girls would like.

He went on to comment candidly on Greek writers that "The best man I've met
here is Katsimbalis (the Colossus of Maroussi), a very good talker with a tremendous
reputation as a writer, though he has never written anything. That is rather typical
here. One gets introduced to 'a distinguished poet,' asks what he has written, + is
told that he has written one poem which has been circulated in MS among his friends.
But they are really the most charming people."[42] He had not yet, apparently, met
Seferis; the earliest correspondence between them that I have found is dated
September 1946.[43]

The only time that Rex ever seems to have lost his temper with Pam in a letter
appears in his missive of 27 February 1946. This letter shows that the calm, jovial
exterior Rex projected at this time belied a certain amount of tension inside. This

explosion seems to have been caused by an aesthetic reason, although under the surface there is Rex's irritation over the lack of a long-awaited letter of appointment from the British Council as well as other annoyances. Pam seems to have suggested that he write a biographical play about an unnamed person. Rex's response was curt:

> this is a short immediate note in reply to your monstrous suggestion. I should have thought you knew me well enough to know that I hate (i) "little plays" + (ii) prostituting my talent except in cases of extreme urgency. . . . Moreover, if there is one kind of "little play" which I dislike more than all the rest, it is the sort which gives the impression that the life of an artist is more important than his work. All "little plays" about artists do this. . . . In short, I will not put pen to paper in the cause. You seem to be mistaking me for Derek Patmore, an incredibly literary lion now in Athens.

Rex seems to have taken out on Pam his dislike, perhaps envy, of Derek Patmore. Rex also was feeling sorry for himself, commenting only half jokingly that "In fact today I'm rather feeling that I'm not being treated with proper respect."[44] At the same time, what he says is true—he had not and would not prostitute his talent by writing sensational or "pop" pieces. That is one reason why he is not better known.

Pam was rightly offended, and Rex on 11 March tried to cover his tracks with an apology, claiming he had been joking: "I'm so sorry that my last letter offended you. Actually I was attempting to be funny,—evidently with no success whatsoever. Least said perhaps soonest mended, but I'm very sorry that my intentions failed so dismally." He was able to report on Frances's safe landing in Athens.[45]

Frances arrived on a plane with military personnel in early March; Anna stayed in Jersey with Frances's mother, while Jonathan was at St. George's and George was deposited with Pam and John at Holtside. Frances's trip began on 2 March at Croydon. She arrived in Rome on 4 March, and in Greece the same day. The weather upon arrival was awful, and the plane had to drop flares so the pilot could see the landing area. Rex did not know what the exact day of her arrival would be, and was told on his way to the Grande Bretagne bar that his wife had arrived. He was glad that things had turned out that way, since he would have been terrified to witness the difficult landing. Once she arrived they enjoyed a round of pleasures, with hefty meat servings a real delight after the wartime hardships in London. As Rex wrote in *Views of Attica* of the celebrations following Easter, ". . . in a round of morning visits or before lunch, one may easily discover that one has eaten half absent-mindedly what in England might in the war years have constituted one's rations for six months."[46]

On 5 April 1946, he wrote to Pam,

Frances's arrival here has rather encouraged me in my worst habits + I have been having another round of parties + late nights comparable to those I had when I first arrived myself. It's all rather silly,—the continual hang-overs + the excited conversation; but, as temporary enjoyment, there's something to be said for it. There are large numbers of very agreeable people here,—a much more brilliant society than that of Raynes Park, + there is something in the excitability of the atmosphere that goes well with the brilliant Athenian air.

Rex went on to comment on the national elections that had been held in March with Western observers present, and which had been boycotted by the Left.

You'll probably have been reading about the elections. These were very quiet. In fact everything happened more or less as predicted, except that there were fewer incidents than one might have supposed likely. The "rightist terror" is greatly exaggerated, at least in Athens. There was a huge EAM (leftist) demonstration in the centre of Athens the day before the elections, + the police behaved very much like the London police. The danger now seems to be that the Royalists will try + get the king back at once,— +that would certainly precipitate a crisis. The trouble is that there is little good-will + very few brains on either side, + the possibility of Russian infiltration from the north doesn't make things easier. The Greeks are almost the best [men?] on earth, I think, but they're in a terrible position between Russia + the West.[47]

On the personal side things were better, with Rex and Frances going to the small resort town of Ayia Marina, on Aegina, an island about four hours from Athens, swimming and visiting the famous Doric Temple of Aphaia there. His feelings about Greece were still more positive than negative, but he told Pam that he could not stay: "I still get tempted to stay here, partly by the climate + food + drink, partly by flattery + the knowledge that, in reasonable conditions, I could be not only a popular but quite a useful member of Athenian society; but what I really want is a home in the country in England + a clear head from which to write."

On 13 May 1946, Rex wrote Greenwood that things were going well with the institute: "I've forgotten whether I told you of our grand opening ceremony, thronged with ambassadors + notables. Since then there have been lots of lectures,—my own little piece on the Medea being a particular success. Now, however, it is getting very hot + lectures are rather a strain." Rex considered coming back to Greece after the summer, but only until Christmas.

Meanwhile that imposter Derek Patmore is nagging the whole time about his scheme of dramatising "Why was I killed?" The fact that he wants to do it shows that there is money in the idea. I've told him that the film and dramatic rights are controlled by Basil Wright + you. I shall next tell him that you are in active negotiation about both. This may conceivably shake him off. I haven't had yet any of the French reviews of The Aerodrome, but gather that they were good.

Fontaine had just published the novel in Paris.

Frances left on Saturday, 18 May; by 19 May, she was back at the military airbase at Croydon. On 10 May Rex wrote Pam that "Frances has rather added to than restrained my demoralisation. She's been very gay indeed + very popular here. I don't know how she'll reconcile herself to water and Raynes Park." He added that he was coming back to England by the middle of June, and that the Council wanted him to return to Greece at least through Christmas; he wasn't sure how much longer he wanted to stay in Greece, partially because of British income tax—"If I'm not out of England for the right number of months I think I may be taxed on all my year's salary (which of course I've spent)." He agreed with Pam that "Things look very black everywhere, + the English country + children are about the only innocent pleasures left to one." He missed George who was staying with Pam and John, in particular. And he added that "Here everything outwardly is very calm, though terrorist activities on both sides seem to be increasing. However nothing in Europe seems to be very calm below the surface. The Russians are behaving very oddly indeed."[48]

On 25 May he wrote a letter to Barbara Morris, Pam's eldest daughter, in which he said that "Greece . . . though absolutely charming, is a little sinister, so far as politics go, + they go a long way here."[49] He looked forward gloomily to three hot weeks and added that he was going to try to take a tour of the islands at the beginning of June with his "beautiful secretary."[50]

Ivor Lewis, an RAF officer, had borrowed a small airplane and taken Rex to Corfu. Rex was scared, but he went. On 26 May 1946, he wrote Barbara Morris that "early this week I flew to Corfu with an incredibly dangerous young pilot. Apart from the appalling risks involved, everything was lovely. . . . Its a most beautiful island, much greener than the islands this way. We bathed in wonderful clean water with trees all over the beach + the snow-covered Albanian mountains in the distance; + we brought back ten pounds of strawberries."[51]

Even as Rex was about to return to England for a summer holiday, finances were a problem. On 30 May 1946, he wrote Pam that "By now, of course I ought to have saved some money, but of course I haven't, +, if I have to pay income tax on my salary, I shall be ruined."[52] Around 10 June 1946, he wrote a final letter to Pam before leaving Athens, "which I'm quite looking forward to leaving, as its very hot + I've absorbed all I can of social life for a time. . . ." But with his own lack of money and English hardships, including food rationing, in mind, he was thinking of asking for a British Council job in Switzerland, "where there are good schools + plenty to eat and drink."[53]

Rex did find England unsatisfactory in many ways, and suffered from the usual traveler's crosscultural discomfort. After a few days in Rome, he arrived in England around 20 June 1946. He wrote John and Pam from Wimbledon "a short note of greeting on arrival in this gloomy country. Indeed the extraordinary depression visible on everyone's face is the first thing that strikes the returning traveller."[54] He was not getting much accomplished except for British Council business. Rex wrote on 8 July to Pam that his life was "absurdly full of organised emptiness. . . ."[55]

We sense a dropping off of Rex's creative vigor during the Greek period, starting in 1946. He was at the very height of his international fame, but that fame was based on reprints of his earlier creative work. *The Cult of Power*, his essay collection (in which only about half of the eight essays had not previously been published or given as lectures), appeared on 5 September. *The Aerodrome* came out in American, French, and German editions during 1946. *The Professor* went into a second impression in the Uniform Edition that the Bodley Head had initiated in 1944 with *The Wild Goose Chase. Why Was I Killed?* went into its fifth impression and first publication in the Uniform Edition. It also was published by the Bodley Head in a second edition for "circulation to the Fighting Forces of the Allied nations," and in French translation. His sonnet, "How sweet only to delight," was reprinted in *A Garland of Prose and Verse*[56] edited by Walter de la Mare, and a passage from *Why Was I Killed?* appeared in *The Treasure Chest: An Anthology of Contemplative Prose*, edited by J. Donald Adams.[57]

Rex's only new literary work during the Greek period was translation, but to turn this criticism into praise, this is certainly one of Rex's major contributions to culture. "Prometheus Bound by Aeschylus," the first part of his translation of this work, appeared in *Greek Horizons*, an Athenian journal, in the summer of 1946; it was billed in the journal itself as the "first publication" of Rex's translation and "a companion piece to his fine translation of Euripides' 'Medea.'" He signed a contract for a full translation of *Prometheus Bound* with the Bodley Head on 29 July 1946.[58] Perhaps most important, during the Greek period he began translating Seferis.

Rex sent Pam a "hurried farewell" on Wednesday, 4 September 1946; he was on his way back to Athens to take up his job again. Greenwood left with Rex on Friday, 6 September, via Dieppe for some business and pleasure in France. On Saturday the 13th Rex would fly to Holland, on the 15th to Rome and on the 19th to Athens. Frances and Rex celebrated his departure from England with some champagne, and Rex could report to Pam that Jonathan had gotten through the School Certificate and had received a gramophone as a present. Anna had experienced a bad attack when visiting Holtside, but was well now. Rex and Frances had decided to give up the house in Wimbledon. Rex half-joked about the possibility of a Russian invasion of Greece.

A letter of 19 September to Greenwood from Athens summed up his trip and its many literary excitements, in Rex's typically modest style. He thanked Greenwood and Fontaine, his French publisher, for a very good week and hoped to repeat it in April. Then he told what followed:

> After you left I had some more rather terrifying times with journalists. . . . I was interviewed on the radio, but rather tongue-tied, + then set off for Holland. I stayed at the Hotel des Indes + had plenty of Dutch gin. The lecture was rather imposing. It took place in the house of parliament + lasted from 8.0 till 10.30. After an interval I read extracts from "Why was I killed?" Queen Wilhelmina was not present, but the Mistress of the Robes was very gracious, as was the Chinese ambassador.

Rex then went on to Paris to see Ludmilla Savitsky, his French translator, and had treated Thérèse Denny, a film friend, to a meal. After some sightseeing in Geneva and Rome, he was delighted to get back to Athens, which he thought "has a good claim to be called the best spot in the world."

He was also in a position to repay old social debts: Maurice Bowra had arrived on the morning of the 19th, and Rex had taken him for lunch in the country, where Bowra caused a stir by remarking "in a very loud voice that the Greek army looked like Bulgarians." Bowra spoke to between fifty and eighty people during one lecture, which was very successful, but in truth his lectures were an excuse for Rex to invite him for days of carousing. Rex at last was able to enjoy life and to do something for his friends.

Rex suggested a visit by Greenwood in March 1947, and commented only semi-jokingly that "The political position, I think, is ugly, but if we're not all killed by then, it ought to be all right." Rex hoped that *The Cult of Power* would do well. He supplied Greenwood with an alternate blurb, which reads in part: "Mr. Warner ranges widely, skating with some dexterity, over his frozen + often inadequate knowledge of Greek + Latin literature, Elizabethan drama + Russian novelists. The book was written for the sake of monetary gain." Rex mentioned that someone he knew in Paris, probably Thérèse Denny, was interested in doing a film of *The Aerodrome*.

Greenwood responded with the first *Cult of Power* reviews, and Rex wrote him back on 7 October from Athens that he had "had a fortnight entertaining Bowra + my digestion is ruined. Bowra himself went off in a rather shaken state. Now, in ten days' time, it will be old Bas[il Wright]. What I do for my country!" Rex went on to complain that "Outside my office now there is a surging mass of chaps waiting to register for courses at the Institute. I've given instructions that good looks + gentlemanly manners should be taken into account as well as intellectual proficiency."

Rex also discussed the institute in a letter of 9 October to Pam, commenting that "I've now got a very good staff +, if anti-British feeling about Bulgaria doesn't rise to exceptional heights, things should go well." In addition to entertaining Bowra, in September he hosted a literary gathering and asked Seferis to name a date for a talk on Cavafy and Eliot.[59]

Frances was going to come in November with George and to stay with Rex until they left Greece for good, and Rex wrote of his preparations for Frances's visit that "I've acquired a large house out of Athens + shall go there as soon as I can find servants. A kindergarten is being organised for English children + we are very close to another English family [the Cardiffs], so old George ought to be all right, + I shall have my bar life considerably curtailed." The suburb was Psychico, still posh and the place for diplomats, and embassies were a reasonable bus ride from the center of Athens. On a later visit to Athens, Rex was to comment that he barely recognized the area any longer because it was so developed.

Rex tells us in *Views of Attica* that Psychico was "a quarter full of modern bungalows and villas, one of the latest and most lucrative examples of Greek speculation in building," yet "a walk of five minutes uphill from this fashionable suburb" would

> bring one into wild and unspoilt country. In the spring there will be anemones growing on the grey rock of the mountain. Flocks of sheep and goats will appear here in as natural an environment as if they were in the hills around Delphi. Beyond, to the north is the plain dotted with hamlets, stretching to Haraklion, Menidi and Parnes. In the north-east is Penteli and Hymettus to the south. Southwestwards is the sea with Aegina rising from the sea.[60]

Rex was able to live better in Greece than he ever had in England, and he relished his ease, as well as the weather and the scenery. Rex mentioned in his letter of 9 October to Pam that Greek politics have been "rather tricky," but that he'd been swimming and "each day is like the one good day that makes an English summer."[61]

IV. REX THE HOST

Rex's relationship with Seferis was developing, and would eventually produce important literary results. On 14 October 1946, he wrote Seferis jokingly that "I'm very glad that you're enjoying the peace of Poros though of course there can be no doubt that to enjoy peace at all is either a rightist deviation or else bourgeois Utopian idealism." He mentioned that John Lehmann would arrive around 31 October. He stated that Lehmann had

> sent me a number of translations of your poems, done by Valaoritis + Bernard Spencer. Many of them seem to me very good, but I hope to have an opportunity of going through them with you when I see you. I'm attempting, in the darkness of my own almost total ignorance, to read them in Greek with the aid of both English and French translations. What I can understand I admire very much. . . . But I am painfully aware of how much I miss through not knowing the language properly.

At this time, Rex was finishing a lecture and working on his translation of Aeschylus's *Prometheus Bound* and commented to Seferis that "Its not so easy for a modern audience as the Media [Medea], + of course the whole thing is incomplete, but its a very fine play. I'd like to show you my translation some time."[62] He conveyed Bowra's greetings, and went on to add quite genuinely that "you are greatly missed here."

On 18 October he wrote Greenwood that he had gone to the airport to meet another friend, Basil Wright, but had found no sign of him, and that he doubted that Frances would ever get to Athens. He informed Greenwood that he had lectured that week on *Prometheus Bound* and had "organised such a distinguished series of lectures that I don't think I need open my mouth again till after Christmas." He was in touch with the Greek publisher Patsifas about a Greek translation of *The Aerodrome*, but without result. He had consulted with the person in Paris about *The Aerodrome* film idea. He asked Greenwood for reviews of *The Cult of Power*, and anticipated a "rather over-done attack in the *TLS*." Rex was quite happy because he was moving to his luxurious new house the next day, and envied Greenwood the availability of French wine "but little else in England just now."

On 31 October he could write Greenwood that Basil had been there for the last week and had been a great success: "Today we had lunch at the embassy (which is very like 'Black Mischief')[63] with the Crown Prince + Princess. Basil was rather alarmed to discover that H.R.H. held exactly the same views as he did on general enlightenment + reconstruction." Rex had taken Basil to Mycenae, Nauplion, and Epidaurus, but Basil had suffered stomach trouble. Rex was still waiting for a publishing memorandum from Patsifas, but "you'll probably find, though, that the whole Greek market has been captured by John Lehmann who is due to arrive tomorrow." In all, "Culture is going ahead by leaps + bounds. All the leading poets + such like are giving lectures here + I have to look as though I understood them. We're also planning a publishing venture by which the translators of Greek poems get nothing at all out of it." Frances had not yet arrived, and Rex was living "like a hermit in a large house with two servants who have nothing whatever to do." He would have threatened the British Council with resigning over the delay "if I were quite sure they would not accept the resignation." He again asked for reviews, especially from the *TLS*, showing how much this one withheld approval meant to him.

By 5 November Frances had not yet arrived and Rex wrote Pam that he was "furious at the way Frances is being kept in England by the incompetence of the Council. . . ." With the delays typical of the time and place, John Lehmann's visit took place only on 1 November, and Rex commented that Lehmann "gets more like a headmaster every day," while Rex himself became "more + more like" Madame Verdurin, Marcel Proust's salon-giving woman of fashion:

> I am very concerned that more of "the little clan" should miss my Tuesdays. On these days public lectures are given, I make a short speech + there is usually a short party afterwards. The "little clan" consists of writers, painters, critics + Lady Norton [wife of the British ambassador to Greece]. The French Institute are rather disturbed at the success of my "offensive culturelle." They are rather tied to the Left, while I make the best of every world + am no doubt regarded as plotting something pretty diabolical.[64]

In his autobiography, John Lehmann explained that he knew that his friend Rex would show him "a good and probably uproarious time, as far as local conditions permitted." This was a true estimate, for Lehmann also wrote, "I have always regretted that I did not keep a diary of this visit, because it was one of the most passionately interesting episodes in my whole life, so crowded with incident that only a day-to-day journal would bring everything back to mind."

Rex

> took charge of me at once, introduced me to all his Greek friends, who always seemed in the highest spirits when in his company, arranged my expeditions and lectures, frightened me by the glowing terms in which he described me as I sat cowering beside him on the platform with a sea of unknown Greek faces before me, and took me off to carouse in tavernas when official duties and ordeals were over. His good humour never failed. The atmosphere in his office when visitors called—and they called very often—was indeed more like that of a taverna than a centre of administrative organization. This the Greeks immensely appreciated, knowing that they could argue exactly as they pleased in his presence, on politics, literature, history and sex, while Rex chuckled continuously at the

quips that flew around and made genial but shrewd ripostes whenever necessary. He imposed authority as much by his sturdy physical build as by his obviously deep classical learning, his devotion to Greek civilization, and his reputation as an outstanding imaginative author.[65]

Through Rex, Lehmann met Katsimbalis, Seferis, and Ghika, as well as the pioneer of modern Greek poetry, Sikelianos. Lehmann wrote,

> One evening in a taverna I was brought to the great poet Angelos Sikelianos, whose *Death-Feast of the Greeks* I had published in *New Writing*. He was in the company of Rex and Lawrence Durrell, the latter over on a visit from Rhodes, where he was working for the British Mission. Sikelianos's health had been undermined by his privations during the war years, but his talk, of poets and poetry and experiences of his life, was full of fascination and wit, and I was struck by the dignity of his bearing, the sweetness of his expression, and the gentle warmth of his manner.[66]

Using a Greek navy boat supplied by the minister of information, Baltazzi Mavrogordato, they visited Seferis on the island of Poros and saw Nico Ghika's cliff-built house (subsequently burned down) on the island of Hydra.

At that time, according to Rex, Seferis had just completed "The Thrush," a poem

> full of the atmosphere of the islands and of those cities on distant coastlines which have always been a part of Greece, and the poem finds a concentration in a submerged wreck in Poros harbour. The meanings and the implications extend from this submarine locality. There are adjectives taken from Homer; there is the light and the texture of paint work on sea-faring boats; there are the leaning statues and the voice of the radio that interrupts itself in the declaration of war and of certain loss; Socrates and Oedipus are in the poem together with the water wagtail, the cicada, the light upon the shutters, and dresses unpacked from old trunks. It is a poem written with incomparable skill, yet more to be admired than the poet's skillfulness is his deep and extensive awareness of the world of the Greeks, a world sharp in every detail yet with every detail significant.[67]

Rex's own writing, however, was not being received that warmly. He wrote bitterly to Greenwood on 8 November about a negative *TLS* review of *The Cult of Power*, "many thanks for the literary suppuration of the Times. I wish I could find out who my enemy is. This was really rather a clever stroke,—to get the material for a leader out of my essay + insert the gibes in the middle." Rex's complaint is justified. The review, which appeared on 19 October, was in the form of a leading article on the letters page.

The writer claimed not only that Rex's fiction "stems rather too obviously from Kafka," but that his essay on "Dostoyevsky and the Collapse of Liberalism," while "thoughtful and earnest," was "not particularly well informed and perhaps misses its opportunities." It attacked Rex at his weak point, namely his lack of specialized knowledge, stating that he had "too little acquaintance with the literary history of nineteenth-century Russia to be able to appreciate the controversial background of Dostoyevsky's thought" (507). But the reviewer admitted that Rex had seized "upon an aspect of Dostoevsky's imaginative argument which lies at the heart of our present anarchy of thought," that is, whether it is possible to have respect for the individual without a belief in a transcendental religious philosophy. This idea had also figured in *Why Was I Killed?* When the distinguished American biographer Mark Schorer reviewed the essays' American edition in September 1947, he pointed out that Rex's use of allegory is entirely different from Kafka's, because Kafka's is open-ended while Rex's is directed toward a clearly discernable object, namely political tyranny. Also unlike the *TLS* reviewer, Schorer found that the Dostoyevsky essay was "considerably ambitious" and "a penetrating essay with a concrete substance," showing the difference between the humanely religious person and the ruthlessly aggressive egomaniac.[68]

In his letter to Greenwood, Rex also attacked the publisher Patsifas, who was all too aware that "By Greek law there is no valid copy right after a ten year period from publication, so its obviously cheaper to wait a bit" and publish *The Aerodrome* for nothing.

By 10 November he was writing Pam, probably having taken the *TLS* too much to heart, that the essays in *The Cult of Power* were not very good, but promising a signed copy anyway. Frances and George were on their way at last. He found life in the big house lonely, and complained that the weekend "has been spoilt by having to have an hour + a half's audience with the King in the middle of Saturday afternoon,— though in a way that was rather interesting." Moreover, he had an exhibition of Ghika's paintings going. Even the King wanted to attend. On the other hand, Rex himself hardly ever lectured, because after fifteen years of secondary teaching, "I have no wish to instruct anyone in anything for the rest of my life."[69]

By 27 November Frances and George had finally arrived, after an exciting trip during which the pilot had flown over the top of a smoking Mt. Vesuvius. Once in Greece George, who would become a biologist, had a wonderful time seeing both an eagle and an octopus and drawing both. Rex was brought up to date about his friends' lives in England. He noted gloomily in a letter to Pam that

> The whole thing makes me think we shall never get back to England at all, or, if we do, only into a prefabricated thing. . . . Life is gradually growing more expensive again here

+ I see no prospect at all of our saving any money. I also see little prospect of the Council being a worth while job. The whole tendency in England is to be afraid of the "highbrow" + to talk aimlessly about the "common man"—whatever that is. The London officials probably disapprove strongly of what I'm doing + want us to spend our time in discussion with groups of boy scouts + trade union leaders, discussing town planning.

Here were, perhaps, the ill effects of the Labour Party, and of the Socialist "revolution" that Rex himself had once wanted. The fact is, Rex always was classically oriented and interested in intellectual matters, and despite a delight in the Marx Brothers and Fred Astaire, he could very rarely write or think in the mass culture vein. Even the ostensibly Marxist *Wild Goose Chase* had used epic devices drawn from classical literature, and it had never been popular with a large group of readers.

But he told Pam that

Meanwhile, however, the sun usually shines; there's plenty to eat and drink; + we're not as worried as we should be about the general situation. It isn't a good situation, but its the fault of Europe as a whole, rather than the fault of England. Greece too is probably behind all other countries in reconstruction because it is split into absolutely irreconcilable groups. I see no hope of things getting better. Perhaps the tendency of the world is now so anti-individualist that there is no place in it for a nation of individuals.[70]

This last comment shows Rex's growing disenchantment with all forms of group think.

Rex wrote Greenwood on 13 December 1946 that "Frances is rather thrilled to have a large house + nothing whatever to do, though now the servants are beginning to quarrel bitterly." Ludmilla Savitsky, who was to become Rex's permanent French translator, had written Rex that she was halfway through translating *The Professor* and felt that the French would understand it better than *The Wild Goose Chase*. Rex confessed to Greenwood that he thought nothing would come of the *Aerodrome* film, because "These film chaps can never keep an idea in their heads for more than a fortnight." The head of the British Council Education Department, named Morgan, had just visited, and Rex found him "stupid + arrogant. He thinks in terms of discussion groups of boy scouts on town planning, + obviously disapproves of everything we do here. What we actually have done in a year is to wrest from the French the intellectual leadership of Greece,—which I regard as a considerable achievement, though it will all be lost if people like Morgan control Council policy." That day Rex put on a reception for the new Byron Professor at the University of Athens, but "The poor man has been ill ever since he came here, he has a huge boil at the end of his nose which makes him look a master-drunkard, he is very superstitious + its Friday the 13th."

Rex introduced Seferis's lecture on 17 December 1946. The manuscript of Rex's introduction is in the Gennadius Library. Rex put a note under it, "A poor speech but meant well." Actually, Rex's introduction is quite good, and stresses Seferis's ability to fuse the Greek and European traditions and the past and the present.[71] Rex undoubtedly gave this manuscript to Seferis as a souvenir.

In his diary Seferis wrote that many people, including Sikelianos, attended his lecture, and that few people understood what he was saying but that many were enthusiastic nonetheless. The non-Greeks were amazed that so many young people had come to listen.[72] Seferis and Rex had by this time become fast friends; Seferis would come out to the Warner house and show George how to fly kites in the Greek manner, with messages directed to the kites themselves, the stars, or the sun, tied to the kites' tails.

The day after Seferis's lecture, Wednesday, 18 December, he and Rex began translating "The Thrush" into English at Rex's house in Psychico. Seferis recorded that "I gave him an extemporaneous oral translation." Rex was working with great enthusiasm, and by Saturday he had already finished the first part. At noon on Monday, 20 January, Rex told Seferis that he had finished the whole poem. "It's strange," he told Seferis; "yesterday as I was writing, the janitor came in—he goes hunting occasionally—and brought me a thrush. A good omen. I wanted to call you." Seferis commented that Rex was the first translator who had not tormented him, and that Rex was aided by his knowledge of ancient Greek and his mastery of English.[73]

On 29 December 1946, Rex wrote Pam that he had given up hope that a film would be made out of *The Aerodrome*, but that it would be published in America on 1 January (actually it came out in late 1946). He and Frances had spent Christmas, with "an illegal Christmas tree, lots to drink + plenty of toys for George. The whole thing cost a fortune but was very enjoyable." The tree was "illegal" because so many trees had been cut down during the German occupation that the government banned further tree cutting. Rex and Frances also enjoyed Christmas morning sitting out in the sun with olives and pink gins.

The somewhat sinister effect that the luxurious life in Greece had on Rex crept into this letter:

> I'm certainly thinking of retracing my steps to the old country, but I can't bear the
> thought of living in a town or in any home that isn't fairly comfortable. And I gather
> from Frances that there are no more good houses about than there used to be. Moreover
> I can see no reason for believing in any stability. This makes one restless, + so I would
> just as soon live a year or two in Belgium or even America. With Greece I'm beginning

to get tired, having achieved everything I'm likely to achieve here in this job + growing more + more aware of the hopelessness of the general situation here. If I were a politician I should find it interesting, but I only find it depressing.[74]

Yet he was doing his job as British Institute Director extremely well. Steven Runciman's excellent performance evaluation dated 16 December 1946 makes that clear.[75] Rex's prestige was no doubt helped on 11 January 1947 when the American *Saturday Review of Literature* ran a picture of him on the front cover to accompany a lengthy and highly laudatory review of *The Aerodrome*, which had just come out in America, written by Ben Ray Redman.

On 15 January 1947, Rex wrote Pam the news that "I'm translating a long poem ['The Thrush'] by George Seferis. As I don't know the language it's rather difficult."[76] Rex's translation of Seferis, who was eventually to win the Nobel Prize, gradually blossomed into a major accomplishment. In achieving it, Rex relied on the aid of native Greek speakers—Seferis himself, and later Theodore Frangopoulos. The aid he received does not diminish Rex's achievement, because it is the second stage of any translation, the polishing of the rough literal translation into lasting English utterance, that determines its quality.

On 20 January 1947, Rex wrote Greenwood

> In the last two days I have improved my health greatly, first by taking a bottle of breakfast wine before dinner instead of gin or whiskey, secondly by translating a long poem of Seferis (200 lines or more). I'm not quite sure what the poem is about, but think my own translation rather good. Would you like to publish it in pamphlet form? Its rather like "The Waste Land" +, if the idea appeals to you, I could probably get Ghika (a very fine Greek painter) to do a cover + illustrations. . . . The advantage of having Ghika is that Seferis would be able to tell him what the poem is about. I'm being urged by Katsimbalis to translate four more long poems, but don't know whether I'll do so or not.

He asked for news of the American edition of *The Aerodrome* and the French edition of *Why Was I Killed?* Rex had heard from Rosamond Lehmann that there might be a cottage in Little Wittenham, near Didcot, that could be rented and had asked her to get it for them: "I'm getting so fed up with the bloody Council that I don't see why I should delay my arrangements for them. But have I got enough money to make residing in England possible? I rather think that before long I should like to write something. I've found the translation very stimulating." George was having a good time, carrying a dead thrush around for two days until Rex persuaded him to bury it.

By 11 February Rex had sent C. J. the "Thrush" translation and mentioned that Lehmann ought to be considered:

> He is shortly bringing out a book of translations of Seferis [*The King of Asine and Other Poems*, published May 1948], for which I've written the preface, + he considers that, in accordance with normal publishing practice, he ought to have the option on anything in the nature of a book by the same author. I've written to him saying that (i) this isn't a book (ii) the force of the argument depends on whether this work is held to be Seferis's or mine, + (iii) that anyway neither you nor I would wish to do anything to prejudice the success of his own Seferis book. Also I suggested that he might get in touch with you.

He left it to Greenwood to decide if he wanted to publish or not, and if not to let Lehmann do it; in any case he did not want to do anything to sabotage Lehmann. Once again Rex's integrity is obvious. Proofs of Rex's *Prometheus Bound* translation had just arrived, along with a German translation of *The Aerodrome* put out by a Zurich publisher in 1946.

Finances continued to be a problem for Rex, even during this relatively flush period. On 14 February he wrote Greenwood that he was overdrawn £317-5-6 at his bank and asked if Greenwood could pay in now or after the new tax year began on 1 April. Rex needed some money because he wanted to bring Jonathan out in April. Jonathan had to go into the army in another year, and Rex wanted him to see Greece first. He asked Greenwood to tell him his financial situation, particularly whether or not he would "be arrested as soon as I set foot on English soil." Rex was planning his permanent return around 20 May, and also asked Greenwood to be on the lookout for a house. The institute was putting on a carnival fancy dress dance on Friday, 21 February, and Rex noted that "Its going to be vastly expensive + the four or five of us who are giving it will be ruined for months. We have eighty guests, including about eight heterosexuals."

V. FAREWELL TO GREECE

By 18 February Rex had been visited by the chairman of the British Council, Sir Ronald Adam, who "seemed fairly impressed with everything + regards me as 'a valuable asset' (perfectly correctly)." Rex was right, for in a confidential memo of 24 March 1947 from Sir Ronald to Mr. Kenneth Jonstone, the head of the European Division (and formerly British Council Representative in Athens), it is said that Rex is "First-class and must not be lost. Will leave Council but might return."[77] Rex extracted a promise of a "pretty good job, possibly in Paris," at some point in the future. The end of his service in Greece was near. Rex and Frances planned on returning to England at the end of May and "if only we could get a house, everything would be very nice, though I shall be sorry to cease living like a gentleman + a capitalist."

The prospect of leaving Greece now began to seem a bit unpleasant. Great Rissington, he had learned from his mother, had the lowest temperature in England, while Rex's Greek house was centrally heated and the sun was out a lot. George had a "vast collection of shells + is very happy. Frances has nothing whatever to do except dress + undress + play a social role." Minding one child was easier than minding three. Moreover, "At the moment we are organising a very extensive carnival party for about 80 people. . . ."[78] Rex had finally arrived at the end of Proust's À la recherche du temps perdu [Remembrance of Things Past] and pronounced it "the novel to end all novels."

On 6 March 1947, Rex wrote Lehmann about the Seferis poem he had worked on: "I hope the question of 'The Thrush' . . . will be settled with amity and justice. . . . I don't mind how it appears myself, so long as it appears in its entirety: though it shouldn't, I think, be included in your book. Seferis himself feels strongly about this, saying, as is quite true, that it is a poem in a very different mood from the others."[79]

On 11 March Rex wrote Greenwood that Jonathan would fly out by TWA from Paris to Athens on 28 March. He wished Greenwood could come too, but Greenwood was apparently going to America. Rex had written Cecil to take a house in Long Wittenham for them from 22 May until the end of July. There was some opportunity for Rex to get to Wisconsin, of whose location he was unsure; his motivation for going to America was to consult American doctors about both Frances and Anna.

Jonathan arrived as scheduled on 28 March, and George was excited by his brother's arrival. Day-Lewis had gotten them the Long Wittenham house, and Rex hoped for a more permanent place by the beginning of August.

On 29 March Rex looked forward to seeing Greenwood in Long Wittenham in July but advised him while in America not to get himself arrested as an anti-imperialist. Lippincott had forwarded Rex the "exploratory" letter about Wisconsin, perhaps from the university, as well as "a very hideous picture of me on the cover of the Saturday Review of Literature, which contained quite a good notice of the Aerodrome." Rex asked Greenwood about the possibility of his sending a refill for Rex's Biro ballpoint pen because the Biro was "quite good for doing crosswords" and refills were apparently unavailable in Greece, a sign of the country's dire situation. Rex agreed with Greenwood that "in war-shattered England" a Seferis pamphlet [of "The Thrush"] would not sell, and he therefore asked Greenwood to try to get Lehmann to publish the poem, since he thought it was good. He asked if Greenwood had any news from E. V. Rieu, the classics scholar associated with Penguin, about a possible translation of Xenophon that Rex might do. Ludmilla Savitsky had told him that the publishing business was not too good but Rex anticipated a royalty from the 1946 translation of *Why Was I Killed?* and proposed spending it on a holiday in the autumn. Rex mentioned too that George Barnes, the organizer of the BBC Third Programme, had been in touch, and that Rex had suggested that the BBC should broadcast his Medea translation, followed by Gilbert Murray's. Rex had recently climbed a very high mountain "+ captured a wild tortoise for George. I've been twice sick on shell fish + have now given them up. I should appreciate a case or two of whisky from the firm to mark my return."

On 29 March Rex noted to Pam,

> Our cultural programme is now drawing to an end. The season closes with one of my own rare appearances. I shall deliver a long + highbrow lecture on "Truth in Literature." Then there'll be a lot of farewell parties + my mission to Greece will be over. On the whole its been very successful but the Council are quite capable of sending one of their usual types here + dissipating the good will overnight. However I think they'll try to avoid this.

Rex's feelings about leaving were mixed: "I shall be quite glad to leave, but I'll always be fond of Greece + shall try to return some time."[80]

Shan Sedgwick, a *New York Times* reporter assigned to cover the British army in the Middle East area, knew Rex and attended one of his lectures. He and his Greek wife, Roxain, remember that the lecture was incoherent, obviously because of alcohol. Sedgwick commented, however, that Rex was "a drunkard in the eighteenth-century sense," meaning that he would never make a fool of himself, however tipsy. Sedgwick went on to comment that Rex was quite popular in Athens, and that "People wanted to be known as knowing him."[81] He was understood to be very interested in the welfare of anyone who studied or worked with him. Tassos Sagos, for instance, remembered that Rex took a great interest in him because of the black Nelsonian patch that he wore over his right eye, which he had lost in the war, and that Rex was always very warm and friendly. So he would be missed.

On 7 April Rex wrote to Lehmann that he was sending a "very good" portrait of Seferis by Ghika, and that he had asked Greenwood to show Lehmann his translation of "The Thrush."[82] Rex and Frances's arrival was scheduled for 22 May 1947.

Rex's last letter to Greenwood from Greece is dated 28 April. In it, he tells him that Jonathan will deliver olives and halva; ouzo was out because there was a large duty on it, and Jonathan might be short of cash. Rex too was short, and complained that everything was getting more expensive in Greece. He was going to lecture on

"Truth in Literature," there would follow a "very spectacular" art exhibition and a concert, and then it would be "goodbye to culture."

He asked Greenwood to get someone to book them rooms in London for their arrival, and he had started to worry about the period after July when they would be out of the Long Wittenham house. It would be quite a time of travels—Rex mentioned that he just received an invitation from the Czechs to visit the country at their expense, and Rex anticipated going in October.

A British Council memo of 2 November 1950 from A. C. Hayter notes that "When he [Rex] left Greece in May, 1947, he asked to be considered for another Council job, but wanted it to be one in England, or nearer home than Greece, because of his children's education and his literary career."[83]

Rex and Frances's last evening in Greece, 20 May 1947, was true to form: the Warners, the Katakouzinoses, and all the couple's other friends went to a taverna, where song and retsina flowed. The good times would not return quite so freely again for a long time. But Rex's bond with modern as well as ancient Greece had been firmly established, to last as long as Rex would. As he flew over Italy, he recalled, the tears came to his eyes because the sunset was not as beautiful as it would have been in Greece.

CHAPTER EIGHT

OXFORD AND BERLIN, 1947-1948

I. OXFORD

Rex left Greece in a hopeful frame of mind. The British Institute directorship, while delightful, had after all been a dead-end job, but he had done it well and had hopes of other employment with the British Council. He and Frances were getting along well, and he had gained self-confidence. He had an international literary reputation. However, he had gotten used to a relatively high standard of living, had cut loose from teaching, and had not done any creative writing (as opposed to translation) in Greece. And a new element suddenly entered his life in the form of Barbara Rothschild (nee Hutchinson). Then came eight months in Germany, coinciding with the beginning of the ten-month Russian blockade of the Western zones and the 25 June 1948 Allied Berlin airlift. As with the Depression, the Blitz, and the Greek civil war, Rex found himself again, however reluctantly, at an unpleasant nodal point in history.

Things began well for the Warners in England, where they arrived on the night of 25 May 1947, even though George had not closed his eyes during the entire trip. They were pleased with the cottage, The Grange, in Long Wittenham, which Cecil had procured for them (although the drains were stopped up at first). On 23 June Rex had to go to Musbury to referee between Cecil and Rosamond Lehmann, who were having a stormy relationship, but the English countryside was wonderful after the heat of the Greek spring. They enjoyed swimming outings with Pam and John and their younger child, Anne, then seven years old. There were good pubs, and lots of drinking (eventually including bitter which Rex had missed, and which had been hard to procure during the first few weeks of their return). George had a tame jackdaw, which he adorned with lipstick. They began to look for a more permanent house and considered Great Rissington and Wargrave.

Rex had lunch with George Barnes of the BBC on 5 June, and reported to Pam on 12 June that "I am still in the stage of sitting in front of blank sheets of paper; but I don't think this is a bad thing. Its a long time since I used my brain at all consciously."[1] Rex also found that "Thackeray is certainly a much nicer man than Dickens, though with less genius. Nothing can be more boring than 'Pendennis.'" He was reading "for some reason, *Garibaldi and the 10,000*" and thought (with some logic) that "1860 was about the last year in which politics were inspiring." Greece and Stalin had taken their toll on Rex's former idealism.

The family moved to an apartment at 11 Holywell, Oxford, during August. Rex wrote Greenwood on 9 August that "Its quite a nice place" but "there's the bloody business of finding somewhere else to live. . . . Meanwhile I've been approached by the British Council about what looks like a good job in Berlin, starting in October. I've written to find out more about it + also to tell them that I know no German,— which might rule me out anyway. But I'm getting so fed up with having nowhere settled to live + no fixed arrangement for the children that I look rather favourably on another move abroad." The apartment was full: Frances's brother David was with them, and so was Anna, and Rex's mother was due the next week. Jonathan had gone on a biking trip to the Hebrides. George was with Pam and John on holiday in Cornwall, where John almost set the house on fire trying to light a bad primus stove.

Despite all irritations, Rex had begun working creatively again. He had composed "a chapter and a bit," probably of *Men of Stones*, although he found it difficult "with all this planning to do, to write regularly." He was going to stay with Greenwood on Sunday, the17th August, because he had a BBC rehearsal at 8:30 and a broadcast of his talk, "The Poetry of Lucretius," at 10:30 P.M. Rex also wrote, "I'm enclosing a letter from a Hun. Can anything be done about it?" Perhaps this was a German publisher interested in one of Rex's books; *The Aerodrome*'s German-language publication in 1946 may have generated some interest.

On 27 August Rex and Frances moved into a "wonderful house, full of Victorian + very comfortable furniture, very quiet + immensely respectable" only a short bus ride from the pubs in Oxford, at 6 Staverton Road. Rex was expecting to get the job in Berlin, rather than in Switzerland or England as he would really have liked. He wrote Pam on 9 September that "I think I'll have to take the job, if it comes off, as life is far too expensive otherwise. Jonathan alone costs about £250 a year." In addition to thinking about the German job, he was continuing work on the novel *Men of Stones*: "I've written five chapters + am hoping that the story will work out. If it does, I can finish the book anywhere."[2]

On Sunday, 4 September, he wrote Greenwood that he'd discovered two beds in the Staverton Road house storeroom, and invited him for Friday evening. He discussed Ken Marshall's life, which was bleak—Marshall had suffered several breakdowns during the three years following the war, and was also on the point of getting divorced.

Rex stayed over in London on the 18th of September with Martin Field, a children's book editor, with whom he caroused a bit. But he wrote Greenwood on 21 September that things had gone downhill from there. The day before, Rosamond Lehmann's dentist had discovered via X-ray that Rex had "a vast submerged wisdom tooth ramming + entangled with some molars" and took his tooth out, along "with a great chunk of jaw," so that on the 21st Rex had "a face like a football + am very unsteady" and needed a series of penicillin injections. If he couldn't work or read, he could still listen to boxing on the radio. Since a translation of *The Wild Goose Chase* was just being published in Prague, the Communist government had offered Rex a trip to Czechoslovakia on 1 October, but now he couldn't be sure that it would happen. There was cause for some happiness, however: it seemed clear that he would get the Berlin job at the end of October. On the 22nd he wrote Greenwood that he was still suffering, but it had gotten better and he could tolerate sherry if not gin.

On 23 September he wrote George Seferis that "I've written perhaps a quarter of a rather queer novel which contains one character who faintly resembles Katsimbalis. This character is the best part of the book." But dental pain continued to intervene and he hadn't "been able to do any work for the last week, but hope to start again soon."[3]

Rex enjoyed being back in England, but he missed Athens:

> It seems almost certain that I shall go to Berlin at the end of October, to the University in the British zone. It will be interesting work + one will not be greatly out of touch with England; but in very many ways I'd much rather be in Athens. Indeed I regret it immensely. I have never in my life been so suddenly + so completely charmed with a country + a people, never made so many good friends so quickly. Early in the summer I met Gide here, + was delighted to hear him speak of Athens just as I felt.

On 11 October he wrote Greenwood from Hotel Alnon in Prague, the Czech trip having come through:

> I have just retired to my well-appointed room in this largest hotel in Prague + have telephoned for a beer + a Slivovitz to send me to sleep. Both are very good. So is the

Slovakian wine, especially the white. Czech gin is not . . . much good + I haven't even tried the whiskey. Food is very good + sound + plentiful, without being particularly exciting. But I believe that there are pleasures in store in Slovakia. So far the Czechs have given me lots of money + walked me off my feet. After the first day's sightseeing I developed enormous blisters + can scarcely move. In the mornings I've been looking at rather boring pictures with an enthusiastic Czech girl + have been left alone otherwise. Tomorrow there's a great cultural expedition to the writers' castle, + the secretary of the writers' syndicate says that he'll get me all the money I want. I'm also being entertained for one day by a progressive town named, aptly enough, Loony. Then I hope for a tour of Slovakia + the High Tatra. So far, so good + I should be back on the 25th.

As his ironic comment about Loony implies, Rex was far from an ideal Socialist guest, although he continued to be seen as one in Eastern Europe because of his past work. But he may have been more positively inclined than some other writers, even though he spoke the truth about the bloody failure of the Communist rebels in Greece, as his letter to Greenwood of 25 October, the day after his return, stated: "The whole trip was great fun + I horrified everyone by telling the truth about Greece. At my final press conference no one asked a single question on the subject. The publishers were very nice + gave me £25 which they didn't owe me. . . . I did Prague, Brno, Bratislava, the Tatras (high + low), + enjoyed it all."

On 28 October he invited Greenwood to a lunch at Long's at 12 noon for Jonathan, to be attended by Frances, Anna, and himself. He was able to report that "I'm getting along slowly with" *Men of Stones*. He complained about the lack of news about the German job, and added, "If only they were paying me all this time, I wouldn't worry."

Rex laid his letter to Seferis of 23 September 1947 aside and continued it about a month later, on 2 November, in Oxford. He was obviously exasperated that the British Council job, while officially slated to begin on 1 October, had not yet begun: "So far as I can make out from Lehmann 'The Thrush' should be published soon; but one never gets anything definite from publishers, the Council or life." He gave the news that "Now I have just returned from a fortnight in Czecho-Slovakia, which was very interesting. I was the guest of the government + made myself rather unpopular by saying that it was incorrect to suppose that 90% of the Greeks supported EAM. What is curious is that people in Europe, with all the aids of modern communications, are more ignorant of each other than they were in the age of Byron." This seems an uncharacteristically naive remark, as if the Communist government of Czechoslovakia suffered from a communications problem rather than from a desire to censor unfavorable news.

In a perspicacious BBC Third Programme radio talk entitled "Reflections on Franz Kafka" which he gave a year later, on 2 November 1948, Rex referred to the Czech trip, and went on to say very interesting things about Kafka:

> Last year in Prague I met some people who had known Kafka and his family. They were rather surprised at the present extent of his reputation and tended to explain away his talent by these arguments: he was a Jew living among Czechs and writing in German; he was, though interested for a time in Zionism, without a clear political faith; he was rather a crank; in particular, his relations with his father were far from satisfactory. This approach to literary criticism, partly psychological, partly political, partly moral, has its own interest but, I think, has no bearing on the problems of truth or of excellence in writing.

Rex found Kafka's work particularly apt for the times: "Its truth and beauty depend, like poetry, on a kind of exaggeration and on an unusual emphasis. Writers, no doubt, should aim at what is called a balanced view of the world; but there is still something to be said for a certain lack of balance where one is interested in the world of the concentration camp and the atomic bomb."[4] A reading of Kafka would be a good preparation for the German scene that Rex would soon encounter, as it had been earlier for Communist Prague.

In his letter of 23 September/2 November to Seferis, Rex puzzled over why he was going to Berlin, since "I dislike Germans intensely." He reported that "The other night, in this very respectable neighbourhood, Frances + I came home, shouting out" Greek phrases "at the tops of our voices."

On 12 November he wrote to Greenwood about a possible drama or film of one of his works by an Eastern European producer, Burian. At 11:30 on Monday, 17 November, Rex was scheduled to see George Barnes and Jo Manton of the Third Programme with his Xenophon *Persian Expedition* translation manuscript in hand, and he asked Greenwood to send Barnes a copy of his *Prometheus Bound*, published that month by the Bodley Head, as well. That night, Rex and Frances entertained Bowra, who had supplied them "with a pheasant, some Chateau-bottled claret + some rather fine port." Rex was trying to finish up a broadcast for the schools on Greek and Roman education. There was still no news from the British Council, and Rex had only the meager proceeds from the BBC and his previous publications to live on.

From 2:30 to 4:30 in the afternoon of Friday, 28 November, Rex recorded a talk on education at Film House, 2 Sheraton St., London. He also had lunch with a BBC "education chap." On 18 December from 6:15 to 6:45 Rex reviewed Henri Troyat's

Firebrand, a life of Dostoyevsky, at Broadcast House. Anna, who was visiting Rex and Frances to see if a surgical procedure could cure her epileptic condition, was scheduled to leave on the 11th; nothing could be done. Rex still had no news from the British Council.

As Christmas approached, on 20 December, Rex begged C. J. openly for some money, stating that he was

> getting rather alarmed at the extent of my debts, possibly as a result of looking at my post when I returned here + finding due £25 rent, £30 hospital, £10 drink. Add to this the £50 I owe the Greek, the £60 I owe Jonny's school, + consider that the overdraft is still about £250, + you get an idea. I'm certainly owed at least £150 by the Council + am writing about it. But meanwhile could something be done as an advance on the new book [*Men of Stones*] + on the Penguin money? [either for *Prometheus Bound*, which was just published in November, or for Xenophon, which would be published in 1949]. Once I get to Germany I shall attempt to live on my salary. The present period is the critical one.

Rex added good wishes for Christmas and then, like Scrooge, wrote, "You can think of us as involved in awful children's parties." One of those was to prove if not awful then at least fateful.

Greenwood responded favorably to Rex's desperate plea for money, because on 24 December, Rex thanked him for a check. The Staverton Road house was now full of decorations and excited children, as well as Rex's mother, who "introduces some order." They had a goose on the 24th and were to have an "enormous" turkey the next day. Best of all, the drink situation was "fairly sound."

II. ENTER BARBARA ROTHSCHILD

Rex was not to get to Germany until January 1948 because of British Council delays. If he had managed to leave earlier, in the early fall of 1947, his subsequent life would have been much different than it was. At some point that fall, through Rosamond Lehmann and Maurice Bowra, Rex met Barbara, formerly Lady Rothschild. The daughter of a known Bloomsbury group family, Barbara played a notable role in the social history of the period (as we shall see in the next chapter). Her former husband was Baron Nathaniel Mayer Victor Rothschild, the heir to the British Rothschild fortune and once chief scientist of Great Britain, who had contributed enormously to the war effort. She had converted to Judaism when she married him, and with him she had had three children—Sarah, Joseph, and Miranda.

On George's birthday, Christmas Day 1947, Barbara brought Miranda to George's party since the children were the same age but had not yet met. Whether George and Miranda got along is not clear, but Rex and Barbara did. It is not difficult to see why. Even when I met her in 1988 at the age of 77, Barbara was immensely charming. Tall and stately, she had an elegance about her. She spoke with a bracing candor—perhaps like Bowra—that was so bold as to be witty. She began our interview by admitting that she was "terrified" of me in my role as a biographer, and she defended herself from what she imagined might be a negative perception of her life by saying that while she had not been good, she had not been boring either.

Frances noticed a flirtation at this birthday party on Christmas Day 1947; after it, Rex talked about Barbara as a beautiful creature, and Frances was sad. But the stirrings were already in progress by then. According to Barbara, she first met Rex at a party given by Graham Greene at his house in Oxford, undoubtedly in the fall of 1947, when Rex was living in the Staverton Road house. Barbara remembered that there were lots of priests and dons there. One of her friends—probably Catherine Walston, Greene's mistress—told her that there was not a single man worth speaking to in the room, but after looking at Rex Barbara responded—"Ah, there's one." While Barbara said that for her Rex was not a grand passion, she also said that he looked like the perfect man, with "splendid, rugged looks, reserve, and knowledge." She of course saw him after the first flush of Greece and at a time when he had resumed creative work. She suggested to Catherine that they make a bet to see which of the two of them could speak to him first. Barbara maneuvered her way through a group of priests and found Rex leaning on the mantelpiece with a drink. Rosamond Lehmann (who probably had been instrumental in getting Rex invited to Greene's party) then came up and unintentionally spoiled this first approach. Another account has Barbara telling one of her friends, "I must have that man."

So Barbara, characteristically, made the first move, but Rex apparently was not far behind, and by the time of George's birthday party the attraction had gone far enough for Frances to notice it. Barbara and Rex saw each other once or twice before he left for Berlin in January. She told him to go there and find out what he felt. That was not hard to discover, because according to her, Rex wrote her hundreds of passionate love letters during his eight months in Germany. "Hundreds" is not an exaggeration, because she stated that he wrote every single day. She would not show me the letters because, she said, she did not want to hurt Frances's feelings. According to Barbara, he saw Barbara as the "perfect woman," and she saw him as the ideal man.

III. BERLIN

Rex's appointment began on 10 January 1947. Frances remembered the train journey to Berlin as long, cold, and slow. Rex and Frances traveled together with George and Anna. They went through devastated towns and a bleak countryside that was an external symbol of their feelings, which had already begun to deteriorate.

Berlin itself was not any better off than the rest of Germany. Trevor Davies, who also served in the British education service after the war, remembered seeing, one year after the war was over,

> acres of ruins, roads littered with rubble, people crossing to Tiergarten by ferry (the bridges had been destroyed), bare-footed men pushing belongings on home-made carts, women piling up masonry, wearing layers of clothes to keep out the cold. The single sheets of the newspapers gave lists of those who had died of cold and hunger, infant mortality . . . rocketed. Children took it in turns to wear the family shoes to go to school, yet English visitors expressed astonishment at their neat and clean appearance. Women took on heavy work so as to get out of the lowest category of food rationing. . . . The juvenile prisons were full to overflowing with young blackmarketeers, made criminal by need.[5]

Frances too recalled that Berlin at this time was ghastly, a complete wreck.

Although a British Council employee with the title of Lecturer in English at the Technical University of Berlin, Rex was actually working for the educational branch of the Allied Control Commission. At first the couple lived with Rex's boss Robert Birley in his house, one of the few houses standing in a formerly affluent area, which was comparable to Hampstead in London. Birley's official title was Educational Adviser to the Military Governor, Control Commission for Germany, and he had a profound knowledge of the literature, history, and philosophy of the country that suited him for this task. Following their stay with Birley came a few weeks of temporary housing and finally the Warners were given a flat at 83 Hohenzollerndamm, in the Grünewald section of Berlin in the British Zone.

Robert Birley's essay, "British Policy in Retrospect," explains the situation in the city of Berlin and in the Technical University at the time. Birley had come to Germany in April 1947 as a successor to Prof. Donald Riddy, who had laid down the lines of British educational policy soon after the war. The Potsdam Agreement had specified that "German education shall be so controlled as completely to eliminate National Socialist and militarist doctrines and to make possible the successful development of democratic ideas."[6] Every month the Educational Committee of the Allied Control

Commission met to work out policies, but accomplished little in practical terms. The French and Russians believed that "re-education" of the Germans was possible; the British did not. The Russians simply planned to annex their sector of the city, which they did. The Americans followed a generous but firm policy, even providing the German history textbook that was to be used in their zone.

The British Military Government, according to Birley, fully controlled education in the British Zone for no more than eighteen months; already in December 1946 they had handed over lawmaking in this area to the state assemblies. The British then went from being controllers to acting as advisers. As such, they helped reestablish a destroyed educational establishment. The British gave advice rather than prescribed solutions to such problems as how to make it possible for students to remain at the university, or how to obtain enough textbooks. In 1947, however, several basic rules were laid down, including raising the status of the teacher training colleges and providing free secondary education. There were many fascinating problems, such as what to do about the education of the children of former Nazi leaders. While Birley understood that "The future of German civilisation" largely depended on the reconstruction of the universities, and felt that "it is, perhaps, our first duty to try to help them," he did not dodge the issues: "For there is no escape from the fact that the Germans, at the time of the Nazis' rise to power, failed to show that almost primitive and unconscious reaction, which is the basis of social morality of ordinary people, of exclaiming that there are some actions which are beyond the pale."[7]

Berlin was not formally divided by the Russians until 30 November 1948, but the Russian blockade of the Western zones began on 18 June when Rex was still in the city. From the outset the Russians had insisted on taking over the University of Berlin (renamed Humboldt University during the time of the East German Republic), and the British insisted on keeping the Technical University of Berlin-Charlottenburg under their control as a retaliatory measure.

At all the German universities, there was a great shortage of teachers and teaching materials, and students had difficulty sustaining themselves while studying. Geoffrey Bird, who served as a British adviser at Göttingen University during this period, mentioned that there were psychological and ideological problems as well:

> I had many informal discussions with students on all sorts of questions, often long into the night. They wanted to know everything possible about the outside world—what had happened before and during the War, how much we considered them responsible for events, why everyone had "turned against them" and what they could themselves do to help to restore democratic government and build up a peaceful and prosperous state. . . .

Their questions were startling in the implication of the state of mind behind them, as when a student asked a visiting British MP in 1946 why we had not yet launched an offensive against the Russians in order to rescue the many thousands of German prisoners of war, whether we intended to do so, and if not why not. The question met with applause from the audience, but not the reply!

Moreover, the students were not familiar with democracy: "They needed guidance in simple democratic procedures, such as electing their officers and committee, setting up committees dealing with problems of accommodation and student welfare, and how to chair a meeting. They were inclined to wait for orders from someone."[8] In Berlin, Rex had the reputation of being a good teacher of English literature, but teaching was not his major preoccupation during this period.

IV. REX'S WINTER OF DISCONTENT

Into this dark and increasingly tense political atmosphere Rex stepped at the very moment that his attention was focused on England and Barbara Rothschild. Taqui Stevens, wife of *Observer* reporter Robert Stevens and herself a Syrian-born writer and intellectual, was one witness to his actions and statements over these months.

She first met Frances and Rex at the Press Club on Fontanastrasse in the Grünewald section of Berlin at an unspecified time after their arrival. Rex was a "name" in the 1940s, and since she had just been reading *The Aerodrome*, she was very excited about meeting him. Her husband, too, admired Rex greatly. He seemed very relaxed and unserious on the surface, but after she knew him better she noticed that he was always red in the face and drinking brandy even at breakfast, and that he was quite fidgety until he had his brandy. Someone commented that Rex's face "looked like a Gloucester ploughland." She noticed, too, that Rex would not expose his actual feelings. He had an ironic, teasing way of talking at this time, and was not particularly nice about George and Anna. She remembered him saying once, "Let's get rid of the children and then we can enjoy ourselves," but this may not have been quite as harsh as it sounds.

Greece was one of the few things he talked positively about at this time. It is Taqui's impression that during their discussions Rex had a way of being scornful about everything except the Greeks. He talked a lot about Seferis and seemed sorry to have left Greece. He did not want to see the Russians come into Berlin, but he did not like the British administration either. This was a somewhat contradictory situation: he was against bureaucracy but he was an "official," if not an actual bureaucrat, himself. Whatever he thought of the Nazi government and party, he was not prejudiced against German individuals and was nice to the servants. He had had servants only in Greece, and perhaps had grown to like having them around. Rex and Frances were given a little car with a chauffeur as well as a German maid, both of whom were delighted to have jobs and to be working in an English household. There was hardly any traffic. George went to a little army school, while Anna attended an international school, which she liked.

In Germany, however, the family was not living nearly as well as they had in Greece; there were no groceries, and they ate army rations gotten from government shops with Control Commission currency, and had to abide by strict rationing rules. They were not allowed to exchange strawberries for oatmeal, for instance. Moreover, the whole atmosphere was very unpleasant. Even privileged German people would ask the British residents for bacon rinds and tea leaves. Frances took German lessons, and the teacher asked for soap flakes and sugar instead of cash payment. There was also a sour, unwashed smell in crowded places. Moreover, signs of despair were everywhere: the club cook's husband was a prisoner of war in Russia, and she would go every day to the train station to see if he had returned.

The Warners and the Stevenses played "Ludo" ("Parchesi" to Americans) to pass the time, and there were some pleasures. Yehudi Menuhin gave a concert, and Rex loved it. He especially liked Mozart's *Eine Kleine Nachtmusik*, which was sometimes played on a phonograph at the club. Around May, Rex traveled by car to Munich to attend a Youth Conference, and he enjoyed getting away from Berlin.

At first Taqui thought that Rex and Frances were happy, especially since they had the two children with them. But after a month together, Frances told her that they were going to break up after they got back to England. Frances was very fraught at this time, while Taqui realized that Rex was showing the strain by too much laughing and drinking, making Frances even more unhappy. According to Frances, Rex's view was that if he was in love with Barbara he ought to have the integrity to act on that rather than to live a lie. He was incapable of just having a fling—if he felt he was in love, then he had to go completely. In Berlin, Rex himself said that when he met Barbara he could not just have an affair. He had to leave Frances or not see Barbara at all; Frances told me that they did not share the same bed for this entire eight-month Berlin period. Paradoxically, the rectitude of Rex's mother may have had an influence on him—even in a romantic affair, he had to follow through on strict principles. Another man might well have remained married while having an affair, and perhaps that would have been easier for all concerned, including Frances and himself.

According to Taqui, he did not consciously care about Barbara's money; he did not care about houses and environments any more than he cared about clothes. Yet at least unconsciously he could not have been indifferent to the idea of living well, even more so than he had in Greece.

There was not all that much writing going on, except perhaps for love letters because of Rex's preoccupation with Barbara, but there was writing. In February 1948 he published a short essay, "The Poetry of George Seferis," in *Orpheus*,[9] and in April a brief travel article, "Where Shall John Go? XV-Greece,"[10] in *Horizon*. His short introduction to the translation of Seferis's *The King of Asine and Other Poems* by Spencer, Valaoritis, and Durrell was published by Lehmann in May.[11] At about this same time, a French translation of *The Professor*, by Ludmilla Savitsky, appeared through R. Martin in Paris. Work on *Men of Stones* continued, and Rex's Xenophon translation was also in the works. Regardless of his problems or concerns, it seems that Rex never went more than a few weeks devoid of writing activity during the major years of his career.

Some long and important letters to Pam Morris from April through June of 1948 give insight into his thinking about his personal situation at this time. Barbara Rothschild's statement that Rex was passionately in love with her certainly finds confirmation in his letters to Pam. From Berlin around April 1948, Rex wrote to Pam that he had just had a week in England with Barbara, "during which I didn't come + see you. I think, however, that you would forgive me for this if you knew how happy I was during this time. I don't know what will happen in the future, but I have certainly found something which I shall never give up." He goes on to comment on his relationship to Frances at this time: "Things here have, of course, been very sad + distressing. I think they are getting better. No more for the moment about this. You'll know that if I hadn't been very deeply serious about it, I should never have acted as I have. Please forgive me for my inability when in England to do anything except what was uppermost in my mind."

Rex finds, though, that "Berlin is getting slightly better, + we're beginning to meet one or two people who aren't appalling. But I'm hoping that we'll be liberated by the Russians before very long. The job here is . . . unimportant + I'm beginning to think that there's no future with the Council. Quite likely I shall try for some good job with the B.B.C. And for the moment I shall try to finish this book. It's already almost like summer here +, once one gets away from the ruins to the lakes, its rather pleasant. But one feels very imprisoned +, though one is at the centre of European politics, I'd rather be somewhere where politics weren't mentioned."[12]

Among the people they met and liked, besides the Stevenses, were Hilda and Peter de Mendelssohn. Peter was also a foreign correspondent, and managed to arrange a tour of Hitler's bunker. Frances remembered this as an awful experience, and even suggested to me that Rex may have eventually retreated into the past as a way, finally, of avoiding the overwhelming politics of the present. Frances said that Rex was at this time in a state of mental torment such that it became very difficult to live together.

She was not in very good shape either. Rex's letter of 27 April 1948 from c/o The Educational Adviser's Office, H.Q., C.C.G. (B.E.), Berlin B.A.U.R. 2 to Pam, explores his situation with Frances in some depth:

> ... as you can well imagine, life hasn't been easy. In fact its been rather hell. I wish, both for her sake + for mine, that Frances could get back to England, + I wish that I'd never come here. Here I am tortured by absence from what I want, by guilt (though I don't really regard it as guilt) + by F.'s unhappiness + my own. It would be much better for us to be away from each other, whatever happens afterwards. As you will have understood by now, what is happening to me is something much more than an "affair." It seems to me that I have at last found everything I want + (though such statements are apt to appear foolish) I'm sure I'm right. In fact, knowing you as I do, I don't think that you will regard such a statement, coming from me, as foolish. In the end I shall certainly live with Barbara married if possible, unmarried, if not. Of course I want to make things as easy as possible for Frances, but the one thing she wants is simply beyond my power to give. This being so, I think it is sure that we shall separate, + I only want to do it on the terms that will be best for her + the children.

He continued, "As it is, life is rather a nightmare. I can't work + am usually intoxicated or in a state. Berlin is awful + I count the weeks till I get back. In many ways, no doubt, things are worse for F. I, at least, know that I could be happy in a moment, if I were free. But things are quite bad enough for me. However the few months will pass."

Considerate despite the passion that was sweeping him and his marriage away, Rex asked Pam to find a place for Frances and the children in Oxford. She would then probably go to Jersey in the summer, and maybe to Brittany at the end of May. Rex added, "I myself couldn't bear this life much longer, + shall be back in July, if not before." Finally he wrote that he was enclosing a testimonial for Ken Marshall, who was then in search of a job, and gave Pam the liberty to rewrite it and "forge" his signature if she felt that was necessary to adapt it to a particular job.[13]

By 26 June Rex was still in Berlin, and wrote this to Pam:

> Life here, with the present political tensions, gets worse + worse, + I'm longing to be away from it. The present plan is for Frances + the children to go to a Leave Centre in the Bavarian Alps about July 13th + stay till the end of the month, then move to England

+ probably stay in Rosamond's flat in London for August. But I'm rather doubtful whether the Bavarian idea will come off, as transport to + from Berlin is bound to be more + more limited. . . . I'd certainly feel much happier if she + the children were out of Germany altogether. As soon as they leave Berlin I shall do likewise, never having enjoyed a city less. Things between F. + me are rather better than they were, but of course it is all very painful, + I really don't think I could stand much more of this life. I think she too will be happier when this period is over. The possible dangers of the Berlin situation don't make things any better. Perhaps things aren't rather serious, but there is always the chance of the Americans doing something foolish.[14]

V. MEN OF STONES

No letters to Greenwood survive from 1948; he probably destroyed them owing to their sensitive personal content. The Lehmann letters are also sparse, and the letters to Pam stress Rex's personal situation. So there is no record of how he was getting on with his novel, *Men of Stones*, originally to be entitled *The Prison*. It is fair to assume, however, that Rex wrote the major portion of the novel during 1948 and possibly early 1949, so it reflects to some degree the tense situation in Berlin, where on 25 June the Allies began an airlift in reaction to a Russian blockade of the Western part of the city. It mirrors earlier events as well.

Men of Stones captures Rex's retrospective reaction to the political situation in Greece and the horrors of World War II, and his own helplessness in the face of these events. In *The Wild Goose Chase* he could present George's quasi-Marxist triumph, however skeptically it is ultimately treated; in *The Professor*, there was a desperate call to action going beyond liberalism; in *The Aerodrome*, Rex took comfort in the English countryside and untidy life itself as an answer to all calls to ideology; in *Why Was I Killed?* he questioned war and juxtaposed the beauty of nature to it; in *Men of Stones*, however, he had no positive call to action, resolution of issues, or hope to offer a warring world. Moreover, his allegorical style is very unconvincing in its vagueness, especially in view of the concrete horrors of World War II massacres and concentration camps that had been revealed by the 1945-46 Nuremberg trials and the accounts of survivors. By the time of this last allegorical novel, politics (or rather any hope of political improvement) for Rex were completely burned out, perhaps like Berlin itself, and allegorical fiction could not compete with a terrible reality.

A prison is set on an island in a beautiful bay, much like the Ionian Sea. The political situation leading to incarceration is "of extraordinary complexity," so that some of the prisoners have been imprisoned by the very regime they thought they were fighting for, while others who opposed the regime are set free for no reason. (Indeed, the Greek civil war had no logic; nor did the extermination of the Jews; nor did Stalin's turning on loyal Communists.) The Governor in the story, who is essentially the Air Vice-Marshal reincarnated, is defeated by the Minister of Information, who is as evil as he is, and no particular words of wisdom are spoken by the relatively civilized Colonel Felson and Mr. Goat (the British Council figures), by Marcus the concentration camp survivor, or by Captain Nicholas, the hardened soldier and bon vivant resembling Katsimbalis or Sikelianos. At the end of the novel the reader is left with a new civil war.

The prison has much in common with a German concentration camp, in that people regardless of age or sex are imprisoned there arbitrarily. Moreover, the prisoners have been turned into automata because the Governor's philosophy is that people are most happy when they are obedient servants who do not question the will of their rulers, who must be seen for this purpose as gods. In *Men of Stones*, Rex tries to explain the success of both Hitler and Stalin, as he had in *The Cult of Power*, on the basis of their destruction of past, generalized ideals of beneficence and their creation of a new godlike worship. The following is from *The Cult of Power*:

> There is to be no longer any truck with the dogmatic and generalised belief in a God to whom all human souls are of equal value; instead there is a human leader to take the responsibility of his own people. There is no more use for the liberal "scientific" notions that the interests of mankind are inseparable. The leader will see to it that his own people get the lion's share. There is no longer any talk of gentleness, of international good will and the like. The armed people confront the world with an independence and virility that scorn such weak notions. Yet among themselves there exists a "real" brotherhood, as distinct from the sentimental professions of the priests and internationalists, a brotherhood of arms.[15]

Toward the end of *Men of Stones*, Dostoyevsky is mentioned by Colonel Felson, the cultural attaché. In his essay on Dostoyevsky, Rex had called attention to Stavrogin, the nihilistic protagonist of *The Possessed*: "The strong man who wins what is considered to be individual freedom—freedom from prejudice, convention, fear of others and of himself—is, in the end, most utterly lost."[16] We recall also that Stavrogin married a crippled, half-witted beggar, just as the Governor keeps a crippled female consort, to demonstrate his unpredictability and disregard for convention. In his essay on Dostoyevsky, Rex had mentioned the "vaulting ambition" that Shakespeare also condemned; and *King Lear*, with its phrase "men of stones" used to describe hard-hearted ambitious people, also figures prominently in *Men of Stones*. Rex was expressing in fictional form his aversion, already stated in his essays, to those who, like Lear, Stavrogin, and Hitler, would set themselves above others and free themselves from "bourgeois" humanistic ideals, including those of the English countryside—life, love, good eating, drinking, and free expression. In all of his original fictional work he really gives us an English village boy's view—strongly tempered by Christianity, moralism, and a knowledge of classical civilization—of systems such as Communism and fascism. While continuing to despise fascism, he had obviously given up all the leftist idealism of his youth but had failed to find anything concrete to replace it.

The vague landscape in part of the novel bears a resemblance to postwar Berlin— "unrelieved misery and devastation."[17] Also, a young officer conjures up the concentration camps that Rex had seen on his mission to Germany just after World War II: "I just went out and was sick. It was partly the smell. One just couldn't get rid of it. You see the people had been dying like flies for about a fortnight. You can't describe it, really, those mounds of bodies with the stomachs caved in, and arms like sticks. And that frightful look in their eyes. And then, worse than anything, the smell. . . . there weren't many of the internees left alive, and they were in an awful state, not human beings at all, just animals" (63). There is also an old nurse whose "line was getting the gold out of people's teeth. No anaesthetics of course."[18] This was the dental assistant he had seen in the prisoner of war camp in Germany.

Rex goes beyond this surface description of some facts to chilling insight as Marcus, the Governor's brother, tells us on the basis of his own experience what it is like to be in a concentration camp:

> One begins to regard it as almost a normal thing that women should be raped over and over again. If any of them make a fuss about it one's feelings are almost of a kind of irritation. One begins to look at those who are being led to death not only calmly, but even with a kind of satisfaction, since one is alive oneself. . . . It may be also that one's mind is incapable of dealing with the very numbers concerned. Two or three people in pain and misery, especially if one knows them, excite our pity; but when you see hundreds going to death, somehow they seem more like animals than human beings, though, in point of fact, they are not animals.[19]

As a believer in the classical Greek and humanistic virtues of love, courage, and loyalty, Rex had to confront the complete moral nihilism of the concentration camps, which he saw with his own eyes during the German trip right after the war. His writing about these things was an attempt to come to terms with them, but he does not give enough detail to force us to confront the experience viscerally rather than intellectually. Moreover, Rex had no response to make to the camps, beyond a rather vague and unconvincing religious belief and abstract ideal of love. He could not face the reality of those camps and his own lack of any answer to them any better than Cecil Grant had faced the philosophical implications of World War I, and Rex's art, in its very vagueness, shows that avoidance.

Rex wrote that a main character was vaguely based on Katsimbalis, and this would be Captain Nicholas, an exiled soldier who had fought in his country's civil war, and who recounts that his father told him to enjoy himself because "You won't have long to do so. The world is in a terrible state. Women are becoming like men and men like women. People eat less and less. In Europe they think about justice in a very bitter way. In America they are always washing and playing games. But there is no justice, and that is why we must be kind" (61). He invites a young officer to his own country, especially to the little wine shops in the city and countryside.

Marcus decides to return with Captain Nicholas to seek a miraculous monastery said to be near the prison. This is the main point of the novel: Marcus's quest for some kind of positive belief is pitted against the Governor's rigid and yet unpredictable ideology. The phrase "the wild goose chase" is used (138) to describe Marcus's attempt and this reminds us of the search of the brothers in Rex's first serious novel. But while George's "wild goose chase" in *The Wild Goose Chase* resulted in the overthrow of an unjust government, in *Men of Stones* the phrase seems apt for Marcus's disappointing quest. Rex was no longer young and idealistic.

Besides Rex's inability to offer any answer to contemporary problems, the new novel seems skeptical about personal matters as well. Mr. Goat is a naive young lecturer in literature attached to a foreign mission, whose job is to have the prisoners act out plays by Shakespeare as a way of reforming them. His immediate boss is Colonel Felson, who serves in Rex's British Council position—director of cultural affairs for a foreign embassy. Mr. Goat is seduced by the Governor's wife, a former guerrilla fighter who is alternately sweet and vicious, whom he improbably falls in love with the day he arrives at the prison. Mr. Goat's guilty abandonment of his earlier, more naive ideals about faithfulness may be an expression of Rex's own guilt with regard to leaving Frances and his family. The disabled "consort" of the Governor may have been inspired by Anna.

In this novel even more than in Rex's other allegories we find a tendency to preach (showing Rex's inclination as the son of a minister and a teacher), but without the counterbalance of enough dramatic action and depth of characterization to compensate the reader for this didactic mood. Rex himself wrote of Dostoyevsky that in *The Brothers Karamazov*, Dostoyevsky's characters "have, in addition to their symbolic character, a new warmth of humanity which makes them appear to us more real and more moving than their prototypes who were often over-intellectualised."[20] Rex's *Aerodrome* is the only place where he fully escapes the pitfalls of didacticism and one-dimensional characterization typical of the "allegorical" novel. But even in *The Wild Goose Chase* and *The Professor* there was far more dramatic action and depth of character than in *Men of Stones*.

When we reach the climax of *Men of Stones*, the acting out of *King Lear*, we find that it takes only two pages, and the dramatization does not contain any ingenuity. The Governor's unfaithful wife is killed and the Minister bombards the prison, and that is it. The action in Dostoyevsky's novels, including the trial of Dmitri in *Brothers Karamazov*, is always completely detailed and brilliantly worked out. In plot as in characterization Rex, especially in this novel, is clearly no Dostoyevsky.

Still, like Dostoyevsky and the Roman historians, Rex understands the godlike dictatorial ruler's belief that he can establish his power precisely by breaking hallowed moral taboos: "What men worship is precisely that which is not bound down to the standards of thought and behaviour which are familiar to them. They cannot revere anything which is situated comfortably within the limits of their imagination."[21] Unfortunately, Rex now has no answer to the power mongers and sees only continued warfare ahead.

This would be Rex's last attempt to use the allegorical method to treat the theme of power hunger among political rulers. This topic had obsessed him from the 1930s until the end of the 1940s, and represented his application of the classical theme of hubris or pride to the modern world's dictators. Perhaps there is also some retrospective self-condemnation here too. For Rex has Colonel Felson, the cultural attaché, refuse to make any political or moral decisions. Here Rex with artistic freedom may have been attacking the political role of neutrality that he himself took in Greece as British Institute director, and that he for the most part defends in the later nonfictional *Views of Attica*, written with British Council cooperation.

But can we blame Rex, as he may have blamed himself, for taking no stand on the problems leading to the Greek civil war and then, in Germany in 1948, possibly to a war between the West and Russia? In reality he could do little to influence these events, whether as British Institute director or as a writer, even if he had found a stand to take on them. He had opposed the Nazis from the start, but what good had that done? World War II and the Holocaust happened just as if he had never written a line. In the 1930s, too, he had advocated Marxism, but then came Stalin. Moreover, the possibility of a better world following World War II that he had tentatively glimpsed in *Why Was I Killed?* had given way to the realities of the Cold War. Rex may have lost interest in politically "engaged" writing because it seemed futile to him. After one uncharacteristically comic novel in which he would make fun of political beliefs in general, he would retreat intellectually into the more distant and therefore less threatening politics of the ancient world.

Rex, Frances, George, and Anna left Germany by train on 14 July 1948. Their experience in Germany had been politically and personally devastating. The trip took a day and a night, so they parted at King's Cross station in London around 16 July. Frances and the children went to an apartment in Oxford for a few months and then, in March 1949, to Jersey. Rex went straight from the station to Barbara Rothschild.

CHAPTER NINE

TACKLEY AND BOGNOR REGIS, 1948-1951

I. REX AND BARBARA

During the years from 1948 to 1958, Rex turned from the politics of the modern world, which had preoccupied him, to the politics of the ancient world. He moved from original novels to translation and historical novels and became an established literary arbiter. He became more conservative, but remained true to the ideals of liberalism and democracy that he had supported all his life. His personal life became more varied, and he was in touch with the elite of English intellectual society.

Rex arrived at Barbara's very elegant house in Tackley, near Oxford, with only his suitcase in hand. She was shocked, even after all the letters, to see him actually appear. One can picture the scene: Rex, having made a momentous decision to leave his family and having suffered through eight months of mental torture with them in Germany with only a short visit to her during that time, approaching Barbara with a more or less passionate phrase, and she, delighted but slightly amazed and amused by it all, responding somewhat less passionately but still very warmly to his presence. Eventually the marriage was to become more routine, with Rex reverting to his habits of steady drinking and outward reserve and Barbara growing increasingly bored until in May 1958 they separated permanently, Barbara having taken up with—of all people—Nico Ghika. But that was in the future.

The couple shared some tastes. Barbara liked walking in the country, and so did Rex. They both enjoyed good food and wine. Although she was used to servants, she could be unpretentious. In her vacation house called Cliff Cottage, at Fishguard, near Newport and St. David's in Wales, Barbara would do her own cooking. She loved Rex's straightforwardness and the fact that he was not superficial. She also felt, rightly, that he had a noble personality—that he was in fact a king, as his name implied. He was also physically large and attractive. He undoubtedly liked her wit and charm, and had no aversion to living well. Rex did not like Mary Hutchinson, Barbara's mother, but got on with Barbara's equally witty brother Jeremy, with whom he would talk cricket and philosophy and joke and drink beer. In the end, however, despite these delights and commonalities that united the couple, the Rex-Barbara episode was a passion without a lasting basis, and Rex's drinking finally got in the way.

It has been said that because of Barbara Rex stopped writing, that the life of luxury did not agree with him and hurt his imagination, and that, essentially, she put him in a golden cage that kept him from achieving what he could have done otherwise. He did lead a life of great luxury with Barbara, and was part of her brilliant social whirl. He had a wonderful study, especially in the house at Woodstock that they were to occupy. Barbara herself said that perhaps Rex needed more of a life challenge, but she also made clear that he liked being "comfortable." In fact, in one of his book reviews dating from this period, he stressed the idea that the production of literature demands some serenity and freedom from worry, including economic worry.

The idea that Rex was harmed by luxury ignores the fact that by the time he was with Barbara, Rex of his own accord had already made his peace with politics. He had made a steadily less rebellious political statement in the course of his first four allegorical novels, going from the radicalism of *The Wild Goose Chase* and *The Professor* to the far more moderate *Aerodrome* and pacifistic *Why Was I Killed?* and finally to the unconvincing *Men of Stones*, which revealed the end of his political idealism. Moreover, through his translations, he had (again, of his own accord) become even more enamored of the Arnoldian virtues of the Greek and Latin classics, and had become more conservative socially and in his artistic tastes. He had given over his earlier and always ambivalent leftist dogmatism already in *The Aerodrome*, although he remained liberal; he was therefore not averse on moral principles to enjoying the good (that is, rich) life.

Life is indeed messy as Roy had learned, and not geometrically perfect or subject to some impossible ideal, as the Air Vice-Marshal (and the Governor in *Men of Stones*) would have it. Stalin, Britain's positive role in World War II, and Communist excesses in Greece had permanently changed Rex's mind about Marxism and Russia. Unlike some liberals who have never forgiven Rex for this change, I can only see it as a wise response to these political currents as well as a natural shift of middle age. Perhaps he felt that after all of the hardships that he had undergone, he was deserving of some pleasure. But he never took money from Barbara, and from all accounts the couple was genuinely happy for five or six years, especially because Barbara completely supported Rex's literary activities, which included reading Dickens's *Little Dorrit* and Milton's *Paradise Lost* aloud with her at the fireplace. Barbara remembered that Rex wrote fluently every day without the need for revision, and that he read the chapters of his books, which she remembered as being wonderfully expressive and lucid, to her as he worked on them.

In fact, this was one of his most productive, if not most vigorously original, artistic periods: he turned out the lighthearted and very funny novel, *Escapade*, in which he gently mocks the social order of an English village and the right—and left—wing politics of his age; the superb travel book *Views of Attica*; mostly well-received studies of Milton and E. M. Forster; and his most famous and ambitious translation, of Thucydides' notoriously difficult-to-translate *Peloponnesian War*, which has sold nearly one million copies. And this is not to mention other translations and a very popular book on the Greek philosophers. He wrote many important reviews for *London Magazine, New Statesman*, and the *Spectator*, and gave BBC talks. He wrote *The Young Caesar*, his first and very impressive historical novel. He wrote the narratives for two Basil Wright films, *World Without End* (1953) about the problem of world poverty, and *The Immortal Land* (1958), about Greece. He also continued the fruitful friendly and professional relationship with George Seferis that would eventually help Seferis win the Nobel Prize. This is not an unimpressive list of accomplishments for a less-than-ten-year period. It was all completed despite (or perhaps with the aid of) a steady diet of alcohol and social life.

There were many interlocking relationships between Rex and Barbara's circles, and a list of their friends reads like a catalog of the British intellectual and social elite of the 1950s. Bowra, for instance, had been a friend of Barbara's as well as of Rex's, while Graham Greene's mistress, Catherine Walston, was one of Barbara's best friends. Rex also met George "Dadie" Rylands, center of a circle at Cambridge, with whom Barbara was friendly. Jill Day-Lewis, widow of C. Day-Lewis, recalls Rex and Barbara bringing Anthony Blunt, the art historian who was later exposed as a spy for the Russians, to the Day-Lewis studio flat around 1951 or 1952. On a trip to China, Rex became friends with Oxford philosopher A. J. "Freddie" Ayer and architect Hugh Casson, while designer and illustrator Michael Ayrton was also among their acquaintances. He wrote a book on Greek philosophy in collaboration with Oxford philosopher Geoffrey Warnock. To this group must be added Day-Lewis and Seferis, as well as other members of Rex's Greek circle, including Katsimbalis and Ghika.

II. BARBARA HERSELF

Barbara, one of the most socially adept women of her generation in England, was used to excitement. Barbara Judith Hutchinson had been born on 22 February 1911 at 18 Cheyne Row in Chelsea South, London. Her father, St. John Hutchinson, K.C., was a great criminal lawyer, and her mother Mary, the former Mary Barnes, was a cousin of Lytton Strachey and a notable figure in the Bloomsbury literary set, which included Leonard and Virginia Woolf and (on the fringes) Lady Ottoline Morrell, who made her house at Garsington a place of pilgrimage for the group. St. John and Mary's house Eleanor, at West Wittering, was also a popular intellectual destination, featuring good food, claret, and much literary gossip. Strachey considered Mary a "wonderful creature."[1] Barbara at the age of seven had been called upon by her mother to mimic Strachey, which she did, much to his distaste. Mary is the heroine in two of Aldous Huxley's novels, and she had her portrait painted by Matisse. She also had a long affair with Clive Bell, the Bloomsbury art critic.

In her life, Barbara had had many lovers; she was not a "good" girl as she readily admitted, but neither was she evil. She was impulsive. On one occasion recalled by Maro Seferis, Osbert Lancaster said something she didn't like, and she smashed his glass. On another, Jill Day-Lewis recalls that on the spur of the moment, she took off her shoes and socks and ran around a riverbank, screaming with delight. At the same time, her wit and sense of social niceties were unique.

From 1933-45, Barbara had been married to Victor Rothschild. Victor, born in 1910, was the 3rd Baron Rothschild, and during his life he was variously the chief scientist of Great Britain, an officer in the secret agency MI5, and head of the Edward Heath government's think tank. In 1944 he earned the George Medal for "dangerous work in hazardous circumstances" and in 1946 he received the MBE (Member of the British Empire) for the same reason, which is believed to be the invention of secret methods of neutralizing bombs placed on ships by enemy agents. He was cleared of being a Soviet spy and the alleged "fifth man" in MI5 at the time of the Kim Philby-Guy Burgess-Anthony Blunt scandal. He was clearly an extremely brilliant and wealthy man—but just as clearly Barbara Hutchinson hurt him deeply, and he never forgave her for it.

He died in March 1990. Although Baron Rothschild was only briefly associated with his family's bank, he had a fabulous fortune and a collection including rare books, Impressionist paintings, and silver. His wealth was probably not easily quantified, but certainly in the hundreds of millions of pounds sterling. He remarried in 1946, to Teresa Mayor, and had three children with her.

With Barbara, he also had three children: Sarah, born in 1934, Jacob born in 1936, and Miranda, born in 1941. But some idea of the intense negative feeling that existed at the time of the divorce from Barbara can be seen in a dispute over Baron Rothschild's will that erupted in 1990. Perhaps her marriage to Rex and what followed figured into the odd terms of the will in some way, but it is difficult to speculate on precisely how. Suffice it to say that both Rex and Barbara, with painful separations from their spouses and with three children involved in each case, were able to understand one another very well in some ways.

When Victor Rothschild died, having worked carefully on his will for the previous six months, Teresa and her three children were left everything, while Barbara's three children were left nothing except one derisory object each—a work box for Sarah, an ink stand for Jacob, and a desk clock for Miranda. Sarah, then fifty-five, stated that behind Lord Rothschild's decision was "her father's refusal to forgive her mother . . . for the break-up of their marriage" and "for finding happiness with someone else." (Rex of course was not the cause of the divorce between Barbara and Victor since he came along later.)[2]

Rex of course had no inkling of the extreme animosity between Victor and Barbara when he came to Barbara, or what Barbara's previous emotional history might portend for his own marriage; nor would he have paid attention to it if he had. Yet in more ways than one, Rex had stepped out of his class in this marriage. It was to end in ashes, just as Barbara's marriage to Victor had, and Barbara rather than Rex made the move that ended it, just as she had begun their romance.

At first, Rex was busy dealing with his own family and friends and what they thought of his decision to leave Frances. The relief of having made the break and escaped the situation of the last eight months was enormous, but his finances and health were not good. Rex seems to have had health trouble after each substantial personal problem—his large, apparently sturdy frame both masking and betraying his emotional sensitivity. On 3 August 1948, he wrote Greenwood that he had "been in bed most of the last week with tonsilitis" but "otherwise everything has been very enjoyable." However he had "A rather alarming letter from my Bank Manager. I imagined I was about £200 overdrawn, but find it is about £600. Is it possible to pay a bit in? Have Penguins yet produced their £100?" (This was an advance on Rex's translation of Xenophon's *Persian Expedition*.) Even though it was written before they were actually married, this letter provides some proof of Rex's independent financial status during the time he was with Barbara. He lived well with her, but paid for all of his own obligations, and continued to provide for his children's education as well.

Despite the distractions, work continued steadily. On 4 August 1948, he wrote John Lehmann that he was going to see John's sister Rosamond soon, and that he was coming to London because he'd been asked to give a Third Programme talk about modern Greek literature. He wanted to use some of Lehmann's translations of Sikelianos because "I've yet to find a good translation of him. I did one myself + Katsimbalis, after reflection, pronounced 'Well, yes: I should say that this is a pretty bad translation. Yes, it is very bad indeed.'"[3] This letter also carries the important news that Rex was hoping to start again in a day or two on his novel *Men of Stones*.

On 11 August 1948, after he had been separated from Frances for only about twenty days, he wrote Pam from Tackley, "In about ten days we shall be in Italy, eating + drinking too; not that there hasn't been a certain amount of this in England." But Rex commented wryly, no doubt referring to his recent domestic history, that although he had managed to write a broadcast on Greece for the Third Programme (which was given on the 27th of August), he was "still stuck in the middle of my article on Moral Planning, which is not really one of my subjects." Possibly he referred here to "The European Spirit in Literature," which was published in 1949.

With regard to Frances, he commented that he had not seen anything of her,

> though I've written once or twice. I don't think she wants to see me now, + I should probably upset both her + the children by doing so. I think that she understands what I feel + that she will be reconciled with it, though it may be that sometimes she thinks that I am the prey of a temporary infatuation. However I think that she knows me well enough to know that if I hadn't been quite certain of my feelings, I couldn't have acted as I have done. Naturally its painful to be causing her pain + to know that all this must have a bad effect on Jonathan. But it seems to me that one simply has to face these painful things. As there isn't the slightest possibility that my feelings about Barbara will alter, I know that it would be better for everyone for the divorce to take place. After that it will be easier than it is now for me to see the children + Frances too.

From past as well as present experience, he was able to say that "It is these indefinite situations that really cause the most anxiety" and he went on to cite the strength of his feeling for Barbara:

> As the subject is of course painful to her, I've never written or talked much to Frances about Barbara; but she must see that my feelings are something much more than physical attraction or the desire to live an easy life. Perhaps well-meaning friends will attempt to convince F. that this is all it is, but the truth is quite different + I think that F sees this. As you know, I love her very much but can't possibly give her the sort of love she wants. Perhaps I am very wicked, but I'm certainly true to what I really feel + know; +, if this is wickedness, I don't mind.[4]

It was certainly hard on Rex's children, particularly George, who was only seven, and wrote Rex some touching letters. Rex would answer at infrequent intervals, which would sometimes be apparent because George would grow and advance but Rex would remember George as he was the last time he had seen him, which was only once every two or three years. He did remember George's birthday always, and would also remember him every year on his name day, St. George's. He would give him a present, such as a large number of books, often in natural history, or when he was a bit older, a check for £25 or £50. Rex liked to say that it was enough to "buy a bottle of champagne and smoked salmon." George remembered receiving a letter from Rex when he was ten in which Rex corrected his spelling, saying "I like bicycles, but I don't 'lick' them." When they would meet, he would perhaps take George to the zoo; Rex's old-time naturalism undoubtedly contributed to George's growing interest in biology.

Although considerably older, Jonathan never forgave Rex for the divorce; as a result of it, George resolved never to abandon his wife and family should he ever get married. But given the circumstances, Rex managed fairly well with his own children and was good to Barbara's children when they would visit.

Barbara also made an effort to be positive about Rex's children and family. Gracie and Dora, Rex's religious aunts from Gloucester, liked her very much, while the intellectual Aunt Ethel liked her somewhat less, but still liked her. Barbara urged Rex to keep in touch with his mother, which he was somewhat reluctant to do, and she seems to have tried her best to be positive toward his family and friends. She thought of Kath as perfectly nice, but pernickety—a very correct and meticulous woman, whose ways maddened Rex. He had to account to his mother for everything, and although relations between them had cooled because of the divorce, she remained a dominant person in his life. On 29 August Rex and Barbara left for Italy, where they stayed until early October, possibly visiting Graham Greene and Bowra.

III. TALKS AND ESSAYS

Rex's Greek friends provided a pleasant sense of continuity with the past during this time of transition. Seferis wrote from Ankara, Turkey, on 14 October 1948 in response to Rex's letter of November 1947, obviously unaware of Rex's new situation. Much had happened to both of them since they last wrote: Rex had experienced Germany, had written most if not all of *Men of Stones*, and had left Frances; Seferis had undergone an operation and had traveled to Constantinople to take up his new duties as ambassador to Turkey. He was glad to be away from Athens, where the air was "stuffy with craziness," since the civil war was off and on. He was amused by contradictory reviews of his work in the Greek papers, but commented on Rex's modern Greek literature broadcast, which had been sent to him in transcript, that he had been "moved by what you have said about me. It is really a strange feeling to be here without anybody with whom one could share the pleasure of a friend's message coming from far away and to have his room crowded with memories . . . of so many things one would like to say or to have said."[5]

Good things were to come from Greece once again for Rex. On 16 September it was suggested by the director general of the British Council that Rex do a book about the Council, and that he go on a lecture tour of Greece to aid his work on this book. The result was to be a trip in the fall of 1949, and the excellent travel book *Views of Attica*, published in October 1950.[6] Katsimbalis came to England on 15 October 1948, and Rex felt that he had never seen him in finer form.

Socializing did not slow down his own work and on 26 October he submitted the script for a Third Programme talk, one of his most perceptive, on Kafka, that he would deliver on 2 November. On the Third Programme on Wednesday, the 20th of October, "The Football Match" from *The Wild Goose Chase* was broadcast from 6-6:20 P.M. with Rex reading it, and he received £17.10 for this; this was then repeated the next day. Rex got the idea for his great Thucydides translation from a commission for the BBC. On 21 October 1948, he argued with E. M. Layton of the BBC's copyright department for a higher fee for a translation of the Periclean Oration from Thucydides because "It is notoriously difficult to translate. I have a good knowledge of Greek + have had the benefit of previous translation; yet I have spent a lot of time + trouble on it." And, conscious of his own worth, he added, "It would not be easy for the BBC to find anyone else equally well qualified to make this translation."[7] This was broadcast on the Third Programme on 7 November, from 9:50-10:10 P.M. Because of this letter, Rex received 45, rather than 30, guineas. A BBC memorandum of 3 November noted that poet Louis MacNeice was interested in working on a broadcast of Rex's Xenophon translation with him.

On 10 November 1948, Lehmann wrote Rex about the typescript of his essay "The European Spirit in Literature," which was to appear the next year in Lehmann's magazine *Orpheus*; he liked the article's thesis about the two sides of European culture, the intolerant and the humanistic.[8] Rex was soon to embark on a book on Milton in which the thesis in this article also figures.

Exactly when Rex finished *Men of Stones* is not clear, but on 18 January 1949 he signed a contract for the novel, which would be published on 14 November. The title *The Prison* has been crossed out on the contract.[9] On 8 February 1949, Rex signed another Bodley Head contract for a translation of *The Hippolytus of Euripides*. This was to be published in January 1950.[10] The Bodley Head also took an option on the next work of translation.

During the same month, Leonard Woolf of the Hogarth Press was looking for an introduction to a translation of Cavafy's poems by John Mavrogordato of Exeter College, Oxford. He first tried E. M. Forster and then T. S. Eliot, who declined on 14 February with the following words: "I have been browsing in Cavafy's poems and find them sympathetic, but it is one thing to read poems in this way and another thing to acquire enough grasp of them as a whole to be able to say anything worth saying about the poetry. Apart from the other difficulty, that I should be dealing with what appears to be a clean and competent but not inspired translation of poems unknown to me in the original."[11] Woolf then applied to Maurice Bowra, who declined because there were some overtly sexual poems included and he was then Warden of Wadham College. Finally, in April Woolf wrote to Rex, who on 5 May 1949 answered from Tackley, agreeing and requesting some biographical material about Cavafy. A letter of 19 May 1949 from Mavrogordato to Woolf says that Rex was a very good choice. By 10 August 1949, Rex informed Woolf that the typescript would soon be ready and that he had enjoyed the translation very much; by 19 August, Rex wrote Woolf that " . . . you may well find that my introduction is very much along the lines of Bowra's. . . . in his last book. I hope however that you won't regard this as an error of a mere copyist. I've often talked about Cavafy with Bowra + our ideas happen to coincide." This was followed by Woolf's acceptance of the piece on 24 August and a letter of 5 November from Mavrogordato stating that Rex's "introduction is admirable."[12] It is admirable. Although Rex had no sympathy for homosexuality, he was able to treat the overtly homosexual Cavafy as a great poet: "His world is the world which most English schoolmasters would describe as 'decadent.' It is a world without any of the obvious epic, lyric or tragic grandeurs. Yet it is a world that existed and exists. It can be examined minutely and dispassionately. And to this examination Cavafy brings a peculiar point of view together with a singular integrity."[13]

Some of Rex's remarks have been cited as recently as 1982 in a book by C. Capri-Karka: "Rex Warner, stressing the poet's realism and acceptance of life, notes that 'if we are to take the poet's own word for it, love affairs of a disreputable character were a source of immense inspiration.'"[14] As usual, however, for Rex, there was relatively little money in writing: for this introduction, he received £20. Yet his previous books were still doing well: *The Aerodrome*, for instance, had gone into a fourth impression of 4,750 copies on 31 May 1947 and Rex had received a royalty of twelve and one-half percent, and more reissues were expected.

IV. REX AND MILTON

On 26 March 1949, he wrote Lehmann from Tackley, "Now I'm attempting to stay here till I've finished my little book on Milton, but am certainly coming to London on Friday the 25th." He mentioned *Views of Attica*, which Lehmann would publish in 1950, and stated, "I haven't yet heard how far the British Council are going to cooperate," possibly referring to a subsidy.[15]

I agree with Barbara Rothschild that Rex's short book on Milton, published in January 1950 but written from around February 1949, contains extraordinary insight into Rex as well as into Milton. For instance, when discussing Milton's divorce pamphlet, Rex sees nothing unusual about the fact that Milton was writing about divorce even during his honeymoon, because "This, to my mind, is exactly what one would have expected Milton to have done. The marriage was clearly a failure; he had made a great mistake, and he would not be slow to recognise it."[16] Upon hearing of Frances's affair in 1939, Rex's immediate reaction was that the marriage had to be over; in leaving Frances for Barbara, his decision was complete and final. Rex expresses through Milton the absolutist side of himself that he received from the evangelical religion and black-and-white world of some of the Luces. But this is not the whole story, for Rex had another side to his personality, one that could compromise and live pleasurably—the Warner side.

Writing of Milton, Rex said,

> The obvious sources of his inspiration were . . . opposed to each other. On the one hand there is the spirit of the Bible, a spirit partly of fanatical intolerance, partly of the purist aspiration towards the One indefinable reality. On the other hand there is the spirit of classical literature, its humanism, its delight in what exists, its pathos and its rationalism, its acceptance of evident contradiction. The existence together of these apparently widely different views of the world, the tensions between them, their different combinations and oppositions from time to time, have, more than anything else, formed and controlled the civilisation of Europe.[17]

This is the same argument that Rex had expressed in his essay on the spirit of European literature. While this view obviously owes much to Matthew Arnold's ideas about Hebraism and Hellenism and their influence on the British character, Rex's choice of them to explain Milton also says something about himself. The battlefield of his inner life may have been formed by Hebraism and Hellenism, by devotion to duty and principles versus devotion to self, pleasure, and art. It is the difference between the

Luces, with their stern evangelism, and the more liberal Warners; it causes the tension between the rigid, dictatorial systems that appear in Rex's novels and the efforts of his life-loving protagonists to evade or destroy them.

In the Milton essay as elsewhere, Rex's writing and his life were intertwined. Milton's divorce was on his mind because he was involved in a divorce. Milton's principles were on his mind because Rex had acted, in his own view, as a man of principle. And Milton's division between principle and pleasure was on Rex's mind because he was similarly divided.

The *TLS* reviewer of 28 April 1950 did not know all of this background nor was he interested; for him, Rex's "enthusiasm and unpretentiousness may be charming, but the result is not criticism and is not likely to further the intelligent appreciation of Milton in our time."[18] In *The Nation*, however, Howard Doughty found that Rex showed how the conflicting elements in Milton were reconciled,[19] and in *The Spectator*, Richard Church was pleased that "Mr. Warner, himself a disciplined classical scholar . . . writes of Milton not only with respect, but with love."[20]

On 9 April 1949, Rex and Barbara left for Italy. They were back by 3 May. Rex wrote C. J. Greenwood from Tackley on 5 May that he was already missing Italian red wine, and he asked for Frances's new address because he wanted to send her lots of books. The real purpose of the letter becomes apparent when he writes, "I hope she's doing something about the divorce,—indeed had hoped that it would all be over by now." Greenwood, who had long been Rex's friend as well as his editor and agent, was serving as Rex's go-between with Frances. Work continued, however. On 12 May Rex wrote Greenwood that he had finished his introduction to Lehmann's edition of Melville's *Billy Budd* and other stories, and his review of E. V. Rieu's *Iliad* translation.

The divorce from Frances came through on 7 July 1949 in the form of an ugly black document. Frances's mother was horrified by it. Rex's mother was very good and helpful to Frances during the divorce, which she too disapproved of, even coming to court to give Frances moral support, and offering the services of the Warner family lawyer. She felt that Rex had acted very badly. In those days, divorce was far less common than it is now, and one had to show fault. The fault in this case was Rex's adultery, which he admitted. Frances, but not Rex, had to appear in court and divorce him even though he was the one who wanted the divorce; C. J. Greenwood witnessed it. Another document dated 26 January 1954 stated that Rex must pay £564 per annum (less taxes) for Frances and £96 per annum for George's support until he reached the age of sixteen.[21]

On Monday, 11 July 1949, Rex and Barbara were married in a small, informal ceremony at the Registry Office at Chipping Norton, with Mary and Jeremy Hutchinson as witnesses. Rosamond Lehmann and Cecil were also present, as were Paddy and Joan Leigh Fermor and Maurice Bowra. Rex's mother was also there. They had a simple lunch, and it was all very pleasant and unpretentious. Rex was forty-four and Barbara thirty-eight, and they gave their residence as the Little Manor, Tackley. For a honeymoon, the couple went to a cottage in County Mayo, Ireland, owned by Alec Wallace, a friend of Barbara's.

Upon their return on a Monday, probably 18 July, Rex wrote Greenwood that "Ireland was wonderful, + the whiskey plentiful." He enclosed some proofs, probably for *Men of Stones*, and noted that the BBC was interested in it. The next day he wrote Greenwood again, telling him that he should show the proofs to Ludmilla Savitzky in France, and suggested Gallimard as a possible publisher. Gallimard was to publish her translation of the book in 1952 and it was to go through no fewer than seven editions in France, more than in any other country. A possible reason for its success there was that France was struggling with the implications of collaboration with the Nazis, much like Mr. Goat with the dictator, and Rex's novel spoke to that anxiety.

By Tuesday, 26 July, he invited Greenwood to stay the night some time that week, because "the servant problem seems to be getting slightly better, with prospects of a highly educated Frenchman to wash dishes." Rex's irony here was apparent: he himself had lived not too far above the poverty line, educated though he was, only a short time ago. He was also worried about Ken Marshall, then very ill, and got involved in a plan with Pam Morris to help him.

V. THE RECEPTION OF *MEN OF STONES*

It must have been very satisfying for Rex to receive a letter of 17 August 1949 from Basil Wright, who had just read a proof copy of *Men of Stones*, and found it the best thing that Rex had ever done, far exceeding Arthur Koestler's works in quality and penetration. Wright felt that Rex had defined a new type of tyrant and had shown that freedom might inevitably disappear, thus summing up the political dilemma of Europe in their period.[22] Wright stressed the universality and prophetic nature of Rex's allegorical novels, and concluded that his latest had been his most mature and poetic.[23] Another positive was a letter Rex received on 1 September 1949 from film photographer Jack Cardiff, who suggested that there might be a way to adapt *The Aerodrome* for the screen. But as with previous proposals, nothing was to come of this.

Then, on 14 November 1949, *Men of Stones* was published. The reviews were fairly positive, and perhaps reassured Rex that he could still do it: this was his first novel in six years. Yet there were frequent ominous notes in the reviews, as some critics detected repetition and exhaustion where Basil had seen only glad things. George Woodcock, an important writer and critic, explained that Rex's "personal myth" was "the castle or aerodrome as symbol of power opposed to the village as symbol of a natural and humane life, the final implicit vindication of compassion" but went on to comment that "with repetition the myth, though more facilely expressed, seems to have become less impressive" because mechanical.[24] For Woodcock, *Men of Stones* "maintains, if it does not increase, Warner's stature as one of the living masters of the allegorical form" (56). The *Atlantic Monthly* reviewer, too, while finding the novel's "theme arresting, its conception audacious," and noting "stretches of brilliant argument, an undercurrent of excitement, and a powerfully suggested atmosphere of the bizarre," thought its philosophy curiously reducible to that of original sin and its realization "seriously flawed" by a diffuse subplot and a loss of intensity.[25] H. F. West, in the *New York Times*, said, "Rex Warner has gone a long way since he wrote the fresh and often amusing 'The Wild Goose Chase' in 1937. But I fear that at times—and this is one of them—he travels in the wrong direction. This is a pity, for he is a writer of talent."[26] Perhaps cruelest of all was R. D. Charques's review in *The Spectator*; Charques wrote that "Mr. Warner fails in dramatic point and coherence. His characters are mere sticks, neither human beings nor effective symbols. And his prose, though careful and measured, has altogether too little life."[27] These reviewers clearly indicate disappointment, a feeling that Rex is repeating himself. It is difficult to disagree with them, and despite Basil's praise Rex may have felt the truth of what they were saying because he was never to write an "allegorical" novel again.

Some cheerful news came from Rex's oldest son Jonathan, who seemed inclined toward the humanities. In the fall of 1949, Jonathan started attending Trinity College, Dublin, and wrote Rex that he was living in his uncle Arthur Luce's rooms there. He was studying English and French and a combination of psychology, logic, and philosophy and had joined the college's historical society as well as the Rugby club. He also told Rex, then planning a trip to Athens for *Views of Attica*, that he envied him the trip and promised to try to visit Tackley on his way back from Dublin at Christmas.

Plans for the Greek travel book were progressing. Rex wanted to include some photographs by Barbara and had written to Lehmann asking him already on 1 September, to say "something which might bolster Barbara's prestige as a photographer. I imagine simply that the book will be illustrated + you hope to use her work."[28] The volume does contain two photos by Barbara along with many more by Lehmann and professional photographer Joan Rayner.

Rex traveled to Greece for his book, with Barbara accompanying him. On the way, they went through Italy and met Graham Greene and Catherine Walston. Although

Rex was an enthusiastic admirer of his, Greene was not particularly pleased by this visit, writing his mother in November that "The weather in Italy was rather awful & Rex & Barbara Warner stayed with us nearly the whole time which we did not intend."[29]

Although Rex enjoyed the trip, the couple's reception in Greece, too, was somewhat awkward. According to Mrs. Katakouzinos, at first there was a rumor that Rex had left his wife for another woman. All of Rex's friends, including the Seferises, the Ghikas as well as the Katakouzinoses, were upset. The rumor—fanciful and wrong, as rumors are apt to be—was that he had met Barbara in Germany, and that she had called him after midnight and said "You are the other half of my soul." Rex's Greek friends thought at first that Rex was attracted only by her money and none of them would invite her. Rex came to Tiggie Ghika alone and begged her to receive Barbara, and she did, even allowing them to stay with her; but the others continued to refuse, at least during this first trip. Yet there were pleasant times too. At Levadia, where there had been little business and no food or wine available in 1945, Rex found good dining and drinking and a busy central square.[30] They returned to England in late November.

Rex's aunt Ethel—who thought Barbara "a sweet girl"—and uncle George stood by him during this time of transition,[31] and Rex's family seemed to adjust to his new life, if with difficulty. On 24 January 1950, Jonathan wrote Rex and Barbara about John Luce's and Uncle Arthur's taciturn praise of the "Extreme Brilliance" that Jonathan had received in his freshman exams. He enclosed his exam paper, eager that Rex should see it. He thanked them for the very good time they gave him and a friend around Christmas and invited them and Barbara's daughter Sarah Rothschild to visit him.

Four days after President Truman approved the production of the hydrogen bomb, on 4 February 1950, Ethel wrote that her reading of *Men of Stones*

> was a non-stop affair, at home, in busses, in an eye doctor's waiting room. I couldn't put it down. Now it is finished I feel a bit weak. Of course it is frighteningly good—I use that word advisedly—and it leaves me feeling amazed at your competence in stating, in such quiet measured sentences, the appalling problems of our time. This has been a bad week for us—all this hysteria about the calculated wickedness of the "hell" bomb—so we are all feeling appalled, wondering if there will ever be any decency in life again, and powerless to do anything. So perhaps your book depressed me because I know we have our Governors over here, but that doesn't mean I don't think it absolutely first class writing. It is, and more power to you old boy. As long as there are people like you who write the truth, there are a few breathing holes for the spirit of man. . . . Bless you Rex, I do love and admire you most sincerely and think you a most creative person.[32]

Although it came from a loving and unobjective aunt, Rex must have felt very reassured by this letter (he kept it). There were other more objective assurances of his literary ability as well: commissions continually came to him, and he was working steadily. In January he had received a contract from Greenwood for three books, including two novels and one work of nonfiction, to be delivered by the end of the year.[33] Moreover, Rex was now part of the literary establishment, and had a say about who would or would not be published in *London Magazine*, for instance. He also became a regular reviewer for the *New Statesman*, another sign that he had "arrived" and was now a taste-maker, with all the danger of stagnation that that implies. Whether or not he formulated it this way, the question was, would he be able to avoid becoming a has-been by finding fresh projects that interested him and others?

The letters in the Michigan State Greenwood collection allow us to trace his literary and other activities at this time. On 7 March 1950, he wrote Greenwood thanking him for an unspecified review of *Men of Stones* (probably writer James Hilton's very favorable *Herald Tribune* piece), and stating that "I expect it will be the same story in America,—good reviews + no sales." Rex asked Greenwood ironically if he had seen his "soulful picture in The Sketch? The next thing to do will be to attend a Hunt Ball." He asked if Greenwood would like to meet for lunch on Monday, 20 March, because he was coming to London "to attend some rehearsals of the Hippolytus," for a 30 April Third Programme performance. (Rex's translation of this play by Euripides had appeared in January.) Also, Barbara would be coming along that evening, and then "About the 26th we're going to Paris for four days with Maurice Bowra." (Needless to say, Rex did not have many excursions with Bowra when he was married to Frances and was relatively poor.) At this point, Rex was halfway through *Views of Attica* and felt that "its not bad."

Rex commented that "we're now in a domestic crisis, as the husband of one of our maids is dying + they both want to return to Italy." There is obviously an irony here, because the lack of servants was never before a crisis (or any) issue for Rex. But the callous, selfish edge to this remark about a servant's possible death, casually inserted without comment into the body of this letter, also leads one to suspect that Rex was adapting all too well to the uncaring high life. He mentioned also, tellingly, that he'd "stopped gin + taken to sherry," always a mark of class at Oxford and elsewhere.

On 20 April Rex informed Greenwood from West House, Barrack Lane, Bognor Regis, another residence of Barbara's, that he was sending him the rest of *Views of Attica*, and asked to have it typed urgently, because he wanted to send it to Lehmann in a week. He said he'd only glanced at a book-length manuscript, Herbert Howarth's "Six Literary Legends," which Greenwood had sent him to read, but mentioned that

Barbara "thought that the chapter on me was very good." He promised to "now slowly begin thinking in terms of novels." He wrote that he hoped "the house is still standing. We've just got rid of our Italian maid who was hopeless + filthy." Rex's comments on servants, again, are telling; this sounds more like Barbara than like Rex. The man who only a few years earlier was living a barely middle-class existence himself more than once sounds insensitive to the situation of other people in the same or worse situations.

On 23 April 1950, he wrote Greenwood from West House with a report on Howarth's manuscript:

> To start with what I know best, namely myself,—I think that he's very perceptive on this subject. No other critic, for example, has even mentioned the importance of Captain Nicholas in "Men of Stones." While reading this chap I felt that he'd seen what I was trying to do, + if he made any mistakes, they were *purely* accidental, not proceeding from any lack of sensitiveness.
>
> With regard to the other essays, I thought that his choice of subjects was very interesting ["except for a rather over-weightedness of Jewish writers" is crossed out here]. It was interesting to find a new estimate of Flecker. The Hardy essay put forward a needed point of view. (I agree with him that Hardy's poetry is now over-valued, but he says more than this.) The essay on Churchill is very good, + says things in a new way. The T. E. Lawrence essay isn't immediately as impressive as the essay by Caudwell, for example; but I think that this chap, in having wider + less definite terms of reference, probably gets nearer the truth than Caudwell. He's constantly saying enlightening things quite quietly + without fuss.
>
> On the other side,—I'm not sure that the essays really hang together by the loose links of legend, the *eastern* Mediterranean, Jewry. Flecker + Lawrence fit in all right; others don't. But perhaps this doesn't matter. All the same if the book is to be judged chiefly as literary criticism, it might be preferable to put the specifically Zionist or Palestinian bits into notes or into an appendix. As the thing stands, there are signs that various essays were written not for the general, but for a Jewish, public. I'd also recommend a rather longer epilogue.
>
> But I do think that this is work to be encouraged. There's a very unusual combination of penetration + of *scrupulous* fairness. I'd certainly recommend publishing it, possibly with some *agreed* alterations. Or perhaps additions. An essay on some aspect of E. M. Forster would fit well + would certainly be done well.
>
> I think I'll write to him to say how I enjoyed his essay on me, + I might make some of these suggestions at the same time.

Rex was perspicacious in thinking that this book was intended for a Jewish audience, because Howarth had published the Lawrence essay in a Zionist magazine.[34] This essay is quite good, and much less thesis-ridden and narrow than Caudwell's view. But since the whole manuscript was not published, it is hard to judge the rest of Rex's criticism. Howarth's essay on Rex was probably "Pieces of History," published in 1958 in the journal *Critique*.[35]

VI. REVIEWS, GREEK MYTHS, AND EURIPIDES' *HELEN*

As an established writer, the time had arrived for Rex to review others as well as to be reviewed himself. The reviews Rex was to publish in 1950 in the *New Statesman* covered books about poetry by F. W. Bateson and William Van O'Connor, a discussion of Yeats's *Collected Poems*, and a Milton biography by James Hanford. Most important, however, was Rex's review of 17 June 1950 of E. V. Rieu's *Homer: The Iliad*, which contained Rex's account of his relationship with Rieu, and gave insight into his philosophy of translation. After praising Rieu's translation as "easy to read, accurate and exciting," he fixes on Rieu's "use of short sentences, determination to use the most modern English possible," and on "the translator's own evident love for his subject and the close, careful attention which he gives to it." Rex mentions that "I was once privileged to do some translation for him and sent him a sample of my work. This, I remember, was returned in a state which somewhat appalled me, so many were the queries, the suggested alterations, the polite but firm insistences on the precise word or turn of phrase. After this experience I was even more careful than I had been before. . . ."[36] Rex was most likely referring to his 1949 Xenophon translation for Penguin. Yet Rex went on to show the faults in Rieu's method also, including being too brief, leaving out words, and altering syntax. It is clear that in translation Rex preferred accuracy above all things, followed by clarity. The connection with Rieu was to be important for his Thucydides translation, since Rieu was his editor.

More evidence of Rex's attitude toward translation as well as his erudition is apparent in another review, of F. L. Lucas's *Greek Poetry for Everyman*, which was also published in the *New Statesman*.[37] After commenting that "it seems possible to make out a reasonable case both for and against almost any translation that has been made," Rex claimed that the most important quality of a classical translator is "the conviction that there is nothing dead about the language which he translates." He criticized Lucas for including "the worst lines Chapman ever wrote" and for choosing a poor meter into which to translate some of the poems.

On 2 May 1950, Rex wrote Greenwood from Bognor Regis that "John Lehmann seems to be tied up with his American agent, but hasn't got anyone in America for the Greek book [*Views of Attica*] yet. I, of course, am not sure of the terms of my contract, but we're going back to Tackley next Monday, + I'll look at it then. We're still without proper domestics, but are getting some more Italians soon after we return." He mentioned that he had enjoyed the BBC's broadcast of his *Hippolytus* on Sunday, 30 April.

Ludmilla Savitsky had agreed to translate *Men of Stones* into French, as Rex wrote Greenwood on 18 May 1950. Rex wanted to go to a party to be given by G. Lyle Blair, with whom he would eventually collaborate on a cricket book, on 27 May, but would probably find it impossible because Mary Hutchinson was coming to visit him and Barbara, and there would be a party in Tackley. He invited Greenwood to come and see Lancashire play. Rex added perspicaciously that he had "just finished Aldington's life of D.H. Lawrence + find it difficult to decide who is most unpleasant, Lawrence or Aldington." Aldington was indeed to become known for his attacks on other writers, including T. E. Lawrence, T. S. Eliot, and Norman Douglas.[38]

The first edition of Rex's *Men and Gods* was published in June 1950 by MacGibbon and Kee. This book, dedicated to Jonathan, is a retelling of the stories of Ovid, and remains one of Rex's best-loved and most popular works. Rex's introductory justification for retelling "Pyramis and Thisbe," "Atalanta's Race," and "The Story of Theseus" is that he felt that all readers should know these stories because they were good in themselves and because they had influenced many English poets. The book met with immediate success in both reviews and sales, and it was still in print in England in 2001. The *Times Literary Supplement*, which had not taken kindly to his Milton effort, found that "Mr. Warner goes back to honest tale-telling; he does not transmogrify, beyond what the story does for him, and the sarcasm, when present, is inclined to be Ovid's."[39] So, too, the *Manchester Guardian*, despite signs of "hasty composition," found Rex's translation to be "accurate, bold, and honest."[40] Moreover, Harold Nicolson wrote, "This is one of the most exact and interpretative renderings of the classics that I have ever read. The book will be a delight to young and old alike."[41] The message, perhaps, was clear to Rex although it was never fully articulated by a reviewer: as a novelist, critic, and political thinker he was no longer so well received as he once had been, but as a translator and classical popularizer he was very much appreciated.

While John Lehmann was in Italy visiting art collectors Harold Acton and Bernard Berenson, negotiations for an American edition of Rex's *Views of Attica*, published by Lehmann, were still going on with Abelard Press. (These did not succeed, but Longmans brought out a Canadian edition of the book in 1951.) Rex mentioned that he had listened to a BBC rerun of his *Hippolytus* translation "again the other night, + thought it rather good. At the moment, till I can think of something more serious, I'm translating another Euripides." This was his *Helen*, to be published in September 1951 by the Bodley Head.[42]

On 20 July, he wrote Greenwood approving a new book by Theodore Stephanides (author of the 1946 *Climax in Crete*, about World War II) that he had been sent to read. Otherwise, he was doing "a lot of mowing + getting better + better at racquet." He was also following cricket. The big family event of the year, however, was to occur in the first half of August, when Barbara would give birth to a child. He invited Greenwood because he didn't expect to come to London until after the birth.

Around this time, Rex decided to join a good men's club in London. He selected the Savile Club, probably because it was an important literary and arts club. His friend Day-Lewis had been a member since 1943, although Cecil would leave it in 1957 for the Athenaeum, E. V. Rieu's club. Among the other members of the Savile were Stephen Spender, Compton Mackenzie, humorist Stephen Potter, director Ralph Richardson, writer Robert Henriques, commentator Eric Linklater, and publishers Max Reinhardt and Sir Francis Meynell. Reinhardt first became aware of Rex through Graham Greene, but the Savile helped solidify what was to become a long association. The club was famous for its snooker playing and for its discussions of affairs of the day, and Rex would come there to relax and talk when he was in London.

But he was too busy with his new family to be at the Savile often. On 4 August 1950, Lucy Warner was born at the Radcliffe Maternity Home. The address on her birth certificate is The Little Manor, Tackley. Rex was forty-five and Barbara thirty-nine, a bit late to be starting anew, but not impossibly so. The birth of a child testified to their feeling for one another.

Lucy's earliest memory of Rex was that he was very warm and loving—perhaps in her he found the daughter that he had not quite had in Anna. He was fun, mowing the lawn and making a nest of the cuttings for Lucy as a child. When she was able to understand it, he would read for her out of *Jack and Jill* magazine. At the Fishguard cottage that Barbara maintained in Wales, Rex taught Lucy the names of the wildflowers and birds. He also taught her the Greek myths. She cannot remember him ever being angry or insincere. He was always there, and always true to himself and her during this early period. Moreover, she remembered that during her early years the relationship between Rex and Barbara approached the idyllic. They were centered on one another.

This closeness, however, did not prevent Rex from taking an occasional solo trip with a friend, as he had also done when married to Frances. On Friday, 8 September 1950, Rex and Greenwood left Victoria Station at 8:20 P.M. and arrived in Dieppe at

2:00 in the morning, sleeping in a train cabin until breakfast time. They stayed over the weekend and left on Sunday or Monday at 1:30 P.M., arriving at Victoria again at 6:15 that night. Probably this was a wine tasting foray. Julia Greenwood remembered that C. J. brought her a funny little souvenir brooch from France, and that Barbara was annoyed that Rex brought her a cheap, nasty-smelling perfume.

By October 1950, Barbara had sold the Manor House in Tackley and she and Rex and Lucy were living in her house in Bognor Regis. They also spent some time in Little Wittenham with Rosamond Lehmann. Rex wrote Greenwood from there on Thursday, probably 26 October, that he'd just seen advance copies of *Views of Attica* and would bring him one when he came to London on United Nations Day to have lunch with his "Burmese uncle," the brilliant scholar Gordon Luce. He proposed meeting with Greenwood and James MacGibbon, of MacGibbon and Kee, who had published *Men and Gods* in June. Rex added that "we're having a much needed rest here. Its an enormous relief to have got rid of Tackley." In October 1951 MacGibbon would publish Rex's *Greeks and Trojans*, his retelling of the main episodes of the Trojan War. The reason for the meeting between Rex, Greenwood, and MacGibbon, which concerned *Greeks and Trojans*, appears in an undated letter still from Tackley probably around summer 1950, in which Rex complained to Greenwood that MacGibbon was offering him an advance of only £200 for another mythology book, contingent on placing it in America.

VII. REX AND FORSTER

Rex's small book on E. M. Forster was published in October 1950. Rex summed up not only Forster's early world, but his own education when he wrote that Forster was "the last survivor of a cultured liberal tradition which is now being swept away by war, by economics and by the internecine struggle of dogmatically opposed ideas. Such a tradition is imagined as gentle, tolerant, and intelligent. It is the tradition of classical literature, enthusiasm for the arts, anti-imperialism, deep respect for the sincerities of personal relationships. . . ." But he found that Forster (like himself) while in this tradition "is also capable of standing outside it, that he is creative beyond the boundaries of a mild tolerance. . . ." What Rex particularly liked about Forster's writing was that "it is a work which, in spite of the wit and subtlety of its style and manner, is both prophetic and intense. It is filled with a passion for truth in personal emotions and relationships, a hatred of what is false or smug. It accepts the size and grandeur of the world, then, with a vigorous modesty, comes to grips with it."[43]

Rex then discussed the meaning of Greece for Forster: "There is the half-mystical world of dryads and powers of nature, there is the world of balance and beauty which we enter in several of the early short stories; there is the enjoyment of the by-ways of history. . . . The modern poet Cavafy is now part of the tradition that began with mythology. Certainly, both as the result of education and experience, Greece has meant very much to Forster."[44] Here Rex hinted at Forster's homosexuality, as he did on the next page when he discussed the weaknesses of the heterosexual love affairs in Forster's novels. Rex thought that Forster felt that "this is one of the things that he ought to like, but doesn't" and that as a result his women characters are lacking.[45] Rex delicately addressed the homosexual issue without allowing it to affect his positive judgment of Forster's work. Rex also found that in Forster's early writing, Greece "is an ideal to be approached with awe and reverence. Possibly with too much awe and reverence . . ."[46] because Forster chose to set his novels in Italy, not Greece.

Rex's summary of Forster's novels reads like a defense of his own education under Cecil Grant:

> It will be seen that their message, if they can be said to have a message, is not easy and is not entirely liberal. Good sense and good will may seem to be his standards, and often he appears to be writing in the liberating tradition of those who in the first quarter of this century believed in the imminent overthrow of injustice, intolerance, and conventional stupidity. But his novels go further than this. They penetrate the boundaries of deep dissatisfaction and despair; and, though they bring back nothing that seems to be either flashily or immediately valuable, no key to understanding, no quick hope for amelioration, nevertheless the mind that has visited his world is wider for the experiences of vision or of nightmare or of both.[47]

Rex was still keeping in touch with family members and on 3 November, he received a letter from Uncle Gordon, who was visiting the School of Oriental and African Studies at London University. Rex had dutifully gone to London to meet Gordon but had apparently missed him. In his letter, Gordon remarked "I read . . . a book on Milton by you lately, and found it quite delightful. I envy you your prose pen no less than your poetic quill."[48] On 10 November his son Jonathan wrote from the Historical Society at Trinity College thanking him for a check. Jonathan had done well in his first-year examinations and had won a prize of £4 for his First Class honors. But Uncle Arthur had been taciturn about this. On the same day Jonathan wrote Barbara as well, thanking her for a letter and sending love to Lucy and Rosamond Lehmann in Little Wittenham. Rex also would hear from his Uncle George at Trent College that he would receive a few hundred pounds upon George's death, and that it should go to Frances and her children, but that he was leaving Rex a "nicely bound copy of Horace's Odes."[49]

VIII. THUCYDIDES AND CRICKET

On Saturday, 4 November, Rex wrote Greenwood that he was going to talk to Denys Kilham Roberts about representing him in America, but he did not mean to replace Greenwood in any way. He thanked Greenwood for "the handsome cheque" and was surprised "that the B.B.C. seem to have behaved properly," possibly by paying well for an upcoming Third Programme rebroadcast of Rex's 1948 translation of the funeral oration of Pericles from Thucydides. He mentioned that the house was full of children at the moment and that he was writing "painstakingly about Liberty," referring to a Third Programme talk on Milton and liberty scheduled for 14 November.

Rex's translation of Pericles' speech was rebroadcast on the Third Programme on Sunday, 12 November 1950. This was to result in what was to be Rex's most popular publication. One of the chance listeners was Alan Glover of Penguin Books, who wrote to Dr. E. V. Rieu that "It struck me as a remarkably good version. I don't know whether it has ever been published, but it did seem to me on the strength of it that if we could get Rex Warner to do Thucydides for the Classics he would make a very nice job of it. . . ."[50]

Two days after the Thucydides broadcast, Rex gave his Third Programme talk on "Milton and the Definition of Liberty," which was later published in *The Listener*.[51] In it, Rex restated the idea behind *Men of Stones*, which ultimately derives from Dostoyevsky: that people find freedom unbearable, and that this leads to dangerous political consequences. Moreover, ". . . we may get somewhere if we abandon those wholly unedifying platitudes which ruled the intellectual roost after the 1914 war. It was—still is—the thing to say that nobody wants war. This is not true. Numbers of people are happiest when there is a war on. Only in wartime conditions is it possible for many people to find what they themselves consider is their full reality—their freedom."[52] Rex's point was that Milton feared that people meant "license" when they said "liberty," but that our recent experience suggested that the problem was that now when they said "liberty" they meant "willing subservience to an inhuman creed or set of values." Rex felt that without "a spiritual, religious, and fundamentally human basis," liberty "may disappear from the surface of the earth." Rex's assertion of human values and his warning against a seemingly idealistic totalitarianism are perpetually valid.

On 26 November, while recuperating from a bad cold, Rex wrote C. J. from Little Wittenham that at a cocktail party at John Lehmann's, probably on 14 November, he had met the producer Rupert Doone who had expressed interest in Rex's *Helen* translation, but wanted to stage it before it was published. Rex had seen Denys Kilham Roberts, and they agreed that nothing should change in Rex's representation. So Greenwood was the one who negotiated the important Thucydides contract with Penguin. By 4 December 1950, Alan Glover had written a memo setting out the terms of Rex's translation of Thucydides: two volumes, to be completed by 31 December 1954. There would be an advance of £150 per volume, "payable half on signature of the agreement, and half on delivery of the manuscript."[53]

Three days after Christmas of 1950, Rex wrote Greenwood from Bognor Regis where they had then moved completely, that "The bedrooms are exceedingly cold here, but everything else is excellent." The house was full of children, but Rex was able to send Greenwood the completed manuscript of the Trojan War book, *Greeks and Trojans*, that he had done for James MacGibbon.

Rex came to London on Wednesday, 10 January 1951, to sign the Thucydides contract with Penguin. Rex was to receive a royalty of £2 per 1,000 copies sold at 1 shilling; 5 percent of the published price of all copies sold if it were published at a price of from 1 shilling 1 pence to 3 shillings; and 10 percent of the published price of all copies sold if it were published at a published price in excess of 3 shillings.[54] These were good terms, and the continuing popularity of Rex's translation was to provide excellent royalties right through the 1990s.

Rex's ability to work did not seem to be affected by the fact that he lived in something of a social whirl. On 20 January 1951, he wrote from West House to Pam, setting forth his itinerary: on that day they would go to Seaford to stay with Barbara's brother Jeremy and his wife, actress Peggy Ashcroft; the next week they would be in London for a "social time"; they would stay the weekend of 17 February with Maurice Bowra; and then there would be a trip to Denmark on 16 March for a week so Rex could give a lecture on Milton. Lucy was left with a nurse.[55]

On 2 February Rex asked Greenwood if he could send the manuscript of *Helen* to Rupert Doone, who wanted to produce it during the very next season but who needed to have a reading "with some prominent producers" now. Rex found Bognor restful after their visit to London and wrote "At last I've discovered the place where all the wild fowl go." Although Rex meant this literally, we might take it symbolically as his recognition that the end of the wild goose chase was not a socialist society but the good life with Barbara.

Rex wrote Greenwood on 6 February that he had missed the post and therefore wanted to deliver the *Helen* manuscript in person on Thursday, 8 February, at 12:15 in Long's, so it could be typed up. He was a bit worried about a new project, writing about the Anglo-Australian Test Match with Lyle Blair, feeling that "I'm not sure it wouldn't be better to write about the Commonwealth tour." This is the first mention of his co-authored book on that subject. Pam Morris was scheduled to visit on 9 February and Beatrix Lehmann (John and Rosamond's sister) was also to be a guest at some point.

The 26th of February was a cold, rainy day at Bognor. Rex wrote thanking Greenwood for sending the *Helen* manuscript back, and offering to correct the typescript for the BBC if necessary. He commented on his Test Match correspondence with Lyle Blair, soon to be published, in cricket terms: "I've sent down a few fast in-swingers to Lyle. He seems to be playing himself in, after having not even seen the first ball."

Blair and the cricket book had been occupying much of his time early in 1951. *Ashes to Ashes: A Post-Mortem on the 1950-51 Tests* was published by MacGibbon and Kee in May 1951. It consists of Rex-Lyle correspondence about the England-Australia Test Match series held in Australia during the winter of 1950-51. Although Rugby was Rex's favorite sport, he also followed cricket closely. According to the introduction to the book, the two writers conceived of it while drinking hot champagne at Lord's cricket field in London in the summer of 1950. The colorful Lyle Blair, who seems to have run away to England from Australia with an opera singer in the 1930s, and was to serve with British Intelligence during World War II, retained his loyalty to his native land's cricket team. From 1955 to 1980 he was the director of the Michigan State University Press.[56] Blair had bet five bottles of champagne to Rex's one that Australia would win the Test Matches over England that year. This in fact happened, with Australia winning four out of five games. They began writing in February and continued until March.

This book is of interest primarily to those who follow cricket closely. From an outsider's perspective, there seems to be a very knowledgeable and sharp exchange between two aficionados of opposing national teams, highlighted by some sarcasm and quiet scorn, all in a positive spirit. But in Rex's letters about the matches, we find some more generally applicable writing, which gives insight into Rex's own character. He held, for instance, that most Englishmen, including himself, would be more interested in the county championships within England than in the Tests, or international matches, and that they would be passionately dedicated to their own counties.[57] Rex specifically mentioned Gloucestershire, and it becomes clear once again just how important Amberley and Stroud were to him.

Also interesting is Rex's enlistment of Milton in the cause of English cricket, after England had won (at last!) the fifth game of the series of five:

Amberley Rectory, Rex's childhood home. Courtesy of Mrs. S.C. Harding.

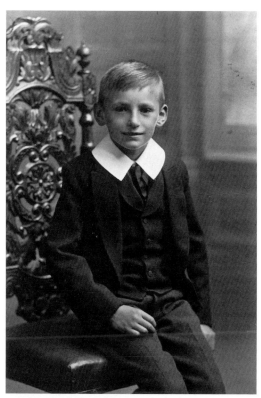

Rex at eight or nine years old, 1913 or 1914. Courtesy of Frances Warner.

Members of the Luce family in 1922, on the 50th wedding anniversary of Rex's mother's parents. Second row, from left (standing), Rex's mother Kathleen, father Frederick Ernest Warner, aunt Dora Luce, uncle Frank Luce, aunt Evelyn Luce, Helen (wife of Charles Luce), uncle Charles Luce; First row, from left (seated), Rex at age 17, great aunt Marie Luce (John James Luce's sister), Kathleen's father John James Luce, Kathleen's mother Alice, Miss Riddiford (family friend), uncle Arthur Luce; On floor, from left, aunt Grace Luce, aunt Ethel Marjorie Luce ("Lucy"). Courtesy of Frances Warner.

Rex and Frances Chamier Grove at Amberley Rectory on their wedding day, 31 July 1929. Courtesy of Frances Warner.

around the age of twelve with his father Frederic Ernest (always called "Ernest" by the family) and *ther Kathleen in the garden of Amberley Rectory. Courtesy of Frances Warner.

x, third from top right, as a Rugby forward at St. George's School, 1919-20. Holding the ball is the *tain of the team, future philosopher Michael Oakeshott. Rex's future brother-in-law, David Grove, is *the top right. Courtesy of St. George's School.

Rex, left, and Cecil Day-Lewis, possibly during Cecil's marriage to Mary King on 27 December 1928. Rex was Cecil's best man, and Cecil returned the favor during Rex's wedding to Frances Chamier Grove. Courtesy of Sean Day-Lewis and Weidenfeld and Nicolson.

From left to right: Rex, Frances Chamier Grove, Mary King, and Cecil Day-Lewis in 1928 or 1929. Courtesy of Frances Warner.

Rex and Frances at Amberley Rectory with Rex's father and mother right after the birth of their first child, Jonathan, in 1930. Courtesy of Frances Warner.

Rex's second wife, the former Barbara Rothschild, and painter Nico Ghika on the Greek island of Hydra in 1958. This was probably taken just after she had left Rex for Ghika. Courtesy of the Benaki Museum.

...eorge Warner, left, and Jonathan Warner in ...reece, 1947. Courtesy of Frances Warner.

Katherine, daughter of Kitty Trevelyan and Rex, in 1947 at the age of seven. Rex did not meet her until she was much older. Courtesy of Katherine Chapple.

Kitty Trevelyan circa 1947. In 1939-40 she and Rex had an affair that resulted in the birth of a daughter, Katherine. Courtesy of Katherine Chapple.

Rex in Scotland circa 1960.
Courtesy of Frances Warner.

Rex at Storrs, Connecticut, circa 1965. Courtesy of Jack Davis.

Rex and Frances, remarried for a little over a year and bound for New York on board the RMS Queen Elizabeth *in September 1967. Courtesy of Paul Ryan.*

Rex and Frances at Sonning, 1929 or 1930. Courtesy of Frances Warner.

Rex and Frances in retirement at Anchor House, Wallingford, circa 1980.

In recalling the events of the fifth Test I am reminded of the words of Milton, who writes, "Methinks I see in my mind a noble and puissant nation rousing herself like a strong man after sleep, and shaking her invincible locks: methinks I see her as an eagle mewing her mighty youth . . . while the whole choir of timorous and flocking birds, with those also that love the twilight, flutter about, amazed at what she means, and in their envious gabble would prognosticate a year of sects and schisms."

He went on to speculate,

If Milton were, as Wordsworth prayed, "living at this hour," he would undoubtedly use such terms as these firstly to glorify the renaissance of English cricket and secondly to describe some of the cricket correspondents now in Australia. The "envious gabble" of these "timorous and flocking birds" has at last been certainly and finally answered. England has, entirely on her merits and with no kind of assistance from fortune, fairly and squarely won.[58]

And once again in the English democratic vein, Rex commented that

Then, too, there is an evident falsity in the argument that only the eye-witness, the back-room boy, the specialist, and the expert can be trusted to give an opinion or to make a decision. It is one of those arguments that look so mathematical and are so plainly wrong. It is the argument of Plato and of Hitler, something very foreign to our own way of life and to our national game. We find, for example, that, though it is obviously absurd to suppose that every voter knows something about economics or foreign policy, nevertheless it is better to assume that he does rather than to leave the whole conduct of these affairs in the hands of a small body of men whose life-work it is to study these problems. And this apparently irrational procedure of ours sometimes works wonders. The man who is not an expert is very often right. Even more often he is partly right, and in almost all cases, his opinion deserves to be taken into account. The fact is that no "expert" can see everything: some, indeed, see very little.[59]

Rex always held that experts should write clearly and understandably and that intelligence can be found in the local pub as readily as in the university.

Pam and John had moved to Woodstock, and Rex looked forward to a drink with them; he was composing his Denmark lecture, "on Milton, of whom I'm now getting rather tired." He also wanted to see his children: "I'm very glad that Frances is coming over to see you + I'm sure it will do her good. She's probably quite right in not wanting to see me. What I'll do is to come to Oxford or Woodstock some time during that week (possibly with Barbara, as there's a lot doing at the house) + then arrange to take out George + Anna, whom I'm longing to see."[60] The Old Town House, an elegant building in the center of Woodstock, was being renovated for them to move into as soon as June.

The 14th of April brought the publication of Rex's *New Statesman* review of Jerome Carpopino's book on Cicero's correspondence. Rex was busy with his own professional and personal life, but he had to call time out to help his friend Cecil Day-Lewis, whose affairs with his wife, Mary King, with his mistress, Rosamond Lehmann, and with a young actress, Jill Balcon, were heading toward an explosion after many months of turmoil.

Cecil had met the very striking Rosamond Lehmann in 1936 at writer Elizabeth Bowen's apartment. Like him, Rosamond was an anti-fascist and Communist, and in the 1940s was to become a very successful novelist, one of whose works sold 600,000 copies. She was also, of course, the sister of John Lehmann, with whom Cecil worked often, and was divorced. From 1941 to 1950 Rosamond and Cecil had been having an affair and even living together although he was married to Mary King. During the war he was in London and his wife and sons were in Devon, but even after the war he continued living with Rosamond at Brimclose while remaining married to Mary. The relationship between Rosamond and Cecil was naturally stormy and Rex was called in several times to save it. Now both the resigned Mary, and the distraught Rosamond, it seemed, would be replaced by a young actress.

Jill and Cecil had met on 4 January 1948, when he was doing a BBC show in which she participated. He was forty-four, she twenty-three. She had hero-worshipped him since 1938 when he had visited her school for a verse-reciting competition. By January 1950 the affair had begun. Jill was the daughter of Sir Michael Balcon, the head of Ealing Studios and the motivating force behind the great Alec Guinness comedies *The Lavender Hill Mob* and *The Captain's Paradise*.

During this difficult time, Rex tried to console Rosamond and to assure her of his and Barbara's support, and he was successful in retaining Rosamond's friendship. Despite Rex and Barbara's loyalty to Rosamond, however, they as well as Charles and June Fenby attended Cecil's wedding to Jill on 25 April 1951. Sir Michael was absent.

On 2 May 1951, Rex was delighted to receive a letter from Seferis, who had been appointed to the Greek embassy in London and had just arrived the past week with his wife and was having trouble finding an apartment.[61] Rex invited the Seferises to 76 Charlotte Street, Barbara's London flat, and the house in which the landscape painter

John Constable died. He revealed that "I'm now translating Thucydides. Very difficult, + terrifyingly up to date."[62] On Wednesday, 16 May 1951, Rex and Barbara met Seferis for the first time since their Greek trip in 1949.

May brought the publication of the cricket book and also Rex's introduction to Lehmann's edition of Melville's *Billy Budd* and other stories. In his introduction, Rex called Melville an allegorical writer, who in *Billy Budd* sought reconciliation between "our formalised humanity" and "what remains primeval."[63] While "the ways of God are in no obvious sense justified . . . the dignity of man is upheld."

On 4 June Rex wrote from Bognor to Greenwood thanking him for Edmund Blunden's *Spectator* review of *Ashes to Ashes* but commenting wryly "I've yet to meet anyone who's bought the book." Blunden called both Rex and Lyle Blair "acute reasoners" but had decided that although Australia won the Test Match, Rex "appears to capture the position" when he preferred a return to local, county matches to professional cricket.[64]

CHAPTER TEN

WOODSTOCK AND GROOMBRIDGE, 1951-1958

I. A NEW HOUSE

During April, May, and June 1951, Barbara had been occupied with the purchase and furnishing of the Woodstock house. By 5 July Rex and Barbara had moved into The Old Town House at 9 Park St., and by the 18th were still sitting among packing cases and were without a telephone—this last much to Rex's delight. This tastefully luxurious dwelling in the center of town still stands. There, Barbara had Italian servants with white gloves serving fine wines and excellent food, and Rex had a magnificent study.

John Lehmann visited the house at the end of July and recorded his visit in his diary:

> Behind the unassuming but very attractive Georgian grey stone facade of this house, only a few yards from the gates of Blenheim Palace, I found tremendous preparations afoot: hammerings, sawings, paintings, a large house with handsome rooms already with beautiful wall-paper laid on the walls and beautiful furniture stacked everywhere; Barbara in the midst of it all, looking pretty and desirable as ever, but a little more matronly, slipping out from time to time to keep an eye on her new baby Lucy, who has the brightest blue eyes and the most remarkable society smile, in a pram in the long finger of garden behind; Rex returning from the pub, as rugged, jolly, imperturbable-seeming and delightful in conversation as ever. We had lunch at the "Bear," talked a

good deal about the Burgess-Maclean business and cracked jokes at one another for a solid two hours. I persuaded Rex to join my "reading panel," and then under the apple-tree he read me passages from his new translation (for the Penguin Classics) of Thucydides.[1]

On 16 July Rex attended a party in honor of poet Edith Sitwell and stayed the night with Greenwood, because Barbara's Charlotte Street flat was unavailable. Two days later, when they were still in the midst of packing cases, he invited Seferis to visit, but mentioned that on Sunday, 29 July, he had to hear his translation of Euripides' *Helen* (which was to be published in September by the Bodley Head) read at the Institute of Contemporary Arts in London. This reading went very well, for Rex wrote Seferis on 1 August that "I was rather nervous of asking you to come + hear the 'Helen,' as I had no idea whether it would be well done. In fact it was extremely well done + I much regretted not having tried to persuade you to come to it."

The Woodstock house was "still rather full of packing cases, but the garden + several rooms are fit for habitation. At the moment we've got all of Barbara's children as well as our joint child, but after this week end will be by ourselves."[2]

On 14 August Rex got a very pleasing letter about *Views of Attica* from Roy Harrod of Christ Church College, Oxford, whom he had met through Barbara. Harrod ranked Rex's writing ability with that of Walter Pater, and called the book one of the finest English works of any age, especially because of its descriptions of the Acropolis and Delphi. Harrod urged Rex not to let the idea of a Thucydides translation drop, because he wanted to see Thucydides rendered in Rex's superb English. And he hoped that Rex was also planning to write something of his own.[3]

On Friday, 17 August 1951, Seferis sent Rex *Listener* and *Tablet* reviews of John Mavrogordato's Cavafy book with Rex's introduction. He thanked Rex for spending a rainy Saturday with him, because "I had lost my father and I needed friends; that was the important thing." And he asked Rex if Forster had ever published anything outside of *Pharos and Pharillon* about Greece or Greeks.[4]

The next day, Rex pointed Seferis to some of Forster's short stories and essays in *Abinger Harvest* and mentioned that he had "just finished doing the whole of the debate on Mytilene. Its one of the best bits of Thucydides."[5] This was substantial progress, since it is in chapter 3 of Book III (of 8), and he had only begun work on 4 May.

In September Rex published his *Helen of Euripides* with the Bodley Head; in October, *Greeks and Trojans* (dedicated to George Warner) came out through MacGibbon and Kee. The introduction to the *Helen* is notable for Rex's statement of Euripides' pacifism, which resembles that of Rex himself in *Why Was I Killed?*:

The themes of going to war for the sake of a phantom, of the unnecessary sufferings of Greeks and Trojans alike, of the advantages of negotiation rather than force in international affairs,—all these recur constantly in the play and must have been applied by the audience to the contemporary situation. Thus there is a keen edge to much that might appear as merely humourous, and it is easier, perhaps, for us in our days to appreciate this than it was for nineteenth-century critics.[6]

On 17 September Rex wrote Seferis that he and Basil Wright (whom Seferis had just met at a party) had been contacted some months ago by a producer named Zervos about a film on Euripides' *Electra*, and then there had been silence. All of a sudden, he had invited them to Greece. Rex felt that "This is all rather exciting, +, even if nothing comes of the film,[7] it will be wonderful to see the Colossus [Katsimbalis]. We want to leave on Oct[ober] 6. . . ."[8] With the quick visas supplied by Seferis, Rex set out from London on Monday, 15 October. A week or so later, Rex, Basil, and Spatch, Katsimbalis's wife, sent Seferis a postcard. Rex's portion reads "They have taken from me the houses that I had; but I like, I love, I adore being in Athens."[9]

By 1 November 1951 Rex was back in Woodstock, and wrote Edith Sitwell that he had just returned "from a fortnight in Greece,—attempting to persuade some awful Greek financiers to put up money for a film based on . . . ancient Greek tragedy. . . ." He mentioned that he "had a wonderful time meeting all my Greek friends." He added that the lack of a telephone was "torture for Barbara but an infinite relief to me. . . ."[10] By Sunday, 5 November, Rex was looking forward to seeing Seferis in London in two days because, along with Louis MacNeice and Seferis himself, Rex was scheduled to give a reading of Seferis's work at the Institute of Contemporary Arts around the 20th.

Having lost his own copy of his translation of "The Thrush," Rex turned to John Lehmann to supply another copy. Rex's letter to Lehmann of 16 November is notable because it mentions for the first time his new novel: "I'm now staying in the country as much as possible till I finish the novel. . . ." This, first entitled *Average Day: An Escapade*, but eventually just *Escapade*, was Rex's only venture into humor. He was obviously trying a new direction, now that his interest in allegory had exhausted itself and he was in a happy mood.[11]

During this period, Rex was free to lead an active social life, including visits to other writers. On 27 November 1951, Rex wrote Seferis that "The Thrush" was his favorite poem of Seferis's, and mentioned that he and Barbara had eaten lunch with poet Edith Sitwell. Also at the end of November, Rex and Barbara visited with Rosamond, who was soon to leave Long Wittenham for London, her son Hugo and his new wife Margaret, and her brother John. According to Lehmann's diary, Rosamond was at work on her novel *The Echoing Grove* until the Warners arrived, and "the party then went with a roar, and we shouted and laughed till long after midnight."[12] This was a cheerful account of a conversation that also dealt with the alleged lack of new writers, the failure of England to recover fully from the war, and the simple need to continue.

By December Rex could look back on a very full year in terms of publication: *Ashes to Ashes*, prefaces to *Billy Budd, Pilgrim's Progress*, and the Mavrogordato book on Cavafy, a translation of Euripides' *Helen*, the retellings *Greeks and Trojans* (the main episodes of the Trojan War) and *Men and Gods* (the Ovid stories), an ongoing translation of Thucydides, three book reviews, and several radio readings. His new family was going well, too, with Lucy a joy. Also, Rex was able to keep up with his other children, whom he could write to and visit. His new life of considerable luxury, travel, and socializing seemed to be moving smoothly along. Rex had what he had always wanted—freedom to write and a location near the English countryside.

Rex began the new year with a letter of 20 January 1952 to E. V. Rieu, informing him that he had finished Book IV of Thucydides about a week earlier, and was having it typed. He added, "I think now that I shall have to leave the remainder alone for a bit, while I employ myself on writing something else. It's not really economically possible to go on giving so much continuous time to Thucydides,—much as I enjoy it." Rex also suggested publishing one volume running through Book IV immediately, and the other when it would be ready. He also requested permission to publish some of the translation in *Colonnade*, a new journal. Permission was granted, for the spring 1952 issue of *Colonnade* included "The Revolution in Corcyra," a part of Book III.[13] In this letter, Rex also consulted Rieu about the meaning of a word that appears in one line of a Homeric hymn quoted in Thucydides III.104.[14]

II. *ESCAPADE*

Partly as a change from the Thucydides translation and partially to earn some money, Rex continued to work on fiction. On 8 February 1952, Rex signed a contract with John Lane The Bodley Head for three entertainment novels, but the only title specified is *Escapade*. The terms of the contract specify that *Escapade* was due on 31 July 1952, that the published price would be in the 9/6d-10/6d range, and that Rex would receive fifteen percent on all copies sold. Moreover, he was to receive a £500 advance, his largest ever. The second and third novels were to follow by 8 February 1954. Tellingly, a typewritten note specified that "This Agreement neither invalidates nor conflicts with the existing Agreement between the Author and his Publisher dated the

27th January 1950, covering three serious novels following *Men of Stones*, but it is agreed that the Three Entertainment novels which are the subject of this agreement shall be delivered and published prior to the works covered by the earlier Agreement referred to above." Clearly, entertainment paid more than seriousness, and Rex was doing his best to earn some money. However, he was never to complete even a second entertainment novel.

On 13 February Edith Sitwell wrote from Italy, congratulating him on having finished translating about one-half of Thucydides.[15]

Two days later there appeared the French publication of *Men of Stones*, translated by Ludmilla Savitzky, who received a prize for this translation. This book enjoyed more success in France than anywhere else, and a French film was also considered at one point.

On 16 February Rex responded to his editor at Penguin, A. S. B. Glover, who had complained about Rex's use of "like" adverbially; he had changed such usages to "as." Rex wrote that Glover's changes were "grammatically correct, yet I think one has the right to sin, if one sins deliberately. Often I find 'like' preferable to 'as' because it seems to me to strike a conversational or excited rather than a scientific or demonstrative note." He had already had this argument with E. V. Rieu during the Xenophon translation, but forgot how it had turned out. Rex won the argument with Glover, who relented, however unconvinced he was.[16]

On 5 March Rex joked in a letter to Seferis that he was in bed with jaundice and "incapable of thought; but still I should have written, since thought was not required."[17] He recovered soon, and his social life went on apace. Jill Balcon was staying with Rex and Barbara at this time. Despite their support of Cecil and their politeness to his new wife, Rex and Barbara remained loyal to Rosamond. Rex wrote Lehmann that he and Barbara had seen an "excellent" *Coriolanus* in Stratford with Maro and Seferis on 15 March, and promised Lehmann some of *Escapade*, confessing his uncertainty over his experiment with comedy: ". . . As for my hilarious novel, I hope to get some of it typed before long + I'll try to find a possible passage or two. But I waver between finding the thing uproariously funny + merely boring. Auditors all laugh, but they may be laughing at me, not it."[18]

On 24 April he wrote to Seferis from Woodstock that he and Barbara would be going to Italy on 2 May for seventeen days: "The main objectives are Venice + Ravenna, + I'm supplementing the travel allowance by giving a lecture over + over again on 'Milton + the Idea of Liberty.' Both subjects will probably bore the Italians immensely." He went on to remark that "The holidays have been very tiring + have driven me from humour back to Thucydides. Even Thucydides isn't very interesting at the moment, though I'm glad to say that both Brasidas + Cleon have been killed."[19] That would put Rex right after chapter 1 of Book V, a little more than halfway through the text. In Italy Rex and Barbara may have stayed with Graham Greene. Back in Woodstock Rex wrote Compton Mackenzie on 12 June congratulating him on an honor, and Barbara added, "I believe we are all dining together with Rosamond . . . which will be great fun."[20]

Rex continued work on *Escapade* and Thucydides. Heinemann published a second edition of *Greeks and Trojans* on 8 July.

Rex wrote Seferis on that day that most of the month would be "complicated with children, mothers + uncles" but that almost every weekend in August would be free. He added, "I'm going on slowly both with my funny book + with Thucydides. Book VI, now. . . ."[21]

Seferis and Maro visited on the weekend of 24 August, and met Day-Lewis, who was also visiting. As Sean Day-Lewis points out, the acquaintance begun during this meeting was eventually to result in 1971 in Day-Lewis's poem "Hellene: Philhellene," devoted to Seferis and Bowra, both of whom died in that year.

Rex's contact with Greece continued to afford him pleasure. On 2 September 1952, he wrote Lehmann thanking him for sending *Zorba the Greek* and stating emphatically, which is rare for Rex, "I've enjoyed it *immensely*." He then recounted his knowledge of the book's author, Nikos Kazantzakis:

> I met Katzantzakis several times in Athens. I remember him declining the offer of a drink (with the words "Je ne veux pas etre l'esclave de mes plaisirs") ["I don't want to be the slave of my pleasures"]. Also I remember him telling a very good story about Sikelianos attempting to raise the dead. But I'd always thought of him as a poet rather than a novelist. I think "Zorba" is really excellent,—full of feeling + clarity, moving, original, + very Greek. I hope its as successful as it deserves to be. If you ever see Kazantzakis, tell him that I have most enthusiastically admired + enjoyed the book. Its conceivable that he may remember me.—As for me, I've stopped trying to be funny. Rosamond listened to large portions of the book [*Escapade*] the other night, + was kind enough to laugh a good deal. I'm also half way through Book VII of Thucydides; so am inclined to relax a bit.[22]

September also saw the third edition of *Men and Gods*, first published in 1950 by MacGibbon and Kee and now by Penguin.

By 25 October Rex and Barbara had just come back from a trip north and he was unimpressed by the country between Birkenhead and Preston. They were going off to see Dorset the next day. On 7 November he had lunch with Frances at Frascati's, and

Greenwood was present. He also met with E. V. Rieu around this time, and apparently declined his invitation to translate Arrian's *Anabasis*, possibly because he had his hands full with Thucydides.

On 3 December 1952, Rex sent the proofs of *Escapade* back to Greenwood. He seemed a little more nervous than usual about this book, his first comic attempt, and his nervousness extended even to proofreading: "I've cancelled all the printer's stylistic improvements, but he may be right about commas. Most of his suggestions then I've left unchanged. Perhaps you might just have a look through + see what you think of them. I must say that I thought the book rather funny when I re-read it, but it remains to be seen whether anyone else will." Jonathan was due to visit on 8 December, and Rex and Barbara were headed for London on the 9th. Rex kept in touch with Lehmann, sympathizing with him on 6 December about the refusal of Wilfred Harvey, the printer who controlled Lehmann's publishing company, to allow Lehmann to buy the company, and consoled him about the termination of his job as director effective 31 December:

> That you who have done more for the writers of your time than any other publisher, should be restricted rather than allowed to expand is a really shocking thing. The thought of it sets me back in the mood of the '30s. . . . Meanwhile I hope you're not unduly despondent yourself. I'd like to hear the facts (so far I've only had an account via Rosamond + telephone + Barbara; it scarcely seemed to make sense,—which I attribute to these modern machines. . . .) But please believe that I am full of sympathy + very shocked. I should like to protest in some way, e.g. by withdrawing "Views of Attica" from the list. But I expect it isn't legally possible, + wouldn't be practically effective.— I'll try to get Greenwood to send you proofs of my funny book [*Escapade*] (you'll either think it funny or not). It's just possible that a chapter might be useful for New Soundings. Both the chapters + the book are short.

He added, "We are in-bound at present + hardly ever seem to get to London."[23] On 14 January 1953, there was a big party for Lehmann, organized by T. S. Eliot, and attended by many of the major writers whom Lehmann had published. This served to raise spirits, and Lehmann was soon to rise from the ashes.

Rex continued to contribute to his first family's economic well being, which kept financial pressure on him despite his luxurious social life and travels. Early in the new year of 1953, he received a bill for Anna's maintenance from the Meath Home for Epileptics in Godalming, Surrey. For the period from 1 October to 31 December, it was £6, 5 shillings and 9 pence. It had become too hard for Frances to take care of Anna all alone.

On Saturday, 24 January, Rex received a letter from Rieu stating that he would be taking the first four books of Rex's Thucydides with him to Penguin on Monday. He thanked Rex for producing a very clear and readable translation of a difficult writer.[24] Rex's first *Spectator* review, which appeared on 23 January,[25] concerned another Greek translation: E. F. Watling's *Sophocles: Electra and Other Plays*. It was accompanied by a note stating that in the future Rex would contribute a fortnightly review to the magazine. At the end of January, Rex and Barbara received an invitation from artist Michael Ayrton and his wife, then living in Essex, to a housewarming and reception celebrating Basil Wright's return from Siam, where he had been working on *World Without End*, co-directed with Paul Rotha. This film, which highlighted UNICEF's work, was simultaneously shot in Siam by Wright and in Mexico by Rotha. Rex wrote the commentary for it, trying to hold these two worlds together. Wright was to write later that the film "seems to have made a considerable impact on the hearts as well as the minds of its audiences. After its first showing on television, many viewers were so affected by the plight of the Thai children suffering from yaws that, unasked, they sent money to the BBC to help towards UNICEF's work." And he went on to comment that "The impact of this film was much helped by Rex Warner's perceptive commentary and a fine score by Elisabeth Lutyens."[26] Rotha, also legendary in the world of British documentary film, stated more generally that "Rex Warner and [Arthur] Calder-Marshall wrote some scripts and wrote them very well."[27]

Around this time, Wright was the producer of another documentary, *The Drawings of Michaelangelo*, for which Ayrton had written the script. Ayrton's reception for the filmmakers was to be held on Saturday, 21 February, and Rex and Barbara were to stay over Sunday night. At the same time, Ayrton asked Rex and Barbara if he might stay over at their place on the night of 4 March because he was lecturing in Oxford.

Friday, 13 February 1953, was a good day for Rex, as he wrote Greenwood. The artist Osbert Lancaster had finished the cover of *Escapade* and was coming to show it to Rex. Rex had also sent the manuscript of *Eternal Greece*, a picture book with text by Rex, to Greenwood with the injunction to have it typed and sent on to Thames and Hudson, who were the publishers. And he wrote that by the next Thursday, "I hope to have a huge (+ final) chunk of Thucydides" to bring in for typing. "I've finished the translation + have only the introduction to do." This magnificent translation begun in May 1951 had taken him under two years, and he had completed it a full year and half before the deadline of 31 December 1954. Finally he asked Greenwood if it would be a good idea "to send 'Escapade' to someone at the Ealing studios? I'm sure it would make a good film." Dilys Powell, who had visited with Rex during the British Institute days in Greece, wrote him on 15 March that he liked *Views of Attica* very much, especially the fact that Rex did not take sides among the Greeks but just liked them. He found Rex's "tranquil love" of the Greeks "completely satisfying."[28]

Escapade was published on 27 April. It tells the story of a female criminal, deceptively named Mrs. Helpless, who causes chaos in a typically English village by alleging that the Canon is Stalin in disguise and that a stalwart Colonel is Hitler, who has not really died.[29] Rex pokes fun at those villagers who see a Communist under every shrub and who belong to the L.R.O.G., the League to Recover Our Greatness. They think the English one of the ten lost tribes of Israel, anointed by God. Rex wrote the story for fun, and it is fun, but it is also more than that. A cricket match in which the town butcher, who is an umpire, renders decisions outrageously in favor of his own team, but who is not challenged because no one will imperil his meat rations by protest, bears some reminiscence to the unjust football game in *The Wild Goose Chase*. Rex's readiness to chide both the anti-Communist villagers and the young radical, Teddy, who is ready to put aside his leftist opposition to marriage because he is in love, shows that Rex is now gently beyond politics, and ready to laugh at both sides of the political divide that he had taken very seriously when a young man. In the English village, rightly named Average, everything goes on as it always has—and Rex, with some humor, obviously approves of that. In *Escapade* we find a Rex who is at ease and living the kind of semirural life that he had always wanted, free of extraordinary stress. The radicalism that had contributed to, but never completely dominated, *The Wild Goose Chase* and *The Professor* now seems an aberration.

Escapade received many good reviews. On 14 June 1953, Lionel Gamlin broadcast a BBC Light Programme in which he recommended *Escapade* as "an uncharacteristic and gay" summer's entertainment. Michael Sadleir in the *Sunday Times* for 3 May 1953 found it "unremittingly funny" and especially praised the "superb cricket match with an epic umpire." The *TLS*, which had often been rough on Rex, now found that

> Mr. Warner writes with evident pleasure, and the charm of his book—which in outline is the kind of thing that has long been doing the rounds of lesser repertory theatres—lies in its poetic evocation of country summer. Altogether *Escapade* belongs on the same shelf as A.G. Macdonell's England, their England and Hugh de Selincourt's *The Cricket Match*. This may seem a strange position for the author of *The Aerodrome*, but it is not one to be despised. (29 May 1953)

But in the left-wing *Manchester Guardian*, Norman Shrapnel opined negatively that the novel shows "what can happen when a serious-minded writer tries to be funny" (1 March 1953). In *Punch* for 10 June, the writer wondered, "How on earth Mr. Warner, a novelist of distinction, could have turned out the kind of farcical morality that was so common twenty or thirty years ago is inexplicable." In the *Tribune*, Mervyn Jones wrote that "It hovers uneasily between social satire and pure farce, but it is too well-mannered for either, rather like the genteel comedies turned out by Ealing Studios." But Rex was never to have a feature film made of his works, although *The Aerodrome* would receive a television treatment much later on.

III. THUCYDIDES AND OTHER PROJECTS

At the end of April, Rex wrote Alan Glover at Penguin that he was glad that the Oxford Local Examinations Board was interested in his Thucydides as a recommended book for an examination on Greek literature that it would be holding in 1956. The translation had been finished since February, but Rex had only just received the typescript of Books V-VIII and had not yet finished writing his introduction. On Wednesday, 6 May, he would be coming to London and would like to meet at the Savile at 12 noon, when he would deliver the manuscript and discuss the question of maps. Another important point was money. Rex wanted to know if he would receive the second part of his advance when he delivered the manuscript: "I hope the book will pay in the end, but at the moment I feel that I've done a great deal of work for a very little money. (Not that I'm the least disgruntled. The work has been fascinating.)"[30] The answer, on 1 May, was that Penguin would try to pay the second part of the advance. Glover also wrote Rex on 29 June that Penguin was hoping that his Thucydides would be published in March 1954; in the event it was June. it was finally published in June]. This must have been enormously satisfying for Rex to hear, although he could not know that this translation would become his most widely known and profitable literary work, with almost one million copies sold by 1997. It was still selling well in both England and America in the summer of 2001.

Rex and Barbara went to Wales on 28 June and stayed through the month of July. On 21 July 1953, Rex wrote Lehmann from c/o Ms. Williams, Dupwell, Newport, Pembrokeshire, thanking him for his invitation to be associated with *London Magazine*, Lehmann's new venture. Rex and Barbara had escaped "beyond the reach of the telephone" and Rex found the place "heavenly." They planned to return to it in September. Around 2 August they were headed to Woodstock because Rex had a lecture to give at Oxford on 11 August and another appointment on 13 August. He mentioned that "I've started writing" another book, "again about Average, but quite different from the last,—in fact rather tragic." This sequel to *Escapade* never progressed beyond one forty-six-page manuscript notebook whose first page is dated 6 July, and which is entitled "Fragment of unfinished novel (sequel to *Escapade*.)" It is held in the University of Texas's Harry Ransom Humanities Research Center.

The sequel, of which Rex wrote five chapters and part of a sixth, uses the same characters as *Escapade*. Rev. Richard Breather, the narrator, appears to be an amalgam of Rex's father and himself: a gentle naturalist and scholar devoted to country living. He proposes to tell us how Sir Fielding Average came into possession "of an ape gifted not only with the powers of speech but a most superior intelligence" (first page) who possesses "a character of the greatest delicacy, reticence + truth" (third page). It is unclear why Rex gave up this funny, well-written fragment. He obviously felt that the reviews of the original were good enough to justify a sequel, but he may have decided finally that he was not meant to be a humorous writer.

The 5th of September saw the third English edition of *Greeks and Trojans*, then published by Penguin. On 28 September 1953, Rex wrote Greenwood from Newport, Pembrokeshire, that despite bad weather he had been enjoying his stay because "For the past two days I've been alone as Barbara has been seeing children off to school. My seal hunting has been tremendously successful + I've discovered a remote beach where there are two young seals that can be approached + stroked." Rex would remain there until 8 October, "after which date, no doubt, it will become sunny."

Rex wrote Glover at Penguin on 3 October that he was "Rather dreading the proofs of Thucydides. It would be very useful if you or Rieu could induce some really good scholar to have a look at them,—not, of course, to find errors, but to give a general impression." He suggested H. D. F. Kitto, who had enjoyed some of the passages that Rex had read during a lecture at Bristol University about two years earlier, when he was starting on the Thucydides translation. Rex added an interesting remark: "Those scholars whom I know at Oxford are pretty unhelpful. One rather has the impression that dons object to anyone outside their circle being interested in this subject." On 7 October Rex wrote Glover that he was very glad that Kitto had consented; Rex had "admired his book on the Greeks very much indeed." Rex would be leaving Wales and returning to Woodstock on 10 or 11 October.[31]

The reviews for *Eternal Greece*, which was published on 26 October, began to appear, and they were mixed. The *Manchester Guardian* for 3 November 1953 felt that it was "A beautifully produced picture book with a sympathetic text by Rex Warner," but the *TLS* found that "His text is a curious ramble. It consists largely of quotations from other writers and selections from his own translations from the Greek, together with his own sentiments as he gazed on the Greek landscape" and that "The text and the pictures are rather casually mated; and . . . the whole book cannot be described as a satisfactory interpretation of the eternal qualities of Greece." But the writer also found that "Much that he says is interesting and perceptive. . . . His delight in Greece is based on an honest appreciation of its classical civilization" and that both the text and the pictures "contain some beautiful and stimulating pages. . . ."[32] Despite the ambiguous reviews, the book has proven worthy enough to be scheduled for republication in 2003.

On 30 October 1953, Rex wrote Greenwood from Woodstock that he had been off on long motor trips, taking Barbara to see her daughter Miranda and his mother to the doctors, but suggesting Tuesday, 3 November, for a meeting. John and Pam "seem to be making a huge success of this educational racket. Much more money in that than in writing or publishing!" They were now running a school in Oxford. Rex had finished reading the Thucydides proofs by 20 November, and was waiting to hear from Kitto about them. By 13 December he was able to send the first 416 pages of corrected proofs; that was as far as he had gotten with Kitto, whom he had visited in Bristol a few days before. On the 14th Glover sent Rex the draft maps so he could indicate the most important places to be included on them. A possible volume of Aeschylus's plays had been under discussion for some time, but nothing conclusive had come of it. On 18 December Margaret Clark of the editorial department of Penguin sent Rex a list of nine minor queries about the proofs, which Rex cleared up on 21 and 29 December.

IV. REVIEWS AND THE CAESAR NOVEL

In addition to his work on *Escapade* and Thucydides, Rex wrote many reviews during this period, and they show his honesty, insight, and ability to keep up with the times when he cared to do so. In the *Spectator* for 4 December 1953, he commented on *The Rebel* by Albert Camus. Rex respected Camus greatly and found that Camus has "nobly protested, as a rebel must, against the appalling and increasingly codified inhumanity of our time." But according to Rex, Camus wrote as a rhapsodist rather than a logician, and had not answered the questions posed by Dostoyevsky's Ivan Karamazov. In writing about Isaiah Berlin's *The Hedgehog and the Fox*, a study of Tolstoy, and Tolstoy's *The Devil* and *Family Happiness* on 1 January 1954 in the *Spectator*, Rex asserted that Berlin, like a fox, had been too quick and superficial. Tolstoy, one of the writers Rex most respected, could not fit neatly into Berlin's theory that artists are either hedgehogs, with one great idea to which they relate everything else, or foxes, who have many ideas but no central one; his theory also had no bearing on the issue of Tolstoy's pessimism. The real problem as Rex saw it was that because Tolstoy lacked a firm religious faith, he could not overcome a feeling of real despair. Rex found in these two novels of Tolstoy both sympathy for humanity and arrogance.

On 12 February Rex reviewed the Incorporated Association of Assistant Masters in Secondary Schools' report on *The Teaching of the Classics*. Rex ended his favorable critique with a recommendation (no doubt self-interested, but not only that) that translations could justifiably be used for students who would never study more than a year or two of Greek and Latin. With the period of meager teacher's pay happily behind him, he still noted "the necessity to pay the teachers something much more than the miserable salaries they get at present. For the best of them are doing the best of all possible jobs."[33]

When Lehmann's *London Magazine* started up early in 1954, Rex was listed on its masthead as a member of the Editorial Advisory Board, along with Elizabeth Bowen, John Hayward, William Plomer, and C. V. Wedgewood. His second review for Lehmann's new magazine was of Kazantzakis's *Christ Recrucified*.[34] Rex found that "Not everyone will . . . concur with what appears to be the author's view that in these days (and perhaps always) 'true' Christianity involves a violent uprising of the poor against the rich. And, though there is something grand in the puritanism of Kazantzakis, there is something offensive in the violence with which it is expressed." Rex was clearly no longer a Marxist, and he himself, if not rich, was living the life of a rich person. But his objection to Kazantzakis's violence goes beyond mere self-interest: he had also witnessed the violence of the Blitz, the Nazi concentration camps, and the Greek civil war.

In April 1954 he reviewed Xan Fielding's *The Stronghold* and Vincent Cronin's *The Golden Honeycomb*, noting that ". . . Mr. Fielding represents a sort of schizophrenia that is to be found not only in Byron but in many travellers of his race. He is far too intelligent, for example, to believe in 'the noble savage' and, in any case, the Cretans are never savage and not always noble. Yet there is something which still exerts its tremendous fascination. . . ."[35] Rex was objective about Fielding, even though Fielding was rumored to be one of Barbara's former lovers. Rex also praised Cronin's style as "perceptive, scholarly and fine. Sometimes it is, perhaps, too consciously 'fine,' but that, in my view of these days, is a fault very much on the right side. I don't like the word 'omnivident'. . . but I have admired very many felicities of language and intricacies of thought."[36] In his older age, Rex still admired "style," but drew the line at pretentiousness.

Rex continued to search for new vehicles for his writing. On 6 May 1954, he wrote to Greenwood from Woodstock, mentioning a fruitful idea:

> I'm writing about the subject which we discussed the other day, namely the possibility of my writing a book on Julius Caesar, which Collins wish to commission.—As I told you,

I'm attracted by the idea + wish I had thought of it myself. But as it is, since the suggestion came from Collins, I feel that, if I do the book at all, I ought to do it for them.—I'm under the impression that, by taking on a commissioned book, I'm not breaking any existing agreement; but of course I don't want to enter into any agreements with other publishers behind your back. Naturally any agreement with Collins would be for this one book alone, + its a book that I'd like to write. Certainly I'd prefer to be writing a novel for you, but I haven't got a novel in me at the moment.

He reassured Greenwood that he had no wish to change his publishers, "But this is an attractive commission. May I go ahead on it without either offending you or breaking any of my existing commitments?"

This letter caused an immediate response from Greenwood, who was very concerned, judging from Rex's reply, also dated 6 May 1954:

The whole of this business is rather awful. I quite see the force of your argument + I expect you see the force of mine. Of course if I could do the book on Caesar for you, everything would be all right. But I don't see how I could possibly do that. It would amount to a very double-crossing action. Because, though the idea may be a sensible one, the fact is that I didn't think of it.

This letter shows a conflict between Rex's personal relationship with Greenwood and his artistic instincts; perhaps most of all it shows how honest and straightforward he was in his dealings with publishers. Such relationships have become more rare as huge conglomerates have taken over trade publishing. Of course a way would be found to enable Rex to go with Collins, and Collins would in fact publish *The Young Caesar* in 1958. Sadly, this is the very last letter that we have from Rex to Greenwood; hopefully they remained on good terms because six months later Greenwood died of throat cancer.

On 29 May Rex wrote Lehmann praising a new poem by Cecil as "the best thing he's done for some time." He liked issue #5 of *London Magazine* very much, especially the poems by Howard Nemerov and Edwin Muir. He mentioned that he would send Lehmann a copy of *The Vengeance of the Gods*, which had been published on 28 May and is Rex's retelling of Greek myths from the plays of Aeschylus and Euripides.[37] The blurb for this book[38] explains that it "supplies an essential background to English literature, now that classics are taught less in schools and *Tanglewood Tales* and Kingsley's *Heroes* are seldom read at home."

Rex thanked Glover at Penguin on 3 June for a copy of the Thucydides translation, and wanted a copy sent to Kitto. He felt that "The size of the volume looks pretty forbidding, but I hope the public won't find it so." Glover responded that Penguin had printed 4,000 copies of the Thucydides. The publication date would be 25 June.[39]

In the June issue of *London Magazine*, the reviewers included Paul Bowles, Stephen Spender, and Rose Macaulay, along with Rex. Rex respectfully discussed T. S. Eliot's play *The Confidential Clerk* at some length, but found that "Mr Eliot himself writes lines which are appropriate to character and situation but which, though very skilful, are not beautiful."[40] Moreover, he found, Eliot was writing something like Greek tragedy without including the gods or epic humans. Rex asked of literature something more elevated than mundane life—as he had when he was writing his proletarian epic, *The Wild Goose Chase*, and his other allegorical novels. He had learned much from Eliot, including even some of his poetic rhythms, but this review shows why Rex never completely followed in Eliot's footsteps.

In the July issue of *London Magazine*, Rex reviewed Middleton Murry's book *Jonathan Swift*, relishing the task considerably because "The strength and violence of" Swift's "satire go beyond anything else of this kind in English. Compared with him a writer such as George Orwell is only faintly protesting against inconsiderable inequities."[41] Rex, tutored by a half-century of political cruelties, shows if anything even more respect for Swift than he had in his 1937 and 1944 essays[42] on him. But Rex could no longer see heroic virtue in either the working or the upper classes. For Rex, the Yahoo episode of *Gulliver's Travels* succeeds brilliantly because "it is not absurd to maintain that man, in spite of his high pretentions, behaves often with a beastliness and loathesomeness that make him absolutely repellent. It is merely a fact that we like to forget."[43]

On 28 August he wrote to Lehmann from Woodstock about what must have been the proofs of Lehmann's autobiography, the first volume of which, *The Whispering Gallery*, was to appear in 1955: ". . . so far I'm enjoying + admiring it greatly. I think that you are excellent on Wystan's poetry +, in general, I very much admire your invariable generosity to everyone,—a different thing from rose-coloured spectacles. Though I must say that I would have wished that I'd reminded you of a Pro than a Con threequarter."[44] Lehmann had written that "Archer's bookshop was also the rendezvous where I at last came together with Rex Warner, who looked—to my first, surprised but admiring glance—more like one of the powerful three-quarters in his own *Football-Match* than the author of it, as I had imagined him."[45] Rex mentioned casually that he would be coming to London to see someone at the BBC on Wednesday, 1 September, and that he had an invitation to go to China.

V. A TRIP TO CHINA

The major intellectual event in Rex's life in 1954 outside of his decision to work on *The Young Caesar* and the publication of the *Peloponnesian War* was his trip to China, which took place from 14 September to 16 October. The philosopher A. J. Ayer gave an account of the trip in the second volume of his autobiography, *More of My Life*, and Rex published two articles about it in the *Sunday Times*.[46] Although these sources give impressions of Red China, Rex's unpublished personal diary[47] is far more informative about the precise progress of the trip.

Regardless of the source we use to trace the progress of this trip, it is important to keep in mind that, as Ayer points out in his memoir, "this was the period at which the [Chinese] Government was at its most liberal, the period when it was building up to the fatal experiment of the hundred flowers. The brutality of the Cultural Revolution, its almost equally disastrous aftermath, and the cynicism which these traumas bred all lay in the future."[48]

In addition to Rex and "Freddie" Ayer, the party consisted of painter Stanley Spencer, architect Hugh Casson, a professor of geology from the University of London named Leonard Hawkes, and John Chinnery, a lecturer on Chinese at the School of Oriental Studies. They were invited to visit by the Chinese People's Society for Cultural Relations with Foreign Countries, the equivalent of the British Council. The list of invitees was drawn from a petition, signed by hundreds of British intellectuals, stating the need for good will between Britain and China; exactly how the invitees were chosen is not clear, according to Ayer. Ayer also states that he and Rex got along from the start, and Stanley Spencer was the odd man out.

Rex's diary tells us that the trip there took the party through Amsterdam, Prague, and Moscow, where he was impressed with the theatrical productions but felt that the paintings of Stalin and other Communist leaders were "Victorian" in their moralism. On 23 September they were stuck at a cold, dreary airfield in Irkutsk, and Rex ironically noted that "In visitors book here there is a statement from [the so-called "Red" Dean of Canterbury] Hewlett Johnson—'spent three useful days here.' How?" Rex also mentioned the "Miseries of travel by air"; in the future, he would always prefer trains and ocean liners to planes. There were other wry moments: when they arrived in Peking, there were flags and a band, but not, it turned out, for Rex's party but for a Rumanian parliamentary delegation.

But Rex is far from critical of China, at least in his diary. He states a phrase such as "our Chinese friends + interpreters" without apparent irony, and was impressed with what he took to be the good mood of the crowds taking part in various ceremonies and demonstrations: such phrases as "A happy + determined people" and "Genuine rejoicings over fore-gone conclusion of election" appear often in Rex's diary. Rex found a film about selling grapes from a farm to a cooperative organization "Naive, but rather charming." Rex witnessed a massive parade of troops, tanks, aircraft, pigeons, and balloons as it went past Mao, Chou En-lai, and Chi Teh, without voicing any skepticism; he found the drive back through the crowds "most moving. Cheers, handclaps + smiles everywhere. The slogans had been obvious . . . but the feeling of the people seems wonderfully friendly, happy + powerful. Trade unionist with tears streaming down." He saw the Dalai Lama at a party for 1,000 guests given by Chou En-lai. Rex notes that Hugh Casson got the Dalai Lama's autograph, but Rex does not comment on China's occupation of Tibet, which had begun in 1950. In the entry recording the huge party, Rex comments, "I'm betting everything I've got on China."

During the trip, Rex may have been worried about having his diary read and censored by the Communist authorities and so did not want to write overtly critical comments in it, but he never comments on that possible worry anywhere in his later newspaper report on the trip (or anywhere else), so it was probably not very pressing. Even if we grant that in 1954 Chinese Communism was newer and happier than it was to be during the then-undreamed-of Cultural Revolution or than it is today, we see in Rex's uncritical enthusiasm in the diary a certain willed blindness to the obvious negativities of Communism, harking back to his hopes of the 1930s.

Yet as Ayer's memoir makes clear (and Rex's diary confirms), a good part of the group's enjoyment of the trip resulted from the superb culinary and liquid entertainment wisely provided for the British delegation by the Chinese:

> Sobriety was not the keynote of our social relations with our Chinese hosts. The Mandarin cooking in our hotel, and in the restaurant in which we were served our farewell banquet, was superb, better than any Chinese food that I have eaten outside of Peking. We were also liberally supplied with a beer, not unlike lager, which the Chinese make themselves and drink in large quantities and with a fiendish spirit called mao-tai, similar to vodka but stronger and coarser. When challenged with the word "gambi" one was supposed to drain one's glass of mao-tai at a gulp. Rex and I were quickly identified as the drinkers in our party, so that we were frequently challenged and never failed to respond. I am proud to say that we always emerged with honor.[49]

It was no doubt difficult to quarrel with such hospitality. Rex was intellectually impressed with the Imperial Palace, the Great Wall, and the Ming tombs, where he felt an "Immense haunting serenity." He also heard enviously of the relatively enormous first print runs enjoyed by Chinese writers.

There was also support from home during the trip, which undoubtedly contributed to his excellent spirits. He had two "lovely letters" from Barbara awaiting him when he returned to Peking from an excursion to Shanghai; and although he does not mention it in his diary, he was probably aware that on 27 September, during the trip, the P.E.N. anthology *New Poems 1954*, which he had co-edited with Christopher Hassall and Laurie Lee, was published. It contains the work of approximately 100 poets including some older (Blunden, Day-Lewis, John Lehmann, Spender, Gwyn Williams) and some younger (Donald Davie, Michael Hamburger, James Michie) names. There were also some poets whose work had not been published before, and some who have not been published since.

The trip back from China, during which they again stopped off at Mongolia and Siberia, was as grueling as the way there had been, but on the whole Rex was pleased with the experience. In China at least he had seen some hope for the humane, rather than the Stalinist, development of Marxism.

Despite his momentary enthusiasm for China, however, Rex was far from ready to relapse into Marxism. A much more meditative view of this trip than appears in his diary can be seen in Rex's two *Sunday Times* articles about it. On one hand he felt that since the Chinese revolution "is likely to prove the most important of modern times," it was a good idea for other nations to help it develop in "friendship and understanding rather than in hostility." The people also seemed to be fairly happy. On the other hand, he rejected literary censorship, finding that "what is a handicap + a danger is for writing to be judged entirely by virtue of its most obvious moral + political significance, + of this danger I am sure that Chinese writers are well aware. Whether the leaders of the party are equally aware of this danger I do not know." Moreover, with a great deal of prescience and also optimism Rex wrote,

> I should guess that the Marxism with which the Chinese are at present indoctrinated will not survive altogether unchanged. Even Mao-Tse-Tung has not got an absolutely orthodox record; + I imagine that Chinese intellectuals will take from the doctrine what is immediately useful rather than swallow it whole + undigested. Poor Marx! one sometimes thinks. For the dialectic has proceeded more dialectically than he could possibly have imagined.

Rex could not foresee the Cultural Revolution and its excesses, but he certainly saw the dangers as well as the hope of China, asking in conclusion, "Will [Chinese Communism] ossify into a narrow orthodoxy of persecution and of intolerance? Will it, secure as it seems to be, reveal the generosity of strength and make contact again not only with the like-minded, but with those whose minds and traditions are unlike? These are questions which cannot yet be answered." Interestingly, between the manuscript version of this article and the published piece he strengthened his criticism of Communism by adding words to one sentence: "I should guess that the Marxism with which all Chinese within reach are at present being indoctrinated will not survive altogether unchanged. . . ."[50] At that time Rex was much more a liberal than a radical despite being capable of momentary political enthusiasm.

Rex's mixed attitude toward Chinese Marxism fits with his October 1954 *London Magazine* review of Arthur Koestler's autobiographical volumes, *The Invisible Writing* and *Dialogue with Death*. Koestler, the author of *Darkness at Noon*, which shows how the Russian Revolution had devoured its own children and succumbed to Stalinism, was one of the most famous intellectuals to have turned away from Communism, as Rex had. So Rex's statements clarify his own views as well as Koestler's:

> But, of course, in the beliefs of those who, like Koestler, became converts to Communism in the early 1930s, there was something more than mere misguided rationalism. In particular there was the wish to "belong," to find oneself in a world of "comrades"; and it was the irrational mixture of dogmatic 'solid rock' with an actual and wistful insecurity that gave such characters both unearthly satisfaction and the bitterest disappointments. As Koestler well shows, all sorts of mental tricks were necessary to convince the believer that all was well—that "the Party" was not only always right but also invariably just and merciful. For what the believer needed was to imagine himself not only intellectually but also morally superior to those who were outside the faith.[51]

We remember Rex's parents futilely trying to argue with him and Frances about Communist ideas. Now he sounded much like they undoubtedly had.

VI. MORE REVIEWING

The November 1954 *London Magazine* brought a lengthy review of Rex's Thucydides translation by none other than Maurice Bowra. Bowra had Rex to thank for a pleasant trip to Athens when Rex had been head of the British Institute, and for more recent hospitality on a Barbara Rothschild scale. He was also adept at Oxonian log-rolling, and Rex was one of his outstanding students. But he retained his integrity, and so his praise for Rex must be taken at face value and must have pleased its recipient immensely:

> Mr Warner has carried out his task with outstanding success. He is far more accurate than his great predecessor Thomas Hobbes and he catches far more of the authentic

Thucydidean spirit than does the facile and evasive Jowett. He writes in modern English and is not afraid of an occasional colloquial phrase in the speeches. But he maintains throughout the essential qualities of intellectual power and precise statement. . . . If we turn to any passage which we admire and remember and look at Mr Warner's version, we always find that he has not only missed nothing but has caught its essential tone and character.[52]

The December issue of *London Magazine* carried Rex's review of Edwin Muir's *Autobiography*, "a good book written by a good man. . . gentle and wise, modest, vivid and illuminating."[53] One feels that Rex would have liked someone to apply these adjectives to him—and indeed those are the ones I would choose were I to describe his essence. Rex was often in touch with Lehmann because of the magazine, and on 7 December Rex wrote him that he had just returned from Wales, where there had been an enormous gale, "But it was very enjoyable + I've at last got pen to paper about J. Caesar." This is the first indication that he had begun *The Young Caesar*.

On 21 December 1954, he wrote from Woodstock to George and Maro Seferis that in a pub he had heard the notes of a Greek song and that this had reminded him of Seferis's "The Thrush," "particularly so because I had just read some passages from the Thrush together with some of my own poetry (which is not so bad as is generally believed) to an extraordinary gathering of people at a place called an 'Ethical Church' in London, where the only pleasant thing was the presence of Dr. Theodore Stefanides. He is a most sweet man, + its difficult to believe the Colossus's stories about his exploits with the girls in Smyrna." He commented that he had seen Katsimbalis in the summer. Rex added, "I am greatly upset about Cyprus + am enclosing a draft of a letter which I'm sending to the *Times* (they probably won't print it). I've already sent one to the Spectator, which they didn't print. Stupidity is a terrible thing." The letter, which was indeed not printed, reads as follows:

Dear Sir: there must be many besides myself who are disturbed by the news which we read every day from Cyprus + from Greece.

As regards Greece (for I can claim no special knowledge of Cyprus) it seems evident that we are risking the loss of something very valuable indeed,—a real friendship, honoured (until now) by both sides, warm, natural, + able, as has been shown, to stand the full brunt of terror + of war.

It would not have been generous (though we should have the credit for generosity) but it would have been right long ago to have [crossed out: consulted our ally about the future of an island which has for many years wished to be united with] discussed with a

Greek government the future of the island of Cyprus. Now it is too late (as has happened frequently in our imperial history) to be generous. Is it too late to be, at least, intelligent?

Is it too late to reiterate the obvious arguments, not from generosity, but from self-interest?

(i) That the efficiency of a military + naval base is improved or impaired by the attitude of local inhabitants.

(ii) That a friendly settlement with regard to Cyprus could easily be reached with any Greek government.

(iii) That such a settlement would improve rather than impair the efficiency of the military + naval base.

(iv) That in the event of Greece being over-run by some enemy, we should, in any case, be in control of the base in Cyprus.

In putting forward these considerations I am not arguing for Enosis. I am arguing for fair + reasonable discussion, as a first step. And I am protesting against what must appear to many, besides myself, as a callous attitude towards a nation which has been [crossed out: since Byron died + before, the nearest, the dearest, to our hearts] for so many years + for so many reasons most near + dear to us.[54]

This certainly shows Rex's sentiments toward Greece, which veered into the emotional, although he had deleted his most intense assertions. Jonathan had served on Cyprus after going to Trinity College and perhaps he was consulted about the situation before Rex wrote this letter. Rex is arguing that instead of getting into a war with the Greek Cypriots under Archbishop Makarios, whose *Enosis* movement wanted to unite Cyprus with Greece despite the fact that half the island had a Turkish population, the British, who controlled two important bases there, should engage in dialogue with him. This is exactly what eventually happened, but only after the British sent the Archbishop into exile and endured a guerrilla war directed against them. Today, of course, the island is partitioned into Greek and Turkish sections.

On 30 December 1954, Rex sent Lehmann a review of the *Collected Poems of C. Day Lewis*, which had been published on 2 December, for *London Magazine*, but Rex agonized about it:

> It's always a ghastly mistake to review the books of one's friends + I fear that Cecil may think the words of censure unkind + the words of praise wrongly delivered. . . . The trouble about this review, to which I've given much thought, is that I may have got the whole thing wrong. It may be that Cecil regards himself, + is, a poet of "illuminations" but I think he will be in the Robert Frost rather than the Dylan Thomas class. All this is

very miserable for me; since I hate to offend a friend, + would probably offend one if I were to come out with a false judgement.

Rex then stated, albeit humorously, the problem that he had been facing since he had married Barbara and altered his class allegiance to some degree: "I may tell you that I had a card from the Chinese Charge d'Affaires. Also that I am addressing a gathering of what I imagine to be old Shropshire business men in the New Year. This is what Cecil would call a 'split mind.' But this is ok with me. I'm becoming used to the fissure."[55] This is an open admission that Rex had come to terms with his new wealthy status and that Socialism had become only an intellectual sympathy at best.

Nineteen hundred and fifty-five saw Rex publishing more reviews. His *Medea* and *Vengeance of the Gods* were reprinted in American editions. He continued to work on *The Young Caesar*. Yet he took time out for Greece, writing on 15 February to Compton Mackenzie to tell him that he had written to the *Spectator* as well as the *Times* about Enosis, "probably in too impulsive language. Anyway no letters were printed." Rex went on to congratulate Mackenzie on a pro-Greek *Spectator* piece.[56]

The February 1955 *London Magazine* included Rex's review of the third volume of Steven Runciman's *History of the Crusades*. Runciman was of course his old boss in Greece, but as in the case of Bowra, Rex's respect for him was genuine and not based on log-rolling. He began by praising Runciman's "fine and distinguished use of the English language. The style is brilliant and appropriate, and it is no exaggeration to say that Mr Runciman is one of the very few who have written literature as well as history."[57] Rex then dwelt on the intricacy of the story that Runciman had told and on the way in which he had raised it from the specificity of history to the universalism of literature: "It is for this union of wisdom with scholarship, of art with science, that Mr Runciman's book seems both admirable and profound, a book which, to quote the words of the great Greek historian, will be 'judged useful' by all who are interested not only in the process of strange and distant events, but in the condition of man on earth."[58] Out of economic necessity and the professional writer's attendant need to turn work out steadily and quickly, Rex was a popularizer and translator of the classics who did no archival, primary research of his own. He was enormously erudite, a very gifted stylist, and a superb presenter of complex ideas simply, but not an original historian or researcher. He generously recognized the superiority of an academic such as Runciman, who had not only some of the style on which Rex prided himself, but also the research to back it up.

The March 1955 issue of *London Magazine* (2, no. 3: 84-86) saw the important review of Day-Lewis's *Collected Poems*, over which Rex had agonized considerably in December. Of all the reviews ever written of this poet's work, it would be difficult to find one that matches Rex's judicious combination of insight and criticism, all based on the most intimate knowledge of the personality and goals of the subject. Rex found that Day-Lewis's oeuvre is "a most impressive achievement and one of the most impressive things about it is the continuity to be observed in a very great variety." Rex argued against criticism of Day-Lewis for accepting many styles, seeing integrity rather than its opposite in that. Rex did have penetrating criticism of his own, however, based on years of knowledge of Day-Lewis:

> Personally I find many things in Mr Day Lewis's poems which jar upon or offend my particular sensibility. I find sometimes a kind of cleverness more suited to parlour games than to poetry. I am not impressed always by the appearance and reappearance of the melodious names of fairly obscure flowers or shrubs. Some of the frequent imperatives annoy, some of the dogmatic statements alarm me.

Yet, Rex added, "even what I deplore seems to me natural, a part of the authentic voice of one of the very few who in a time of disorder has continued to write admirably, and, in his own way, consistently."

Rex's summary of Day-Lewis's qualities is unsurpassed:

> For the writing is indeed admirable, and, when one sees so much of it gathered together in one volume, the faults one sees, or thinks that one sees, become (as in the case of Hardy's poems) rather endearing than repulsive. For here is a poet who has attempted to live a life and to record it, accepting but not overlooking the difficulties of a world half-realized; one greatly gifted with the power of arranging words and finding them, sensitive to impressions, yet searching (as a rule vainly) for an over-riding faith.

Moreover,

> . . . very many fine lines could be chosen to illustrate the melodies and the deep pieties of this poet. But there is more to him than melody or the piety that can look reverently at childhood, heroism, or at the countryside. He is one of the few who, loving the past, has tried to love the present without arrogance or affectation, and who has come back to tell the story. It may be that in the contemplative moods of "Word Over All" and of the "Elegy Before Death" Mr Day Lewis is at his best. But even in the slow movements of such poems as these the poetry is that of contrast and can be the better appreciated when one can remember different moods, different speeds and other poems. This volume

suggests that Mr Day Lewis's reputation will rest not on a few poems, however excellent, but on an already long and a still growing achievement.

Rex did not claim that Day-Lewis was the greatest poet of the century, or that he was without fault; and his solid, hard-won assessment seems truer than ever at this point in time.

VII. THE GOALS OF THE HISTORICAL NOVEL

Rex did a review of Robert Graves's *Count Belisarius* and *Homer's Daughter* in the July 1955 *London Magazine*. Graves, perhaps already annoyed by Auden's criticism of him in the poem about Rex's son in *The Orators* and no advocate of Auden's poetry in any case, would not forgive Rex for this review. When the time was ripe, with the publication of Rex's *The Young Caesar*, he exacted his revenge (see chapter 11). Regardless of the issue with Graves, what was Rex's view of the historical novel during the very time he was writing his own?

Essentially, Rex felt that accuracy in detail is not the most important quality of an historical novel. Rather, what counts is that the novel "should be alive, that the characters and the period in which they once existed should seem to us, however unfamiliar, real, so that, when we lay the book down, we can imagine that this was a period in which we might have lived, these were people whom we might have known."[59] Moreover, "In order to produce this effect of reality the author is not only entitled, but bound to take certain liberties and to exercise great ingenuity. For the historical documents themselves cannot, in the nature of things, be adequate for the purpose of the historical novelist, whose business it is not to record, but to recreate."

Unlike the historian who also recreates the past, however, the historical novelist

> is entitled to produce characters out of his sleeve and to pretend to know about the weather. ... Much more difficult are the problems which confront the author when he comes to create or conjecture, as he must, the thoughts, feelings and words of imaginary, and in particular, real characters. Here a demand for perfect accuracy is impossible. We simply do not know what Napoleon or Belisarius felt or said on numbers of important and unimportant occasions. Yet in a novel they must feel or say something, and in a novel which is based on history their feelings and sayings must be, from both a human and historical point of view, at least credible. Perhaps this is as far as one can go in one's demand for accuracy and one must approve all authors who possess sufficient skill to make their inventions credible.

Although Rex praised Graves for creating this atmosphere of credibility while adhering for the most part to fact, he also accused him of claiming that Belisarius was blinded—questionable historically—so that he could create a horrific blinding scene. Moreover, Rex did not find Graves's argument that a woman wrote the *Odyssey*, in his *Homer's Daughter*, very convincing.[60] In effect, he politely accused Graves of sensationalism without calling it that, and he would not be forgiven for it.

In the August 1955 *London Magazine*, Rex reviewed Kenneth Muir's book about John Milton and Roger Sharrock's about Bunyan, both subjects close to Rex's own concerns.[61] But it was in his review of Margaret Yourcenar's *Memoirs of Hadrian* in the October issue that Rex made another important statement about the historical novel, finding that "In attempting to understand him [the Roman emperor Hadrian] she has come to love him and perhaps to love him too much, though this is not a defect in this particular form of art, for we may assume that he loved himself and that, in recalling his past life, he will, as a man of taste and distinction, not go out of his way to incriminate himself."[62] Yet Rex in this review continued to feel that Yourcenar's portrait of Hadrian remained too one-sidedly positive. He would try in his own *Young Caesar*, even though it is narrated by Caesar himself, to show Caesar's faults as well as his strengths. Rex also remarks that Yourcenar's style sometimes passes from a fine precision to a boring lifelessness. He faced and avoided just that difficulty when crafting his own highly distinctive prose.

VIII. *THE YOUNG CAESAR*

By 3 September, he wrote Lehmann from Freelands, a new house in Burford, Oxfordshire, the leasehold of which Rex and Barbara had taken (and which would subsequently be occupied by Douglas Hurd, who would become home secretary in the Margaret Thatcher government, and foreign secretary in John Major's government). The previous occupants of the house had been Liz and Robin Fyfe, whom Rex had known in Greece and who would later figure prominently in his personal history. He stated that he was writing about the Cataline Conspiracy while the carpenter was working on the house. On 14 September he stated that he was trying to avoid London until he had finished the Caesar novel, and sent Lehmann the first and last chapters of Book II ("The King of Bithynia" and "Funeral Speeches") for consideration by *London Magazine*; a piece from the book would be published in the magazine more than a year later. He would finish writing the whole manuscript probably at some point in October.

Meanwhile, on 23 September, Mark Bonham-Carter of Collins wrote to Seymour Lawrence of the Atlantic Monthly Press, initiating a correspondence about the possible

American publication of Rex's Caesar novel. On 4 October Lawrence replied that he had met John Lehmann, who was reading the Caesar manuscript (undoubtedly the two chapters Rex had sent him) and liking it; Lawrence stated that at the Atlantic Monthly there was much enthusiasm for the book, based partially on admiration of Rex's previous work as a novelist. He made a $250 option offer for the first consideration of the work, if Rex agreed. On 10 October Bonham-Carter wrote Lawrence that he would speak to Rex when he next saw him.[63]

On 10 October Rex wrote from the Savile Club to thank Lehmann for a copy of *The Whispering Gallery*, which had just been published. He mentioned conspiratorially, "Last night went to a subversive Cypriot dinner" with Compton Mackenzie, a Professor Falls, and journalist Tom Driberg. Rex had placed his mother Kathleen in a nursing home and found, "The whole thing has been rather harassing."[64]

Whatever his views on Cyprus, Rex was becoming more conservative in his literary tastes, preferring the classics to almost all contemporary fiction. Like many people, Rex also came to favor nonfiction as he got older. In the November *London Magazine*, he praised Chekhov's letters (although not Lillian Hellman's edition of them) very highly, finding in Chekhov a robust personality and good sense, but in the December issue he saw nothing to like in three recent novels—*That Uncertain Feeling* by Kingsley Amis, *The Day of the Monkey* by David Karp, and *The Stepmother* by R. C. Hutchinson. He admitted to not having read Amis's *Lucky Jim*, which had (justly) been something of a sensation. The only recent novel he liked was a thriller by Robert Harling, *The Enormous Shadow*, based on the Burgess and Maclean case.

There might have been some envy feeding into Rex's distaste for most recent fiction. Whether good or not so good, the younger novelists were having their say and getting published, while Rex's Caesar book was proving to be a great strain. Rex had to accept the limits of historical fact in a way that he had not had to do with his purely imaginary fictions, and moreover, the editors had to be convinced that the book was good. On 16 November he wrote Lehmann apologizing for an article on the 1930s writers that he had done for Lawrence Branden's feature service: "I may say that the whole article was written when, owing to acute stomach disorder, I was scarcely able to hold a pen. After finishing J. Caesar (Vol. 1.), I seemed suddenly to collapse inside,—possibly from sheer relief at not having to think about Romans day and night. Am now much better though still conscious of the fact that I've not read all Cicero's Letters."[65] Rex only thought that he was finished with the first Caesar novel. In fact, he was not to finish until April 1957 because of the changes in the original that the publishers' readers wanted.

Despite Rex's disclaimer about his article on the 1930s writers (a typescript of which is included with his 16 November letter to Lehmann), it contains some important historical paragraphs, and reveals that he felt personal pride in the 1930s as a time, unlike the 1950s, when he was in the forefront of new literary thinking:

> Because of its later developments the movement has been represented as having been from the beginning an attempt "to bring politics into poetry" or as something akin to "social realism." Such a view is entirely mistaken. It was a movement designed, if the word "designed" can be used at all, to make poetry and prose alive and precise in the contemporary world. There was much, and perhaps an exaggerated, fervour in the use of images taken from modern life. Here Eliot and Joyce had already preceded the younger writers. Only gradually, and as a result not only of certain powerful influences from the poets and prose-writers themselves but also of the whole trend of history, did it become apparent to many that literature was, in some sense or other, "engaged" in the wider movements of society.
>
> It is now fashionable in some circles to decry those writers of the 'Thirties who not only "had ideas" but were interested in seeing these ideas implemented in practise, who strove for a new and wider form of communication and who, in attempting to find it, were often impelled to take part in politics, usually on the extreme left. Probably we are still too close to the period to be able to judge it with any finality; but it is worth pointing out that the problems raised at that time are still with us and have not yet been solved.[66]

This last line is one of Rex's repeated defenses of the 1930s, but which problems he is referring to are not clear—perhaps poverty. No matter how much Rex enjoyed good living as a well-deserved rest from a life of poverty and schoolmastering, he would never renounce or apologize for his early work or beliefs. And in fact until his retirement he was never able to rest from his constant writing, even when the strain began to show, as it did in the 1950s.

Meanwhile, Bonham-Carter and Lawrence were making progress on the publication of the Caesar novel, but it was not smooth. By 5 January 1956, Lawrence wrote Bonham-Carter that he was interested in the book for early fall publication but hadn't yet received a reader's report on the manuscript. On 11 January, however, Lawrence wrote saying that a report he had just received had made it seem that a good deal of revision would be necessary.

In the March *London Magazine*, Rex wrote about one of the few contemporary novelists of whom he approved—Graham Greene, who was, of course, of his own generation. Rex praised Greene's *The Ugly American* because "he perpetually questions the rules, thinking, not without reason, that they may be, however cordially or rigidly acknowledged, unfair."[67] In the May 1956 *London Magazine*, Rex reviewed an edition of Gibbon's letters with great delight, finding that Gibbon's "great 'compositions' command our admiration and respect" while "from the letters we recognize his humanity."[68]

In the July 1956 issue he reviewed F. R. Cowell's *Cicero and the Roman Empire* and Michael Grant's *Tacitus on Imperial Rome*. At the very time that he was working on his *Young Caesar*, Rex here revealed his view of Caesar. Liberal critics who (mistakenly) feel that Rex deserted their cause and "sold out" to wealth sometimes also grotesquely accuse him of a taste for dictatorship because he liked Caesar. Nothing could be further from the truth. Rex pointed out that the debate between Cicero's theory of political freedom and Caesar's determination to achieve order and efficiency

> continues and it is not relevant to the central issue to point out that Cicero, as a man, lacked the practical abilities which his theories demanded, or that Caesar had a very much more attractive character than those possessed by Hitler or Mussolini. It may be more relevant to reflect that it was in the end Caesarism which triumphed, that his assassination merely plunged Rome back into the disorder and bloodshed from which for a short period he had preserved her, and that what finally gave peace and security to the empire was not political liberty but efficient administration. Yet neither is the end of the story. The story is a tragedy. There is no reason in the nature of things why liberty and efficiency should be incompatible. Yet in the generation of Cicero and Caesar, as in others, they proved to be so.[69]

Rex saw no conflict between democracy and good order, but Caesar lived in an age when it was not possible to have both at the same time, and so had to act accordingly. His tolerance of Caesar's one-man rule under those special conditions cannot be construed as support for the principle of dictatorship.

Rex undoubtedly incurred the further wrath of liberal critics when, tackling the problem of literature under a dictatorship, he wrote the following in this review:

> Under the veiled dictatorship of Augustus literature positively throve and it throve as an activity sponsored by the state. Even more surprising to liberal minds is the fact that some of the greatest of this literature is propagandist. . . . The liberal of today must be puzzled to find that while he may have good reason to claim that the great flowering of literature in ancient Athens was either caused or stimulated by the birth of democracy, the fine flower of Roman literature seems to have blossomed in grateful welcome of a dictatorship; and I am afraid it is impossible to say that the flower is not fine. Such reflections as these will lead one to doubt the common assumption that literature

necessarily thrives best in periods of greatest political free speech. Indeed such assumptions are untenable. . . . Yet in the idea of freedom itself there is something necessarily and eternally inspiring. It would seem that a writer, even if he is not free, must believe himself to be as free as possible.[70]

Rex here in his own way states the truth that art can thrive under a wide variety of conditions, and that no easy formula can explain the connection between artistic productivity and the politics of a given society.

While Rex was reviewing others, he himself was being reviewed. Bonham-Carter wrote to Sam Lawrence on 20 March about the Caesar manuscript that there was too much about Marius and Sulla, that it ended at the wrong point in Caesar's career, and that the average reader would not understand Rex's references to Roman political practices and terms, including for instance praetor, quaestor, and tribune. Bonham-Carter also reported that Rex was thinking of rewriting it in the first person, and that he himself approved of this change. So Rex began with a third-person account, as if writing a biography, and then decided on first-person narration to make it a fictional autobiography. Despite these unexpected problems, Rex enjoyed some small triumphs: E. V. Rieu offered to put him up for membership in his own Athenaeum Club, and announced that Scott-Kilvert, the editor at Penguin, had accepted a plan for Rex to translate Plutarch's Roman biographies.

On 25 April 1956, reader R. E. Reynolds of the Atlantic Monthly Press submitted a trade editorial report on the first draft of Rex's Caesar book. He felt that it was a distinguished work, and his recommendation was to accept, subject to some conditions, such as the addition of more historical background, the simplification of some incidents, and the provision of dates (he pointed out that there was not one date in the book). But Reynolds contradicted Bonham-Carter by completely rejecting the idea of first-person narration.[71] So much for the objectivity of criticism! Yet there was a very important unstated issue here. Caesar himself wrote in the third person, as Rex had, so a third-person narrative not only would put Rex into competition with the superb writing of Caesar himself but would make the book seem like a biography to the modern reader who was unfamiliar with Caesar's own convention. On the other hand, a first-person account would automatically remind readers of Robert Graves's *I, Claudius* and the work of Margaret Yourcenar.

Full of praise, Reynolds went on to recommend the book for the press's annual award, feeling that it was better than any other such work and that it was, in effect, a classic, with permanent value. Another Atlantic Monthly reader's report relating to the prize and signed only "m1" is also favorable, calling the book the very best entry in the contest and chiding the English publishers for overly harsh criticism. This reader agreed that the book should not be changed to first-person narration because it would lose power and sincerity if it were projected into Caesar's head, but the reader also agreed that the beginning had too much about Marius and Sulla and not enough about Caesar. This element in fact remains the one weakness in the published novel.

The editorial saga continued, with the publishers' readers arguing over whether or not Rex should recast the book in the first person. The first American readers proved far more admiring of Rex than the readers at Collins, but only at this early point; opinions about the book were to diverge drastically, even at the Atlantic Monthly itself. On 23 April 1956, E. M. Beck of the Atlantic Monthly Press wrote that the book should be accepted because it was a superb biography with wonderful style and fascinating background detail relating to ancient Rome and its major personalities. Beck also felt that it would be an error to change the narration to first person, and went on to opine that the book was the best entry in the nonfiction contest, although he felt that it needed some reworking.

A trade editorial report by Seymour Lawrence from around this time follows Reynolds, Beck, and "m1." Lawrence put Rex's work in the "accept with revisions" category and felt that although it had been submitted as a rough first draft, it had the stature to be worthy of the Atlantic Non-Fiction Award. Lawrence felt that the revisions needed should place more emphasis on Caesar himself and less focus on the minor characters. It was Lawrence who suggested the title *The Young Caesar* and he stated that he was happy to recommend it for the award and for publication under the Atlantic-Little Brown imprint. On 1 May 1956, he urged his agent in London, Edward Weeks, to obtain the Caesar manuscript from Collins because four readers, including himself, saw it as a strong work.

But not everyone at Little, Brown agreed with Lawrence's enthusiasm for awarding Rex's book the nonfiction award. On 7 May 1956, A. J. Thornhill wrote a trade editorial report agreeing that the book was distinguished, but opining that its commercial appeal would be limited and that some necessary conditions for the award were not fulfilled. The question of nationality crept in, with Thornhill openly stating that he wanted the prize to go to an American author. He was joined in this by another Little, Brown, reader, N. Bradford, who also found that the book was too erudite and called for its complete rejection.

The upshot of all this disagreement was that on 9 July, Lawrence wrote Bonham-Carter stating that no prize at all would be given for the Atlantic Non-Fiction Award, but that three of the best submissions out of the hundreds received, including Rex's, would be published and that therefore he wanted to transform his option into a final contract.

He reiterated his opinion that the book should remain in the third person. On 17 July Bonham-Carter wrote Lawrence that he was passing his comments on to Rex. Around this time, however, Rex definitively decided to recast the book in first-person narration.

Also around July 1956, through a mutual friend, Marcus Dick, Rex made contact with Oxford philosopher Geoffrey Warnock, whom he had met only casually before that time. Rex had been slogging away at *The Greek Philosophers* for Mentor, but (according to Geoffrey Warnock, whom I interviewed) felt that his Greek philosophy was a bit shaky. He therefore asked Warnock, who was twenty years younger and a specialist, to advise him on the book. Warnock is not billed as a co-author, but is thanked in the introduction for practical help. According to Warnock he actually did more than half of the work, and the royalties were split 50/50. This may well be the case, but Warnock accepted these conditions when he agreed to work with Rex.

Rex wrote about Democritus and Parmenides, while Warnock dealt with Plato, Aristotle, Plotinus, and the Epicureans. They worked independently, and by the autumn of 1957 the book was finished. Warnock, who greatly admired Rex for *The Professor* and *The Aerodrome*, said that Rex had admitted to him at that time that he had more or less given up on pure creation. He had run out of steam as a serious novelist. In fact, Warnock felt that Rex was a slightly sad figure at that time because Rex did not value his own work. According to Warnock, Rex would become very enthusiastic about the Greeks and romanticize them because he found them congenial to his personality: he respected physical as well as intellectual accomplishments, and liked tough, energetic people. Warnock visited Rex and Barbara in Wales during the time of the writing, and remembered that Rex insisted on going for a swim on a particularly rough day. He also remembered a rather glamorous dinner party, which included the actor Michael Redgrave, given by Rex and Barbara at an old Welsh pub; Redgrave seemed to be an old friend of Rex's, judging from the way he behaved toward him. It was an enjoyable visit and the couple seemed to be at ease. Warnock and his wife, also a known academic, visited at the very elegant Freelands. He and Rex talked a good deal about cricket. One evening Rex read one of his excellent translations of a poem by Seferis, and they discussed it. Barbara enjoyed the company of academics, and Warnock found that she had a very strong personality and was a very skilled hostess. He recalled hearing about a perhaps apocryphal and typically outrageous remark of Bowra's to Rex and Barbara when they were newly married: "I don't know how long this will last. 3 times a day + all that drink. No good."

Rex continued reworking the Julius Caesar manuscript in first-person narration. On 11 August 1956, he wrote Lehmann from Cliff Cottage, in Wales, that he and Barbara would be there until the middle of September, and that he was "getting along quite well with my Caesar. Its easier to work here than anywhere else I know. I asked

Mark [Bonham-Carter] to send you the King of Bithynia chapter. If you think it's worth having I think it would be best in its original form."[72] This chapter would be published in the December 1957 issue of *London Magazine*, but it was published in the first person, so Rex's suggestion that it be published in "its original form," which would be third person, was not accepted by Lehmann.[73] On 24 August Mark Bonham-Carter reported to Seymour Lawrence that the book was progressing, but slowly, partly because of other writing in which Rex was engaged, meaning his work with Warnock on the Greek philosophers. On 31 August Lawrence had worked out the terms for the Caesar book: an advance of $1,000 against royalties of 10 percent to 7,500 copies, 12 1/2 percent to 15,000 and 15 percent thereafter.

On 4 September Rex wrote from Cliff Cottage, expressing sympathy for Lehmann's mother's illness, and adding, "I know well how disturbing these things are, having had a very anxious time with my own mother about two years ago. . . ." He went on to complain that "its years since I saw anything really striking from a young English writer. . . ." He revealed that he and Barbara had just acquired a Corgi puppy that they had named Dai, and that "By nature I like other people's dogs + eschew possession. But I'm rather fond of this animal."[74] As a child Rex had been very fond of pets, so it is not as surprising as he claims here that he should decide to own a dog.

In the same month, Rex's review of Colin Wilson's *The Outsider* was published. Rex was perhaps an odd choice as a reviewer of this book, which was almost the Bible of the Angry Young Man generation of writers in England. That movement, which included novelist Alan Sillitoe and playwright John Osborne, among others, was as irreverent as Rex's generation had been. Its complaints about the failure of the welfare state were viewed by the writers of Rex's age—who, with their Socialist sympathies, had fought for that state—almost as distastefully as Marxism had been considered by T. S. Eliot in Rex's generation. Yet Rex did his best to be objective, finding the book "remarkable for its enthusiasm" and "not a performance, but a genuine exploration." At the same time, Rex's pique was obvious: "He seems to imply that there is something particularly 'adult' in living in a world without values. . . . He is certainly much too intelligent to believe that just because the most insensitive 'bourgeois' types tend to say 'yes' to life, therefore everyone who says 'yes' is insensitive and a 'bourgeois'; yet somehow he contrives to give this impression." Rex also felt that the "Outsider" or alienated individual was nothing new—that there had been outsiders throughout history. He also noticed that most of mankind was excluded from the purview of the book. Finally, he tried to be fair when he wrote that "it is unjust to blame the book simply because one believes its scope to be less wide than do the publishers; nor is it any criticism of the author to suggest that it is a book which is being, by some eminent reviewers, absurdly over-valued."[75] Rex underestimated the social discontent that began around the time of this book's publication, and which would run through the 1960s—but he would be forced to confront it himself in due course on an American campus.

IX. WORK WITH SEFERIS

Rex would soon go to Greece for a short time in connection with a possible Basil Wright film. This was a busy trip during which he had no meal time free, and was in Athens itself for only four days. In a mood of nostalgia, Rex had tried to visit the British Institute building only to find darkened windows and a policeman at the door.

On 15 November Rex wrote George Katsimbalis to ask if he liked Rex's improvement on Katsimbalis's translation of Seferis's poem "Helen," and suggested that they should wait to hear Seferis's opinion before trying to publish it. He added generously, "Incidentally most of the best lines [are] yours." But the points Rex made in this letter convincingly refute anyone who would claim that he did not earn his reputation as a translator just because he worked from rough literal translations done by Katsimbalis and others:

A few points. Page 1. a I've put "The nightingales will never let you go to sleep at Plateus" ["Platres" in published version] deliberately into

a jumbling or singing rhythm. Caesura after "let." In fact like certain Cretan songs. Is this right?

b I really prefer your "fumbling" to my "turning over"; but "fumbling" seems a bit too animal-sexy.

c I presume "last sword" means the suicide of Ajax.

Page 2. "Melodious nightingale." Your "troubadour" is very good, but it definitely recalls French romance. "Bardic" would recall Welshmen. "Melodious" is anyway a Greek word. "Coloured" we might find a better word; but not "azure." . . . "Everywhere" isn't emphatic in English. . . . .Page 3. I wish one would find a better word than "garment"; but I can't. "Shirt" isn't right for a woman. Kimon Friar, I think, had "chemise," which is totally vulgar + Greek American.

Rex concluded this portion of his letter by adding that

the whole poem is wonderfully beautiful. I wish we could have made it perfect,—I mean as good as Seferis made it.—If you've got any ideas about dealing with the translation, do go ahead, since its mostly yours. My whim is first to offer it to John Lehmann (who may be already committed to Kimon Friar's inferior work), +, failing him, to either 'Encounter' or the Spectator. I've already written to Lehmann, but had no reply. He's always very angry with me when I go abroad, because I always enjoy it more than he does. Really he's rather impossible.—So please don't let me hear any more: 'Rex is the laziest man I know.'

Rex invited Katsimbalis and his wife Spatch to England and Wales, where they could "translate the whole of Seferis, drinking whiskey every afternoon + seeing all the time the most beautiful mountains in Europe outside Greece. The people, too, are delightful, either sea-captains or Arcadians. No Oui-Ouis, no Lehmanns."

Rex added that he was "attempting to get on with my life of Julius Caesar," and that "I can't live without Greece." He concluded by saying that he was thinking of coming to Rhodes for about four months the next year and by sending regards to the Ghikas.[76]

In the November issue of *London Magazine*, Rex defended the Victorians

who, in any case, have usually been their own best critics. Certainly it is unfair to blame them for a smug stability simply because we happen to know that the volcano on which they lived was about to erupt. We often mistake for smugness something that was merely formal and sincere; and, in our own age of instability, are tempted to envy or deplore what we are unable to achieve ourselves. Moreover there is an important sense in which we tend to expect more from life—more security, more pleasure, more satisfaction—than ever did these wealthy, religious and high-minded exemplars of the Victorian middle-class.[77]

Rex was probably thinking of his own uncles and aunts, most of whom were both religious and high-minded, if not wealthy.

Seferis wrote Rex from Athens on 2 December thanking him for his "Helen" translation and correcting a line or two, including one in which Rex had written "messengers coming up to him to tell him" and which Seferis thought should be "messengers coming up to tell him." He also enclosed a word-by-word translation of the poem "Engomi" (the title of which is the name of a village northwest of Famagusta, Cyprus). He complimented Rex, stating that "you are the only man with whom I enjoy collaborating on translations of my work."[78]

Rex wrote Lehmann from Cliff Cottage on 1 December promising to go to a party of Lehmann's on 19 December, but he was not sure about Barbara because they were expecting a visit from Barbara's daughter Miranda around then. Gasoline rationing was on because of the 31 October-6 November Suez Campaign and its aftermath, but Rex made no political comment. On 11 December he wrote Lehmann from Freelands about the Seferis poem, "Let me remind you that my own translation was quite accidental. It was forced on me by Katsimbalis." He goes on to report that "I've now heard from Seferis who is kind enough to say that I am the person he prefers above all others in the matter of translating his work. He's sent me a word for word translation of another of his new ones, a rather mystical one called 'Engomi' (a place name). I'm having a go at this + hope to get it 'authorised' in due course. . . ."[79] Here, then, is Rex's usual method of translating Seferis's poems, which is confirmed by his lengthy correspondence in the Seferis files in the Gennadius Library in Athens: Seferis (or someone close to and consulting with Seferis) would give Rex the literal translation and leave it to Rex to smooth it into superb English. Seferis would then review Rex's version, discuss fine points with him, and finally approve or "authorize" it. It is a very good translation method because the reader benefits from both the original poet's understanding of the work and the final, excellent English form. Rex devoted a great deal of effort to the Seferis poems and that made all the difference between bare, literal translations and superb, Nobel-Prize-winning English versions. He deserves the title of "translator" as much as Kenneth Rexroth and most other Western translators do.

On 23 December he sent Katsimbalis his own version of "Engomi," as well as a literal translation by George Savidis that was sent to him by Seferis, adding,

> I've probably made a lot of mistakes + I wish we could discuss it together. For instance "ringlets" in line 3. I imagined he was thinking of the kind of sky when all the clouds are twisted into small curls like the . . . fleece of sheep; but he may not have been thinking of this at all. There are plenty of other points too. "Tattoo" for instance + "humming." I don't think that "running" in English gives the necessary feeling of *sound*. Altogether I do these things much better if I've had them explained in person by you or by Seferis or by both.

Rex found that Greece was behaving well about Cyprus. The weather in Burford was "thick fog, cold + rain" and the petrol shortage was immobilizing them, but "if we can get to pubs it will be all right. The Welsh are sensible enough not to take government regulations seriously" and stayed open when they were supposed to be shut.[80]

On 13 January 1957, Rex expressed delight that Seferis liked his "Engomi" effort. He went on to tell Seferis that he'd love to try some more translation, and

> am very keen on the idea of getting together a small anthology. So if Savidis or Katsimbalis can be encouraged to send me translations adapted to my ignorance, I'd be delighted.

I'm still not sure whether "Helen" will appear in the London Magazine or in Encounter. Its becoming rather an apple of discord between John Lehmann + Stephen Spender. One only requires another editor for a real judgement of Paris. I'm leaving them to sort things out, being reluctant to draw upon myself the wrath of any goddess. I'll certainly try to improve the "Salamis." The most difficult bit is at the beginning. . . .

He concluded by mentioning that he was going on with his "life of Caesar + have nearly finished a translation of Plutarch (Marius, Sulla, Cicero, Pompey, Crassus, Caesar)."[81]

Eleven days later, he wrote Lehmann from Cliff Cottage that "I'm very glad you will publish the 'Helen.' George himself, I think, is rather fond of the 'Engomi'; but I rather agree with you. I think it would be all right in a book, but stands with some difficulty by itself." He added that "I'm getting on fairly well with Julius Caesar, very well with Plutarch + am also restudying Greek philosophy in aid of the New American Library + my own pocket." They would be back in Burford in about ten days, but were planning to "abandon" it "+ get a small place in London."[82] On 15 February Rex was sent a contract at Freelands for the Caesar book. He had hoped to deliver the manuscript in January, but then needed more time.

During February, Rex translated several Seferis poems from literal translations supplied by George Savidis. He was going to send his translations on to Seferis for approval, and on 27 February he again mentioned to Seferis the idea of publishing the poems as a book and wanted to approach John Lane the Bodley Head (which had just come under new management) about it. He suggested an introduction by himself, Bowra, or Katsimbalis. Spender wanted Seferis's "Salamis in Cyprus," in Rex's translation, for *Encounter*.

By 17 April, Rex had received copies of the May *London Magazine*, which included his and Katsimbalis's translation of Seferis's "Helen." Except for the work of Colin Wilson, who was "rather an ass," Rex had enjoyed this issue, and asked Lehmann to send dozens of copies to Seferis and Katsimbalis. Rex had just finished a solitary week at Cliff Cottage with Dai, his Corgi dog, and Barbara and her daughter Miranda had arrived. He commented to Lehmann that he was "sending through the many thousand words I've written on Caesar and Plutarch's lives. Then I've got to do a book on Greek philosophy. I wish I could have about two years without writing or reading anything."[83] Rex's fatigue is apparent; he probably could have used several years off, to rest his mind—but because he did not want to live on Barbara's money and had to pay child support, he could not afford to do so. By the end of April or early May, he had completed the revised Caesar novel, part of which would be published by Lehmann in December

1957 in *London Magazine*. Instead of the year he had anticipated when beginning the book, it had taken him from December 1954 until April 1957 to write and revise. On 7 May he sent Lehmann Katsimbalis's address, and mentioned that Seferis would become ambassador in London, and he added that he was only beginning to concentrate on the Greek philosophy book. The Caesar novel had proved particularly exhausting because it had involved a complete rewriting in first person. But that had been a success. E. M. Beck, the Atlantic Monthly reader who had opposed this change when it was first suggested by Bonham-Carter, wrote in a trade editorial report of 28 May 1957 that he now completely approved of it, and compared the success of the new, autobiographical format to the work of Margaret Yourcenar. On 5 June 1957, another Atlantic reader, P. H. Davison, found the first-person narration brilliant.

English readers, however, still did not take a wholly positive view of the work. On 5 June Bonham-Carter suggested a few more revisions to Rex, but Rex wasn't having any of it and the book was sent to another reader for adjudication. On 28 June 1957, Rex wrote from Cliff Cottage to Lehmann that " . . . As for the book, as a whole Mark [Bonham-Carter] still seems to want me to cut out a lot of the first book, + I'm pretty sure that he's wrong. I think that Veronica [Wedgewood] is reading it now + I hope she'll support me rather than Mark."[84] She did: on 10 July she wrote Bonham-Carter that the book was remarkable, the first-person narration excellent, and Rex's style very appropriate.[85]

Rex wrote Lehmann on 28 June that he was getting on with his book on Greek philosophy "+ praying for the speedy return from America of Geoffrey Warnock who, unlike me, really understands the subject."[86] On 5 July he wrote again to Lehmann about his Greek philosophy book, this time stating that "I think Geoffrey Warnock (just back from America + collaborating with, or rather guiding, me in Greek philosophy)" would be a useful contributor to *London Magazine*.[87] These remarks seem to support Warnock's comment to me that he played a large role in the writing of the book.

Rex liked the July issue of *London Magazine*, which featured an article by Isaiah Berlin. About the chapter of *The Young Caesar* that he had sent to Lehmann and which was published by him in December 1957, Rex wrote, "Incidentally, I'm not imagining him [Caesar] as *writing* his memoirs, only as reflecting on his life." He mentioned that the only immediate problem he faced was "large enormous houseflies which can only be avoided by plunging into the sea."[88] Rex wrote from Cliff Cottage to Seferis on 8 July that it was wonderful there in Wales, and that they were going to Stratford on Avon to see Shakespeare's *Cymbeline*. They planned to stay in Newport until the beginning of September with many children in the house. Then in the middle of September they were traveling to Greece for two months because Rex was possibly going to be involved with documentary and mythological films that Basil Wright wanted to make. Rex informed Seferis that Basil "was in Athens in the good days lecturing + showing films at the British Institute + went out again with me later, when we tried unsuccessfully to get the finance for a film based on the Oresteia."[89] He wanted to bring Basil to meet Seferis on 31 July. The fate of *The Young Caesar*, even after all of the revisions, still seemed uncertain to Rex.

In the meantime, Rex's translation of Plutarch's *Roman Lives* was moving through the publishing bureaucracy. E. V. Rieu wrote the Penguin editor on 5 August that Rex had done a very interesting and readable translation, but had avoided all annotation of it. This lack of annotation and Rex's very concise introductions were to be a constant complaint about him during his many years of work with Penguin. Rex wanted the title to be *Plutarch: The Fall of the Republic: Six Roman Lives*. Rieu wanted the names of the men mentioned. When the book was published in 1958, the title was *Fall of the Roman Republic: Six Lives by Plutarch (Marius, Sulla, Crassus, Pompey, Caesar, Cicero)*. On 14 August Seymour Lawrence wrote Rex at Freelands that he would be in London for three weeks from 15 September on and wanted to meet him. On the 18th Rex responded that he would like to meet Lawrence, but that he would be leaving for Greece on a "sort of film job" on 14 September, and would be there until the end of November. On 21 August he wrote Lawrence that the dedication of the novel should be "To Barbara." Seymour Lawrence remained a firm advocate of Rex's and was eventually instrumental in getting him to the United States. But championing Rex's work was not always easy. At the publishing house, opinions about this novel would remain divided to the end, and even beyond: in an undated Atlantic Monthly Press note an anonymous person said that he found *The Young Caesar* a complete bore and refused to use it for the magazine.[90]

In a letter to Seferis of 26 August 1957 from Cliff Cottage, Rex wrote that on the 31st they were returning to Burford, their home base now, and that they would be in London on the 12th and 13th before leaving for Athens on the 14th. Seferis had helped smooth Basil's way, and Rex was grateful for that. He went on to say that "At the moment we have my son George (with whom you used to fly kites on the Turko Russo) staying with us. I haven't seen him for more than a day on end for nine years + it is delightful to be seeing him now." He looked forward to a discussion of Seferis's poems when he returned from Greece.[91]

On 10 September he wrote Seferis regretting that he wouldn't see him before going to Athens, but thanking him for what he had done for the film project; Wright, in Greece, was very hopeful. Rex would be joining Basil in the Peloponnese on 1 October, after they saw Rhodes together. Rex would be taking Seferis's poems, because

"They tell the truth with passion, like Thucydides." Rex expected to be back around the middle of November. He hoped to see Maro in Athens. A postcard from Greece dated 23.9.57 to Seferis at the Greek Embassy in London informs him that Rex was having a great time with Katsimbalis. The upshot of this work was to be the Basil Wright documentary *The Immortal Land*. The art adviser for it was Michael Ayrton, and when the film came out in 1958, Rex's narration was spoken by Michael Redgrave and John Gielgud, among others. *The Immortal Land* won the Council of Europe Gold Medal and the Greek Sculpture First Prize at the Bergamo Film Festival.

X. ADRIFT ONCE AGAIN

However well Rex was doing with Basil and Katsimbalis, he was not doing well with Barbara, although he did not know it. This trip to Greece was to be very fateful in terms of his personal life, for the erosion leading to the breakup between Rex and Barbara occurred during this time. There are several versions of what happened, depending on whom one listens to. Barbara Rothschild did not comment directly on these events during my interview with her, and Nico Ghika declined to be interviewed. But my information has come from other eyewitness sources.

Tiggie, Ghika's wife, grew increasingly unhappy during this marriage to a man fifteen years her junior; people who did not know them would ask if she were his mother. She began to drink, and when she did, she became verbally abusive toward Ghika. On the other hand, drinking was a connection between her and Rex; they liked to drink together.

Barbara by this time had been accepted with some reluctance by Rex's Greek friends, even though they liked Frances. Tiggie liked Barbara and was instrumental in getting Barbara accepted in Athenian society. She even allowed the Warners to stay with them during their several visits to Athens. On the fateful trip to Athens in the fall of 1957, Rex and Tiggie hit it off really well, and were drinking together in the living room of the Ghika house over the course of several days. Since this was boring for Barbara, who was not an alcoholic, she would go up to Ghika's atelier and watch him work on his striking paintings.

One evening at a taverna dinner during which the Warners, the Katakouzinoses, the Ghikas, and the Katsimbalises were present, a drunk Tiggie publicly attacked Nico Ghika, saying that he was "nothing" and using other abusive language. Ghika, quite naturally, did not know how to respond. Barbara was embarrassed and felt sympathy for Ghika, who spent the night at the Katakouzinoses' apartment.

Shortly afterward, when Rex and Barbara were back in England at the end of November, Ghika went on an exhibition trip to America and then to India. He begged Tiggie to go with him, but she refused. Barbara must have learned of this, and she sent him a telegram and met him in Washington, and then they went to India together. Tiggie did not know anything but Rex, judging from his correspondence, was planning to go to India around this time. He never did, probably because Barbara said that she wanted to go alone, or even that she no longer wanted to go to India, but only alone to Washington.

When Ghika returned from India, he went to Tiggie and told her about his adventure. He claimed that it was just an escapade and that he was finished with Barbara. Barbara probably told Rex at this point, probably around late November or early December. The result was that Tiggie threw Ghika out of the house, and Barbara eventually left Rex.

Rex's letters reflect his state of mind. On 24 December Rex wrote Seferis from Freelands wishing him a happy Christmas. But the typically undemonstrative Rex closed with an unusual note clearly referring to the fatal events during and following the Athens trip: "Last time I'm afraid I was rather hysterical + more boring than usual. Please forgive me."[92]

On 14 January 1958, Rex wrote Lehmann from Cliff Cottage that "I'm now, as you see, in retirement, solitary except, I'm glad to say, for the dog. I haven't been feeling well for some time + apparently my blood pressure isn't right, so I was told to have a rest. This I'm certainly doing, + enjoying it very much. It's entirely cold + stormy, but I build up huge fires, cook large steaks for the dog + myself + enjoy looking at the sea + talking to the sea captains."[93] During his two-week solo stay in Wales, he seemed to have recovered his mental balance, and he was looking forward to the scheduled publication, in March, of *The Young Caesar*. But physically he was deteriorating.

XI. THE RECEPTION OF *THE YOUNG CAESAR*

At this juncture, on 15 January 1958, Rex filled out a prepublicity biographical form for the Atlantic Monthly Press. As always, Rex was able to deal with his own writing coolly and professionally. He responded to the request to give a brief account of himself as follows:

> I started writing early. At Oxford I was a friend and contemporary of C. Day Lewis + W. Auden. Here most of the writing was poetry. I wrote my first novel when I was about 23 and immediately destroyed it. I then wrote the much more ambitious "Wild Goose Chase" for which I had the greatest difficulty in finding a publisher. When

published, it got surprisingly good reviews. This + some of the other novels have been said to be imitations of Kafka. Not true, though I do admire Kafka. But I've been more influenced by Dickens, Dostoievsky, Fielding + ancient Greek.

Asked about his writing habits, he responded:

> I write best in the morning, say 9.30-12.30. Like everyone else, I do things I don't like (such as talks on the radio) best under pressure. Otherwise I like to have plenty of time, though I work, as a rule, fast. Writing is a very great pleasure indeed. I think that ordinary continuity is the best way of "sustaining a mood."

Here we see once again the still point in the midst of turmoil that Rex's writing was to him, except at times when he was writing only for money.

Asked about special research for the Caesar book, he wrote that

> Most of the research is pretty obvious. There is
>
> (i) the contemporary Latin literature: Caesar himself. Cicero, Catullus, Lucretius.
>
> (ii) Plutarch. Here I was rather glad to have the opportunity of doing this thoroughly. While writing about Caesar, I was also translating for the Penguin Classics the lives of Marius, Sulla, Crassus, Pompey, Cicero + Caesar himself.
>
> (iii) other minor ancient sources
>
> (iv) modern histories.

In response to the question, "Did the plot or overall plan change as the work grew?" he answered frankly, "Yes. That was why it took so long. Originally I wrote the whole book in the 3rd person (as Caesar himself used to write). But it then appeared that no one followed this convention. So I rewrote the whole in the 1st person."

Asked to state what "you feel you have accomplished" in writing the book, Rex said

> I think that the other lives of Caesar pass over his youth much too quickly. I've tried to convey what the impact on Caesar himself must have been of his long years of indebtedness, difficulty + danger; + of the real squalor of Roman politics. Hence, I think, one can explain the odd mixture in him of ruthlessness + clemency, of charm + dynamic violence. I also hope that I've shown that Caesar's times were not unlike our own.[94]

This is why Rex steadfastly (and perhaps mistakenly) refused to cut the first section of the book, in which the times of Sulla are explained at length; and Caesar's youth is what Rex, unlike other writers on Caesar, has given us as the explanation of his later life.

Work and the friendship that came with it were to prove Rex's salvation at this difficult moment. He was able to write Seferis on 16 January asking about the meaning of the word "Hagahianapa" because Penelope Gilliatt, features editor of *Vogue*, wanted to know since they wanted to publish "Hagahianapa. I." He told Gilliatt that it was a place name (it is a village on the southern coast of Cyprus), and accepted her proposed division of £15 between Rex and Seferis if Seferis agreed. He wrote Seferis that "I'm having a hermit's life here, companioned only by the dog, and am rather enjoying it. You must come here for a few days in the spring, when it is one of the most beautiful places on earth." Rex also commented that he was feeling much better and that "it is very good for one to be silent."[95]

On 27 January Seymour Lawrence sent Rex a good advance review of the Caesar novel and informed him that they'd sold the rights for a paperback reprint edition to the New American Library. He asked Rex for a signed copy, and was very enthusiastic indeed. Lawrence wrote to Bonham-Carter the same day asking when he intended to publish the novel. He was also eager for a second Caesar novel. On 6 February Rex wrote Lawrence, "I'm afraid I can't report much progress yet on Vol. 2. I feel that I want to soak myself in the material for a bit longer. In fact, with this end in view, I'm now doing a translation of Caesar's War Commentaries for the New American Library. This will be quite a useful diversion while I'm writing my own book."[96]

During the weekend of 1-2 March, Rex checked into the Lindo Wing of St. Mary's Hospital in London for a week-long checkup. On Wednesday, 26 February, just before he went to London, Rex wrote Lehmann from Westwell that he wanted to give him a copy of the American edition of *The Young Caesar* if he could get out of the hospital for a meeting.[97]

The first reviews were very good indeed. *Kirkus* for 15 January opined that "The narrative (and one may hope that there will be a second volume describing Caesar's maturity) carries the validity and significance of an historical document; it is fictional biography of a high order,"[98] and the *Library Journal* said that "Mr. Warner tells the story vividly and accurately in a style befitting both a poet and an author who deals with classical languages."[99] Some negative reactions were to come later. Ironically, this novel remained dedicated "To Barbara."

Rex's letter of Wednesday, 5 March, to Pam from the Lindo Wing told her that he was enjoying the treatment very much, and he commented that "I'm sure you'll have seen that things have been going very badly between Barbara + me + I'll tell you all about it when I see you. Meanwhile don't bother about me. I'm not without love + am rapidly getting better."[100]

On 10 March he wrote Seferis from the Lindo Wing, touchingly thanking him for cigarettes and for visiting him, which "did me much good." Rex was "drugged into normality" and felt peculiar. There had been a reading of Seferis's poetry the day before, Rex's birthday, but he had forgotten about it completely. He loved the treatment he received at the hospital, comparing it to a return to the womb.[101] On 12 March Rex rejected a request from Rieu to do a list of chief dates for the Plutarch book, pleading his stay in the hospital and asking him to get someone else to do it. (This was a wonderful excuse, since he never liked to do any of the editorial extras that Penguin requested him to include.) He also claimed that he was in hospital only for a checkup and that there was nothing much wrong with him—a bit of an understatement, since his blood pressure was dangerously high.

On 13 March Sam Lawrence sent Rex a message addressed to Burford: "Best wishes on publication day." There would be other good news about *The Young Caesar*, which had been so exasperatingly long in coming to fruition. A note of 4 April from Atlantic Monthly to Little, Brown by one Edwin Seaver states that the book had been selling between 300 and 500 copies a week for three consecutive weeks. On 21 April Lawrence wrote to Bonham-Carter that more than 5,000 copies had been sold, and that the weekly sales pattern was very good.[102]

XII. EXIT BARBARA AND ENTER LIZ

Things with Barbara were coming to a head. She apparently offered Rex the possibility that they live together while she went on seeing Ghika; Rex refused. On 30 April Seferis noted in the second volume of his diary that he was told that Rex was still not well, and that Barbara was living elsewhere. He asked himself "What's going on?" And on 2 May he noted, "In the morning Barbara: they're separating. What a waste of humanity."[103]

The hospital apparently recommended longer treatment, for in May Rex checked himself into Burrswood, a sanitarium in Groombridge, Kent. At this juncture, on 11 May 1958, Rex's mother Kathleen died in Charnwood House, Gloucester. Although senility is listed as one of the causes of death on the certificate, and Rex's relationship with his mother had been correspondingly difficult during these last years, he must have felt more alone than ever. On 16 May Rex wrote from Burrswood thanking Seferis for writing him. The closeness of the relationship is apparent from Rex's comment that Seferis was one of the very few people to whom he had wanted to talk about this personal crisis earlier, but that, typically, he had not talked to anyone.

I know that you would understand how I have been feeling, complex as these feelings are + you would probably help me to escape from this egotism of contemplating one's own wounds. As it is, I ought to be much better now, but somehow the body drags a long way behind the mind + it seems to be the body rather than the mind that is subject to hallucinations. My blood pressure remains high + I still find it very difficult to work. But they are trying out some new drugs + injections that may do good.

Rex enjoyed Burrswood, about four miles from Tunbridge Wells, finding it populated entirely by women except for himself. He was in a contemplative mood, stating that "I would rather talk than wish about all the rest" and that it was difficult to get the matter of his relationship with Barbara into perspective.[104]

On 26 May he wrote a similarly frank and unusually open (for Rex) letter to Pam Morris: "I agree that in these things pride always plays a most distorting part, + I know that I have a particularly awful kind of pride. It lies around one's heart like ice + prevents any good there may be from getting through." He then mentioned Liz Fyfe, who had done some cooking for Rex and Barbara. Undoubtedly she had heard about his marital problems when he was living alone and, separated herself, had come to his aid. Frances was later to credit her with having saved Rex's life. So Rex moved from woman to woman, being cared for like a big, vulnerable whale that is beached.

Rex continued, "I've talked a lot about this with Liz + its largely because of her that I am, I hope, getting rid of my pride + seeing things more clearly. I can see for instance that I do love Barbara (its impossible not to love when one has loved) + that I always shall love her. I hate the idea of having caused her pain + I'm worried about her future, as I much doubt whether Ghika is the right person for her."

Rex explained that he had written Barbara

to say all this, but haven't heard whether the letter offended her or not (it was probably unwise of me to mention the last point); but I hope the letter gave her pleasure + I certainly feel better myself for having written it. Yet while writing it, + afterwards, I felt that, though it is perfectly true that I still love her, it is also true that what is really important has somehow gone,—I mean the real confidence that is the most important part of love. I think I've got out of all the resentment I did feel + that I've escaped at least partly from my absurd pride + wounded vanity, yet still I haven't got back to the important things I felt before. It's difficult to explain. There were so many occasions where things between Barbara + I could have easily been mended, + all these occasions somehow went wrong in such a way that one almost believes that this was "meant" to happen.

Rex went on to say that

> I know that I could live with Barbara, but I don't think that for either of us it would be more than a half life, + it might be more for me than for her because I think that I need to be able to trust people more than she does. I do trust Liz absolutely + know that between her + me all the really important aspects of love are shared + reliable. One can only see what will happen + hope for a future at the moment. Obviously for me the important thing is to get well + I think that at last I'm beginning to do so.

Rex planned to go back to Westwell after leaving Groombridge in another ten to fourteen days. He would be able to see Lucy there and to be near Liz, but because of the separation and possible future divorce legalities, "The stupid thing is that we can't live there openly without some chaperone; but this might be arranged." Rex concluded on a humorous note, pointing out that "I've been for long the only male in the establishment + one of the nurses has fallen passionately in love with me. This makes life interesting but difficult."[105]

During his stay at Burrswood and at some point after 13 May, Rex also wrote Seymour Lawrence that "I wish I could report further progress on Vol. 2. Unfortunately I've been ill for some time and am at present in a nursing home, trying various things to get my blood pressure down. I'm glad to say that the remedies seem to be working at last and I hope to be all right quite soon." On 26 May Seymour was able to tell Rex the cheering news that almost 6,000 copies of his novel had sold, that the critics seemed to like it very much, and that orders for it from libraries, schools, and universities were steady.[106]

On Thursday, 29 May, Seferis visited Rex and commented in his diary,

> To Groombridge to see RW. Too much drinking and domestic melodrama. He's been there 15 days. Big park and lots of flowers. Very quiet, little lakes, ponds. Large house but looked quite melancholy. Inhabitants right now are all elderly women. He's the only male there. One lady has talked to him about faith healing. Rex told me today was an extraordinary day. She performed some faith healing attempts by hand on a sick person. She tries to give this therapy to cancer patients.

They had gone to a pub in Groombridge and talked:

> He spoke in a measured way, typical English style. His wife has left yesterday or today to join her lover—is 48 years old. He himself tied up in a sentimental affair or rather with a woman, mother of 3 children, whose husband is almost mad. Without money. He

himself as well without any money, not to mention whatever he gets from his first wife + mother of two—three children—more children with Barbara—a world of children. And he's sick. A very lovable human being.

So Barbara had left Rex on 28 or 29 May 1958 to join Ghika.

Rex stayed at Groombridge until Thursday, 12 June, and then took a car trip with Liz through Wales to Scotland. He wrote Seferis on 10 June that the reason for the trip was "partly by way of an introduction to normal life, partly to investigate some places where the cost of living is said to be low." He told Seferis that he would be back in Burford by 1 July, and thanked him for his visit: "I much enjoyed seeing you the other day + it was most kind of you to come + visit me here." He added touchingly, "Believe me, these things make a great difference + I'll always be grateful to you."

Rex went on to say that he was feeling much better than when he had arrived at Groombridge, "whether as the result of religion, injections or rest, + for the first time am being allowed to reduce the amount of drugs I'm having. It is ridiculous how one is impeded by one's body, but clearly it has to be taken seriously."[107]

The separation had certainly taken its physical and mental toll on Rex; Liz may well have saved Rex's life by taking care of him when he needed it most. During this time of crisis, Seferis too had shown his mettle and had become perhaps Rex's closest friend next to Day-Lewis. High blood pressure, exacerbated by alcohol, would remain a problem for Rex until the end of his life.

Even today, there are two schools of thought about Rex's separation from Barbara, depending upon whether one listens to his partisans or hers. According to his, he was simply betrayed by someone, Ghika, whom he regarded as among his good friends, and to whom he had shown many favors. According to the friends of Ghika and Barbara (including Stephen Spender), Rex was simply not able to handle a sophisticated woman like Barbara and to give her what she wanted. He was a minister's son and a schoolmaster and was not cut out for the 1950s version of "jet setting." Barbara's own claim, that despite his great attractions she simply tired of his drinking, has much to recommend it. Frances, too, had grown tired of it after only a few years of marriage.

Luckily for Rex, his friends remained loyal. Rex's deep friendship and intellectual relationship with Seferis, and his growing relationship with Liz Fyfe, form a new chapter in what seems an epic life along the lines of a Greek drama.

CHAPTER ELEVEN

KILMARTIN AND LOCH CRAIGNISH, 1958-1962

I. WRITING TO SURVIVE

Rex had gone from riches to rags in one short step. With Liz Fyfe and her two children he first lived in a small apartment in a town in Scotland, which was quite a change from the magnificent luxury of the Old Town House in Woodstock. With Barbara's desertion, he had taken a severe mental and physical blow. His health, particularly his blood pressure, continued to be bad. Writing for money became a matter of absolute necessity. Never a "popular" writer, Rex's income came from his translations rather than from his novels. Yet the critical success of *The Young Caesar* led him to write *Imperial Caesar* and to continue with his explication of the classical world in two additional novels. The Seferis translation was successfully concluded. Despite these significant intellectual successes, Rex had to fight doggedly to survive financially until an offer from an American college opened up new vistas.

After he left Groombridge, he spent two weeks visiting Scotland with Liz, and he decided to move there if he could afford it. But in the meantime he was in Freelands. Most reviews of *The Young Caesar* in both England and America continued to be good, with the *Springfield Republican* calling it "An exceptionally brilliant and penetrating biographical novel."[1] Even the usually dour *TLS* stated grudgingly that "Though the picture of Caesar himself is pale and disappointing, this is a scholarly reconstruction of an exciting period in history, and some of the minor portraits, especially that of Cicero, are sketched with deep understanding."[2]

On 26 May, however, Robert Graves, who had not forgotten Rex's criticism of his historical novels in *London Magazine*, opened fire in the *New Republic*. He claimed that Rex had nothing new to contribute in light of Caesar's own memoirs, and that "If I were reviewing *The Young Caesar* as serious history, I should check every reference against the original texts, but it does not merit that treatment." Graves went on to state, insultingly, that "He does not know his stuff, and writes unconvincingly."[3] There was no other completely hostile review, which reveals the malice behind this one.

The Young Caesar contains superb sketches of all the main players of Julius Caesar's time in Roman history —the people's hero Marius; the dictator Sulla who spares Caesar's life because he sees something in him; Brutus; and Caesar himself, who comes across as an unapologetic but on the whole benevolent dictator. As N. H. Reeve perceptively points out, Rex's distinction between positive and negative dictatorship is that made by Christopher Caudwell in his study of T. E. Lawrence. Sulla, the bad dictator, uses his power for personal aggrandizement; Caesar, on the other hand, while ruthless, acts out of necessity and to prevent worse evils than his dictatorship.[4] But while Caesar in Rex's presentation has some justification for his actions in view of the times, he is helpless, in the sequel *Imperial Caesar*, to prevent the hardening of his rule into totalitarianism. He comes arrogantly to feel, even in the first volume, that he is indispensable. If he knew he were to be assassinated, he tells us shortly before his assassination, he would "deplore the stupidity of my assassins more than my own fate."[5] Yet while he is sometimes arrogant, Caesar is honest about his use of brutality to attain power. The result is that Rex's Caesar comes off as a clear-sighted dictator who makes a case for himself as the only real alternative in very troubled times. Even when we do not agree with his actions, we can understand them. Was Caesar's greatness "an admirable or a disastrous thing?" Rex asks us at the beginning of the novel.[6] It is not an easy question to answer, and Rex does not tell us what to think about it. We are left to judge Caesar's self-justification for ourselves.

In addition to a clear-eyed view of Caesar and the whole Roman world, with its vicious political intrigues, cruelties, and extravagances, Rex provides timeless philosophical wisdom through the mouth of a Caesar who regrets, for instance, that "human nature is always apt to destroy that which is greater than itself,"[7] while acknowledging that people desperately want the assurance that they themselves are too weak to provide, especially during difficult times. Caesar also asks, skeptically, whether anyone has ever "attained power by means which were entirely honourable and dignified?"[8] Through Caesar, Rex identifies the difficult challenge of politics in all ages: the need to "carry out in practice the essential aims of combining liberty with authority, revolution with continuity, discipline with initiative."[9] The fineness of Rex's Caesar novels, ultimately, is that, in the pure, clear, austere style of his maturity—akin to that of the Milton he admired—and with a complete lack of sensationalism, he offered the skeptical wisdom of a lifetime, informed not only by profound study of the classical period, but by two world wars, the Depression, the Holocaust, the Greek civil war, and the Cold War. Neither rulers nor ruled escape without criticism in Rex's mature vision. In contrast to his youthful hope for a better world, in both Caesar novels he presents idealism in politics as very much a wild goose chase. Collins published the English edition of *The Young Caesar* in June 1958 and on 28 July *The Greek Philosophers* appeared through the New American Library.

Rex wrote Seferis from Freelands on 29 July 1958 that he would have liked to have had him and Maro down for a visit but was unable to do so. He was about to go off to Cliff Cottage and could not invite more guests because "the house will be full: Rosamond (Lehmann) is coming to stay, + there will also be Liz + me + three children."[10] These were probably Lucy, and Liz's two young children, Marcus, then ten, and Mariella. They were to stay there for June and July. He had not heard anything of Basil Wright's (and his) Greek film *The Immortal Land*, but expected that it would be shown soon. He also mentioned that he would like to move to Scotland if he could afford it. At this juncture, Seymour Lawrence's note to Rex that his book had earned Rex $3,045.52 through 30 June must have been very satisfying.

Rex had plenty of work to do. On 31 August he gave a television talk on British artist Graham Sutherland. Rex wrote Lawrence on 21 September from Cliff Cottage about his second Caesar novel that "I'm afraid I'm still in no position to give a firm date for the completion of the sequel. I've been spending the summer in translating Caesar's War Commentaries + have nearly finished the job. In a month or two I should have some sort of an idea of what the new book may be like." He also informed Lawrence that he was now in the hands of the literary agent David Higham.[11]

II. HOW TO TRANSLATE

On 26 September Rex's *Three Great Plays of Euripides: Medea, Hippolytus, Helen* was published by the New American Library; by 1964, it would go into five printings. This edition was a reprint of Rex's English editions, published in 1944, 1950, and 1951, respectively. In response to a question in 1962 by Ian Scott-Kilvert about why he chose to translate Euripides rather than Aeschylus or Sophocles, Rex responded that Euripides was more sympathetic for a modern audience, and said the following:

> Also I think he's easier to do, apart from the choruses. I mean, the ideas are very modern
> indeed and easily recognized by any modern audience, whereas the ideas of Aeschylus
> take a bit of understanding, and one wants a bit of knowledge of the background and
> everything, and also, of course, a much grander style altogether; whereas Euripides
> conforms to what Aristotle says, I think, that the iambic is the nearest thing to prose and
> the particular sort of poetry that Euripides uses is a sort of fifth-century poetry of ideas
> which is similar to everything we are used to in England.[12]

In response to another question about whether Rex was thinking of a stage or radio production, he answered, "I think I was chiefly thinking of having them read and making them readable, but there is no reason why they shouldn't at the same time become playable. I was very conscious that, particularly with Euripides, it is perfectly playable in modern terms, and in fact more modern than many modern things are."[13] Rex also said that he always tried to get as close to the rhythm of the original as possible: "I think it's easier to do the dialogue of a Greek tragedy. I use a long line, a semi-Alexandrine thing, based on a six-foot line rather than a blank verse line, which is certainly more familiar in English. I think if one could, it would be better to do the same thing in the choruses, but they are too difficult. One can't get that into an equivalent at all in English; and after all, one misses the dancing."

Rex stated his philosophy of translation when he said,

> One can't exactly make oneself like the original, simply because one knows one's not so
> good as Aeschylus or Sophocles, but one can at least try and give the words, which is
> about all one can do. All translation of poetry is bound to be defective, I think. But give
> what the poet's *meaning* is first, because there's a great danger, if you start making it like
> your own favourite poem or poet, you may make something which pleases you, but gives
> a totally false idea of the original; whereas the meaning does give you something, anyway.[14]

In these opinions, Rex was very close to Auden, who thought that translations should be "as philologically literal as the differences between the two languages will permit"; and that "a reader who knows both languages well enough to judge must be convinced, firstly, that the departure was necessary and, secondly, that the change made by the translator was the best of all possible changes." For Auden, as for Rex, the best translation "is the one which, first of all, does not have the air of being a translation"[15] But Rex was at some distance from Day-Lewis, who felt that a translation itself must be an original work of art, and who wrote that "a translation cannot be poetry in its own right unless it has been subdued to the imaginative process of its original; nor can it be a faithful translation unless it is in some sense an original poem."[16] Quite possibly Rex would have agreed most with T. E. Lawrence, who while translating Homer wrote that "In translating you get all the craftsman's fun of play with words, without the artist's responsibility of the design and meaning. I could go on translating for ever: but for an original work there's not an idea in my head."[17]

Rex's continuing translation work and his other writing allowed him to move to Scotland. But he had not adjusted to it when he wrote to George Seferis on 8 October 1958, from Sonachan House, Port Sonachan by Dalmally, Argyll, that

> one might well feel like Euripides in Macedonia, except that there is no barbarian king + that the dogs are quiet. I have a small + cheap flat here with Liz + her two children + we shall be here certainly for four months, meanwhile looking round for something permanent. If I can make sufficient money this will be for me a perfect solution + I think I shall be able to work + get well quickly.

Rex got on well with the Fyfe children, and Mariella attests that she loved him very much and that her time with him was one of her happiest.

This letter also contains calmly stated information about Barbara and Rex:

> I spent a few days at Burford before driving up here. Barbara had just got back + I saw her in much less strained circumstances than before. I am very fond of her + would do anything for her,—except that it has been found impossible to live with her. But this time we were able to speak without ill feeling, + that will be a good sign for the future of Lucy. If you see Barbara, do be kind to her. She is rather oversensitive to public opinion +, apart from public opinion, is frightened of what she thinks may be the opinions of you + of Katsimbalis.[18]

Rex's peculiarly passive construction, "it has been found impossible to live with her" leaves the question of whose choice it is to live apart unclear. Is Rex saying that he finds it impossible to live with her, or she with him?

Rex goes on to discuss his translation of Seferis's poems: "If you can get Xydis to send me something here I'd be delighted to go ahead with it." He sent Seferis a copy of *The Greek Philosophers* and his Plutarch translation, and lamented his distance from London, where Basil Wright's *The Immortal Land*, with Rex's commentary, was to be shown on 12 October. Rex's changed circumstances are clear when he has to state that "We could almost certainly provide a room" for a possible visit by Seferis, and "in any case, there is a good hotel quite near." But Rex ended by saying that "The country is the most wonderful I know + would sometimes remind you of Greece." He asked for some poems to translate.

His contacts with Sam Lawrence continued apace, now partially through David Higham, who wrote Lawrence on 6 November that Rex accepted an advance of $1,500 for the second Caesar book. On 28 November Lawrence suggested three titles to Rex: Caesar the Emperor, The Imperial Caesar, and The Emperor Caesar. Rex responded on 5 December that he did not like any of the titles, proposing instead Caesar the Dictator or Caesar, Perpetual Dictator. (These original suggestions for the title, including the obviously negative modern connotations of the words "Dictator" and "Perpetual Dictator," indicate clearly once again that Rex meant to emphasize the problems of dictatorship, not to praise dictatorship.) He was able to report that "I've started on the actual writing + am trying not to get too heavily bogged down in Gaul. I think the Civil War is really more interesting."[19] On 21 December he wrote Lawrence from Sonachan House that "Most of the past year I've been fairly ill, but am definitely getting better now. I think I told you that I've got started on the new Caesar volume. This is a fine place for working + I hope I'll get ahead fast with it." Sam Lawrence replied on 29 December with a suggestion of the titles Caesar the Tyrant or Caesar Tyrannus. This was countered by Rex with a letter of 7 January 1959 with Caesar Imperator or Imperial Caesar, "But I think Imperator is better."[20] Most important, Rex could report that the manuscript was going along steadily. On 14 January Seymour Lawrence voted for *Imperial Caesar*, which is more accessible to an audience not trained in Latin, and which keeps Rex's stress on dictatorship. It was in fact to be the final title.

On 11 January 1959, Rex wrote Seferis from Sonachan House that he was coming to the Savile Club from the end of January to 6 February and hoped to see him, especially to "spend an hour or so in looking through some of your poems." Rex apologized that "I'm afraid I've been rather lazy about them, but have translated one or two out of the Levesque book[21]. . . . But I doubt whether I've done them any better than they've been done already." He praised the beauty of Scotland, especially the "bright sun + snow on the mountains," and went on to say that "I'm living a very quiet life + am very gradually getting this blood pressure down."[22]

But Rex's health was far from good. In a letter to Pam Morris (20 January) he wrote that "I saw my doctor in Glasgow yesterday + for the first time he's detected some improvement, so that I can start having rather less drugs. I've been feeling well, except for the rather numbing effects of these drugs of which I've been having a huge daily dose for about two months." He explained the reasons for his upcoming trips to London, namely two literary committee meetings, probably for the British Council and *London Magazine*, and appointments with publishers. The meetings would pay his train fare—otherwise he could not do it. But he asked if Pam and John could come up so they could meet. The letter also contains the news that "I've suggested meeting Barbara [Rothschild/Warner] in London on either Feb 2 or 3. She hasn't told me anything about her plans. I hope she's still in favour of sending Lucy to Knighton House, which I'm sure would be the best thing for her."[23] The separation was very hard on Lucy, and Rex continued to be concerned about her. February saw the publication of Rex's review of Mary Renault's *The King Must Die*, a retelling of the story of Theseus, the mythical figure who was the king and then protector of Athens. Rex found that the author was at times brilliant, but he could not accept her version of Theseus. Still, she had fulfilled her function as a reteller: "We cannot in fact know 'the real' Theseus. But an artist can make him stand for something real and thus throw light both on the world in which he dimly existed and on our own world."[24] Since Caesar was a real person, Rex was able to base his novels on solid documentation, but nonetheless this statement holds true for them as well.

III. LIFE WITH LIZ

In late March 1959 Rex, Liz, and her children were able to move to The Old School House, a very small cottage in Kilmartin. Rex later described this as "a fairly squalid little furnished house,"[25] which cost him £1 a day. On 21 March Rex wrote Sam Lawrence with the new address, and announced, "Caesar is coming along. I should think I've done 1/3 of the whole, or perhaps more. Too early to know if its any good or not."[26] He also wrote Seferis on that day that he expected to be in The Old School House for three or four months. Kilmartin "is in beautiful country. I'm trying to become a Scot + am learning how to fish. So far I have not caught anything." He invited Seferis to see the Highlands. By this date, Rex had translated some Seferis poems for an anthology by John Lehmann. He would have liked to go to a showing of Compton Mackenzie's films, but it was far and Rex was recovering from the flu.[27]

Instead of just "three or four months," Rex and Liz lived in The Old School House for a year, until April 1960, when they moved to the banks of Loch Craignish, near Ardfern, where Rex—with the aid of a loan from Rosamond Lehmann—had bought some land from Jean Campbell, Liz's sister, and had built a house. Rex and Liz were becoming something of an established couple. Rex never married Liz, but she took his name during the time they were together. An attractive woman, she had been an actress but at the time they met she was working as a cook and housekeeper for "Tiny" Seligman, the wife of a merchant banker. Tiny was a friend of the actress Sylvia Copeland, who was a friend of Liz's from before she married Robin, and who got her the job. Liz had a strong character, and according to rumor, in her marriage to Robin she had been the dominant partner. If Liz had a tendency toward domination, it would certainly cause some dissonance, as would the couple's financial insecurity and Rex's lack of interest in marriage at this time. Liz died in 1984, and I was unable to interview her.

Mariella remembered that during the Kilmartin and Craignish periods Rex was very disciplined. He would shut himself away and work from 9:30 A.M. to 1 P.M. every day and "In the afternoon he would put on his deerstalker hat and call his Corgie Dai, take his walking stick and go for a long walk, whatever the weather." She remembered him translating Greek poetry, probably Seferis's, most of the time. After the walk, he would go back and work until drink time, and he preferred English beer to Scottish. "He was a keen ornithologist and always carried his binoculars on his walks. At that time in 1959 there was a pair of Hen Harriers and a pair of Golden Eagles at Craignish."[28]

On 3 April 1959, Rex wrote Lehmann from The Old School House, Kilmartin by Lochgilphead, that "I seem to have had continual flu for the last month" and he complained that "I've done no work at all lately except for toying with a few of Seferis's poems; but I suppose that if one survives this terribly dangerous period of the spring, there may be hope."[29]

The next day, Rex wrote thanking Seferis for a copy of Philip Sherrard's *The Marble Threshing Floor* (1956), which contained an essay on Seferis. Rex had read the essay and found "that I often disagree with Sherrard but . . . he is always interesting +, unlike most critics, makes one think." He also asked Seferis to get George Savidis working again on the literal translations. He commented that his own French was more suited for the translation of poetry than of prose.

He noted that

> I've just finished writing for the London Magazine a review of Kazantzakis' "Odyssey." I think that Kimon Friar has done this translation extremely well (so far as I'm able to judge). The poem itself is often very moving, but is it not almost absurdly exaggerated? What I remember of Kazantzakis bears no relation whatever to this Odysseus who, though sometimes impressive, is often a sort of parody of a Cretan swashbuckler who somehow contrives, through Bergson, to be also a sage + an ascetic. But there are some splendid purple passages.[30]

On 15 April he wrote to Compton Mackenzie, congratulating him on a television broadcast about Greece, and commenting, with obvious pro-Greek partisanship, that "The Missilonghi bit was very moving indeed + will have done much good." He said that Kilmartin was a "delightful village" and that "I'm still loading myself with drugs for this beastly blood pressure, but everyone has always told me it would take a long time" to bring it down.[31]

On 14 May Rex wrote Seferis that he had at last "summoned up the energy to use a typewriter." That was an improvement, but on the other hand, "It remains to be seen what you think of my efforts. I've often been doubtful of the precise sense intended + have very much wished that you or Katsimbalis were available for consultation. Probably I've made great numbers of mistakes. . . ." He was "still writing away about Julius Caesar + shall be very glad when I've finished. I never want to think of another Roman again." His health was improving, "but this disease is obviously a slow thing to cure. But I can be patient as I don't expect to be very normal for about another year." Rosamond Lehmann, always mindful of Rex's support during her difficulties with Cecil and probably more sympathetic to him than ever now that he had been abandoned by Barbara, was coming to visit on 22 May.[32]

IV. SEFERIS AND CAESAR

On Sunday, 21 June 1959, Seferis wrote him apologizing for not responding earlier to Rex's 14 May letter and typescript. Seferis had just received from Savidis a word-for-word translation of "Stratis Thalassinos Describes a Man," which he was sending on to Rex. He wanted to know if Rex thought that the poem would mean anything to an English reader. Rex apparently said "yes," because it is included in the Seferis volume with the title "Stratis the Sailor Describes a Man," although it is not among the Rex-translated Seferis poems published in 1959 in *London Magazine*, which included "Hagianapa," "Memory (2)-Ephesus," "Euripides the Athenian" (August 1959) and "Engome" (December 1959). Seferis thanked Rex for these translations, commenting, "On the first reading I felt that you added a great deal to what I was used to up to now."[33] He hoped that they would be able to complete the typescript of the entire book of his poems by the end of July or the beginning of August 1959. Although it would take a little longer than that, this was not a bad estimate.

Just what Rex added to the literal translations of Seferis and others is clear from an English manuscript translation of "Euripides the Athenian" in what appears to be Seferis's own hand[34]:

He grew old between the fire of Troy
and the stone-quarries of Sicily.

He liked caverns on the beach and the pictures of the sea
He saw the veins of men
Like a net of the gods, in which they catch us like wild beasts;
he tried to pierce it.
He was difficult, his friends were few
the time came and the dogs tore him to pieces

Rex's published version of the work above is:

He lived and grew old between the burning of Troy
And the hard labour in Sicilian quarries.

He was fond of rocky caves along the beach;
Liked pictures of the sea;
The veins of man he saw as it were a net
Made by the Gods for trapping us like beasts.
This net he tried to pierce.
He was difficult in every way. His friends were few.
The time arrived and he was torn to pieces by dogs.[35]

Rex's version adds both explanation and elegance, as we see, for instance, in the difference between the first translation's "fire of Troy" and Rex's "burning of Troy" and the first translation's bare "stone-quarries of Sicily" and Rex's "hard labour in Sicilian quarries."

It must have been particularly galling to Rex to hear from Seferis in the 21 June letter not only that Kimon Friar had enjoyed a grand success with his Kazantzakis translation, but also that he had written Seferis about preparing a collection of Seferis's poetry for publication by Simon and Schuster. Seferis reassured Rex that he had told Friar that Friar had no rights and that he had already chosen Rex as his translator. Seferis also consulted Rex about the inclusion of some of Seferis's poems in a collection being edited by Sherrard and Keeley, asking if it would interfere with the book.

On 24 June Rex responded to Seferis's query about Sherrard and Keeley: "My first reaction to Keeley's proposal is to be rather against having so many of your poems published in another book. Also I wonder what the book is." And he added about another rival, "I'm sure you're getting some very high-handed soliciting from Kimon Friar. I review his 'Odyssey' in this month's London Magazine."[36] Rex's review of Friar's translation of Kazantzakis's *Odyssey* sequel is positive, but it was written before he knew that Friar was a rival for Seferis's work. Given Rex's integrity, that knowledge probably would not have made a difference to his review; but human frailty being what it is, it might have. At least partially because of the Friar threat, Rex came to see Seferis at this juncture, and had a good dinner meeting with him in London on 9 July.

In the midst of beautiful weather on 29 July, Rex wrote about the difficulties of translating Seferis's "Neophytos," a poem about which he would say in a letter of 2 August to Seferis, "Incidentally it seems to me to express rather well my own feelings about Ghika."[37] (This must be a reference to the poem's use of a line from Shakespeare, where Othello, suspecting his wife's infidelity, says, "You are welcome, sir, to Cyprus. Goats and monkeys." Goats and monkeys are signs of lust, and like Othello, Neophytos is enraged.) Rex was trying to make some money by doing "a few short adaptations of the Iliad for the B.B.C. Schools programme." Soon after this, he received a semiannual statement from Sam Lawrence, with the welcome news that Rex's first Caesar novel had earned royalties of $1,499.06 for the first six months of 1959.[38]

On 27 August Rex was ready to send off the last of the poems in "Mythistorema," the first section of the published book. He asked Seferis's help with a Greek phrase which did not conform to his learning in school that "all trees are feminine." Seferis had enjoyed his trip to Athens and on Sunday, 20 September, he sent Rex an anecdote about Katsimbalis: Katsimbalis had told of a woman who said that she wanted to be his last love; he had shouted at her, "Why last? Why last?"[39]

Rex's work on the second Caesar volume continued to occupy him. On 25 September he wrote Sam Lawrence from The Old School House that "I'm getting within sight of the end of Vol 2 +, barring accidents, should certainly be able to let you have the typescript by the end of the year. Whether its any good or not I don't know, as I'm too close to it. But I do think that the story (particularly the story of the Civil War) would make a good film." The house was coming along well and he hoped that Sam could visit.[40] On 28 September 1959, Max Reinhardt of the Bodley Head wrote to Seferis expressing interest in publishing Rex's translation of the poems.[41] Rex wrote to Seferis from Kilmartin on the 29th that he had not "looked closely yet at the suggested emendations of the poems"[42] and he felt that it would be best if Seferis could come up and they could work together. By 15 October Rex still had made no progress, because he'd been working on "various odd money-making jobs" and was also "working hard on this endless book on Caesar (which is nearly at the end)." He would be going to London for a week or more at the end of December because he'd "been asked to work on the script of a film of Iphigeneia, which Michael Cacoyannis is doing." His health seemed to be improving, and he was hoping for a good report from his doctor, whom he would visit in three weeks.[43]

Rex was "getting gradually towards the end of Julius Caesar. After that, + by way of relaxation, I'm thinking of translating the Confessions of St. Augustine. It depends on whether an American publisher will pay enough money." An American publisher would. Rex's translation appeared in April 1963 through the New American Library.

On 13 October 1959, Rex wrote Pam that he had to turn down her invitation because "I'm very busy . . . finishing my Caesar book + am also meant to be having a quiet time medically, as I'm trying to reduce the amount of drugs I'm taking." (Rex was translating Caesar's *Commentaries* for the New American Library and working on *Imperial Caesar*, but here he is referring to the novel.) He was definitely better, "though this damned blood pressure is a slow business." He praised his (unnamed) doctor in Glasgow. He also mentioned that building operations on the Craignish house would start that very week. Rosamond Lehmann would be visiting for a week beginning 16 October. He was enthusiastic, saying that the house would be "on the sea in a wonderful position."[44]

The pressure of Kimon Friar's attempt to translate Seferis was still urgent. Perhaps wanting to move Rex along, Seferis wrote Rex on 25 October 1959 that Friar, obviously not ready to give up, had written to ask permission to publish a book of his own translations of Seferis's poems, and Seferis asked Rex, perhaps disingenuously, "I wonder if it would not be feasible to allow him to publish his work in America only reserving the right for the United Kingdom for your translation which I consider as you know the most important."[45] Friar, having done so well with his *Odyssey: A Modern Sequel* translation, was now encroaching on Rex's own territory, and given Friar's fame his appeal was obviously tempting to Seferis, however loyal he remained to Rex.

Rex was at a crucial moment, and his reply shows him at his best in terms of diplomacy, while he fought for his own translation:

> First, with regard to Kimon Friar, I think that the advantages of his suggestion are these:
>
> 1. He is obviously an extremely energetic + successful literary entrepreneur + also has had great (+ deserved) success with his Kazantzakis translation. Consequently it's quite likely that a book of his translations of your work would sell more copies + get more notices in America than a book of translations by me.
>
> 2. I cannot think of any other advantages. Disadvantages seem to be:
>
> 1. It might be a good thing to have an, as it were, authorised translation of you in the English language. If you prefer mine to Friar's, then mine would be the one.
>
> 2. My own American publisher (the Atlantic Monthly Press) are, I know, anxious to publish my (I should say "our") translation. They would probably not be interested if there were a translation of you available in America.

3. I imagine that from a general publisher's point of view, it is better to have the same translation (whether K. Friar's or mine) for both England + America. John Lehmann or Max Reinhardt might give useful advice on this.

—These are all the points which occur to me. Of course the decision is yours + you must do what you think best. Only I'd certainly recommend discussing it with some English publisher. You needn't think that, whatever you decide, I shall be offended. As you know my attitude is quite simple. I enjoy translating your poems + I'd like to see them as widely read + in as good a translation as possible.[46]

Of course, Rex himself was being a bit disingenuous here—his stake in the translation was economic as well as aesthetic. He needed the money, however little it would be, and he also did not want to have this promising and prestigious project snatched out from under him by Friar. But there was more to it, also, including friendship and professional pride. Despite his denials, Rex would undoubtedly have been deeply hurt had someone he considered one of his very best friends and one of the few writers whom he genuinely admired, Seferis, decided to entrust his work to one of Rex's rivals.

On the positive side, Rex was able to say that he was working on the last chapter of the Caesar volume, and "I may finish the whole thing in ten days' time + will then return, with great relief, to your poetry." Moreover, the "builders have at last started putting up a house here, in spite of continual rain + storm. Its in a perfect place + you + Maro must come + see it in the spring."

On 7 November Rex delightedly announced to Seferis that "I've now (thank God!) finished my book on Caesar + have sent the MS away to be typed. So at last I've got some time." Feeling pressure from Kimon Friar's competition, he insisted on finishing the Seferis translation quickly, stating that "The awful business of translation is that, of course, one could easily go on for ever trying to make improvements, + no book would ever be published. This would, no doubt, suit old Kimon Friar."[47]

By 11 November Rex was working on "Spring AD" and "Days of June 1941" and sent Seferis some literal translations from Savidis for his comment. Rex thought that Savidis's "choice of words is admirable." Rex also felt that "if we soon stop translating, the book will be well-balanced. Mythistorema + the Thrush will make long pieces, between + after which the shorter poems will go well. I suggest that the order should follow that of the Greek edition."[48] Rex would be flying from Glasgow to London on 27 December, and would arrive by lunchtime. On the 11th, he also reminded Sam Lawrence that Sam had expressed an interest in publishing the Seferis poems. He stressed that he was working with Seferis himself on the translations: "He + I have worked through each one of them,—a fact which will, I hope, make up for

my own rather elementary knowledge of modern Greek."[49] Rex also mentioned that
Seferis preferred Rex's translations to those of Friar.

On 12 November 1959, he wrote Seferis from The Old School House, Kilmartin,
referring to his rivalry with Friar: "I only hope you won't regret the Kimon Friar
decision. I admire Friar, rather as one might admire a monster, for his extraordinary
ability to force people to read everything he writes. And as he doesn't really write
anything,—only translation,—he's all the more remarkable." The pressure under which
Rex and Seferis were working (albeit for different reasons) shows when Rex writes,
"I quite agree with you that we should try now to get things done as quickly as possible;
+ now I'm relieved of Caesar, things will be easier for me."[50] Rex had to worry about
literary rivalry and the necessity of constant writing for money, while Seferis had the
pressures of his job as ambassador. Yet they produced a wonderful translation.

Rex enclosed "all the poems on which you've sent me notes, together with
your notes. In most cases I've accepted your suggestions word for word; in some
there are differences. But it seems likely that for the majority of these poems, if not
all, we can now reach a final agreed version." He hoped to have the book to the
publisher by January or February. On the same day, he wrote Sam Lawrence that he
wanted to send the Seferis poems quickly, but "the trouble is that Seferis is determined
to get every word right, + this delays matters. However I shall be in London for the
new year + shall be seeing a lot of him there; so I'm hoping to get an established text
by February."[51] Rex was still waiting for the typescript of the second Caesar novel.
Sam Lawrence was eager to receive it, given the performance of *The Young Caesar*:
more than 6,000 copies had been sold in the bookstores by 24 November, and it was
still moving steadily.

Rex made steady progress with the translation despite his complaint about Seferis's
exactitude. On 21 November he wrote Seferis that he would send "Spring AD" and
"Days of June 1941" to Seferis for approval the next week. By 24 November, he could
write that as soon as he had received Savidis's comments on "Santorin," "Mycenae"
"In the Manner of G.S.," "Our Sun," "Interval of Joy" and "Mr. St.T. Describes a
Man," and Seferis and himself had solved the problems with those, they would be in
a position "to produce a typescript which could be shown to a publisher, I think."[52]

Collaboration was not always easy, however. On 26 November Rex wrote Seferis,
"I agree. We ought not to have left out 'The Return of the Exile.' It's a very fine poem.
But of course there are more very fine poems, + if we go on like this, we shall never
finish + you will never give any attention to the British bases in Cyprus or whatever it
is that is occupying you. Not a bad prospect, all the same."[53] Rex would later apologize
for this remark, which may show the irritation of the professional writer, wanting

completion of the project in order to supplement his meager income or because of the constant pressure to move on to the next project, with the more financially secure diplomat who was collaborating on the translation with perfection in mind. On the other hand, in fairness to Seferis, it was Rex who had delayed the project earlier when he was trying to finish his second Caesar novel.

Despite these minor irritations, compared to other literary collaborations this one was very smooth, and Rex and Seferis remained close friends until the end of Seferis's life. The translation would bring both of them great honor, and many good things would come from it, not least publicity in England and America. In the 26 November letter to Seferis, Rex wondered which poem they would choose for a scheduled Third Programme broadcast of Seferis's work, and suggested that "Orestes" would read well. Sam Lawrence had written that he was looking forward to seeing the manuscript of the Seferis poems in February. Rex continued, "Whether we'll have it ready by then, God knows. But I think it is a good thing that he gets on well with Max Reinhardt. Also he might put some of the poems into the Atlantic Monthly magazine before publishing them in book form." Lawrence was an interesting person himself; Rex wrote Seferis that "I think I told you that he claims to have been the first person in America to have printed one of your poems. He was, I think, editor of some university magazine."

Rex continued, "For the next week or so I shall be busy correcting the typescript of my Caesar. There are also daily visits to the new house, which now has a roof on." He looked forward to having dinner with Seferis on 29 December. On 1 December Rex was able to send the *Imperial Caesar* typescript to Sam Lawrence, with the modest note that "My impression, while reading it through, is that it tends to get rather less boring as one goes on with it."

On 3 December Rex wrote Seferis that "I've had about three letters from you which I haven't acknowledged because I've been very busy correcting typescript of my J. Caesar + getting copies sent off to England + America. It was somehow a very tiring task + I went to bed for a day at the end of it. But what an infinite relief to have got the thing off my hands!" He had also heard from Savidis, who enclosed some literal translations, including "Return of the Expatriate," which Rex translated as "Return of the Exile."

He added, "One rather difficult thing for us to decide is this. Shall we aim at getting the book finished in the next two months, or shall we wait for another 6 months or more + make it a bigger book? There are still many poems that I'd like to include. This is a difficult problem + perhaps one that we might discuss with Max Reinhardt."[54] So now Rex, too, was willing to consider a longer book.

He apologized for his irritable 26 November remark about deadlines, writing that

> I had the impression from your letter that you might have been offended by whatever I
> said (meaning to be funny) about your great amount of work on the poems preventing
> you from attending to your normal duties. If you were offended, please forgive me. Of
> course I did not mean such a thing seriously,—though indeed it would be better to be
> writing poetry than listening to [British Secretary of State for Foreign Affairs] Selwyn
> Lloyd. I'm tremendously grateful for the great care + trouble you're taking. Indeed this
> is another reason why I think we should consider continuing the task a little longer.
> Having given so much thought, we should try to get things as perfect as possible.[55]

He concluded jocularly that if Seferis "saw the room in which I work, you'd be impressed
at there being any order at all (there isn't much) in my procedure." Confident and relieved
that the translation was almost finished, and perhaps impressed by the genuine importance
of the work now that he could see it as a whole, Rex was ready to consider slowing
down, even if it would mean a delay in receiving much-needed income.

He also wanted to make up for any irritation that he had caused Seferis. On 6
December Rex wrote Seferis that he had just received a contract from the BBC for the
use of his translations in a Third Programme broadcast of Seferis's poetry that had
been organized by Louis MacNeice. He generously offered Seferis the use of more of
his translations without requesting payment for them from the BBC. Seferis, too, was
in a positive and celebratory mood; he and Maro planned a dinner party on 5 or 6
January for Rex, Day-Lewis, and other mutual friends.

Artistic matters were going well for Rex all around. Seymour Lawrence wrote
Rex on the same day expressing his appreciation of *Imperial Caesar*. The confidential
readers' reports that followed were just as complimentary. P. H. Davison wrote in a
trade editorial report that it was even better than the first novel, while E. M. Beck in a
similar report on 18 December wrote that the book was an outstanding literary and
historical achievement.[56]

On 16 December 1959, Rex sent Seferis copies of his translations of "Engomi"
and "Salamis in Cyprus." He felt there should be a separate section for the Stratis the
Sailor poems. He was now translating "A Word for Summer," which "I like very
much + which Katsimbalis has done well." He followed this up with a letter of 17
December, restating that he agreed that there should be a special Stratis section of the
book and he would write to Savidis asking for translations of the poems. Rex
commented that "There is a great purity + fidelity about his versions (+ also about
those of Katsimbalis) + they are certainly much the best material to work on. I think

(though you will know better) that if this section is included with the poems we have already . . . the book will really be representative of your work."

He liked the idea of a dinner party "very much, unused as I am to social life. Day Lewis + his wife have to be kept apart from Rosamond Lehmann. Otherwise I'd have suggested that you might ask her + John. It would be nice to see Basil W. I suppose you ought to invite his mother (though it is not for me to give you advice on diplomacy). . . ."[57]

On 18 December Rex responded delightedly to Sam Lawrence's favorable letter of the 14th about *Imperial Caesar*, because, as he explained,

> I never have a very clear idea of the merits of my own books immediately after writing them, though sometimes, when years have passed, I think that some of them are not too bad. Also the writing of the Caesar book was rather exceptionally difficult. I was quite ill for a good deal of the time + often wondered whether I would be (as they say up here) "spared" to finish it. There were also difficulties in the nature of things. I wanted to make the book accurate as history (+ of course a good lot more is known about the elder than the young Caesar) + at the same time wanted occasionally to be imaginative.

He thanked Sam for a complimentary *Atlantic Monthly* subscription and then asked him, expressing how out of step with the literary and historical times of the "Angry Young Men" he had become, "why do the reviewers still bother with Colin Wilson?"

Rex also hoped to send Sam the Seferis poems soon, but he explained that "We keep on adding to what we have got, + indeed I think it would be better to have a book that is really representative of his work than a mere short anthology." The house construction was proceeding apace. On 29 December, in contrast to the many editorial revisions in *Young Caesar*, Sam responded only that he wanted a glossary and for Caesar to say rather less often that "This was my most dangerous moment."[58]

V. LIKE A PHOENIX

All in all, this was not a bad way to end 1959 and one of the most pleasurable and painful decades of Rex's life. Like a phoenix, he seemed to be rising from the ashes, although he was still far from solvent financially.[59] The year 1960 was to be an excellent one for Rex in terms of publication—the second Caesar novel, the translation of Caesar's *War Commentaries*, the Seferis poems translation, one review for the *TLS*, and an article on Cleopatra for the *New York Times Magazine*. Given this productivity (which was to result in a major literary award), 1960 was probably Rex's best year since 1941, demonstrating his powers as a creative artist and as a translator from the ancient and modern Greek. As always, Rex's writing had pulled him through his personal travails. On 12 January 1960, Seferis wrote Rex that he hoped he had had a good return trip to Scotland. On 14 January Rex responded that he had "got some sort of a chill in Glasgow, where there was thick fog + ice, + have not been so well for a few days. Quite all right now. I enjoyed our talks + work as I always do—And the party was a very good one. I found it moving to meet again the friends of 1945. Very emotional." He asked what Seferis thought of his version of "Pentheus."[60]

Their written discussion of the poem "Pentheus" (which immediately follows "Euripides the Athenian" in the published collection), is now in Gennadius Seferis file 96/7. It sheds light on the process of translation. Rex's original version was

> Asleep he was filled with dreams of
> fruit and leaves;
> awake he was not permitted to pick
> one berry.
> Sleep + wakefulness together took his
> limbs
> + shared them out in fragments
> to the Bacchae.

In notes on the manuscript page, Rex suggested that "instead of 'to the Bacchae' we might have 'to the raving women.'" But Seferis complained that there were too many words in Rex's version and added, "I think I prefer *Bacchae* to *raving women*" and included his own literal version:

> Sleep was (stuffing) filling him with dreams of
> fruit and leaves;
> wakefulness (prevented him from) did not permit
> him to pick
> even (one) a berry;
> Both of them shared out his limbs to
> the Bacchae—

Rex answered, "I agree there are too many words in my version. The trouble is that there is no precise opposite to 'sleep' in English. 'Wakefulness' has a hint of 'trying to keep awake' or 'keeping awake under compulsion.' On the other hand, 'asleep' +

'awake' are precise opposites. What about this?" And he included what would be the published version of the poem (except for minor variations of upper and lower case and one plural):

> Asleep he was filled with dreams of fruits and leaves;
> Awake he was not permitted to pick one berry.
> Sleep and wakefulness shared out his limbs to the Bacchae.

On 24 January Rex wrote Seferis that he had just begun translating St. Augustine and found him an interesting change from Julius Caesar. Seferis wrote on 31 January that he wanted Rex to settle the matter of a preface for the poetry book with Reinhardt, and Seferis would go along with any conclusion they reached. He asked Rex to tell him about the notes he had in mind. Seferis was soon going to view some specimen pages with Reinhardt and was delighted that the work was near its end. And he suggested, with obvious relief, that in the future they could discuss translating St. Augustine.[61]

On 5 February 1960 Rex, who was working on a review of a new book, *The Anger of Achilles: Homer's Iliad*, by Robert Graves, commented bitingly to Lehmann that Graves "believes that there are only three poets: (i) Graves (ii) Skelton (iii) Sassoon. . . ."[62] In his actual review of Graves's book, Rex struck back at Graves for his attack on *The Young Caesar*, echoing the theme in this letter. He exacted full revenge, beginning,

> Robert Graves is remarkable not only for being an excellent poet himself, but for a quite
> extraordinary insensitivity to the poetry of other people. So far as the poetry of the British
> Isles is concerned, his criticism sometimes leads one to believe that, in his view, the only
> poets of importance are Robert Skelton, himself and some of his brother officers of the
> First World War. . . . Then there is the question of a poet's war record. Ideally, it would
> seem, a poet should be Welsh and a Fusilier. Certainly he must have served with the
> infantry somewhere or other. Thus, in a recent article, Robert Graves pours scorn on poor
> Vergil who, it seems, could not even slope a spear, but commends the rough and fragmentary
> Ennius because it is assumed that he must have behaved well in the Punic Wars.[63]

He goes on to call Graves "the Great White Fusilier," mocking Graves's book *The White Goddess*. This is one of the few times Rex ever engaged in name-calling. He went on to indict Graves for "very limited understanding of Homer" and for producing therefore an *Iliad* reading not like that of Homer but like that of Robert Graves.[64] As we shall soon see, Rex let Gilbert Murray off far more lightly for a similar (and greater) offense.

Seferis wrote Rex approvingly on 11 February about his translation of some poems and said that he had discussed the contract with Reinhardt—the terms were to be fifteen percent, divided between them. He also discussed Rex's possible introduction and notes, and he offered some gossip as well: "Last week Mrs. [Mary] Hutchinson asked us to dinner with Barbara, Joan [Rayner], the Nations and Ghika. There was also an interesting Frenchman [Pierre] Leyris the translator of Eliot and G. M. Hopkins."[65]

On 14 February Rex wrote Seferis from Kilmartin, enclosing the notes on the last two poems and on "Pentheus." He stated that he would now go through all of the poems carefully and suggested that they could be published in chronological order. If this final work met with Seferis's approval when Rex returned it to him, Seferis could send the whole manuscript on to Max Reinhardt. He apologized for being rather slow, but "I've had to do a lot of proof reading + revision of my Caesar book for America." The weather was cold but sunny, and Rex was having an awful time with the builders.[66]

Lehmann sent Rex an inscribed copy of the second volume of his autobiography, *I Am My Brother, Autobiography II*, and on 15 February 1960 Rex responded to this gift by praising Lehmann's role in advancing the cause of literature. Rex and Liz kept having difficulty with the house builders and were "still living in great discomfort, but within a month should really be in the new house. Its more than two years now since I've had my own books around me or a room in which to work alone. But if all goes well, those hardships are coming to an end." He also noted that "The book of Seferis poems is now very nearly complete. There will be quite a few that you haven't seen + I think the whole collection deserves to impress."[67]

On 17 February 1960, Rex wrote Seferis about splitting the royalties from the poems, and added, "I was interested in your dinner party + wonder what your impressions were of Barbara + Ghika,—perhaps difficult to express in a letter. I hope for Barbara's sake that things are going well. I can't (even with the aid of St. Augustine) feel very Christian about Ghika."[68] The wound of losing Barbara still hurt, as (no doubt) did Rex's fall from high estate and good dinner party chat to exile and financial exigency in Scotland.

On 26 February Rex commented to Lehmann about *I Am My Brother*:

[F]or the last few days your Confessions have been more often in my hand than those of St. Augustine, which I should be translating. Now that I've finished it I feel that I've thoroughly enjoyed something fresh + sincere. I think its even better than Vol I + I can even forgive you for handing me down to posterity as the only literary character in Europe whom you were unable to recognise at one of your own parties. Or is the implication that I was gate crashing?

Rex especially liked the war sections. He complained about having to hurry the builders, who had promised that the new house at Craignish would be ready by last Christmas. He also seemed to have gout, which was "extremely painful."[69]

That same day, Seferis wrote that he had just received Rex's "translator's note," which Seferis suggested should be the foreword or preface to the volume. Seferis stated that the order of the poems in the volume should be the order in which they were originally published. Seferis translated the motto for the epigram for the "IV From Logbook I" section of the poems as "we remain on the same spot (place) awaiting orders"; at the top of the letter itself, Rex had written what would be the actual published translation: "Hove-to. Awaiting instructions."[70] This he had gotten from a retired naval commander.[71] Seferis passed on the news that Savidis and his wife would be coming in a few days. As a postscript, he noted that in Greece poems had lowercase letters at the beginning of lines, but he felt that it would be better to keep capitals in English.

On 29 February 1960, Seferis's birthday, Rex sent Seferis a telegram wishing him many leap years. And in a letter of that date Rex expanded on that theme, "Sometimes it seems rather typical of you to get born on a day that is outside the normal flow of time. Or was it the fault of Julius Caesar + his calendar reform?" Seferis sent Rex some notes for the poems and Rex mentioned that he had made a few alterations to them.[72] The published version includes Seferis's notes, with attribution.

On 3 March Seferis wrote him with corrections of Rex's notes which were the final pages of the volume, and added, "I'm happy we finished the job—under the conditions we were working it is an achievement. It couldn't have been accomplished without your friendship."[73]

Rex responded the next day that he would try to send Seferis the complete typescript that very day and that Seferis could then forward it to Max Reinhardt. He then commented, "It seems incredible that the task is nearly over + in a way I wish I was starting it all over again. I personally have gained greatly, since I can now read the poems with more pleasure in Greek than in English. We can still make minor alterations in the proofs; but the whole is there, for better or for worse,—an alarming thought."[74] Rex complained to Seferis about the builders in a letter of 7 March discussing Rex's notes for the Seferis poems, and on 9 March, Seferis responded, adding this very wise postscript: "Don't spoil your health with builders. They are, all of them, the same. I know them."[75]

On 11 March 1960, he sent Seferis his translator's note, and commented that he had received the contract for the poems from Max Reinhardt and had sent it back signed. Demonstrating his usual lack of interest in business, he said, "I don't really understand these things, but it seemed to me a very fine" contract.[76]

VI. IN CRAIGNISH HOUSE AT LAST

The *War Commentaries* came out on 30 March, and *Imperial Caesar* on 17 May. In between, on 1 April, Rex published a magnificent tribute to his old teacher, Gilbert Murray, in the *TLS*. Rex mentioned that "At the time of his death 400,000 copies" of Murray's Euripides "translations had been sold and Allen and Unwin are now issuing them in a new series of paperback editions. . . . It cannot be denied that Murray made more of a theatrical success of these plays than anyone else has done before or since." Rex defended Murray even as he criticized him for inaccuracies: "It may not be Euripides, but it is certainly magnificent."[77] He had not been ready to grant Robert Graves this same freedom.

On 3 April 1960, Rex wrote from Kilmartin to Seferis that "we could now get into the new house [at Loch Craignish] if only the cooking machinery had arrived. Of course the builders have made a complete mess of this." He added that "It seems very strange to be writing a letter containing no reference to your poems."[78] The translation had truly been completed, and in retrospect the collaboration seemed as trouble-free as possible, with each man supplying his best effort. Three days later, he congratulated Seferis on an honorary doctorate given him by Cambridge. He looked forward to seeing him and Maro in May in the new Craignish house. "We have a spare room with two beds (no carpet). In all probability we shall move into the house ourselves next week, though we can't get the rooms painted + papered till the end of April. So, if you want to come later rather than earlier in May, there would be less smell of paint." Rex also mentioned that the manuscript of the poems had been delivered, and hoped for proofs before May.[79]

Rex stated that he had his son George with him. George, who had graduated from a public (i.e., private) school, Victoria College in Jersey, had just been accepted into London University and was up for a visit. Rex had paid for George's education. George remembered visiting Rex and Liz at Kilmartin and that they had a small house in a row of houses. George talked to Mariella Fyfe, while Rex and Liz were working crossword puzzles. As George saw her, Liz was the opposite of Barbara—intellectual and down to earth, and not a fancy dresser.

On one of his visits, perhaps this one, George Warner met Tony Bland, who was Rex's nearest friend at this time—an aspiring writer, who was also a friend of Day-Lewis. Bland was living at a place called The Ferry House in Ardpatrick, near Tarbert on Loch Fyne, about 25 miles south of Kilmartin. He remembered that in Kilmartin Rex had a favorite pub, where he would order a double whiskey and "the landlord used to pour him a treble and would say 'Och, man, I have a very shaky hand.'" He also recalled that on one occasion during a rough sea journey he and his former wife needed Dramamine, but Rex was able to keep going on whiskey—usually a bottle a day. Rex and Tony seemed to joke a lot, and George told them that they were not serious, that they just trivialized everything. So they wrote a never-published play together, in which a character named George suddenly appears and tells the characters to be serious.

Rex moved into Craignish House on 12 April, and asked Lehmann if he had read "a long + rather pompous article by me in the April 1 Times Lit Sup on Gilbert Murray."[80] Ironically, while Rex was attacking himself for immodesty and pomposity, one of the critics of his *Imperial Caesar* found on 15 April that "Mr. Warner has used almost ascetic restraint. We may applaud him for his integrity and modesty, while regretting a somewhat dry account as the result."[81] Even worse, the *Library Journal* critic R. R. Rea wrote on 1 May, "Lacking descriptive coloration, personal characterization, or artistic imagination, this book has few virtues as either fiction or history. Caesar was troubled by insomnia (the ostensible excuse for this book); Warner's readers will not have the same difficulty. Purchase recommended only upon demand."[82] Luckily, these were not to be the only opinions, but they must have depressed a Rex trying to fight for economic and even physical survival.

Rex proudly sent Seferis his new address on 14 April, delighted because he had a study to himself and his books conveniently available for the first time in more than two years. On 24 April 1960, Rex wrote Seferis from Craignish House, Ardfern, telling him that the house would be fit for a visit by 21 May. In any case, there was no good hotel for miles and "Also the Scots in their hotels force you to eat meals at the most absurd times + like you to get up for breakfast." There was another problem: "The Scots are rather like the Greeks (except for you + Socrates); they don't like to admit that they don't know what you ask them, + consequently are able to give misleading answers." He was glad that Seferis liked his piece on Murray, and the weather was good, with a cuckoo singing since dawn.[83] Rex would come with his car, which he called "the Achilles horses," to meet Seferis at the port of Ardrishaig on Loch Fyne at 12:45 on 21 May.[84]

Rex and Seferis, then Greek ambassador in London, and dressed in a deerstalker hat and an ulster, visited Tony Bland and his wife at Ardpatrick, in the evening of Sunday, 22 May 1960. They talked about Katsimbalis and Proust and Tony was shown the proofs of Rex's translation of Seferis's poems.

In general, however, Rex did not say much about his writing to Tony, except to admit that he preferred his early novels to his historical work on Caesar. Always generous, he gave Tony the manuscript of *Imperial Caesar*.[85] He also showed Tony what Tony thought was the manuscript of *The Wild Goose Chase*. This was probably the notebook for the work, because Rex gave the manuscript away in the 1930s for a left-wing cause. Tony commented that "At the beginning the whole book had been worked out with mathematical precision and the interesting thing is, that he never made any alterations in his manuscripts. They just seemed to flow on." Rex did indeed work out *The Wild Goose Chase* philosophically if not in terms of plot before writing it, while *The Aerodrome* was carefully plotted in advance; all of Rex's manuscripts, with rare exceptions, show very little revision.

In his diary for Monday, 23 May 1960, Seferis has left a record of his visit.[86] Rex's house was new and unfinished. Seferis could hear the painters whistling and the beating of the brushes outside of their room. On the afternoon of Sunday the 22nd, a neighbor named Gilbertson, a fisherman who had been wounded in the war, came for a drink. Other neighbors visited. At night came the visit to Tony Bland, and on the way home, according to Seferis's diary, the loch was as still as a lake, with clear water and "fresh green islands." It rained on the night of the 22nd. From his bedroom, he could see the loch. To the right of a road running near the window were some caves and a little island. A green boat, which happened to be owned by George Orwell's brother-in-law, was docked there in the morning. To the left of the road was a ruined boat with grass growing through it; this Rex named "The boat of Stratis Thalasinos," after Seferis's character Stratis the Sailor.

They went around the area on Tuesday, 24 May. They looked at an old grave, and Mariella Fyfe asked if Seferis liked seeing the bones of her ancestors. Seferis found Liz "a lady snob" and added, "But nobody knows if she's like that naturally or because of psychological compensation" for their poverty. Rex mentioned islands that disappear and reappear in the fog as being part of the local mythology; this reminded Seferis of stories about the island of Santorini.

Wednesday, 25 May, was the last day of the visit and they talked about Frank Macasline, the London *Times* reporter in Athens from 1947-52, who had wanted to leave Greece but never could seem to tear himself away. Rex related that he had gotten teary-eyed himself in discussing Greece with Macasline.

By Tuesday, 14 June, Rex was celebrating the fact that his house now had a stove, although he and Liz needed chairs, knives, and glasses because some neighbors and Rosamond Lehmann were coming for a dinner party. Rex was looking forward to a copy of a book by Keeley and Sherrard, *Six Poets of Modern Greece* (1960), for review in the *TLS*.

VII. *IMPERIAL CAESAR* TRIUMPHS

Rex's literary career was proving resilient. *Imperial Caesar* began to get good reviews. In the *New York Times*, C. A. Robinson wrote that the book was a "grand success" and found that it was so accurate historically "that it takes rank with the best accounts of Caesar—John Buchan's biography, for example."[87] In the *New York Herald Tribune*, Pierson Dixon wrote that "Every line of the book strikes a note of authenticity. The most authentic thing is the taut tenseness of the narrative style which conveys the magnetic personality of the man himself."[88] This is very true. Rex had not spent at least a year translating Caesar without deriving some intellectual benefit from the experience. As in *The Young Caesar*, Rex's Caesar comes off as a worldly, decisive, and tough thinker and actor on the stage of history. But as he grows more and more dictatorial and out of touch with the people, he becomes less sympathetic.

Caesar's harshness almost always arises from political necessity rather than from personal pleasure: for instance, in *The Young Caesar* he condemns the cruelty of the slaughter of animals in the arena, but admits allowing the continuation of these "games" in order to gain the favor of the brutal masses. But in *Imperial Caesar*, he seems even more calculating, more inclined to believe in his own course of action as the only one, more callous about the cruelty he inflicts in the name of necessity, and more rigid. The Aduatuci tribe in Gaul first submitted to Caesar, and then made a treacherous attack on his army. Because Caesar felt that he had "no reason" to show mercy in this case, "The whole population were sold as slaves. I was told that the number was 53,000."[89] The matter-of-factness of this statement despite the large number of people involved, combined with Caesar's explanation that he wanted to make sure his men received some financial profit from the campaign, makes him unsympathetic to the reader at this point. N. H. Reeve even finds some similarity between the older Caesar and the Governor in *Men of Stones*, who feels that he can prescribe what is best for mankind.[90]

But Rex's triumph in both Caesar novels is to cause a tension between our judgment of Caesar's increasingly rigid and arrogant character and our lingering, if ambiguous, sympathy for him. When, for instance, Caesar is shown the head of the dead Pompey, his bitter rival, "I burst into tears and for some time was unable to speak. I have been asked since to explain these tears, and there are some, I know who will regard them as hypocritical. . . . Yet, still my tears were sincere. I wept at the horror, the pathos, the incongruity of the thing. How could Pompey the Great be reduced to a severed head lying on wood? I wept for the misery and disorder of our world in which, so far as the individual is concerned, nothing whatever is certain."[91] Despite some egotism in this statement, there is also humanity and universal fellow-feeling, as there is when Caesar comments, just as he is about to leave for the Senate meeting on the Ides of March, that "as I know well at this age, I may die at any moment from an accident or an inevitability of illness. I may even, I suppose, be assassinated."[92] Moreover, Caesar is largely justified in his claim that he has "never betrayed a friend and never acted savagely towards a

Roman enemy."[93] Thus Caesar retains his claim on our affections, however ambiguous or diminished, to the very end.

As in the case of *The Young Caesar, Imperial Caesar*'s poignancy is heightened because it is cast in the form of Caesar's reflection on his life during the last, sleepless night before his assassination. The Warnerian crystal clarity of style is here. So is Rex's unflinching political vision found, for instance, in Caesar's insistence that "it is a fact of nature that most men desire to look up to something more powerful than themselves, something capable of affording protection, of rewarding good actions and of punishing and preventing what is wrong. . . . From youth to old age they will always demand an assurance that cannot be found in their own natures."[94] But while acknowledging this need, Rex views it less sympathetically than does the Caesar who exploited it.

There are personal, biographical touches too, even in the Caesar novels. In *The Young Caesar*, a Rex taught by his daughter Anna's epilepsy acknowledges that Caesar's similar affliction may have increasingly caused changes in his conduct and manners. In *Imperial Caesar*, Caesar's stoic, touching acknowledgement of his mortality also speaks for a Rex who was often desperately ill when he was writing this novel. On a lighter, more ironic note, we hear Rex with a lifetime's experience of writing speaking through a Caesar who says that "I have observed that in general, writers, poets and orators show even less generosity towards each other than do rival practitioners of other professions."[95]

On 12 July Rex wrote from Craignish House to David Wight, the editor of the literary magazine X, rejecting his request that Rex write something about Rider Haggard, because he had promised Lehmann to do so a long time ago. Rex claimed that "The only person I know who can discuss Haggard with me on equal terms is Maurice Bowra," and referred Wight to him.[96]

In the July-September issue of *Poetry Review*,[97] Rex's translation of Seferis's "Salamis in Cyprus" was published. Rex was working steadily, because he mentioned to Seferis on 10 August that he had "just finished Book 10 of St. A[ugustine's *Confessions*]. Three more books to do. I think by now I've had about enough of saints; but if I ever translate another one I'll try an eastern one."[98] This translation was to be followed, as the Caesar *Commentaries* were, by a related novel. Also, Rex's little book on E. M. Forster was reissued on 22 August for the second time by Longmans, with revisions by one John Morris, who updated the bibliography but left the rest largely intact.

On 28 August Rex wrote Seferis, who was in Greece, from the Savile Club that a producer named Skouras "has suddenly come to life again + I'm getting a well-paid job on the script for at least 3 weeks." He had spent the last day "here in an almost continuous whirl of film people. One of them rather easily surpasses you + Katsimbalis in the matter of Christian names. He is called George St. George + is a Georgian." Rex would probably go to Athens on 15 September. He added, happily, "In the first review I saw of my Caesar book the reviewer compared me to a Rolls-Royce. Not as good as the Colossus, but not bad."[99]

In September, Rex was in Greece working on a film script that he hoped would be an authentic treatment of a classical subject. But that was not to be: the producer, quite naturally, wanted pop sex and violence and Rex was not the man to provide that. In his entire career, he had never written down to an audience no matter how hard-pressed for money he had been. *The Greek Philosophers* is a concise and solid exposition, not a simple-minded work; Rex's retellings of classical tales in *Men and Gods* are intended for children, but children of the more advanced grades and forms. Even *Escapade*, Rex's one excursion into the semi-popular, is like a witty Alec Guinness/Michael Balcon film, while *The Kite* is an intelligent boys' thriller (and it would be republished in both the Hamish Hamilton Books for Children and a school edition in 1963).

Rex's reputation in America, which had begun with *The Wild Goose Chase* and had continued with his translations and historical novels (which were published by Little, Brown and the New American Library even before they were issued in England), continued to grow. Students in American graduate schools in the 1950s were reading his novels in their courses on the British thirties and contemporary British fiction. On the strength of *Young Caesar* and *Imperial Caesar* and his translations, he was called upon by the *New York Times Magazine* to write an article on Cleopatra, which appeared on 9 October 1960.[100] The occasion for the article was to add to the publicity surrounding the new film, starring Elizabeth Taylor and Richard Burton, but Rex would not see the film for several years; when he finally did see it, he thought it hilarious because of its inaccuracies. Rex's writing in the *Times Magazine* was both colorful and accurate; in many ways, he was at his best in this piece:

> As for the other side of her reputation—that of a "Bad" woman, a voluptuary, a coward, a nymphomaniac—most of this comes straight from the propaganda service of Julius Caesar's official heir, the cruel, treacherous, clever and immensely resolute Octavius, who ended up in a blaze of respectability as the Emperor Augustus. It aimed at setting up a sort of color bar between the virtuous matrons of Italy and the lascivious oriental mistress of the degraded Roman Mark Antony. Octavius' propaganda, tasteless and untrue as it was, proved extremely successful.[101]

Rex wrote happily of the fact that Cleopatra was of Greek origin, and of the cultural glory of Alexandria. Was he thinking of Barbara when he quoted Plutarch's view of

Cleopatra?: "Her beauty, as we are told, was not in itself absolutely incomparable; it was not of the kind that strikes beholders dumb; but when one was with her one felt an irresistible charm, there was a kind of spin or stimulus about the way she looked and the way she could sway others by her talk and a kind of ambiance which made itself felt when she was with people."[102]

On 16 October Rex wrote Seferis from Craignish House that the weather was "absolutely perfect." He reported happily that his favorite swan "Lohengrin has returned, along with 23 other swans, many of which are constantly flying about over the loch." Moreover, he had received his six copies of the Seferis *Poems* the previous week. "I think the book looks good, though I'd have preferred thicker paper, as it appears now to be smaller than it really is—What do you think?"[103] The book does look rather unprepossessing. It is of unusual width, which gives it a certain elegance, but at the cost of appearing like a very slim volume. Yet there are more than fifty poems, and a great deal of work involved.

Rex told Ian Scott-Kilvert around 1965 why he was attracted to Seferis and wanted to translate his work in the first place:

> I always liked the poetry from the first one I saw, which I think was "The Argonauts," and I had a go at that immediately I saw it, knowing even less Greek than I know now. There is a quality about him which I think is unique, and the kind of themes that come into him the whole time, exile, loss, tragedy, certainly, and yet there's an enormous vitality in it all, and he sees the interpretation of the past and the present in a way that very few others do. I suppose it's really because I myself have a very strong feeling about Greece in general, and the thought that it's just the same as it was, but different, and Seferis is one of those who certainly feels that himself. I suppose it's something like that. But, of course, it's hard to say, because one simply likes the poetry and I'm also a great friend of his and am extremely fond of him and so I like it all the more.[104]

What Rex did not say is that Seferis was one of the few contemporary writers— Auden, Forster, and Day-Lewis were among the others—for whom he had the highest respect.

In his foreword to the Seferis volume, Rex explained the obstacles to good translation:

> It is always, of course, difficult (some would say impossible) to translate poetry from one language into another. But additional difficulties will confront anyone who attempts to translate modern Greek poetry into modern English. A Greek poet can use a word that

is stamped with modernity and put next to it a word straight from Homer or from Byzantium or from the Cretan poets of the seventeenth century. And Seferis, eminent as he is as a European poet, is preeminently a Greek poet, conscious of that Greek tradition which shaped, and indeed created, the tradition of Europe, but which, in very modern as in very ancient times, has often developed differently.[105]

Moreover, Seferis "will never use two words where one is sufficient, and each word has its weight, its colour or what he calls its 'halo'" and "one will find that it is more difficult to translate a word than a sentence. The work becomes a particularly delicate work of precision. And of course one is never satisfied with the result."[106]

A comparison of Rex's translations with the Edmund Keeley and Philip Sherrard translations of Seferis's work—some of which preceded Rex's—shows that Rex had his own style. The choice between the translations depends largely on personal taste, because both are clearly literary and evocative, and differ mainly in fairly small points. On the whole, Rex's translation uses simpler vocabulary, but Rex is ready to use more words if that will make Seferis more clear. For instance, in "Stratis the Sailor by the Dead Sea," Rex translates

> Down to the river Jordan
> Came three holy monks,
> And tied up to the bank there
> A small red sailing ship.[107]

Keeley and Sherrard write,

> To the River Jordan
> three monks brought
> a small red caique
> and moored it to the banks.[108]

Rex uses "small red sailing ship" instead of "caique," and calls the monks "holy." Rex's "Salamis in Cyprus" translation reads

> Greed, dishonesty, selfishness,
> The drying up of love.
> Lord help us to root out these things.[109]

where Keeley and Sherrard have

> greed, dishonesty, selfishness,
> the desiccation of love;
> Lord, help us to root these out . . .[110]

In "Euripides the Athenian," Rex uses seventy-eight words to Keeley and Sherrard's sixty-four; the original Greek has fifty-seven. Rex's years of work as a schoolteacher and his task of explaining the classics to a broad audience helped make his translations of Seferis, a difficult poet who is known as the T. S. Eliot of Greece, very accessible. Keeley and Sherrard's translations have a harder edge, but may demand a little more knowledge and effort from the reader.[111]

Rex was planning to go to Stratford on Avon on 3 November to see actress Peggy Ashcroft in *The Taming of the Shrew*. She was going to get Rex a room there and then drive him to London on the 4th, where he would be staying at the Savile. He would bring his six copies of the *Poems* and wanted Seferis to inscribe one for him. The other five he suggested "we might both sign + send back to such people as Savidis, Katsimbalis, Osbert [Lancaster] etc."[112] One is struck by Rex's humility before Seferis, and also by his integrity and modesty. In his preface, he immediately and openly acknowledges the help not only of Seferis, but of Savidis and Katsimbalis as well, and specifies the poems for which they provided him literal translations.

VIII. FROM STRENGTH TO STRENGTH

The Atlantic Monthly Press was going to bring out an edition in 1961, and the poems were doing well not only with the reviewers, but with poets themselves. On 1 December he wrote Seferis that he "was very glad to hear of John Betjeman's good opinion. Some time you must let me know what Eliot thought."[113] On 2 December the *Times Literary Supplement* referred to Rex's "graceful English" translation of Seferis. In *The New Statesman* of 17 December, poet Louis MacNeice claimed that Rex had sometimes been "forced into awkwardnesses through trying not to repeat the earlier translators of Seferis" including Spencer, Durrell, and Valaoritis, and Keeley and Sherrard. But he also said that Rex was a "very good translator" and that he deserved the most praise of all the Seferis translators because his collection was the most extensive to date. MacNeice is right on both counts. In "M.R.," for instance, Rex does seem to be straining to avoid repeating the Spencer, Durrell, and Valaoritis translation, which reads:

> The garden with its fountains in the rain
> You will see it only through the low window
> Behind the blurred pane. Your room
> Will be lit only by the flame from the hearth
> And sometimes the distant lightning will reveal
> The wrinkles on your forehead, my old Friend.[114]

Rex's version reads

> The garden with its fountains in the rain
> You will only see it looking through the low window
> Behind the blurred pane of glass. Your room
> Will have no light but the fire-light on the hearth
> And sometimes in flashes of distant lightning will stand out
> The wrinkles on your forehead, my old Friend.[115]

Rex's version is certainly not bad, but the first version is more economical; there is no need for Rex's "pane of glass" where "pane" will do quite nicely; "will stand out/The wrinkles" is more awkward than the first translation too. At the same time, as in the case of the Sherrard and Keeley comparison, Rex's translation adds extra explanation, and therefore clarity. For Rex, the literal meaning and accessibility were always the most important elements in any translation. In the *New York Times Book Review* for 18 January 1961, Dudley Fitts, a noted translator and poet, wrote that "Rex Warner's selection" of Seferis's poems "is the fullest in content and the most sensitive in handling. It is exactly what one would expect from Mr. Warner, a Hellenist and a poet in his own right."[116]

On 9 December 1960, Rex wrote Seferis enclosing the *Times Literary Supplement* commentary, which compared Seferis to the ancient Greek poets Hesiod and Pindar and he commented, "who can have thought that you are like Hesiod?" Rex complained that "There have been howling gales here for a week, but the Scots still believe that they are very fortunate + that most of the English are drowned in floods." He enclosed a photo.[117] Seferis must have responded with a photo of himself, because on 21 December, Rex wrote him jokingly, "Truly a magnificent picture, full of significance. I contemplate it daily + wonder whether Hesiod would approve." He added the information that Sam Lawrence, his Atlantic Press editor, agreed with them that the book should be clothbound and printed on thicker paper. Rex also mentioned that he had "a very nice message from [T. S.] Eliot," no doubt about the translation. And Rex signed the letter "Odysseus (Capt. Rtd [retired])."[118]

On 8 January 1961, Rex wrote Lehmann that he was coming to London later in the month for an unspecified film job because he needed a change, and that Rosamond was staying with them.[119] On 11 February 1961, Rex wrote Pam, asking if she and John could put him and Liz up in Oxford on 13 March."[120] He was again going to visit England, quite happily.

On 8 February, he also wrote Seferis that he and Liz were planning a trip south in early March and commented humorously that "as we are relying on Achilles' horses, it seems very doubtful whether we shall arrive; but, if all goes well, we should reach London on March 5." They would stay with unspecified friends on the 5th and 6th, but after that Rex would be at the Savile and Liz would stay with Rosamond Lehmann. He hoped to get tickets for *The Duchess of Malfi* from Peggy Ashcroft, but otherwise was open for a meeting with Seferis. On the 11th and 12th he planned to visit Lucy at her school in Dorset. Touchingly, he then writes of a local pub personality: "Here the main, + sad, event has been the death of old Neil Vernal of the Kilmartin pub. He had the most enormous funeral that has ever been seen in these parts,—just what he would have liked best." Rex commented that the American edition of the Seferis poems would be out in early May and asked if Seferis was having a happy collaboration with his French translator. Then, for the first time, he mentioned a new project for himself: "I'm now toying with the idea of writing a life of Pericles."[121] He would do this, publishing the novel in 1963.

Rex's career as a writer of historical fiction received a gratifying boost when he was informed on 10 February that he had won the 1960 James Tait Black Memorial Prize for *Imperial Caesar*. This prize, founded in 1919, is one of the most prestigious and financially rewarding in England, comparable to the American Pulitzer Prize, and is awarded annually for the best novel and the best biography. Winners from the late fifties included Rose Macaulay, Anthony Powell, and Angus Wilson, and later winners included Muriel Spark, Christine Brooke-Rose, and Margaret Drabble. In 1935 Robert Graves had won the award for *I, Claudius*. Surprisingly, this was Rex's first high-level British literary award. Badly in need of an ego-boost as well as money, he was delighted with the recognition and the cash, but typically he took it in stride, writing Pam on 11 February that "I don't want to be reminded of it today. Last night I celebrated it in the pub by giving drinks to all the Scots, who in their turn gave me drinks. So far today I've only managed a lightly boiled egg." Rex mentioned that his eldest son Jonathan had another child (he was to have eight) and that it was "About time he stopped."[122]

In high spirits Rex wrote Seferis on 21 February congratulating him on his receipt of the Foyle's booksellers' prize for their volume, and adding that "I can think of quite a few reasons why you should have it rather than I,—the conclusive reason being that you wrote the poems. It's very good too that you are the first foreign poet to get the prize. Indeed the whole thing is very good. I do wish I could get there for the lunch; but it doesn't seem possible." Rex could of course afford to be genuinely generous, since he had won an award in his own right. Interestingly, one of the reasons that he could not come to the lunch was that he was due to appear on 2 March "in a sort of Brains Trust for the Argyll Agriculture Society. Apparently one doesn't have to know about agriculture,— only poetry, foreign affairs, psychology, life, etc! Wouldn't Socrates be horrified?"

Rex mentioned the James Tait Black award only in his second paragraph, as if it would be bad form to brag, and yet wanting to let Seferis know about it: "Incidentally, I've got a prize myself,—for the best novel of 1960—Its called the James Tait Black prize + is awarded by the Edinburgh Professor of Rhetoric and Literature. I don't know who he is, but he must be a nice chap (probably English). Anyway I get £200 (more carpets). We ought to have a photograph of ourselves holding our cheques." The Regius Professor of Rhetoric and Literature at the University of Edinburgh in Rex's time was John E. Butt, who had acceded to the chair in 1959. It may have helped Rex's candidacy that Rex was resident in Scotland, although the prize is awarded to a novelist or biographer living anywhere in the United Kingdom.

Rex then facetiously commented that it was just as well that he would not be at the Foyle's lunch because "As you know, if I once start reading your poetry, its impossible to stop me—No business man or writer would get away. You might lose your job.

AMBASSADOR'S POEMS CAUSE STRIKE AMONG CATERING WORKERS—
TYPICAL GREEK AGGRESSION ON ENGLISH WAY OF LIFE (Daily Express)"[123]

Rex's good humor may refer to an incident at the British Institute when Rex read for too long a period, or to some other occasion. It is gratifying to see Rex in such a good mood, enjoying his friendship with Seferis and his prize, which was both deserved and very welcome. The secret of Rex's resilience was his love of literature and dedication to his craft. His writing was, perhaps, his best friend of all: it had enabled him to survive Barbara, to ameliorate his financial difficulties, and now to go from triumph to triumph. But he was far from financially secure, and his health was not good.

On 26 February he wrote Seferis that his plans had changed and that he would spend ten days from 15 March to 26 March at a health spa near Godalming, "one of these places which are chiefly frequented by fading beauties + ailing furies + where one is given nothing to eat or drink except hot water + lettuce."[124] In a letter to Pam of the same day, he mentioned hot water and orange juice, and said that he would use some of his prize money to pay for it. Rex was plagued by chronic ill health from the time Barbara left him until he got to Maine. While he had high blood pressure, drank too much, and obviously did not respond well to the cold, damp climate of Scotland, there also seems to be a psychosomatic element, or he would not have felt well so quickly in the similarly cold (but admittedly less damp) climate of the northern United States. He proposed to see Seferis in London either on the 13th or 14th or the 26th, and hoped to see Pam and John at some point too.

At Seferis's suggestion, he had considered applying for the Byron Professorship at the University of Athens but decided against it because, as he wrote Seferis on 14 April, "I don't really like the idea of lecturing + teaching or the general rush + excitement of university life. If there were only some quiet cultural job like the one I had before it would be different, but I don't expect there is." He asked if there were some organization that would invite him for a month or so in Greece while he was engaged in writing his "life" (in reality a historical novel) of Pericles. He wanted to "investigate the size of Samos, which was admirably defended by the philosopher Melissos (who believed that there was no such thing as motion) against Pericles + Sophocles."

Spring in Argyllshire that year was cold and wet, but "the flowers are wonderful + the loch is full of ducks + swans." Moreover, the health cure and drying out near Godalming must have done Rex some good, because "I haven't started to get fat again yet + retain a tremendous taste for lettuce + oranges." On the bad side, "Achilles' horses have been out of action for a week. They can't survive much longer."[125] Rex did not continue all of the good habits he learned at the spa. On 15 April he wrote Lehmann, mentioning that Cyril Connolly, Ian Fleming, and Godfrey Wirer had also stayed in the same spa. He was still eating oranges and salad, "both of which I used to hate," but "otherwise have relapsed into my old ways."[126]

Around this time he heard from Sam Lawrence, who would be coming to Great Britain at the end of June and would be staying over a weekend with Rex in July. This was to be a fateful visit, for out of it would come a position for Rex in America; after almost half a century, his desire to see America would come to fruition. Lawrence was a great admirer of both Rex and Seferis, and wanted his personal copy of the Seferis volume, which he had published, signed by the author and the translator.[127] Rex had not yet received a copy of the American edition but was expecting one at any moment.

Rex's reputation was on the upswing in America as well as in England, but he still lacked money as he had all his life except when he lived with Barbara. Rex wrote

Seferis that John Wain had suggested that Rex should appear with Seferis on the Mermaid Theatre stage in July, but that he did not have the money for the trip. He would manage to get to London only in June when he could get a British Council or other committee to pay his fare.

In a letter of 4 May to Seferis, Rex stated that "I'm just beginning to write my book on Pericles. I'm doing it by way of an imaginary work of your fellow townsman Anaxagoras. So if you can tell me anything about him or about Clayomenae, I'd be grateful. Katsimbalis once, in great excitement, pointed out to me Clayomenae, but it turned out that what he was pointing at was Halicarnasius." Now it was raining all the time, and the "ship's dog" was always soaking wet. "I've now got a crommach [walking stick] + go for long walks with the dog, while Liz despairingly plants roses in the garden."[128]

Pam's daughter Anne was getting married. On 8 May he vowed to come to the wedding, although "Its difficult to get south very often + also do one's work; + also George is coming here for most of June." Tony Knowland and his wife, Pam's other daughter Barbara, had settled in Oxford near Pam and John. Again Rex commented on the rain and storm and added, "Even the Scots are depressed."[129]

Rex was growing increasingly bored in Scotland. The distance from London and his friends began to tell on him, and there was little input of ideas. On 17 May he wrote to Seferis that "I sit at my desk trying to imagine Pericles + I fail dismally. Or I walk on the hills with the ship's dog, searching for ideas. No ideas come + I go to sleep in the sun. But I've known these periods of impotence before . . . so perhaps they will be all right in the end."[130]

By 28 May the new novel was still being difficult, but it had begun to flow. Although he was tempted to visit the Morrises on 16 June, he had decided to wait for Anne's wedding. Not only was George going to visit, but "I'm just beginning to get going on my new book, which I've found very difficult up to now. And I know well enough that even a flying visit south would disrupt everything. The least enjoyment now seems to disintegrate me."[131] On 5 June Rex told Seferis that the main source for his characterization of Anaxagoras in the Pericles novel was Burnet's *Early Greek Philosophy*. Rex added that "I'm still finding it difficult to get going on Pericles, but maybe my brain will work in the end."[132]

He was pleased to have received £220 in royalties for the Seferis poems. "This was only for the period up till December + is, I consider, not bad." He wanted to do some traveling with his son George, but the decrepit state of "Achilles' horses" made it difficult. George remembered these visits positively although he was impressed by Rex's lack of money during this period.

On the weekend of 24-25 June, Rex and Liz went to the island of Iona with the Knowlands. During that trip, Rex had a toothache and water on the knee and the sea was very rough, but the way back was beautiful.

Finally, Rex would manage to get to London, after having put in a reasonable amount of work on the Pericles novel. On Friday, 30 June 1961, Rex wrote Seferis that he planned to come to London on the morning of 18 July and to stay at the Savile Club. But "Early on the 19th I go to a dentist + have a lot of teeth out. They are meant to be replaced by the evening, but I may by then be feeling miserable."[133] He wanted to go see Lucy on Friday, 21 July, at her school in Dorset and stay until the 24th, when he would return after lunchtime. On the 27th he would go to Oxford for Anne Morris's wedding. He was looking forward to seeing Sam Lawrence at Craignish House on 8 July.

I have found no record of Sam's visit itself, but probably because of it Rex was offered a job at Bowdoin College in Maine. Concerned about Rex's drinking, Liz implored Sam Lawrence to get Rex something to do in America. Always fond of Rex, she generously put his health above her relationship with him. Despite his reluctance to return to teaching, Rex of course was easily induced to go along with the idea, given his mounting debts.

On Tuesday, 25 July 1961, Rex wrote Seferis, then in Greece, from the Savile Club, that on Sunday, 23 July, probably while Rex was visiting Lucy in Dorset, he "suddenly felt rather ill + collapsed into bed for three days. I've only just got back here. The doctor said I was suffering from exhaustion (strange, considering the little that I do). He also pleased me by saying that my liver was quite all right. In fact I expect the loss of all those teeth was more of a shock than I realised. Anyway I'm better now, + am soon going back to Scotland." On Friday the 21st, Rex had attended a party in London with Seferis, and hoped that "I behaved myself. Not that I think I was drunk, but I did find myself behaving oddly before the short illness. Now I'm as normal as I ever am."[134]

For the first time, he mentioned a project that was to come to fruition in 1966, a translation of Seferis' essays: "Of course I'm prepared to co-operate in any way you think fit about the prose book,—though, if it were done as we did the poems, I think Savidis should get at least half the credit for the translations."

He also mentioned a possible trip to India scheduled for November. Writing to Pam Morris from Craignish House on 7 August, he explained that this would be a six-week trip for the British Council. He apologized for missing Anne's wedding because he had been sick, and "am still not in very good form. The doctor I saw rather surprised me by saying that my liver is all right. So I suppose it must be something else. Gall bladder? Ulcers? Anyway I'm going to see the doctor here + perhaps get some X-rays." He had lots of work to do, but was doing it "slowly + inefficiently."[135]

On 18 August Rex wrote Seferis in Greece that the weather was bad, and he had discovered that he had gout again, in addition to his other ailments. But there was some good news too. His dog Dai had won a first and a second prize at the Argyll Agricultural Show. He had been reviewing *The Complete Poems of Cavafy*, translated by Rae Dalven, for the *TLS* anonymously and begged Seferis to keep that confidential, because "I don't want to make enemies." He explained: "I didn't think much of the translation or of the Introduction by Auden. But it's good anyway to have more Cavafy in English."[136] In the published review, Rex's criticism of Auden shows his independence and his own expertise: "It is unfortunately doubtful whether the reader will be greatly helped by Mr. Auden's introduction. . . . Indeed it is difficult to imagine what Mr. Auden can mean by 'politics in the original Greek sense.' Is it the politics of Homer, of Pericles, of Aristotle? Nothing could be more remote from Cavafy than any of these." He faults the homosexual Auden for misunderstanding Cavafy's homosexuality: "Here again Mr. Auden does not help our understanding when he writes: 'The erotic world he depicts is one of casual pickups and short-lived affairs.' These are sometimes part of the theme, but from such themes emerges a splendour of which Mr. Auden seems unaware. Has he not read 'Myres' or 'The Mirror in the Hall?'"[137]

In the letter to Seferis, Rex asked for permission to use his translation of Seferis's "Mycenae" in a second edition of *Eternal Greece* that Thames and Hudson would publish in December 1961. He sent regards to Katsimbalis and stated that he would be in London during the last week of October, en route for India. Seferis answered from Greece on 2 September 1961 with a long letter detailing his own trip to Delphi and then to the island of Amorgos, where he had no newspapers and no telephones to distract him. He enjoyed his visit to the monastery there except for a strong wind which threatened to blow the party off a mule path into the sea below. He would be sorry to leave the island, which was spoiled by a rich French tourist with a yacht she didn't like or need. He looked forward to seeing Rex in London at the end of October.

Rex's poor health and financial problems persisted. On 22 September 1961, Rex wrote Pam that he had been seeing a doctor "about all my digestive + other troubles + have had a week of gruelling tests. Final results won't be known until next week + I'm sure the bill will be enormous." In London he was discussing a possible film commentary that he might write. But he would be back in November for a British Council meeting. Pam had offered to pay Liz's fare to London too, an offer Rex accepted gratefully because "It would be good for her to get a holiday + I'm getting rather broke."[138]

After receiving the doctor's diagnosis, Rex was in a good mood because he felt that at last there would be some progress against his persistent feeling of ill health. He wrote Seferis on 3 October, referring to Seferis's poem "The King of Asine," that

I've just come back from a week in London, having been persuaded to take my health seriously + to see a good doctor. The result is rather good. I was examined, like the citadel Asine, from every angle, + it was discovered that all organs were all right. But (a thing I had never imagined) I am full of malaria + may have had this disease for years. I've also got some colonic thing called, I think, diverticulosis; but this can be cured by diet. And the malaria can be cured by quinine. I'm now taking great doses of this for a period of ten days,—unpleasant, but, I hope, effective. I'm seeing the doctor again about the 24th or 25th. In spite of the quinine I'm feeling rather cheerful, indeed hopeful for the first time in years.

Rex could have contracted malaria on one of his trips to Greece.

Another reason for Rex to be in a good mood is that he had received another prize— "one of the Guinness awards (£50) for the translation of the King of Asine. This is delivered at a ceremony in the Goldsmiths' Hall on Oct. 31."[139] The first prize of the Guinness Awards, which were related to the Cheltenham Poetry Festival, went to Sylvia Plath that year. Rex received the translation award. Although not as prestigious as the James Tait Black Award, this was still a fine recognition of Rex's work as Seferis's translator, and must have further strengthened his position with Seferis. Rex also felt secure enough in a *London Magazine* review to criticize renowned poet and critic William Empson's book, *Milton's God*, which he found "exasperating because for most of the time what is being discussed is not Milton's God at all, but Mr Empson's." He faulted Empson for a "Certain vulgarity of writing" and for imposing a Benthamite, Utilitarian vision on a Milton who would most likely not have subscribed to Jeremy Bentham's philosophy.[140]

In a letter to Seferis of 10 October 1961, Rex wrote that he had learned of a disgruntled servant's burning of the Ghika family's home on the island of Hydra, with the loss of many artistic treasures. He commented with genuine feeling, "Very sad. I've always thought that that servant of Ghika was a dangerous character." Rex was finding it hard to work because of the quinine that he'd had to take, but had finished the treatment: "Tomorrow I shall go back to Pericles. With the best will in the world I can't help feeling bored with the great name."[141] Rex had clearly begun to feel exhausted by the historical novels, but knew that he had to push on with them for financial reasons. On 20 October he wrote Pam that his divorce from Barbara—the decree nisi—had gone through at the end of July, but that neither he nor his lawyers had been informed until recently and "I'm meant to pay £164 (which I haven't got). . . . I shan't pay anyway."[142]

Rex traveled to London to see his doctor and dentist and on 24 October he wrote from the Savile Club to Pam that he was "having a terrible medical time—Two days ago I was given another go of malaria drugs. The result was that I got completely tight after two drinks + yesterday collapsed entirely in a pool of sweat. I rang up my doctor today to say that I was nearly dead, + he just said 'It is to be expected'" but that there would be improvement soon. Rex comments, "All very well; + today I am a bit better, though going rather slowly on the drugs. Anyway I hope I'll reach Oxford all right on the fourth + by then I'll only be having two of these ghastly tablets a week."[143] There is no more mention of India, and apparently the trip never took place, owing to Rex's health problems.

On 7 November Rex thanked Pam for her hospitality to Liz and him. Ten days later he wrote Pam with some anxiety that he had left behind his Pericles manuscript, a book about Pericles, two small books called "Looking at something or other" and a small notebook.[144] The two books were part of a series to which Rex was considering contributing. He and Liz had returned to Scotland on Monday the 13th and he was living a sober life. George would be visiting in early January, and Pam's daughter Anne was expected then too.

On 26 November he wrote Seferis about the possibility that *London Magazine* might publish some more translations. Also, the British Council wanted Rex to record some of his own poems and some of the Seferis work, and he was hoping that it might pay his way to London for that purpose. The recording would be not only for the British Council, but also for the library of recorded poetry at Harvard. He was feeling much better than he had in London, because he was apparently cured of malaria and was enjoying writing his book on Pericles and also "a small child's handbook on birds."[145] This was *Looking at Birds*, to be published by Hamish Hamilton on 26 November 1962. Richard Hough, Rex's former student, was involved with this series and wrote in 1992 that "We offered authors a £100 advance (£1,000 in today's money) for a text varying from 2,500 to 7,500 words, and any number of well-known writers contributed—Gerald Durrell on zoos, Rex Warner on birds, Air Chief Marshal Sir John Slessor on aircraft, and stories by Rosemary Sutcliff, William Mayne, Dorothy Clewes and a host more."[146] But Rex felt that he could do better work than historical novels and children's books, despite the recognition he received for them, and his letter to Seferis continued, "Some day I hope to write something worth writing, but now I have to make money as I can, as I'm in rather a mess financially. This was to be expected. I'm only surprised that I've been solvent for the last three years." There was snow on the mountains, and his dog had attacked but not injured a child named Christian, which he found ironic.

The financial situation was getting worse. On 2 January 1962, Rex wrote Pam Morris that "It would be wonderful if a house turned up in Oxford. I'll probably have to sell this house in the end, as the financial position is pretty desperate. The trouble is that I doubt whether I could sell it without even further loss." He said that Anne and her husband David Norrington could visit whenever they wished. They would have more fun if they could come by car, but there could be no predicting what the roads would be like. Rex himself had had "two nerve racking drives in the last two days." He commented about an acquaintance that he had met at a New Year's party that "I don't know her surname, only that of her stepfather. All these divorces are very confusing."[147]

But things were looking up, too, as always in Rex's life when his writing would win him benefits at crucial moments. Difficulty was magically overcome by an offer of a trip or a job. On 2 January 1962, Guido A. Waldman wrote Rex that final arrangements had been made with Cassell for the inclusion of Rex's *Peloponnesian War* in their Belle Sauvage Library. Royalties would be ten percent to 3,000, twelve and one-half percent to 6,000 and fifteen percent thereafter. Moreover, there would be an advance of £125.[148]

On 26 January 1962, he wrote Seferis that owing to the "kind offices" of Steven Runciman, he had obtained a free trip to Greece, which included Liz, on "some sort of educational cruise." They were to leave London on 4 February and return on 18 February. They would have only two days in Athens, but Rex hoped to see Katsimbalis anyway.

Then comes a very important piece of news: "In the autumn I think I shall take a job that has been offered me at an American university for the academic year. It would mean leaving Liz + the children behind for at least some months, but it seems the only possible way of ever paying my income tax."[149] Sam Lawrence had managed to get Rex an offer from Bowdoin College, and Rex had decided to accept. His dream of working in America, alive since the days of his tutoring of the Pell children in the 1920s, would come true. Rex ends the letter on another upbeat note: "I'm getting within sight of the end of Pericles." This was a relief for Rex, because he regarded writing that novel as a chore, and it is probably the least successful of the historical fictions.

Rex seems to have gotten back from the Greek trip on 18 February. He had met Katsimbalis in Athens and generally had a good time. Papers in the Bodley Head Archive at Reading University show that two days after his return, Rex signed a contract at Craignish House for an unspecified nonfiction work to be delivered on 31 August 1963 and for a novel to be entitled *The Converts* on the same date. He received £500 per book as an advance and was to receive fifteen percent of the published price for each in royalties.

On 29 March Rex wrote his editor at Hamish Hamilton that he had just sent the bird book to be typed, adding with typical humility that he found while writing it that "I really didn't know much about the subject, but have tried to disguise my ignorance." He was worried about the reissue of *The Kite*, scheduled for 1963, "mainly because all the villains are Greeks +, since I wrote it, I've become a terrific phil-Hellene. Could one say 'German' for 'Greek' throughout? And why not get rid of the Egyptians too? There must be some quite decent Arabs somewhere."[150]

The editor answered on the 25th that he couldn't understand why Rex was concerned about the bird book; he had found it fascinating and needed to do only minimal editing. It would go to the printer that very day.[151] And well it should have. Despite his disclaimer, after a lifetime of bird watching, Rex knew quite a bit about birds. He also knew how to express his knowledge in a striking way, sure to appeal to children: "The wood-peckers have a curious bucketing flight. The lark goes up like a slow singing rocket. Wild duck move their wings like garden shears."[152]

Rex wrote Max Reinhardt on 25 April that he had a letter the day before from Sam Lawrence about the Pericles book, which Sam liked. Rex had told Sam that he had signed a contract with Max for two books, one of which would be a novel about St. Augustine. He wanted Max to handle the negotiations, and he wanted a $1,500 advance from Sam Lawrence. Rex planned to be in London for at least a week from 15 May for a job writing a television commentary for a film about Greece. He felt that he would start on the St. Augustine book first: "I'm afraid it will mean a lot of reading, so the book may take some time, but I'm rather excited by the idea of it + I don't think anyone has done much with this subject before." At the moment he was working on a "sort of Greek anthology" but this would not take long.[153]

This anthology was never published, but the typescript exists in the University of Connecticut's Warner collection. Composed of pieces of Rex's favorite reading woven together with some comments of his own, it contains some intriguing personal notes. The first section, entitled "Heroes and Heroines," begins by stating, "The first Greek poetry I ever attempted to read in the original was the Odyssey. I was then about twelve and had to look up nearly every word in the dictionary. I found everything very difficult; proceeding as one did at about fifteen lines an hour, it was only gradually that one grasped the fact that Homer is telling a good story" (1). But eventually, the "character of the hero began to emerge," and he was more than merely satisfactory, because he "constantly finds himself in serious trouble (as one did oneself at school) and he invariably (unlike oneself) comes out of every difficulty with flying colours" (2). Rex also notes that "Among the most recent versions of Homer's hero is the creation of the contemporary Greek poet, George Seferis. Seferis calls his character 'Stratis the Sailor.' He is a traveller and an exile" (14).

Rex recalls too that when young he thought of Achilles and Hector just as he thought of them later in life. About Achilles, he states that Robert Graves "very perversely" finds him the villain of the piece, and then disputes Graves's opinion (17). He still sees Helen "as I saw her in one of the illustrations of the first book of Greek myths which I read. She has long black hair and is looking mournfully from the walls of Troy at the fighting heroes. The artists succeeded in convincing me that she was not only beautiful but blameless, in fact wronged" (21).

Part Two includes pieces of literature about real "Men and Women," such as Alcibiades and Alexander; Part III is about "Places and Travel," in which Rex assumed "the objectivity of the lover rather than that of the scientist," and attempted to "describe isolated scenes and characters rather than try to paint a broad and comprehensive picture. . . ." There is also a section on "Life, Love and Death." Since this whole work forms largely a pastiche of *Views of Attica, Eternal Greece*, and Rex's translations, it is possible to understand why it was not published; but it still has merit and is pleasant to read.

He wrote Seferis on 1 May, to say that the weather in Scotland had been perfect for the last ten days. Rex's face had even been blistered by the sun, and he had never seen the Scottish countryside look so beautiful. Liz had taken the children south when she had landed a job at a school for the term, "partly in order to get the children into other schools, partly to effect some necessary economies." Rex was "rather selfishly, enjoying the sun + solitude. Cooking + cleaning take me about 20 minutes a day, so that I have plenty of time for work + for taking the ship's dog for walks."[154]

He was grateful to Liz and liked her children, but he was not in love with her. Going to America for a year might offer a handy way out of the relationship, although Rex did not say this anywhere.

He wrote that he would be coming to London on 15 May for a fortnight and would spend a week of that working on the television film about Greece.

Rex's editor at Hamish Hamilton wrote him on 13 June that he was pleased he liked Humphrey Price-Jones's drawings for the bird book, which are quite elegant. He suggested quite seriously that Rex do a *Look at the Greeks* for Hamish; like the bird book, it would be only about 8,000 words but the subject could be handled that briefly, as Peter Green's *Look at the Romans* proved. Rex thanked the editor at Hamish Hamilton on 20 June for sending him *Look at the Romans*. He thought a similar book on the Greeks could be done fairly easily, but he could not take it on at that time because he was behind with many other things. Perhaps in a year or so, but he advised him to look for someone else. He would be going to America at the end of August. He asked after *The Kite* reissue and hoped that "you've changed all the Greeks into Germans. They have far more sinister names anyway."[155]

Two days later, Max Reinhardt wrote Rex that the Atlantic Monthly Press would commission both the Pericles and the St. Augustine historical novels with a $2,500 advance. The royalties would be ten percent to 7,500 copies, twelve and one-half percent to 10,000, and fifteen percent thereafter. Max felt that the royalty rate should be improved to ten percent at 5,000, twelve and one-half percent to 10,000, and fifteen percent above that and asked Rex if they should accept the offer. On the 20th, Rex responded that he liked the Atlantic offer and agreed with Max that the royalties should be improved. Displeased with the services of David Higham, whom he sometimes called "old lavatory brush" because of his moustache, Rex added "You do a great deal better for me than any agent ever has done + I think I shall gradually liberate myself from the lot of them." Rex was pleased that the Bodley Head's Ford Madox Ford novels were getting good reviews; he himself had only read the Tietjen books, "which I think are excellent." He mentioned that a mutual acquaintance named Monty liked to talk about Ford, claiming that "he was the greatest liar he's ever known."[156]

IX. UNFINISHED BUSINESS

On 26 July 1962, he wrote Seferis again from Craignish House, telling him that he would be sailing for America on the *Queen Mary* on 30 August, and that he would come to London on the 25th. He was afraid he would miss Seferis, who was leaving for Greece.

> I wanted to come earlier, but simply couldn't afford it. Indeed my economic position is rather desperate + it looks as though I'll have to sell the house in order to get to America without too many debts. I seem to have taken on a great deal more than I can manage. However, once I do reach America I think I shall be all right.

He went on to say that "I've now had nearly three months by myself, with one visit from my son George, who was in very good form. I must say that I now enjoy the solitude +, with a view to writing about St. Augustine, have been studying the heresies of the early Church. . . ."[157] Liz and Rosamond would be coming up in August to say good-bye.

The film about Greece for which he had done the script and commentary, entitled *Land of Heroes*, had been aired on television on 17 July, and he had watched it "in the company of an archaeologist + two doctors from a lunatic asylum. They all seemed to like it."[158] This film would eventually lead to his being awarded the Greek Order of the Phoenix.[159] Also, although Rex didn't state it, a Danish paperback reissue of *The Aerodrome* had been contracted for, around 1 August. But there was still not much money.

Rex provided his address at Bowdoin College, "where I have the honourable, but rather bogus, title of Professor." He went on to comment, "All I have to do is to teach the Greek + Latin classics in translation." It is fair to say that Rex did not do much preparation, probably figuring that his many years as a secondary school teacher would serve him well enough.

Even though Rex might miss Seferis who was finishing his ambassadorship, "Long absences seem to me to make no difference to friendship, + I hope to get to Greece again some day, if, as the Scotch say, I am 'spared.'" Rex was not only spared, but would go from strength to strength in America, which proved kinder and more appreciative than he ever could have wished.

Just before Rex left for America, he decided to tie up all the loose ends he could. He summoned up his courage, and on 28 August 1962, wrote one of the most important letters of the thousands that he wrote during his life. It reads, in full:

> My dear Frances—I'm off to America on Thursday, + must write to you before I go, though I find it very difficult to say what I want to try to say—I would like you to know that I love you as much as I can have done, + probably more; also that I think I always have felt this—I can see now that even when I thought I was most happy with Barbara, I was always miserable about you; though I tried to disguise this from myself. I knew that I was doing wrong + I have certainly suffered for it—I don't mind this, but I do mind the fact that you + the children have suffered even more, + of course I can never forgive myself. As it is I don't want to live with anyone except you, + I can see that I've always thought of you as the only wife I've ever had. But I can't do anything about this, partly because I wouldn't dare to ask you to marry me again + for you to risk still further disappointment, + partly because I must try to do my best for Liz for as long as she wants me. I'm very grateful to her for being so kind when I was really very ill, but I haven't any deeper feelings than that. She doesn't understand me + probably I don't understand her; but we get on more or less all right + at least I've been useful in supporting her children, for whom, of course, old Fyfe hasn't yet paid a penny. It is really this that makes the situation as it is economically impossible. I'll have to sell the house to pay back debts + in a year or two I expect to be straight, which will be an enormous relief, as I take these things rather seriously, while Liz doesn't seem to mind how much money she owes. She's now got a very nice job with some friends, which gives her a cottage + enough money to support the children; so I shall be free to try + disentangle myself from debts by earning a bit extra in America. Frankly I'm absolutely longing to get away. I feel that probably I'm no use to any woman, + I don't even want to be of much use to anyone except you.
>
> I suppose I ought to tell you about my will, which I ought to have made years ago, when I really was almost dead. I've left the house + furniture (except books) to Liz; the books to Jonathan; everything else to you for life + to Jonathan + George equally after

your death. "Everything else" may only mean a few miserable royalties, but one never knows with books.

I loved seeing you in London, but I didn't feel any differently then from what I've always felt. If I appeared to do so, it was only because I may have been less disguised. I can understand perfectly how you can never not feel resentment for me, + it is only right + natural that you should—I'm very grateful for whatever love you feel for me + wish so much that I deserved any of it.[160]

Rex then gave his address, and noted that "it is correct (though rather ridiculous) to address me as 'Professor.'" The letter continued, "Don't write if you don't want to. But do, please, believe that I'm not only grateful to you for most of the good things of my life, but also miserable about my own ingratitude or stupidity or worse. But most of all that I still love you as much as ever + only wish I could do something to make you happy." Rex concluded with, "This is a very inadequate sort of a letter, but I think you'll understand roughly what I'm trying to say. It's so good anyway to be able to write to you more freely than I could when I was pretending to be someone else."

America promised Rex a new start in many directions.

CHAPTER TWELVE

BRUNSWICK, 1962-1963

I. FIRST IMPRESSIONS OF AMERICA

Rex's very happy year at Bowdoin in Brunswick, Maine, is well documented in the unpublished forty-seven-page manuscript, "An Englishman at Bowdoin," which he wrote during the summer of 1963.[1] America, which he had wanted to visit since the time he worked for the Pell family while still a student at Oxford, had now become a reality, and he enjoyed it greatly after some inevitable adjustments. Best of all, he continued to be productive in terms of both novels and translations.

In "An Englishman at Bowdoin," Rex recalls that early in 1962 he received a letter from Pres. James S. Coles of Bowdoin offering him the Tallman Professorship for one year. He had never even heard of Bowdoin, but he eventually realized that Sam Lawrence had set this job up for him by speaking to Prof. Larry Hall, who was another of Sam's authors. Hall, who had published the novel *Stowaway* and the short story "The Ledge," would become one of Rex's best friends on the faculty. Rex attempted to understand the salary offered, although "I of course got the pounds wrong" when he tried to translate from dollars. Regardless of the salary, he would have come after five years of poor health, straitened financial circumstances, and no prospects for change of any kind in Scotland. He saw no future with Liz and wanted to get back together with Frances.

In a thoroughly diplomatic vein, Rex praises America continually in his Bowdoin memoir, which was written at the request of President Coles, but there is genuine feeling behind everything he says. He was very grateful for his rescue from Scotland, and was determined to enjoy himself. No European view of America as wicked could keep him from appreciating the country, even in the early 1960s, the time of incipient American Vietnam involvement and protest. He did not think, like some in England in the 1960s, that "all Americans are eager for war, self-righteous, materialistic, uncultured, ridiculously rich or abjectly poor, all cities to be governed by bribery + corruption, all negroes persecuted + all food tasteless" (3).

When he first received the letter of appointment, Rex worried because he had not taught on any level for fifteen years. To Professor Dane, chair of the Classics Department, Rex honestly assessed himself as "in no sense of the word a scholar," but he stretched the truth a bit by claiming that he had translated from the Greek and Latin only because he enjoyed it. In fact he was a hardened professional writer working out of necessity.

Rex admits in his memoir that he was "somewhat apprehensive at the prospect of meeting American students," although he had known one American at Wadham. This student had played Rugby for the College XV "+ did it very well except that in moments of excitement he would emit a blood-curdling yell + hurl the ball vast distances forward,—a most intelligent idea, had it not been in direct contravention to the rules of our game." During the 1962 fall semester Rex met this old friend on a trip to Washington for the first time in thirty-five years and had "resumed our friendship as though we had parted only yesterday."[2]

Apart from this unnamed friend, Rex's image of Americans had come from the movies, where "there is of course a tendency to represent" American youth "as ferocious, lecherous, luxurious or suicidal + it never occurred to me to reflect that our own youth is usually represented in the same media in the same ways."[3] Rex did not have to ponder the issue of American youth without examples. He shared a cabin with two American students and had another American student at his table during the voyage to the United States. One of these boys was good at meeting girls, so soon Rex was in the middle of a large group of American college students of both sexes, and "had one of the most enjoyable trips I have ever had in my life."

After learning delightedly that the students spoke the same language that he did, he also discovered that

> At least two of these students were exceptionally intelligent + well read. Their manners were excellent + though they may have been surprised at my ignorance of many books which they themselves regarded as vitally important, they treated me with great forbearance, either lending me the books themselves or instructing me in their purport. When, after a few drinks, I ventured to make a few literary pronouncements myself, they would listen with apparent

interest, almost as though they expected me to say something intelligent. We talked about all sorts of subjects. The talk was easy, delightful +, for me at least, instructive. Among them I felt, as I have felt so constantly during my stay at Bowdoin, at home. This is not a feeling I have ever experienced in any other foreign country except Greece. (5)

High praise indeed from Rex!

He found the view of the Statue of Liberty and Manhattan from shipboard "one of the finest on earth" and although he did not like New York, he felt immediately at home when he arrived in Boston. As he wrote in this unpublished memoir, "The almost excessive kindness + honesty of the taxi driver who drove me from the air port contrasted very sharply with anything I had experienced in New York + fully reestablished what faith I have in human nature."[4] He remained "under the protection" of Sam Lawrence, and stayed at "that excellent + hospitable institution" the St. Botolph's Club, which reminded him of the Savile in London as a place distinguished for a friendly and civilized atmosphere. And he was entranced by the swan boats in the park. He ate clams for the first time in his life, and then became deathly sick. He was to learn that he could safely compensate for this inability to eat clams with any amount of Maine lobster. But by far his most important culinary discovery was Jack Daniel's "fine old sour mash Tennessee whiskey."[5]

While in Boston Rex went to visit the site of the Boston Tea Party, since he had studied this event in school. He reflected that he felt no shame as an Englishman because America had gotten its own back on Britain by exporting the first female member of parliament, Lady Acton, who wished to impose Prohibition on England. "Had anything come of this, I think that my countrymen would have reacted with the same fervour as that shown by Bostonians on the question of tea."

A few days later, a car arrived to bring Rex up to Bowdoin. He remembered vividly the drive up from Boston to Maine. "Nothing was quite as I had expected + yet everything seemed somehow + strangely familiar. I looked for mountains, yet none were visible. This was because I had judged Maine from a small-scale map + so formed the erroneous conclusion that it was the size of a small English county" (7). He found the maples a "staggeringly beautiful sight" but his driver told him that they were not yet at their best. He thought that the New England architecture would be undistinguished, and was surprised to see beautifully "appropriate" white frame saltbox houses. They arrived at the Moulton Union on campus where Rex stayed at first, and he washed up before meeting President Coles, thinking about how he might escape early if he did not like the meeting.

For Rex was apprehensive about President Coles, despite his charming letters. He did not believe, as he had in his childhood, that all presidents looked as forbidding as the bearded Lincoln or Grant, but he did fear that American college presidents were businessmen with little interest in learning. He imagined them "as hard-faced, unsleeping, efficient, perpetually fund-raising + largely inarticulate." If they were married, their wives "would be shut away somewhere where they could not impede their husbands' vast financial operations" (9). In fact, James Coles was a decent man who chatted gaily about numerous subjects, while his wife proved very hospitable. Rex's preconceptions vanished, never to recur.

Early during the fall semester, Coles gave a reception to introduce new faculty members to their colleagues, and Rex found this a daunting exercise. Lined up in a row with other new faculty, outfitted in tight English shoes and a heavy English dinner jacket totally unsuited to good American heating, and flanked by Coles and his wife and a Professor Kumber on the other side, he shook "hand after hand for hour after hour, uttering from time to time" (11) whatever words he could think of.

After five years in "the remote highlands of Scotland where one's friends tend to live forty or fifty miles apart from each other" (35), Rex was amazed at the friendliness shown by the people at this reception and by his new colleagues as he went from one party to the next. He got to know Larry Hall and Louis Coxe, a poet, very early on, since he drank tea or coffee on campus every morning when they did, and Hall had written Rex earlier. Larry Hall remembers that he took Rex sailing, having been told that he was a great outdoorsman. He was surprised, therefore, when Rex leaped into an eight-foot dinghy, nearly capsizing it. Rex even discussed his personal life with Larry Hall, saying that Barbara Rothschild had first agreed to be the guilty party in the divorce, as was required in those days, but that she had then asked him to assume that role, and that he had done so to oblige her.

At the time of the Cuban Missile Crisis, from 21 October to 28 October 1962, Rex's conversations with the other professors became very serious. Rex heard Kennedy's speech about this dangerous American-Russian confrontation during a lively party at Larry Hall's house, and like everyone else was momentarily sobered by it.

Attending parties at the houses of the Halls and the Coxes, he soon found a mutual bond of literature and sport. It took Rex awhile to understand football, but he became a genuine aficionado. He had seen it played in the Marx Brothers films in the 1930s and was eagerly looking forward to his first game.

He writes in his Bowdoin memoir that an Englishman watching American football for the first time "will have to get rid of a lot of his usual prejudices." For starters,

> What first offends an Englishman is that the players go into battle heavily (to our minds) armoured + that they are constantly being reinforced by fresh troops from the side lines. We have no body protection + a team of fifteen men will play unchanged through the

game. If one or more are injured, then the teams will remain one or more short. Thus one's first impression of the great helmets + the covered knees of American players + of the reserve forces always ready to be moved up into line is that here is yet another example of that luxury + effeminacy + lavish expenditure in the American way of life of which one had been told.

However, "Before long one can see that these suspicions are unjustified. There is indeed nothing effeminate about the game." Rex wondered about whether or not the protective clothing were really necessary, and volunteered the information that in his youth he had received concussions three times while playing Rugby.

Next, "one is amazed at the sight of the ground itself. What, one wonders, are all these lines for? . . . And should not football be a game of speed + movement rather than of mere attrition?" However, "It soon becomes evident that there is a point to all this, indeed that there is an added element of excitement when an inch more or less can make an important difference at any part of the field."[6] Rex was also amazed that the players were allowed to pass the ball forward, which is not permitted in Rugby.

As Rex watched every home game at Bowdoin he felt increasingly attracted to football and suffered serious disappointment when the season was over. Moreover, he watched football on television every Sunday afternoon in the company of Larry Hall and others, and "soon become as ardent a supporter as any of the incomparable Mr. Y.A. Tittle + the New York Giants." He even managed, "by intelligent betting" to turn his enthusiasm "to commercial advantage," although the currency used for bets was green shopping stamps rather than money. Larry Hall played a special role in Rex's sports education: "Watching football on television in the company of Larry Hall is indeed something to remember. His excitement somehow communicates itself to the screen + to the whole atmosphere of the room. It is positively Celtic + he would make a notable contribution to any Scotch or Welsh crowd at any Rugby International. And that, I should point out, is saying something."[7] As for Louis Coxe, what Rex liked about him was not only his ability to write good narrative poetry, but his

delight in the kind of literature which one was enouraged to read in one's boyhood + which is not now, in fashionable circles, widely esteemed. We soon recognised that we were both able to quote long passages from Macaulay's "Lays of Ancient Rome," Tennyson's "Revenge," + "Lady of Shalott," Chesterton's "Lepanto" + indeed much else, + our pleasure in this knowledge was so great that we began, at the least provocation, to chant these remembered verses antiphonally before any audience that happened to be around.[8]

Larry's wife would say "Anyone for Tennyson?" and Rex and Louis would recite "The Lady of Shalott" by heart.

Like Rex, Coxe was well informed about the popular music of the 1930s, but Rex found that Mrs. Coxe surpassed both of them in this area of knowledge. So while Rex and Coxe could remember a verse or two from "A Blue Room," "Marqueta" (shades of *The Wild Goose Chase*, where Marqueta is an important character), "I Met Her in Monterey," or any of the Ginger Rogers-Fred Astaire songs, Mrs. Coxe could remember the entire songs from beginning to end. In a letter of 20 April 1988 to me, Edith Coxe stated that Rex's favorite song was Rodgers and Hart's "Dancing on the Ceiling." He felt friendly enough with the Coxes to explain his personal history to them, including his marriage to Frances, his falling madly in love with Barbara, and then his life with Liz. He flirted with the faculty wives and they all liked him, even though he would flood the whole bathroom in their houses if he took a shower or a bath. He was generous and always sending money to his children. He was proud of his friendship with Auden and spoke a good deal of Day-Lewis, or "Day" as he called him. He was also witty and raffish. Once, when he was visiting a friend in Brunswick, he said to his host, "One need not rise with the fucking lark here, need one?"

II. REX AS A FACULTY MEMBER

Rex worried about his first classes since he had not taught since departing from Raynes Park in 1945, but he found the experience of teaching delightful rather than daunting. In the fall he taught one course on Greek literature in translation. With clear self-knowledge, Rex knew that "what talent I have for teaching is best exercised among small groups of people who can be encouraged to ask questions + by discussion in fact teach themselves. I have always found it difficult to speak as it were ex cathedra, since everything I say from this kind of elevation always appears to me either perfectly obvious or extremely dubious" (13).

But in his fall Greek course, Rex had seventy students. Although they rarely all appeared at the same time, Rex never had few enough for a discussion group and was therefore forced to "behave in a more orthodox + pontifical way than is really natural for me."[9] One reason for his popularity, Rex discerned with great honesty, is that "A visiting professor will naturally be reluctant to give anybody very bad marks, + I myself, however much I strain after an ideal rectitude, find it very hard to award any mark lower than C to anyone who is a good football player."[10]

Rex's lectures were well received and he liked the attitude of his Bowdoin students very much. Moreover, he found it possible to defend the study of the classics to a wide and receptive audience—stating in his memoir as he no doubt had during his lectures that "It seems to me that nowadays we suffer more from over- than from underspecialisation, + that this is one of the reasons why to my mind the study of the classics is more than ever necessary today." Rex preferred the broader American curriculum, too, stating that while an English student may know more about one or two subjects than an American when he goes to college, "he is also lamentably ignorant of many other subjects. By the end of the educational process the American graduate has caught up in his main subject + will still have the advantage of having had a wider education."[11] On the negative side, Rex saw too much attention paid to grades, which were of necessity inaccurate in any case—it was possible for him to recognize the outstanding and the very bad paper, but the middling papers were difficult to distinguish from one another.

Sadder and more important, he saw "many students who have undoubtedly . . . shown keen interest in their work, but who find themselves debarred almost wholly from expression + partially from thought simply because they have not acquired the facility to use their own language in written words." He attributed this to the large number of students each high school teacher had to face but also to "the fact that Latin + Greek are now rarities instead of necessities in education, + it is certainly true that most of those who in the past have used English with distinction never did 'English' as a subject at school." He points out with typical balance, however, that while "Greek is a most valuable aid to the writing of English, I think it impossible to maintain that this discipline is essential."[12]

Despite these problems—which would be echoed today by most professors of English at American universities—Rex found much good writing at Bowdoin. The student magazine, *The Quill*, presented excellent work, as did another student journal, *Orient*. All departments supported the goal of good writing, and the library was excellent. Rex felt, therefore, that with regard to the students' writing problems, "the answer lies more in the general state of our society. . . . That education should be functional + utilitarian is a wide-spread delusion so that there is a tendency to forget what has been variously described as 'the Muses' or 'the greater glory of God.'" The antidote to this forgetfulness of the broader purposes of a liberal education is study of the classics in the original or in translation, because "even from a strictly utilitarian point of view it will inculcate accuracy + precision in thought + expression, but, much more important than this, it will encourage a student to find delight in words + to enter into a depth of experience where it will soon become evident that life is bigger +

history longer that it is made to appear in newspapers or on television sets."[13] Here Rex appears in one of his final and most endearing roles, defender of the classics.[14]

This is where Rex first mentions Paul Ryan, a devoted classicist who would become one of his best friends and correspondents and whose mutual correspondence with Rex supplies many of the details in the following chapters. Rex writes of Paul, who lived in his apartment building on Federal Street in Brunswick, that "We soon got into the habit of calling on each other in our rooms + for me, after my long isolation in the wilds of Scotland, it was indeed a pleasure to find someone with whom I could again talk about the classics. Even better was it to find someone who knew so much more about them than I do, + even better still someone who, in the English tradition, knew English literature as well as he knew the classics." Even Paul's acquisition of a retriever puppy who, according to Rex, exerted a more tyrannical pull on Paul than a wife or lover, did not interfere with their conversations.

On 12 September 1962, Sam Lawrence introduced Rex to the poet John Malcolm Brinnin during a lunch at the Ritz in Boston. This was to be important in terms of Rex's next job, at the University of Connecticut, where Brinnin was then a professor. Brinnin, who was about eleven years younger than Rex, was delighted to meet him because he had been teaching Rex's novels at Vassar as early as 1942 and felt that Rex's poetry as well as his fiction had been underrated.[15] Brinnin had run the famous Poetry Center at the Young Men's Hebrew Association in New York from 1949-56, and knew most of the major British and American poets. This lunch was followed by a dinner party given by Sam and his wife, Merloyd, for Katherine Anne Porter, Brinnin, and Rex at their house on Beacon Hill.

On 3 October 1962, Rex wrote from Apartment C, 86 Federal Street, Brunswick, Maine, to Pam Morris giving his first impressions of the United States, and explaining his personal situation. "Now I shall be here a year, + so far am enjoying it a good deal, living my favourite solitary life with plenty of excellent lettuce + fruit, cigarettes cheaper than in England + whiskey stronger." Moreover, things were going well in Scotland too: "I've not yet heard definitively about the house in Scotland but am fairly sure it's now sold, which is a great relief. Its the first step toward eventual solvency."

At Bowdoin everything was a delight: "I like the people here very much + my work is pretty easy, just waffling away on Greek + Latin literature, with an occasional lecture, for some of which I get very well paid. I've plenty of spare time + an excellent library accessible." This life was very good for his health, too: "When I feel like a good meal I cross the road to a hotel established in the house where Uncle Tom's Cabin was written. Also, touching wood, I am for the first time in about 7 years no longer feeling permanently ill." Was it the climate of Scotland that had harmed Rex, or the economic difficulty and the shock of his second divorce? He commented that "Ever since I've been here the weather has been wonderful + I'm wearing summer clothes all the time. The trees changing colour is one of the best sights I've seen. Though they say that in a month we'll be under snow until May. However the houses are warm + I've no complaints. At the moment I feel that I wouldn't mind settling down here; but I don't expect that this will last."[16] Early on, Rex was in demand on the lecture circuit, and spoke on Seferis at Brown University on 18 October.

The fall reminded Rex of fall in England, but there were more reds and scarlets in Maine, and also, to his delight, a great variety of birds. Rex's superb *Look at Birds* was published by Hamish Hamilton in London on 8 November 1962 and then reprinted in 1963 and 1967 and published in a revised edition in 1970. Rex's comments in his Bowdoin memoir reflect the same enthusiasm that he reveals in that book, even when he gently comments on the difference between the American and British birds that are called "robins": "What is known to Americans as a robin bears only the smallest resemblance to our national bird + we are inclined, when it is pointed out to us, to reply 'No, that is not a robin. It is too long, too fat + too lacking in character to deserve that distinguished name. Also it is the wrong colour.'" Rex is completely correct here, because the American robin is a type of thrush, whereas the British (and European) bird is not a thrush.

There were also completely new birds:

> It is good, at this time of life, to find new things under the sun + I used to go about for days enjoying the memory of my first view of a scarlet tanager or a Baltimore oriole. Particularly exciting was a humming bird which I saw with President Coles at Port Clyde. In my ignorance I had believed that this species was unknown in North America. (43)

Rex did not see as many animals as he would have liked, largely because he did not go hunting, "+ this was partly from laziness, partly because I have no gun, partly because I do not like killing things + partly because, if I even try to do so, I nearly always miss"(44). He kept hoping that a moose would show up in Federal Street, where he lived, or on the campus of Bowdoin, but he had no luck.

He was really having a wonderful time. To Seferis at his Greek address, 20 Agras, Athens, he wrote on 26 October that he had met Seferis's niece ("whose eyes remind me of you") at Brown University, "where I delivered a lecture on the Poems. I hope to repeat the performance elsewhere. So far I'm enjoying everything here enormously— I'm at a small + good university + like both the students + professors very much. I've plenty of time for working on St. Augustine + have a very easy job lecturing 3 times a week on Greek literature (in translation)." To Seferis he also commented that during the past seven years in England and Scotland he had "often felt happy but never for a single day well" and added, "I can't describe how good it is to feel a recrudescence of whatever powers I used to have—It's been rather miserable for all these years being always conscious that one was only half, + precariously, alive—though of course it is always precariously so."[17] Since Rex was in Scotland for only three years, his reference to seven years of bad health indicates that even before the breakup with Barbara in 1958, he felt far from well. He passed on the information that Sam Lawrence was interested in Seferis's memoirs, and Rex said that he had not only recommended Savidis as an excellent translator for that project, but that he would be "glad to be of any help I could be to him, just as he did for me" with regard to the poems. Rex's reference to his work on St. Augustine covers not only his translation of the *Confessions*, but also the novel that he would soon begin writing.

On 22 November Rex ate Thanksgiving dinner at John Brinnin's house, along with Howard Moss and William Read. But when they sat down to dinner at 5 P.M., they learned that Rex had just had an earlier Thanksgiving dinner, which ended at 3 P.M.! That same day, Max Reinhardt wrote Rex that he had sold rights to the St. Augustine novel that Rex was planning to Norstedt's of Sweden, which also published Rex's two Caesar books.

Rex wrote Max Reinhardt on 26 November 1962 telling him that he had begun on his St. Augustine novel "though God knows how long it's going to take. There's 50 times more material than there was about Caesar or Pericles."[18] He thought that the title should be *Alypius*, after the "chap who was a friend of Augustine," but in fact the final title would be *The Converts*. For Christmas Rex would be going to New York and Washington and "I'm still finding this the most enjoyable place I've been in for years. As its impossible to get any news about cricket, I've become a football fan + spend every Sunday afternoon watching the N.Y. Giants on T.V."[19] On 7 December Rex had a long lunch with John Brinnin at Locke-Ober in Boston.

On 23 December Max cordially answered Rex's letter, stating that Rex owed (probably for advances) the Bodley Head £317.11s.9d as of 30 June 1962. He said he liked the title and looked forward to planning for the book's arrival in 1964. He joked that when the St. Augustine novel was ready Rex would be able to get another advance and would "soon be a rich man." After a life of writing, Rex really had very little in terms of money to show for it. It was the age of the blockbuster novel and the big film, and Rex was too serious a writer ever to work successfully in either genre.

Still, the troubles of Scotland seemed to be behind him now as he embarked on one of the most successful phases of his life and career. On 5 January 1963 Rex wrote to Seferis in Athens:

Here I'm enjoying myself enormously. It is more Hyperborean than Scotland (perpetual snow from now till May), but the houses are warm, the people charming + there is more intellectual life than I've found for a long time. I've just been travelling (Vermont, Boston, New York, Washington, Baltimore) + often lecturing about you. This is easy for me (since the lectures are mostly readings) + it may be that the effect will be to sell copies of the Poems. (In fact, Sam Lawrence, whom I often see in Boston, is very pleased at the way they're going. Not many copies, but many more than are usually sold).

In Washington, Rex stayed "at the grandest club I have ever seen (the Cosmos). Vast high rooms, through which glide exquisitely beautiful [waitresses] carrying trays of drinks past sleeping senators." In Baltimore, Rex "ate a terrapin (vary nasty) + in Boston I bought the most beautiful fur hat (better than Kruschev's or Macmillan's) that has ever been seen." In Brunswick, "I enjoy long conversations about literature with a brilliant young classical scholar who lives in the same building, + only yesterday we talked over a bottle of excellent Retsina." This was, of course, Paul Ryan.

Moreover,

For some reason I'm beginning to feel well for the first time in years + am taking very seriously the thing I'm trying to write about St. Augustine. Indeed, I haven't been happier since 1945-46 + all I'd like is to come to Athens to see you + the Colossus. As I'm getting more + more lecturing, perhaps you would suggest that the Greek government should give me a free trip in order to convince me that Greece is really all right.[20]

On 23 January Rex's *Pericles the Athenian* was published. This is not his best historical novel. In Anaxagoras, he had not found the most exciting persona to narrate the story of fifth-century Athens, which becomes ponderous instead of exciting and alive. Moreover, in retelling the story of the Peloponnesian War, Rex was competing with Thucydides, one of the greatest narrators who ever lived. N. H. Reeve, who was greatly appreciative of the Caesar novels, found that *Pericles the Athenian* lacks urgency of feeling, because "The hero's already shadowy life is narrated by the philosopher Anaxagoras, whose own fussy and pedagogic nature merely distances his subject still further. Here the history that is told gains very little from being 'fictionalised'" and the result "is an efficient historical reconstruction almost completely devoid of the productive interplay between method and material that helped vitalise the latter and protect it from staleness."[21] Reeve echoes in his own way the views of Christopher Ricks in the *New Statesman*, who wrote that "Pericles himself turns out to be unimpeachable, gazing with the blank rectitude of a marble bust. . . . Rex Warner's story is told through the pebbly mouth of Pericles' friend, the philosopher Anaxagoras. The style is so bland that it seems urged on by a passion not so much for the past as for the pastiche. . . . Anaxagoras' sonorities tend to crowd out Pericles."[22] An anonymous TLS reviewer, as eager as any of his predecessors for Rex's blood, wrote snidely that Rex's novel cures the reader of a longing to see the Parthenon as it originally was "if that would entail reclining for hours before watered wine listening to Pericles justify his foreign policy."[23]

At his best, Rex was able to make ideas come alive; at his worst, his novels become abstract and unconvincing. When he was writing *Pericles the Athenian* in Scotland, he was contending with fatigue, ill health, and economic worry. But given Rex's respect for and knowledge of *Pericles*, he could not write about him without saying something valuable. Despite its lack of force, *Pericles* is not without its virtues, including Anaxagoras's clear exposition of his own philosophy that "What appears is . . . a mere vision of the unseen. At first impression, our ordinary, unaided senses are too weak to enable us to judge the truth. But that does not mean that truth is inaccessible to us."[24] Aided by this philosophy, he goes beneath the surface of the question of whether or not Pericles was a wise leader, since Pericles was in large part responsible for the war that caused Athens' decline. Despite his unexciting quality, Anaxagoras succeeds in allowing the reader to understand the reasons for Pericles' decisions and to feel that his death was a tragedy.

On 30 January 1963, Rex asked Prof. Leonard F. Dean for two weeks to make up his mind about a one-year visiting job in the English department at the University of Connecticut that Dean had just offered him. He would serve as a replacement for John Malcolm Brinnin. Rex would see Brinnin (who was going to try out poet Robert Lowell's old job at Boston University during the coming year) over the weekend, and hoped to find out from him if he were suitable for it. (Of course the answer was "yes," since Brinnin, after having sounded Rex out about the Connecticut job, had recommended him for it.)[25] In this letter, Rex informed Professor Dean that he would give a talk on Tuesday, 5 February, at Connecticut College and stay a few nights because he hoped to see W. H. Auden (who had been resident in America for many years) there. Rex wrote Seferis on 8 February that "it was great fun" seeing Auden after all those years. Rex "found him physically much changed, but in other respects the same as in 1926,—very charming, very intelligent + rather absurdly dogmatic."[26]

When Rex got home from the trip, he found a large package from the Greek embassy in London, containing "the insignia of a Commander of the Phoenix," one of Greece's highest honors. Rex commented gratefully to Seferis in his 8 February letter that

> no other honour (of this sort) that I can think of could have given me more pleasure. No doubt this is another thing I owe to you. It's really made me absurdly delighted. My

infatuation for Greece cannot really be logically defended; it exists, like love. And, as with love, the slightest recognition of it brings great pleasure. Not that "slightest" is a word that can be used of my dizzy elevation to the taxiarchy.

Rex took this high honor in his stride, as usual.

Rex was planning to go to the University of Iowa in the spring, where he would meet fellow Seferis translator Edmund Keeley. He was planning to stay on in the United States and "have already been offered another pretty good job." On 18 February Rex replied to Leonard Dean, saying he would be interested in the visiting job for the 1963-64 academic year. A letter to Dean on the letterhead of the *New England Quarterly*, based at Bowdoin, by Herbert Brown, chair of English and managing editor, and dated 7 March 1963, gives Rex a very positive—and truthful—reference. Brown states that Rex is not an academic scholar or a brilliant public speaker but has a wonderful personality, knows how to interest students, and cares about them. These comments proved to be absolutely accurate for Storrs as well, where Rex would serve for not one but for eleven years.[27]

Springtime approached. Like everyone else, Rex was looking forward to it because, whatever the virtues of American snowplows and heating, a winter of snow that lasts from October to May is monotonous. Rex had been warned that in Maine the seasons went abruptly from winter to summer, with a short interval of rain. But in 1963 he found the change from winter to spring to be gradual and beautiful. It created some nostalgia for England but Rex also found enough new species, such as ladies' slippers in Maine and dogwood in Washington, D.C., to make America botanically attractive.

On 14 March 1963, he wrote Max Reinhardt from Federal Street, boasting good-naturedly that it was "Quite true that I'm now a Commander (or Taxiarch) of the Order of the Phoenix. I've got a very beautiful cross + ribbon which I don't suppose I'll ever be able to wear. But I'm looking forward to telling friends at the Savile that Hellenic decorations rather outclass all their trashy . . . stuff." Rex was still enjoying himself very much but his work had been slowed up lately by "a lot of lecture employments which, though lucrative, do take up time." He looked forward to his year at the University of Connecticut, after which "I should be reasonably solvent." He felt that "Old Pericles has had some quite good reviews here + seems to be selling satisfactorily. I don't think it's a very good book myself, but musn't say so openly. Alypius is coming along, but I think the book is going to take some time, as I really see possibilities in it. If it comes off it will be all right." He was going to have dinner with Sam Lawrence next week, and he was "pushing up the sales of old Seferis by my constant lectures on him to adoring college kids."[28] In referring to "quite good reviews" for *Pericles*, Rex may have put a positive slant on the fact that the reviewers, having been prepared by Rex's two previous historical novels, were polite. They praised his "competent re-creation of an age,"[29] or his "unusual evocation of the Athens of Pericles" which painlessly provided "background material"[30] necessary for the average reader.

He continued to enjoy John Brinnin's company. On 1 March he had a rather "bibulous evening" with him at St. Botolph's Club, and on 24 March Brinnin and Rex ate in Concord at the Concord Inn. On 27 March the two of them went to hear a speech by Stephen Spender at Kirkland House, Harvard, after which the House Tutor Peter Stansky gave a party that included Rex, Brinnin, and I. A. Richards, among others. Rex found Spender's talk "curiously ineffective"[31] on this occasion.

On 1 April 1963, Rex wrote Pam Morris that he had accepted the job at the University of Connecticut. His hope was that "Another year out here might even leave me solvent." He was able to plan a trip to England for Christmas because the fares would be very cheap then. He had been earning a lot of extra money by lecturing, most recently in Iowa, but it had been tiring: "Indeed I'm only just recovering from celebrating Greek Independence day in Iowa City." There were no romantic involvements to report, and he found that "at my age friendship seems more appropriate (+ satisfying) than anything else." He commented that "Liz may come over for a short time in the summer. I hope she's getting on all right + would like to do more. But it's really impossible for me to take up the sort of life we had in Scotland which resulted in my being £500 in debt very rapidly. I've now paid most of this off but it was very worrying at the time."[32]

On 13 April his translation of *The Confessions of St. Augustine* was published by the New American Library. He continued to do well with his students, and wrote in his Bowdoin memoir that he was entertained at numerous fraternity houses. He found the atmosphere very friendly and open but also polite: "Behaviour was decorous (I don't suppose that it always is), conversation free + natural." He even found the singing of college songs moving, especially when many doing the singing of these songs at graduations were aged alumni, and commented that "In England we are more, + perhaps unduly, reticent about our loyalties. Not that, as is often supposed, we are unemotional, but we will go to almost any lengths to express our emotions in some way that is intellectually unintelligible."[33]

Rex was intrigued with fraternities, and saw both good and ill in them, conceding that at some point in one's life, it might be useful to be a member of a small, tightly knit group but that the quality of life in that group should be the determining factor as to its worth. He concluded that fraternities might have value for the first two years of a student's career, but that after that more independence was desirable. Rex found that "there is nothing in itself wrong with small groups + partially closed circles. Indeed life would be meaningless without them. The theoretical friend of the world is usually friendless + the cosmopolitan is a man without a city. Yet the lovers who feed solely on their own personalities are prone to indigestion, + the best city is that one which, while retaining its own personality, will be open to the world."[34] This may be Rex's best statement of his own philosophy of life now that he had almost arrived at the age of sixty. To be oneself yet open to the world—that is precisely what was good about Rex. And part of his openness was that he did not see any difference whatsoever between American and English undergraduates.

On 8 April Max wrote to Rex suggesting that he do two children's books—histories of Greece and Rome and what ideas they have passed down to us. Max's idea was that these books would be intended for older, upper form children in grammar and secondary schools and for the general reader. He would be coming to the United States at the end of October and hoped to see Rex then. On 19 April Max wrote again, urging Rex to stay with the Bodley Head and not to go over to Weidenfeld, as Rex had apparently suggested he might do. He again pushed the children's book idea.

When the end of his employment at Bowdoin approached, Rex was sad about it. He had become an ardent defender of America and its inhabitants: "I think that I may claim that my ignorance, when I came here, both of America herself + of American colleges, was, if almost total, not, as often happens with ignorance, rigidly prejudiced. I was prepared to see, + almost to believe, anything. It will, I hope, appear from what I write that, if I have not seen much, I have enjoyed + admired everything I have seen."[35] Rex went on to attack those Englishmen who were "professional anti-Americans." Rex's letters amply demonstrate that the sentiments he expressed in this memoir were genuine.

He was allowed to keep his apartment for the summer, and he had the University of Connecticut appointment to look forward to. Yet he would be sorry to leave Bowdoin. The pile of 100 final exam essays that crowded his desk made him feel positive rather than the opposite. He was inclined to give everyone higher grades than they deserved, and had to fight this inclination. At commencement he felt melancholic because he was in a place which "only nine months ago had seemed so strange, but which had never been anything but friendly + inspiring + had now become endearingly familiar."

On 11 June Guido Waldman of the Bodley Head sent the welcome news that Mrs. Helen Macy, the manager of Limited Editions and the Heritage Book Club, wanted to issue Rex's translation of *Prometheus Bound* and that Rex would receive $500 for this. On 15 June Rex answered that the offer seemed okay, and suggested that he do an introduction for more money. She had paid him $200 or $250 (Rex could not remember which) previously for his introduction to the *Oresteia*.

During the summer of 1963, Liz came over to visit. Edith Coxe saw that Liz very much wanted to stay with him, but Rex was not interested. Larry Hall remembered Liz as stylish, highly intelligent, and noticeably younger than Rex. Asked by Larry why he was not more positive about his relationship with her, Rex said that he had made up his mind to go back to Frances, and with Liz at some point he might lose perspective and say something unwise like "I love you" and become more or less permanently committed. Larry Hall felt that Liz was perhaps too bohemian for Rex at that later stage of his life. Rex was also moving into a new, uncertain situation in Connecticut.

On 24 August Rex wrote Professor Dean that he would stay on in Maine till 9 September, and he included his book list for the fall semester: for English 211, Modern British and American Poetry, he wanted G. M. Hopkins and Hardy "if they're not too ancient." These might be substitutes for Pound and Lowell. In English 112, Classical and Medieval Western Literature, he wanted to stay with Latin and Greek and would teach the *Iliad* in the Lattimore translation and the *Odyssey* in Rieu's Penguin. He would also teach the *Oresteia* in the Penguin or University of Chicago edition, Sophocles' Theban plays in Penguin, his own Thucydides, and his Mentor *Three Plays of Euripides*. Rex added, modestly, that if it looked ostentatious of him to teach his own translations, he could find another translation of the Euripides, but he doubted whether he would make "more than 50 cents out of the whole transaction" if he used his own. For the graduate course, he would do the *Iliad, Odyssey, Oresteia*, and Thucydides and also use H. D. F. Kitto's book on the Greeks, as well as Kitto's *Form and Meaning in Drama*. Rex found that the boys at Bowdoin had learned a lot more from Greek than from Latin literature, "+ I quite agree with them."[36]

Unbeknownst to him, Rex was embarking on some of the best teaching and most pleasant personal years of his life.

CHAPTER THIRTEEN

STORRS, 1963-1974

I. 1963-1966

Rex's eleven years at the University of Connecticut were among the best in his life both professionally and personally. The university is situated about 35 miles east of Hartford on a grassy, gently hilly campus including a beautiful pond. In Rex's day, the town of Storrs was more like a village, consisting only of a small shopping center and one movie theater, and the professors and staff still live in the woods surrounding the campus. In this idyllic setting, Rex found himself among an appreciative community of scholars and students. He was well paid and continued to be productive. He also regained stability in his personal life by remarrying Frances.

As at Bowdoin, Rex was in a very collegial department in which he was greatly respected. The English Department emphasized creative writing as much as scholarship, and took a flexible attitude toward curricular offerings. On the practical side, Rex earned a relatively large salary—$11,340 for a nine-month term—and was free to write at his leisure. Even though this was less than the $13,000 he had made as Tallman Professor at Bowdoin, it was certainly better than anything that he had ever earned in England. Intellectually, Rex was delighted to teach the Greek and Latin classics to a new generation. He had gone from seeing (albeit half-heartedly) the classics as a hindrance to understanding the modern world in *The Professor*, to presenting them in his classes as providing an excellent perspective on contemporary problems. And in an ironic turn, like his own chief character in *The Professor* he had become a professor himself, and was often at odds with the callow student radicalism around him.

The English Department at Connecticut was a fairly prestigious one, among the top forty English departments in the United States during Rex's time.[1] It included not only John Malcolm Brinnin, but also Stephen Crane's biographer, R. W. Stallman.[2] In the late 1960s, poets Stephen Spender and Charles Olson taught courses there. During 1963-64, Rex supplied the need for a highly visible writer, since Brinnin was on leave. Irving Cummings, a Renaissance scholar in the department, remembered that he had read Rex's work in his graduate courses at the University of Wisconsin in the 1950s, and was thrilled to be working with him.[3]

An eminently clubbable man, Rex quickly made friends as he had at Bowdoin, not only with senior professors such as Robert Stallman but with assistant professors, such as modern literature scholar Joseph Cary and romanticist Jack Davis. He was also a great favorite with the women on campus, and people reckoned that he had been quite a lady-killer when young. Dr. Francelia Butler, who had served as the *International Herald Tribune* correspondent in Paris just before the German occupation prior to becoming known as a scholar of children's literature, remembered Rex for his terrific sense of humor. After she went on for a long time extravagantly praising a female faculty member of whom she was not very fond, Rex commented, "I've always wondered about her myself." She recalled that once in the crowded office that he shared with Joe Cary, Rex had to sit on a footstool and had remarked, "I feel like Goldilocks."

Rex's love of American musical comedy, including especially *Oklahoma*, as well as his drinking made him an excellent party companion. Jack Davis once saw Rex put away three bourbons, some wine, and a liqueur at one sitting, which caused him to slur his speech but affected his gregariousness in a positive manner. Soon after he came to Connecticut, Rex's doctor discovered that he had had a stomach ulcer for years; undoubtedly his ill health in Scotland and earlier had largely been owing to this problem, which was aggravated by alcohol consumption. But even after this revelation about an ulcer—which Rex had suspected while living in Scotland—he did not cut down on his drinking.

Rex's colleagues and friends noticed that behind the bluff exterior there was suffering. Rex did not consider himself a distinguished man of letters, and perhaps felt that he had not realized his promise. This appears obliquely in the tribute that he was to publish for E. M. Forster's eighty-fifth birthday, when he stated with wry insight that of most of us it could be said, as it is of many schoolboys, that "he could do better if he tried."[4]

Yet Rex immediately brought intellectual recognition to the university. On 17 November, following the announcement of Seferis's receipt of the Nobel Prize for Literature, Rex's article "The Nobel Poet: His Themes are Greek and Universal" was published in the *New York Times Book Review*. Rex praised Seferis for being able, like Yeats, to "write political poetry which is not 'politics,' but poetry,"[5] a goal that had often eluded Rex himself in the 1930s. The review included Rex's translation of Seferis's poem, "Our Own Sun."

This visibility certainly helped the English Department make a momentous decision about Rex's future. On Friday, 22 November, the day that President Kennedy was shot, a departmental committee including Charles Owen, Joseph Cary, Jack Davis, and William Moynihan discussed Rex's candidacy for a University Professorship. This professorial chair was the University of Connecticut's newest and highest honor. Other prospective candidates for the position in the past had been the noted critics Alfred Kazin, Daniel Aaron, Sherman Paul, and poet Richard Eberhardt. When Rex's name was put forward there was no disagreement among the English Department committee members. As University Professor, Rex would teach as little as one course a semester (about half the usual teaching load) and earn a salary approximately one and a half times his visiting salary.

When the university approved this appointment early in 1964, Leonard Dean began the process of getting Rex a visa waiver from the executive secretary of the Waiver Review Board in Washington, D.C., so Rex could stay in the United States longer than the two years allowed by the International Educational and Cultural Exchange Program. It was to be a long struggle.

Over the Christmas break of 1963, Rex visited his son George, who was pursuing doctoral research on crustaceans in Jamaica. Rex had not seen George since Rex had left for Bowdoin in the summer of 1962, and their meeting on that occasion had been memorable for the wrong reasons: George had visited Rex in Craignish on his motorcycle, had found only whiskey and gherkins to eat in the house, and had then contracted tonsillitis and been forced to spend his holiday in the hospital. This time, Rex stayed at the Mona Hotel in Kingston, and had a tour of the island in George's old car. George remembered that during this trip, Rex confessed that he had "ballocksed" things up in his life, and he asked George if he thought that there was any chance that he and Frances might be reunited. This was a good way for Rex to find out what reaction, if any, Frances had to his letter of August 1962. In fact, George was ignorant of the letter, but he replied that he thought there might be some possibility of a reconciliation, and that he, personally, would be delighted if there were one. For some years after the divorce of 7 July 1949, Frances had lived with the Jersey man with whom she had originally had the affair in the 1930s, but she was no longer living with him by 1958, long before Rex's interview with George. Rex would obviously have some wooing to do, but things were looking up.

Rex continued to actively seek new translation as well as writing projects. Edmund Keeley did not have the time to do a translation of Seferis's essays, so Sam Lawrence suggested that Rex do the job. Rex admitted to Seferis that he did not know enough Greek, but that with the help of someone such as Katsimbalis or Savidis he would be able to do it.[6] Sam Lawrence proposed giving Rex a $750 advance, which could be used to pay a literal translator, and Rex suggested Theodore Frangopoulos as "the best person available."[7] Frangopoulos who had aided Rex before, wanted full credit this time, and since he would help Rex much more than he had with the Seferis poems, Rex thought it only fair that both their names should appear on the book. On 12 March 1964, Rex thanked Seferis for sending the essays in Greek.

But Rex was not making as much progress on old projects as he would have liked. He complained to Seferis that he was irritated by Xenophon's pro-Spartan attitude, and was therefore finding the *Hellenica*, which he was translating for famed editor Betty Radice at Penguin, hard going. By 18 March, Rex had "hardly got any distance" with the St. Augustine novel.[8]

Travel often interfered with his work. Early in March he stayed with Edmund Keeley in Princeton, and used the opportunity to visit Auden in New York. Rex lectured widely on "Julius Caesar and the Idea of a Dictator." In that lecture,[9] he follows the same direction as in his Caesar novels, presenting Caesar as a more attractive ruler and personality than Hitler, Stalin, or Mao, particularly because he invented no clearly defined ideology and never put himself in the place of God. He also read some Seferis poems in Buffalo, and published a piece on Greek travel in the *New York Times Magazine* on 26 April.[10]

That summer Rex traveled to England, where he met Barbara (probably concerning straightforward matters such as Lucy's education), definitively ended his relationship with Liz, and saw Frances. The question was how Frances would respond to his letter and to his desire for a reconciliation as reported to her by George. Rex spoke to Frances at Anchor House, Wallingford, on the occasion of the birth of a set of twins, on 13 June, to Rex and Frances's son Jonathan and daughter-in-law Marigold. Rex came out back suddenly as she was hanging up clothes and asked, "Is there no hope?" She answered, "Certainly there's hope." But it was to be another year before they would see each other again, and yet another until they remarried.

Things were looking up all around. On 3 June Connecticut Senator Dodd wrote Leonard Dean that the Department of State had recommended to the attorney general that a waiver for Rex be granted. On 28 July Rex wrote Lyle Blair that A. L. McLeod, a literary scholar, and Elizabeth Curry, a Ph.D. candidate in literature, were interested in his work.[11] Although he found the *Hellenica* very boring, he had almost finished translating it. Around 20 August, the task was accomplished. Just one day before he left England on 12 September, he escorted John Brinnin, then visiting London, to lunch with writers Patric Dickinson and Roger Senhouse at the Savile Club; it was a small repayment for Brinnin's many kindnesses to him in America.

From the S.S. *France* he wrote on 12 September to Seferis that he had begun on the essays. Xenophon had been delaying him, but now he could work, and Frangopoulos's translations were "very helpful. Sometimes he writes a meaningless sentence, but usually he's very good. I'm aiming, as I did, with the poems, to keep the sense as exact as possible. . . ."[12] Rex would soon feel that he was working on this project only out of affection for Seferis, because it was difficult and his entire advance had gone to Frangopoulos.

The republication of *The Kite* in May and June 1963, meetings with Auden in America and Frances in England, the inclusion of Rex's "Hymn," "Sonnet" ("The brightness, the peculiar splendour"), "How sweet only to delight," and "Light and Air" in Robin Skelton's *Poetry of the Thirties* (published 29 October), and then the reappearance of his best college friend, Day-Lewis, in America, may have made Rex feel something like a time-traveler into the past.

Cecil had arrived at Harvard University for a semester's visiting position on 29 September. As soon as he could get away from a crowded series of lectures at Harvard and along the East Coast, he came to visit Rex. On 3 December he wrote his wife Jill describing the situation of Rex, who was renting the house of Americanist Milton Stern and taking care of the family dog:

> Rex has gone out to take a 2 1/2 hour seminar on Thucydides, and I am sitting alone, except for his dog Corky, in his charming house, which is deep in a wood of birch and hickory with nothing in view but trees, squirrels and chipmunks. Yesterday I talked to Rex's class in the afternoon, and in the evening had a huge and excellent audience for my poetry reading. Tonight R. and I got out to yet another dinner engagement. He is extremely popular here, and goes around bellowing with laughter, and flirting with the professors' wives. Everyone seems to have read *The Buried Day* and teases him about his young self as described in the book.[13]

During this visit, he demonstrated how to build a good fire by lying on Rex's floor and blowing on his fireplace to get the fire going.

Rex needed a lot more housekeeping help than that. He never cleaned up a house, and Marilyn and Ken Wilson remember that the Sterns' stove was awful when Rex got through with it. Also, his favorite solo meal was sardines on toast, and what hospitality (outside of whiskey) he could offer was not clear. Leonard and Dorothy Dean had dropped in on Rex during the year, and found that he had worn a path from his chair to the refrigerator. Rex would be in a corner drinking whiskey while Corky would snooze nearby.

On 25 January 1965, Rex submitted the typescript of the *Hellenica* to Betty Radice. Writing of his own introduction to the volume, he commented humorously:

> I hope I've concealed my secret desire to warn readers off the reading of such dull matter. There are a few good bits, + I have a certain affection for Xenophon. I imagine him as a retired Colonel, a churchwarden, living in the Highlands for the grouse and salmon, who, long ago as a junior officer, had done something really spectacular in India + who, as an undergraduate, had made friends with Bertrand Russell without understanding much about philosophy. So, for a cover, I can suggest nothing better than a hunting print.[14]

Rex's introduction, published with the book in 1966, makes his sentiments clear: "Few, if any, historians can be placed in the same class as Thucydides. Xenophon certainly cannot."[15] Rex rejected Betty's request that he do indexes for his Thucydides, his Xenophon *Persian Expedition*, and his Plutarch translation, but he did not want to quarrel because "I shall always be grateful to Penguins + to Dr. Rieu (even though he didn't think I was sufficiently saintly to translate Augustine's 'Confessions')."[16]

A bout of flu in early February slowed Rex down, but he was moving ahead with the Seferis essays. By 5 March, he was almost finished. He shrewdly noted to Max that "There is great charm, of course, in the way George writes, but he doesn't write like a critic of the American school + may be blamed for this."[17]

Elizabeth R. Curry, who teaches at Slippery Rock University in Pennsylvania, sent Rex a copy of her newly completed Wisconsin Ph.D. dissertation on him. In response, Rex wrote on 5 March a fascinating four-page retrospective view of his career.[18] In a very relaxed mood caused by a few nips of bourbon, Rex stated that he felt slightly embarrassed by *The Kite*, which he had written for a badly needed £100, and he admitted that the ending of *Why Was I Killed?* is sentimental and unsatisfactory. He mentioned that "The original 'Wild Goose Chase' was about half as long again + had digressionary essays in the Fielding manner, among other things. I sent the MS to some sale in favour of Spain + never heard what happened to it." He disagreed with her criticism that he lacked a sense of the visual, and went on to correct a genuine error in her dissertation:

> About the only thing in your interpretation that I can say is definitely wrong is your statement that the landscape in "Men of Stones" is unreal, or fairy like. In fact the prison is a fairly accurate description of an old Venetian castle (known as Bourtyi) near Nauplia

in Greece. In old days it was the residence of the Venetian hangman. Now it's a rather expensive hotel. When I was there with some friends someone said "What a place for a production of Shakespeare," + that was the germ of the idea of the book. The concentration camps + scene of the church bells are things I saw in Germany.

Rex also candidly explained the problems attending the reception of *Escapade*: "Some who had admired me were shocked at the idea of me trying to be funny. And one very kind + good writer (Richard Church) once came up to me + said 'Some people think that you were just trying to write a funny book, but I saw what the point was.' He gave me an approving + mysterious look + I didn't dare ask 'What was the point?.'" Rex was hurt by Curry's statements that his eye was unimaginative and that his criticism could not be taken very seriously, but he was clearly delighted to have his work studied by a young scholar.

The 9th of March 1965 was Rex's sixtieth birthday. Cecil's poem "For Rex Warner on his Sixtieth Birthday" is wonderful for its perceptive accuracy. He begins by referring to his "Transitional Poem" of thirty-five years before, where he had called Rex "The hawk-faced man who could praise an apple in terms of peach and win the argument." He calls the young Rex the "unsophisticated son of a Modernist clergyman, who came down/ From a Cotswold height with the larks of Amberley/And the lays of Catullus running wild in his head." According to the poem, his friendship for Rex, like all good friendships, could be picked up again after any interval of absence, and although Rex was "bulkier" than he was when young, he remained "in focus with the young self I knew first":

> Scholar, wing three-quarter, and bird-watcher:
> Self-contained, yet an affable bar-crony:
> A mind of Attic dash and clarity,
> Homeric simpleness, and natural charity
> For all but intellectual cliques and their baloney.

There is more of Rex in these five lines than in anything else that has been, or probably will be, written about him. Day-Lewis's characterization of Rex's writing style as "intrinsic, dry and firm" is perfect. So is his delineation of Rex's "tonic skepticism, cordial address" and "Understanding" nature.

On the 9th, Rex thanked Cecil for the poem:

> I was inexpressibly moved + delighted by your birthday poem for me. This chap McLeod sent me a copy of it, as apparently his book, or booklet, will be delayed a bit by publishers' inefficiency. Certainly this amply makes up for all the birthday presents you've neglected

to give me. Indeed I feel "I don't deserve it." If I could be objective about it (which I can't) I should also say that its a singularly fine poem in itself.

I liked the phrase "though bulkier." Much better than "fatter," "more cumbrous" or other equally true descriptions. A good thing too to have got in the wing-three-quarter aspect. But was it beyond you to have adapted metrically that fine phrase from the Stroud News: "Perhaps the most dangerous man in the West of England"?

Rex follows his signature on this letter with a mordant P.S.: "You showed an unusual sense of restraint in not bringing in communism, fascism or lechery."[19]

The poem appears at the beginning of *The Achievement of Rex Warner*, a collection of critical essays edited by A. L. McLeod and published by Wentworth Press in Sydney, Australia, in 1965. This was the first collection on Rex since the *Focus I* symposium of 1945, and this new recognition must have felt very good to him.

In the foreword to McLeod's collection, John Lehmann recalled Rex's "infectious chuckle against a background of London clubs, country houses and country pubs in Oxfordshire or Berkshire, and Greek *tavernas*. No one I have ever met has a greater capacity for merriment, for dissolving everything under the sun—politics, war, literature, love, the intrigues of bureaucratic man and the pains of economic man—into laughter" (14). Lehmann saw Rex as British Institute Director as "an official who loved human beings." He recalled the moment when as "a young editor eagerly searching for material for the first volume of *New Writing*" he was shown the typescript of *The Wild Goose Chase*, and felt that "a new dimension" had come into English fiction. Like Day-Lewis's poem, Lehmann's view of Rex, unsurprisingly, is very accurate.

The collection contains the pieces from the *Focus I* issue, and also a selection of later pieces on Rex. There is V. S. Pritchett in 1947, saying that Rex was "the only outstanding novelist of ideas whom the decade of ideas [the 1930s] produced" and "the only English novelist to make original imaginative use of the three-cornered struggle between Fascism, Communism, and Democracy" (36). There is an Indian critic, Darshan Singh Maini, comparing Rex's attentiveness to his topics to "the unsleeping devotion of an ascetic" and finding Rex's understanding of contemporary politics no less penetrating than Orwell's or Koestler's, "while his poetic sensibility is far richer" than theirs (40). Another Indian critic, Prema Nandakumar, praises *Why Was I Killed?* There are pieces by Elizabeth Curry and A. A. De Vitis, who had also written a Ph.D. dissertation on Rex at Wisconsin, and who find Rex's novels significant because "they insist on the dignity of human life and the moral integrity and political responsibility of the individual" (54). A. L. McLeod thinks Rex "not a great poet, but . . . an accomplished, polished, stimulating, and satisfying one" (82). Finally, classicist

David Grene stresses the difficulties under which modern translators of Greek and Latin labor: ignorance of the original languages and cultures on the part of the audience and the inability of the translator to hear the languages spoken. But Grene feels that because of Rex's career as a writer rather than as an academic, "he has kept a freshness and delicacy of approach which have served his translations well. He is never pedantic; he is never dull and rigid in his renderings—I am thinking particularly of his translations of the tragedies. For those who know the original, there is also always evidence of a real confrontation of mind between the Greek author and Warner the translator" (85).

Rex's growing academic reputation as a writer and translator was surely very satisfying. In the meantime, however, another tribute was being paid to Rex's writing career without his knowing it, this time by novelist Angus Wilson, who on 18 March responded to the request of the Bodley Head's James Michie for an introduction to *The Aerodrome* by commenting, "Warner is quite as well known as I am and a senior man—what right have I to preface his book?"[20] Michie responded that during the last three years, *The Aerodrome*'s sales had been only 200 copies a year, and that he hoped to revive it with a new look. Wilson responded that he "used to love" the book and was willing to write the preface if Rex wanted him to do so. Rex was very pleased to agree, and when submitting his preface in July, Wilson wrote Michie that he hoped that it "does some justice to this wonderful book."[21]

By 12 April, Rex had finished all of the Seferis essays except for one on Pirandello, and "Letter to a Foreign Friend," which he requested from Keeley, who had already translated the work with Nanos Valaoritis.

Family matters were also coming along well. Rex had heard from Lucy, and George Warner had taken to photographing sharks under water, claiming that they were really very mild creatures.[22] Best of all, on 28 April he met with Frances on her way back from George in Jamaica, at the Plaza Hotel in New York, which he considered an F. Scott Fitzgerald atmosphere suitable to their ages. They had not yet decided on the remarriage that would follow, but they were moving toward that end. They invited George's friend Alan Ainslie, who was then in New York, to dine with them so Rex could make it up to him for giving him only whiskey and gherkins when he had accompanied George on a visit to Scotland. On 8 May Rex was able to report to Seferis that he had spent "four very good days" with Frances.[23]

From 6-16 June, Seferis visited at Princeton, and he probably went to Storrs at least once during this period. Rex undoubtedly took him to the restaurant of the Matsikas family, The Marlborough Tavern, where Rex had immediately become a hero when he spoke some words of Greek and displayed his Order of the Phoenix. At this restaurant, Rex very much enjoyed a record entitled "Sing Along in Greek with Tetos

Demetriades and His Friends," although his favorite popular song during this period was country singer Roy Acuff's "Great Speckled Bird," which he would listen to over and over again. By 2 July, Rex had sent Seferis a typescript of the essays.

By then, Rex was in Maine in a cottage by the sea that he had rented from Tom Cornell, who taught art at Bowdoin. When it was learned that Cornell had castrated his own tomcat in order to avoid paying veterinary fees, Rex (or perhaps Louis Coxe) had christened the place "Catcutter's Cove."

On 7 July Rex was able to report to Max that he was making progress with what he called the Alypius novel, after Augustine's friend, the narrator of the story.[24] He proudly related that "I've just completed a pretty lurid scene in a brothel which James [Michie] will, I hope, like."[25] This scene (in chapter six of the published novel) relates an incident in which Augustine, with the help of several prostitutes, reenacts a parody of a traditional Roman wedding and then along with them witnesses his friend's intercourse with a prostitute. It is the sexiest Rex ever wrote. Perhaps his impending remarriage to Frances inspired him. He delighted in scandalizing the assembled company later by reading it at a faculty party in Storrs.

Michie was looking for an American publisher for *The Aerodrome*, and was turned down by Viking and even by Sam Lawrence, who had left the Atlantic Monthly Press to set up his own company, and who feared that Rex's lack of audience in the United States would affect sales.[26] Sam visited Rex in August, and was pleased to see that St. Augustine was moving forward. He urged Rex to get out of his contract with Peter Davison at the Atlantic Monthly so he could publish it, never apparently realizing that his refusal to publish *The Aerodrome* would doom his chances of getting the Augustine work. Rex had no intention of leaving the Atlantic Monthly. He liked Peter Davison, and he had a contract with the Atlantic for an autobiographical work as well as for the novel.

In addition to the continued interest in and even competition for his work, Rex had another reason to be happy: Ken Wilson, then chair of the English Department, was in need of a teacher, and Rex, always loyal to his friends, suggested Tony Knowland, his old Frensham Heights student and husband of Barbara Morris. So Tony and his wife Barbara and six-year-old daughter Rosalind would be in Storrs during the 1965-66 academic year.

Tony arrived a month before his wife and child and stayed with Rex, then occupying Leonard Dean's house at 10 Westwood Road. He noticed that Rex's schedule for writing during this period involved getting up at 8, having two cups of coffee (with a cigarette between the cups) and a piece of toast, and watching the Chet Huntley and David Brinkley news show on TV. He would go upstairs at 10 A.M. and write until 12 noon, which would be a cocktail hour as well as lunchtime. On Saturday he would watch football, but on Sunday as on all the other days he would stick rigorously to this writing schedule.

Rex received the galley proofs of the *Hellenica* on Friday, 22 October, and commented in a letter to Paul Ryan that "It's even more boring than I thought."[27] By 5 November, the Augustine novel was coming along slowly but steadily, and Rex predicted a spring completion date. "Bits of it are all right," he wrote Max, but as always when he was working on something he had no firm idea of its merits.[28] Rex wrote Seferis that his new novel was "too sexy to please the religious + too religious to please the sexy." Rex also disliked Augustine's mother, St. Monnica, "more + more + so will alienate the great mother-loving public. Is there anyone left to buy the book?"[29] On 22 November Peter Davison wrote James Michie that Rex had given him the manuscript of the first half of the novel, and that Rex hoped to finish it by the end of the summer.

By 2 December, Rex had the typescript of the essays back from Seferis who "had them since late May, but seems to think he's been rather quick about it all," as he wrote Max. Luckily Seferis had approved of everything, and now Rex had only to organize Seferis's proposed footnotes and write an introduction. Rex was clearly tired of the task, confiding in Max that "It will be wonderful to get this laborious + non-profit-making job finished."[30] In a happy mood, Rex celebrated Christmas Eve at the restaurant of the Matsikas family, who presented him with a huge bottle of Old Grand Dad.

The New Year of 1966 was to prove an exciting one for Rex personally and professionally. By 2 January, he was up to the death of Praetextatus, or about two-thirds through the Augustine novel. Max Reinhardt visited for a weekend in February, and discussed the new novel with Rex and the *Aerodrome* reissue with Peter Davison; he wrote Rex afterward that the weekend revolutionized his life because he started drinking bourbon instead of scotch during his visit. The rights of all of Rex's novels had reverted to the Bodley Head, and Max suggested that Davison take *The Wild Goose Chase* as well as *The Aerodrome*, but Davison wanted to see what happened to the new *Aerodrome* in England first.

Reviews were mixed. In the *Spectator* John Davenport wrote that the novel was "extremely interesting" and "deeply felt and beautifully written," but also "sentimental" and a "brave failure" because Roy's return to Bess did not answer the problems of fascism as represented by the Aerodrome.[31] In the *New Statesman* Robert Taubman was surprised that the book had once been considered important, and even disputed Angus Wilson's more modest claim that it was a good adventure story, finding that "the cardboard ideas are juxtaposed, but they supply no action."[32]

But Rex had his new projects to occupy him. The *Hellenica* was published in April and he wrote Max on 2 May that he was reading galley proofs of the Seferis essays, finding that "They read to me better than I thought they would. They are the work of a poet rather than of a literary critic, + that seems to me a damned good thing." The Atlantic Monthly Press would publish the essays in November. Rex had about four more chapters of the Augustine novel to do, and hoped to finish it by August.[33] He ended up finishing it by 16 July. He wrote Max, "Of course its not as good as I'd hoped, but what book is?"[34] But he was very happy to have finished it at last.

On 9 August, in response to a request for a blurb for the new novel, Rex supplied Max with this description:

> "Alypius" contains the story of Augustine up to the time of his conversion. The story is told in the form of a kind of diary imagined to be written by his friend Alypius in Rome +, later, in Milan. Alypius is some years younger than Augustine + has been his pupil in Carthage. He is an intelligent, earnest + diffident young man + has the utmost admiration for Aug. He, Aug. + another African friend, Nebidius, are eager in the search for wisdom + certainty + are profoundly dissatisfied with the various creeds,—religious or political— which they encounter. At the beginning of the book they are Manichaean converts already finding this system unsatisfactory. They end, of course, as Christians. Augustine's story is shaped or complicated by his relationships with two women,—his pious + devoted mother, Monnica, + his mistress, whom I have called Lucilla. He is torn between these two + he is also for long kept back from becoming a Christian by his inability to go without sex combined with his belief that sex is wrong in itself (or at least that his unauthorized kind of sex is,—though in fact he's been faithful to her for 15 or 16 years). His conversion is very clearly associated with his sudden +, as he believes, miraculous freedom from all sexual desire.

Rex also noted that he had first become interested in St. Augustine when he had read the *Confessions* in Latin as an undergraduate. He found that one of the strangest aspects of Augustine's period was the new cult of virginity.[35]

Although Rex expressed disappointment with this novel on several occasions, he need not have worried. This is his best historical novel, and the best piece of work he had done since *The Aerodrome*, twenty-five years ago. The reason may be that Rex renewed himself by dealing with love and religion instead of with power. Moreover, by showing Augustine's conversion agony through the eyes of a friend, he brought a new angle to it, adding tastefully to what Augustine had written in his own *Confessions*. The moment of Augustine's conversion provides a quiet but forceful climax that allows the reader to feel the power of Augustine's experience while at the same time remembering the pain and cruelty of his separation from the mistress who loved him.

Rex and Frances were married on Friday, 19 August 1966, in the house of a friend in Maine, and the reception took place at Rex's rented cottage.[36] As Rex never tired of pointing out facetiously, in the eyes of the Pope he and Frances had never been other than married. The wedding was a quiet ceremony, conducted more or less according to the rites of the Church of England by a postmaster who had been an Episcopalian minister until he lost his parish (but not his license) "through living in what is regarded as sin." Rex felt that Graham Greene would have loved the ceremony because of its unorthodox character. There were only a few friends present. The cottage was a wonderful setting for the reception, with pines and rocks everywhere, and the high tide coming right up to the front door, frequently producing horseshoe crabs. In a letter of 7 September to Pam Morris, Rex reported that on the night of the wedding, "There was a full moon, lots of champagne + the honeymoon had already been under way for some time."[37]

As always, Rex's best writing bears some relationship to the immediate circumstances of his life, if in this case an inverse one. He had been working on the Augustine novel during the years when he was considering living with Frances again. Augustine gives up his beloved mistress for what he conceives to be the demands of his new religion, but Rex was regaining love and in a sense moral and even religious rectitude and a healing of his own conscience with his remarriage. For Frances, too, there was the sense of a new start. At least in terms of its emotional force and meaning, it was a kind of conversion, or reconversion, if not a particularly religious one. Another new beginning took place when Rex and Frances's youngest son George got married soon after they did, also in August, to a Jamaican woman named Monica (no relation to Augustine's mother!). They would soon visit Rex and Frances in Storrs.

Rex's American gamble had worked. He had achieved not only financial and professional stability, but worthy colleagues and students and the respect becoming an important, senior writer. Now the way was clear for personal happiness as well. Remarkably, both he and Frances seemed to achieve it.

II. 1966-1974

In *Life* Webster Schott wrote that *The Aerodrome* had been ignored for too long in the United States (although he mistakenly implied that U.S. publishers had not published it prior to this). He liked every aspect of the book, stating that "Most new fiction is typing. Warner's is writing—precision, economy, resonant language. Warner plots beautifully. He shapes characters who live. He worries about human values."[38] A *Time* review, which appeared on 23 September 1966, was very complimentary too, stating that "Anyone rereading [*The Aerodrome*] will be struck by how firmly Warner's tolling cadences have lodged in the echo chamber of the mind, and how rewarding it is to hear them again" (109).

Despite this good start, however, the second American appearance of Rex's novel was to prove a bitter disappointment. Little, Brown misplaced all of the copies of the book in a warehouse, and had no copies available to take advantage of the excellent publicity afforded by the reviews. By the time the publisher located the books, enthusiasm had cooled. This was the first serious case of a publisher's incompetence that Rex ever had to face.

Rex could not dwell on the failure of *The Aerodrome*, hurtful as it was. There was still what was now called *Meditations of Alypius* to see through the press, and the editors at the Atlantic Monthly Press and at the Bodley Head were not entirely convinced of its value. A trade editorial report of 21 September by an unnamed Atlantic editor praised the novel but added "I see no gain in not admitting at once that this is a static and meditative novel; we will gain more, I would argue, from admitting this in its title, than by pretending there are novelistic virtues here that simply don't exist."[39] William Abrahams at the Atlantic wanted the insertion of chapter titles to relieve monotony, and Rex accepted them.

The title was a more difficult problem. Rex wrote Seferis on 2 October from the house of Professor Balaji Mundker who was on leave in India, informing him that he wanted to dedicate the book to him. He mentioned that "there is much discussion as to what it should be called. I would prefer 'Alypius' or 'Meditations of Alypius'; but their suggestions range from 'So Great a Darkness' to 'The Element of Passion.'"[40]

On the Greek Style: Selected Essays on Poetry and Hellenism was published on 7 October. In the *New York Times Book Review* for 6 November, Kimon Friar opined that Seferis's prose was "simple, direct, precise and logical, cutting through verbiage and tributary temptations to unfold with a disarming humanity those fundamental truths which the shibboleths of generations tend to distort and hide" (50). But he did not say a word about Rex's translation, nor did the other general reviewers, most of whom, as might be expected, were respectful but not enthusiastic about the book.

Yet this work of translation, which cost Rex so much effort, could only help his reputation among scholars.

Socially, Rex was also getting around, attending a party with Frances at the home of Peter Davison and his wife Jane, where there was a reception for Sean O'Faolain as well as for Peter Stansky and William Abrahams, whose co-authored *Journey to the Frontier: Julian Bell and John Cornford: Their Lives and the 1930s* had just been published. Among the other guests were Howard Mumford Jones, Louis Kronenberger, Justin Kaplan, Edwin O'Connor, Ben and Felicia Kaplan, Robert Manning, Charles Morton, and Jack and Moire Sweeney. This was followed by dinner with John Brinnin and Bill Read. From 21-28 October Rex attended a tribute to Auden hosted by the Graduate English Club at the University of Vermont. He discussed Auden's poetry on 23 October, and took part in a panel discussion.

Rex was becoming something of a New England, if not a national, celebrity. The *Hartford Courant* magazine for 23 October 1966 carried a long article about Rex by staff writer Victoria Walmus, complete with a picture of him strolling in the woods near the Mundker house on Dunham Ponds Road. Walmus did an excellent job of noticing details, such as Rex's hatred of typewriters, preference for fountain pens for manuscripts and ball points for crossword puzzles, and his way of writing on the right-hand page of his ledger notebooks while leaving the left-hand page free for additions and corrections. She quoted him as saying that "I've never been rich, exactly . . . ," which was not a bad summary of his position during the Barbara period. He also told her that "publish or perish" was "absolutely ridiculous" as a principle, and asked, "After all, why the hell should people write books . . . there are too many of them being written anyway" (11). By the end of the year 1966, Rex was translating another book himself, though: Plutarch's "Moralia," or treatises on various subjects, for Penguin.

While Rex had by now realized that he would not achieve the celebrity of Stephen Spender or the constant academic recognition and genuine permanence of Auden, he had received national recognition in the United States for *The Aerodrome*, and his translation program was progressing. In England Rex's historical novels continued to do quite well. *Young Caesar* had sold 8,000 and then 10,000 copies in a reprint of 1959; *Imperial Caesar*, 7,500, 10,000, 11,500 and 14,000 copies, and its most recent reprint had been ordered in 1961.[41] In February 1967 Collins published a one-volume edition of these two books. Also, on 14 February, the Royal Shakespeare Company wrote to David Higham Associates, requesting permission to use Rex's Thucydides translation in a club performance to take place on 26 February.[42] The pleasure of writing seemed to increase now that it was just that, a pleasure, rather than the grim obligation that it had been in Scotland.

During the spring semester of 1967, Rex was seeing a lot of Stephen Spender, then an English Department visitor, and found him excellent company. Spender would later write that *The Converts* was one of the best historical novels that he had ever read. But the reviewers were not as impressed.

In England, *The Converts* was published on 28 April, and reviewed briefly in the *TLS*. The reviewer felt that Rex had made Alypius "so real and representative a creature of his time that the reader can readily be seduced into accepting that these 'reflections' are authentic documents," but that on the other hand "Much of the passion and agony of Augustine is lost."[43] These mixed remarks were far better than those that appeared on 9 June in *Time*, which practically reversed the fine reception it had given to *The Aerodrome*. The reviewer opined that Alypius was verbose and too philosophical, and that Lucilla, Augustine's mistress, would have been a better narrator. Since Augustus had written his own confessions, "Who needs Alypius?" asked the reviewer. Luckily, on 15 June the *Library Journal*, always on Rex's side, found the book "vivid" and informative and recommended it for large public libraries. In the *Weekly Catholic* of Anchor Fall River Massachusetts on 29 June, Rt. Rev. Msgr. John S. Kennedy praised the authenticity of the book and accurately wrote that Rex "is a writer whose novels, although never enjoying exceptional sales, have won high praise from discriminating readers and reviewers." In the *New York Times Book Review* for 30 July, Samuel Hynes said that the book was a "novel of ideas, the playing of a fine intelligence upon the theme of faith and its consequences" and that "in a novel like this the ideas are the action."[44] The novel was later listed in the *New York Times Book Review* as one of the outstanding books of the year. The royalty period ending 31 December 1966 netted Rex £705. 8. 3 from Max. Not bad, surely, but a confirmation of Monsignor Kennedy's statement. True to his parents' professions, Rex remained essentially a teacher and a preacher, and it is perhaps surprising that he achieved as much success as he did in an age of blockbuster conglomerates demanding sensationalist entertainment.

An important aspect of Rex's legacy is his fame in foreign countries. People in France, India, and Hungary, among other places, frequently know more about him than do readers in the United States or England, not least because of his one-time reputation for leftism. On 11 July Rex wrote the Hungarian translator Elek Mathe, who had translated *Pericles*, and who was now interested in translating the two Caesar novels and *The Converts*. Mathe also wanted to translate a proposed Augustus novel that Rex had agreed to do for Peter Davison, who had convinced him to write that rather than his autobiography.

In August 1967 there appeared a brief statement by Rex on the Vietnam War, in a book entitled *Authors Take Sides on Vietnam: Two Questions on the War in Vietnam Answered by the Authors of Several Nations*, reminiscent of the thirties' title *Authors Take Sides on the Spanish Civil War*. Rex's brief contribution states the following: "1. I am, like most of my American friends, opposed to the intervention of the U.S. in Vietnam. 2. I lack sufficient knowledge to attempt to say how precisely the conflict should be resolved. Among those who seem to me to be thinking intelligently on the subject are Senator Fulbright, Walter Lippmann and General de Gaulle."[45] Stephen Spender said during a visit to the University of Connecticut in spring 1970 that the attitude among American intellectuals, torn between love and dislike of their country, reminded him of the situation in England in the 1930s, and probably Rex would have agreed with that, but not vehemently. He was no longer given to vehement politics, he liked America very much, and remained a mild Labor Party leftist until the end.

During the early fall of 1967, Rex sold Narayan Cutting, a student who had just arrived from Bombay, his little gray Saab. He wanted only $500 for it, although its mileage was just 24,000, and Rex also generously offered to reimburse Cutting for any necessary repairs right after purchase. Upon opening the glove compartment during his inspection of the car, Cutting found the Barbara Rothschild/Warner divorce papers. Rex had commented, "They make wonderful reading Mr. Cutting. Read them again and again." He also told Cutting, "I have gout. People say it's from drinking. But I don't drink Mr. Cutting, and I never fool around." It was clear that all of this was ironic, for Rex admonished the student never to do business with someone who did not drink.

Around 7 November, Rex realized "a life-long dream of crossing the Rockies by luxury train." He had been invited to Santa Barbara by H. D. F. Kitto to give his Julius Caesar and dictatorship talk, and Frances was staying behind to work in a Montessori school run by Edie Cary. On 14 November he reported on the trip to Max. He had gone on the California Zephyr from Denver to San Francisco, and regretted that the day of the fine train would soon pass in America. Rex told Max that he preferred New England to California, though he liked the luxury to be found in California. To Pam's daughter Anne Norrington, he explained that "The Hippie quarter in San Francisco was rather un-English + I didn't go to an Amateur Topless Contest which was advertised. . . . The native Californians are deranged. The women do Yoga in the afternoons + then get back to normalcy on Martinis. Here everything seems rather agreeably sane."[46]

On 28 December 1967, Max asked if Rex would like to write a 50,000-word Thucydides book for the Bodley Head's children's department, which produced books for readers aged eleven through fourteen. It would follow the style of *Men and Gods* and be a retelling of the *Peloponnesian War*. Max wanted the book to sell at about 18 shillings to one guinea to bookshops and libraries and in a cheaper edition to schools.

Nineteen hundred and sixty-eight saw less work by Rex, and less recognition than in the years immediately preceding. The Augustus novel never developed, and neither was there an autobiography (outside of the few pages in my possession). Some of his less creative projects, such as the children's Thucydides, moved ahead but in retrospect we can see that a peak (if a somewhat lower one than those during his best years in the 1940s) had quietly passed. Cecil, on the other hand, had received the post of Poet Laureate on 2 January 1968 and celebrated it with a six-stanza patriotic poem, "Then and Now," in the *Daily Mail*. Rex commented wryly that "old Cecil . . . is exhorting his countrymen to work harder. If I were in his shoes I'd be going straight out to the West Indies to celebrate Imperial Cricket."[47] Certainly Rex was struck by the irony of the former Marxist rebel Day-Lewis having become Poet Laureate and the anti-academic and similarly rebellious Rex having found refuge as a distinguished professor at an American university; in the same vein both writers, having risked all on literary careers, had won their gamble.

If not quite as impressively as Day-Lewis, Rex was granted some recognition of his own achievements. On 14 March 1968, he traveled to McGill University to lecture.[48] There he "pronounced the Faculty Club with its worn leather armchairs 'just like White's,' addressed waitresses in impeccable French but with an utterly unchanged accent, and charmed everyone he met in Montreal," according to Harriet Duer, one of his former doctoral students, who was present.[49] On 24 March Rex wrote Max that Montreal was "the best city this side of the Atlantic, though, like most of the rest, its probably hell in the summer." Most impressively, he was awarded a D.Litt. *honoris causa* at commencement exercises at Rider College in New Jersey on 28 July in the presence of Dr. Franklin Moore, the college's president, and dean of Arts and Sciences A. L. McLeod, who had nominated Rex for this honor. In his speech, Rex deplored the need to defend the classics in a technological world.

When Rex returned to Storrs after a summer spent in Maine and Cape Cod working on the abridged retelling of Thucydides for Max and on Plutarch's essays for Betty Radice, he found a wonderful new idea in the air—a "Semester of the Thirties," scheduled for February through May 1969, in which Rex, Day-Lewis, Auden, Spender, and John Lehmann would participate. Rex wrote Lehmann that it would be fun because they might get to see some good Buster Keaton and Laurel and Hardy films.

The thirties and the sixties were coming together for Rex personally. He wrote Seferis on 16 October about Lucy that "it's wonderful to be young + able + to think of salvation in terms of Che Guevara or Chairman Mao. With us it was Marx + Freud,— though we'd also read Thucydides."[50] Seferis and Maro visited a month later, just in time for Keeley to finish translating Seferis's "Letter to Rex Warner," which was written between 1965 and 1968. In this poem, Seferis recalls first meeting Rex in a war-torn Greece and then in the university, where "studious children learn/to unravel wise books/ and the labyrinth of love." He praises Rex for celebrating Homer and nature, and recalls Rex's good nature and his service to Seferis as a translator. Perhaps the best lines in the poem are "Our life is always a separation/and a more difficult presence."[51]

Having suffered from many political vicissitudes, Seferis could sympathize with Rex's consternation over the new student radicalism. Rex wrote him on 1 December, commenting,

> Only a very small number are involved, but as any reader of Thucydides, or Lucian, knows, a very small number can cause much havoc. Already we have a rather Corcyrean

situation, where words alter their meanings + logic becomes of the Alice-in-Wonderland sort. The man in Dostoievsky who said "If there is no God, how can I be a major?" expressed, as Stavrogin remarked, "a rather interesting idea"; but now the formula is "If Joe Cary, Jack Davis and Charles Owen are not fascist monsters, how can I be a Maoist?"[52]

It is amusing to see Rex—now a liberal—confronting the young of the rebellious sixties just as his parents had faced the Marxist sympathies that he and Frances felt.

Rex's productivity during 1968 had tapered off into the Plutarch translation and the Thucydides retelling. Betty Radice considered him "one of our best translators, always fluent and readable"[53] and he still worked hard every day—finishing the Thucydides on 4 February and delivering the polished typescript of it to Max Reinhardt on 24 June—but his creative powers were declining and he had no economic spur to force him to accept all offers. In 1969 a third English edition of *The Vengeance of the Gods* (Heinemann Educational Books) and a third U.S. edition of *Men and Gods* (paper, by Avon) were published. There is no more mention of a novel about Augustus, but Rex had one important book, *Men of Athens,* still in him, and the Semester of the Thirties, planned by Americanists Milton Stern and John Seelye, among others, promised a bout of reunions and fun. In letters to Lehmann, Rex delighted in speculating that although the cold weather had dampened the enthusiasm of the Students for a Democratic Society for demonstrations, Stephen Spender, who remained more radical than either Rex or Lehmann, would no doubt "revive their flagging energies."[54] Rex and Spender would have much to talk about because Spender's daughter, also at St. Clare's School, was a friend of Lucy's.

On 7 February Rex summed up his past and present political position for scholar Elizabeth Curry:

> In my near-Communist days I certainly thought of myself as a revolutionary +, in a sense, I still do. But it's true that I respect tradition + I did even then, though I pretended not to. I think that my friends + I were always concerned for human values + we saw them threatened by capitalism and fascism. For some time we believed in the propaganda that communism (Russian model) is automatically +, according to Marx, "scientifically" supporting the threatened values. This belief was shaken by the pact with Ribbentrop that started the war + since then one's seen enough to know that "revolution" can be as oppressive as anything else.

Rex's admission that he had always respected tradition although he had "pretended not to" is extremely important for the understanding of *The Wild Goose Chase* and *The Professor,* as I have tried to show.

Rex went on to comment on present campus politics:

> As for "academic freedom," the S.D.S. don't seem to have grasped the meaning of either of the two words. I sympathize with their dislike of a materialistic, impersonal, uncertain, sentimental society, but I hate their conviction of their own moral rectitude which, together with their preference for "actions" to be taken against what is most defenceless, reminds one of the Hitler youth. Of course there are good elements among them, but also too much hysteria + hatred. Some of their stupidities I tolerate easily enough, probably because I was guilty of the same sort of thing myself. We used, for instance, to feel ashamed because we weren't exactly "proletarian," + today they seem guilty about not being black. I like to think we were more rational too, but perhaps we weren't.[55]

The thirties meet the sixties in this statement. Rex had not betrayed his past political commitments, but was speaking with the voice of maturity. He had learned that capitalism was not all bad, and that the "oppressed" were not all good. Fascism could be found on the left as well as on the right. He did not think like this at the age of twenty-five, nor did he expect the Students for a Democratic Society to do so now.

The parties assembled for the Semester of the Thirties, which was supported by a Ford Foundation grant of $30,000. Early in February, just before the action began, Rex sent Betty Radice the typescript of the Plutarch essays. The core course of that semester got under way on 3 February and concluded on 27 March. In addition to this course, which was team taught, there were lectures and colloquia on three topics: Literature and Social Commentary, History and Public Affairs, and The Arts, and these went on into May. Sessions were devoted to both British and American topics. So it was that during the last week of February, in a grand coup for the conference organizers, Rex, Auden, and Spender met at the University of Connecticut. The immediate occasion was Spender's sixtieth birthday, which fell on Friday, 28 February. Auden's sixty-second birthday had been on 21 February, while Rex's sixty-fourth would be on 9 March.

It had been a long time since Oxford in the 1920s, and the path had been full of vicissitudes, but all three writers had emerged triumphant. America, especially, had been kind to all of them. Rex's career did not, on the face of it, appear any less distinguished than the careers of the other two, but he had less public fame, possibly because he had never really sought it. He was not a great writer, like Auden, capable of blinding insights, but he was a worthy, serious, and honest writer of absolute integrity. Also, owing to his decent and optimistic temperament and his excellent friendships and now reunited family, Rex seemed always to remain young. He took interest in what young people said, whether or not he agreed with them, and he joked and enjoyed life. Auden, on the other hand, had lapsed into a somewhat decadent drunkenness in New York, having been deserted by his long-time lover Chester Kallman. Like Rex, he too was now more conservative in politics, having declared himself at one point in favor of American involvement in Vietnam. Here, as in Rex's case, one sees the émigré's attachment to America and perhaps a reaction against his own support of Marxism during the 1930s. Auden had become religious, and had even preached sermons; Rex never became religious, and when Philip Toynbee in a review of *The Converts* claimed that he had, Rex denied it.

There was a History and Public Affairs Symposium on the Spanish Civil War on Saturday, 1 March, moderated by Hugh Hamill. Among the participants was Stephen Spender, who commented on a talk by Prof. Stanley Weintraub of Pennsylvania State University. Spender made the point that the political opinions of Shaw, Eliot, and Yeats about Spain were simply ignored by the younger writers not only because these three were not anti-fascist but because they did not seem to really care about contemporary politics. Spender also pointed out that more English writers had died in Spain than in the Second World War. He felt that Auden's poem "Spain" was the best political poem written this century.

On 4 March Rex presented the Wilbur Cross Library of the university with many of his manuscripts, including those of *The Converts* and his *Hellenica* translation. The university's president, Homer D. Babbidge Jr., was present, as were librarian John P. MacDonald, Stephen Spender, and John Lehmann. Their photo appears in the *Connecticut Daily Campus* for 7 March.[56] The presentation of manuscripts was preceded by a luncheon in Rex's honor at the Faculty Alumni Center.

That afternoon in the Faculty Lounge in the Student Union Building, at four o'clock, Lehmann spoke about "Poets and Poetry of the 1930s." When introducing Lehmann's talk, Rex said that "we don't . . . have schools of writing in England. Publishers make theirs up. There were sorts of parties that he used to have in London and I don't know how he got the drink for them because there wasn't any in England, but they were nice occasions. One used to meet writers from all over the world there." Lehmann traced the way in which some of the poetry of Spender, Auden, and Day-Lewis became increasingly dogmatic and Marxist while at the same time these poets were writing other, apolitical poems, which were their best. And then he spoke of how, during the Spanish war, the peak of left-wing commitment passed. From Rex's poem, "The Tourist Looks at Spain," he quoted the line "Spain has torn the veil of Europe" as illustrative of the early days of the war when the issues seemed crystal clear. He referred to "the brilliantly allegorical demonstration of Rex Warner's *The Aerodrome*" as an example of the turn against power politics on any side that occurred after the Spanish war.

In response to Spender's point during the discussion period that the thirties saw a movement into politics of people who were brought up hating politics but saw no alternative, an unnamed speaker, who was almost certainly Rex, agreed completely and said that "One was sort of brought up hating politics. I still do but one was forced into it." Rex also pointed out, however, that "one did not want the way one was brought up" and so became political for that reason too. He also stated why a lot of "proletarian literature" was bad writing: ". . . one wanted some form of maybe salvation, which we happened to find in something unreal, I think. I mean an idealized picture of save the worker and then the worker for some reason was good. We ought to have [had] enough sense to see that some workers are good and some are not good." Rex also found similarities in the politics of the 1960s: "There is possibly a parallel in our days and the present days (now) in that you find everybody rightly concerned about the injustices under which the black citizens suffer and that, therefore, all blacks are good."[57]

Spender maintained that one must not "confuse the life of the revolution with the revolution" and that even if a dictator is bad, the idea of the revolution that brought him to power can be good. He liked the idea, current in the 1960s, of "permanent revolution." Rex agreed with Spender that their generation had been mistaken in thinking that it would be easy to connect revolutionary causes with genuine political freedom. However, Rex disagreed with him about "permanent revolution," because while revolutionaries may be trying to get "a life of justice and peace, the things everybody wants," revolutions "nearly always" end up in the hands of bureaucrats. Commenting on Graham Greene, speaker #3, possibly Rex, said that Greene "was a Communist for one day. He handed in his ticket in one day." To this, Spender responded that Greene "is a kind of anarchist, perhaps, or a conservative," and speaker #3 corrects that to "Puritan Anarchist." Speaker #3 insisted that Greene's *The Power and the Glory*, despite Spender's grudging praise of it, was "extremely good." Speaker #1 commented that "in America, the S.D.S. movement right now is extremely anti-intellectual" because its members thought dogmatically and did not prize any kind of dialectic. And then Speaker #3 concluded that "You can't do at all without a sense of history and you haven't got it at that age." What emerges from these scattered remarks, imperfectly recorded and largely unlabelled except for the utterances of Spender and Lehmann, is Spender's continued leftism and the more moderate liberalism of Rex and Lehmann, tempered by age. If Speaker #3 is Rex, as seems likely, his respect for Graham Greene's work emerges clearly. In fact, he taught Greene's work and was directing two doctoral dissertations on Greene that were successfully completed during that very semester: Jane Manly's "Graham Greene: The Insanity of Innocence" and Carl Sternberg's "The Quest for Justice in the Fiction of Graham Greene."

After the conference, Lehmann went to the Humanities Research Center at the University of Texas and sold some manuscript materials, including Rex's correspondence with him. Rex remarked in a letter of 2 April to him that "I like the thought of you standing in the vaults of the Humanities, contemplating the records of your past. Somehow it reminds me of Sir Henry Curtis in 'King Solomon's Mines,' + I hope you got away with a few diamonds."[58] Rex and the Thirties had passed into history. But he was still alive and kicking.

If Rex was less active in terms of publishing during his last years at Connecticut, he had become a very fine teacher and dissertation director. Part of Rex's success in these areas stemmed from his more than fifteen years of teaching secondary school in the 1930s and 1940s; he also empathized with college students because his own daughter Lucy was looking for a college and in the spring of 1969 was visiting with an eye toward attending the University of Connecticut. Although she had not gotten on with her sociology teacher at St. Clare's School because, in Rex's words, he "perhaps, was lacking in enthusiasm for Che Guevara," she agreed with Rex that "student militants would be better occupied in attacking a number of other things before their universities."[59]

Rex spent the summer and fall of 1969 in England, where he was on sabbatical. He wrote Paul Ryan, whom he had helped land a teaching job at Connecticut, that he hoped Paul would have some reasonable classes and "that you'll manage to support, as I did, the looks of horror aimed at one by beautiful girls when they find that one is not Mr. Cary." Talking about George Brandon Saul, the resident Yeats scholar who was close to retirement, Rex added, "I shall hope for grateful looks when it's discovered that I'm not Prof. Saul." But in fact Rex remained enormously popular with students.

His English residences became places of pilgrimage for both colleagues and students. In June 1969 when he was living in Charlbury, on the outskirts of the Cotswolds, he and Frances had been visited by his former chair, Leonard Dean, and his wife Dorothy, along with their daughter and son-in-law. Then had come a party of graduate students. The Warners had visited Basil Wright, the Cardiffs (friends from Greek days), and Michael Ayrton. Otherwise, Rex was whiling away the time reading Nero Wolfe mysteries and a life of Field-Marshall Wavell, who Rex—with his taste for the unusual detail—considered "by far the best general of the war + probably the only general who regarded [Francis Thompson's] 'The Hound of Heaven' as the best poem ever written." The gaiety was interrupted on 21 August by hand surgery—proof that "writer's cramp" was a genuine occupational hazard when writers used to write.

When Rex returned to Storrs after his trip with Frances on the HMS *Franconia*, he taught his ten-student graduate seminar in Greek Literature in Translation. I was in that class. Rex did not come in with brilliant prepared remarks, and he frequently slurred his words, making his sentences hard to understand. But there was an indescribable thrill in studying Thucydides with the translator of the Penguin text that we were using. He responded to any question or remark with respect, so the questioner got the impression that he was actually asking Rex something new, rather than something that Rex had heard or thought of a thousand times before. He never treated any student with anything other than the utmost respect; at most he might respond humorously to an opinion he did not agree with. He also would stop after he answered the question, and there would be an embarrassing silence until one of the students picked up the thread and asked another question or made a comment. Rex loved to tutor another generation in the classics, writing Seferis that "it's a pleasure to find the young people getting enthusiastic about Thucydides + Euripides."[60] It was group tutoring rather than lecturing, but that is entirely appropriate at the graduate level.

Harriet Duer, who finished her doctorate in 1970 with a dissertation on Evelyn Waugh that Rex liked very much, recalled waiting for Rex's arrival in September 1963, thinking that he would probably be very aloof. Instead, when he did arrive, she and the other graduate students found that he "adapted to life at Storrs as if he had always lived there." She studied classical literature in translation with him during the fall semester of 1963 and the modern British novel during the spring semester of 1964. He was easy-going as a person but

> He assumed we'd all read practically everything, or so it seemed at the time. We hadn't, of course, but spent the rest of the year reading to a demanding standard which was never explicitly imposed, but somehow always expected. The excitement of reading Thucydides especially sticks in my mind, as does a particularly moving memory of Rex reading Auden's "Shield of Achilles" with a clear but never spoken sense of special knowledge.

Her husband Leslie Duer, who also studied with Rex, found that "A great thing about Rex was that he took one on absolutely level terms. There wasn't one voice for colleagues and another for students." He remembered "Rex in carpet slippers padding around a drinks party" for Cecil Day-Lewis when he visited Storrs. Rex "would stop to greet a drop-in graduate student (me, in this case) with the same hospitality" that he would show any of his colleagues.

Harriet remembered that for her, "Rex was the ideal dissertation adviser. His encouragement and good advice were freely given. He wholly lacked any grimness toward scholarship—the competitiveness and anxiety that so often seem to characterize graduate study. Working for him was fun, and I think that is how he regarded his work, too." Her husband recalled rolling up to Rex's house one afternoon to deliver a seminar paper, "expecting a little conversation and a quick departure but finding instead sardines on toast, a whiskey, three hours that passed as if they had been as many minutes, and by a considerable distance, more knowledge about what I had written than I had come in with."[61]

Bill Lannon, one of Rex's students at Bowdoin whom he had convinced to come to Connecticut for his M.A., and who became a college teacher himself, recalled Rex's style during his M. A. oral examination. His attitude was that the exam should be a pleasant chat, and he prefaced it by saying to his fellow examiners, in Lannon's presence, "Let's ask Lannon some difficult questions and then go and have a drink." Rex also helped me greatly in preparing for my own doctoral oral. But the relationship did not end there; nor did it with many of his other students. We would keep in touch until he died, and I like the others would make a pilgrimage to his and Frances's house in Wallingford many times.

Rex's productivity had slowed, but a reprint of the 1947 U.S. edition of his essays, *The Cult of Power*, had been published in February 1970 by Kennikat Press[62] and his "children's Thucydides" had come out in London on 26 March 1970. For a change, the *TLS* for 16 April had published a very positive review of the Thucydides book, *Athens at War*, saying that his method of retelling even where he included his own explanations as part of the text, was "abundantly justified by results" and that all eighteen-year-olds should read Thucydides before being allowed to vote, a sentiment with which Rex would certainly have agreed.[63]

Moreover, he had begun thinking about *Men of Athens*, one of his best books, which he would write for Michael Raeburn, the editor at Rainbird Books, which was acting as a packager for the Bodley Head. On 20 April he wrote Seferis that in the summer he would "probably start writing one of those rather unnecessary books about Athens in the 5th century. I think I shall concentrate not so much on what went right as on what went wrong + on the courage + vision of people like Sophocles + Thucydides (+ even Nicias) who could believe in apparently lost causes."[64]

By Monday, 22 June, he was getting on very slowly with the book, and blamed himself for getting out of practice, as he had by not writing anything for a year previously. Frances was in England, where she purchased Anchor House, Jonathan and Marigold's old dwelling, and Rex was amusing himself by reading Trollope's *The Way We Live Now* aloud with the Davises.

The *New Haven Register's Sunday Pictorial* carried a cover story about Rex on 28 June. The writer, Robert Holland, a former undergraduate student of Rex's at Connecticut, quoted Rex as saying that "I don't believe things have changed awfully much since earliest times" and Holland went on to say that Rex's novels, too, were timeless. To explain Rex's lack of fame, Holland ventured the good idea that *The Aerodrome* failed to catch on as much as it might have because the middle of World War II was the wrong moment for an attack on the military. But Rex did not seem to mind, because he was "always moving on to something else and he even gives you that feeling when he's just sitting, talking. He perches up near the edge of his chair, leaning forward, concentrating on your questions or what you have to say, then leaping suddenly up to answer the phone and coming back to perch again and resume the conversation precisely where it was interrupted" (8). Holland noted too that "always, despite the intensity, his great good humor comes through. He knows how to enjoy and he likes very much to laugh." These observations are absolutely accurate.

Holland, however, got some of his facts wrong: he made it seem that Rex had written *The Wild Goose Chase* after returning to England from Egypt rather than (mostly) before he left England for Egypt; that he had spent five years in Greece instead of two; and made it seem as if Rex had been struggling from the time he got back from Greece through the Scottish period, omitting the Barbara years. But about Rex's character he was rarely mistaken. He quoted Rex as saying that he "might have stayed in Greece the rest of my life, but I got sort of tired. I suppose it was my puritanical nature came to the fore. I mean, whenever you're enjoying things so tremendously. . . ." This would fit Barbara Rothschild's theory about Rex—that the puritanical and fun-loving sides of his nature were perpetually at war.

Holland, quoting Rex again, also provided a clue as to why he never wrote the autobiography that Peter Davison had once wanted him to do: "I have this old contract to do an autobiography, but I don't think I'll ever get to it. I've always felt that sort of thing should be about somebody who's done something interesting. Like St. Augustine or someone." Holland concluded that "The modesty is not false, nor is it meant to generate a mood of tragic greatness in the listener. It is simply Rex Warner and his way of dealing with Rex Warner" (10).[65] Robert Holland was later to publish a novel, *The Hunter*, in a copy of which he has a hand-written dedication thanking Rex for teaching him to stick to the point. Rex's many successful students prove that his casual teaching style was not laxity. It was really an attempt to help students relax so that they could focus more directly on his high expectations.

Frances wrote Rex from Wallingford on 8 July that in the company of her friend Taqui Stevens she had met Agatha Christie, who also lived in the town, but that Christie did not know Rex's writing.[66] Rex's new writing was still going slowly. He wrote Frances on 20 July from Leonard Dean's house in Damariscotta, Maine, that he was making some progress, but "It's very difficult to say anything new about chaps like Aeschylus." By 1 August Rex was beginning to write quickly, and regretted that he would soon leave the Deans for John Brinnin's house in Duxbury, Massachusetts, and then Martha's Vineyard, where he had taken a house and would await Frances's arrival from England.

On Sunday, 23 August 1970, Rex wrote Paul Ryan that Frances had joined him in the Martha's Vineyard house. Despite the fact that the Carys and the Davises were visiting, Rex had written "about 25,000 words, mostly about Aeschylus + Pericles, but said little that is new." He hadn't seen a newspaper for weeks and felt better for it, but his blood pressure remained troublesome.

The 1970-71 academic year passed smoothly. On 10 April 1971, Elizabeth Curry came to interview Rex. One of her questions related to Graham Greene, who Rex described as "a very great writer, certainly" and, perhaps surprisingly, "much more of a Protestant writer than a Catholic one." When asked why Rex had given up writing his allegorical novels and had turned to historical ones, he responded that he had said all that he had to say in the allegorical framework, while "in the historical things I suppose I was reverting to something that has always been in the back of my mind," namely the exercise of power in the classical world. Rex felt that his St. Augustine novel "didn't come off quite right—but the Caesar books and the Pericles were, I think, not too bad." Most critics would agree about the Caesar books, but not about the Pericles; Rex himself had not thought it very good when it was published. *The Converts* is better than Rex thought it was.

Then Dr. Curry asked the most interesting question of all: "Your Caesar in his mature years deeply questions whether he is good or bad. Yet you as an author never for a moment allow the reader to doubt that Imperial Caesar is a great man. You personally like great people, yet you sometimes deplore the common results of greatness. Can you explain this conflict and show how it operates in your allegories?"

Rex answered, "Yes, I see what you mean, and of course I believe it's wrong to think of *The Aerodrome* as a total attack on the great man, the Air Vice-Marshal. In the end, if forced to choose between the kind of model of the village and the heartless efficiency of the Aerodrome, then one chooses the model of the village. But I'd rather have it that one wouldn't be forced to make that particular choice. I was exaggerating again." The ideal for Rex would be a combination of the efficiency (but not the dictatorship) of the aerodrome with the humanity (but not the sloppiness) of the village. Rex's love of the village supplies one of the meanings of the subtitle, "A Love Story." Asked whether a person could legislate equality—a favorite topic of the American 1960s and 70s—the former Marxist sympathizer Rex answered that "you certainly can't legislate equality. In fact, you don't find equality."

Dr. Curry went on to explore the topic of whether a belief in common goodness was possible after Hitler, and Rex answered that it was still possible to believe in the basis of a common goodness of humanity "so long as at the same time one sees that under certain conditions the same human nature will behave absolutely abominably. It's rather important to see the conditions under which what is good will come out." Rex's personal philosophy at this point came close to Sir Richard Francis Burton's:

self-cultivation with due respect for the rights of others. As Rex put it, "one is much happier when one is enjoying oneself, without doing injury to others." He said nothing about trying to save the world.

To a question about his American reputation, Rex responded that he didn't know why he didn't sell well in the United States, but he shrewdly suspected that it "may be my consciously slightly archaic style. . . . I don't try to make things easy, anyway. I know that's unfashionable." Having just finished *Men of Athens,* Rex said, "It's not bad: it's again dealing with the problems of power, mostly." His future plans as a writer—which revealed his true professionalism—were only that "one would like to write something better than one has written before."[67]

The only other book he was to complete was a small anthology of G. M. Hopkins's poetry—always a favorite with Rex—that he was also doing for Max Reinhardt. His personal life was also narrowing. Around Easter 1971 he wrote to Seferis, who would die on 21 September, what was to be his last letter to the poet. In it, he recalled the "good days" when "we went with you + Katsimbalis to the Easter service below the Acropolis + then to a great feast with the mother of the Colossus [Katsimbalis]." Rex was relieved to have finished *Men of Athens* because he would then have time to reread the *Iliad* and Chaucer, "both more sane than anything one reads in any newspaper."[68]

Rex and Frances went to England for the summer and moved into Anchor House. After only one month there, he had read Oliver Warner's *Trafalgar,* three Agatha Christies, and Jane Austen's *Persuasion,* which, as he commented in a letter of 19 June to Paul Ryan, he felt left something to be desired "though of course it's ten times better than anything written by the Bronte girls." On 5 July Rex wrote Paul Ryan that he had just read with sorrow of Maurice Bowra's death the day before at Wadham College.

Yet he had his many grandchildren living near him in Wallingford and Reading, and literature continued to provide entertaining surprises. On 19 July he wrote Paul that he had two climbing roses in his garden, a "Dorothy Perkins" and an "American Pillar," and that they had helped him "elucidate some early lines of Auden" that he had always found difficult:

> And may the Giant American Pillar
> Fertilise Dorothy Perkins + kill her.

George Eliot's *Daniel Deronda,* which Rex had finally begun after many false starts but had not yet finished, "seems to me extremely good—if you like that sort of thing." The meaning of this last remark is not clear, but it may refer to Rex's difficulty with reading very long novels at this point. It might be that Rex was reading this book because of my interest in Israel; I had gone to Israel immediately after finishing my doctorate, and would keep in touch with him intermittently from there from this summer on. On 26 July, when he finished the novel, Rex wrote Paul that he had done some very interesting "research" on *Deronda*: he had discovered that Michael Ayrton's grandmother, "a beautiful, impoverished Jewish refugee with whom George Eliot was much impressed," was the model for the character Mirah in the book; rather than a singer, she had been an electrical engineer.

In other literary commentary, Rex wrote that if he

> happened to rewrite Book VI of the Aeneid, I would only make one basic alteration. I should make Aeneas beg the sybil to show him everything except members of his own family + in particular to keep him away from any descendants of Ascanius. Instead he could exchange war stories with Hector + Achilles, + have interesting discussions with Orpeus + Musaeus. Ovid could no doubt do a good scene with Dido ("Well, anyway, it was good while it lasted").

Rex returned from England in the fall of 1971 by himself and was immediately struck by asthma. This proved unusually dangerous, for his upstairs neighbor in the house on Horse Barn Hill Lane, a Doctor McGowan, gave him some medicines which when combined with bourbon were nearly lethal: Rex fell into a deep sleep caused by the interaction of the medicines and alcohol, and his pipe set the sofa smoldering. Fortunately, McGowan smelled the smoke, came downstairs, and put the fire out. Unfortunately, Rex wrote Paul, who was no longer at Storrs, when Frances arrived the next day she did not "show the gratitude that she ought to show my Deliverer (whose views on race + Women's Lib. conflict with hers)."

Rex's ill health—not only asthma, but a suspected second stomach ulcer—was the cause of his negative response to Max's telegram of 21 September, asking if Rex wanted to do the Seferis obituary for the *TLS*.[69] But Rex's previous work was paying off, for on 17 September, a formal agreement for Bodley Head to buy 10,000 copies of *Men of Athens* from Rainbird, the packager, at £1.25 per copy was signed. On 30 October it was agreed that Rex would receive an advance of £1,250 for the book. *Men of Athens* would be published in October 1972, and his sixty-four-page Hopkins anthology *Look to the Skies!* in November 1972.

The pre-publication sale of *Men of Athens*, however was not without problems. On 12 November editor J. B. Blackley at the Bodley Head wrote to Michael Raeburn of Rainbird expressing disappointment over what he saw as a lack of energy in the text and attempting to revise his order for 10,000 copies downward.[70]

On 17 November, because he had a "general bias against what is called here 'Eng. Lit. Crit.,'" Rex responded negatively to James Michie's suggestion that he might consider a critical book on Hopkins. But Rex had discovered that Jesuits don't wear pants by performing some detective work on Hopkins's poem "Epithalmion": "You'll remember how the chap who is undressing first of all discards 'his bleached both + wool-worn wear'; last of all he 'offwrings' what appear to be enormous boots, which obviously would have been taken off earlier if he were wearing pants. No doubt I'd get a Ph.D. if I were to write this up."[71] A look at the poem will show that Rex is right.

Rex urged Michie to continue his own work on translation. He called poet Louis Zukofsky, then visiting Storrs, an impostor, since he had "translated Catullus without the aid of the slightest knowledge of Latin" and apparently became "very angry with people who suggest that it's not a bad idea to know what the words mean." It might be argued that Rex had done the same with Seferis, but he did know ancient Greek, had two years of contact with modern Greek, and had the assistance of the poet himself as well as good literal translations. I have found no record of whether or not Rex and Zukofsky ever actually met.

On 7 December Michael Raeburn vigorously responded to Blackley's negative letter about *Men of Athens*, writing that the book was a very vigorous exposition of the conceptions that lay behind the achievements of fifth-century Athens. Moreover, Rainbird had two confidential reports on the manuscript, one from noted classical translator Michael Grant and the other from Raeburn's brother David (an expert on Greek drama). Grant had written that Rex was a "good, persuasive and eloquent writer" and David Raeburn that *Men of Athens* was a sensitive and convincing piece of work.

Just before Rex and Frances left for England for the summer, Cecil Day-Lewis died on Monday, 22 May 1972. The loss of Cecil must have been extremely painful, all the more so since it followed the deaths of Bowra and Seferis by less than a year. Luckily for Rex, he had a large family and new friends for support, as well as the continued friendship of the Morrises. In September Rex and Frances would attend the memorial service at St. Martin's in the Fields, along with Spender and other luminaries.

On 7 July Rex had been given an advance copy of *Men of Athens* and wrote Paul Ryan that the publishers had done a good job, "Except that there must be some ghastly Women's Lib. girl in the office who keeps on introducing things into the captions to the effect that women were treated disgracefully in Athens." Interestingly, in *Men of Athens* Rex deals with this issue in his Aristophanes chapter:

> The fact that women play such an important part and that Lysistrata herself is one
> of the most impressive figures in all comedy does not, of course, indicate that Aristophanes

was a feminist or remotely interested in Women's Liberation. The Athenian women seem to have been perfectly well able to look after themselves without the vote and it is difficult to see how there arose the notion, still often held, that they were ever an oppressed class of mouse—like creatures somehow resembling the more insipid of Dickens' heroines. Certainly the women presented on the Athenian stage, whether comic, like Lysistrata, or tragic, like Clytamnestra or Antigone, are so far from being insipid that they are at least as impressive as any of the men; and this is, after all, what anyone who has ever met an Athenian woman would imagine to be the case.[72]

On 12 September writer John Julius Norwich conducted a BBC interview with Rex about other aspects of *Men of Athens*. Rex explained that the underlying theme of the twelve essays that make up the book is "this tremendously important experiment in democracy, in man thinking he can control himself and the world around him. Starting with an enormous wave of optimism after defeating the Persians. . . . And then a gradual diminution of confidence, until you get to the end of the period where these ideas which promised so much have somehow got debased, largely through the war."[73] Rex stressed that there was no real anti-war sentiment in Athens in a modern sense, only the anti-war sentiment of those who are fighting; so Aristophanes is not a modern pacifist of the anti-Vietnam variety. Here, as with his distinction between the Greek attitude toward women and modern views, Rex performed a useful service in interpreting the ancient world for us.

The reception of *Men of Athens* began to gather steam around September. It is his best and final word on Greece. Organized around biographies of the great men of the fifth century, Rex's work gives the reader a very positive sense of what humanity, while always prone to error, is capable of achieving; it is not only a study of what we once were, but of "what we are or may become," as Rex writes in his first chapter.

Rex brings us close to the period by offering fresh comparisons and perspectives based on a lifetime of reflection. For instance, in discussing Thucydides, Rex shows how in *The Peloponnesian War* he may have used the Hippocratic method of medicine as a model for describing not only the plague but the spiritual sickness of Athens itself. He shows how Aeschylus can be compared to Shakespeare and Shelley, and how Sophocles was like Milton. Euripides is illuminated by Rex's knowledge of Seferis. Rex devotes a whole chapter to the architect Phidias and the building of the Parthenon. If one were to teach this period in an introductory class, it would be difficult to find a better book. While Rex's text ensures that *Men of Athens* is more than a coffee table book, it is beautifully produced and a pleasure to hold and read.

On 20 September the novelist Mary Renault wrote George Rainbird that "Rex Warner has I think done a magnificent job of the text, wide-ranging in scope and perception, balanced in judgement. You could not, I'm sure, have made a better choice; I can think of nobody better equipped for this particular assignment, certainly not I."[74] On 28 September Stanley Mayes reviewed the book on the BBC "Book Talk" show. He found that Rex's study of the nine great men of Athens—Aeschylus, Sophocles, Euripides, Aristophanes, Plato, Socrates, Pericles, Phidias, Thucydides—was distinguished for his "fresh presentation of the kind of impact these men made on their contemporaries, and what they can still tell us about own problems two-and-a-half-thousand years later."[75] When Rex wrote to Paul Ryan on 30 September, he was obviously pleased with the good reviews that were beginning to come, but was still modest enough not to pay too much attention to them, commenting ironically that "One reviewer of my Athens book was kind enough to say, quoting Dryden on Chaucer, that I am a perpetual fountain of good sense,—a view which, up to now, has only been held by Petter." Here Rex referred to Petter Juel-Larssen, a professor of music at Storrs who remained one of his most devoted colleagues.

While the Athens book was going well, James Michie dissuaded Rex from doing a book on Defoe as he had suggested some months earlier, and tried to get him to write a "Plain Man's or Everywomen's Guide to Greek Lit.," for which he predicted enormous sales. This book, like the Defoe, the Augustus novel, and the autobiography, was not to be.

September also brought a "revised edition" of Rex's Thucydides translation. In fact, the revisions seem largely limited to Moses Finley's new introduction and notes while Rex changed very little in his own work. The book would be reprinted again in 1974, 1975 (twice), 1976, 1977, and twice in 1978, and it remains in print in 2001. Could it be that the Vietnam War, as the *TLS* reviewer on 1 December would say of the Thucydides chapter in *Men of Athens*, was causing students to see the similarities between the failed expedition to Sicily and that war?

The reviewer went on to state that "The late Sir Maurice Bowra's *Periclean Athens* (1971) was excellent, and so, in a different way, is Rex Warner's book, which is dedicated to Bowra" (1466). To be compared favorably to Bowra, and in the *TLS*, was perhaps the highest accolade Rex could receive. Moreover, the reviewer so truly wrote that Rex "was not only a highly sensitive and well-informed observer of the ancient scene: he writes admirable English." These qualities, however, did not translate into high sales for *Men of Athens*, and by 15 June 1973, the Bodley Head had sold only 4,000 copies out of the 10,000 it had purchased from Rainbird.[76] So Rex's writing career ended more or less as it had begun, with intellectual praise and somewhat disappointing sales.

Rex's last few years at Storrs were quiet, but there were some high points, such as his fall 1972 trip to Athens for the British Council. He found Maro Seferis and Alekko

Xydis (an "old pal" from 1945) waiting at the airport. The council representative, Ian Francis, put on a party for Rex at his house at Psychico, and those present included folk singer Dora Stratou, Rex's literal translators Theodore Frangopoulos and George Savidis, and others. He would also meet Shan and Roxain Sedgwick and Paddy and Joan Leigh Fermor. He had the most fun, perhaps, with his friend Katsimbalis, who (as Rex wrote to Paul Ryan) said, "They have sold in Germany 70,000 of [Henry Miller's] 'Colossus of Maroussi.' What have I got out of it? One fuck. A very bad one, with a hideous Italian girl." Katsimbalis had become extremely rich but complained about that, too, saying, "I swim in riches. What do I profit? I am a corpse."

On 1 February 1973, the University of Connecticut *Chronicle* reported Rex's statement that "It was jolly nice not doing anything for awhile." While far from being a literary lion, Rex around this time had a radio interview with a Pittsburgh station, but was annoyed that he had missed Thomas Hughes's *Tom Brown's Schooldays* on PBS as a result of the interview.

After a quiet spring semester in Storrs and summer in England, Rex, now back in Storrs for the beginning of the 1973-74 academic year, wrote department chair Bill Moynihan that

> I'm afraid that the time has come for me to resign as from the end of this academic year the post I've held at this University with so much pleasure for the last decade or more. I reach the age of 69 next March. But I can't send this formal letter without thanking you and all my many friends in the department for having made these years some of the happiest in my life.

Rex did not particularly want to retire, but Frances wanted to return to England to be near their grandchildren. Except possibly for the years at Oxford University and in Greece, the Storrs period had been the most enjoyable of his life.

Auden, yet another old friend, died on 28 September 1973. Rex contributed soon after to a collection edited by Stephen Spender, and published in 1975. There, Rex recalled the Oxford years fondly, and did not comment on any of Auden's later aberrations and social cruelties. Rex had been the hurt recipient of at least one of these callous thrusts when at some point he and Spender had visited Auden in New York and Auden had asked Rex rudely what he was doing there. Rex's memoir showed that he preferred to dwell on happier times.

His sense of self-deprecating humor continued to help him through life. After the 1973 war and the Arab oil embargo he felt that the situation in the Middle East looked bad, but as he commented in a letter to me in Israel, "you'll be glad to know that my short-term (not long-term) predictions are nearly always wrong. I remember long ago spending a whole day proving conclusively that Hitler could not be such a fool as to attack Russia just then. He invaded the next day."[77] On 4 February 1974, he wrote that he had recently been "promoted" to Honorary Fellow of Wadham College, and that the main advantage of this honor was that it entitled him to free dinners whenever he happened to be in Oxford.

Rex's final advisee was an M.A. candidate who wanted to do a thesis on tragedy but could not seem to manage it. He bequeathed this student to Charles Owen and was bemused when watching Owen's struggle to cope with him. But Charles forgave Rex, for before he and Frances left, there was a large retirement party for Rex, Edward Manchester (another English professor), and Robert Stallman at the Owen house. A sheaf of poems, signed by the whole department, was given to the retirees. Faculty member and writer Donald O'Hara referred to Rex as "Limey and Latinist;/ Distinguished novelist," while Barbara Rosen compared him to an Odysseus who "took your ten years' exile on this shore,/and called Penelope from Ithaca" and who "learned an alien tongue." But perhaps the high point of the party was Bill Moynihan's presentation to Rex of an autographed photo of Y. A. Tittel, Rex's favorite football player. These were the days when collegiality was still an important value in university departments, but even in those days the Connecticut department was unusual. Stephen Spender wrote in his diaries that he found the Storrs department "the most congenial English Faculty I was to know in all my years of teaching in America."[78] And Rex had been one of the most congenial members of that congenial faculty.

CHAPTER FOURTEEN

WALLINGFORD, 1974-1986

I. CLOSING THE CIRCLE

Rex and Frances's arrival in Wallingford was very good; they found the pub—the Row Barge—right across from the house in St. Leonard's Lane covered with Union Jacks and signs of welcome, and in the pub Rex was embraced by young and old, including some pretty girls. It was an auspicious beginning, and Rex adjusted to retirement very well; in a sense, he had already retired when Frances purchased Anchor House and when he had stopped writing for publication a few years earlier. Despite his liking of American football, electric gadgets, and Boston, he wrote Paul Ryan on 1 June that England still possessed some solid advantages—"vegetation, flowers, song-birds, food, cricket, pubs, excellent colour TV (on which the other night we saw a magnificent performance of last year's Glyndebourne 'Marriage of Figaro'), architecture, trains—to list a few." Rex had come back to where he started—he had completed the circle by returning to a quiet village in the center of England, this time as an honored elder in his own right, happily married and with numerous children and grandchildren.

The pub became Rex's cultural center, and he wrote bemusedly that "The best elements in the Row Barge are very Aristophanic. They hate politicians, wars, highbrows, women's lib., foreigners (except Americans whom they know), tax collectors, etc. + at the same time are very patriotic, admiring . . . Nelson, Wellington + Churchill. . . ."— It is as if the people in the pub were a Greek chorus to Rex's own values, which did include a more cosmopolitan culture than theirs and a teasing tolerance of the eccentricities of others.

Happy in this old-new environment, Rex would continue a program of voracious reading and correspondence, punctuated by a few trips abroad and visits from friends and relatives. Rex's taste in reading ran strongly to the literature he loved as a boy— Conan Doyle, Stevenson, and Rider Haggard in particular—augmented by biographies and histories. He also read deeply in Dickens, Trollope, and Conrad. He often read himself to sleep with 50 or 100 lines of the *Iliad* in Greek. Rex was saddened by the death of humorist P. G. Wodehouse in 1975, writing Paul Ryan that "he, alone of authors, sometimes ousts Homer from my bedside when I've retired." He worked the *Times* crossword puzzle regularly, but was chagrined to find that a puzzle that took him several hours to complete had been polished off by the English champion in five or ten minutes. He met Max Reinhardt in London once or twice, but nothing came of it. Rex made a start on his autobiography—a brilliant start—but never progressed very far with it. He was ready to do more Penguin translations, but was not given the chance. He did, however, review books on the BBC and give speeches at festivals, and was himself interviewed.

On Saturday, 2 November 1974, page 8 of the *Arts Guardian* carried an interview with Rex by Hugh Hebert, because he was scheduled to give his talk on Julius Caesar and dictatorship the next Friday at the Cheltenham Festival of Literature. Lucy, by then married, and her husband Richard would drive up to hear Rex speak. In the interview Rex mentioned that when *The Aerodrome* was first published, the Air Ministry wanted to take legal action against him, but could not; this was why he added the disclaimer in the beginning of the book that all events were imaginary and that he really had "affection and respect" for the villages of England and the Royal Air Force. Rex felt that his novels had gone out of fashion because they dealt with ideas in the context of fantasy, an unpopular combination. In response to a question about where he saw contemporary danger, Rex said "in some so-called scientific slogan which ends up destroying the really important things—whether the banner is left-wing, right-wing, no blacks or only blacks." The trouble was, Hebert paraphrases Rex as saying, that "history never quite repeats itself—the attack never comes from exactly the same direction."

Rex had become an authority on the past as well as on the present. On 26 May 1976, Jill Black of the Bodley Head asked him what he thought about the Samuel Hynes book, *The Auden Generation: Literature and Politics in the 1930s*, and why he thought *The Aerodrome* was not discussed in it. Rex responded on 8 June at some length, praising Hynes's book but subtly pointing up its flaws:

> It's not Sam Hynes' fault that I find it rather heavy going. This, I suppose, is partly because I was there at the time + partly because I've listened to so many words of English + American criticism. Everything that Sam Hynes says is right + yet I'm left with a feeling

that there's something lacking, that, while it was like this, it wasn't quite like this. Things were more alive, because they were only changing + there were more differences + shifts than can be got into a critical framework, however good.

So far as my own work is concerned, he's been very kind to "The Professor," though I think that "The Wild Goose Chase," with all its many faults, is more interesting. "The Aerodrome" as you say, is just outside his period, + also, perhaps, it doesn't quite fit in with his general theory. The essays in "The Cult of Power" (also outside his period) say many of the things he says + also some others.[2]

Rex did not like grand theories, especially when (as is all too often the case) they are not quite correct.

Around 1 July, Rex went into the hospital for a prostate operation, but when he got there, the doctors found that he also had a urinary infection and a barely functioning liver. He stayed for eight days, loaded with drugs and deprived of all alcohol, a regimen that he was forced to maintain at home too. Back at home, he wrote Paul Ryan on 13 July in shaky handwriting that he did not "mind the abstinence at all, though they told me that I would be afflicted with horrible cravings . . . As it is, I'm gradually mending + even go to the Row Barge most evenings for 2 or 3 . . . orange juices." The doctors had certainly done the right thing by demanding abstinence, because Rex was indeed an alcoholic. Even at this point in his life, if there were two bottles of wine on the table during a family meal, the family would drink one even if they didn't want to because otherwise Rex was sure to drink both. And when he was forced to be abstinent, his son George says, he was much sharper mentally and did not slur his words. On the other hand, one can ask whether or not alcohol made Rex a more genial companion, and there is no sign that it impeded his writing. It may well have oiled the wheels of imagination. When he wrote Paul on 15 August, Rex's handwriting was back to its normal sharpness, he was allowed to drink table wine, and he was re-re-reading Jane Austen, "who, like Homer, always surprises one with previously undiscovered excellencies."

On 15 September 1977, Rex wrote congratulating me and my wife on the choice of a Greek name, Daphne, for our daughter, and commented that "the girl was right in running away from Apollo, a very unreliable god." He also had read from Genesis halfway through the Psalms and provided his fullest explication of the Bible ever:

> After those interminable books of the Law it was a relief to get some action. David seems to me about the only heroic figure + a very fine poet. In fact he's about the only good man in the first few thousand years, apart from Joseph (whom his brothers attempt to assassinate) + Moses (who, for some utterly incomprehensible reason is supposed to

have "sinned" + is banned from the Promised Land). The Lord behaves disgracefully throughout (especially to Saul) + one is not surprised to find that the Israelites, whose incompetent leaders have taken 40 years over an easy 3-weeks' march, take the first opportunity to go whoring after strange gods, to which they quickly revert as soon as David + Solomon, who alone succeeded in governing with reasonable efficiency, are gone (+ who wouldn't, with people like Elijah + Elisha about?). It's a relief to get to Job (an Alexandrian + Greek-educated I imagine). But captivity does a world of good, as is shown by the prophets and late Psalms. In fact it would be possible to maintain that the Jews are only at their best when they are outside Israel. I doubt, however, whether this thesis would go down well at your University.

For Rex, at least on the surface, Hellenism always won out over Hebraism. But if one looks at his return to Frances and his family, as well as at his interest in the Bible itself, the balance is not completely one-sided, despite his provocative opinions here. He was perhaps unconsciously fighting against his evangelical aunts and even his parents when rendering these opinions. Moreover, by 4 October he had gotten beyond the Psalms, as far as Ecclesiastes, and wrote Paul Ryan that "After the long record of crime, duplicity + rabid nationalism, interspersed with a few (a very few) good heroic stories, there is a great improvement, starting with the Psalms."

The years from 1978 on brought more reading, occasional visits and outings, family holidays, continued harmonious relations with Frances, and more sickness. Also, he continued to be republished. In 1978 another reprint of Rex's Milton pamphlet appeared, via Norwood Editions of Pennsylvania. On 12 April 1979, his Seferis poetry translation, unchanged from the original, appeared through Godine in Boston. In 1980 Valentine Cunningham's compilation, *The Penguin Book of Spanish Civil War Verse*, included Rex's "Arms in Spain" and "The Tourist Looks at Spain." In 1988 Cunningham would publish *British Writers of the Thirties*, which remains the best book on the period; it contains many references to Rex.

In March 1979 he wrote me during my sabbatical in California after I had mentioned a professor in Santa Barbara who thought that Rex had defended dictatorship in his lecture on Julius Caesar there so long ago. Rex replied that "There are no doubt a few Californians who aren't crazy, though your friend who thought that I was defending Mussolini wasn't one of them." Rex was very interested in the San Diego Zoo, advising that Giant Pandas, together with seals and flamingoes, were favorites with children, "though I remember that our second son, George, now a Zoology lecturer at Reading University, was mad about small mammals, such as an odd-looking creature called Bosman's Potto." Rex felt that "There's a lot to be said for the life of a naturalist" and he recalled from his reading of *Father and Son* that the father of Edward Gosse overcame the Darwinians' attack on Genesis by "the hypothesis that in the course of the six-day creation God spared a few moments to create the fossils of various irregularities in rock formations just in order to test the faith of Darwin."

On 4 April 1980, Rex, then seventy-five, wrote me apologizing for a long silence. He was under the weather and could not see much without a magnifying glass. But he had hopes of getting new glasses that would enable him to read and to cross the road. Soon after Christmas 1979 he had had a cataract operation and

> As they'd discovered that I had diabetes, I had to have a local anaesthetic, for which our enlightened Health Services provided a beautiful girl to hold my hand. The trouble about diabetes is that if you follow strictly the doctor's orders, as I did, you soon get rid of all the sugar in the blood + begin to suffer from hypoglycemia (too little blood-sugar). This leads to mental derangement which, in its turn, can be easily cured by eating a lump or two of sugar. But this simple + natural remedy is a closely guarded secret. However, after a day + night of semi-lunacy, I found a doctor who revealed his secret + have been perfectly ok ever since.

On 28 December 1980, he wrote Alan McLeod that Frances had just gotten back from a two-month stay in the hospital for skin grafts after having dropped a heavy object on her leg.[3]

In his letter of 4 April, Rex praised my idea of "writing on forgotten and worthy literature," but he suggested that "another good theme would be the performance of some very good critics in persuading people that good things aren't worth reading, e.g. Dryden on Chaucer, Johnson on 'Lycidas,' Eliot on Milton + Shelley, most people (except T. E. Lawrence) on the Romantics + William Morris."

Rex was not forgotten, however. In 1981 Joseph Cary corresponded with him about a piece on his work that Cary would publish in *The Dictionary of Literary Biography* in 1983. In that article, Cary sees a tension between the one and the many or the ideal and real as motivating all of Rex's political writing. During the correspondence, which remains in Cary's possession, Rex revealed that *Why Was I Killed?* was the "only one of my books which my mother liked,—I expect because of its 'religious' atmosphere. In fact there's more of a sort of religion in all the other books, even in the historical ones." This book had never been filmed, although it was originally conceived as a film. Would Rex ever achieve the ultimate accolade for a writer of our period—having his work filmed? The answer was shortly to come, and it was positive.

II. *THE AERODROME* IS FILMED

Rex wrote to Anne Norrington on 4 October 1981 that he was "throwing caution to the winds + going to London tomorrow (first time in 4 years) to have lunch with Max Reinhardt. He'll no doubt tell me more about the BBC thing; but I'm pretty sure that they have signed up a script writer already + he will no doubt show his originality by producing something utterly unlike the book."[4] This was a real *Aerodrome* film proposition at last, after many false starts. Practically every five or ten years a company would suggest producing the novel, but nothing had ever come of it. Now, on 17 September, a "Licence to Televise Material Not Specially Written for Television" was signed by the BBC and the Bodley Head. It specified that the BBC had paid £3800 for the rights to turn *The Aerodrome* into a television dramatization of approximately 120 minutes.[5]

By 10 August 1982, a revised script had been submitted to the BBC by Robin Chapman. In an article he wrote a year later, Chapman discussed the problems of his dramatization. Before agreeing to adapt any book, Chapman said that he had to like, even admire it. He had decided that *The Aerodrome*'s complicated family relationships would be better understood if the work were shown in one, rather than several, episodes.[6] The shooting would be done on location, from 6 September to 22 October 1982. The producer was Kenith Trodd, the director Giles Foster, the designer Geoff Powell, and the photographer Ken McMillan.

Undoubtedly because of the film interest, *The Aerodrome* was published in paperback in 1982 by Oxford University Press. This time the introduction was by Anthony Burgess, who recounted his own first reading of the book. He was "enthralled" and at each re-reading became

> progressively more amazed at its prophetic qualities. Eight years older than *Nineteen Eighty-Four*, its claim to be regarded as a modern classic is as sound as that of Orwell's novel, but one can see clearly why it has to be rescued periodically from popular oblivion. It lacks the "popular" elements of Orwell's book—sex, overt brutality, explicit and recognizable ideology. It is subtle, ambiguous and restrained. It is also optimistic. (9)

In a letter of 4 January 1983 to me, Rex mentioned the BBC film, which he had not yet seen but which was supposed to be shown in April. All he knew was that it had an "extremely good producer." I was teaching a course on neglected literature, and Rex was quick to add, "But you can still keep most of my other books in your neglected literary series. Though its true that the Italians have put out a new edition of *The Wild Goose Chase*, + that, no sooner had they done so, they won the World Cup."

He also wrote me about my publication of a book on Charles M. Doughty, author of *Travels in Arabia Deserta* and a major influence on T. E. Lawrence, the subject of my dissertation. Rex admitted that he had never read *Arabia Deserta* cover to cover (like most people), adding wryly "I wonder if Lawrence ever did."

On 2 February 1983, he thanked me for a copy of my Doughty book but corrected my "use, or misuse, of the word 'cohort' (pp. 22 + 113). A cohort is an established formation in the Roman legion + can never be used except to denote a pretty large number of highly disciplined soldiers. The word is largely misused in the US + is becoming so here too,—the result of the decline in the study of the classics." Rex was still doing his share for literary study, even though he could barely walk more than 100 yards and could not see very well. In April he was able to give a Seferis reading at the Cambridge Poetry Festival, and had been touched to see how many students liked Seferis's work. But when I asked Rex if he would contribute to a collection on Doughty that I was putting together, he responded that "I find that I'm getting lazier + lazier in the matter of writing anything at all. . . . And I get terrified at the idea of any 'dead line.'"[7]

In May he wrote Joseph Cary thanking him for a copy of his article, which had now appeared. He admitted that, as Cary had claimed, *Men of Stones* was not an aesthetic success, because "I'd failed in that book to get across the really strong impression I'd received from my trip to Germany in 1945 as a War Correspondent (substantive rank of Captain) before I went to Greece." Ever considerate, Rex asked Cary to tell Prof. Milton Stern, who as a temporary resident in Anchor House had come to know the Row Barge and its habitués, that the landlord, Ray Hoddenott, had died of cancer.

At some point in October, Will Sulkin, the Oxford University Press editor who was responsible for the publication of *The Aerodrome*, drove Rex and Frances to London for a private showing of the BBC film, which Rex thought very good. Rex wrote me on 9 December that he had been

> enjoying (if that is the word) some local acclaim lately as there have been several articles about me with reference to the film of The Aerodrome which is on TV next week. What is remarkable is the way most journalists get everything wrong + especially the simplest facts. . . . A woman from the Daily Express rang me up the other day + commented on my daring + originality in dealing with the theme of incest. I told her that (i) I wasn't dealing with the theme of incest + (ii) that this subject had been very often + very well handled about 500 BC.

(Rex was of course referring to Sophocles' *Oedipus Rex*.) Rex humorously noted that only one of the airplanes used in the film was real and that the rest were props made of wood.

The *Aerodrome* film was to be shown on Tuesday, 13 December. That same day, Richard Boston published an interview with Rex in *The Guardian*. Rex revealed that at the time he wrote *The Aerodrome*, he had picked up his knowledge of flying from a magazine in a barber shop, which provided "a specialist vocabulary of words like 'aerolon' which he liked the sound of" (11). He described himself as twice-disillusioned: once when he gave up his religious faith and the second time after the Molotov-Ribbentrop pact. At the moment he was Socialist-Democratic-Partyish, if reluctantly. Boston found him more "like an individualist anarchist."

Even the triumph of at last having had his best novel filmed was distorted by some unfavorable reviews. In the *Financial Times* for 21 December, Chris Dunley found that the film was "visually a marvelous piece of work," but "Unfortunately— and I suspect this goes straight back to Rex Warner's book—the characters were no more than socio-political ciphers" (11), and he claimed that the funeral scene was clichéd.

In the *TLS* for 23 December 1983, Peter Kemp found that in the film, "the novel's already rather simplistic opposites are exaggerated into a crudely gaping dichotomy, often achieved by distorting what is in the book." Instead of the novel's forbidding airbase and unimpressive town, the airbase had become "a starkly symmetrical compound of clanging iron grilles and giant concrete runway" contrasted "with insensitive tastelessness" to a quaint Cotswold village. Kemp went beyond attacking the film, stating that Rex's novel itself was only "precariously integrated." Its main strength, however, was "the solid immediacy with which Warner establishes his rural world." But according to Kemp, even these "delicately caught natural effects were lost in the film's loudly artificial atmosphere" (1432a).

Moreover, the few viewers who commented did not do so favorably. In the BBC Daily Duty Office Log for 13 December, it is recorded that there were four callers within minutes of the start, who pointed out that "the aircraft used were of a later period," but all except one were "happy with the explanation for that." Four people found the film offensive or boring without explanation, and one, a teacher in Harlesden, "considers this just the sort of thing to provoke greater violence and less tolerance in the playground and the street." The teacher's reason for thinking this is not recorded.[8]

Whether or not Rex paid much attention to these reviews and the log is difficult to say; probably he thought the film making, at long last, triumph enough. Rex's very last bout with newspaper reviewers had yielded the usual results.

III. HAIL AND FAREWELL

Around the end of 1984, Rex had another prostate operation, and was in a nursing home for three weeks. He wrote Paul Ryan on 4 January 1985 in an almost illegible hand that the operation had been very unpleasant, with many blood transfusions necessary. Rex's last letter to Paul is dated 17 January 1985. In a good mood, he joked that a certain professor was "delighted to discover that 'Emeritus' did not mean 'without merit,'" but Rex added that "no doubt it soon will." He had received two cases of Mouton Rothschild wine and would try to preserve at least one case until Paul appeared on a planned visit in the spring. On 8 March he comforted Anne Norrington, who had just lost her father John Morris. He himself had the "sobering prospect" of being eighty the next day, but was "bearing up pretty well."[9]

On 5 September 1985, Rex wrote me in a steady but very small hand that he had just finished Alan McLeod's collection of essays *A Garland for Rex Warner: Essays in Honour of His Eightieth Birthday*, which had appeared during the summer, and appreciated McLeod's work on it. With his usual kindness, he thanked me "for the nice things you said about me" in my contribution to the collection. Then, typically, he immediately added the self-deprecating and also very sly, "Let's hope that some of them are true." Outside of this limited fame, things were going very quietly for Rex. He was getting worse and worse at walking and not much better at seeing.

I did not know that this would be the last letter he would write me, but so it was. In October he had a stroke combined with pneumonia and bronchitis. It came on suddenly without warning, and affected his right arm and leg, making writing and walking difficult. He was at Wallingford at the time, but was taken about ten miles away to Reading Hospital, a very dreary place with crowded beds. He was upset that he was not in Wallingford, and made jokes about it. Lucy saw him in Reading and felt that he was terribly alone and vulnerable despite the support of his family. But he soon was allowed to go home, although he had to use a frame, or walker, to get about.

During Christmas 1985 Edie Cary came to Anchor House for one day and was the last American friend to see him alive. Around that time Katherine (married with the last name of Chapple) had done a tape of herself reading poetry. He listened through the tape with her, a bottle of champagne at his side. He put her right about the pronunciation of some of Yeats, and was very humorous about it. He did not often express his love, but did so in surprising ways, she feels. For instance, he said on this occasion "My dear, it's so lovely to hear your voice." About a year earlier, he had given Daniel Warner, his grandson, his binoculars, telling him that they've "seen many good birds." Since his cataract surgery around that time, he had had very poor sight.

A few months after the first stroke in October 1985, Rex had a second, more crippling one, and an ambulance had to be called. He recovered somewhat in the Wallingford hospital, and was taking some physiotherapy treatment. But then, on 22 May 1986, he had a third stroke. Rex went to the hospital in Wallingford, where he lingered for several weeks, first in a small ward and then in a private room. His speech was not affected, and he remained fully alert. He was very grateful for all the attention he received in hospital, and was very nice to all the nurses. He was able to quote Horace in the original while in hospital, and corrected the grammar of the physiotherapist shortly before he died, something involving the use of "me" and "I."

Lucy told Marigold Warner that at the same time that Rex was in the hospital, Barbara Rothschild (now Barbara Ghika) was in a nursing home also, and that perhaps this was a sympathetic vibration. Lucy saw Rex three or four days before he died, and read him *Lycidas*; he had not been able to read for about six months, which was a terrible trial for him. He said, "That's pretty good stuff." Katherine Chapple saw Rex the day before he died. Katherine said that she did not want to come to his funeral. He joked that he would be bored if she did not come, and said that "we'll put a note in the Times saying 'Rex has died + Katherine has not come to his funeral.'" When you love someone, she told me, you never believe they're dying. She said, "I'll see you tomorrow, Rex." He took her hand and kissed each of the fingers, individually. He also kissed Monica's hand.

Rex was very thin right at the end, and George and Monica did not want to take their children to see him. Frances was with him most of the time, but had to go home and come back. Once he said, "I'll come with you" and Frances gently responded, "You're not awfully well." He was alert and sensible until the end, and said once to her, "How long do they give me?" Frances and Marigold were present when Rex, breathing with difficulty, died in the late afternoon of Tuesday, 24 June.

Vicar Good was at first unsure about a service for Rex because Rex was not a frequenter of St. Leonard's or any other church. But he gave an insightful funeral oration on 30 June, in which he stated,

> He was in the tradition of the scholar country parsons of the 19th century where I think he would have been at home, sitting loosely but thoughtfully in the area of theology, quietly writing, studying and conversing with the locals yet always probing to find the motives behind all human action.
>
> He loved his time in Greece and America where he became the centre of an enthusiastic group. He was indeed a dominus. He never achieved the acclaim that was due to him perhaps because he never sought it. He couldn't be bothered with it. He lived

simply and quietly here in Wallingford since he retired. He felt that he had said everything that he wanted to say and refused to write further just for the sake of it.

The service was attended by a large, mostly family crowd, some of whom George Warner had not seen in years. Except for Jill Day-Lewis, no figures from the literary world were present, probably because they did not know about the funeral, although Rex's death was reported in both the London *Times* and the New York *Times*. After the service, a smaller group went to the Oxford Crematorium. Frances had decided that cremation would be right; Rex's father, after all, had approved of that. Rex's ashes were scattered among the trees.

When George came back to Anchor House after the cremation, there was already a party in progress among all the friends and relatives. Joining the close relatives of the families of George and Jonathan were Taqui Stevens, Frances's friend from Germany, June Fenby and her daughter, and Frances's sister Marion's daughter. George felt that it was good, because the cremation had been solemn and the party was happy, like a wake. He went out and bought some whiskey to make the party even happier. No doubt Rex would have approved.

IV. REX'S LITERARY CONTRIBUTION

With the publication of Alan McLeod's collection of essays, *A Garland for Rex Warner*, as with the *Aerodrome* film, Rex had the satisfaction of receiving a substantial sign of recognition before he died. McLeod had published his 1960 critical book, *Rex Warner: Writer, an introductory essay* and a previous collection, *The Achievement of Rex Warner* (1965), in Sydney, Australia, and the new collection's publication by the Literary Half-Yearly Press of Mysore, India, indicated once again that Rex's reputation was international in scope.

The new essays, like those in the older collection, showed genuine enthusiasm for Rex's work. Maria Theresa Chialant of the University of Naples compared *The Aerodrome* with Orwell's *1984*, not unfavorably. Andrew Cramp, the writer of a 1984 British doctoral dissertation on Rex, found that despite its faults, *The Wild Goose Chase* was an "interesting and adventurous eclectic experiment" (19). Elizabeth Curry explored Rex's anatomy of the wise and unwise uses of power in the historical novels. James Flynn, the author of a 1974 University of Washington dissertation on Rex, analyzed the reasons for the failure of *Men of Stones*. H. H. Anniah Gowda of the University of Mysore treated *Why Was I Killed?* as a Hindu-like search for the meaning of existence. Daniel Lamont, author of a

1973 Canadian doctoral dissertation on Rex, saw *The Professor* as a critique of academic intellectuals. Marian McLeod found points of interest in Rex's juvenilia and in the first edition of Rex's boys' novel, *The Kite*, compared to recent abridged editions. I found that Rex's classically modeled style in *The Wild Goose Chase* saved the novel from its excess of topical revolutionary fervor and made it permanently valuable as literature. Alan McLeod thought *Escapade* worthy and amusing.

In the preface to the collection, Alan McLeod rightly pointed to Rex's growing reputation in academia and elsewhere. McLeod noted that Rex had had enthusiastic advocates in the 1940s, and dissertations (A. A. De Vitis, Elizabeth Curry) and articles in the 1950s and 1960s. There had been three dissertations—by James Flynn, Daniel Lamont, and Andrew Cramp—in the 1970s and 1980s. To these works can be added the excellent chapter in Richard Johnstone's *The Will to Believe* of 1982, Joseph Cary's insightful encyclopedia piece, and N. H. Reeve's fine *The Novels of Rex Warner* (1989), among other critiques. Moreover, Rex's work continues to be republished. In 1986 a paperback edition of *The Professor* came out through Lawrence & Wishart, and in 1990 a paperback of *The Wild Goose Chase* appeared through Merlin. His works flourish especially in translation, including a Norwegian edition of the Caesar novels in 1989, and several recent editions of the historical novels in Spanish. In 1998 Frances Warner was approached about *The Wild Goose Chase* as a possible film project. In 2000 that novel and *The Aerodrome*, as well as numerous translations, remained in print in America, while in England, *The Professor, The Aerodrome, Men and Gods, Greeks and Trojans*, and several other works were available. *Eternal Greece* has been scheduled for republication in 2003. Moreover, Rex's name perennially turns up in the *Arts and Humanities Citation Index*, especially because of his translations. His Thucydides continues in print in both England and America and had sold almost 1,000,000 copies by mid-1996.[10]

Rex was one of the most important public advocates of the classics in the mid twentieth century—a title he would have worn with honor, since he was tireless in promoting the classics and, especially toward the end of his career, believed them to hold the key to understanding the present. He was also one of the very best translators from Greek and Latin this century, with a wonderfully clear English style that, according to all commentators, manages accurately to convey the feeling and content of the originals. The cadenced, crystalline clarity of the Thucydides translation will not soon be bettered.

There is also every reason to believe that Rex will increasingly be viewed as an important, if not major, twentieth-century novelist. *The Wild Goose Chase* and *The Professor* are historically important and still readable, and he produced at least one minor classic, *The Aerodrome*, which remains perennially relevant. He is mentioned in a large number of literary histories, and his influence shows up in sometimes unexpected places: Alan Tate, for instance, once claimed that Rex's fiction influenced the American writer John Hawkes. Angus Wilson and Anthony Burgess have testified to how important *The Aerodrome* was to them. The historical novels also seem permanently valuable, especially for those who want insight into the periods they cover, and for Rex's uncanny ability to enter convincingly into the minds of Caesar, Pericles, and Augustine. In 1985 Stephen Spender wrote in a *TLS* survey of neglected books that

> Rex Warner is justly famous for two novels, *The Wild Goose Chase* and *The Aerodrome*, allegories of the ideological conflicts of the 1930s. His later novel, *The Converts* (1967) seems to have attracted far less attention than these but to me it seems his greatest achievement, perhaps the best historical novel I have read. . . . Rex Warner portrays his scenes with such intelligence and sympathy that, re-reading the *Confessions* after *The Converts* one does not feel that he has sensationalized the material nor cheapened the ideas leading into Augustine's tremendous autobiography.[11]

Frank Kermode has spoken of the gritty honesty of Rex's thirties novels, Samuel Hynes has repeatedly praised them, and in Valentine Cunningham's *British Writers of the Thirties* (1988), Rex has an honored place, although not quite the place that I believe he will increasingly assume as his work is reconsidered. The Auden-Spender-Day-Lewis group, insofar as it was a group at all, should properly be called the Auden-Spender-Day-Lewis-Warner group, and not particularly in that order although Auden will always head the list.

Rex's importance as a writer goes beyond the formal and the stylistic. Yes, he wrote very well, giving new life to the cliché "wild goose chase," revitalizing a seldom-used expression like "fiercer than tigers,"and coining memorable phrases such as "the cult of power." Yes, he was capable of complex plotting, as *The Aerodrome* shows. Yes, some of his characters, such as George of *The Wild Goose Chase*, the Professor of *The Professor*, and Roy and the Air Vice-Marshal of *The Aerodrome*, are memorable. But he also had something very meaningful to say.

I have been reminded of his moral prescience on many occasions, sometimes quite unexpectedly. In *The Wild Goose Chase* he wrote of kings who receive blood transfusions from live peasants, killing them. In *The Jerusalem Post* of 13 May 1995, Red army veteran David Kuzminsky recalls that, upon entering Berlin in 1945 with the Russian army vanguard, he found a group of Russian children, much to his astonishment. The children "had been dragged from their homes in White Russia and the Ukraine, or taken from concentration camps, and put into a children's home in

Berlin called the 'SS Heimschule.' Next door was a hospital for wounded SS officers. The children provided live transfusions during operations. Blood was siphoned from their arms and pumped into the bodies of the SS men." There had been 120 Russian children at the beginning of this monstrous project; when Kuzminsky entered, there were twenty-six left alive.[12]

Rex understood and unequivocally spoke against Hitler from the very beginning, and was disgusted by appeasement. To suggest that he actually condoned dictatorship, except under the most extreme and exceptional circumstances, is wrong. He understood the false allure of dictatorship for many people, and constantly spoke against it. In all of his novels, he is for humane qualities and against that which would denigrate or deny those qualities. Understanding Caesar (and Pericles and St. Augustine for that matter) is not the same as justifying all of his actions.

Moreover, Rex's human values grew out of his literary values and vice-versa; at least for Rex, there was no gap between the two, no ability—all too common—to read or write literature and act inhumanly. For him, literature—especially classical literature—pointed the way to humane actions, for those wise enough to read it well. The classics were not intended only for academic study and for parsing in some dry fashion, but were to be read and used as guides to right action. For him the classics were constant companions; they were alive.

Entwined with his Arnoldian classicism was a strong dose of the moderate, tolerant Christianity of his father and the Luce and Warner uncles. Even when Rex's work appears in the guise of secular radicalism, it reveals the very same decency and respect for people that his family had passed on to him. His love of the English village is a love of nature, moderation, and erring humanity, and that, ultimately, was his religion.

Rex was one of the last representatives of the old Victorian literary ethos that included novels read aloud for pleasure, a love of the classics, and a genuine life in literature. He had absolute integrity in his own writing and in his love of the writing of others, never descending to sensationalism, even when he badly needed money. With Rex's departure, we say goodbye not only to a person, but to an era.

BIBLIOGRAPHY

COLLECTIONS OF PRIMARY MATERIALS

PUBLIC COLLECTIONS. THE FOLLOWING REPOSITORIES HAVE THE MAJOR PUBLIC
REX WARNER CORRESPONDENCE, MANUSCRIPT, AND FILM HOLDINGS. I HAVE
IDENTIFIED INDIVIDUAL ITEMS BY LOCATION AND (WHEREVER POSSIBLE)
FILE NUMBER IN MY ENDNOTES.

BBC Written Archives, Caversham (RW correspondence and contracts)

Betty Radice Archive, Bristol University Library (RW correspondence)

Bodley Head Archive, Reading University Library (RW-Max Reinhardt and other
correspondence, contracts, and reviews)

The Gennadius Library of the American School of Classical Studies, Athens (Seferis
files: RW-Seferis correspondence and manuscripts)

Hamish Hamilton Archive, Bristol University Library (RW correspondence)

Harry Ransom Humanities Research Center, University of Texas (RW-John Lehmann
and other correspondence, Atlantic Monthly Press RW readers' reports, RW
notebooks and manuscripts)

Henry W. and Albert A. Berg Collection, New York Public Library (RW correspondence,
notebooks, and manuscripts)

National Film Archive of the British Film Institute, London (RW films)

Penguin Books Archive, Bristol University (RW correspondence)

Pennsylvania State University Libraries (RW manuscripts and RW-Alan McLeod and
other correspondence)

Special Collections, University of Connecticut (RW correspondence, notebooks, and manuscripts)

Special Collections, Michigan State University Libraries (RW-C.J. Greenwood correspondence and RW notebooks and manuscripts)

PRIVATE COLLECTIONS

Letters and manuscripts in possession of Anne (Morris) Ambrose

Letters in possession of Elizabeth Curry

Letters in possession of Joseph Cary

Letters in possession of Paul Ryan

Letters and manuscripts in possession of Stephen Tabachnick

Letters and manuscripts in possession of Frances Warner

SCHOOL MAGAZINE REPOSITORIES

Raynes Park School, Wimbledon

St. George's School, Harpenden

Wadham College Library, Oxford

REPOSITORIES CONTAINING A FEW ITEMS

Hogarth Press Archive, Reading University Library

Special Collections, Brigham Young University

Special Collections, Cambridge University

Special Collections, State University of New York at Buffalo

PUBLISHED WORKS

Alan Munton and Alan Young's Rex Warner chapter in their *Seven Writers of the English Left: A Bibliography of Literature and Politics 1916-1980* (New York: Garland, 1981) is admirably accurate and comprehensive with respect to Rex's articles and reviews as well as his books and reprints of his books. A. L. McLeod's *The Achievement of Rex Warner* has a useful bibliography, including Rex's contributions to radio and television, but it runs only to 1965. The following list owes much to their excellent work, which has been extremely helpful, but includes numerous items supplementing it. Other items supplementing Munton and Young's and McLeod's work that I have located, whether in manuscript or print, may be found in my text or endnotes. The following list of primary material is limited to important publications in volume format. I have used these editions in my text.

BOOKS

The Aerodrome. Intro. Anthony Burgess. Oxford: Oxford University Press, 1982. Originally published London: John Lane the Bodley Head, 1941.

Ashes to Ashes: A Post-Mortem on the 1950-51 Tests. London: MacGibbon and Kee, 1951.

The Converts: A Historical Novel. Boston and Toronto: Little, Brown, 1967.

The Cult of Power: Essays. London: John Lane the Bodley Head, 1946.

E. M. Forster. Writers and their Work, No. 7. London: Longmans Green for the British Council and the National Book League, 1950.

English Public Schools. London: Collins, 1945.

Escapade: A Tale of Average. London: The Bodley Head, 1953.

Eternal Greece. Photos by Martin Hürlimann. London: Thames and Hudson, 1953.

The Greek Philosophers. New York: New American Library, 1958.

Imperial Caesar. London: Collins, 1960.

John Milton. London: Max Parrish, 1949.

The Kite. Oxford: Basil Blackwood, 1936.

Look at Birds. London: Hamish Hamilton, 1962.

Men of Athens. New York: Viking, 1972.

Men of Stones: A Melodrama. London: The Bodley Head, 1949.

Pericles the Athenian. Boston and Toronto: Little, Brown, 1963.

Personal Impressions: Talks on Writers and Writing. Edited by Marian B. McLeod. Sydney: Wentworth Press, 1986.

Poems. New York: Knopf, 1938. Originally published London: Boriswood, 1937.

Poems and Contradictions. London: John Lane the Bodley Head, 1945.

The Professor. Intro. Arnold Rattenbury. London: Lawrence & Wishart, 1986. Originally published London: Boriswood, 1938.

Views of Attica and Its Surroundings. London: John Lehmann, 1950.

We're Not Going to Do Nothing. London: Left Review, 1936.

Why Was I Killed? A Dramatic Dialogue. London: John Lane the Bodley Head, 1943. Published in the United States as *Return of the Traveller*. Philadelphia: J.B. Lippincott, 1944.

The Wild Goose Chase. Intro. Andrew Cramp. London: Merlin, 1990. Originally published London: Boriswood, 1937.

The Young Caesar. New York: New American Library, 1959. Originally published Boston and Toronto: Little, Brown, 1958.

SOME WORKS BY REX WARNER APPEARING IN TRANSLATION

L'aérodrome: une histoire d'amour. roman. [The Aerodrome]. Trans. Ludmilla Savitzky. Paris: Editions de la revue Fontaine, 1945.

El aerodromo. [The Aerodrome]. Buenos Aires: Editorial Losada, 1949.

Láerodromo. [The Aerodrome]. Torino: Einaudi, 1959.

Aru kyoju; jiyu shugisha no higeki. [The Professor]. Trans. Kazuo Nakahashi. Tokyo: Iwanamishoten, 1955.

La caccia all'Oca selvatica. [The Wild Goose Chase]. Trans. Carlo Fruttero. Torino: Enaudi, 1953.

César imperial. [Imperial Caesar]. Trans. Marta Alvarez de Toledo. Buenos Aires: Editorial Sudamericana, 1990.

La chasse á l'oie sauvage. [The Wild Goose Chase]. Paris: Gallimard, 1954.

La dernière semaine du professeur A: roman. [The Professor]. Trans. Ludmilla Savitzky. Paris: Editions Robert Marin, 1948.

Der Flugplatz. [The Aerodrome]. Zürich: Büchergilde Gutenberg, 1946.

Hombres de piedra. [Men of Stones]. Trans. Maria Antonia Oyela. Buenos Aires: Emecé, 1951.

Hommes de pierres: mélodrame. [Men of Stones]. Trans. Ludmilla Savitzky. Paris: Gallimard, 1952.

Hvorfor blev jeg droebt? [Why Was I Killed?]. København: Grafisk, 1946.

Flyplassen. [The Aerodrome]. Oslo: H. Aschehoug, 1951.

El joven César. [The Young Caesar]. Buenos Aires: Editorial Sudamericana, 1990.

Julio César: roman. [The Young Caesar]. Buenos Aires: Emecé, 1960.

Kugun kichi. [The Aerodrome]. Trans. Kyoichi Ono. Tokyo: Daviddosha, 1955.

Liemu fosuta. [E.M. Forster]. Trans. Tado Kozu. Tokyo: Kenkyusha-shuppan, 1956.

Marná honba: roman. [The Wild Goose Chase]. Praha: Prace, 1947.

Nuori Caesar. Suomentanut Hannes Korpi-Anttila. [The Young Caesar]. Helsinki: Werner Söderstrom, 1959.

Pericles el Ateniense. [Pericles the Athenian]. Trans. Roberto Bixio. Barcelona: Edhasa, 1989.

Pourquoi ai-je été tué?. [Why Was I Killed?] Trans. Jeanne-Marie Rivet. Paris: Editions de la Revue Fontaine, 1946.

Professoren. [The Professor]. København: Grafisk, 1948.

Die Tugendhafte Republik: Caesars Jugenderinnerungen. [The Young Caesar]. Trans. Gerd van Bebber and Ernst Sander. Hamburg: Hoffmann und Campe, 1959.

Den Unge Caesar. [*The Young Caesar*]. Trans. Ingeborg von Rosen. Stockholm: P.A. Norstedt & Soners, 1990.

Het vliegveld een liefdesgeshiedenis. [*The Aerodrome*]. Brussels: A. Manteau, 1946.

Wenn keine andre stimme spricht. [*Why Was I Killed?*]. Hamburg: Rowohlt, 1948.

Die wildgansjagd. [*The Wild Goose Chase*]. Zürich: Büchergilde Gutenburg, 1949.

TRANSLATIONS AND RETELLINGS

Aeschylus. *The Prometheus Bound of Aeschylus.* Trans. Rex Warner. London: The Bodley Head, 1947.

Athens at War: Retold by Rex Warner from 'The History of the Peloponnesian War' of Thucydides. New York: E.P. Dutton, 1971. Originally published London: The Bodley Head, 1970.

Augustine, Saint. *The Confessions of St. Augustine.* Trans. Rex Warner. New York: New American Library, 1963.

Caesar, Julius. *War Commentaries of Caesar.* Trans. Rex Warner. New York: New American Library, 1960.

Euripides. *The Helen of Euripides.* Trans. Rex Warner. London: The Bodley Head, 1951.

———. *The Hippolytus of Euripides.* Trans. Rex Warner. London: The Bodley Head, 1949.

———. *The Medea of Euripides.* Trans. Rex Warner. London: John Lane the Bodley Head, 1944.

———. *The Vengeance of the Gods.* London: MacGibbon and Kee, 1954.

Greeks and Trojans. London: MacGibbon and Kee, 1951.

Ovid. *Men and Gods.* London: MacGibbon and Kee, 1950.]

Plutarch. *Fall of the Roman Republic: Six Lives by Plutarch (Marius, Sulla, Crassus, Pompey, Caesar, Cicero).* Trans. Rex Warner. Harmondsworth: Penguin, 1958.

———. *Plutarch: Moral Essays.* Trans. and Intro. Rex Warner. Harmondsworth: Penguin, 1971.

Seferis, George. *Calligram.* Trans. Rex Warner. Richmond, Surrey: Miniature Press, 1960.

———. *Poems.* Trans. Rex Warner. London: Bodley Head, 1960.

———. *On the Greek Style: Selected Essays in Poetry and Hellenism.* Trans. Rex Warner and Th. D. Frangopoulos. Intro. Rex Warner. Boston and Toronto: Little, Brown, 1966.

Thucydides. *Thucydides: The Peloponnesian War.* Trans. Rex Warner. London: Cassell, 1962. Originally published Harmondsworth: Penguin, 1954.

Xenophon. *Xenophon: History of My Times (Hellenica)*. Trans. and Intro. Rex Warner. Harmondsworth: Penguin, 1966.

——. *Xenophon: The Persian Expedition*. Trans. Rex Warner. Harmondsworth: Penguin, 1949.

EDITIONS AND INTRODUCTIONS

Aeschylus. *The Oresteia*. Trans. E. D. A. Morshead. Intro. Rex Warner. New York: Limited Editions Club, 1961.

Ayrton, Michael. *The Testament of Daedalus*. Fore. Rex Warner. London: Methuen, 1962.

Bunyan, John. *The Pilgrim's Progress*. Ed. Rex Warner. London: News of the World, 1951.

Cavafy, C.P. *The Poems of C. P. Cavafy*. Trans. John Mavrogordato. Intro. Rex Warner. London: John Lehmann, 1951.

Hopkins, Gerard Manley. *Look Up at the Skies!* Ed. and Intro. Rex Warner. London: The Bodley Head, 1972.

Horace. *The Odes of Horace*. Trans. James Michie. Intro. Rex Warner. New York: Washington Square Press, [1965].

Hürlimann, Martin. *Athens*. Intro. Rex Warner. London: Thames and Hudson, 1956.

Melville, Herman. *Billy Budd and Other Stories*. Intro. Rex Warner. London: John Lehmann, 1951.

New Poems 1954. Ed. Rex Warner, Christopher Hassall, and Laurie Lee. London: Michael Joseph, 1954.

Seferis, George. *The King of Asine and Other Poems*. Trans. Bernard Spencer, Nanos Valaoritis, Lawrence Durrell. Intro. Rex Warner. London: John Lehmann, 1948.

SOME ANTHOLOGIES CONTAINING WORK BY REX WARNER

Adams, J. Donald, ed. *The Treasure Chest: An Anthology of Contemplative Prose*. New York: E. P. Dutton, 1946.

Allott, Kenneth, ed. *The Penguin Book of Contemporary Verse*. Harmondsworth: Penguin, 1950.

Auden, W. H., and C. Day-Lewis, eds. *Oxford Poetry 1927*. Oxford: Basil Blackwell, 1927.

Bessie, Alvah, ed. *The Heart of Spain: Anthology of Fiction, Non-Fiction and Poetry*. New York: Veterans of the Abraham Lincoln Brigade, 1952.

Cunard, Nancy et al., eds. *Authors Take Sides on the Spanish War*. London: Left Review, 1937.

Cunningham, Valentine, ed. *The Penguin Book of Spanish Civil War Verse*. Harmondsworth: Penguin, 1980.

Day-Lewis, C., ed. *The Echoing Green: An Anthology of Verse Book II*. Oxford: Basil Blackwell, 1937.

————, ed. *A Lasting Joy: An Anthology*. London: Unwin Books, 1973.

————, ed. *The Mind in Chains: Socialism and the Cultural Revolution*. London: Muller, 1937.

Day-Lewis, C., and John Lehmann, eds. *The Chatto Book of Modern Poetry 1915-1955*. London: Chatto and Windus, 1956.

Day-Lewis, C., and L. A. G. Strong, eds. *A New Anthology of Modern Verse 1920-1940*. London: Methuen, 1941.

de la Mare, Walter, ed. *A Garland of Prose and Verse*. New York: William Morrow, 1946.

————, ed. *Love*. London: Faber and Faber, 1943.

Grigson, Geoffrey, ed. *Poetry of the Present: An Anthology of the Thirties and After*. London: Phoenix House, 1949.

Horlock, Muriel, ed. *It Seems to Us: A Book of Thoughtful Opinions*.: London: Longmans, Green, 1958.

Kronenberger, Louis, ed. *Atlantic Brief Lives: A Biographical Companion to the Arts*. Boston: Little, Brown, 1971.

Lehmann, John, ed. *Folios of New Writing*. London: Hogarth Press, Autumn 1940.

————, ed. *Folios of New Writing*. London: Hogarth Press, Autumn 1941.

————, ed. *New Writing*. London: Hogarth Press, Autumn 1936.

————, ed. *New Writing*. London: Hogarth Press, Autumn 1937.

————, ed. *New Writing*. London: Hogarth Press, Christmas 1939.

Morrish, Hilary, Peter Orr, John Press, and Ian Scott-Kilvert, eds. *The Poet Speaks: Interviews with Contemporary Poets*. London: Routledge and Kegan Paul, 1966.

O'Donnell, Margaret J. *An Anthology of Contemporary Verse*. London and Glasgow: Blackie, 1953.

Osborne, E. Allen, ed. *In Letters of Red*. London: Michael Joseph, 1938.

Plumb, Charles, and W. H. Auden, eds. *Oxford Poetry 1926*. Oxford: Basil Blackwell, 1926.

Roberts, Denys Kilham, Gerald Gould, John Lehmann, eds. *The Year's Poetry 1935: A Representative Selection*. London: John Lane the Bodley Head, 1935.

Roberts, Denys Kilham, [and] John Lehmann, eds. *The Year's Poetry 1936: A Representative Selection*. London: John Lane the Bodley Head, 1936.

Roberts, Denys Kilham [and] Geoffrey Grigson, eds. *The Year's Poetry 1937*. London: John Lane the Bodley Head, 1937.

Roberts, Michael, ed. *New Country: Prose and Poetry by the authors of 'New Signatures.'* London: Hogarth Press, 1933.

Rodman, Selden, ed. *The Poetry of Flight*. New York: Duell, Sloan and Pearce, 1941.

Skelton, Robin, ed. *Poetry of the Thirties*. Harmondsworth: Penguin, 1964.

Smith, Janet Adam, ed. *Poems of Tomorrow: An Anthology of Contemporary Verse Chosen from 'The Listener.'* London: Chatto and Windus, 1935.

Smith, L. E. W., ed. *Speculations 2*. London: Methuen Educational, 1971.

Smith, P. G., and J. F. Wilkins, eds. *The Sheldon Book of Verse,* III. London: Oxford University Press, 1959.

Spender, Stephen, ed. *W.H. Auden: A Tribute*. London: Weidenfeld and Nicolson, 1975.

Spender, Stephen, and John Lehmann, eds. *Poems for Spain*. London: Hogarth Press, 1939.

UNESCO. *Freedom and Culture*. Intro. Julian Huxley. London: Wingate, 1951.

Woolf, Cecil, and John Bagguely. *Authors Take Sides on Vietnam: Two Questions on the War in Vietnam Answered by the Authors of Several Nations*. London: Peter Owen, 1967.

Wyatt, Woodrow, ed. *English Story: Fifth Series*. London: Collins, 1944.

SELECTED SECONDARY WORKS PARTIALLY
OR WHOLLY ABOUT REX WARNER

This section lists studies entirely about Rex Warner as well
as useful works with a chapter or one or more brief mentions
concerning him. Reviews of his work and his newspaper interviews
are cited in the text and notes only.

Allen, Walter. *Tradition and Dream*. Harmondsworth: Penguin, 1965.

Anonymous. "Rex (Ernest) Warner 1905-1986." *Contemporary Literary Criticism* 45 (1987): 426-41, Detroit: Gale, 1987.

Bergonzi, Bernard. *Reading the Thirties*. London: Macmillan, 1978.

Bowra, Maurice. *Memories, 1898-1939*. London: Weidenfeld and Nicolson, 1966.

Carpenter, Humphrey. *W. H. Auden: A Biography*. London: Unwin, 1983.

Cary, Joseph. "Rex Warner." *British Novelists 1930-1959, Part 2. Dictionary of Literary Biography*, Vol.15. Ed. Bernard Oldsey. Detroit: Gale, 1983.

Churchill, Thomas. "Rex Warner: Homage to Necessity." *Critique: Studies in Modern Fiction* 10, no. 1 (1968): 30-44.

Clark, Jon, ed. *Culture and Crisis in Britain in the 30s*. London: Lawrence and Wishart, 1979.

Cramp, Andrew. "Three British Novelists of the Thirties: Elizabeth Bowen, Patrick Hamilton, Rex Warner." Ph.D. diss., University of Loughborough, 1984.

Cunningham, Valentine. *British Writers of the Thirties*. Oxford: Oxford University Press, 1989.

Curry, Elizabeth R. "Rex Warner on the Allegorical Novel, Power Politics, and the Contemporary Scene: A Personal Interview." *Genre* 5 (1972): 404-15.

————. "Theme and Method in the Allegorical Novels of Rex Warner." Ph.D. diss., University of Wisconsin, Madison, 1963.

Daniel, Peter. *Frensham Heights, 1925-49: A Study in Progressive Education*. N.P., 1986.

Day-Lewis, C. *The Buried Day*. London: Chatto & Windus, 1960.

Day-Lewis, Sean. *C. Day-Lewis: An English Literary Life*. London: Weidenfeld and Nicolas, 1980.

De Vitis, Angelo A. "The Religious Theme in the Novels of Rex Warner, Evelyn Waugh, and Graham Greene." Ph.D. diss., University of Wisconsin, Madison, 1953.

Drenner, Don V. R. "Kafka, Warner and the Cult of Power." *Kansas Magazine* (May 1952): 62-64.

Flynn, James H. "Politics in the Novels of Rex Warner." Ph.D. diss., University of Washington, 1974.

Fraser, G. S. *The Modern Writer and His World*. London: Andre Deutsch, 1964.

Gerber, Richard. *Utopian Fantasy: A Study of English Utopian Fiction Since the End of the Nineteenth Century*. London: Routledge and Kegan Paul, 1955.

Gorliere, Claudio. "Rex Warner." *Paragone* 2 (April 1951): 76-80.

Hopkins, Chris. "A Source for Rex Warner's *The Aerodrome*." *Notes and Queries* 40, no. 238 (1993): 1, 68-69.

Hoskins, Katherine Bail. *Today the Struggle: Literature and Politics in England during the Spanish Civil War*. Austin: University of Texas Press, 1969.

Hough, Richard. *Other Days Around Me: A Memoir*. London: Hodder & Stoughton, 1992.

Howarth, Herbert. "Pieces of History." *Critique: Studies in Modern Fiction* 2, no.1 (1958): 54-64.

Hynes, Samuel. *The Auden Generation: Literature and Politics in England in the 1930's.* New York: Viking, 1977.

Johnstone, Richard. *The Will to Believe: Novelists of the Nineteen-Thirties.* Oxford: Oxford University Press, 1982.

Karl, Frederick R. *A Reader's Guide to the Contemporary English Novel.* London: Thames and Hudson, 1963.

Keeley, Edmund. "Letter to Rex Warner." *Encounter* 34, no. 2 (1970): 1968-69.

Kermode, Frank. *History and Value: The Clarendon Lectures and the Northcliffe Lectures, 1987.* Oxford: Clarendon, 1988.

Lamont, Daniel R. "The Novel and Society: A Discussion of the Novels of Christopher Isherwood and Rex Warner, 1928-1941." Ph.D. diss., Queen's University, 1973.

Lehmann, John. *In My Own Time: Memoirs of a Literary Life.* Boston: Atlantic Monthly Press, 1969.

Maini, Darshan Singh. "Rex Warner's Political Novels: An Allegorical Crusade Against Fascism." *The Indian Journal of English Studies* 2, no. 1 (1961): 91-107.

McCormick, John. *Catastrophe and Imagination: An Interpretation of the Recent English and American Novel.* London: Longmans, Green, 1957.

McLeod, A. L. *Rex Warner: Writer.* Sydney: Wentworth, 1960; 1964.

———, ed. *The Achievement of Rex Warner.* Sydney: Wentworth, 1965.

———, ed. *A Garland for Rex Warner: Essays in Honour of His Eightieth Birthday.* Mysore: The Literary Half-Yearly Press, 1985.

McLeod, A. L., and Eleanor Wyland. *A Concordance to the Poems of Rex Warner.* Lock Haven, Penn.: N.p., 1966.

Munton, Alan, and Alan Young. *Seven Writers of the British Left: A Bibliography of Literature and Politics, 1916-1980.* New York: Garland, 1981.

Needham, Joseph. *Moulds of Understanding.* London: Allen and Unwin, 1976.

Neumeyer, Peter F. "Franz Kafka and England." *German Quarterly* 40 (November 1967): 630-42.

Perez Minik, Domingo. "*El aerodromo* de Rex Warner." *Revista de Letras y Ciencias Humanas* 38 (1983): 7.

Rajan, B., and A. Pearse, eds. "A Symposium on Franz Kafka and Rex Warner." *Focus* I (1945).

Reeve, N. H. *The Novels of Rex Warner: An Introduction.* Basingstoke: Macmillan, 1989.

Rotha, Paul. *Documentary Diary: An Informal History of the British Documentary Film, 1928-1939.* New York: Hill and Wang, 1973.

Seferis, George. *A Poet's Journal: Days of 1945-51*. Trans. Athan Anagnostopoulos. Cambridge: Harvard University Press, 1974.

Spears, Monroe K. *The Poetry of W. H. Auden: The Disenchanted Island*. New York and London: Oxford, 1968.

Spender, Stephen. *Journals 1939-1983*. Ed. John Goldsmith. New York: Random House, 1986.

———. *World Within World*. London: Hamish Hamilton, 1951.

Strong, L. A. G. *Green Memory*. London: Methuen, 1961.

Tindall, William York. *Forces in Modern British Literature, 1885-1946*. New York: A.A. Knopf, 1947.

Vaughan, Paul. *Something in Linoleum*. London: Sinclair-Stevenson, 1994.

Weintraub, Stanley. *The Last Great Cause: The Intellectuals and the Spanish Civil War*. New York: Weybright and Tally, 1968.

Wiedemann, Thomas E. J. *Thucydides, The Peloponnesian War, Book I-Book II, Ch. 65: A Companion to the English Translation by Rex Warner, with introduction and commentary*. Bristol: Bristol Classical Press, 1985.

Williams, Raymond. *Culture and Society 1780-1950*. London: Chatto and Windus, 1967.

Wright, Basil. *The Long View*. New York: Alfred A. Knopf, 1984.

Wright, Patrick. "Berkshire to Beijing." *The Guardian Saturday Review*. 17 March 2001. Pages 1-2.

OTHER USEFUL WORKS

Annan, Noel. *Our Age: English Intellectuals between the World Wars—A Group Portrait*. New York: Random House, 1990.

Blythe, Ronald. *The Age of Illusion: England in the Twenties and Thirties, 1919-1940*. London: Hamish Hamilton, 1963.

Bowra, Maurice. *Homer*. New York: Scribner's, 1972.

———. *Sophoclean Tragedy*. Oxford: Oxford University Press, 1967.

Caudwell, Christopher. *Studies in a Dying Culture*. London: John Lane The Bodley Head, 1938.

Day-Lewis, C. *A Hope for Poetry*. Oxford: Basil Blackwell, 1934.

Day-Lewis, C., and Charles Fenby. *Anatomy of Oxford*. London: Jonathan Cape, 1938.

Forster, E. M. *Alexandria: A History and a Guide*. Garden City, N.Y.: Anchor, 1961.

Fox, Ralph. *The Novel and the People*. New York: International Publishers, 1945.

Grant, Cecil. *A School's Life: Addresses*. London: Marshall Brothers, 1913.

Grant, Cecil, and Norman Hodgson. *The Case for Co-Education*. London: Grant Richards, 1913.

Green, Henry. *Pack My Bag: A Self-portrait*. London: Hogarth, 1952.

Green, Martin. *Children of the Sun: A Narrative of "Decadence" in England after 1918*. New York: Basic Books, 1976.

Hearnden, Arthur, ed. *The British in Germany: Educational Reconstruction after 1945*. London: Hamish Hamilton, 1978.

Hewison, Robert. *Under Siege: Literary Life in London, 1939-1945*. New York: Oxford University Press, 1977.

Holroyd, Michael. *Lytton Strachey: A Critical Biography*. New York: Holt, Rinehart, 1968

Hollis, Christopher. *Oxford in the Twenties: Recollections of Five Friends*. London: Heinemann, 1976.

Keeley, Edmund. *Cavafy's Alexandria: A Study of a Myth in Progress*. Cambridge: Harvard, 1976.

Levin, G. Roy. *Documentary Explorations: 15 Interviews with Film-Makers*. Garden City: Doubleday, 1971.

Lloyd-Jones, Hugh. *Blood for the Ghosts: Classical Influences in the Nineteenth and Twentieth Centuries*. London: Duckworth, 1982.

Mackenzie, Compton. *Sinister Street*. New York: D. Appleton, 1930.

Mendelson, Edward. *Early Auden*. New York: Viking, 1981.

———. *Later Auden*. New York: Farrar, Straus, 1999.

Miller, Henry. *The Colossus of Maroussi*. Norfolk: New Directions, 1941.

Powell, Anthony. *Infants of the Spring: The Memoirs of Anthony Powell*. New York: Holt, Rinehart, 1977.

Radice, William, and Barbara Reynolds. *The Translator's Art: Essays Honor of Betty Radice*. Harmondsworth: Penguin, 1987.

Raizis, M. Byron. *Greek Poetry Translations: Views, Texts, Reviews*. Athens: Efstathiadis Group, 1981.

Savory, Theodore. *The Art of Translation*. Philadelphia: Dufour, 1960.

Seferis, George. *Collected Poems*. Trans. Edmund Keeley and Philip Sherrard. Princeton: Princeton University Press, 1981.

Simons, Judy. *Rosamond Lehmann*. New York: St. Martin's Press, 1992.

Smith, D. *Socialist Propaganda in the Twentieth-Century British Novel.* London: Macmillan, 1978.

Spender, Stephen. *Forward from Liberalism.* London: Gollancz, 1937.

———. *Trial of a Judge.* London: Faber, 1938.

Stansky, Peter, and William Abrahams. *Journey to the Frontier: Julian Bell and John Cornford: Their Lives and the 1930s.* London: Constable, 1966.

Stevenson, John. *British Society 1914-45.* Harmondsworth: Penguin, 1984.

Symons, Julian. *The General Strike: A Historical Portrait.* London: Cresset Press, 1957.

Waugh, Evelyn. *A Little Learning, An Autobiography: The Early Years.* Boston: Little, Brown, 1964.

West, Francis. *Gilbert Murray—A Life.* London: Croom Helm, 1984.

Wilson, Duncan. *Gilbert Murray OM 1866-1957.* Oxford: Clarendon Press, 1987.

Zervos, Christian, and Dora Iliopoulou-Rogan. *Ghika.* Athens: Adam Editions, 1991.

NOTES

ACKNOWLEDGMENTS

1. Because they are in the possession of Mrs. Ambrose, I have identified these letters in the endnotes by "Ambrose" and the number that she has assigned each letter. These numbers, however, are largely arbitrary and do not arrange the letters in any order, or follow any particular order within the letters themselves.

2. See Sean Day-Lewis, *C. Day-Lewis: An English Literary Life* (London: Weidenfeld and Nicolson, 1980), xiii.

INTRODUCTION

1. C. Day-Lewis, *The Buried Day* (London: Chatto and Windus, 1960), 123. A small treatise could be written about Day-Lewis's changing attitudes concerning his own inclusion or omission of the hyphen in his name. For the purpose of consistency, I have opted to retain the hyphen in his name throughout the book, except where it has been omitted in a direct quotation.

CHAPTER 1

1. Rex Warner, one of four "Essays July-1917," 6, Berg Collection, New York Public Library.

2. The manuscript, consisting of only seven 7 1/2 x 11 3/4-inch lined pages, is in my possession.

3. Frederic was always called by his middle name, Ernest, in the family, but in this biography I have used his first name to avoid confusion.

4. Rex Warner, "Essay on Gloucester" in "Essays July-1917," 7, Berg Collection, New York Public Library.

5. Ibid., 6.

6. Ibid., 10.

7. I owe Pam Weatherley a debt of thanks for many of these facts.

8. Letter of 3 October 1988 to author. See also Close's *A Village of Parts: A History of Amberley Parish* (Cheltenham: n.p, 1986), 26, 27.

9. Rex Warner, autobiography manuscript, pp. 3-4.

10. Warner, "Essay on Gloucester," 7-8.

11. This is the second of the "Essays July-1917" in the Berg Collection. The story is about a Protestant aristocrat murdered in the time of Catholic Queen Mary who as a ghost commits the murder of two students in his turn.

12. M. A. J. Tarver, *Trent College, 1868-1927; A Rough Sketch* (London: G. Bell, 1929), 103-17.

13. Warner, "Essay on Gloucester," 11.

14. I am indebted for much of my information about the Warner family to John Basil Goode, Rex's cousin, born 28 April 1906, and to Mrs. Frances Warner. Daniel F. Poffenberger, a professional genealogist, supplied me with many of the documents upon which my history of the Warner and Luce families is based.

15. Rex Warner, one of four "Essays July-1917," Berg Collection, New York Public Library; written while he was at St. George's School, Harpenden.

16. Rex Warner, *Views of Attica and Its Surroundings* (London: John Lehmann, 1950), 27.

17. R. B. McDowell and D. A. Webb, *Trinity College Dublin 1592-1952: An Academic History* (Cambridge: Cambridge University Press, 1982), 353.

18. McDowell and Webb, *Trinity College Dublin*, 490.

19. Ibid., 490-91.

20. J. S. Furnivall, "G.H. Luce-in the Round," *New Burma Weekly*, 24 January 1959, p. 113.

21. John Luce and A. B. Griswold, "In Memoriam Gordon Hannington Luce, C. B. E., D.Litt.," *Artibus Asiae*, Separatum 42, no. 1 (1980): 115-18; D. G. E. Hall, "Obituary Gordon Hannington Luce," *Bulletin of the School of Oriental and African Studies* 43, part 3 (1980): 580-88; *New Burma Weekly* 4, no. 4 (24 January 1959).

22. The notebook is in the possession of Mrs. Frances Warner.

CHAPTER 2

1. Pam Weatherley, *A History of St. George's School Harpenden* (Harpenden: St. George's School Association of Parents and Staff, 1991), 24.

2. In the possession of Mrs. Frances Warner.

3. Weatherley, *A History*, 22.

4. Ibid.

5. In my possession.

6. V. Boyce, "In Memory of Cecil Grant," *The Georgian*, Special Supplement (1946): 33.

7. Weatherley, *A History*, 14-15.

8. Ibid., 16.

9. Letter of 22 November 1988 from James Will to author.

10. Cecil Grant and Norman Hodgson, *The Case for Co-Education* (London: Grant Richards, 1913), 307.

11. *Georgian* 17, no. 1 (spring 1922): 3.

12. *Georgian* (spring term 1922): 10.

13. *Georgian* 17, no. 1 (spring term 1923): 3.

14. This is the third essay in "Essays July-1917," Berg Collection, New York Public Library.

15. *Georgian* 13, no. 2 (July 1919): 44.

16. *Georgian* 16, no. 3 (winter term, 1922): 46.

17. *Georgian* 17, no. 3 (winter 1923): 49.

18. Page 32.

19. *Georgian* 16, no. 2 (summer term, 1922): 22.

20. *Georgian* , 15, no. 2 (summer term, 1921): 29.

21. John Cox, *75 Not Out*, vol. 1 (n.p., n.d.): 32.

22. Letter of 14 October 1988 to author.

23. Letter of 23 November 1988 to author.

24. Letter of 23 October 1988 from Dr. Sheila Hines to author.

25. In the possession of Mrs. Frances Warner.

26. *Georgian* 9, no. 27 (December 1915): 110.

27. In the possession of Mrs. Frances Warner.

28. *Georgian* 13, no. 24 (December 1914): 64.

29. *Georgian* 11, no. 32 (July 1917): 19.

30. In "Essays July-1917," 28.

31. *Georgian* (July 1919): 40.

32. *Georgian* 13, no. 2 (July 1919): 39-40.

33. Ibid., 55.

34. Undated holograph in the Berg Collection, New York Public Library.

35. *Georgian* 13, no. 2 (July 1919): 13.

36. *Georgian* 17, no.1 (summer 1923): 13.

37. Rex Warner, "The Greek and Latin Classics," in *Rex Warner Personal Impressions: Talks on Writers and Writing*, ed. Marian B. McLeod (Sydney: Wentworth Press, 1986), 59.

38. Other American connections that might have influenced Rex: the American Admiral Sims appeared at a Speech Day after the war, and St. George's had an association with a private school in Rhode Island. Mr. Howe's report followed a visit there.

39. Margaret Budd recalled this during the memorial service for Dr. Watts.

40. *Georgian* 11, no. 33 (December 1917): 13.

41. Rex Warner, "Sonnet," five holograph poems, Berg Collection, New York Public Library. The other poems are clearly labeled age fifteen, and this one seems to be written at the same time.

42. *Georgian* (spring 1923): 6.

43. *Georgian* 17, no. 1 (spring 1923): 11.

44. Reported in *The Georgian* 17, no. 3 (winter 1923): 43-45.

CHAPTER 3

1. Letter of 31 August 1989 to author.

2. Letter of 17 September 1989 to author.

3. Tom Hopkinson, *Of This Our Time: A Journalist's Story, 1905-50* (London: Hutchinson, 1982), 94-95.

4. Cecil Day-Lewis, *The Buried Day* (London: Chatto & Windus, 1960), 175.

5. Evelyn Waugh, *A Little Learning: The First Volume of an Autobiography*, vol. 1 (London: Chapman & Hall, 1964), 168.

6. Letter of 25 August 1989 from Robert Hodges to author.

7. Letter of 17 September 1989 to author.

8. Letter of 30 August 1989 from Lance Garrard to author.

9. Day-Lewis, *Buried Day*, 161-62.

10. Anthony Powell, *Infants of the Spring: The Memoirs of Anthony Powell* (New York: Holt, Rinehart, 1977), 143.

11. Andrew Cramp, "Prose Fiction in the 1930s: A Study of Elizabeth Bowen, Rex Warner and Patrick Hamilton" (Ph.D. diss., Loughborough University, 1984), 357.

12. Waugh, *A Little Learning*, 168-69.

13. Powell, *Infants of the Spring*, 143.

14. Maurice Bowra, *Memories, 1898-1939* (London: Weidenfeld and Nicolson, 1966), 149.

15. Letter of August 1989 to author.

16. *Wadham Gazette* 3, no. 3 (January 1988): 55-57.

17. Christopher Hollis, *Oxford in the Twenties: Recollections of Five Friends* (London: Heinemann, 1976), 19.

18. The book *Oxford of Today* (New York: Oxford University Press, 1923), published as a guide for prospective American Rhodes scholars coming to study at Oxford, describes precisely

what would be expected in these examinations in Greek and Latin literature, which would be taken in the student's fifth term. This helps us appreciate Rex's magnificent achievement. In this book, Laurence A. Crosby writes that the Honours Moderations in Greek and Latin Literature "demands of the candidate a thorough and critical knowledge of Latin and Greek texts, and a thorough command of Latin and Greek prose composition. It is the most difficult of the Intermediate Examinations. . . . The subjects of the examination include:

1. Translations of passages from Homer, Virgil, Demosthenes, and Cicero's orations.

2. Translations of passages from Greek and Latin authors other than the above named.

3. Portions of Greek and Latin authors specially offered; candidates are required to offer three books selected from a prescribed list and to answer questions bearing upon their contents, style and literary history.

4. Questions are also set in Greek and Latin grammar, literary criticism and antiquities.

5. Candidates must offer one of the following subjects:

History of the Greek Drama, with Aristotle's Poetics.

History of Attic Oratory.

History of Roman Poetry to the end of the Augustan Age.

History of Latin Prose Style.

The Elements of Deductive Logic.

Comparative Philology as applied to Greek and Latin with a special knowledge of Greek or Latin Philology, or the Historical and Analytical Syntax of the Greek and Latin Languages.

Outlines of the history of Greek Sculpture.

Homeric Archaeology.

The elements of either Greek or Latin textual criticism.

The detailed study of a Greek or Roman Site.

6. Latin Prose Composition.

Papers are also set in Greek Prose Composition, and in Greek and Latin Verse Composition; candidates who omit either or both of these papers are strongly recommended to offer additional work under other parts of the examination." Crosby notes that "in the assignment of Honours account is taken of the total amount of work offered by the candidate and of the average of excellence attained by his papers as a whole" (69). He goes on to remark that "Honour Mods contains something like the American courses in Greek and Latin literature in the detailed study of certain prescribed texts; it includes, however, a far wider range of supplementary reading both in the ancient authors and in modern literary and textual criticism bearing on them. A man who has done well in Honour Mods has an intelligent acquaintance with the whole field of Greek and Latin literature, and a real command of the essentials of grammar and prose composition" (72-73).

19. Letter of 30 August 1989 to author.

20. Letter of 1989 to author.

21. Letter of 28 August 1989 to author.

22. Julian Symons, *The General Strike: A Historical Portrait* (London: Cresset Press, 1957), 62.

23. Ibid., 67.

24. Hollis, *Oxford in the Twenties*, 27.

25. Day-Lewis, *Buried Day*, 171.

26. Cecil Day-Lewis, *Starting Point* (New York: Harper, 1938), 58-59.

27. Letter of 1989 to author.

28. Letter of 12 September 1989 to author.

29. Letter of 12 October 1989 from Cyril Davies to author.

30. Quoted by L. Wilson in a letter of 21 September 1989 to author.

31. Rex Warner and Gabriel Carritt, "Auden at Oxford," *W.H. Auden: A Tribute*, ed. Stephen Spender (New York: Macmillan, 1975), 48.

32. Warner and Carritt, "Auden," 48.

33. L. A. G. Strong, *Green Memory* (London: Methuen, 1961), 185-86.

34. Day-Lewis, *Buried Day*, 166.

35. From the Star Inn, Alfriston, Sussex, Michigan State Special Collections, MS 45.

36. These letters of recommendation are in the possession of Mrs. Frances Warner.

37. Allison Danzig, *The Racquet Game* (New York: Macmillan, 1930), 114-15.

38. Ibid.,114-15.

39. In the possession of Mrs. Frances Warner.

40. Cramp, "Prose Fiction," 357.

41. Ibid., 359.

42. In Sean Day-Lewis, *C. Day-Lewis: An English Literary Life* (London: Weidenfeld and Nicolson, 1980), 310.

43. In the possession of Mrs. Frances Warner.

44. Richard Boston, "Warner's Warning," *Guardian*, 12 November 1983.

45. In the possession of Mrs. Frances Warner.

46. Dated 15 January 1958. Among 20 ALS concerning Rex Warner's *Julius Caesar* novels, Harry Ransom Humanities Research Center, the University of Texas at Austin.

CHAPTER 4

1. Humphrey Carpenter, *W.H. Auden: A Biography* (London: Unwin, 1983), 128.

2. Ibid., 129.

3. Letter of 24 October 1983 to author.

4. Rex Warner, *The Wild Goose Chase* (London: Merlin, 1990), 113.

5. In my possession at the time of writing.

6. Dated 15 September 1931. In the possession of Mrs. Frances Warner.

7. Page 634.

8. Rex Warner, "Holiday," *New Statesman* (29 March 1930): 804-5.

9. Ibid., 805.

10. Andrew Cramp, "Prose Fiction in the 1930s: A Study of Elizabeth Bowen, Rex Warner and Patrick Hamilton" (Ph.D. diss., Loughborough University, 1984), 361-62. At least one of these notebooks is in the collection of Rex's manuscripts in the Michigan State University Library's Special Collections.

11. Alan Munton and Alan Young, *Seven Writers of the English Left: A Bibliography of Literature and Politics, 1916-1980* (New York: Garland, 1981), 169.

12. Cramp, "Prose Fiction," 361.

13. Ibid.

14. In my possession at the time of writing. This letter is undated except for "Monday," "Tuesday," and "Thursday," but I have been able to fix it at around October 1931 because of its internal evidence, including its mention of the recent publication of Day-Lewis's *From Feathers to Iron*, which took place in September 1931.

15. In a letter to Professor Peter Neumeyer written long after this time, Rex wrote:

> I certainly came across Kafka first in the Muir translation (I can't read German anyway). The first I read was *The Castle* and it impressed me very much. I think . . . that it impressed me even more stylistically than psychologically. Indeed Edwin Muir once wrote to me to say that to him my work seemed, while using some of the methods of Kafka, to be directed in a quite different direction, being rather extravert than introvert. I rather agree—though of course these terms are pretty difficult to apply with any accuracy. The sort of things which delighted me in Kafka I had already observed in Dickens and in Dostoievsky. Indeed if I were asked what novelist had chiefly influenced me, I should name these two and Smollett and Fielding before Kafka.

Quoted in Peter Neumeyer, "Franz Kafka and England," *The German Quarterly* 40, no. 4 (1967): 634-35.

16. Warner, *Wild Goose*, 100.

17. In the possession of Mrs. Frances Warner. Although dated only "Tuesday," this letter, written in Cheltenham, is very similar in format to Day-Lewis's other letters from around this period. And since Day-Lewis in a P.S. invites Rex for the weekend, it had to be written before Rex left for Egypt.

18. I have fixed this date and ship as follows: A copy of Lucretius's *De Rerum Natura* in Rex's personal library is dedicated "For Rex Wells 18 February 1932." This was from Wells Coates,

Frances's sister Marion's first husband, and undoubtedly given to Rex as a departure present. The shipping news informs us that the *S.S. Rawalpindi*, a P & O liner, sailed for Bombay on 19 February 1932. It would of course pass through the Suez Canal on the way to Bombay, and passengers for Egypt could disembark then. This fits with Frances's memory that Rex left in "early spring," because the *Rawalpindi* did not sail again from England until 10 June.

19. Rex's reappearance in England shows up in Mary Day-Lewis's diary as a visit of 1-4 July 1934, at which time his address is given as Amberley Rectory. I thank Sean-Day Lewis for showing me these diary dates.

20. Cramp, "Prose Fiction," 358.

21. This and the subsequent Day-Lewis letters to Rex in this chapter are in the possession of Mrs. Frances Warner.

22. From "Egyptian Kites," in Rex Warner, *Poems* (New York: Knopf, 1938), 32.

23. From "Khamseen," *Poems*, 27.

24. From "Nile Fishermen," *Poems*, 29.

25. Frances remembers that she came to Egypt when Anna was three months old, that is, in January or February 1933, and that Rex was living in Alexandria then. Day-Lewis's letter of 3 October 1932 is still addressed to Rex in Minia.

26. Gwyn Williams, *ABC of (D.)G.W.: A Kind of Autobiography* (Llandysul, Dyfed: Gomer Press, 1981), 65.

27. ALS to John Lehmann 1936-1945, Harry Ransom Humanities Research Center, University of Texas, Austin. ALS indicates "autograph letters signed" here and elsewhere in these notes.

28. Ibid.

29. "Choruses from 'The Dam,'" in *New Country: Prose and Poetry by the Authors of 'New Signatures,'* ed. Michael Roberts (London: Hogarth Press, 1933), 252.

30. Ibid., 251.

31. Ibid., 253.

32. Rex Warner, "Hymn," in *New Country*, 256.

33. Rex Warner, *The Kite* (Oxford: Basil Blackwell, 1936).

34. Rex Warner letter to Alan McLeod, 11 December 1965. Rex Warner manuscripts and letters to Alan McLeod, Pennsylvania State University Rare Books Room, #1997-0038R.

35. Warner, *Kite*, 13.

36. Ibid., 14.

37. Ibid., 42.

38. Ibid., 132.

39. Ibid., 30-32.

40. Marian McLeod, "Juvenilia and *The Kite*," in *A Garland for Rex Warner: Essays in Honour of His Eightieth Birthday*, ed. Alan McLeod (Mysore: Literary Half-Yearly Press, 1985), 72.

41. As Marian McLeod points out, it is the only book in its series to have been reprinted, and as recently as 1963. Her article contains an excellent comparison between the original 1936 edition and the abridged 1963 edition in the Hamish Hamilton "Big Reindeer Books" series for children.

42. Warner, *Kite*, 43-44.

43. Ibid., 214.

44. Ibid., 214-15.

45. Ibid., 125.

46. E.M. Forster, *Alexandria: A History and a Guide* (Garden City, N.Y.: Anchor, 1961), 103-4.

47. Ibid., 181.

CHAPTER 5

1. Mary Day-Lewis's diary shows that Rex visited on 1 July-4 July 1934; on 13-14 July when he visited again, his address is given as 33 Midvale Road, St. Helier, Jersey (Frances's parents' address); when he visited on 15-17 September 1934, his address is Middle Park Cottage, Frensham Heights School.

2. In the possession of Mrs. Frances Warner.

3. Quoted in Peter Daniel, *Frensham Heights, 1925-49: A Study in Progressive Education* (n.p., n.p., 1986), 44.

4. Ibid., 121.

5. Ibid., 122.

6. Richard Hough, *Other Days Around Me: A Memoir* (London: Hodder & Stoughton, 1992), 125-26.

7. Daniel, *Frensham Heights*, 126.

8. Ibid., 48.

9. Ibid., 58.

10. Rex Warner, *Poems* (New York: Knopf, 1938), 52. The contents of this American edition are identical to those of the 1937 Boriswood edition, but the pagination is different.

11. Hough, *Other Days*, 18.

12. Janet Adam Smith, comp., *Poems of Tomorrow: An Anthology of Contemporary Verse Chosen From 'The Listener'* (London: Chatto and Windus, 1935).

13. ALS from Rex Warner to John Lehmann, 1935-60, Harry Ransom Humanities Research Center, University of Texas at Austin.

14. Published in *Poems* (New York: Knopf, 1938), 30-31.

15. ALS from Rex Warner to John Lehmann, 1935-60, Harry Ransom Humanities Research Center, University of Texas, Austin.

16. *Poems*, 4. First published in *The Year's Poetry 1935: A Representative Selection*, comp. Denys Kilham Roberts, Gerald Gould, [and] John Lehmann (London: John Lane the Bodley Head, 1935), 97.

17. Part of the manuscript of his revised *Poems*, which appeared under the title *Poems and Contradictions* in 1945. Michigan State University Library Special Collections, Greenwood collection of Rex Warner material, MS 50.

18. Denys Kilham Roberts [and] John Lehmann, comps., *The Year's Poetry 1936: A Representative Selection* (London: John Lane the Bodley Head, 1936), 66.

19. ALS to John Lehmann 1936-1945, Harry Ransom Humanities Research Center, University of Texas, Austin.

20. John Lehmann, *In My Own Time* (Boston: Little, Brown, 1969), 159.

21. ALS from Rex Warner to John Lehmann 1936-1945, Harry Ransom Humanities Research Center, University of Texas, Austin.

22. This pamphlet, published by the *Left Review*, has Day-Lewis's name on it, and is claimed for Day-Lewis in Geoffry Handley-Taylor and Timothy d'Arch Smith, *C. Day-Lewis, The Poet Laureate: A Bibliography* (Chicago: St. James Press, 1968), but according to Munton and Young, "The British Library catalog now accepts that this pamphlet was written by Rex Warner." Alan Munton and Alan Young, *Seven Writers of the English Left: A Bibliography of Literature and Politics, 1916-1980* (New York: Garland, 1981), 175. Rex told Munton and Young that he had written the pamphlet because Day-Lewis was too busy. A letter of 19 February 1938 from Rex to Lehmann (ALS to John Lehmann, 1936-45) offers possible evidence that Munton and Young are right. Rex writes there that ". . . The two themes which appeal to me at the moment are (i) Pacifism (a reply to Huxley's arguments) (ii) a plea for less realism in the novel." No doubt the immediate cause of this letter is the publication in late 1937 of Huxley's "Ends and Means," which extended his earlier pacifist argument. But in any case this letter offers clear evidence that Rex was directly concerned with Huxley's arguments for pacifism, albeit over a year after "We're Not Going to Do Nothing" was published. But it is also notable that a poem by Rex attacking pacifists had already appeared in 1935:

> On lovely levels, whining in a wash of gold
> pacifists, pale as porridge, are burying bugles,
> who feel no fight, who are learned liberals.
> Blow, bugle, blow! Let loose, lungs, over the meadows
> to tell these twisters that war is being waged
> cruelly in complete peace and pleasant pastures.

This poem, "Pacifists," published in the *Left Review* 1, no. 10 (1935): 396, seems to have been influenced by Tennyson's dreamy and apolitical "The Splendor Falls," which contains the phrase "Blow, bugle, blow." By adapting Tennyson's as well as Hopkins's mannerisms for political purposes, Rex seems intent on playing on the tensions between a secure Victorian past and the political uncertainties of the present.

Some internal indications that Rex did indeed write "We're Not Going to Do Nothing" are the historical allusions (on page 11) to the Roman empire, Augustus, and the battles of Marathon and Salamis—but Day-Lewis knew his classical allusions too and so this is less than conclusive. More to the point, we find references to Plato and to Huxley as an idealist thinker on page 12, as well as to Ivan Karamazov, and Rex was far more adept at philosophizing than Cecil was. Moreover, he was a devoted student of Dostoyevsky at this time.

There is a lack of unique Warnerian stylistic traits in this pamphlet, but it was only journalistic, not a carefully crafted work of art.

23. Stephen Spender, "Fable and Reportage," *Left Review* 2, no. 14 (1936): 782.

24. Michigan State University Library Special Collections, MS 61, Julia Greenwood's introduction to the collection of Rex's papers.

25. Hough, *Other Days*, 125.

26. Michigan State University Library Special Collections, Greenwod collection, MS 61.

27. Hough, *Other Days*, 126.

28. Almost all of Rex's letters to Greenwood that appear in this and subsequent chapters are from MS 45 of the Greenwood collection of Rex's materials, Michigan State University Library Special Collections.

29. The *Poems* contract states that the title is to be mutually agreed upon, that the book shall be published in 1937, and that royalties are to be 10 percent of the published price of the first 1,000 copies and 15 percent on all sales thereafter. A £10 advance is to be paid on the date of publication and Rex is to receive six free copies. The publisher is entitled to 10 percent of what the author receives for broadcast rights, but there is an addendum dated 22/10/45 that states: "Mr. Greenwood says apportion B/C in future at 2/3 author 1/3 Pub." Obviously Rex's stock had gone up from the time of his first publication in 1937 to 1945, when his poems' broadcasting rights were worth something to the publisher.

According to the terms of the *Wild Goose* contract, the final version of the book is to be delivered "no later than May 1, 1937." Rex's royalties are to be "10% of 1st 2000 sold, 15% of the following 5,500 copies sold, and 20% of all sales in excess of 7,500." He is to receive an advance of £40 on 1 July 1937, and Boriswood is to receive an option on his next two full-length works of prose. The Rex Warner contracts file in Reading University Library's Bodley Head Archive contains many of his other contracts as well.

30. ALS from Rex Warner to John Lehmann 1936-1945, Harry Ransom Humanities Research Center, University of Texas, Austin.

31. *Twentieth Century Verse* 1 (January 1937): [8].

32. These editions have identical pagination, although the Merlin edition has the Cramp introduction and lacks the wild goose poem but not the epigram at the beginning.

33. Michigan State Greenwood collection, MS 49.

34. As stated previously in note 32, the original 1937 Boriswood and the 1990 Merlin editions have identical pagination, but the poem that begins the Boriswood edition has been omitted from the Merlin.

35. "Hymn" appears on page 201 of the typescript.

36. Michigan State Greenwood collection, MS 49, p. 20.

37. When I was working on my T. E. Lawrence dissertation with Rex in 1970-71, he mentioned casually once that he had done some unpublished writing about Lawrence a long time ago. He had no idea where it was. Imagine my delight when I discovered in 1989 a manuscript of thirty-five 8-inch x 13-inch ruled notebook pages, grouped with a similar thirty-two-page manuscript about the Norwegian North Pole explorer Fridtjof Nansen, in MS 53 of the Greenwood collection at Michigan State. These manuscripts were two chapters of a never-completed book on adventurers, probably part of the prospectus for the book that Greenwood decided not to publish for some reason. I estimate the date of the manuscript as 1937 or 1938 for certain external and internal reasons.

The external evidence is that Rex would probably not have been emboldened to submit a prospectus for a nonfiction work until his other, fictional and poetic work had achieved some success—and that would have been 1936 at the earliest, with *The Kite*, and probably 1937 when the *Poems* and *The Wild Goose Chase* were published. A second external reason is that in the manuscript description of that novel that he wrote for Greenwood on 3 May 1937 (quoted in text), he mentions Lawrence—showing not only that he had read Lawrence's *Seven Pillars of Wisdom* by that date, but that he was thinking about Lawrence around that time.

The internal evidence that Rex's manuscript chapters on Lawrence and Nansen were written circa 1937 or 1938 is that Rex does not mention the Lawrence discussion in Christopher Caudwell's *Studies in a Dying Culture*, published in 1938, although Rex usually mentions his sources and he would undoubtedly have known of that book's publication fairly quickly. The sources that he does mention are Robert Graves's 1927 biography of Lawrence and Liddell Hart's of 1934. Moreover, in the Nansen chapter in particular, Rex displays the overt sympathy for Marxism, and especially for Nansen's efforts to aid Bolshevik Russia in the face of Western intervention, that marked Rex's affinities in the middle and later thirties until the signing of the Molotov-Ribbentrop Pact in August 1939. In addition, Rex, who at St. George's had served on an Armenian relief committee, writes in the Nansen chapter that "the sufferings of the Armenians are without parallel in history." Rex visited the Nazi concentration camps in 1945 right after World War II and was permanently horrified by what he saw there. Not to minimize Armenian sufferings, it is fair to assume that he would have at least mentioned the Holocaust in this statement were it written during or after World War II. All of this evidence, taken together, indicates that Rex's Lawrence chapter was written before 1945 and most probably before, or early in, 1938.

38. Andrew Cramp, "Prose Fiction in the 1930s: A Study of Elizabeth Bowen, Rex Warner and Patrick Hamilton" (Ph.D. diss., 1984), 361.

39. Cecil Day-Lewis, *The Buried Day* (London: Chatto & Windus), 216.

40. Christopher Caudwell, *Studies in a Dying Culture* (London: John Lane, 1948), 39. Originally published in 1938.

41. Chris Hopkins, "A Source for Rex Warner's *The Aerodrome*," *Notes and Queries* 40, no. 238 (1993): 1, 68-69.

42. N. H. Reeve, *The Novels of Rex Warner: An Introduction* (London: Macmillan, 1989),145. But it is worth noting that on 23 April 1950, Rex sent Greenwood a reader's report on a still-unpublished critical work by Herbert Howarth entitled *Six Literary Legends*, in which Rex commented that Howarth's "T.E. Lawrence essay isn't immediately as impressive as the essay by Caudwell, for example; but I think that this chap, in having wider + less definite terms of reference, probably gets nearer the truth than Caudwell." This statement shows that Rex by this date preferred a liberal and relatively unideological view to Caudwell's Marxist perspective, and that he was not consciously at least thinking of Caudwell when he described Caesar in his novel later on. Rex does not mention Caudwell in his Lawrence chapter, so he probably read him after he wrote it, perhaps in the very late 1930s.

43. *The Cult of Power* was published in 1946, but some of the ideas in his essays in that book appear as early as 1937 elsewhere in his work.

44. For perceptive commentary on Brown's ideas, see Valentine Cunningham, *British Writers of the Thirties* (Oxford: Oxford University Press, 1989), 320.

45. In a letter of 22 September 1982 to Alan McLeod, Rex commented that Don Antonio is meant to be a caricature of Italian writer Gabriele d'Annunzio (1863-1928), who glorified the instincts. Rex Warner manuscripts and letters to Alan McLeod, Pennsylvania State University Rare Books Library, Pennsylvania State University Libraries, #1997-0038R.

46. Rex Warner, *The Wild Goose Chase* (London: Boriswood, 1937), 441-42.

47. In the letter of 22 September 1982 to McLeod cited earlier, Rex states that the first king is meant to be a caricature of Sir Oswald Mosley (1896-1980), who resigned from the Labour Party and after a visit to Mussolini's Italy founded the British Union of Fascists, which supported Hitler.

48. Warner, *Wild Goose*, 15.

49. From Hermocrates' speech to the Syracusans in Thucydides, *The Peloponnesian War*, trans. Rex Warner (London: Cassell, 1962), 388.

50. Warner, *Wild Goose*, 440.

51. See Winston Weathers, "The Rhetoric of the Series," *Contemporary Essays on Style* (Glenview, Ill.: Scott-Foresman, 1969), 21-27.

52. *Peloponnesian War*, 9.

53. For a more detailed look at Rex's use of stylistic devices in this novel, see Stephen E. Tabachnick, "In Pursuit of The, Wild Goose Chase," in *A Garland for Rex Warner*, ed. A.L. McLeod (Mysore, India: Literary Half Yearly, 1985), 77-88.

54. Joseph Needham, *Moulds of Understanding* (London: Allen and Unwin, 1976), 50. First published in *The Cambridge Review*, 20 May 1938, p. 412.

55. London *Times*, 1 October 1937, p. 8.

56. Harold Strauss, *New York Times Book Review*, 23 January 1938, p. 2.

57. Herbert Howarth finds Rex "an eighteenth century classicist, insistent on the use of a rational prose" in "Pieces of History," *Critique* 2 (1958): 63. Walter Allen writes that "The prose, good as it is, has a formal quality that removes it from the contemporary scene" and attributes it to neoclassical models, in *Tradition and Dream* (Harmondsworth: Penguin, 1965), 262. Thomas Churchill's description, albeit written about *The Aerodrome*, is perhaps the best: "There is a sonorousness, a distance and nostalgia—something uncanny-civilized about the prose. The style is always mixing moods and toying with one's sense of time; Warner's balanced periods take one back at least to the 18th century, yet invariably reveal a contemporary spirit, a real gentleness and virile humor that sounds most amused when confronted by pretension and that which is bizarre in human behavior," "Rex Warner: Homage to Necessity," *Critique* 18 (1967): 32.

58. V. S. Pritchett, *New Statesman*, 25 September 1937, p. 448.

59. Alick West, "Wild Goose Chase," *Left Review* 3, no. 10 (1937): 630-31.

60. Cramp, "Prose Fiction," 369.

61. Day-Lewis, *Buried Day*, 219-20.

62. N. H. Reeve, *Novels of Rex Warner*, 46.

63. See also, for instance, Rex's interview with Elizabeth Curry, in which Rex, discussing *The Aerodrome*, admitted that around that time "the democracies were pretty hopeless and did nothing.... And one did feel something of an attraction toward some clear-cut way of looking at things, which is what the Air Vice-Marshal represents." But Rex added immediately, "But if that's going to be at the cost of cutting one's human relations. . .then it's too great a cost, and the idea doesn't take one anyplace." "Rex Warner: on the Allegorical Novel, Power Politics, and the Contemporary Scene: A Personal Interview," *Genre* 5, no. 4 (1972): 407.

64. Rex Warner, "Arms in Spain," *Left Review* 3, no. 3 (1937): 139.

65. Cramp, "Prose Fiction," 363-64.

66. Rex Warner, "Education," in *The Mind in Chains: Socialism and the Cultural Revolution*, comp. Cecil Day-Lewis (London: F. Muller, 1937), 26-27.

67. Ibid., 36.

68. Montagu Slater, "Prometheus Unbound," *Left Review* 3, no. 6 (1936): 364.

69. Rex Warner, "Jonathan Swift: Defender of Liberty," *Left Review* 3, no. 5 (1937): 268.

70. Stephen Spender, "Poetry," *Fact* 4 (1937): 24.

71. From "Poem" in *Poems*, 62.

72. Ibid., 62.

73. "Nile Fishermen," *Poems*, 28-29.

74. Louise Bogan, "Revolution in Wonderland," *The Nation* 146, no. 5 (29 January 1938): 129-30.

75. *The New Yorker*, 15 January 1938, p. 64.

76. Edgell Rickword, *Left Review* 2, no. 7 (April 1936): 339-40.

77. The "Directions" read as follows:

I wish my body *to be cremated* for the following reasons:

(1) as a protest against materialistic theories of "the resurrection of the body";

(2) as being the only sanitary + wholesome way of disposing of it;

(3) as objecting to the veneration of graves and gravestones.

(Let me rather leave a memorial in the hearts of those who love me).

My ashes I should like sprinkled on the ground provided for that purpose near the crematorium.

Most of the Service I should like held in Amberley Church—*no flowers, no mourning worn*—and no melancholy hymns and music.

Service from New Prayer Book. Ps. 23, and for Lesson 2 Cor. 4.16-5.10 Hymns 171, 524. with regard to music I would suggest "Oh rest in the Lord" "But the Lord is mindful"— "The Londonderry Air." . . . but nothing gloomy or depressing.

I would like Mr. Ratcliffe to act as undertakers and some of my many Amberley men friends to act as bearers.

Eve of S. Michael. All Angels 1933.

78. Rex Warner, "Visit to a Mine," in In *Letters of Red*, ed. Eric Allen Osborne (London: Michael Joseph, 1938), 265-72. Why the chapter was omitted is not clear because it contains hilarious cartoon-like images of policemen: "Some wore dinner jackets and had hung toy balloons to the manes of their horses or to the barrels of their rifles. . . . He looked into the officer's eyes, and was fascinated by them, for they were not the eyes of an ordinary man. The pupils expanded so far as almost to fill the sockets when the

policeman drew in his breath and contracted again to pin-points when he exhaled" (269). The anthology also includes reprints of Rex's essay on Swift and "Arms in Spain."

79. Manuscripts of the *Poems* are included in the materials of the Greenwood collection at Michigan State (MS 50), indicating that Greenwood, to whom Rex had sent them, held on to them. Rex later stated that he had donated the manuscript of *The Wild Goose Chase* to an auction for leftist causes.

80. Letter of 10 January 1938 from Rex to Lehmann, 49 ALS to John Lehmann 1938-1969, Harry Ransom Humanities Research Center, University of Texas, Austin.

81. ALS from Rex Warner to John Lehmann 1936-1945, Harry Ransom Humanities Research Center, the University of Texas, Austin.

82. "Modern English Poetry," *International Literature* (Moscow) 7 (July 1939): 80-85.

83. ALS from Rex Warner to John Lehmann 1936-1945, Harry Ransom Humanities Research Center, the University of Texas, Austin.

84. This letter, however, is not in the Rex Warner materials at Michigan State, but among the letters in the possession of Anne Ambrose.

85. Sean Day-Lewis, *C. Day-Lewis: An English Literary Life* (London: Weidenfeld & Nicolson, 1980), 111.

86. ALS from Rex Warner to John Lehmann 1936-1945, Harry Ransom Humanities Research Center, the University of Texas, Austin.

87. Ambrose, #49.

88. Author interview with Mrs. Frances Warner.

89. ALS from Rex Warner to John Lehmann 1936-1945, Harry Ransom Humanities Research Center, the University of Texas, Austin.

90. N. H. Reeve, *Novels of Rex Warner*, 58.

91. Stephen Spender, "An Open Letter to Aldous Huxley on his 'Case for Constructive Peace,'" *Left Review* 2, no. 11 (1936): 540.

92. *Left Review* 3, no. 15 (1938): 904-9.

93. Michigan State University Library Special Collections, MS 51.

94. Rex Warner, *The Professor* (London: Boriswood, 1938; London: Lawrence & Wishart, 1986). The original 1938 hardback and the 1986 paperback have identical pagination.

95. Warner, *Professor*, 13.

96. Rex makes ironic comments about schoolmasters at several points in the novel, for instance where he refers to cheers that were given "musically by the rich women and somewhat hoarsely by the schoolmasters" (49).

97. Warner, *Professor*, 104, 106, 107, 118, 119.

98. Ibid., 127-28.

99. Ibid., 222.

100. Ibid., 223.

101. *Times Literary Supplement*, 28 October 1938, p. 20.

102. Christopher Isherwood, "The Man of Honor," *The New Republic* 97, no. 1266 (8 March 1939): 138.

103. Henry Lappin, *Evening News* (Buffalo, N.Y.), Saturday Magazine sect., 18 February 1939, p. 7.

104. *People's World*, 11 March 1939, p. 10.

105. Ralph Thompson, *New York Times*, 20 February 1939, p. 15.

106. Richard Johnstone, *The Will to Believe: Novelists of the Nineteen-Thirties* (Oxford: Oxford University Press, 1982), 54.

107. Samuel Hynes, *The Auden Generation: Literature and Politics in England in the 1930's* (New York: Viking, 1977), 313-14.

108. Frank Kermode, *History and Value: The Clarendon Lectures and the Northcliffe Lectures* (Oxford and New York: Clarendon Press, 1988), 70-71.

109. Sean Day-Lewis, *C. Day-Lewis: An English Literary Life*, 121-22.

CHAPTER 6

1. The letters from Rex to Greenwood that appear in this and other chapters are almost all from MS 45 of the Michigan State Greenwood collection of Rex Warner materials.

2. Rex Warner to E. W. Martin, 30 October 1946, from Athens. Rex Warner manuscripts and correspondence collection, Rare Books Library, Pennsylvania State University Libraries, #1997-0038R.

3. Letter in possession of Anne Ambrose; Ambrose, #258.

4. From "Hymn," in Rex Warner, *Poems* (New York: Knopf, 1938), 71-72. Except for pagination, the 1938 Knopf edition is identical to the 1937 Boriswood editon of the *Poems*.

5. Rex Warner, Sonnet XIV, in *Poems and Contradictions* (London: The Bodley Head, 1945), 50.

6. Ibid., 52.

7. Ibid., 54.

8. Ambrose, #92.

9. The date of this letter might be 1938, but the references to soldiers indicate that it is 1939, since Britain's entry into World War II was on 30 September 1939. Also, Rex's dissatisfaction with his family, never expressed in any other letter, would seem to reflect domestic discord. So 1939 seems the most probable date.

10. Ambrose, #134.

11. Peter Daniel, *Frensham Heights, 1925-49: A Study in Progressive Education* (n.p., n.p., 1986), 146.

12. Ambrose, #204.

13. ALS from Rex Warner to John Lehmann 1936-1945, Harry Ransom Humanities Research Center, University of Texas, Austin.

14. Ambrose #155.

15. Ambrose, #153.

16. Ambrose, #181.

17. In the possession of Mrs. Frances Warner.

18. Ambrose, #219.

19. Ambrose, #87.

20. Ambrose, #158.

21. Ambrose, #244.

22. In the possession of Mrs. June Fenby.

23. Ambrose, #246.

24. Ambrose, #252.

25. Ambrose, #270.

26. Rex Warner, *The Aerodrome* (Oxford: Oxford University Press, 1982), 15-16.

27. Inserted in MS 52, Michigan State University Library Special Collections, Greenwood collection of Rex Warner materials.

28. Is this Rex's very free translation, or mistranslation, of the phrase "della mala coltura" from Canto XII, 1. 199 of Dante's *Paradiso*, which John Sinclair, for instance, translates as "of bad tillage"? See *The Divine Comedy of Dante Alighieri: III Paradiso*, trans. John D. Sinclair (New York: Oxford University Press, 1961), 180-81. Perhaps Rex had another reference to Dante in mind, but I have been unable to find it. I thank George Economou for this reference.

29. Warner, *Aerodrome*, 13.

30. Following are the outline and notes in the manuscript notebook inserted in Michigan State MS 52:

The Aerodrome

The Squire (an ex-Colonel) & wife

The Rector-son, wife, daughter

Tom, Dick, Harry one of them a nervous wreck (noise)

The Church Army leader

The Air-Marshall never appears

Air Vice-M (his daughter) He sometimes explains

The Sky Pilot

The Flight Lieutenant (possessed?)
The Aircraftsman— The technical instructor—
Women at aerodrome must talk of 'creative work'
The Church
The Manor
The Pub

The Pub
The Officers Mess
[After "*Marriage of Heaven + Hell*," Rex notes in schematic form that] "The Air Force represents the devil (Individual morality) Celibacy—Indifference + hatred of body. Shrinking from sex, except in violence [.] Intellectual dogmatism [.] Success—with ambition) [.] Discipline as escape. Despair. Intellectual ruthlessness [.] The village represents material for love Instinctive loyalty (often stupid) [.] Care of animals + plants— Acceptance of sex—Independence of 'systems,' but acceptance of necessity-Hope in posterity + memory of ancestors—Pity" [.]
[He then writes]:
From a distant viewpoint it is impossible to know whether the aerodrome is there or not. Those who live in the village know that it is there.

Rector's adopted son discovered between aerodrome + village. His parents (Air Marshall + landlord's daughter) Somehow I had always imagined that my parents, if they lived together at all + if they were still alive, must be living at a considerable distance from the scenes in which I was brought up as a child, + perhaps in some other country

---

Or his father is really the King. He thinks it is the Air V.M.—thus fearing incest. The King 'is perfectly nice, perfectly just'

The Flight-L. murders the Rector
'Who were your fathers + mothers? Some of you may know. Forget it then. You are yourselves, poised for a brief + startling flash of light between two annihilations. Ownership, locality, are the words of those who stick-in-the-mud. So is 'marriage.'
    Love? His affections do not that way tend
The utmost freedom with the utmost discipline—
    The meanest of lies—beauty is Truth
    The cult of cruelty (Dante)
1. Description of village on 21st birthday party or Man

drunk lying in a marsh—Disclosure of birth—Murder of

2. Scene at Fair—Merry-go-round

Final chapt. O ubi Campe.

Pursuit of parents represents reintegration with world.

The Rector is tradition, murdered by F.L.—

(The priest who slew the slayer + shall himself be slain)

Themes (i) Pursuit of parents

       (ii) Escape from cycle of murder

L. By what right have you taught him all this—

R. By the right of justice + honour—

   L goes to window, opens it + looks out—'F.H. Oh very good!'

'Rumble book'—book of fines for pilots who use their engines in the glide on to aerodrome. Kept in Mess.

[There follows the draft manuscript of the first chapter]

                               Landlord's wife + Airmarshall

      Roy   Fl. L.   Elizabeth

'Be wholly convinced of yourselves, poised as you are for a brief + startling flash of light between two annihilations. yes, it is yourselves I mean'

Reflections (1) after dinner party

              (2) when about to enlist

              (3) before service

              (4) before marriage

              (5) after infidelity

2. Breakfast next day. Nothing said of the incident.

or

2. I was sitting in the Church. I had enlisted.

3. The agricultural show. Flight L. looses bull, interferes with machinery of roundabout

---

2. Surely those high walls could contain, I thought, nothing but death + the instruments of death. I was on the point of enlisting.

---

2. Rector's confession overheard: He has murdered the previous incumbent (an aeroplane designer—his father-in-law)—His wife also overhears conversation (&, possibly, the bell ringers)

3. Agricultural show. Death of Rector

4. The Squire. Government proposal to buy his property. The Landlord's daughter

5. Investiture of Fl. L. as Rector. Church Dinner Sermon (with arrow pointing to chapter 7 and question mark)

6. Death of Squire. Infidelity of Landlord's wife. Urges [?] in pub. Revelation

7. I enlist [and an arrow enters Church Army Sermon? here]

8. Training

9. Disaffection in village

10. Visit of Air marshall—previous incumbent—Secrets of birth

Priests	Mothers	Sons
The Rector	Rector's wife	Roy
The Air marshall	Landlord's "	Fl. L.
The Fl.L.	Squire's sister	Landlord's d.
Capt. Webb		

Rector—Landlords wife.
    Landlord's daughter
Airmarshall—Rector's wife
    Roy
Airmarshall—Squire's sister
    Fl.L.

There are also notes for the last several chapters of the book, worked out in greater detail. In all these pages of Rex's notebook we watch the genesis of his thinking and learn the clear meaning for him of the Aerodrome: it is an antiseptic and dictatorial man-made substitute for life's muddle, including its personal pain and disorder—which Rex himself was experiencing at the moment and which he still chose over any possible substitute.

31. Ambrose, #212.

32. Ambrose, #245.

33. Michigan State Greenwood Collection, MS 45.

34. Letter of 2 December [1940] to Greenwood.

35. Ambrose, #2.

36. ALS from Rex Warner to John Lehmann 1936-1945, Harry Ransom Humanities Research Center, University of Texas, Austin.

37. John Lehmann, ed., *Folios of New Writing* (autumn 1941): 112. The precise publication date is not clear, and this poem seems to have been written after George's birth, judging from its content. But Rex may have only been imagining George's birth and growth, based on the experience of his other children.

38. Letter of 6 June to Pam Morris (Ambrose, #96).

39. Ambrose, #105

40. Ambrose, #266.

41. Rex Warner, "On Subsidizing Literature," *Folios of New Writing* 4 (autumn 1941): 182-91.

42. Rex Warner, "The Cult of Power," *Daylight* 1 (1941): 59-71. Published in January 1942.

43. Ambrose, #136.

44. Michigan State Greenwood Collection, MS 45, dated only Sunday.

45. Rex Warner radio contributor files, BBC Written Archives, Caversham, WAC ref RCONT1.

46. *Herald Tribune*, 30 January 1947, p. 19.

47. Warner, "Subsidizing Literature," 182-91.

48. Michigan State Greenwood collection, MS 52.

49. Undated, Tuesday Wimbledon, Michigan State University Library Special Collections, Greenwood collection, MS 45.

50. Paul Vaughn, *Something in Linoleum* (London: Sinclair-Stevenson, 1994), 3.

51. Rex Warner, *The Spur* 6, no. 1 (1942): 1-2.

52. Letter of 27 June 1991 to author.

53. Vaughn, *Something*, 110.

54. Ibid., 107.

55. Rex Warner, "The Cult of Power," in *The Cult of Power* (London: John Lane the Bodley Head, 1946), 11.

56. Ibid., 18.

57. Ibid., 21, 27-28.

58. Ambrose, #26.

59. Ambrose, #148.

60. Ambrose, #249.

61. Ambrose, #116.

62. Ambrose, #100.

63. Ambrose, #253.

64. Ambrose, #232.

65. Letter of 8 July 1991 to author.

66. Ambrose, #230.

67. Letter of 27 June 1991 to author.

68. Letter of 1 September 1988 to author.

69. Letter of 27 June 1991 to author.

70. Rex Warner, "Opening Hour: A London Interior," in *English Story, Fifth Series*, ed. Woodrow Wyatt (London: Collins, 1944), 154-60.

71. Ibid., 158.

72. *The Spur* (December 1942): 25-26.

73. Ambrose, #91.

74. Rex Warner, *Why Was I Killed?: A Dramatic Dialogue* (London: John Lane the Bodley Head, 1944), 188-89. Originally published in October 1943.

75. Ibid., 190-91.

76. Ibid., 188.

77. Ibid., 119.

78. Ibid.

79. Ibid., 125.

80. *Times Literary Supplement*, 23 October 1943, p. 509.

81. Alan Munton and Alan Young, *Seven Writers of the English Left: A Bibliography of Literature and Politics, 1916-1980* (New York: Garland, 1981), 184.

82. Rex Warner radio contributor files, WAC ref RCONT1, BBC Written Archives, Caversham.

83. Ibid.

84. Norman Cousins, *The Saturday Review* (10 June 1944): 18.

85. Diana Trilling, *The Nation* (10 June 1944): 686.

86. In a letter of 11 December, probably 1943, to John Morris, Rex complained that "I haven't received the documents about the Atlantic Charter. I'm doing a film on the subject, + another unlikely commission is a book on the Public Schools for the Britain in Pictures series. I get £50 for this, but unfortunately have to find something out about the bloody institutions first." At the conclusion of this letter, Rex wrote "It really looks as if this bloody war might end some time now. The relief will be enormous. I feel my whole character + feelings hardening + ossifying as it continues + look forward to peace like a re-birth, whatever happens afterwards" (Ambrose, #214).

87. Ambrose, #81.

88. Letter of 18 October 1988 to author.

89. According to the terms of the contract, Rex was to receive 12 percent on the first 2,000 copies, and 15 percent on all copies after that, with an advance of £50 upon signature of the contract, which is dated 3 September 1943.

90. U.B., *The Spur* (December 1943): 13.

91. Letter of 3 August [1943] to Greenwood.

92. Michigan State University Greenwood collection, MS 45. Dated only Saturday, Wimbledon.

93. Rex Warner, "The Uses of Allegory," *Penguin New Writing* 17 (1943): 139-48.

94. Rex Warner, "The Uses of Allegory," in *The Cult of Power*, 116. Originally published in *Penguin New Writing* 17 (1943): 139-48.

95. Warner, *Cult of Power*, 120.

96. *The Spur* (December 1943): 18.

97. ALS from Rex Warner to John Lehmann, 1936-45, Harry Ransom Humanities Research Center, University of Texas, Austin.

98. Warner, *Cult of Power*, 21.

99. Ibid., 23.

100. Ibid., 25.

101. Ibid., 24.

102. Ibid., 27.

103. Ibid., 36-37.

104. Ambrose, #184.

105. Ambrose, #72.

106. Ambrose, #262.

107. Ambrose, #38.

108. The terms were 12.5 percent on the first 2,000, 15 percent of the published price of the next 5,000, 20 percent above 7,000, with an £50 advance and an option on Rex's next nonfiction work. The published price, when the book appeared in 1946, was 8s.6d.

109. ALS from Rex Warner to John Lehmann 1936-1945, Harry Ransom Humanities Research Center, University of Texas, Austin.

110. *The Spur* (summer 1944): 19.

111. Ibid., 20.

112. Ibid.

113. Michigan State University Greenwood Collection, MS 45 dated Tuesday, West Woodhay.

114. Ibid., dated Saturday.

115. Ambrose, #151.

116. Rex Warner radio contributior files, WAC ref RCONT1, BBC Written Archives, Caversham.

117. ALS from Rex Warner to John Lehmann 1936-45, Harry Ransom Humanities Research Center, University of Texas, Austin.

118. Rex Warner, "What's the Point of Poetry?" in *Personal Impressions: Talks on Writers and Writing*, ed. Marian McLeod (Sydney: Wentworth Press, 1986), 9.

119. Ibid., 10.

120. Ibid., 14.

121. Ibid., 10.

122. Ambrose, #51.

123. Rex Warner radio contributor files, WAC ref RCONT1, BBC Written Archives, Caversham.

124. Copy in my possession.

125. Ambrose, #95.

126. Ambrose, #202.

127. Ibid.

CHAPTER 7

1. Rex Warner, *Views of Attica* (London: John Lehmann, 1950), 71.

2. Letter in possession of Anne Ambrose; Ambrose, #140.

3. Ambrose, #90.

4. Amikam Nachmani for the United Nations Special Committee on the Balkans, 1947-52, *International Intervention in the Greek Civil War* (New York: Praeger, 1990), 1.

5. Quoted in Robert Eisner, *Travellers to an Antique Land: The History and Literature of Travel to Greece* (Ann Arbor: University of Michigan, 1991), 214-15.

6. Nachmani, *International Intervention*, 10.

7. See Eisner, *Travellers*, 211-13. The film *Ill Met by Midnight* (1956), based on Stanley Moss's 1950 memoir of the same title, recounts this exploit, but Moss's account has been challenged by Leigh Fermor.

8. Frances Donaldson, *The British Council* (London: Cape, 1984), 146.

9. Warner, *Views of Attica*, 70.

10. Ibid., 74.

11. Ibid.

12. Donaldson, *British Council*, 147.

13. Warner, *Views of Attica*, 75.

14. Letter of 28 August 1989 to author.

15. Letter of 5 March 1989 from Patrick Leigh Fermor to author.

16. Warner, *Views of Attica*, 19.

17. Ibid., 60.

18. Ibid., 93.

19. Gennadius Seferis file 91/2.

20. Rex Warner, "The Love of Rites and Remote Places," *Life* (January 1964): 18.

21. Rex Warner, *Rex Warner Personal Impressions: Talks on Writers and Writing*, ed. Marian B. McLeod (Sydney: Wentworth Press, 1986), 19.

22. Dated "Athens 1946," Gennadius file 91/2, p. 4.

23. Pp. 10-11.

24. He continued as editor until 1952.

25. Warner, *Personal Impressions*, 16-17.

26. Warner, *Views of Attica*, 77.

27. Letter of 3 May 1989 to author.

28. Warner, *Views of Attica*, 37.

29. Ibid., 78.

30. Ibid., 22-23.

31. See also his enthusiastic comments about his first view of the Acropolis in his August 1948 radio talk on Greek writers, published in *Personal Impressions*, 15-16.

32. Ambrose, #70.

33. Ambrose, #264.

34. Ambrose, #76.

35. Ambrose, #229.

36. Warner, *Views of Attica,* 82.

37. Ibid., 101.

38. Ibid., 103.

39. Ibid., 108.

40. This is a perspicacious document by a seasoned judge of ability, although as Runciman himself wrote, it was still too early in Rex's career in the B.C. to make definite judgements:
    1. Performance of the duties of his post. B It is not yet time to give an opinion, as the individual is not yet fully [?]
    2. Personality. A
    3. Judgement. B
    4. Power of taking responsibility. C
    5. Initiative. B
    6. Accuracy. A
    7. Tact. A
    8. Zeal. A
    9. Power of supervising staff. B
    10. Linguistic ability in relation to country. C Learning Greek
    11. Extra mural activities and relations. A
    In the "General Remarks," Runciman added: "Mr. Warner has only been in Greece for two months and it is too early to assess his work. I can only say that he has made an excellent impression on the British and Greeks whom he has met. He lacks administrative staff confidence, but would work well with an efficient second-in-command." From Rex's British Council personnel records.

41. Ambrose, #231.

42. Ambrose, #117.

43. Gennadius Library Seferis File IV 109/18.

44. Ambrose, #65.

45. Ambrose, #113.

46. Warner, *Views of Attica*, 65.

47. Ambrose, #109.

48. Ambrose, #102.
49. Ambrose, #118.
50. Ibid.
51. Ibid.
52. Ambrose, #127.
53. Ambrose, #115.
54. Ambrose, #242.
55. Ambrose, #108.
56. Rex Warner, "How Sweet Only to Delight," in *A Garland of Prose and Verse*, ed. Walter de la Mare (New York: William Morrow, 1946).
57. Excerpt from "Why Was I Killed?" in *The Treasure Chest: An Anthology of Contemplative Prose*, ed. J. Donald Adams (New York: Dutton, 1946).
58. The price would be about 7 shillings 6 pence, and Rex was to get 12 1/2 percent on the first 2,000 copies, 15 percent above 2,000, and a £50 advance.
59. This, dated 23 September 1946, is the first of a series of letters in the Gennadius Library from Rex to Seferis, stretching right up to the time of Seferis's death.
60. Warner, *Views of Attica*, 135.
61. Ambrose, #112.
62. Gennadius Seferis file IV 109/18.
63. Rex refers to Evelyn Waugh's 1937 novel *Black Mischief*. He greatly enjoyed and respected Waugh's writing.
64. Ambrose, #111.
65. John Lehmann, *In My Own Time* (Boston: Atlantic Monthly Press, 1969), 440.
66. Lehmann, *In My Own Time*, 444.
67. Warner, *Views of Attica*, 167.
68. Mark Schorer, "Essays on Sundry Dilemmas of Modern Man," *The New York Times Book Review*, 14 September 1947, 4.
69. Ambrose, #50.
70. Ambrose, #196.
71. In full, Rex's introduction is as follows:

> Again tonight we are honoured in having to speak to us a very great Greek writer. Again I am in the somewhat curious position of introducing to you a poet with whose work you are much better acquainted than I am. I do, however, know enough of the work + the thought of Seferis to know that we shall be listening to the words of one who is in the very front rank of those,—rare enough in Europe today—who combine the most acute sensitivity with the most acute critical intelligence.

The claims made for the ancient Greeks—that they were able "to see life steadily + see it whole" is a bold claim. It may well be doubted whether anyone has been able to do this. Yet the attempt to do so is a necessity both for art and for civilisation. And perhaps today, when so much of life seems to have lost its balance + when even the scientists give us contradictory explanations of the world, the difficulties of a steady + a complete view of things are greater than they ever were. Good + fine things are difficult, as Plato said.

My understanding of the work of Seferis, limited as it is, leads me to think of him as one who, with an infinite care for the depth and variety both of the Greek + of the European tradition, seeks to fuse these traditions in a poetic vision + in a general understanding. He is one of those who see the present more clearly because they see it penetrated by + interfused with the past. Such clear vision is a necessity for civilisation, though it is easier for the half-blind to come to definite conclusions.

The English poet T. S. Eliot has been throughout his life conscious of the same problem. So, I should say, in a rather different way, has Cavafy. And it is a rare privilege to hear these poets discussed by one who is uniquely able to understand them.

72. George Seferis, *A Poet's Journal: Days of 1945-51*, trans. Athan Anagnostopoulos (Cambridge: Harvard University Press, 1974), 70.

73. Seferis, *A Poet's Journal*, 71.

74. Ambrose, #200.

75. Performance of the duties of his post. A

  2. Personality. A

  3. Judgment. C

  4. Power of taking responsibility. C

  5. Initiative. A

  6. Accuracy. B

  7. Tact. A

  8. Zeal. A

  9. Power of supervising staff. C

  10. Linguistic ability in relation to country. C-

  11. Extra mural activities and relations. A

Runciman remarked that "Mr. Warner is proving an immense success at his job. He is an extremely popular figure in Athens, where his obvious distinction and his personal friendliness impress all types and classes. His personality has done a great deal to build up the Institute to be a feature in Athens life. He is not himself an administrator, but he has good [rapport] and is in every way most co-operative. Mrs. Warner is an additional asset." He added, however, that "I do not think Mr. Warner is ready or would wish for a Grade I post." From Rex's British Council personnel records.

76. Ambrose, #144.

77. Supplied to me by the British Council.

78. Ambrose, #64.

79. The manuscript of this translation, written on British Institute paper, can be found in Seferis file 91/2 at the Gennadius Library; it contains very minor variants from the published poem.

80. Ambrose, #68.

81. Interview with Shan and Roxain Sedgwick conducted for me by Prof. Clayton Reeve, 19 June 1989. I thank Professor Reeve (as well as the Sedgwicks) for this interview.

82. ALS to John Lehmann 1936-1945, Harry Ransom Humanities Research Center, University of Texas, Austin.

83. Copy supplied to me by the British Council.

CHAPTER 8

1. Letter in possession of Anne Ambrose; Ambrose, #29.

2. Ambrose, #239.

3. Gennadius Library, Seferis File IV 109/18.

4. Rex Warner, *Rex Warner Personal Impressions: Talks on Writers and Writing*, ed. Marian B. McLeod (Sydney: Wentworth Press, 1986), 25.

5. Trevor Davies, "A British View of Education in Berlin," in *The British in Germany: Educational Reconstruction after 1945*, ed. Arthur Hearnden (London: Hamish Hamilton, 1978), 212.

6. Robert Birley, "British Policy in Retrospect," in *The British in Germany*, ed. Hearnden, 46.

7. Harald Husemann, "Anglo-German Relations in Higher Education," in *The British in Germany*, ed. Hearnden, 98, 163, 162.

8. Geoffrey Bird, "The University," in *The British in Germany*, ed. Hearnden, 150-51.

9. Rex Warner, "The Poetry of George Seferis," *Orpheus* 1 (1948): 76-82.

10. Rex Warner, "Where Shall John Go? XV—Greece," *Horizon* 17, no. 100 (1948): 295-301.

11. Rex Warner, introduction to George Seferis, *The King of Asine and Other Poems*, trans. Bernard Spencer, Nanos Valaoritis [and] Lawrence Durrell (London: John Lehmann, 1948), 7-15.

12. Ambrose, #122.

13. Ambrose, #141.

14. Ambrose, #71.

15. Rex Warner, *The Cult of Power* (London: John Lane the Bodley Head, 1946), 19-20.

16. Ibid., 44.

17. Rex Warner, *Men of Stones* (London: John Lane the Bodley Head, 1949), 57. The typescript of this novel is in the Michigan State Greeenwood collection, but I am unaware of the whereabouts of the manuscript.

18. Ibid., 67.

19. Ibid., 78-79.

20. Warner, *Cult of Power*, 63.

21. Warner, *Men of Stones*, 125.

CHAPTER 9

1. Michael Holroyd, *Lytton Strachey: A Critical Biography*, vol. 2 (New York: Holt, 1968), 216.

2. Sarah Daniel (nee Rothschild), now resident in Cambridge, said in 1990 that she had spoken to Jacob, who took the view that they should rise above it and not contest the decision, and added "But that's not so easy. Jacob of course inherited £93 million from his relative Dollie de Rothschild less than two years ago. What's happened won't make any difference to him financially. I have spoken to Miranda and she is very upset. Without money left to me by my mother [Barbara], who died last September [1989], I would be in a very difficult financial position today." Sarah went on to say that "I have lived in Cambridge for 30 years and always thought I was on good terms with him. I certainly loved my father and believed that he loved me. I saw him most weekends and he used to take a great interest in my son Tom, who got a good university degree. I was probably closer to my father than my brother and sister were. Indeed he seldom saw my sister because she spends most of her time abroad. . . . It is not for me a question of money. . . . It is having been deceived by him. It hurts very much." *Daily Mail*, 18 June 1990, pp. 1, 3.

3. ALS from Rex Warner to John Lehmann 1938-1969, Harry Ransom Humanities Research Center, University of Texas, Austin.

4. Letter in possession of Anne Ambrose; Ambrose, #101.

5. In the possession of Mrs. Frances Warner.

6. The manuscript for this work is in the Harry Ransom Humanities Research Center, University of Texas, Austin HANLEY II.

7. Rex Warner radio contributor files WAC ref RCONT1, B.B.C. Written Archives, Caversham.

8. This typescript is now in the Lehmann collection at the Harry Ransom Humanities Research Center at the University of Texas, Austin.

9. The publication price was set at 8 shillings, 6 pence, and the terms are royalties of 15 percent on the first 5,000, 20 percent on the next 5,000, 25 percent of the published price on all copies sold above 10,000, and a £250 advance. Rex Warner contracts file, Bodley Head Archive, Reading University.

10. The price was set at around 7 shillings, 6 pence, with Rex to receive 12.5 percent of the published price on the first 2,000 copies and 15 percent on all subsequent copies, as well as a £50 advance.

11. Reading University Library Hogarth Press Archive, file 592.

12. Hogarth Press Archive, file 592, Reading University Library.

13. Rex Warner, introduction to *The Poems of C.P. Cavafy*, trans. John Mavrogordato (London: Hogarth Press, 1951), 1.

14. C. Capri-Karka, *Love and the Symbolic Journey in the Poetry of Constantine Cavafy, T. S. Eliot, and George Seferis* (New York: Pella, 1982), 23.

15. ALS from Rex Warner to John Lehmann 1938-1969, Harry Ransom Humanities Research Center, University of Texas, Austin.

16. Rex Warner, *John Milton* (London: Max Parrish, 1949), 34.

17. Ibid., 15-16.

18. *Times Literary Supplement*, 28 April 1950, p. 255.

19. Howard Doughty, *The Nation*, 6 May 1950, p. 429.

20. Richard Church, *The Spectator*, 17 March 1950, p. 348.

21. In the possession of Mrs. Frances Warner.

22. In the possession of Mrs. Frances Warner.

23. Basil's esteem for Rex's work is also clear in his substantial history *The Long View* (New York: Knopf, 1974), in which he remembers "the appalling Professor Pothimere in Rex Warner's *The Wild Goose Chase*" (279) and refers to *The Wild Goose Chase* and *The Aerodrome* and Auden and Isherwood's *The Dog Beneath the Skin* as "seminal works of the Thirties" (677).

24. George Woodcock, *Tomorrow*, May 1950, p. 55.

25. *Atlantic Monthly* 185 (April 1950): 87.

26. H. F. West, *New York Times*, 19 February 1950, p. 34.

27. R.D. Charques, *The Spectator*, 23 December 1949, p. 902.

28. ALS to John Lehmann 1938-1969, Harry Ransom Humanities Research Center, University of Texas, Austin.

29. Norman Sherry, *The Life of Graham Greene, Volume 2: 1939-1955* (New York: Viking, 1995), 307.

30. Rex Warner, *Views of Attica* (London: John Lehmann, 1950), 93.

31. Letter of 20 December 1949 from Ethel to Rex, in the possession of Mrs. Frances Warner.

32. In the possession of Mrs. Frances Warner.

33. Rex Warner contracts file, Bodley Head Archive, Reading University.

34. Herbert Howarth, "Silence in Zikhron," *Jewish Frontier* (June 1947): 14, 25-29.

35. Herbert Howarth, "Pieces of History," *Critique* 2 (1958): 54-64.

36. Rex Warner, *New Statesman*, 17 June 1950, p. 622.

37. Rex Warner, *New Statesman*, 24 February 1951, pp. 224, 226.

38. But see Fred D. Crawford, *Richard Aldington and Lawrence of Arabia: A Cautionary Tale* (Carbondale and Edwardsville: Southern Illinois University Press, 1998) for a defense of Aldington with regard to his views on other writers as well as T. E. Lawrence.

39. *Times Literary Supplement*, 21 July 1950, p. 450.

40. *Manchester Guardian*, 21 July 1950, p. 4.

41. Harold Nicolson, jacket blurb for *The Vengeance of the Gods* (London: MacGibbon & Kee, 1954).

42. The contract, dated 4 August 1950 and now in the file of Rex Warner contracts in Reading University's Bodley Head Archive, put the published price at 7/6d, with royalties of 12.5 percent for the first 2,000, 15 percent above the first 2,000, and a £50 advance, with an option on Rex's next work of translation.

43. Rex Warner, *E.M. Forster* in Writers and Their Work, no. 7 (London: Longmans, Green, 1950), 5.

44. Ibid., 8.

45. Ibid., 9.

46. Ibid., 8.

47. Ibid., 28.

48. In the possession of Mrs. Frances Warner.

49. Ibid.

50. Bristol University Penguin Archive, DM 1107. Alan Glover's letters quoted by permission of Penguin Books.

51. Rex Warner, "Milton and the Definition of Liberty," *The Listener*, 11 January 1951, pp. 58-59.

52. Rex Warner, *Rex Warner Personal Impressions: Talks on Writers and Writing*, ed. Marian B. McLeod (Sydney: Wentworth Press, 1986), 29.

53. Bristol University Penguin Archive, DM 1107.

54. Ibid.

55. Ambrose, #30.

56. See Maurice Hungiville, *From a Single Window: Michigan State University and Its Press, 1947-1997* (East Lansing: Michigan State University Press, 1997).

57. Rex Warner and Lyle Blair, *Ashes to Ashes: A Post-Mortem on the 1950-51 Tests* (London: MacGibbon and Kee, 1951), 11-12.

58. Ibid., 66-67.

59. Ibid., 70-71.

60. Ambrose, #47.

61. In the possession of Mrs. Frances Warner.

62. Letter from Rex to Seferis, 6 May 1951. Gennadius Library, Seferis file IV 109/18.

63. Rex Warner, introduction to Herman Melville, *Billy Budd and Other Stories* (London: John Lehmann, 1951), xi.

64. Edmund Blunden, *The Spectator*, 8 June 1951, p. 760.

CHAPTER 10

1. John Lehmann, *In My Own Time* (Boston: Little, Brown, 1969), 482.

2. Seferis file IV 109/18, Gennadius Library.

3. In the possession of Mrs. Frances Warner.

4. Ibid.

5. Seferis file IV 109/18, Gennadius Library.

6. *The Helen of Euripides* (London: Bodley Head, 1951), 9.

7. Nothing apparently did, nor of an undated holograph and ms. by Rex entitled "Lion of Sparta" (in the Berg Collection), clearly the dialogue for a film about Leonidas, the king of Sparta who defeated the Persians under Xerxes at Thermopylae. It is a pity that "Lion of Sparta" does not seem to have been produced, because Rex's fifty-six-page typescript is quite good, and expertly imagines the political and military tensions on the Greek and Persian sides before, during, and after the battle. It might have been written during the 1950s when, judging from his letters, Greek producers were in contact with Rex about possible films on classical subjects.

8. Seferis file IV 109/18, Gennadius Library.

9. Ibid.

10. ALS to Edith Sitwell, Harry Ransom Humanities Research Center, University of Texas, Austin.

11. The notes and manuscript of this novel are in the Harry Ransom Humanities Research Center, University of Texas, Austin, HANLEY II.

12. Lehmann, *In My Own Time*, 484.

13. Thucydides, "The Revolution in Corcyra," trans. Rex Warner, *Colonnade* I, no.1: 37-43.

14. Bristol University Penguin Archive, DM 1107.

15. In the possession of Mrs. Frances Warner.

16. Bristol University Penguin Archive, DM 1107.

17. Seferis file IV 109/18, Gennadius Library.

18. ALS from Rex Warner to John Lehmann, 1935-60, 19 March 1952, Harry Ransom Humanities Research Center, University of Texas, Austin.

19. Seferis file IV 109/18, Gennadius Library.

20. ALS to Compton Mackenzie, Harry Ransom Humanities Research Center, University of Texas, Austin.

21. Seferis file IV 109/18, Gennadius Library.

22. ALS from Rex Warner to John Lehmann 1938-1969, Harry Ransom Humanities Research Center, University of Texas, Austin.

23. Ibid.

24. In the possession of Mrs. Frances Warner.

25. Rex Warner, *Spectator,* 23 January 1953, p. 100.

26. Basil Wright, *The Long View* (New York: Alfred A. Knopf, 1984), 329.

27. Paul Rotha, *Documentary Diary: An Informal History of the British Documentary Film, 1928-1939* (New York: Hill and Wang, 1973), xiv.

28. In the possession of Mrs. Frances Warner.

29. Stalin died on 5 March 1953, too late for Rex to include this fact in his novel, but it makes no difference to the action since Stalin, like Hitler, never, of course, actually appears in Average.

30. Bristol University Penguin Archive, DM 1107.

31. Ibid.

32. *Times Literary Supplement,* 27 November 1953, p. 766.

33. Rex Warner, *Spectator,* 12 February 1954, p. 188.

34. Rex Warner, *London Magazine* 1, no. 2 (March 1954): 86.

35. Rex Warner, *London Magazine* 1, no. 3 (April 1954): 79.

36. Ibid., 80.

37. ALS to John Lehmann, 1938-69, Harry Ransom Humanities Research Center, University of Texas, Austin.

38. Rex Warner, *The Vengeance of the Gods* (London: MacGibbon & Kee, 1954).

39. Bristol University Penguin Archive, DM 1107.

40. Rex Warner, *London Magazine* 1, no. 5 (June 1954): 78.

41. Rex Warner, *London Magazine* 1, no. 6 (July 1954): 75.

42. Both are entitled "Jonathan Swift: Defender of Liberty," but they have different content. The first appeared in the June 1937 *Left Review* and the second in the October 1944 *Our Time.*

43. Rex Warner, *London Magazine* 1, no. 6 (July 1954): 77.

44. ALS to John Lehmann, 1938-69, Harry Ransom Humanities Research Center, University of Texas, Austin.

45. John Lehmann, *In My Own Time: Memoirs of a Literary Life* (Boston: Little, Brown, 1969), 162.

46. Rex Warner, "Peking the City of Smiling Discipline," *Sunday Times,* 31 October 1954, p. 7; and "The New Puritanism in New Dress," *Sunday Times,* 14 November 1954, p. 7.

47. In the possession of Mrs. Frances Warner.

48. A. J. Ayer, *More of My Life* (London: Collins, 1984),111.

49. Ibid., 112.

50. *Sunday Times*, 14 November 1954, p. 7. The ms. quotations are from "Account of a Visit to China," AMS w/A emendations, Harry Ransom Humanities Research Center, University of Texas, Austin. The ms. should be dated October or November 1954 rather than c. 1953 as at present.

51. Rex Warner, *London Magazine* 1, no. 9 (October 1954): 77.

52. Maurice Bowra, *London Magazine* 1, no. 10 (November 1954): 90-91.

53. Rex Warner, *London Magazine* 1, no. 11 (December 1954): 77, 80.

54. Seferis file IV 109/18, Gennadius Library.

55. ALS to John Lehmann, 1938-69, Harry Ransom Humanities Research Center, University of Texas, Austin.

56. ALS from Rex Warner to Compton Mackenzie, Harry Ransom Humanities Research Center, University of Texas, Austin.

57. Rex Warner, *London Magazine* 2, no. 2 (February 1955): 85.

58. Ibid., 88.

59. Rex Warner, *London Magazine* 2, no. 7 (July 1955): 74-75.

60. It has been claimed by George Steven Swan, in "Who Was Homer's Daughter?: Robert Graves and T.E. Lawrence" (*Focus on Robert Graves and His Contemporaries* 2, no. 2 [spring 1994]: 17-23) that Graves based his characterization of Princess Nausicaa, the narrator of *Homer's Daughter*, on the personality of T. E. Lawrence, and that Rex was obtuse in his review for not noticing this. I feel that Rex did not notice the alleged resemblance between Nausicaa and Lawrence because, contrary to what Swan claims, it is very unlikely that it exists. See my "T.E. Lawrence and Robert Graves: A Friendship?," *T.E. Notes* 9, no. 1 (1998): 1-8.

61. Rex Warner, *London Magazine* 2, no. 8 (August 1955): 75.

62. Rex Warner, *London Magazine* 2, no. 10 (October 1955): 77.

63. ALS concerning Rex's Julius Caesar novels, Harry Ransom Humanities Research Center, University of Texas, Austin. This file contains at least forty items, including letters, readers' reports, and other material relating to these novels.

64. ALS from Rex Warner to John Lehmann, 1938-69, Harry Ransom Humanities Research Center, University of Texas, Austin.

65. ALS to John Lehmann, 1938-69, Harry Ransom Humanities Research Center, University of Texas, Austin.

66. ALS from Rex Warner to John Lehmann, 1938-69, Harry Ransom Humanities Research Center, the University of Texas, Austin.

67. Rex Warner, *London Magazine* 3, no. 3 (March 1956): 79.

68. Rex Warner, *London Magazine* 3, no. 5 (May 1956): 75.

69. Rex Warner, *London Magazine* 3, no. 7 (July 1956): 77.

70. Ibid., 77-78.

71. ALS concerning Rex Warner's Julius Caesar novels, Harry Ransom Humanities Research Center, the University of Texas, Austin.

72. ALS from Rex Warner to John Lehmann, 1935-60, Harry Ransom Humanities Research Center, University of Texas, Austin.

73. The title was changed from "The King of Bithynia" to "Julius Caesar: My First Voyage Abroad," *London Magazine* 4, no. 12 (December 1957): 36-44.

74. ALS from Rex Warner to John Lehmann, 1938-69, Harry Ransom Humanities Research Center, the University of Texas, Austin.

75. Rex Warner, *London Magazine* 3, no. 9 (September 1956): 55-56.

76. Seferis file IV 109/18, Gennadius Library.

77. Rex Warner, *London Magazine* 3, no. 11 (November 1956): 79.

78. In the possession of Mrs. Frances Warner.

79. ALS to John Lehmann, 1938-69, Harry Ransom Humanities Research Center, University of Texas, Austin.

80. Seferis file IV 109/18, Gennadius Library.

81. Ibid.

82. ALS from Rex Warner to John Lehmann, 1938-69, Harry Ransom Humanities Research Center, University of Texas, Austin.

83. ALS from Rex Warner to John Lehmann, 1935-60, Harry Ransom Humanities Research Center, University of Texas, Austin.

84. Ibid.

85. ALS concerning Rex Warner's Julius Caesar novels, Harry Ransom Humanities Research Center, University of Texas, Austin.

86. ALS from Rex Warner to John Lehmann, 1935-60, Harry Ransom Humanities Research Center, University of Texas, Austin.

87. ALS from Rex Warner to John Lehmann, 1938-69, Harry Ransom Humanities Research Center, University of Texas, Austin.

88. ALS to John Lehmann, 1938-69, 5 July 1957. Harry Ransom Humanities Research Center, University of Texas, Austin.

89. Seferis file IV 109/18, Gennadius Library.

90. ALS concerning Rex Warner's Julius Caesar novels, Harry Ransom Humanities Research Center, University of Texas, Austin.

91. Seferis file IV 109/18, Gennadius Library.

92. Ibid.

93. ALS from Rex Warner to John Lehmann 1938-1969, Harry Ransom Humanities Research Center, University of Texas, Austin.

94. Included among the ALS concerning Rex Warner's Julius Caesar novels, Harry Ransom Humanities Research Center, University of Texas, Austin.

95. Seferis file IV 109/18, Gennadius Library.

96. ALS concerning Rex Warner's Julius Caesar novels, Harry Ransom Humanities Research Center, the University of Texas, Austin.

97. ALS to John Lehmann 1935-1960, Harry Ransom Humanities Research Center, University of Texas, Austin.

98. *Kirkus*, 15 January 1958, p. 45.

99. *Library Journal*, 1 March 1958, p. 766.

100. Letter in possession of Anne Ambrose; Ambrose, #182.

101. Seferis file IV 109/18, Gennadius Library.

102. ALS concerning Rex Warner's Julius Caesar novels, Harry Ransom Humanities Research Center, University of Texas, Austin.

103. George Seferis, *Diary 1 October 1956-27 December 1960* (Athens: Ikaros, 1990), 70-73. [In Greek.] I thank George Economou for translating this and other passages of Seferis's diary for me.

104. Seferis file IV 109/18, Gennadius Library.

105. Ambrose, #1.

106. ALS concerning Rex Warner's Julius Caesar novels, Harry Ransom Humanities Research Center, University of Texas, Austin.

107. Seferis file IV 109/18, Gennadius Library.

CHAPTER 11

1. *Springfield Republican*, 18 May 1958, p. 9C.

2. *Times Literary Supplement*, 4 July 1958, p. 373.

3. Robert Graves, *The New Republic* 133 (26 May 1958): 17.

4. N. H. Reeve, *The Novels of Rex Warner: An Introduction* (Basingstoke and London: Macmillan, 1989), 145.

5. Rex Warner, *The Young Caesar* (New York: Mentor, 1963), 125.

6. Ibid.,10.

7. Ibid., 124.

8. Ibid., 256.

9. Ibid., 151.

10. Seferis file IV 109/18, Gennadius Library.

11. ALS concerning Rex Warner's Julius Caesar novels, Harry Ransom Humanities Research Center, University of Texas, Austin.

12. Rex's statement in "Rex Warner," *The Poet Speaks: Interviews with Contemporary Poets*, conducted by Hilary Morrish, Peter Orr, John Press, and Ian Scott-Kilvert. Gen.ed. Peter Orr (London: Routledge and Kegan Paul, 1966), 265. The interview with Rex by Ian Scott-Kilvert took place on 20 February 1962.

13. Ibid., 265.

14. Ibid.

15. W. H. Auden, "The State of Translation," *Delos* 2 (1968): 30.

16. C. Day-Lewis, "On Translating Poetry" (Abingdon: Abbey Press, 1970), 4.

17. T. E. Lawrence, letter to E. M. Forster of 28 August 1928 in *The Letters of T. E. Lawrence*, ed. David Garnett (London: Cape, 1938), 625.

18. Seferis file IV 109/18, Gennadius Library.

19. ALS concerning Rex Warner's Julius Caesar novels, Harry Ransom Humanities Research Center, University of Texas, Austin.

20. Ibid.

21. Robert Levésque, *Seferis: choix de poèmes traduits et accompagnés du texte grec avec une préface* (Athens: Ikaros, 1945).

22. Seferis file IV 109/18, Gennadius Library.

23. Letter in the possession of Anne Ambrose; Ambrose, #37.

24. Rex Warner, *London Magazine* 6, no. 2 (February 1959): 68.

25. Letter of 13 October 1959 to Pam Morris; Ambrose, #269.

26. ALS concerning Rex Warner's Julius Caesar novels, Harry Ransom Humanities Research Center, University of Texas, Austin.

27. Seferis file 77, Gennadius Library.

28. Letter of 6 October 1988 from Mariella Piggott to author.

29. ALS from Rex Warner to John Lehmann 1935-1960, Harry Ransom Humanities Research Center, University of Texas, Austin.

30. Seferis file 77, Gennadius Library.

31. One of 3 ALS from Rex to Compton Mackenzie, Harry Ransom Humanities Research Center, University of Texas, Austin.

32. Seferis file 77, Gennadius Library.

33. Ibid.

34. Seferis file 96/7, Gennadius Library.

35. George Seferis, *Poems*, trans. Rex Warner (London: Bodley Head, 1960), 117.

36. Seferis file 77, Gennadius Library.

37. Ibid.

38. Sam Lawrence to Rex, 14 September 1959, ALS concerning Rex's Julius Caesar novels, Harry Ransom Humanities Research Center, University of Texas, Austin.

39. Seferis file 77, Gennadius Library.

40. ALS concerning Rex Warner's Julius Caesar novels, Harry Ransom Humanities Research Center, University of Texas, Austin.

41. Seferis file 96/7, Gennadius Library.

42. Seferis file 77, Gennadius Library.

43. Ibid.

44. Ambrose, #269.

45. Seferis file 77, Gennadius Library.

46. Letter of 28 October 1959, Seferis file 77, Gennadius Library.

47. Seferis file 77, Gennadius Library.

48. Ibid.

49. ALS concerning Rex Warner's Julius Caesar novels, Harry Ransom Humanities Research Center, University of Texas, Austin.

50. Seferis file 77, Gennadius Library.

51. ALS concerning Rex Warner's Julius Caesar novels, Harry Ransom Humanities Research Center, University of Texas, Austin.

52. Seferis file 77, Gennadius Library.

53. Ibid.

54. Ibid.

55. Ibid.

56. ALS concerning Rex's Julius Caesar novels, Harry Ransom Humanities Research Center, University of Texas, Austin.

57. Seferis file 77, Gennadius Library.

58. ALS concerning Rex's Julius Caesar novels, Harry Ransom Humanities Research Center, University of Texas, Austin.

59. In an undated manuscript in the Berg Collection entitled "Notes on revisiting Greece," Rex somewhat desperately sketches out four more possible publication projects, none of which seems to have come to fruition. The prevalence of Scottish subjects and a reference to Seferis as ambassador to England (which he was from 1957 to 1962) show that these suggested projects date from around this time. The projects are very briefly outlined. The first project was a book giving his personal impressions of Athens and the writers he knew there; the second was to be an article about the Clyde, "One of the world's great waterways with a lot of interesting local traffic," which would focus on three or four ships; a piece showing "The contrast between the pomp + severity of Edinburgh + the bustling vitality + crudity of Glasgow"; and possibly an article about the clan massacre at Glencoe, and how "A MacDonald may still throw a pint of beer at the head of a Campbell."

60. Seferis file 77, Gennadius Library.

61. In the possession of Mrs. Frances Warner.

62. ALS from Rex Warner to John Lehmann 1935-1960, Harry Ransom Humanities Research Center, University of Texas, Austin.

63. Rex Warner, *London Magazine* 7, no. 6 (June 1960): 64.

64. Ibid., 65.

65. Seferis file 77, Gennadius Library.

66. Ibid.

67. ALS to John Lehmann 1938-1969, Harry Ransom Humanities Research Center, University of Texas, Austin.

68. Seferis file 77, Gennadius Library.

69. ALS from Rex Warner to John Lehmann 1938-1969, Harry Ransom Humanities Research Center, University of Texas, Austin.

70. In the possession of Mrs. Frances Warner.

71. Letter of 4 March 1960 to Seferis, Gennadius file 77.

72. Seferis file 77, Gennadius Library.

73. Ibid.

74. Ibid.

75. Ibid.

76. Ibid.

77. Rex Warner, *Times Literary Supplement*, 1 April 1960, p. 202.

78. Seferis file IV 109/18, Gennadius Library.

79. Ibid.

80. ALS to John Lehmann 1935-1960, Harry Ransom Humanities Research Center, University of Texas, Austin.

81. *Kirkus* 28 (15 April 1960): 336.

82. R. R. Rea, *Library Journal* 85 (1 May 1960): 1826.

83. Seferis file IV 109/18, Gennadius Library.

84. Letter from Rex to Seferis, 12 May 1960, from Gennadius file IV 109/18.

85. Unfortunately, it seems to have been misplaced.

86. George Seferis, *Meres* [vol. 7, 1 October 1956-27 December 1960] (in Greek) (Athens: Ikaros, 1990), 200-1. I thank George Economou for translating passages from this work for me.

87. C. A. Robinson, *New York Times*, 12 June 1960, p. 6.

88. Pierson Dixon, *New York Herald Tribune*, 12 June 1960, p. 3.

89. Rex Warner, *Imperial Caesar* (London: Collins, 1960), 77.

90. Reeve, *Novels of Rex Warner*, 149.

91. Warner, *Imperial Caesar*, 312.

92. Ibid., 383.

93. Ibid., 7.

94. Ibid., 15.

95. Ibid., 378.

96. Rex Warner Works V-Z, Letters, Miscellaneous, Harry Ransom Humanities Research Center, University of Texas, Austin.

97. Rex Warner, *Poetry Review* 52, no. 3 (July-September 1960): 140-41.

98. Seferis file IV 109/18, Gennadius Library.

99. Ibid.

100. Rex Warner, "Cleopatra Still Lures and Baffles Us," *New York Times Magazine*, 9 October 1960, pp. 50, 51, 55, 58, 60.

101. Ibid., 50.

102. Ibid., 51.

103. Seferis file IV 109/18, Gennadius Library.

104. Warner, *The Poet Speaks*, 266.

105. Rex Warner, foreword to *Poems*, by George Seferis, trans. Rex Warner (London: Bodley Head, 1960), 5-6.

106. Ibid. 6.

107. Ibid., 84.

108. George Seferis, *Collected Poems 1924-1955* (Princeton: Princeton University Press, 1967), 291.

109. Seferis, *Poems* (1960), 111.

110. Seferis, *Collected Poems* (1967), 381.

111. I obviously do not agree with M. Byron Raizis, who in his *Greek Poetry Translations* (Athens: Efstathiades Group, 1981) finds that Rex's English "is not always acceptable to readers on both sides of the Atlantic." This may be true of the one line ("I met old John. He stood me an ice.") from Rex's translation of "In the Manner of G.S." that Raizis quotes, but I have not noticed that problem elsewhere, nor does Raizis give any other examples. Raizis also claims, without giving any examples at all, that Keeley and Sherrard's 1967 versions "sound more poetic" than Rex's, and "of course communicate the Greekness of the poem more directly" (178). In answer to this, I would point out that whether one version "sounds more poetic" than another is a matter of individual taste, since as I have tried to show, both Rex's and the Keeley-Sherrard versions are poetically worthy, if different. As for the "Greekness" of the poems, Raizis may well be correct, but it is a fact that Seferis approved all of Rex's translations after examining them in detail. Rex was indeed a pioneer in the translation of Seferis's poems, but his work cannot be written off on that basis, as Raizis tries to do.

112. Letter of 16 October 1960 to Seferis, Gennadius Seferis file IV 109/18.

113. Gennadius Seferis file IV 109/18.

114. George Seferis, *The King of Asine and Other Poems* (London: Lehmann, 1948), 23.

115. Seferis, *Poems* (1960), 16.
116. Dudley Fitts, *New York Times Book Review*, 18 January 1961, p. 10.
117. Seferis file IV 109/18, Gennadius Library.
118. Ibid.
119. ALS from Rex Warner to John Lehmann, 1938-69, Harry Ransom Humanities Research Center, University of Texas, Austin.
120. Ambrose, #186.
121. Gennadius Seferis file IV 109/18.
122. Ambrose, #186.
123. Seferis file IV 109/18, Gennadius Library.
124. Ibid.
125. Ibid.
126. ALS to John Lehmann, Harry Ransom Humanities Research Center, University of Texas, Austin.
127. Seymour Lawrence's papers and other materials are a special collection in the University of Maryland library.
128. Seferis file IV 109/18, Gennadius Library.
129. Ambrose, #22.
130. Seferis file IV 109/18, Gennadius Library.
131. Ambrose, #188.
132. Seferis file IV 109/18, Gennadius Library.
133. Ibid.
134. Ibid.
135. Ambrose, #187.
136. Gennadius Seferis file IV 109/18.
137. Rex Warner, *Times Literary Supplement*, 25 August 1961, p. 566.
138. Ambrose, #28.
139. Seferis file IV 109/18, Gennadius Library.
140. Rex Warner, "Review of William Empson's *Milton's God*," *London Magazine* 1, no. 7 (October 1961), 81, 83, 85.
141. Seferis file IV 109/18, Gennadius Library.
142. Ambrose, #20.
143. Ambrose, #21.
144. Ambrose, #5.
145. Seferis file IV 109/18, Gennadius Library.
146. Richard Hough, *Other Days Around Me: A Memoir* (London: Hodder & Stoughton, 1992), 146.

147. Ambrose, #180.
148. Bodley Head Archive, Reading University, BH23.
149. Seferis file IV 109/18, Gennadius Library.
150. Hamish Hamilton Archive, DM 1352, Bristol University.
151. Ibid.
152. Rex Warner, *Look at Birds* (London: Hamish Hamilton, 1962), 73-74.
153. Bodley Head Archive, Reading University, BH23.
154. Seferis file IV 109/18, Gennadius Library.
155. Hamish Hamilton Archive, University of Bristol, DM1352.
156. Bodley Head Archive, BH23, Reading University.
157. Seferis file IV 109/18, Gennadius Library.
158. I have been unable to view *Land of Heroes*. Since Rex mentions the archaeologist, this might have been the same as a film entitled "Ruins of Greece," the twenty-two-page typescript of which is in the Berg Collection of the New York Public Library. But this is doubtful, because the typescript seems to deal largely with twentieth-century Greek politics, and ends with praise of the British intervention during and after World War II: "British intervention no doubt saved Athens for Greece and Greece from a revolutionary minority."
159. Rex Warner to Alan McLeod, 23 September 1964, Rare Books Library, Pennsylvania State University Libraries, #1997-038R.
160. In the possession of Mrs. Frances Warner.

CHAPTER 12

1. University of Connecticut Special Collections Rex Warner papers.
2. "An Englishman at Bowdoin," 4.
3. Ibid.
4. Ibid., 6.
5. Ibid., 7.
6. Ibid., 28.
7. Ibid., 39.
8. Ibid., 40.
9. Ibid., 13.
10. Ibid.
11. Ibid., 14.
12. Ibid., 15.
13. Ibid., 17.

14. As Rex himself understood, the academic classics establishment did not want to notice the efforts of freelancers and others outside of academe. A typical example is Hugh Lloyd-Jones, *Blood for the Ghosts: Classical Influences in the Nineteenth and Twentieth Centuries* (London: Duckworth, 1982), a compendium of biographies of classicists including Gilbert Murray and Bowra. Rex does not even merit a footnote.

15. Letter of 11 September 1988 from John Malcolm Brinnin to author.

16. Letter in possession of Anne Ambrose; Ambrose, #30.

17. Seferis file IV 109/18, Gennadius Library.

18. Rex's two notebooks containing the manuscript of the St. Augustine novel (Denbigh Commercial Books D1/100 Faint, with long, blue-ruled paper) are in the University of Connecticut special collections at Storrs. The date at the beginning of the first notebook is November 1962, showing that this is about when Rex began planning and writing what was to be his last novel. The second notebook, which begins with page ninety-seven of the manuscript, is dated 10 October 1965, revealing how long it took him to make progress with this, perhaps his finest historical novel. A third, undated, notebook contains an intense, year-by-year notation of events in Augustine's life and approximately forty-one pages of other notes for the novel, as well as the lecture that he had been giving on Seferis and a review of Gore Vidal's *Julian*.

19. Bodley Head Archive, BH23, Reading University.

20. Seferis file IV 109/18, Gennadius Library.

21. N. H. Reeve, *The Novels of Rex Warner: An Introduction* (Basingstoke and London: Macmillan, 1989), 150-51.

22. Christopher Ricks, *New Statesman* 605 (8 February 1963): 207.

23. *Times Literary Supplement*, 8 February 1963, p. 89.

24. Rex Warner, *Pericles the Athenian* (Boston: Little, Brown, 1963), 5.

25. Letter of 11 September 1988 from John Malcolm Brinnin to author. Also letter of 30 January 1989 from Leonard Dean to author.

26. Seferis IV 109/18, Gennadius Library.

27. Brown's letter is in Rex's University of Connecticut English Department personnel file.

28. Bodley Head Archive, BH23, Reading University.

29. J. G. Harrison, review of *Pericles the Athenian*, *Christian Science Monitor*, 21 February 1963, p. 11.

30. Edward Tribbe, review of *Pericles the Athenian, Best Sellers*, 15 February 1963, p. 421.

31. Letter of 11 September 1988 from John Malcolm Brinnin to author.

32. Ambrose, #9.

33. "An Englishman at Bowdoin," 31.

34. Ibid., 32.

35. Ibid., 1-2.

36. Courtesy of the University of Connecticut English Department.

CHAPTER 13

1. According to Elga Wasserman and Ellen Switzer, *The Random House Guide to Graduate Study in the Arts and Sciences* (New York: Random House, 1967), 52.

2. The complete faculty roster for 1963-64 was as follows: Professors L. F. Dean, J. A. S. McPeek, G. B. Saul, R. W. Stallman; Associate Professors J. M. Brinnin, N. Friedman, C. A. Owen Jr., K. A. Spaulding, M. R. Stern, T. W. Wilcox, K. G. Wilson; Assistant Professors R. A. Blanshard, E. W. Carlson, J. B. Cary, W. R. Clark, J. M. Davis, H. I. Goldstone, J. E. Grant, G. T. Hemphill, C. A. McLaughlin, W. T. Moynihan, W. Rosen, W. C. Spengemann; Instructors P. Brotkorb Jr., I. P. Cummings, J. L. Foster, J. D. Hankins, E. W. Manchester, C. Rees, H. S. Weil Jr. (*University of Connecticut Bulletin and General Catalog*, 1963-64), 240.

3. This and other information from the members of the University of Connecticut English Department was gathered from interviews with them during 13-15 November 1988.

4. Rex Warner, "A Passage to India and Beyond: For E. M. Forster on his 85th Birthday, a Friendly Tribute and Reassessment," *The New York Times Book Review*, 18 December 1963, pp. 1, 18.

5. Rex Warner, *New York Times Book Review*, 17 November 1963, p. 5.

6. Letter to George Seferis, 4 January 1964, Gennadius file 97/8.

7. Letter to George Seferis, 23 February 1964, Gennadius file 97/8.

8. Letter to Max Reinhardt, 18 March 1964, Max Reinhardt "Miscellaneous Correspondence," Bodley Head Archives, Reading University.

9. The manuscript of which is in the University of Connecticut Warner collection.

10. Rex Warner, "A Dream of Marble, A Symphony of Light," *New York Times Magazine*, 26 April 1964, pp. 78-79, 99-100.

11. Letters to C. J. Greenwood and three letters to Lyle Blair, Michigan State University, C. J. Greenwood collection of Rex Warner materials.

12. Seferis file IV 109/18, Gennadius Library.

13. C. Day-Lewis quoted in Sean Day-Lewis, *C. Day-Lewis: An English Literary Life* (London: Weidenfeld and Nicolson, 1980), 258-59.

14. Betty Radice Archive, DM 1187, Bristol University.

15. Rex Warner, introduction to Xenophon, *A History of My Times* (Harmondsworth: Penguin, 1966), 7.

16. Betty Radice Archive, DM 1187, Bristol University.

17. Max Reinhardt, "Miscellaneous Correspondence," Bodley Head Archive, Reading University.

18. A copy of which she has kindly supplied to me.

19. Letter in possession of Jill Day-Lewis.

20. Bodley Head Archive, BH 277, Reading University.

21. Ibid.

22. Letter to George Seferis, 12 April 1965, Gennadius IV 109/18.

23. Seferis file IV 109/18, Gennadius Library.

24. One of Rex's sources for this novel was in his home library: Sister Marie McNamara's *Friends and Friendship for St. Augustine* (Society of St. Paul, State Island, N.Y.: Alba House, 1964). This book has a long section on Alypius, and Rex has folded down pages 97-98.

25. Bodley Head Archive, Reading University, BH 275.

26. Ibid., BH 222.

27. Paul Ryan has generously supplied me with copies of Rex's letters to him.

28. Max Reinhardt, "Miscellaneous Correspondence," Bodley Head Archive, Reading University.

29. Seferis file IV 109/18, Gennadius Library.

30. Max Reinhardt, "Miscellaneous Correspondence," Bodley Head Archive, Reading University.

31. John Davenport, *The Spectator*, 24 June 1966, p. 796.

32. Robert Taubman, *New Statesman*, 18 February 1966, p. 232.

33. Max Reinhardt, "Miscellaneous Correspondence," Bodley Head Archive, Reading University.

34. Ibid.

35. Bodley Head BH Editorial 409, Reading University.

36. In a letter of 18 August 1966 to Max, Rex writes: "Frances + I, after more Kafka-like impediments about documents, are actually getting married tomorrow." (Max Reinhardt, "Miscellaneous Correspondence," Bodley Head Archive, Reading University.)

37. Letter in possession of Anne Ambrose; Ambrose, #161.

38. Webster Schott, *Life Magazine*, 26 August 1966, p. 10.

39. Bodley Head Archive, BH Editorial 409, Reading University.

40. Seferis file IV 109/18, Gennadius Library.

41. Bodley Head Archive, BH Editorial 409, memo of 10.11.66 from John Hinchingbrooke to Max Reinhardt, Reading University.

42. Bodley Head Archive, BH Editorial 409, Reading University.

43. *Times Literary Supplement*, 25 May 1967, p. 433.

44. Samuel Hynes, *New York Times Book Review*, 30 July 1967, p. 26.

45. Rex Warner, in *Authors Take Sides on Vietnam*, ed. Cecil Woolf and John Bagguley (New York: Simon and Schuster, 1967), 73-74.

46. Ambrose, #22.

47. To Max Reinhardt, "Miscellaneous Correspondence," Bodley Head Archive, Reading University.

48. Rex Warner to Alan McLeod, 13 March 1968, Rex Warner manuscripts and correspondence, Rare Books Library, Pennsylvania State University Library, #1997-0038R.

49. Letter of 10 April 1988 from Harriet Duer to author.

50. Seferis file IV 109/18, Gennadius Library.

51. George Seferis, "Letter to Rex Warner, Resident of Storrs, Connecticut, U.S.A. On His Sixtieth Birthday," *Collected Poems* (Princeton: Princeton University Press, 1981), 432-37.

52. Seferis file IV 109/18, Gennadius Library.

53. Letter to D.A. Russell, 2 February 1969, Betty Radice Archives, Bristol University, DM 1187.

54. ALS to John Lehmann 1935-1969, Harry Ransom Humanities Research Center, University of Texas, Austin.

55. Letter to Elizabeth Curry, 7 February 1969.

56. *Connecticut Daily Campus*, 7 March 1969, p. 4.

57. Typescript transcription, The Semester of the Thirties, tape #156, University of Connecticut Archives.

58. ALS from John Lehmann to Rex Warner 1938-1969, Harry Ransom Humanities Research Center, University of Texas, Austin.

59. Letter to David Norrington, 4 May 1969, Ambrose, #11.

60. Letter to Seferis, 20 April 1970, Gennadius IV 109/18.

61. Letter to me, of 10 April 1988. I can confirm these remarks. I remember coming down to the white two-storied house on Horse Barn Hill Lane where I would be greeted warmly by Rex and Frances. I was always amazed at Rex's sheer size—he was just about as tall as I (6'1"), but quite a bit bigger. He weighed around 300 pounds at this time, but he never gave the impression of being fat. He seemed genuinely pleased to see me, even though I was bringing work for him. I would give Rex my latest chapter and possibly a related book of criticism or biography and then discuss the problems that I had faced when writing the chapter. Then, sitting next to me on the edge of the couch in his living room in sight of a large desk covered with papers in an alcove with a pleasant view, he discussed the points in my previous chapter that he had noted in the margins. I remember him bowing his head as he listened attentively to my explanations, and how his advice would always be given with a supportive quality or a joke. He would sometimes retell an anecdote about T. E. Lawrence, the subject of my dissertation, that he had heard from someone—bookseller Ken Marshall, for instance—who had known Lawrence. It was obvious that

Rex knew more about British history and literature in the 1920s and 1930s than I could learn from any published source, but he listened to my ideas with care.

I suffered a crisis of self-confidence when I discovered that a doctoral dissertation, completed at another university the year before mine, had dashed my hopes to have written the first dissertation on Lawrence of Arabia as a writer. Hearing my despondent voice on the phone, Rex invited me over. He then put me at ease by declaring that the competing dissertation was everything about American criticism that he disliked: it was too Freudian, too smoothly symmetrical, too thesis-laden. A large whiskey helped convince me that he was right, although I realized that he was trying to soothe me and to make it possible for me to finish. But more important perhaps was the principle that Rex tried to instill that while being first could sometimes be important, it was not of ultimate importance; the really important thing was to do good work. This was a special session, but I looked forward to every session with him as a privilege from which I would return heartened, enlightened and chock-full of authentic information about Lawrence. When Frances was present, the drink was hot tea rather than whiskey.

62. A letter from Alice Jaray of Kennikat to the Bodley Head states that 508 copies had been printed and bound; of these 473 were available for sale. There was an advance of $250 and the royalty rate was 10 percent. The list price was $7.50; 20 October 1969, Bodley Head Archive, BH 595, Reading University.

63. *Times Literary Supplement*, 16 April 1970, p. 424.

64. Seferis file IV 109/18, Gennadius Library.

65. Robert Holland, *New Haven Register Sunday Pictorial*, 28 June 1970, pp. 7-10.

66. In the possession of Mrs. Frances Warner.

67. Elizabeth Curry, "Rex Warner on the Allegorical Novel, Power Politics, and the Contemporary Scene: A Personal Interview," *Genre* 5, no. 4 (December 1972): 404-15.

68. Seferis file IV 109/18, Gennadius Library.

69. Letter to Max Reinhardt, 22 September 1971, Bodley Head Archive, BH 723, Reading University.

70. Bodley Head Archive, BH 767, Reading University.

71. Bodley Head Archive, BH 723, Reading University.

72. Rex Warner, *Men of Athens* (London, Sydney, Toronto: Bodley Head, 1972), 233.

73. Typescript, p. 4., WAC ref RCONT1, BBC Written Archives, Caversham.

74. Quoted in a memo from Max Reinhardt to Euan Cameron, 16 October 1972, Bodley Head Archive, BH Adult Publicity: Reviews 473, Reading University.

75. Bodley Head Archive, BH Adult Publicity: Reviews 473, Reading University.

76. Bodley Head Archive, BH 767, Reading University.

77. Letter to author, 14 December 1973.

78. Stephen Spender, *Journals 1939-1983*, ed. John Goldsmith (New York: Random House, 1986), 259.

CHAPTER 14

1. Letter to Paul Ryan, 29 January 1976.

2. Bodley Head Archive, BH 959, Reading University.

3. Rex Warner manuscripts and correspondence, Rare Books Library, Pennsylvania State University Libraries, #1997-0038R.

4. Letter in the possession of Anne Ambrose; Ambrose, #9.

5. In the possession of Mrs. Frances Warner.

6. London *Times*, 13 December 1983, p. 11.

7. Letter to me, 14 November 1983.

8. In the possession of Mrs. Frances Warner.

9. Ambrose, #39.

10. Letter of 5 June 1996 from Peter Carson of Penguin Books to author.

11. Stephen Spender, in "Neglected Fictions," *Times Literary Supplement*, 18 October 1995, p. 1191.

12. Sue Fishkoff, "With the Red Army at the Elbe," *Jerusalem Post International Edition*, Week Ending 13 May 1995, p. 12A.

INDEX

N

U

V